WORKS ISSUED BY
THE HAKLUYT SOCIETY

———

THE VOYAGE OF GEORGE VANCOUVER, 1791–1795

VOLUME I

SECOND SERIES
NO. 163

HAKLUYT SOCIETY

Plate 1. Captain George Vancouver.
The authenticity of this portrait has been questioned. The evidence is discussed in the appendix.

GEORGE VANCOUVER

A Voyage of Discovery to the North Pacific Ocean and Round the World 1791–1795

With an Introduction and Appendices

VOLUME I

EDITED BY

W. KAYE LAMB

THE HAKLUYT SOCIETY
LONDON
1984

G
420
.V22
V3
1984
V.1 / 52,309

Published by the Hakluyt Society
c/o The Map Library,
British Library Reference Division
London WC1B 3DG

To the Memory of my Wife
WESSIE TIPPING LAMB
Silent Partner in this Enterprise

CONTENTS

PREFACE

The primary sources relating to Vancouver's voyage of discovery are widely scattered, and I am greatly indebted to the many institutions and individuals who made it possible for me to assemble copies of virtually all of them. Most of the copies were received as microfilms, and from them full-size paper prints were made, as this was the only form in which they could be consulted and compared quickly and easily. The prints ran into the thousands, and I am grateful to the Canada Council for two research grants that paid for most of them, and also provided me with the sets of hydrographic charts that made it practicable to trace Vancouver's survey of the Northwest Coast in detail.

The largest collection of papers relating to the expedition is in the files of the Admiralty and Colonial Office in the Public Record Office. Vancouver reported to and corresponded with both departments. Unfortunately the original of his own journal has disappeared; the brief logs he kept as a young lieutenant serving in the Caribbean are all that have survived. These are in the National Maritime Museum, and the Museum's Director, Dr Basil Greenhill, kindly sent me copies of them. The official logs compiled by members of the expedition were deposited with the Admiralty, and although some have vanished, more than a score are available. Microfilm copies of them and of all other relevant papers were provided by the Public Record Office. The most informative of the logs is probably that kept by Peter Puget, which frequently expands into a journal, and by a happy chance it can be supplemented by his rough journal – often more frank and informative than the official version – which is in the Department of Manuscripts of the British Library.

The Department of Manuscripts also possesses the greater part of the journal of Archibald Menzies, one of three highly informative private accounts of the expedition. The Library's text runs to February 1794. An additional part, carrying the narrative forward for another year, is in the National Library of Australia. Mrs Fanning, in charge of the Library's manuscript collection, very kindly gave me a complete photostat copy, which supplements the photostat of the earlier section which had already been provided by the British Library.

The other private accounts are those kept by Edward Bell, a treasured possession of the Alexander Turnbull Library in Wellington, New Zealand, and the narrative in the form of a series of letters written by Thomas Manby, now in the Coe Collection of Western Americana in Yale University Library. I am much indebted to both libraries for their courtesy in allowing me to secure copies.

Miss Suzanne Mourot, until recently Mitchell Librarian in the State Library of New South Wales, drew my attention to a substantial volume in the Brabourne Papers that consists of correspondence and memoranda relating to Vancouver's voyage. She very kindly gave me a microfilm copy. Sir Joseph Banks and Archibald Menzies figure largely in the collection which, amongst other things, throws some light on the Camelford affair that caused Vancouver much distress in his last years. Menzies items of considerable interest are also included in the Banks Papers in the Sutro Library in San Francisco. Mr Richard Dillon, its librarian, sent me copies. The Provincial Archives of British Columbia contributed copies of papers presented to it by the Menzies family, and facsimiles of transcripts of letters from Menzies to Banks which had been secured many years ago from the Royal Botanic Gardens at Kew.

The key documents required to unravel the Camelford story are in the Cotes Papers, in the National Library of Wales, which made facsimiles available. Camelford also figures in the Sir Robert Barrie Papers in the Perkins Library at Duke University. Barrie and Camelford were friends both during and after the expedition, and his letters to his mother, copies of which the Perkins Library sent me, include interesting comments on Camelford, Vancouver, and various aspects of the voyage. Mr Tom L. Brock, of Victoria, B.C., very kindly gave me copies of Vancouver and Barrie letters in his collection, and checked several points in his transcripts of the Gardner Papers.

Copies of individual Vancouver letters were received from widely separated sources, including the Scottish Record Office in Edinburgh, the Huntington Library in San Marino, California, the Provincial Archives in Victoria, and both the Library of the University of British Columbia and the City Archives in Vancouver. Miss Agnes Conrad, State Archivist of Hawaii, gave me facsimiles of the two statements Vancouver left in the islands for the guidance of future visitors. Mrs

Cynthia Timberlake and Miss Dorothy Barrère of the Bernice P. Bishop Museum, in Honolulu, helped me to fill in the background of Vancouver's three sojourns in Hawaii. Mrs Timberlake also arranged for me to borrow a copy of the 'Index to Hawaiian Ethnological Data in Vancouver's *Voyage of Discovery*' compiled by Miss Margaret Titcomb. Amongst other things this helped to sort out the confusing references to persons and places in the *Voyage* and various logs, due to the fact that Hawaiian was still an unwritten language. Transcripts of a Vancouver letter and other papers relating to the Northwest Coast in the Mexican Archives were available in the Public Archives of Canada, in Ottawa.

The maps and drawings relating to the Vancouver expedition deserve a separate study, and the obvious person to undertake it is Lieut.-Commander A. C. F. David, R.N., of the Hydrographic Department at Taunton, Somerset. The largest collection of surviving charts and sketches is at Taunton, and Commander David became so interested in them that he is compiling a check list of all known items both there and elsewhere. His help in identifying draughtsmen and artists has been invaluable. Some charts and a few sketches are in the Colonial Office records, and a number of the logs in the Admiralty's collection contain drawings and sketch maps. A substantial collection of drawings (originals or copies) by Heddington and Humphrys has found its way to the Bancroft Library at the University of California, in Berkeley.

Dr Helen Wallis kindly checked the collections for items in the Map Room of the British Library. The Provincial Archives in Victoria has copies of almost all the maps prepared by fur traders who visited the Northwest Coast before Vancouver's voyage in the versions published by Dalrymple in 1789–91, and Mr Geoffrey Castle, map librarian, sent me facsimiles of them.

Surgeon Vice-Admiral Sir James Watt shared with me his conclusions regarding the cause of the deteriorating health from which Vancouver suffered during the voyage, and which caused his death at the early age of 40. I wish also to mention Sir James' kindness in checking a source which I had been prevented from consulting during my last visit to London.

Several years' residence in Vancouver as Consul General for the Netherlands aroused the interest of Mr Adrien Mansveldt in Captain Vancouver's family background. Patient searching solved the mystery, and thanks to him we have information about the Van Coeverden family in Holland, and know that contacts continued between them and the Vancouvers in England.

I owe a very special expression of thanks to Mrs J. M. White, until recently Head of the London Office of the Public Archives of Canada. She was tireless in her efforts to trace elusive items and was almost invariably successful in her searches. Among the points she investigated for me were Vancouver's relations with the Board of Longitude, the outcome of the court martial held to investigate Vancouver's charges against Henry Phillips, carpenter of the *Discovery*, and Vancouver's efforts to secure for himself and his crews a fair share of the prize money due them for the capture at St Helena of the Dutch East Indiaman *Macassar*.

Mrs Anne Yandle and her staff in Special Collections at the Library of the University of British Columbia were always helpful, and Mr C. R. Tharalson and his staff in the History Department and Northwest Room of the Vancouver Public Library assisted me on many occasions.

I owe a debt to the Honorary Secretaries of the Hakluyt Society which it is a pleasure to acknowledge. In the early stages of the preparation of this edition Professor Eila Campbell was most helpful, and as publication approached Dr Terence Armstrong provided a quite invaluable link between the author and the Press.

Finally, I wish to express my special appreciation of the interest taken in the project by Dr Glyndwr Williams. I am well aware of the amount of time he must have devoted to reviewing my introduction and notes, and his great knowledge of the period made his comments and suggestions particularly helpful and valuable.

W. KAYE LAMB

VANCOUVER, BRITISH COLUMBIA, APRIL 1982

ILLUSTRATIONS

† Indicates engravings reproduced from a set of the 1798 edition of *A Voyage of Discovery* in the British Library (1889 R 42), by permission of the Library. Original captions, where retained, are indicated by quotation marks.

PLATES

xiii

SKETCH MAPS

All base maps by Michael E. Leek

ABBREVIATIONS USED IN
INTRODUCTION AND NOTES

MANUSCRIPT LOGS AND JOURNALS

Baker   Joseph Baker, Third, Second and First Lieutenant, *Discovery*. 22 Dec. 1790–1 July 1795. PRO Adm 55/32 and 33.

Ballard   Volant Vachon Ballard, A.B., midshipman and clerk, *Discovery*. 1 March 1791–2 July 1795. PRO Adm 55/29.

Bell   Edward Bell, clerk, *Chatham*. Personal journal 1 Jan. 1791–26 Feb. 1794. Alexander Turnbull Library, Wellington, New Zealand.

Heddington   Thomas Heddington, midshipman, *Chatham*. 1 Feb. 1791–2 July 1795. PRO Adm 55/15 and 16.

Hewett   George Goodman Hewett, surgeon's first mate, *Discovery*. Marginal notes and comments in his copy of the 1798 edition of the *Voyage of Discovery*, now in the Provincial Archives of British Columbia, Victoria.

Humphrys   Henry Humphrys, midshipman and master's mate, *Discovery*; Master of the *Chatham*. 16 Dec. 1790–27 Nov. 1794, *Discovery*; 27 Nov. 1794–17 Oct. 1795, *Chatham*. PRO Adm 55/26.

Johnstone   James Johnstone, Master and Second Lieutenant, *Chatham*. 2 Jan. 1791–20 May 1792. PRO Adm 53/335.

Manby   Thomas Manby, A.B. and master's mate, *Discovery*; Master of the *Chatham*; Acting Third Lieutenant, *Discovery*. [15] Dec. 1790–5 June 1792, *Discovery*. PRO Adm 53/403 ff. 187–245. 27 Sept. 1792–8 Oct. 1794, *Chatham*. PRO Adm 51/2251. 8 Oct. 1794–2 July 1795, *Discovery*. PRO Adm 53/403 ff. 246–300.

Manby Letters   —Personal journal in the form of narrative letters intended for his friend John Lees, of Dublin. Sections dated 18 Feb. 1791 to 22 June 1793. Incomplete. Original in Coe Collection of Western Americana, Yale University Library.

Menzies   Archibald Menzies, botanist and acting surgeon, *Discovery*. Personal journal, 1 Dec. 1790–16 Feb. 1794. BL Add MS 32641. 21 Feb. 1794–18 Feb. 1795. Manuscript Collection, National Library of Australia, Canberra.

Mudge   Zachary Mudge, First Lieutenant, *Discovery*. 4 Jan. 1791–1 Oct. 1792. PRO Adm 51/4533 pt. 52.

Orchard   H. M. Orchard, clerk and midshipman, *Discovery*. 1 Dec. 1792–30 Nov. 1794. PRO Adm 55/31.

Puget   Peter Puget, Second and First Lieutenant, *Discovery*; commander of the *Chatham*. 4 Jan. 1791–14 Jan. 1793, *Discovery*. PRO Adm 55/27. 13 Jan. 1793–March 1794, *Chatham*. PRO Adm 55/17.

Puget, rough journal —BL Add MS 17542–45, 17548. Supplement the official log as they include entries as late as September 1795.

Scott   James Woodward Scott, midshipman, *Chatham*, midshipman, *Discovery*, A.B. and midshipman, *Chatham*. 3 March 1791–Aug. 17, 1791, *Chatham*. PRO Adm 51/4534 pt. 3. Aug. 18, 1791–6 Oct. 1793, *Chatham*. PRO Adm 55/14. 6 Oct. 1793–19 Feb. 1794, *Discovery*. PRO Adm 55/14. 20 Feb. 1794–March 29, 1795, *Chatham*. PRO Adm 55/14.

Sherriff   John Sherriff, master's Mate, *Chatham*. Aug. 18, 1791–6 June 1795. PRO Adm 53/334.

Stewart   John Stewart, A.B., midshipman and master's mate, *Discovery*. 1 Jan. 1791–11 July 1791. PRO Adm 51/4533, pt. 54. 12 July 1791–28 July 1794. PRO Adm 55/28. 29 July 1794–2 July 1795, PRO Adm 51/4533 pt. 55.

Swaine   Spelman Swaine, master's mate, *Discovery*, Master, *Chatham*, Acting Third Lieutenant, *Discovery*. 18 Dec. 1790–30 Aug. 1792, *Discovery*. PRO Adm 51/4532 pt. 1. 31 Aug.–26 Sept. 1792, *Chatham*. PRO 51/4532 pt. 1. 26 Sept. 1792–2 July 1795, *Discovery*. PRO Adm 51/4532 pt. 2.

Whidbey   Joseph Whidbey. A brief log kept while the *Discovery*, of which he was Master, was under the command of Captain Roberts. 1 Jan.–May 20, 1790. PRO Adm 52/2262 pt. 6. A near duplicate follows, possibly kept by John Sykes.

PRINTED SOURCES

BCHQ	*British Columbia Historical Quarterly*
DNB	*Dictionary of National Biography*
OED	*Oxford English Dictionary*
OHQ	*Oregon Historical Quarterly*
PNQ	*Pacific Northwest Quarterly*
WHQ	*Washington Historical Quarterly*
BL	British Library
BM	British Museum
NMM	National Maritime Museum
PRO	Public Record Office

———

Cook, *Journals*   The Journals of Captain James Cook on his Voyages of Discovery. Edited by J. C. Beaglehole. 3 vols. in 4, Cambridge, 1955–69. (Hakluyt Society, Extra Series, XXXIV–XXXVI)

Vancouver,   George Vancouver, *A Voyage of Discovery to the North Pacific Ocean, and Round the World*. 3 vols. and atlas, London, 1798.

INTRODUCTION

I

PREPARATIONS

The Years with Cook

IT would be interesting to know who brought young George Vancouver to the attention of Captain Cook when Cook was mustering the crew that was to sail with him in the *Resolution* on the second of his three great voyages. Appointments as midshipmen were much sought after and were secured in most instances through personal or political influence. John Elliott, a fellow midshipman in the *Resolution*, noted his own experience in his memoirs. It was thought 'it would be quite a great feather, in a young man's Cap, to go out with Captn Cook, and it requir'd much Intrest to get out with him; My Uncle therefore determined to send me out with him in the Resolution'. The uncle, John Wilkinson, had influence with Sir Hugh Palliser, controller of the navy; Palliser passed the boy on to a kinsman, Robert Palliser Cooper, who was Cook's first lieutenant in the *Resolution*, and Cooper introduced him to Cook, 'who promis'd to take care of me' and did so.[1] Vancouver's friend at court was probably someone known to his father, John Jasper Vancouver, who had retired recently after serving for over 20 years as deputy customer at King's Lynn, Norfolk. The position of customer (collector of customs) was a sinecure and the deputy was the functioning official. King's Lynn was then a major port, and Vancouver's father had many links with politics and the maritime world. He had received his appointment from Charles Turner, head of the most influential local Tory family, and was himself described as 'a small-made man and a very active Tory'.[2] Godwin states that 'contemporary political satires lampoon him as "Little Van", but without malice'.[3]

George Vancouver joined the *Resolution* at Deptford Yard on 22 January 1772. Elliott remembered him as aged 'about 13½, a Quiet

---

[1] Quoted in J. C. Beaglehole, *The Life of Captain James Cook* (London, 1974), p. 299.

[2] From notes on a family tree in the possession of Mrs Caroline Bundy, a descendant of Vancouver's brother John. Copy in PAC.

[3] George Godwin, *Vancouver. A Life* (London, 1930), p. 2.

inoffensive young man'.[1] Actually Vancouver was a year older, for
he was born at King's Lynn on 22 June 1757, the sixth and youngest
child of John Jasper Vancouver and his wife, Bridget Berners. She was
descended from an old Essex and Norfolk family that traced its ancestry
back to Sir Richard Grenville, of *Revenge* fame. As the name suggests,
the Vancouvers were of Dutch origin. They were descended from the
titled van Coeverden family, one of the oldest in The Netherlands. By
the twelfth century, and for many years thereafter, their castle at
Coevorden,[2] in the Province of Drenthe, was an important fortress
on the eastern frontier. George Vancouver was aware of this. In July
1794, he named the Lynn Canal 'after the place of my nativity' and
Point Couverden (which he spelled incorrectly) 'after the seat of my
ancestors'. Vancouver's great grandfather, Reint Wolter van Coeverden,
was probably the first of the line to establish an English connection.
While serving as a squire at one of the German courts he met Johanna
(Jane) Lillingston, an English girl who was one of the ladies in waiting.
They were married in 1699. Their son, Lucas Hendrik van Coeverden,
married Vancouver's grandmother, Sarah, whose surname has not yet
been discovered. In his later years he probably anglicized his name and
spent most of his time in England. By the eighteenth century the estates
of the van Coeverdens were mostly in the Province of Overijssel, and
some of the family were living in Vollenhove, on the Zuider Zee. The
English and Dutch branches kept in touch, and in 1798 George
Vancouver's brother Charles would marry a kinswoman, Louise
Josephine van Coeverden, of Vollenhove. Both were great-grand-
children of Reint Wolter van Coeverden.[3]

Training under Cook was recognized as being rigorous but rewarding.
Beaglehole justly remarks that 'It would be difficult, indeed, to imagine
a better education for a young seaman than three years in the
Resolution.' Elliott provides a glimpse of the programme: 'In the Early
part of the Voyage, Capt.[n] Cook made all us young gentlemen, do the
duty aloft the same as the Sailors, learning to hand, and reef the sails,
and Steer the ship, E[x]ercise Small Arms &c thereby making us good

[1] Quoted in Beaglehole, *Life of Cook*, p. 299.
[2] Spelling of the name of the town varies.
[3] These and other details were brought to light by the research of Adrien Mansvelt,
formerly Consul General for The Netherlands at Vancouver, B.C. His articles include:
'Vancouver: A lost branch of the van Coeverden Family', *B.C. Historical News*, VI (1973),
20–23; 'Solving the Captain Vancouver mystery', and 'The original Vancouver in old
Holland', both in *Vancouver Sun*, 1 September 1973.

Sailors, as well as good Officers'.[1] Later came training in observing, surveying and drawing. The boys were doubly fortunate because the astronomer of the expedition was William Wales, one of the leading scientists of the day. He had assisted Dr Nevil Maskelyne, the Astronomer Royal, in preparing early editions of the *Nautical Almanac*, and when he returned to England in 1775 was appointed master of the Mathematical School at Christ's Hospital. He was a gifted teacher, and Vancouver remembered him with gratitude and affection. In 1793, while exploring Observatory Inlet, he named the west point 'after my much-esteemed friend Mr. Wales, of Christ's Hospital; to whose kind instruction, in the early part of my life, I am indebted for that information which has enabled me to traverse and delineate these lonely regions'.

The *Resolution* and her companion ship, the *Adventure*, sailed in July 1772 and returned three years later, having circled the globe and done much else. Both outward and homeward they called at the Cape of Good Hope for rest, repairs and supplies. From the Cape the general strategy of the voyage was conditioned by the seasons. The Antarctic summers were devoted to the main purpose of the expedition, the search for the legendary southern continent; the winter months, which forced abandonment of this search, provided time for exploratory voyages through the islands of the South Pacific. The first of the southern sweeps probed the waters south of the Indian Ocean as far as ice and weather permitted; the second carried the search farther eastward into the South Pacific; the third and last explored the South Atlantic. The tropical islands visited on the winter cruises included Easter Island, the southern group of the Marquesas, Tahiti, Tonga, the New Hebrides (which Cook named), and New Caledonia and Norfolk Island (both of which he discovered and named). New Zealand, which Cook had circumnavigated in 1770, in the course of his first voyage, became the base from which these southern and tropical sweeps were made, and it was from New Zealand that he sailed finally for home by way of Cape Horn and the Cape of Good Hope.

The voyage had been a quite extraordinary experience for a teenage boy, and gave Vancouver a training and maturity that were to stand him in good stead. He evidently kept a journal, but it has disappeared, along with most of the personal records relating to his career. Two pen and ink charts now in the British Library are the only original

[1] Quoted in Beaglehole, *Life of Cook*, p. 299.

Vancouver documents relating to the voyage known to have survived.[1]
One anecdote may be added. On 30 January 1774, the *Resolution*
reached the farthest south attained by the expedition – south latitude
71° 10'. Shortly after Vancouver's death the *Naval Chronicle* noted that
'Captain Vancouver used to say, that he had been nearer the South
Pole than any other Man for when the immortal Cook in latitude 72,
was stopped in his progress by impenetrable mountains of ice, and was
prepared to tack about, he went out to the very end of the bowsprit,
and waving his hat, exclaimed *Ne Plus Ultra!*' But unknown to
Vancouver there was a rival claimant. The supernumeraries on board
included Andreas Sparrman, the Swedish physician and botanist, who
wrote later: 'In order to avoid the bustle and crowd on the deck, usual
in such operations, I went below to my cabin to watch more quietly
through the scuttle the boundless expanses of Polar ice. Thus it
happened, as my companions observed, that I went a trifle farther south
than any of the others in the ship, because a ship, when going about,
always has a little stern way before she can make way on the fresh tack
when the sails fill.'[2]

Cook's second voyage ended at Spithead late in July 1775. He retired
briefly to the position of captain at Greenwich Hospital, but returned
to active service within a few months when it was decided to send a
third expedition to the Pacific. It sailed in July 1776. Cook again
commanded the *Resolution*, but Vancouver joined the *Discovery*,
Captain Charles Clerke, which replaced the *Adventure* as companion
ship.

In several respects this voyage is of special interest in relation to
Vancouver's own expedition, which would sail fifteen years later. Except for Vancouver's short survey of the southwest coast of Australia,
both expeditions followed much the same route to the Northwest Coast
of America, travelling by way of the Cape of Good Hope, New Zealand,
Tahiti and the Sandwich (Hawaiian) Islands. Various remarks in
Vancouver's narrative show that he was very conscious that he was
following in Cook's track, and the veneration in which he held him
is also very evident. The voyage gave rise to the maritime fur trade
on the Northwest Coast, the development of which was one of the

---

[1] Add MSS 31360. One shows part of the east coast of New Caledonia; the other is
a chart of New Georgia.

[2] *The Naval Chronicle*, I (*1799*), p. 125; Andreas Sparrman, *A Voyage round the World
with Captain James Cook* (London, 1953), p. 112. Both are quoted in Beaglehole, *Life of
Cook*, p. 365n.

chief reasons for Vancouver's expedition. Cook found that sea otters were plentiful, and when his ships reached China, crew members who had traded somewhat casually for their skins discovered that they fetched high prices. When this became known, with the publication of accounts of the voyage, traders quickly appeared on the coast. Two of Cook's geographical discoveries – Nootka Sound and the Sandwich Islands – were highly important later to the trading ships. Nootka provided an excellent summer base, as it offered sheltered anchorages at which wood, water and timber were all readily available. The Sandwich Islands, with their semi-tropical climate, were an ideal winter refuge to which ships intending to return in the spring for further trading could retreat when cold and stormy autumn weather temporarily ended the commerce in furs.

Although the strategy each followed was quite different, the primary purpose of both Cook's third voyage and Vancouver's expedition was to search for the Pacific outlet of the long-sought Northwest Passage. Cook's instructions reflected the fact that in 1774 the Admiralty had learned from the Hudson's Bay Company that Samual Hearne, one of its servants, had reached the Arctic Ocean at the mouth of the Coppermine River. Although Hearne's estimate of the position of the river's mouth – 71° 54′ north latitude – was found later to be about 200 miles too far north, it indicated rightly that any passage from the Pacific to the Atlantic must be in high latitudes. The search therefore changed to one for a passage across the top of North America instead of one through the continent as heretofore. This impression was heightened the same year by the publication of an account by Jacob von Stählin of alleged Russian discoveries in the northern waters between Asia and North America. Stählin included a map that showed the Northwest Coast leading to a broad, unobstructed channel that gave direct access to the Arctic.[1] Cook was therefore instructed to begin his search at 65°. He was to reach the Northwest Coast at about 45°, which he did, then 'put into the first convenient Port to recruit... Wood and Water and procure Refreshments', which he did at Nootka Sound, and then to hurry northward, 'taking care not to lose any time in exploring Rivers or Inlets, or upon any other account' until he reached 'the before-mentioned Latitude of 65°'. But Cook's search for a passage was a failure. Stählin's broad channel did not exist, and Cook did not reach

[1] *An Account of the New Northern Archipelago, Lately Discovered by the Russians in the Seas of Kamtschatka and Anadir* (London, 1774). The map is reproduced in Cook, *Journals*, III, opp. lxiv.

6

65° until he had rounded the long obstruction of the Alaska peninsula and had reached Bering Strait. Following the Alaskan coast, his ships sailed on until they reached their farthest north at 70° 44′ and encountered ice that was 'quite impenetrable' and extended 'as far as the eye could reach'.[1] Clerke fared no better when he brought the ships back to the Arctic in 1779, after Cook's death.

Cook's instructions and the bad weather that drove him offshore combined to make his survey of the southern part of the Northwest Coast a cursory one. Except for Nootka Sound he saw nothing between Cape Flattery and 55° north; the innumerable islands and inlets are represented on his chart by a single unbroken line. Hence arose the need for Vancouver's expedition. Faith in the tales of Juan de Fuca and de Fonte still persisted, and there remained the possibility that somewhere on this unexplored part of the coast a search might reveal the entrance to a passage that led to an outlet in the Arctic west of Hearne's Coppermine River. In any event, the maritime fur trade and the interest in the coast that it had engendered had developed to a point at which the British Government wished to know much more about the area. Cook's voyage had been devoted essentially to exploration and discovery. Vancouver, by contrast, was instructed to make a detailed survey from 30° to 60° which would both provide the information the Government was seeking and settle once and for all the question as to whether or not a Northwest Passage existed within the temperate region. Beaglehole senses that Cook was a surveyor at heart; he hazards the guess that 'he had a tinge of regret' that his later charts 'were not really surveys in the technical sense' and adds: 'after all, what is his north-west American coast but a magnificent, an epoch-making, reconnaissance? It needed Vancouver.'[2]

Vancouver joined the *Discovery* as an A.B. on 27 February 1776, and was rated a midshipman on 18 March. The ship sailed on 1 August, and caught up with the *Resolution*, which had left three weeks earlier, at the Cape of Good Hope. Once again Vancouver's log has disappeared, and the only references to him in other journals relate to the expedition's tragic second visit to the Sandwich Islands, in January and February of 1779.

The two ships anchored in Kealakekua Bay on 17 January, and on the 26th Vancouver was a member of a small expedition that set off to explore some distance inland. The party of seven included Robert

---

[1] Cook, *Journals*, III, 417. The date was 18 August 1778.
[2] Beaglehole, *Life of Cook*, p. 702.

Anderson, gunner of the *Resolution*, and David Nelson, the botanist. It had been 'sent by Captn Cook...to examine the Productions of the Island'[1] but an additional objective was an ascent of the high 'Snowy Mountain' – Mauna Loa – which could be seen from the ships. Captain King describes the journey in some detail.[2] Thick underbrush, lack of trails through it, scarcity of water and cold nights that had to be passed with little or no shelter, defeated the party and they turned back while still a considerable distance from the mountain. Archibald Menzies was to encounter but overcome the same difficulties when he climbed Mauna Loa in 1794.

King notes that the party 'carried no arms of any kind'; at the time there was no reason to be apprehensive. The natives were curious, but friendly and helpful. Carpenters sent ashore to cut plank had had a similar experience. No doubt this treatment was a reflection of the extraordinary deference with which Cook had been greeted – so extraordinary that it is assumed that he was regarded as the incarnation of the god Lono. In spite of this, King was uneasy, and he was relieved when the ships had been troubled by nothing more serious than some petty thieving when they left the bay on 4 February. Remembering Cook's experience in Tonga he wrote that day in his journal: 'It is very clear...that they regard us as a Set of beings infinitely their superiors; should this respect wear away with familiarity, or by length of intercourse, their behaviour may change'.[3]

King had no expectation that his theory would be put to an early test, but serious damage to the foremast of the *Resolution* forced Cook to return to Kealakekua Bay within a week. A change in the attitude of the natives was apparent immediately; as Beaglehole expresses it, their propensity to theft was now matched by a propensity to mischief. A week's reflection may well have given rise to doubts about Cook's divinity. Doubtless the damage to the mast contributed to the change: 'Should the ship of a god have suffered damage at all?'[4] And there may have been a change in Cook as well. He was weary, irritable and perhaps unwell; the delay caused by the damaged mast exasperated him.

Matters came to a head, appropriately enough, on Friday, 13 February. Several items were stolen from the *Discovery*; Thomas Edgar,

[1] Samwell's journal, 26 January 1779. Cook, *Journals*, III, 1169.
[2] Cook, *Journals*, III, 520–24.
[3] *Ibid.*, 525.
[4] Beaglehole, *Life of Cook*, p. 663.

the ship's master, and Vancouver, with two men, manned the small cutter and pursued the thief. Near the shore they were joined by the *Resolution*'s pinnace, but unfortunately the latter ran aground on some rocks. Neither the cutter nor the pinnace was armed, and their crews fared badly when the natives attacked with stones and clubs. 'I not being able to swim,' Edgar recorded, 'had got upon a small rock up to my knees in water, when a man came up with a broken Oar, and most certainly would have knock'd me off the rock, into the water, if Mr Vancouver, the Midshipman, had not at that Ins^t Step'd out of the Pinnace, between the Indian & me, & receiv'd the Blowe, which took him on the side, & knock'd him down.'[1] Later Vancouver was knocked down a second time, and if a friendly chief had not managed to intervene, it is probable that he would have lost his life.

Cook was on shore at the time, and he had hurried along the beach in a vain hope that he could intercept the thief when he landed. He was not molested by the crowds of natives that had assembled, but it was evident that their attitude toward him had changed drastically. He was well aware of this; King records that when he returned to the *Resolution* 'the Captn expressed his sorrow, that the behaviour of the Indians would at last oblige him to use force; for that they must not he said imagine they have gaind an advantage over us'.[2]

The next day saw the tragic clash with the natives in which Cook was killed. Firearms were used, but ineffectively. Vancouver took no part in the fracas, but he did assist in the great effort made to secure Cook's remains. In the course of the negotiations a friendly chief came on board ship, and King makes the interesting observation that he 'seemd rejoiced to see Mr Vancouver... who best understood them'.[3] This suggests that Vancouver had already developed the keen interest in the Hawaiians and their islands that was to be a major preoccupation during his own expedition.

The Caribbean

Vancouver completed his second voyage around the world when Cook's ships arrived in the Thames on 7 October 1780. The *Discovery* was paid off three days later, and Vancouver applied at once to be examined for promotion to lieutenant. A minimum of six years' sea

---

[1] Edgar's journal, 13 February 1779. Cook, *Journals*, III, 1360.
[2] Cook, *Journals*, III, 530.　　　　　　　　　　　[3] *Ibid.*, 554.

service was called for, a requirement he met by a wide margin. His passing certificate, dated 19 October, shows that he had served a total of 8 years 3 months and 3 weeks in the *Resolution* and *Discovery*.[1]

The American Revolutionary War, in which both France and Spain had become involved, was still in progress, and Vancouver was not left unemployed for long. In December, just two months after his return, he was appointed to the sloop *Martin*, Captain William Wardlaw. After spending more than a year on escort and patrol duty in the Channel and the North Sea, the *Martin* was ordered to the West Indies. It was there that Vancouver was to spend the rest of his career before embarking on his great voyage of discovery.

The *Martin*, now commanded by Captain William Merrick, sailed from Plymouth on 11 February 1782 and by early March she was in the Caribbean. Her first assignment there was to assist the *Invincible*, a 74-gun ship of the line, in convoying ten merchant ships to Port Royal, Jamaica, the naval base for the West Indian Station. The entries in the surviving fragment of Vancouver's journal[2] describing his service in the *Martin* are brief, but they become somewhat more informative in April, when she was sent with supplies intended for the garrison on Swan Island, north of Honduras. She arrived on the 11th, only to discover that the island had been devastated a month before by the Spaniards. Vancouver records that they 'found no Inhabitants the Garrison & Houses Burnt'. Later one man turned up who described how the Spaniards 'Besieged the Island destroyed the Fort carried off the Guns and took the People as Prisoners except him & a few Negroes who escaped in the Bush.'

On the return voyage to Jamaica the *Martin* met with a further adventure. On 19 April she encountered a Spanish ship, hailed her captain, and 'desired him to shorten sail immediately. He answered he would, but he fired a broadside at us which we immediately answered & both ships kept continually firing for near four hours.' The action broke off at nightfall but was renewed the next morning, when the Spaniard finally struck her colours. A prize crew took her to Jamaica.

This was one of the few actions in which Vancouver participated, and the mission to Swan Island probably caused him to miss a famous battle. On 29 April, when nearing Port Royal, the *Martin* met Rodney's squadron, which on the 12th, off Dominica, had won the celebrated

---

[1] In the *Resolution* 3 years 7 months 2 weeks and 4 days (27 Jan. 1772 to 28 Aug. 1775); in the *Discovery* 4 years 7 months 3 weeks and 10 days (26 Feb. 1776 to 10 Oct. 1780).

[2] N.M.M., ADM/L/M 16B. The entries extend from 9 Dec. 1781 to 16 May 1782.

victory known as the Battle of the Saints over a powerful French fleet commanded by the Comte de Grasse.

Little more than a fortnight later Vancouver left the *Martin* and on 17 May joined the *Fame*, a 74, as 4th lieutenant. His journal for the thirteen months and a half he spent in her is complete, but the entries are again brief.[1] In July Admiral Hugh Pigot arrived to take command of the station, and he immediately took his whole fleet of 37 ships to New York, to avoid the hurricane season in the Caribbean; an unwritten agreement with the French, who also moved their ships to the north, made this practicable, even in wartime. When they returned in October, the British ships spent most of their time keeping a watchful eye on the French possessions in the Leeward Islands. These patrols ended when news arrived that a preliminary peace had been signed in Paris. The King's proclamation was read on 5 April 1783, and on the 22nd the *Fame* sailed for England. She arrived at Plymouth early in June and was put out of commission on 3 July.

Vancouver now experienced his only lengthy period on half pay. With the coming of peace the number of ships in commission was reduced drastically, and vacancies were few and far between. At last, late in November 1784, after nearly eighteen months of waiting, he had the good fortune to be appointed to the *Europa*, the flagship of Rear Admiral Alexander Innes, the new commander-in-chief in the West Indies, and by February 1785 he was back at Port Royal.[2]

Only a few ships were now based there, and little of interest happened during the rest of the year. But, so far as Vancouver personally was concerned, it was a different story in 1786. In January Admiral Innes died, and in the summer Commodore Sir Alan Gardner (later Admiral Lord Gardner), who was to become a good friend and patron of Vancouver, arrived to succeed him. This relationship began in September, when the Commodore shifted his flag from the *Experiment*, in which he had arrived, to the *Europa*. Gardner was a progressive commander, who believed in activity that would keep his crews interested and efficient. The success of the American Revolution had ruled out further cruises to New York to escape the Caribbean hurricanes; instead, the squadron took shelter from July to November in the inner harbour of Kingston, adjacent to Port Royal. But Gardner was resourceful; he had only two ships of the line – the *Experiment* and

---

[1] N.M.M., ADM/L/F 115. Log of the *Fame* 17 May 1782 to 3 July 1783.

[2] N.M.M., ADM/L/E 155. Vancouver's log of the *Europa*. The entries begin on 24 Nov. 1787, when he was appointed 2nd lieutenant and end on 8 Aug. 1789.

Europa — but he hit upon the plan of shifting his flag from one to the other, keeping one ship in harbour while the other cruised in coastal waters. Nevertheless service on the station cannot have been exciting. The only occasion when the *Europa* was far from Jamaican waters was in January 1789, when she sailed south to Cartagena, on the coast of Colombia.

Alexander Dalrymple was not appointed as the Royal Navy's first hydrographer until 1795, but the Admiralty already recognized the need for more charts and more accurate surveys. In 1786 all ships were instructed to make surveys of the harbours they visited, and Gardner took steps to carry the directive into effect. In September Joseph Whidbey joined the *Europa* as master, and in the fall of 1787 he and Vancouver were instructed to survey Port Royal and Kingston harbours. This began an association between the two that was to continue for the rest of Vancouver's years afloat. The assignment was a considerable one, as the harbours were extensive and the survey was to include the complicated pattern of shoals lying offshore. The resulting chart, dedicated to Gardner, was published in London in 1792 for Whidbey and Vancouver. That they took pride in it is shown by a note regarding the New Channel that appears on the engraving: 'This Channel was Surveyed, Buoyed, and first used by order of Rear Admiral Affleck in 1791, by In°. Leard and Stephen Seymour, who proved the Original Survey by Mess.rs. Vancouver & Whidbey to be very correct.'

The death of Admiral Innes had been followed later in 1786 by that of Captain Marsh, of the *Europa*. He was succeeded by Captain James Vashon, with whom Vancouver was soon on terms of friendship. At this period the health record in the Caribbean was appalling; scurvy and yellow fever took a fearful toll. Vancouver had had first hand experience of this, as a fever epidemic had caused many deaths in the *Fame* on her voyage back to England in 1783. Nevertheless, with ships scarce and young unemployed lieutenants legion, some of the latter were willing to take the risk of serving on the station because deaths in the officer ranks might offer opportunities for promotion. Whether or not Vancouver ever had this in mind we do not know, but deaths and the patronage of his commodore and captain did bring him important promotions. On 24 November 1787 he was commissioned 2nd lieutenant of the *Europa* and less than three months later, on 13 February 1788, he became her First Lieutenant, or second in command.

The *Europa*'s lengthy spell of service in the West Indies, which had lasted the better part of five years, ended in the summer of 1789. Rear Admiral Affleck arrived early in July to take over command from Gardner, and a week later the *Europa* sailed for home. By the middle of September she was back in England.

It had been a highly important commission for Vancouver. He had won promotion and had had considerable experience as second in command of a ship of the line. He had gained the regard and patronage of Sir Alan Gardner, who within a few months would become a member of the Board of Admiralty. And, almost as if coming events had cast their shadow before, he had met in the *Europa* the men whom he would select to serve as his officers on his expedition to the Pacific. Peter Puget had been one of her midshipmen for more than four years; Joseph Baker served in her for a short period. Joseph Whidbey was her master for three years. Finally, Zachary Mudge, already a lieutenant, had gone out to the West Indies with Admiral Affleck, but after a stay of only a few days had returned to England in the *Europa*.

The Northwest Coast

Much had happened on the Northwest Coast during Vancouver's years in the Caribbean. Britain's interest in the Pacific had quickened, and she showed no inclination to recognize Spain's blanket claim to sovereignty of the west coast of the Americas all the way from Cape Horn to the Far North. But the first threat to that sovereignty that worried the Spaniards came not from Britain but from Russia, whose traders were advancing through the Aleutian Islands and were obviously headed for the mainland of Alaska. Spain reacted to alarming reports by sending exploring expeditions north from Mexico in 1774 and 1775. The first was commanded by Juan Pérez, in the frigate *Santiago*. The name of his second in command, Estéban José Martínez, was to become very familiar to Vancouver. The expedition reached Alaskan waters, but did not venture sufficiently far to secure the information about Russian activities that Madrid was seeking. However, on 8 August, when sailing southward along the coast of Vancouver Island, Pérez made a discovery of some significance: he sighted the entrance to Nootka Sound, which he named Surgidero de San Lorenzo. He did not land, but his crew traded with the natives. Later, when supporting their claim to the coast, the Spanish would point out that this discovery anticipated Cook's visit by four years, and they would note further that two silver spoons stolen by the Indians from Martínez were sold to

Cook's expedition, thus providing tangible evidence of a previous Spanish presence.[1]

The *Santiago* sailed northward again in 1775, this time commanded by Bruno de Hezeta and accompanied by the little schooner *Sonora*. Off what is now the coast of Washington the two ships lost contact, and so many of the crew of the *Santiago* were suffering from scurvy that Hezeta decided to return to San Blas. On the way he sighted the mouth of the Columbia River, which he assumed was a bay. Meanwhile the *Sonora* sailed northward in an effort to reach the expedition's objective, latitude 65° N. Mount Edgecumbe was sighted, just beyond 57°, and the *Sonora* struggled on to 58° 30′, before adverse winds, sickness and other difficulties forced her to turn about. It was an astonishing voyage for a ship no more than 33 feet in length and reflected the remarkable qualities of her commander, Juan Francisco de la Bodega y Quadra,[2] whom Vancouver was to know well and appreciate seven years later.

Cook had received some information about these voyages before he sailed from Plymouth in July 1776, but he was quite unaware that Madrid had reacted strongly to the news of his departure and had sent instructions to the Viceroy of New Spain that, if available forces permitted, he was to be intercepted, arrested and imprisoned for infringing Spanish territorial rights. But it was a case of blind man's buff, for the Spaniards had no inkling of Cook's whereabouts, and in any event an expedition was not ready to sail from Mexico until 1779, after Cook had left the Northwest Coast. In Alaskan waters its two ships, one commanded by Quadra, and the other by the commander of the expedition, Ignacio de Arteaga, followed to a great extent in Cook's footsteps, but found no evidence of his presence. Arteaga took formal possession in what is now Port Etches, on Hinchinbrooke Island, at the entrance to Prince William Sound, beyond 60° N – the farthest north point to which the Spaniards ever laid claim by act of possession. He then sailed along the Kenai Peninsula. No Russians were encountered, and it was assumed that their activities were confined to the Aleutians. This reassuring conclusion, and the fact that Spain had become involved in war with Great Britain, resulted in the suspension of plans for any further exploration.

[1] King, Clerke and Samwell all mentioned the purchase in their journals. Cook, *Journals*, III, 1103, 1329, 1401.

[2] Hereafter referred to as Quadra. Strictly speaking he should be referred to as Bodega, but as Vancouver and most books and British documents refer to him as Quadra, this name has been used in the introduction and notes.

The lull that followed was broken by the coming of peace in 1783 and the publication in 1784 of the official account of Cook's third voyage, with its revelation that valuable furs were plentiful on the Northwest Coast of America. Surprisingly, France was the first to take an active interest. Early in 1785 it became known that an elaborate official scientific exploring expedition, more or less on the Cook model, would sail for the Pacific under the command of the Comte de la Pérouse. It put to sea from Brest at the beginning of August. In England it was the mercantile community that responded most promptly. A group headed by Richard Cadman Etches, a London merchant, determined to try and anticipate the arrival of the French on the Northwest Coast. To command their two ships they enlisted the services of Nathaniel Portlock and George Dixon, both of whom were experienced mariners and familiar with the terrain, having sailed (with Vancouver) in the *Discovery* on Cook's last voyage. The Etches venture enjoyed official favour, which may have accounted for the names of its vessels, the *King George* and *Queen Charlotte*, and it had some official assistance in securing trading licences from those two well-entrenched monopolies, the South Seas Company and the East India Company. The former nominally controlled access of British vessels to the western coast of the Americas, where the furs the expedition sought would be obtained; the latter reigned supreme over British trading in China, the market in which they would have to be sold. After some delay the licences were forthcoming, and the ships, like La Pérouse, sailed in August 1785.

The expedition was not intended to be an isolated effort. Etches later placed great emphasis on the fact that it was intended to establish permanent factories on the coast, and that Portlock and Dixon had received specific instructions to this effect. In the light of Cook's discoveries, Nootka Sound was regarded as a likely site for one post, and Prince William Sound seems to have been in mind for another. At no point does anyone seem to have been at all worried about Spain's claim to sovereignty.

Etches believed that he was sponsoring the first British trading expedition to the Northwest Coast, but unknown to him projects were afoot in China and India. In this same month of August 1785 the brig *Harmon*, Captain James Hanna, the pioneer of the maritime fur trade, anchored in Nootka Sound. She had sailed from Macao in April. In December James Strange, who was associated with the East India Company, and hoped to persuade it to participate in the fur trade, left

Bombay with two ships. They arrived at Nootka late in June 1786. And John Meares, representing a Bengal Fur Company, sailed with two ships from Calcutta in March and was off the coast in the late summer. In July the *King George* and *Queen Charlotte* arrived, and as Hanna made a second voyage that year, there were seven traders on the coast in 1786. Most of them, like Etches, cherished the belief that they were first on the scene, but two random interceptions disillusioned them. On 19 July, when in Cook Inlet, to his surprise and chagrin, Portlock heard the report of a gun. 'It was now very evident', he wrote later, 'that some nation or other had got to this place before us, which mortified me not a little.'[1] He had encountered one of the first parties of Russians to reach the inlet. Late the following month, when Strange was in Prince William Sound, the *Sea Otter*, one of Meares' ships, appeared suddenly, to give what Strange termed 'the *coup de grace* to my future Prospect of Success in this line of Life.'[2] Strange returned to India and took no further part in the fur trade, but Meares and the Dixon–Portlock expedition persisted. The *Sea Otter* sailed with furs for China, while Meares himself, in the *Nootka*, not realizing the severity of the winter he would be facing, unwisely decided to pass it in Prince William Sound. Many of his crew died of scurvy, and he was in dire straits when Dixon chanced upon him in the spring. Dixon and Portlock, who had visited the Sandwich Islands with Cook and had experienced their mild climate, had wintered there – the first traders to do so – and had then returned to the coast for a second season. There they were joined by two additional ships sent out by Etches and his associates, the *Prince of Wales* and the *Princess Royal*. The former was commanded by Captain James Colnett, who had sailed with Vancouver in the *Resolution* on Cook's second voyage, and who was later to become embroiled with the Spaniards at Nootka Sound. His officers included Archibald Menzies, the surgeon-botanist who would sail in the *Discovery* with Vancouver, and James Johnstone, who would serve in the *Chatham* and head many of Vancouver's surveying parties.

Portlock and Dixon devoted most of their time to northern waters – Cook Inlet, Prince William Sound, the coast of the Alaskan mainland and the Queen Charlotte Islands. They saw the entrance to Nootka Sound, but weather conditions were unfavourable and they did not enter. Their failure to establish a factory there or elsewhere later became

[1] Nathaniel Portlock, *A Voyage Round the World* (London, 1789) p. 99.
[2] Quoted in Vincent T. Harlow, *The Founding of the Second British Empire 1763–1793*, I (London, 1952), p. 430.

a matter of heated controversy with Etches. He would declare that 'their conduct from leaving the Channel of England was a continual series of misconduct, disobediance of their Instructions, pusilaminity and shameful waste of the property committed to their care.'[1] Dixon contended that none of his crew volunteered to man a post, and that they could not be required to serve, as they had signed on for three years.

When promoting his first expedition, Etches had found a 'warm and strenuous patronizer'[2] in the influential person of Sir Joseph Banks, who identified himself publicly with the project by christening the *Queen Charlotte*. His position as President of the Royal Society, which he held for forty years, kept him in contact with the leading figures in the scientific world, and most of the prominent politicians were well known to him. He had sailed with Cook on his first voyage, and would have sailed with him again if it had been practicable to meet his exorbitant demands for accommodation. Etches turned to him in 1788, when he learned that Portlock and Dixon had not built the projected factories on the Northwest Coast. Banks had supported the plan to establish a convict colony in New South Wales, for which the first Botany Bay fleet had sailed in May 1787, and Etches proposed that a somewhat similar plan should be adopted for Northwest America. When Banks objected that the cost would be too great, Etches replied that the convicts would have to be accommodated somewhere else, if not on the coast, and that the only extra expense involved would be 'a small arm'd vessell commanded by a Lieutenant'[3] that could stand by during construction; and he added the suggestion, interesting in the present connection, that 'After having attended to the forming of the Establishment, she might make a *regular survey* of the whole of the Coast, and the Islands, from King Georges [i.e., Nootka] Sound to Cooks River.'[4] When the Etches proposal first came to light in 1942, F. W. Howay, the authority on the maritime fur trade, hazarded the opinion that 'it may be that we have here the seed out of which' the Vancouver expedition grew.[5]

---

[1] Etches to Banks, 19 May 1792. F. W. Howay (ed.), 'Four letters from Richard Cadman Etches to Sir Joseph Banks', *BCHQ*, VI (1942), p. 137. The original letters are part of the Banks collection in the Sutro Library, San Francisco.

[2] Etches to Banks, 6 May 1790. Tomas Bartroli (ed.), 'Richard Cadman Etches to Sir Joseph Banks', *B.C. Historical News*, VIII (1975), p. 16. The original letters are in the library of the Royal Botanic Gardens at Kew.

[3] This and many others details are given in letters from Etches to Banks, 17 and 20 July 1788. *BCHQ* VI (1942), pp. 130–34.

[4] Etches to Banks, 20 July 1788. *Ibid.*, p. 133.   [5] *Ibid.*, p. 133n.

So much has been written about the fur trade that this has tended to obscure the fact that the British Government had two other interests in the Pacific which, at this time, it regarded as of greater importance. One was the southern whale fishery; the other was freedom of access to the ocean, and the right to establish bases and trading centres on some of the many coasts and islands included in Spain's vast blanket claim to sovereignty. Trade rather than territory had become Britain's main objective; to further it, trading posts and harbours in which ships could refit and their crews refresh themselves had become essential. The British took a dim view of prescriptive rights; they contended that no claim to territory was valid until confirmed by effective occupation. They were willing to keep clear of Spanish settlements, but contended that their ships should have freedom to range along the lengthy stretches of unoccupied coastline in North and South America, and to establish trading and supply centres there.

The southern whale fishery came into being as a result of the revolt of the American colonies. Samuel Enderby, its leading figure, had hitherto operated whaling ships based on Boston; in 1776 he and others dispatched a dozen whalers from London. The South Pacific, where sperm whales were plentiful, soon became the new industry's main objective. There were difficulties with the East India Company, which controlled access to it by way of the Cape of Good Hope, but with official support some concessions were secured, and the fishing limits were gradually extended. In 1786 an Act for the Encouragement of the Southern Whale Fishery stimulated the trade; in 1792 there would be no fewer than 59 ships involved. The whalers soon discovered that seals were plentiful along the South American coasts whose skins and blubber were valuable commodities to supplement oil and whale-bone.

By coincidence, British whaling ships on the Southeast Coast of South America and British fur traders on the Northwest Coast of North America were involved at almost the same time in incidents that related to Spanish territorial claims. In April 1789 the whaling ships *Sappho* and *Elizabeth and Margaret* entered Port Desire, on the Patagonian coast, where their crews proceeded to take seals while the ships secured water and made repairs. Presently a Spanish frigate, accompanied by two other armed vessels, hove in sight, made inquiries about their business and objected to their presence and activities. To questions posed by the Spanish commodore, the British captains replied, in keeping with British doctrine, that they were not aware that the coast belonged to Spain, 'but looked upon it as a desert coast which no country claimed'.

In keeping with Spanish territorial contentions, the Spaniards replied that 'All foreign nations must abstain from frequenting the Seas, Coasts and ports of all these Provinces and their districts as the pretext of fishing whales is invalid'.[1] The whalers were given six days to complete repairs and refreshment, but they were ordered to stop taking seals, and the 7,000 skins they had already gathered were confiscated. In October, after they returned to England, the London Committee of Southern Whalers submitted a strongly worded memorial to the Board of Trade, which held an inquiry and subsequently sent a memorandum to the Foreign Secretary which characterized the Spanish action as 'preposterous' and was intended to be the basis of a representation to Madrid.

It was not known until some months later that in the summer of 1789 British ships had been seized at Nootka Sound by the Spaniards, but there was already considerable uneasiness in London about freedom of trade and settlement on the Northwest Coast. Word had been received that Spain was preparing to send to the Pacific an elaborate scientific exploring expedition analogous to those of Cook and La Pérouse. Under the command of Alejandro Malaspina it sailed from Cadiz at the end of July. The British feared Russian encroachments on the coast as well as Spanish claims. In this same month of July George Dixon sent a letter to Evan Nepean, then Under Secretary of State, that may well have had considerable influence. Dixon had been in touch with Alexander Dalrymple, who was anxious to see the continental fur trade pushed westward from Canada and Hudson Bay to the Pacific Coast, whence furs could be shipped directly to the China market. It was Dalrymple's opinion, Dixon wrote, 'that a Ship should be sent by Government as soon as possible round Cape Horn and a Settlement made on the other Side.... His Reasons for this are. The Russians having got full Possession of Cooks River, [and] Prince Wm. Sound; and he makes no Doubt but they will soon have Settlements to the Southward, as they are in Possession of all the Information Mr. Etches is enabled to give, who is at Petersburg on that Business at the present Time. The Americans last Year had a Ship on the Coast...two were under Portuguese Colours, and I am told of one under Swedish to say nothing of the Spaniards who we are sure are extending their Settlements Northwards.' He concluded: 'Upon the whole, I am afraid if something is not done and that immediately this Valuable Branch of Commerce will be lost to this Country and in Consequence of that Loss the Traders both from Hudson's Bay and Canada will find

[1] Quoted in Harlow, *Founding of the Second British Empire*, I, p. 316.

themselves in a bad Neighbourhood [when they extend their operations to the Pacific Coast].'[1]

Meanwhile Spain, also fearful of a Russian push southward from Alaska, had taken steps to counteract it. The alarm was first raised early in 1786, when La Pérouse visited Chile and there displayed a map that purported to show four permanent Russian posts on the coast, one of them at Nootka Sound. Madrid ordered the Viceroy of New Spain to explore the sites listed by La Pérouse, but owing to various complications, including the death of the Viceroy, the expedition did not leave San Blas until March 1788. A minor event that was to have major consequences was the illness of the intended commander, which necessitated his replacement by a junior, Estéban José Martínez, who had been second in command of the *Santiago* when Spain first sent an exploring party northward in 1774. Martínez sailed with his two ships directly to Prince William Sound and then proceeded westward along the Alaskan coast and islands as far as Unalaska. Russians at the posts visited were friendly and hospitable; gifts were exchanged and each party dined and wined the other. But the Spaniards secretly performed formal acts of possession at six points, and although the rumour that the Russians already had a post at Nootka Sound proved to be groundless, the Spaniards were thoroughly alarmed by hearing that they planned to establish a settlement there in 1789, as soon as additional ships and personnel arrived from Kamchatka.

Upon hearing this report, the new Viceroy immediately ordered a second expedition prepared that would anticipate the Russians, occupy Nootka, and establish a fortified post there. Though some doubts had arisen about Martínez' qualities as a commander, circumstances again made it necessary for him to be given the command. The expedition sailed from San Blas in the middle of February, entered Nootka Sound on May 5, and at once set about the construction of fortifications and barracks.

Unknown to either the Spaniards or the Russians a third plan to establish a post at Nootka was about to be carried into effect. Early in 1789, in China, Meares and the representative of Etches & Company decided to merge their fur trading operations. Etches had never abandoned his hope of seeing a post built at Nootka; in July 1788 he had told Banks that 'an Establishment is what I have long had at Heart, not only as an Individual, but as a National interest.'[2] Meares had been

---

[1] P.R.O., C.O. 42/72, f. 243.
[2] Etches to Banks, 17 July 1788. *BCHQ* VI (1942), p. 131.

at Nootka himself in 1788, had built the schooner *North West America* there, had acquired possession of some land, and had erected a building of some sort, the precise character of which would later become a subject of international dispute. With the formation of the combined concern, a permanent post at Nootka became an immediate objective, and the snow *Argonaut* sailed from China under the command of Captain Colnett, carrying materials, supplies and a work force that included Chinese artisans.

Colnett and Martínez were clearly on a collision course, and their meeting quickly resulted in a resounding clash. Martínez was an ardent nationalist, determined to maintain Spain's claim to the sovereignty of the entire coast from California to Prince William Sound, with a proposal for a Spanish establishment in the Sandwich Islands thrown in for good measure. Colnett held the view that an unoccupied coast was open to all comers and contended that in any event this part of the coast belonged to Britain by virtue of the discoveries of Captain Cook. It was not an argument likely to carry much weight with an aggressive Spaniard who had sailed along the coast in the *Santiago* and had been off the entrance to Nootka Sound in 1774, four years before Cook's visit. Both Colnett and Martínez appear to have been arrogant and quick tempered. It has been suggested that Martínez might merely have compelled Colnett to leave the sound, which the force at his disposal would have enabled him to do. But personal antagonism and the probability that Colnett would simply have established his post elsewhere made him take the extreme course of seizing the *Argonaut* and two of the united concern's other vessels, the *Princess Royal* and *North West America*. Colnett, the two larger ships, and most of their crews were then taken to Mexico.

Some months before any word of these events was received in London the British Government had ordered the preparation of a new exploring expedition which, according to Beaglehole, was first intended 'either to examine sites for colonies in West Africa or to survey the north-west coast of America'.[1] The needs of the southern whale fishery soon took precedence over Africa, and the objectives of the expedition became a search for bases for the whalers in the South Pacific, to be followed by a survey of the Northwest Coast. In both areas it would be supplementing Cook's explorations.

[1] Cook, *Journals*, II, 875. Bell states that the *Discovery* was 'to survey the Mozambique Channel'. Bell, note following 1 April 1791.

A suitable merchant ship of 330 tons under construction in the Thames shipyard of Randall & Brents was purchased, and when she was launched on 19 December 1789 was named *Discovery*. She was not only named after one of Cook's ships but was to be officered by men who had sailed with him. Captain Henry Roberts was appointed to the command; George Vancouver and Richard Hergest were her first and second lieutenants. All three had served on Cook's second and third voyages. Vancouver owed his appointment to Sir Alan Gardner, who, he noted later, 'mentioned me to Lord Chatham [the First Lord] and the Board of Admiralty; and I was solicited to accompany Captain Roberts as his second'.[1]

Presently a companion vessel was chosen. Edward Bell, who served in her as her clerk, relates the circumstances: 'The intention of Government at the first was not to send out two Established Vessels, but to send out in the Discovery the frame of a small Shallop, to be set up when the occasion required it, and to be manned and victuall'd from the Discovery; but after this frame of the small Vessel was stowed away, it was found there was not sufficient room left, for a requisite proportion of Stores & Provisions, this Scheme was therefore abandoned, and it being deem'd necessary for the service on which we were to be employ'd to have a second Vessel smaller than the Discovery, the Chatham Brig, then a Tender lying at Deptford was chosen, as best calculated for the purpose required'.[2] Doubts about the usefulness of the shallop may also have influenced the change. Roberts must have known that on both his second and third voyages Cook had been provided with two small vessels in frame which had never been used.[3]

---

[1] Vancouver, I, vii.

[2] Bell, note after 1 April 1791.

[3] The shallop was of 42 tons, about twice the size of those provided for Cook. Whidbey's log shows that she was stowed on board the *Discovery* between March 8 and 14, and returned to the yard on March 19–20. She was later sent in the transport *Pitt* to Port Jackson, where she was assembled, named *Venus*, and 'was probably the first seagoing vessel launched in Sydney.' For a time she was employed in carrying stores to Tasmania, but in June 1806, while at Port Dalrymple, she was seized by her convict crew 'and carried off to New Zealand where most of the runaways were murdered by the Maoris.' See notes by John Earnshaw in his edition of *A Letter from the South Seas, by a voyager in the Daedalus, 1792* (Cremone, N.S.W., 1957). Earnshaw identified the *Discovery* 'supposed author' of the letter as William House, boatswain of the *Discovery*, who was invalided to Australia in the *Daedalus*, and the identification is certainly correct. In 1793, when about to explore Portland Inlet, Vancouver was to express regret 'that we had not one or two vessels of thirty or forty tons burthen, calculated as well for rowing as for sailing, to assist us in this intricate investigation, by which means much dispatch would have been given to our survey, and our labours would have been carried out with much less danger and hardship than we had constantly endured.' Vancouver, II, 329.

Roberts joined the *Discovery* on 1 January 1790 and Vancouver and Hergest 'came on board' on the 6th. For the next few months the fitting out and provisioning of the *Discovery* and *Chatham* proceeded steadily. The proposed expedition seems to have attracted some attention; in April the *Discovery* was visited by both the Duke of Clarence and the Duke of York.[1] But by that time plans for her employment had been changed drastically. Late in January the first scanty news of the seizures at Nootka had reached London. The British Government reacted sharply, but only the national honour seemed to have been damaged, and the release of the ships and a suitable apology were expected to resolve the matter. But over the next couple of months the broader issue of Spain's blanket claim to the Northwest Coast came to the fore, and a tentative decision was taken to challenge it directly by establishing a British post on the Northwest Coast. Documents drafted late in March 1790 give details of the proposal. One notified Roberts that the service for which the *Discovery* was originally intended had been postponed, that she would be 'employed on a particular Service in a more distant part of the world', and that initially he was to make his way to Port Jackson, the convict settlement in New South Wales.[2] A long draft dispatch from W. W. Grenville, the Secretary of State (soon to be created Baron Grenville) to Governor Arthur Phillip of New South Wales, informed him that the *Discovery*, accompanied by the much larger *Gorgon* instead of the *Chatham*, would be proceeding thither, and that the two ships would then 'be employed upon an expedition on the north-west coast of America' one purpose of which would be to form a settlement 'for assistance of his Majesty's subjects in the prosecution of the fur trade'. Initially it was not expected to consist of more than thirty persons; these might include 'a few of the most deserving of the convicts'. Defence was not forgotten; at least half the settlers were to be soldiers. Commodore Cornwallis, commanding the East Indies Station, was being instructed to detach a frigate, which would rendezvous with the *Discovery* and *Gorgon* at the Sandwich Islands, take command of them, and accompany them to the Northwest Coast.[3]

The full scope of the plan was revealed only in secret instructions intended for the captain of the frigate. The Spaniards had established

---

[1] Whidbey, April 1 and May 1, 1790.

[2] Draft dispatch to Roberts, March 1790. P.R.O., H.O. 28/61, f. 249.

[3] Grenville to Phillip, March 1790. Printed in full in *Historical Records of Australia*, Series I, 1 (Sydney, 1914), pp. 312–14.

themselves at Nootka Sound; no doubt with a view to avoiding a pointless confrontation the British settlement should be farther north, in Fitzhugh Sound or Queen Charlotte Sound. It was understood that Malaspina's expedition had been sent from Spain 'for the purpose of...exploring the Coast contiguous to Nootka Sound'. The British had a much more comprehensive survey in mind, but proposed to omit that part of the coast. The ships were to 'examine the whole of the Coast Northward from the Latitude of 51 degrees [the latitude of Queen Charlotte Sound], to Cook's River, which is in the Latitude of 60 degrees, and South from the Latitude of 49 degrees, to Cape Mendocino in the Latitude of 40 degrees, carefully examining such Rivers or inlets within the said limits, as you shall judge likely to afford a communication with the interior part of the Continent'. It was pointed out that the *Discovery* had been 'fitted, stored and appointed for the purpose of executing Nautical Surveys' and that she was 'commanded by an officer [Roberts] peculiarly qualified for such an undertaking.'

But there was to be no compromise on trading or freedom of access to the coast. The captain was informed that a ship had been seized by Martínez at Nootka, and if he found that 'on the pretence of a claim asserted by the Crown of Spain to an exclusive Trade on that coast' Spanish ships had since 'captured any Ships or Vessels fitted out by His Majesty's subjects, or committed any other act of hostility on their persons or property' he was commanded to 'demand immediate restitution of such Ships or property, and the release of their Crews if they should be confined, His Majesty being determined to support the right of His subjects to a free and uninterrupted intercourse with the whole of the American Coast lying to the North of the Latitude of 40 degrees, except such parts only as may be actually settled and occupied by any other European power'. Finally, great care was to be taken 'not to molest, disturb, or afford any just ground of complaint to the Subjects of His Catholic Majesty', but if any attack were made on his squadron, or on British ships under his protection, or on the settlement, he was 'to resist it to the utmost, and...endeavour to destroy or capture the Vessels making such attack'.[1]

The resemblance between this project and the suggestion made to Banks by Etches in 1788 may have been a coincidence, but this seems unlikely. Banks and Grenville were friends; knowing Banks' great interest in exploration, Grenville consulted him about plans for other

[1] For the complete text see P.R.O., H.O. 28/61, ff. 273–279v.

expeditions and no doubt discussed this project with him as well. Grenville was in a key position, both personally and officially. He was a cousin of William Pitt, the Prime Minister, and of John Pitt, second Earl of Chatham, who was First Lord of the Admiralty. He himself was the Secretary of State, through whom cabinet decisions regarding exploring expeditions were transmitted to the Board of Admiralty and thence to the Navy Board. As we shall see, Banks, through Grenville, was to have much to do with the arrangements for the Vancouver expedition when plans for it were being finalized in 1791.

In the event, none of the dispatches drafted in March 1790 were sent. Early in April John Meares arrived in London, and it became known that not one but three British-owned ships had been seized at Nootka. Meares had left China as soon as he learned of the seizures, and by the middle of April his famous memorial was in the hands of the Government. This set forth his grievances and gave what was not recognized at first as being a greatly exaggerated impression of the losses suffered by Etches, himself and their associates. While Meares approached the Government, Etches turned to Banks, expressing confidence that he would support the justness of their claim for compensation not only for 'the immediate property seiz'd' but also for their 'great and certain prospects'. Remembering Banks' interest in exploration, he referred to the 'Importance of the discoveries' they had made and to 'the great probability' that they would have been able to reduce 'the prospect of a [Northwest] passage to a certainty' within 'a Season or two'.[1]

In the light of Meares' charges relations with Spain deteriorated, and on April 30 the Cabinet ordered mobilization of the formidable fleet that became known as the Spanish Armament. Inevitably the departure of the *Discovery* for the Pacific was cancelled and by the middle of May most of her complement were being transferred to combat ships. Sir Alan Gardner, Vancouver's friend and patron, left the Admiralty temporarily to take command of the *Courageux*, a 74 in the Channel Fleet. Vancouver joined her as 3rd lieutenant, but by September he had been promoted to 1st lieutenant. Whidbey, once again serving with Vancouver, became her master.

Though preparing energetically for war, the Government was aware

---

[1] Etches to Banks, 6 May 1790. *B.C. Historical News*, VIII (1975), p. 15. Two years later, in a letter to Banks dated 19 May 1792, Etches was to advance the extraordinary claim that Colnett had 'made a complete survey of the N.W. Coast from 38 to 60 N. lat'. *BCHQ* VI (1942), p. 138.

that it had caught Spain at an awkward moment, when she was unlikely to be able to muster allies, and they were hopeful that a swift show of strength and a firm stand would produce the concessions they were seeking. An able diplomat, Alleyne Fitzherbert (who would be created Baron St Helens for his services) was sent to Madrid to take charge of negotiations there, and five months later, on 28 October 1790, the Nootka Sound Convention was signed. It gave Great Britain virtually everything she sought. The national honour was vindicated: the ships seized were already in the process of being repatriated, and Spain agreed to compensate Meares and Etches for their financial losses. Early in the dispute Spain had herself raised the matter of the southern whale fishery, an activity in which she took little interest, but which she claimed was being used as a screen for illicit trade with the Spanish colonies. The convention gave the whalers the liberty of action they wanted, and Britain agreed to see that illicit trade was held in check. As for the Northwest Coast, the convention made fatal inroads on Spain's prescriptive claims to exclusive sovereignty. Henceforth British and Spanish subjects were to be equally free to trade and establish posts anywhere north of the areas already occupied by Spain.[1]

One provision to which the Spaniards agreed only with the greatest reluctance was an undertaking to restore 'the buildings and tracts of land' that Meares claimed he and his associates had possessed at Nootka Sound in 1788, and which allegedly had been taken from them by Martínez in 1789. From Britain's point of view this was a vital matter, for, in the words of Vincent Harlow, 'The only effectual way of countering the Spanish claim to the exclusive possession of the North-West Coast (up to 61° N.) was to demonstrate that British subjects had actually formed an establishment there and to insist upon the traditional British argument that this constituted a valid title, transcending claims of prescriptive right which were not so supported by occupation.'[2] To secure clear evidence of this from Meares proved to be difficult, and uncertainty as to precisely what buildings and tracts of land had been involved complicated matters greatly for the British Government and later presented difficulties for Vancouver.

One point of importance was left undetermined: the convention did not set the northern limit of Spanish sovereignty on the coast. The

---

[1] For the text of this and the later conventions relating to Nootka Sound see William Ray Manning, *The Nootka Sound Controversy* (New York, 1966), a facsimile reprint of part XVI of the *Annual Report* of the American Historical Association for 1904.

[2] Harlow, *Founding of the Second British Empire* I, p. 464.

British had made some mention of 40° north latitude, and for a time the Spaniards had the Strait of Juan de Fuca in mind. They recognized that it would not be possible to carry the limit as far north as Nootka Sound, but they did not give up easily. As Vancouver was to discover when he arrived on the coast, the years 1790–1792 were the period of greatest activity in Spanish exploration, both in the Strait of Juan de Fuca and north of Nootka Sound.

Projects and Preparations

Preparations for an expedition to the Pacific were resumed promptly after the signing of the Nootka Convention. Chief emphasis was now to be placed on the Northwest Coast. The Government was anxious to know much more about the area to which it had gained free access, and to make that interest evident. In addition, it had become necessary to send an emissary to Nootka to receive back the 'buildings and tracts of land' that had been seized by Martínez in 1789, and which, according to the term of the convention, were to be 'restored' to British possession.

During the war scare the *Discovery* and *Chatham* had served as receiving ships for impressed seamen. On November 17 the Navy Board instructed the Deptford Yard to put them 'into a proper state to proceed on a Voyage to remote parts.' The next day this was followed by an urgent order 'to hasten the fitting [of] the Discovery and Chatham Tender as much as possible giving them the preference to all other Works.'[1] Captain Roberts had continued in command, but a change was in the offing. Vancouver had been called to London, where he reported to the Admiralty on November 20. No doubt his appointment as commander of the expedition was discussed immediately, but it did not become official for nearly a month. Roberts was notified on December 13 that the *Discovery* would be paid off the next day, and on the 15th Vancouver received his commission as her new captain. Gardner had probably recommended him, but the change seems to have been due to a decision to revive the original proposal for a voyage to the coast of Africa. A note from Archibald Menzies to Banks, undated but certainly written at this time, is relevant: 'About three o'Clock this afternoon I saw Capt. Roberts – he told me that some new arrangement had taken place at the Treasury in consequence of which he resigned the Command of the Discovery to Captain

[1] P.R.O., Adm 106/2625.

Vancouver (formerly 1st Lieut. of her)...Capt Roberts is to have another Vessel, & to go out in the Spring'.[1]

One person greatly concerned about the change in command was Archibald Menzies, who had been engaged by the Treasury as a naturalist for the voyage as it had been first planned in 1789; whether or not he would be re-engaged to accompany Vancouver remained to be seen. But he agreed that it was desirable that the *Discovery* should be recommissioned, for it meant that 'Captain Vancouver had the pleasure of naming his own officers & entering the full complement of Seamen, an indulgence that ought always to be allowed on any similar occasion, as the success of an Expedition of this nature may greatly depend on the harmony & good understanding which is more likely to subsist among those of the Commanders choosing'.[2]

When selecting his officers Vancouver looked back to the Caribbean and the *Europa*; all three of his lieutenants and the *Discovery*'s master had served in her – Mudge only briefly, but Peter Puget, Joseph Baker and Joseph Whidbey for several years. The lieutenants were a young group; Mudge was only 20, but he had gained his commission in 1789, whereas Puget and Baker, the 2nd and 3rd lieutenants, though a few years older, only received theirs just before they joined the *Discovery*. Mudge had entered the Navy at the age of 10 as servant to Sir John Jervis (later Earl St. Vincent), who continued to take an interest in his career. He had been a lieutenant in the *Perseus* in the Irish Channel during the Nootka crisis. Puget had made a voyage to the East Indies, lasting eighteen months, as a midshipman in the Indiaman *Prince William Henry*. By the time he returned, in June 1790, the *Discovery* was serving as a receiving ship and he joined her as a master's mate. In November he passed his examinations for lieutenant. Details of Baker's employment after he left the *Europa* are lacking, but he received his commission on December 18. Whidbey, at 35 one of the oldest men

---

[1] Banks Collection, Sutro Library, San Francisco. PN1:16. As this note indicates, Roberts was not in the West Indies at this time, as is usually stated, with the implication that he was superseded because of his absence. That Africa was to be on the itinerary of Roberts' expedition is shown by a letter from Menzies to Banks written at Simon's Bay on 10 August 1791. Francis Masson, the botanist, then making his second visit to South Africa to gather plants for the Royal Botanic Gardens at Kew, had accompanied Menzies on some of his own excursions there. Reporting this to Banks, Menzies added: 'If Capt. Robert's Expedition should take place I think Mr. Mason would be the best hand to accompany him, as he is so well acquainted with the African plants'. Brabourne Papers, Mitchell Library, Sydney. Vancouver was acquainted with Masson, as the latter had made his first voyage to the Cape, in 1772, with Cook in the *Resolution*, in which Vancouver was serving.

[2] Menzies, preliminary note to his journal.

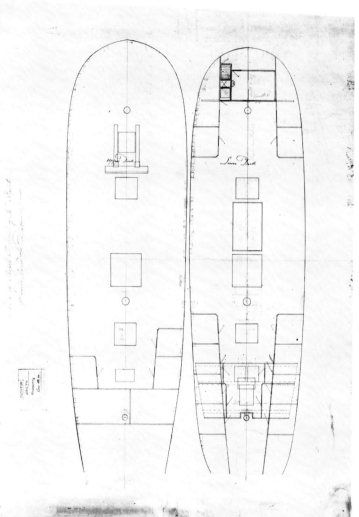

Plate 2. Plan of the *Discovery*.

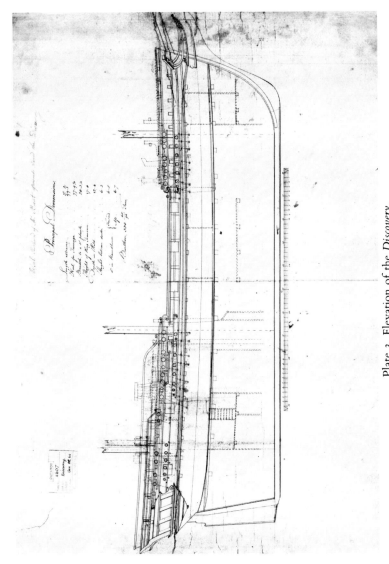

Plate 3. Elevation of the *Discovery*.

Plate 4. The *Discovery* as a convict hulk at Deptford in 1828.

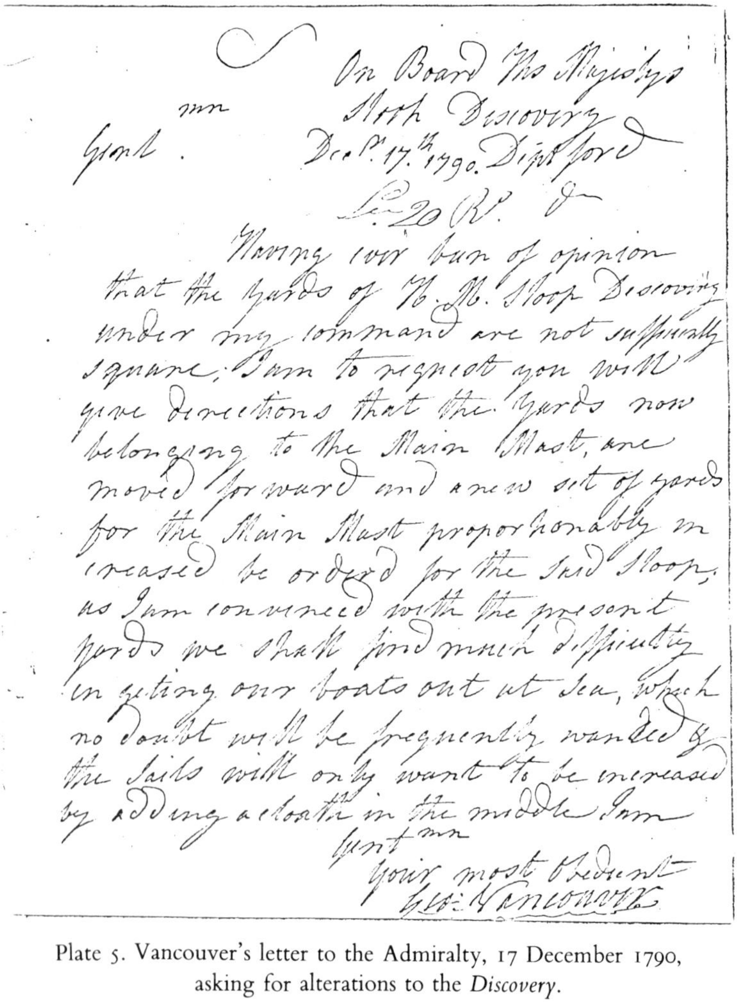

On Board His Majestys
Sloop Discovery
Dec.r 17.th 1790. Deptford

Gent.mn

Having your Board of opinion
that the yards of H. M. Sloop Discovery
under my command are not sufficially
square; I am to request you will
give directions that the yards now
belonging to the Main Mast, are
moved forward and a new set of yards
for the Main Mast proportionably in
creased be ordered for the Said Sloop,
as I am convinced with the present
yards we shall find much difficulty
in geting our boats out at Sea, which
no doubt will be frequently wanted &
the Sails will only want to be increased
by adding a cloath in the middle I am
Gent.mn
your most Obedient
Geo: Vancouver

Plate 5. Vancouver's letter to the Admiralty, 17 December 1790,
asking for alterations to the *Discovery*.

in the ship, but one upon whom Vancouver depended heavily, returned to the *Discovery* in his former capacity of master as soon as Vancouver assumed command. All four were to serve him loyally and well in the strenuous years that lay ahead.

It seems likely that Vancouver had little if any say in the selection of the officers of the *Chatham*, none of whom is known to have had any previous association with him. Her commander, Lieutenant William R. Broughton, aged 28, may have owed his appointment to the influence of Captain John (later Admiral) Knight. As a midshipman Broughton had served under him in the American Revolutionary War, and had been taken prisoner with him in 1776, when they attempted to destroy a schooner that had run ashore on the coast of Massachusetts. He had just served again under Knight, who was captain of the *Victory*, in the Spanish Armament.

About Broughton's second in command, Lieutenant James Hanson, little seems to be known except that he had been promoted to that rank in 1790. By contrast, a good deal is known about James Johnstone, master of the *Chatham*. He had been in the Navy since 1778, and had served for a time in the West Indies, after which he was a midshipman and master's mate in the *Assistance* on the Halifax Station. He then joined the merchant service and sailed in the *Prince of Wales*, commanded by Captain Colnett, which Etches and his associates were sending to the Pacific to participate in the maritime fur trade. She spent the summers of 1787 and 1788 on the Northwest Coast, and then proceeded to China, where Johnstone assumed command and brought her home to England. Returning to the Navy, he was given charge of a squadron of ships in ordinary at Plymouth. His knowledge of the Northwest Coast would obviously be of value to Vancouver's expedition, but he owed his appointment to Lord Chatham, First Lord, and Philip Stephens, Secretary of the Admiralty, who, Menzies states, 'have his interest at heart, and are not unacquainted with his merits, by their being so solicitous for his coming out on the Voyage'. Lord Chatham had made 'a particular request' to Vancouver that Johnstone should have 'the preference for being first promoted', and this request Vancouver duly honored when Hanson left the *Chatham* at Nootka Sound. But later, when Vancouver sent Broughton to England with dispatches, and an opportunity for a second promotion occurred, Vancouver gave the command of the *Chatham* to Puget and not to Johnstone, as Menzies thought he should have done, 'for besides his being equally capable to Command her, his [Johnstone's] long experience & great knowledge of this coast in general, and of Marine Surveying in particular of which the other knows little or nothing, should give a decided preference in his favour'.[1] But Vancouver really had no alternative; Puget was the senior lieutenant, and at the time Johnstone held that rank only in an acting capacity.

Vancouver certainly recognized Johnstone's abilities and made good use of them. When it became evident that a survey of the coast could only be carried out effectively by parties sent off in the ships' boats, he depended heavily on Whidbey, but by the second and third seasons Johnstone was commanding almost as many of the excursions. Some 46 boat parties were sent out, and Whidbey and Johnstone between them led 38 of them. In view of Menzies' remark about Puget's deficiencies, it is interesting to note that although he was in charge of many of the survey parties during the first season, he was almost invariably accompanied by either Whidbey or Johnstone.

Menzies could speak with authority about Johnstone, for he had served with him both in and out of the Navy. Menzies came from a Scottish family of gardeners and botanists, but in addition to botanical studies at the Royal Botanic Garden in Edinburgh and at the University of Edinburgh, he had qualified as a surgeon. He entered the Navy as assistant surgeon of the *Nonsuch*, a ship that took part in Rodney's great victory over de Grasse in 1782. He then served in the *Assistance* on the Halifax Station from 1783 to 1786, where Johnstone was a shipmate. In the course of his travels Menzies collected plants and seeds whenever opportunity offered and in 1784, at the suggestion of Dr. John Hope, professor of botany at Edinburgh, he sent a parcel of seeds to Banks. A correspondence followed and other parcels were sent, the last from Chatham, where the *Assistance* was being paid off in August 1786. From Chatham Menzies also sent a note to Banks which read in part: 'I am informed that there is a Ship a private adventurer now fitting out at Deptford to go round the World – should I be so happy as to be appointed Surgeon of her, it will at least gratify one of my greatest earthly ambitions & afford one of the best opportunities of collecting Seeds & other objects of Natural History for you & the rest of my friends.'[2] The ship was the *Prince of Wales*, bound for the Northwest Coast. Menzies was aware that Banks advised the King on the development of the Royal Botanic Gardens at Kew, and that he was

---

[1] Menzies to Banks, Monterey, 14 Jan. 1793. Brabourne Papers, Mitchell Library, Sydney.

[2] Menzies to Banks, 21 August 1786. Royal Botanic Gardens, Kew.

sending trained collectors to distant places to secure new plants and seeds. Banks duly used his influence with Etches to secure him the desired appointment. On the *Prince of Wales* Menzies found Johnstone, and by the time the ship arrived back in England in July 1789, they had been shipmates, first in the *Assistance* and then in the *Prince of Wales*, for the better part of six years.

Menzies soon heard about the expedition that was expected to sail shortly in the *Discovery*, under the command of Captain Roberts. Banks was also interested, and used his influence to have the Treasury appoint Menzies to accompany it as naturalist. Then came the postponement due to the controversy with Spain and the changes in plan and command when preparations were resumed. Uncertain of his position, Menzies 'requested leave of the Treasury to go out as Surgeon of the Discovery, promising at the same time that my vacant hours from my professional charge, should be chiefly employd in their service, in making such collections & observations as might tend to elucidate the natural history of the Voyage'. To this the Treasury agreed, but for reasons unknown to Menzies Vancouver objected, and he sailed in the *Discovery* as supernumerary naturalist and botanist, as had been intended originally.

Vancouver's objections may well have been due to irritation with some action by Banks, who was apt to assume that if he took an interest in a project this gave him the right to interfere. Amongst other things a glass frame twelve feet by eight had been built on the after part of the *Discovery*'s quarter deck and furnished with boxes and flower pots in which Menzies was expected to bring home new and curious plants for the gardens at Kew. 'This Frame', Menzies noted, 'was built from a particular plan of Sir Joseph Banks Bart. who in his great attention to this & every other accommodation showd such a particular zeal for the success of my department as deserves my most grateful acknowledgement.'[1] At times this 'great attention' may well have been irritating for Vancouver, just as Banks' demands for accommodation on the *Resolution* had irked Cook in 1772. Menzies was very much Banks' man; the instructions that came to him just before the *Discovery* sailed were signed by Banks, who had drafted them at the request of Lord Grenville. And Banks had arranged that in order to safeguard Menzies' position the Lords of the Admiralty should send Vancouver specific instructions, outlining the facilities he was to accord Menzies – instructions of which Menzies knew nothing at the time. At some point

· ¹ Menzies, December 1790.

[1] Menzies, December 1790.

Vancouver evidently met Banks with objections instead of the deference he felt was his due, for in a letter that followed Menzies to Nootka Sound Banks wrote: 'How Captain Vancouver will behave to you is more than I can guess unless I was to judge by his conduct towards me which was not such as I am used to receiving from Persons in his situation'; but, Banks added, if he should place obstacles in Menzies' way 'the instances whatever they are will of course appear as they happened in your Journal which as it will be a justification to you will afford ground for impeaching the Propriety of his conduct which for your sake I shall not Fail to make use of'.[1]

As will appear, late in the voyage both the glass frame and Menzies' journal were to be causes of serious differences with Vancouver, but for the most part the two got along well. Ironically, the illness of the surgeon of the *Discovery* compelled Vancouver to conscript the services of Menzies and accord him the status of surgeon-naturalist which he had sought in the first place.

With the possible exception of the two surgeons, Menzies was the only man in the two ships who would today be considered to have had training in science. In this respect the expedition differed from Cook's. True, Cook found scientists a bothersome lot, and each succeeding expedition had had fewer of them. Nevertheless the ships' companies on the third voyage had included an astronomer sent by the Board of Longitude, a botanist nominated (like Menzies) by Banks, and an official artist. In addition, Lieut. James King and William Anderson, surgeon of the *Resolution*, had exceptional backgrounds and were very well informed and perceptive observers. On second thoughts, Vancouver asked for an astronomer, but William Gooch, chosen for the appointment by the Board of Longitude, was killed before he could join the expedition. For the pictorial record Vancouver had to depend upon the considerable but amateur talents of his officers and midshipmen. Mudge and Baker each produced a sketch of two, but most of the surviving drawings are the work of midshipmen John Sykes, Henry Humphrys and Thomas Heddington.

The descriptions of distant lands and primitive peoples scattered through Vancouver's narrative reflect this lack of trained observers. Vancouver intended to supplement them in a concluding chapter, but John Vancouver, who completed the narrative after his brother's death, found that most of the notes recording his 'many curious observations' were 'too concise and too unconnected for me to attempt any

[1] Banks to Menzies, 10 August 1791. Brabourne Papers, Mitchell Library, Sydney.

arrangement of them'.[1] Many of the details relating to natural history in the printed text seem to have been derived from Menzies' journal or from Menzies himself. And it may be added that even Menzies' journal is far from being a complete record of his observations. The surviving manuscript is a revised copy, intended for publication, and while it includes many notes and comments on natural history, these can only be a selection from the much more voluminous memoranda he must have jotted down along the way.

The authorized complement of the *Discovery* included only three master's mates and six midshipmen, but the number of 'young gentlemen' on board when she sailed was fifteen. To avoid exceeding the authorized number some of them were ranked as able seamen and all of them moved from one category to another in the course of the voyage. Appointments as midshipmen were usually secured by influence, and there were few if any exceptions in the *Discovery*. The Hon. Thomas Pitt, who was to cause Vancouver much trouble, was perhaps the best example. He was the son and heir of Thomas Pitt, Baron Camelford, who was closely related to the Prime Minister and the First Lord of the Admiralty. While young Thomas was voyaging with Vancouver his sister, Anne, would marry Lord Grenville. The Hon. Charles Stuart was a son of the Earl of Bute. Thomas Manby was a friend of the Marquis of Townshend and had found a naval patron in Rear Admiral Leverson Gower, in whose flagship, the *Illustrious*, he had served during the Nootka crisis. Both Robert Barrie and Henry Humphrys were nephews of Sir Alan Gardner. John Stewart was the nephew of Rear-Admiral Stewart. Spelman Swaine was a protégé of the Earl of Hardwicke. John Sykes was the son of James Sykes, the Navy Agent in London who looked after Vancouver's affairs. (Both Swaine and Sykes had been in the *Courageux* when Gardner commanded her and Vancouver was her First Lieutenant, which may also have influenced their appointments.) The name of Volant Vashon Ballard suggests that he was related to Captain Vashon, who had commanded the *Europa* in the West Indies, and Robert Pigot may well have been related to Admiral Pigot, who arrived in the Caribbean to become commander-in-chief shortly after Vancouver joined the *Fame*. No doubt similar links would explain the other appointments if the details were known.

The complement of the *Discovery* was 84. In addition she carried a lieutenant of marines, a corporal and fourteen privates, bringing the

[1] Vancouver, I, xxxii.

total to 100. Of the crew, 38 were rated as able seamen, but this number included six midshipmen and a 'widow's man', a fictitious personage whose pay and maintenance accumulated for the benefit of the widows' pension fund. Menzies, who was not entered on the official muster roll until he became acting surgeon in September 1792, kept the actual total to 100. The authorized complement of the *Chatham* was 37, plus a sergeant of marines and seven privates, making 45 in all.

In an age when many of the seamen had been forced into service by a press gang, desertions were numerous. Before the ships set sail from Falmouth the *Discovery* had lost sixteen men, and five had 'run' (as desertion was termed in the muster roll) from the *Chatham*. Surprisingly, each ship lost a warrant officer. Richard Richards, the boatswain, absconded from the *Discovery*, and it was soon found that there were substantial deficiencies in the boatswain's stores. The *Chatham* lost her carpenter. The total of 21 deserters from the two ships may seem high, but it was proportionately considerably lower than the loss suffered by Cook when he was setting out on his third voyage. In 1776 there were 36 desertions from the *Resolution* and 22 from the *Discovery*, or 58 in all, from complements totalling 182, excluding marines. Vancouver's loss was 21 from a total of 121.

In addition to the desertions, ten men were discharged from Vancouver's *Discovery* and five from the *Chatham* owing to illness, unsuitability, or assignment elsewhere. One seaman had been lost overboard from the *Discovery* on the passage from the Thames. A total of thirty-seven replacements thus had to be secured before the ships finally sailed on their great voyage.

Vancouver joined the *Discovery* at Deptford Yard on 16 December 1790. Although she had not been dismantled when the expedition was postponed, a good deal remained to be done before she would be ready for sea. Vancouver evidently had one or two alterations in mind that he was specially anxious to have made, notably to the yards of the fore and main masts, which he considered were 'not sufficiently square'. The day after he assumed command he asked the Navy Board to 'give directions that the Yards now belonging to the Main Mast are moved forward and a new set of Yards for the Main Mast proportionately increased be order'd'. He had a sound reason for the request, for he was convinced that 'with the present Yards we shall find much difficulty in getting our boats out at sea, which no doubt will be frequently wanted'. Lest the Navy Board (which ordered the changes to be made immediately) should be deterred by the possibility that they might necessitate new sails, he added that the present suit would 'only want to be increased by adding a cloath in the middle'.[1]

One defect Vancouver did not succeed in having corrected. The head of the ship was 'materially too slight and too low' with the result that it was damaged by heavy seas before she reached Teneriffe and much of it had been washed away entirely by the time she arrived at the Cape of Good Hope. 'This business', Vancouver reported from the Cape, 'was frequently mentioned by the Officers of the Discovery on her former equipment, as also at her late fitting out, but was entirely discountenanced by the Officers of the Dock-Yard; as likewise I believe, by some persons at the Navy Board.'[2] The head and bowsprit were raised somewhat at the Cape, but this did not end the problem, as the head continued to give trouble throughout the voyage. Another instance of shoddy refitting, this time in the *Chatham*, came to light when a wave smashed against her stern not long after the ships left the Cape of Good Hope. Johnstone, her master, commented: 'Nothing could appear more insufficient than the part that was stive in, those who had fitted it could never have dreamt that it was to be exposed to the least force. It was nothing but a mere blind, a piece of half inch deal just kept in its place by a Small ledge on each Side, equally Slight.'[3]

In one of the last entries in his journal Cook charged that 'the cordage and canvas or indeed any other stores made use of in the Navy' were not 'of equal goodness with those in general use in the Merchant service'. Most of the time this did not become apparent because the quality of items was 'seldom tried, for things were generally Condemned or converted to some other use by such time as they are half worn out. It is only on such [very extended] Voyages as these we have an opportunity to make the trial where every thing is obliged to be worn to the very utmost.'[4] Vancouver would have endorsed this opinion; but some things failed very early. A new cable in the *Chatham* parted the first time it was used, costing her the loss of an anchor, and later all the similar cables that had been supplied were replaced. Loss of anchors was a most serious misfortune, owing to the impossibility of replacing them. Vancouver was shaken in July 1793 when an anchor that 'appeared to have been composed of very bad materials, and to have been very ill wrought' broke when it was dropped and struck

[1] Vancouver to the Navy Board, 17 December 1790. P.R.O., Adm 106/1434.
[2] Vancouver to the Admiralty, Teneriffe, 6 May 1791. P.R.O., Adm 1/2628 f. 631.
[3] Johnstone, 21 August 1971.   [4] Cook, *Journals*, III, 482.

a rock. 'Such were the anchors with which we were supplied for executing this tedious, arduous, and hazardous service....A loss of confidence in the stability of these our last resources, must always be attended with the most painful reflections that can occur in a maritime Life.'[1]

The *Discovery*, of 330 65/94 tons burthen, was larger than Cook's ship of the same name but considerably smaller than the 462-ton *Resolution*. According to a sheer plan her extreme length was 99' 2", length on keel 77' 9⅝", breadth 28' 3¼" and depth of hold 12' 4". Height between decks was 6' 2", increasing to 6' 7" in the roundhouse, at the after end of the quarter deck. She was copper-fastened, sheathed with plank and coppered over to give maximum protection to her hull. When well laden her draught was about 15' 6".[2] Her armament consisted of ten 4-pounders and ten swivels. Vancouver notes that 'construction of her upper works, for the sake of adding to the comfort of the accommodations...produced an unsightly appearance, and gave rise to various opinions unfavorable to her qualities as a sea-boat', but these fears proved groundless.[3] Bell states that 'her accommodations for the Officers & Ships Company were excellent'[4] – a much more important consideration than mere appearance on a long voyage in unfrequented seas. Johnstone commented on her 'Projecting Sides', which afforded 'great Convenience & Room for working'.[5] In sum, she was evidently very well suited for the voyage she was about to undertake.

It was quite otherwise with the *Chatham*, which was abused by most of those who had much to do with her. Johnstone, her master, described

---

[1] Vancouver, II, 309. The *Discovery* was equipped originally with ten anchors. Whidbey records their weights, and as these details are rarely available they are given here.

Cwt	grs	lb	Cwt	grs	lb
21	2	0	13	1	1
21	1	7	8	0	0
21	1	7	7	0	12
21	0	6	5	0	23
20	3	7	3	2	7

The anchors stowed in the bow were referred to as bower anchors, and the 'best bower' was usually the largest of them.

[2] John Charnock gave slightly different dimensions in *A History of Marine Architecture* (London, 1802), III, 263: length on gun deck 96', length on keel 79', breadth 27' 3¾", depth of hold 14'; tonnage 337.

[3] Vancouver, I, p. 2.

[4] Bell, note after April 1, 1791.

[5] Johnstone to J. Berteret, Cape of Good Hope, 12 August 1791. Abstract in Brabourne Papers, Mitchell Library, Sydney.

her as 'without a doubt the most improper Vessel that could have been pitched upon...& for sailing we have not been a match for the Dullest Merchant Vessel we have met with'.[1] Bell referred to her sourly on one occasion as 'our *Dung Barge*'. She was a brig-rigged tender and seems to have been chosen simply because she was idle and available. Charnock gives her dimensions as length on keel 53' $1\frac{3}{4}''$, breadth 21' $6\frac{3}{4}''$, depth of hold 10', and tonnage 131.[2] She was armed with four 3-pounders and six swivels. She was both very crank and a poor sailer. When bringing her round from the Thames to Falmouth, Broughton found her so unstable that he was anxious to secure additional ballast there. Vancouver, impatient to get away, sought a temporary solution by transferring 662 rounds of 4-pounder shot to her hold, but this proved to be quite inadequate. Bell records that when near Madeira she encountered 'such a sudden violent Squall...that we were laid on our Beam ends – and it was expected by many that either the Vessel would upset, or the Masts be carried over the side however being expert in taking in the Sails and getting her before the Wind, the danger was [soon] over'.[3] In the light of this experience about 23 tons of shingle ballast were taken on board at the Canaries. This improved her stability but had little effect upon her rate of sailing, which was a constant source of exasperation to Vancouver. The logs record innumerable signals urging her to put on more sail, to which she was able to make little response. In spite of this, when by choice or by stress of weather the two ships became separated, the *Chatham* had a disconcerting habit of invariably arriving at the appointed rendezvous before the *Discovery*.

Their rate of sailing naturally depended upon wind and weather. Puget estimated the distance from Falmouth to Teneriffe to be 1920 miles, which was traversed at an average rate of 74 miles per day. This was a slow passage, which Vancouver blamed on the poor sailing of the *Chatham*. From Teneriffe to the Cape of Good Hope, 5701 miles, the average daily run rose to over 93 miles, and from the Cape of Good Hope to New Holland (Australia), 5119 miles, it increased sharply to 122 miles. Across the Tasman Sea the ships attained an average of just short of 150 miles per day. But such runs were quite exceptional.[4]

---

[1] *Ibid.*

[2] Charnock, *History of Marine Architecture*, III, 1802, 275.

[3] Bell, April 1791.

[4] The best daily run noted for the *Discovery* was 178 miles, on 27 November 1791, when sailing alone between New Zealand and Tahiti. This compares well with Cook's *Resolution*, which covered 183 miles in 24 hours in November 1774 – according to Clerke, 'the greatest distance we've ever reach'd in this ship.' Cook, *Journals*, II, 583n.

The Admiralty had some expectation that Vancouver would be able to complete the survey of the coast in two seasons, but the capacity of his ships was limited, and a supply ship was to be sent out to meet him at the Sandwich Islands, or, failing that, at Nootka. On 29 March 1791, just three days before Vancouver left Falmouth, the Admiralty instructed the Navy Board to charter a suitable vessel as storeship. The choice fell upon the *Daedalus*, of 310 65/94 tons, owned by Alexander Davison, Nelson's friend and agent. Like Cook's last two ships, she was Whitby-built. Lieutenant Richard Hergest, a particular friend of Vancouver's, who before the Nootka crisis had been Second Lieutenant of the *Discovery* under Roberts, was appointed agent of the *Daedalus* (as the lieutenant in command of a transport was then called).

The *Discovery* and *Chatham* were provisioned generously. Menzies notes that 'it was the study of every one concerned, to fill up deficiencies that were complained of, or even hinted at, in former voyages of this nature'.[1] The ships left Falmouth laden to capacity. At the last minute Vancouver requested one or two additional items, but explained that they would have to be brought to him in the storeship: 'these articles may appear in themselves trifling and easy to be taken with us but we are with those and every other article in proportion so full so exactly like an Egg that there is no room to stow away one single Box more in any part of the Ship'.[2] The lack of stability that plagued the *Chatham* was attributed in part to the great number of casks she was carrying on deck.

Careful arrangements were made for the future needs of the expedition. At the Cape of Good Hope all provisions and stores that had been expended were to be replaced, and the *Daedalus* was to join the ships in the autumn of 1792 with supplies expected to meet all requirements until September 1793. By that time the *Daedalus* would have made a round trip to New South Wales and have returned with whatever additional supplies Vancouver had requisitioned. In the event she caught up with the *Discovery* south of San Francisco in October 1793. With a third season of surveying required, instead of the two the Admiralty had envisaged, Vancouver took her with him to the Sandwich Islands, and from her holds was able once more to provision his ships fully with most items as late as February 1794.

It was not forgotten that native peoples would expect gifts, and that it would be necessary to barter with them for provisions. Bell

[1] Menzies, January 1791.
[2] Vancouver to Nepean, Falmouth, 12 March 1791. P.R.O., CO. 5/187, f. 65.

comments on this point: 'Government were exceedingly liberal in providing the Vessels with assortments of every kind of Trade [goods] for the purposes of providing the Ships' Companies with refreshments among the Indian nations we may touch at, and facilitating their friendship & esteem; no less a sum that £8000 Stg was appropriated to this purpose, and there was indeed so much of it, that we left a considerable quantity to be brought after us in the Storeship.'[1] When the *Discovery* was first being outfitted in the early months of 1790 Banks had been consulted, in this and in many other matters, and asked to suggest specific items that should be sent for barter. He in turn asked Menzies for suggestions, a sensible move, as Menzies had spent two seasons on the Northwest Coast recently and had first-hand knowledge of trading conditions there. On April 4 Menzies sent Banks the following note, which illustrates the difficulty of anticipating native preferences:

Sir Joseph

I have here subjoined agreeable to your request, a list of such articles as I think will answer best for Trading on the West-coast of N. America; but any Vessel going there ought to be supplied with Two Black Smiths & a Forge together with the necessary Utensils for working Iron, Copper & Brass into such forms as may best suit the fickle disposition of the Natives.

At Nootka we found Copper the article most Sought after & in this we were very deficient having little or none on board. At Prince Williams Sound the Natives preferred Iron & put very little value on Copper or any thing else – they were so over stocked with Beads as to ornament their Dogs with them. At Queen Charlottes Isles & Banks's Isles, Iron, Cloth, Beads and Brass & Copper trinkets answered best. At Cape Edgecombe, Iron Frying-pans – Tin Kettles – Pewter basons & beads formed the chief articles of Trade. Ornamental lofty Caps covered with Brass or Copper would be good presents for the Chiefs & Warriors.

I have the honor to be with due respect
Sir Your most obed.^t Humble Serv.
Arch. Menzies.[2]

---

[1] Bell, note after 1 April 1791. His estimate was considerably lower than the sum provided by Parliament, which was £10,329. 15. 4. Many of the items had been loaded on the *Discovery* when she was first being outfitted early in 1791. Vancouver was able to make suggestions of his own, and 'calicoes, copper, nails, vermillion, and red baize were added to the goods for the Indians.' – Barry M. Gough, *Distant Dominion, Britain and the Northwest Coast of North America* (Vancouver, 1980), p. 120.

[2] Menzies to Banks, 4 April 1791, and subjoined lists. Banks Collection, Sutro Library, San Francisco. PN:17. Banks' more formal list is in the Brabourne Papers, Mitchell Library, Sydney.

Menzies' list is supplemented in Banks' papers by two others, one in rough form, in Banks' own difficult handwriting, and the other probably the first part of a draft of the list finally sent to Grenville. All three largely duplicate one another, and they undoubtedly tabulate the suggestions from which the goods supplied to the expedition later in the year were selected. The variety of merchandise suggested is astonishing. It includes axes, hatchets, adzes, chisels, hammers, nails, saws of several kinds, files, rasps, gimlets, pocket knives, spades, shovels, pick axes, sickles and augers. A large quantity of bar iron was a major item, along with brass and copper both in sheets and in the form of kettles, goblets, bracelets and such trinkets as buttons and thimbles. Frying pans, tin kettles, pots and jugs, and pewter pots, basons and spoons were other items. Scissors, needles, thread, scarlet cloth, coloured linen, feathers, red and blue gartering, red caps, ear-rings, and blue, red, white and yellow beads were included. Menzies suggested 'Scotch Tartan or particoloured blankets', and he also listed 'Daggers & Old Bayonets' and 'Muskets & other fire Arms with Powder shoot [*sic*] & balls', but it is doubtful if the latter items were supplied. Banks' list included a thousand 'Medals of H. Majesty', the intention being that they should not only please the natives, but leave an identification of the expedition's visits, another item not provided.

Entertainment as well as gifts and goods for barter were to be offered to the natives. The marines drilled and paraded on many occasions and the *Discovery* was provided with a good supply of fireworks. Sky rockets, water rockets, Roman candles, Bengal lights and Catherine wheels were included in the assortment. They seldom failed to impress and astonish, and, occasionally, to frighten.

Vancouver's instructions were put into final form very late in the day. Thanks to the Nootka Sound Convention he was to be a diplomat as well as an explorer, and was to receive back from the Spaniards the properties they had seized in 1789. For three days in February 1791 Meares was questioned at length by the Cabinet, under oath, in an effort to secure specific details of the buildings and lands of which he claimed he had been dispossessed. He stated that he had given Chief Maquinna 'considerable Presents for leave to build a House' at Nootka, that the building could accommodate about 35, and that it stood in about an acre of land, enclosed by a fence and ditch. He claimed further that to the south, at Port Cox, in Clayoquot Sound, Chief Wickananish had agreed to allow him to erect a permanent trading post.[1] 'Buildings and tracts of land' at Nootka and Port Cox were mentioned in subsequent exchanges with Madrid, but the evidence given was exasperatingly vague. In the end Vancouver had to be informed that 'as the particular specifications of the parts to be restored may still require some further time' it was intended that the King's orders 'for this purpose' would be sent to him by the store ship due to sail during the summer. As will appear, the 'particular specifications' were never in fact forthcoming.

On February 11, while Meares was under interrogation, Lord Grenville sent to Sir Philip Stephens, Secretary of the Admiralty, a draft of the instructions it was proposed to give Vancouver. In essentials the final text followed this closely, but there were one or two interesting modifications. The draft referred in sceptical terms to the Northwest Passage, which more than once had been spoken of as the major object of Vancouver's quest: 'the discoveries of Captain Cook & of the later Navigators seem to prove that any actual Communication by Sea, such as has commonly been understood by the name of a North West passage cannot be looked for with any probability of success'. These lines were struck out, but the following sentence, which refers to communication across the continent rather than a passage through it, was retained. One of the 'principal objects' of the expedition was to secure 'accurate information with respect to the nature and extent of any water-communication which may tend, in any considerable degree, to facilitate intercourse, for the purposes of commerce, between the north-west coast, and the country upon the opposite side of the continent, which are inhabited or occupied by His Majesty's subjects'.

The coast was to be explored from latitude 30° N to Cook's River (as Cook Inlet was then thought to be), and Vancouver was to devote 'particular attention' to 'the supposed straits of Juan de Fuca'. If no water communication of the kind sought was found south of Cook's River, the instructions took the view that there was 'the great probability that it will be found that the said river rises in some of the lakes already known to Canadian traders [from Montreal], and the servants of the Hudson's bay company'. This expectation was based on the explorations and maps of Peter Pond, of the North West Company, and it is surprising to find his theory still accepted in official circles as late as February 1791. Pond built the first trading post in the

[1] Harlow, *Founding of the Second British Empire*, I, p. 465.

fur-rich Athabasca country and later visited Great Slave Lake. After he read the published account of Cook's third voyage, he became convinced that Cook's River was the mouth of the large river (the Mackenzie) that flows out of the western end of the lake. By 1787 he had prepared maps reflecting this opinion. In January 1790 Evan Nepean, Under Secretary of State, and well known to Vancouver, had received a note from David Ogden, of London, enclosing a copy of an excited letter from his son, Isaac Ogden, of Quebec, reporting that he had had several conversations with Pond and that he was confident 'the source of Cook's River is now fully discovered and known'.[1] But in December 1790 word reached London that Alexander Mackenzie had descended the great river that now bears his name, and had found that it emptied into the Arctic, and not the Pacific, as Pond had surmised. Grenville may have been confused by receiving a copy of Pond's map in January 1791 from Lord Dorchester, Governor-in-Chief of Canada, who made no mention of Mackenzie's expedition and its implications in his brief covering letter.[2]

Although the Admiralty recognized that Vancouver's survey would have to be so conducted 'as not only to ascertain the general line of the sea coast, but also the direction and extent of all such considerable inlets...as may be likely to lead to, or facilitate, such communication as is above described', there seems to have been a suspicion that Vancouver was somewhat of a perfectionist, and might well make the survey more detailed than its purpose required. He was specifically instructed 'not to pursue any inlet or river further than it shall appear to be navigable by vessels of such burthen as might safely navigate the Pacific Ocean', and the Admiralty thought that two seasons should suffice for it 'if carried out with a view to the objects stated, without too minute and particular an examination of the detail of the different parts of the coast laid down by it'. In the event three seasons were required, and as the prodigious task was concluded, Vancouver admitted that he had searched for a passage or water communication 'with a degree of minuteness far exceeding the letter of my commission or instructions; in this respect I might possibly have incurred the censure of disobedience, had I not been intrusted with the most liberal, discretionary orders, as being the fittest and most likely means of attaining the important end in question'.[3]

---

[1] For Ogden's letter in full see Henry R. Wagner, *Peter Pond. Fur Trader and Explorer* (New Haven, 1955), pp. 86–96.   [2] Quoted in Wagner, *Peter Pond*, pp. 37–8.
[3] Vancouver, III, 295; entry for 19 August 1794.

Vancouver's interest in the Sandwich Islands has been mentioned. At the time his instructions were drafted this interest was evidently shared by Grenville. In a note accompanying the draft letter to the Admiralty, Grenville expressed anxiety that Vancouver should be dispatched promptly 'as every hour's delay is now important to the material object of examining the Sandw. Islands, & for that reason I am extremely anxious for his sailing as soon as possible'.[1] In the final text Vancouver was 'required and directed, to proceed without loss of time...to the Sandwich Islands in the north pacific ocean, where you are to remain during the next winter; employing yourself very diligently in the examination and survey of the said islands'. Vancouver's interest in the islands was to increase as he became better acquainted with them, but preoccupation with long wars in Europe was to cause them to fade from attention in London.

The Nootka Sound controversy had pushed the South Pacific and the southern whale fishery into the background, but they were not entirely forgotten. Vancouver was instructed to return home by way of Cape Horn, and in the event of time permitting he was to begin an 'examination of the western coast of South America from the south point of the island of Chiloe, which is about 44° south latitude', and 'ascertain what is the most southern Spanish settlement on that coast and what harbours there are south of that settlement.'

The instructions included no passage corresponding to the formidable paragraph in which Cook was directed to report in all possible detail on virtually every aspect of the regions he would be visiting. This task was assigned to Archibald Menzies, whose instructions were prepared by Banks at Grenville's request. Their intention was as broad as those given to Cook, as the opening sentence indicates: 'The business on which you are employed being of an extensive nature as it includes an investigation of the whole of the Natural History of the countries you are to visit, as well as an enquiry into the present state & comparative degree of civilization of the inhabitants you will meet with, the utmost degree of diligence & perseverance on your part will be necessary, to enable you to do justice to your employers, and gain credit to yourself.' The detailed directions that follow are interesting both in themselves and for the way they reflect the strong utilitarian bent of Banks' thinking. Menzies was to note the nature of the soil and the 'probable climate', with a view to the possible establishment of settlements, and to try to gauge whether the grains and fruits

[1] P.R.O., H.O. 28/61, f. 394. Undated.

43

cultivated in Europe would be likely to thrive; he was 'to enumerate all the Trees, Shrubs, Plants, Grasses, Ferns and Mosses' and to bring home seeds, dried specimens and in some instances live plants, for which the plant frame on the *Discovery*'s quarter deck had been provided; he was to watch for evidence of deposits of metals and coal, to note 'what sort of Beasts, Birds, and Fishes [were] likely to prove useful, either for food or commerce', and to note places where whales and seals were numerous. He was to 'make diligent enquiry' about the 'manners, customs, Language and Religion' of the natives, and to note 'particularly the art of dyeing, in which Savages have been frequently found to excell.' Banks realized that he was asking a great deal, and left much to Menzies' 'discretion and good sense', but he was directed always to act 'as you judge most likely to promote the interest of Science, and contribute to the increase of human knowledge'.[1]

As we have seen, Banks had his doubts about the way in which Vancouver would treat Menzies, and the Lords of the Admiralty sent Vancouver both a copy of Menzies' instructions and an additional order requiring and directing him to afford Menzies 'on all occasions, every degree of assistance in the performance of his Duty, which the Circumstances of the Expedition will admit'. In particular, boats were to be made available to him, he was to receive merchandise to enable him to deal with the natives, his need for water for plants was to be kept in mind, and every care was to be taken to keep the plant frame in good repair, and to prevent 'Dogs, or any other Animals' from getting into it.

These instructions were marked 'secret' and for a considerable time Menzies knew nothing of their contents. Cook, we are told, had the 'reputation of keeping his officers in the dark' and, like him, Vancouver seems to have tended to keep his own counsel. Only on rare occasions did he consult his officers. As Menzies had been in touch with Banks, he probably knew more than they did about many matters. Bell comments that at the beginning of the voyage its object 'was in a great measure kept a secret, no one could positively pretend to a knowledge of our immediate destination, further than the Cape of Good Hope; although it was generally believed that we were sent out to receive Nootka from the Spaniards, and at the same time to examine and survey the North West Coast of America; More I knew not at this time, except

---

[1] Banks to Menzies, 22 February 1791. Quoted from Menzies' own copy, now in the Provincial Archives, Victoria, B.C. Oddly enough, it was addressed to 'Mr. Alexander Menzies' instead of Archibald, a mistake corrected in Menzies' own hand:

that we should most likely be employ'd in the expedition at least Three Years & a half'.[1] As it turned out, four years and a half would have been a more accurate estimate.

One lengthy sentence in Cook's instructions for his third voyage must have struck him as being unnecessary:

At whatever Places you may touch in the course of your Voyage, where accurate Observations of the nature herein mentioned have not already been made, you are, as far as your time will allow, very carefully to observe the true Situation of such Places, both in Latitude & Longitude; the Variation of the Needle; Bearings of Head lands; Height, Direction, and Course of the Tydes and Currents; Depths & Soundings of the Sea; Shoals, Rocks &cᵃ; and also to survey, make Charts, and take views of, such Bays, Harbours, and different parts of the Coast, and to make such Notations thereon, as may be useful either to Navigation or Commerce.[2]

No passage of this kind was included in Vancouver's instructions, but the sentence summarizes so well what Cook did and Vancouver was expected to do that it is worth quoting.

At one time it was intended that Vancouver should be given detailed instructions regarding the way in which his survey was to be carried out. This was one of the numerous matters that Grenville discussed with Banks, and the latter was asked to secure opinions on the subject. Two of the memoranda received have survived. One was prepared by a geographer, Major James Rennell; the other was drafted by none other than Captain Bligh, of *Bounty* fame, who had served as master of the *Resolution* on Cook's last voyage. Both were evidently forwarded to Grenville, but Banks' copy of Bligh's contribution is endorsed 'not made use of'. In view of Vancouver's training and experience, both appear to be exercises in the obvious. More interesting·is Banks' covering letter to Grenville, written late in February 1791, evidently promoted by a mistrust of marine surveyors in general and presumably of Vancouver in particular. 'I have added instructions for surveyors', he wrote, 'which are intended...to secure to Government what they always ought to be possessed of a series of proofs of the degree of accuracy with which it [the survey] has been done to which they may at any future time refer. The Temptation of Substituting Conjecture for Fact in Laying down the shores of an unknown Country is so great especially at times when from the circumstances of winds & weather

---

[1] Bell, note after 1 April 1791.   [2] Cook, *Journals*, III, ccxxii–iii.

it is dificult [sic] to approach near to the Land that I doubt whether any surveyor has ever wholly resisted it.' Banks' solution was to require the surveyor to record every detail in a specially designed book of record. The result of its use would be 'that the employment of Conjecture will be all but impossible'.[1]

There is no evidence that Vancouver actually received either surveying instructions or the special book of record. Admiral Bern Anderson surmises that he was probably guided by the 8th edition of *The Practical Navigator and Seaman's Assistant*, by John Hamilton Moore, published in 1784, and outlines the techniques it describes. It seems more likely that he was guided chiefly by his own experience with Cook and later with Whidbey in the West Indies. On long stretches of the coast – notably those of California, Oregon, Washington and parts of the Alaskan mainland – it was only possible to make a running survey of the kind he had seen Cook conduct on his second and third voyages. This was carried out mostly from the *Discovery*. A careful record of course and distance was kept as the ship moved forward; compass bearings of headlands and other prominent coastal features were taken from successive positions of the ship, and when these were plotted on a sheet, the point at which the bearing lines intersected indicated the position of the feature, relative to the vessel's track. To ascertain its true position, allowance had to be made for the variation of the compass, which it will be noticed Vancouver ascertained very frequently. The coastline between prominent features was filled in by visual observation, and as an additional aid to future navigators, drawings were often made of features or short segments of the coast that were of special interest.

Soon after Vancouver entered the Strait of Juan de Fuca it became evident that most of the surveying would have to be carried out by the ships' boats. He had decided that the only way to ascertain conclusively whether or not important passages or water communications inland existed was to trace the continental shore. Sheltered as it was by innumerable islands and broken by numerous inlets, it was quite impossible to follow it in detail in the ships. In these confined waters, it was practicable to make a much more detailed survey, and to supplement the observations taken from the boats by others taken on shore. References to surveying techniques in Vancouver's own narrative are few and far between, but some are found in other journals. One early example is in Menzies' journal for 18 June 1792. At daybreak

[1] Banks to Grenville, 9 February 1791. Banks's draft of this letter and copies of the two memoranda are in the Brabourne Papers, Mitchell Library, Sydney.

that morning he accompanied Johnstone, who was setting out from Birch Bay to fill a gap in the survey that still existed to the south: 'We rowed across & landed upon the Easternmost of a group of small Islands where we staid [for] breakfast & where Mr. Johnstone took up his first bearings, after which we proceeded to the South Westward landing here & there as occasion required it to continue the Survey.'

Notes in Banks' papers show that Vancouver was provided with copies of all the journals and charts that might prove useful to him. The list includes the voyages of Cook, Portlock, Dixon, Meares and Bougainville (the latter to be in English).[1] Bit by bit the maritime fur traders had produced rough maps that revealed some of the major geographical features of the Northwest Coast. Some of their sketches and several derived from Spanish sources were published by Dalrymple in 1789–90, in time for Vancouver to take copies with him for such guidance as they could offer. They included four maps of harbours made by Johnstone, drawn when he was on the coast with Colnett in 1787. Vancouver evidently checked these sources carefully, and from time to time cites observations by Cook, Meares and others; but he never accepts them as substitutes for his own.

The routine followed in the preparation of the expedition's charts is fairly clear. As already noted, most of the boat expeditions were commanded either by Joseph Whidbey or James Johnstone. Both were highly competent and experienced surveyors. A few of Johnstone's sketches have survived,[2] recording exploration carried out by his boat parties, and they are models of clarity. Whidbey's would have been on a par. These sketches were handed to Joseph Baker, 3rd lieutenant of the *Discovery*, who added their findings to a fair sheet he maintained in the ship. This step may have been taken for the first time in June 1792, when the ships were anchored in Desolation Sound. Vancouver had absented himself 'from the present surveying excursions, in order to procure some observations for the longitude here, and to arrange the charts of the different surveys in the order they had been made. These, when so methodized, my third lieutenant Mr. Baker had undertaken to copy and embellish, and who, in point of accuracy, neatness, and such dispatch as circumstances admitted, certainly excelled in a very high degree.'[3] Baker was a key figure throughout, and after the ships returned to England he was Vancouver's natural choice to

[1] Banks' list also included such maps as were available of the west coast of New Holland and the Fiji Islands.

[2] Now in the Hydrographic Department, Ministry of Defence, Taunton, Somerset.

[3] Vancouver, I, 322.

prepare for the engravers the charts that were to be published in the atlas volume that accompanied the 1798 quarto edition of the *Voyage of Discovery*.

Throughout his survey, and in the charts in which it resulted, major emphasis was placed upon the continental shore. Indeed, this was all that Vancouver claimed to have determined with any exactitude. Although his explorations resulted in the discovery of many islands and other features, this was incidental. He referred explicitly to the fact in June 1794, when he had just concluded the survey of Prince William Sound. This had been completed, he wrote, insofar as it 'respected the boundary of the continent; but the numerous islands, islets, rocks, and shoals, which are contained within this space, being considered as secondary objects, did not fall within the limits of our service for accurately ascertaining or delineating; yet these have been noticed with every degree of circumspection, that circumstances, and the nature of our researches, would allow, without swerving from our principal object, viz. *the survey of the shore of the continent*'.[1]

Inevitably the survey had limitations and errors, and despite Banks' fears, Vancouver showed little inclination to conceal them. To cite an example: thick foggy weather had prevailed in August 1792 when the ships were examining inlets between Fife Sound and Smith Sound, along the north shore of Queen Charlotte Sound, at the northern end of Vancouver Island. In 1793 some re-examination was possible, but Vancouver warned that 'the coast, islands, islets, rocks, &. &c.... excepting the western extremities' were still 'to be considered as likely to have been erroneously described as well in respect to their positive, as relative positions'. But he emphasized that he considered himself 'answerable only for the certainty of the connection of the continental shores' which he believed had been 'traced in such a manner, as to ascertain the fact beyond all possible dispute'.[2] As it happened, Vancouver was over confident in so thinking, for his chart of this part of the coast failed to include Seymour Inlet and Belize Inlet, which share an outlet in common. But this outlet is both very narrow and completely screened by an island; and in any event the omission was of slight importance.

Menzies, though not involved professionally, had watched the progress of the survey closely, and had accompanied many of the boat excursions. As it was nearing completion the expedition's most unfortunate error came to light – its failure to explore Dry Strait,

[1] Vancouver, III, 187.   [2] *Ibid.*, II, 257.

48

which links Sumner Strait with Frederick Sound, a mistake that had resulted in considerable loss of time and much unnecessary labour. Shaken by this, Menzies seems to have feared that other errors might well come to light: 'These and other instances ought to teach us to speak with the utmost diffidence of our having all along tracd the continental shore, notwithstanding that every degree of precaution was in general made use of, yet such was the expeditious nature of the service, performed often in obscure & inclement weather & such the difficulty of tracing all the windings of such an intricate laybrinth through a region so dreary & broken that it is impossible to pronounce such a laborious task as infallible.'[1]

Cook's first and second voyages took place just as two means of solving the age-old problem of how to determine longitude were coming into use. For centuries mariners had been dependent upon dead reckoning, an estimate of the position of the vessel based on compass readings and the distance the vessel was thought to have travelled, as measured by the log. Currents and other variables that were often difficult to detect made accuracy impossible, and errors were sometimes horrendous. A classic example was the experience of Anson's ships when they rounded Cape Horn in 1741. They narrowly escaped crashing ashore on the cliffs near Cape Noir when they were under the impression that they were 300 miles to the west, heading north in the open Pacific. What was required was some means of ascertaining accurately the difference in time between Greenwich, from which longitude was calculated, and the ship or feature whose location it was desired to determine. As the earth revolved through 360° in 24 hours, each hour of difference would represent 15° of longitude.

The first of the new methods, based on the measurement of lunar distances, was developed by Dr Nevil Maskelyne, who tested it on a voyage to St Helena in 1761. The angular distance between the moon and the sun, or the moon and one of the fixed stars, was determined by observation, and the time when the observation was made was compared with the time at which the same lunar distance would have been observed at Greenwich. In 1765 Maskelyne was appointed Astronomer Royal, and he immediately set about simplifying the system, and eliminating a vast amount of calculation, by publishing the annual *Nautical Almanac*, in which the Greenwich readings were calculated every day of the year, at three-hour intervals, and printed

[1] Menzies, 19 August 1794.

in advance. When Cook sailed on his first voyage in 1768, the period covered by available editions was still limited, which moved him to remark, two years later, that 'unless this Ephermeris is publish^d for some time to come more than either one or two Years it never can be of general use in long Voyages'.[1] By the time he sailed on his second voyage, in 1772, advance editions covering three years were available, and he was also able to secure 'as much as may be printed' of a fourth.[2] Similarly, in 1791, Vancouver could be provided with advance data for years to come.

The second new means of determining longitude was the marine chronometer, a timepiece that could maintain a high degree of accuracy over a long period, in spite of the violent motion and wide variations in temperature and climate to which it would be subjected on long voyages in small ships, such as those of Cook and Vancouver. The purpose of the chronometer was to provide a constant record of Greenwich mean time, so that whenever local time could be determined by observation, the difference between the two, and hence the longitude, could be ascertained. The lunar method continued in use for many years after the chronometer was introduced, for, as Vancouver's experience was to show, even the best of timepieces could fail. None kept time with absolute accuracy and it was necessary to resort to the lunar method for comparison, in order to determine the rate at which they were gaining or losing. The *Discovery* was provided with a portable observatory, and whenever it was possible to set this up on shore scores of observations were taken to check both the rate of going of the chronometers and the various calculations that had been made for longitude.

The chronometer had come of age in 1759, when John Harrison, who had been experimenting for decades, completed his fourth timepiece – known to history as H4 – which Rupert Gould has rightly called 'the most famous chronometer that ever has been made or ever will be made'.[3] After exhaustive tests lasting until 1764 its excellence was officially acknowledged, and Harrison was awarded the prize that had long been offered as a reward for a successful marine timepiece. In 1767 a copy of H4 was ordered from Larcum Kendall, an accomplished instrument maker, and this duplicate – K1 – sailed with

[1] Cook, *Journals*, I, 392.

[2] *Ibid.*, II, 722.

[3] Rupert T. Gould, *The Marine Chronometer. Its History and Development* (London, 1960), p. 49.

Cook in the *Resolution* on his second voyage. It performed magnificently, and Kendall received orders for two more chronometers, this time to his own design. The last of these, K3, was completed in 1774, and the Board of Longitude decided that both K1 and K3 should go with Cook on his third voyage – K1 again in the *Resolution*, and K3 in the *Discovery*, in which Vancouver first made its acquaintance. The two watches differed considerably. K1, which had an orthodox watch face, was elaborately decorated, with a back plate that was a work of art. K3, which cost only £100, as compared with £450 for K1, was severely functional, and its curiously designed face had three dials, recording hours, minutes and seconds. Both watches have survived and are now on display at the National Maritime Museum.

Chronometers were essential for Vancouver's expedition, and the Board of Longitude decided that K3, which had spent most of the 1780s in Newfoundland waters, should be assigned to the *Discovery*. For the *Chatham* they provided a chronometer – no. 82 – made by John Arnold. Harrison had made only four chronometers; Kendall only three. As the number suggests, Arnold hoped to produce them in some quantity and make them generally available, an amibition shared by a rival instrument maker, Thomas Edenshaw. Initially Vancouver had decided that it was not necessary to include an astronomer in his expedition, but by the time the ships reached Teneriffe he had changed his mind, and, as Bell notes, 'wrote home from this, applying for one to be sent by the opportunity of the Storeship'.[1] The Board of Longitude responded by sending the unfortunate William Gooch, who was killed by the natives in the Sandwich Islands. With Gooch the Board sent three additional chronometers, two by Arnold (nos. 14 and 176) and a pocket timepiece by Edenshaw. The choice of watchmakers may be a further reflection of the influence of Sir Joseph Banks, as he was a strong supporter of Arnold.

Gooch's death meant that Vancouver and Whidbey continued to have major responsibility for observations taken in the course of the voyage. Vancouver kept a careful record of them, and after the expedition returned to England he sent the books in which they were tabulated to the Board of Longitude. Unfortunately they were returned to him and have since disappeared. The only records that survive are those in the printed *Voyage*, supplemented occasionally by a note in other logs. No doubt the records sent to the Board included a report on the performance of the five chronometers as well as the record of

[1] Bell, May 1791.

astronomical observations. Here again only the entries in the printed narrative survive, but these are sufficiently numerous to indicate how the various watches behaved. All five gained in varying degrees, as shown in the table in the appendix. Kendall's K3 performed well, but after the *Discovery* arrived on the Northwest Coast the rate at which it gained time increased sharply. It stopped on 9 June 1794, 'but on applying a gentle horizontal motion, it was again put into action'. Vancouver came to place much reliance on Arnold's no. 14, which ran very steadily, increasing its rate by less than five seconds per day over a period of eighteen months. Arnold's no. 176 gained at a higher rate and at times erratically, while the much less complete records relating to his no. 82, in the *Chatham*, show some even wider variations. Edenshaw's pocket watch, which Vancouver had come to regard as an 'excellent piece of workmanship...highly intitled to praise', stopped in April 1793, and when restarted ran for only a few days. Although the chronometers were immensely helpful in navigation, this record shows how indispensable it was that they should be checked carefully and their rates of going determined by astronomical observations. And it is interesting to note that the calculation of longitude by dead reckoning was not abandoned. Many of the logs of the voyage have entries recording the longitudes as determined in all three ways – by chronometer, by lunar distance, and by dead reckoning.

Vancouver's latitudes are very close to modern readings, but it is otherwise with his longitudes, in spite of all the care he took to ascertain them. When he reached the coast of California in 1792 his first step was to try and fix accurately the location of the point from which he was beginning his survey northward. He himself, Whidbey, Puget and others on the *Discovery* took a total of eighty-five sets of lunar observations, each set consisting of six readings. After allowing for a change in the rate of going of the chronometer, Vancouver concluded that the position of the ship at noon on April 18 was 236° 25' east longitude (123° 35' W). Actually this was too far to the east, and would have placed the *Discovery* about 15 miles inland. This was a portent, for in spite of his efforts, and regardless of whether they were determined by Vancouver himself or by the masters of his ships, the positions assigned to geographical features in his narrative are virtually all too far to the east. In his biography of Vancouver, Admiral Anderson states that this error 'was one in celestial navigation' and adds that it was 'a function of latitude, as the error increases uniformly with the latitude'.[1] But a comparison of 157 positions as given by Vancouver for features between Cape Mendocino and Chirikof Island with modern readings shows that his longitudes do not increase uniformly. True, the error is largest in the north, in the region of Cook Inlet and Prince William Sound, where it averages 38 minutes, or nearly two-thirds of a degree (about 22 miles at that latitude), and in the south, in the Puget Sound area, it is only about 15 minutes, or one quarter of a degree. But in between there are many positions in which the error is less than 15 minutes, and two sequences, each of five locations, in which one of the ten is the correct position and the other nine are all from $2\frac{1}{2}$ to 7 minutes *west* of the modern determination.[2]

These discrepancies were not due to any lack of effort. At Port Discovery, where the ships spent some time while the boats were exploring Puget Sound, no fewer than 220 sets of lunar observations were taken, and at Nootka Sound, where the ships arrived at the end of August, the number taken was 106.[3] By that time Vancouver was becoming aware of what was happening. The observations at Nootka gave its location as 233° 31' 30" east, which, he noted, placed it 'about 20' 30" to the eastward of the longitude assigned to it by Captain Cook, and about 10' to the eastward of Senor Malaspina's observations; whence it should seem to appear, that our instruments for the longitude were erring on the eastern side'. But he decided not 'to subscribe to the longitude as settled by astronomers of superior abilities' as 'such a concession would have been attended with a very material inconvenience, in deranging the position of the different parts of the coast that have already been surveyed, and laid down by our own observations. For this essential reason I have been induced to retain the meridian of Nootka, as ascertained by our own observations.'[4] Although, as noted,

[1] Bern Anderson, *Surveyor of the Sea: The Life and Voyages of Captain George Vancouver* (Seattle, 1960), p. 201.

[2] Between Cape Mendocino and Cape Flattery the error to the east varied from 9 to 17 minutes; Cape Flattery itself was placed 22 minutes too far to the east. In the Puget Sound area the error varied from 13 to 17 minutes. For a few readings farther north it increased sharply to half a degree or more. Then came the readings in which the error was very small, or even erred to the west. All other positions (some 50 in all) given during the 1793 surveying season average about 9 minutes too far to the east. From Port Conclusion, where the survey was completed in August 1794, to Cape St Elias the average error is about 15 minutes, and as noted, the positions between the cape and Chirikof Island are on the average about 38 minutes east of the true location.

[3] At Salmon Cove, in Observatory Inlet, Whidbey, Baker, Orchard, Ballard and Pigot took the astonishing total of 346 sets of lunar observations in July and August of 1793.

[4] Vancouver, I, 412.

the extent of the error varied on different regions of the coast, in each of them it was sufficiently consistent not to falsify to any serious degree the relative positions of the various features to one another. Admiral Anderson, who navigated the coast frequently from Puget Sound to Alaska, makes the interesting comment that even today 'navigational charts of the coastal waters of upper British Columbia have a small error in orientation of some of the channels, and traces of Vancouver's original survey can be found on them'.[1]

[1] Anderson, *Surveyor of the Sea*, p. 201. In an article on 'Captain Vancouver and the Lunar Distance', *Journal of Navigation*, xxvii (1974), p. 493, N. W. Emmott, remarks on the fact that Vancouver expresses all his results in terms of east longitude and adds: 'It is interesting to note that when the astronauts visited the Moon they did not bother with east or west longitudes; it was all east to them as it had been for Captain Vancouver.'

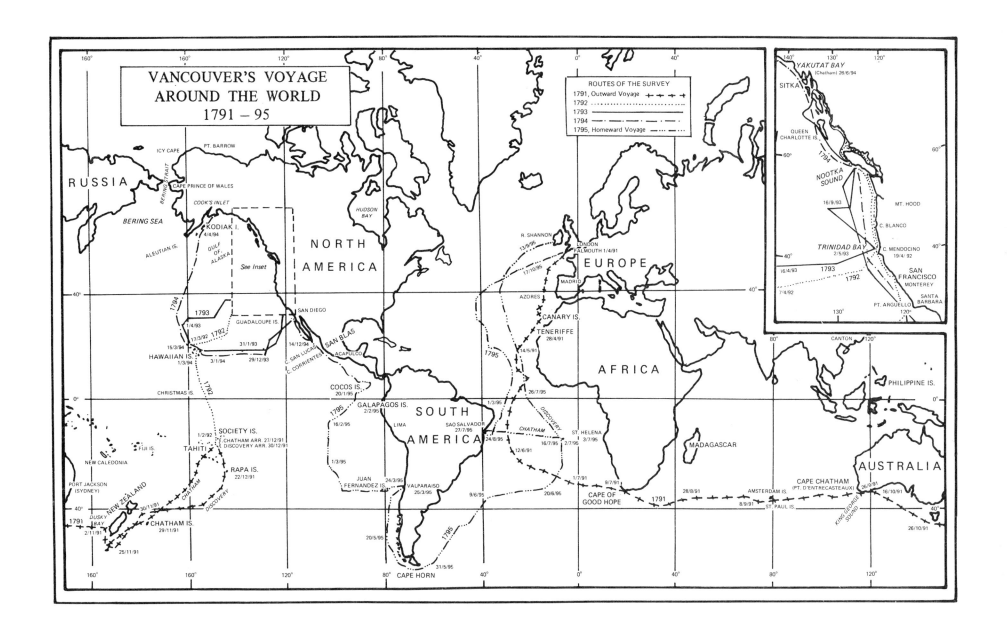

VANCOUVER'S VOYAGE
AROUND THE WORLD
1791 — 95

ROUTES OF THE SURVEY
1791, Outward Voyage ++++++
1792
1793
1794
1795, Homeward Voyage

II

THE VOYAGE

The South Seas

THE voyage of discovery was beset at the beginning by delays that Vancouver found exasperating. The ships were to proceed from the Thames to Spithead, and thence to Falmouth, their final port of departure. The *Discovery* was ready to leave Longreach late in January, but she encountered such bad weather that she was ten days on the way to Spithead. As Vancouver feared, the storm demolished the bumkins and a considerable part of the head. While repairs were in progress, Vancouver was called to London, where (in midshipman Barrie's words) he became 'very ill...but not so as to retard our Voyage'.[1] This is the first hint that Vancouver's health was not of the best. Writing in March from Falmouth, he assured Evan Nepean, who was evidently concerned about the matter, that he was gaining strength every day, and in a note written on the eve of sailing reported that his health was 'wonderfully improved'.[2]

The *Chatham* did not get away from Woolwich until late in February. She met with even more tempestuous weather than the *Discovery*, which forced her to take shelter and resulted in damage that had to be made good at Spithead. The consequence was that she did not reach Falmouth until March 31. She had proved to be so unstable that Broughton was worried about her safety and was anxious to secure additional ballast. But this would have involved further delay, and Vancouver insisted upon the makeshift solution of transferring to her the *Discovery*'s 4-pounder shot. The ships sailed the next morning – April 1, All Fools' Day, a circumstance that was recalled jocularly from time to time.

Vancouver had been left free to choose his route to the Pacific, and he decided to proceed by way of the Cape of Good Hope – a choice dictated by his wish to visit New Holland, as Australia was then known.

---

[1] Barrie to his mother, 13 Feb. 1791. (Sir Robert Barrie MSS, William R. Perkins Library, Duke University, Durham, North Carolina.)

[2] Vancouver to Nepean, Falmouth, 12 Mar. and 31 Mar. 1791 (P.R.O., C.O. 5/187).

On the way he intended to call at Madiera for wood, water, wine and fresh provisions. Due to bad weather and the tenderness of the *Chatham*, he went to Teneriffe instead, where the roadstead at Santa Cruz promised to be a convenient place to secure the ballast Vancouver now realized was essential. 'The Chatham', he reported to the Admiralty, 'was so exceedingly crank as to entirely prevent her carrying the common necessary sail, which in course infinitely retarded our progress; and in which state, it was self evident fact, she never would have been able to encounter the South East trade.'[1]

At Santa Cruz the *Chatham*'s stability trouble was in great measure corrected by taking on 23 tons of shingle ballast, but the visit was marred by an incident that could very easily have had disastrous consequences. On Sunday, May 1, some of the seamen and marines were given shore leave, and having imbibed too freely they began to quarrel. A Spanish sentinel tried to separate them, but, in Bell's words, this 'inflamed the Sailors still more (for they have an unalterable hatred for a Spaniard)'.[2] The sentinel called for reinforcements and a violent clash followed. Vancouver, Baker and Whidbey, who were also on shore, hastened to the scene in an effort to stop the fighting, but failed completely and were roughly handled. Vancouver (who was not in uniform) was thrown into the harbour, Baker was beaten about the head and Whidbey sidestepped a bayonet that had been thrust at him with such force that it broke on the stone wall behind him. Fortunately everyone eventually got off to the ships without serious injury. Vancouver lodged a complaint with the governor, who expressed regret but contended, quite correctly it would appear, that the sailors and marines had been to blame for the fracas.

Puget, Bell and Menzies all described the affair in their journals but Vancouver did not mention it in his report to the Admiralty. This must have caused him some embarrassment later, for accounts of it travelled to England in letters (written by Menzies and Baker amongst others), and it was noted in the London papers. Worried about her son's safety, Barrie's mother sent an inquiry to her brother, Sir Alan Gardner. On July 9 he replied: 'I...am happy to inform you that I have reason to believe that the Paragraph in the papers...is without foundation, as a letter has been received from Captain Vancouver dated the 5th of May...which does not mention a syllable of the matter, and if any dispute had happened between his people and the Spanish Inhabitants I am confident he would have given the Admiralty an account of it.'

[1] Vancouver to Stephens, Santa Cruz, 5 May 1791 (P.R.O., Adm 1/2628).
[2] Bell, May 1791.

But a fortnight later Gardner wrote again, sending his sister a letter 'received from my friend Capt. Vashon, who received it a few days ago from Mr. Baker...and as it contains a particular account of the Fracas that happened at Teneriffe between Captain Vancouver's men and the Spaniards, I have sent it to you for your perusal'.[1]

Vancouver chose to reach the Cape of Good Hope by much the same route that Cook had followed in 1776. Prevailing winds and currents made a roundabout, almost semicircular course, stretching far to the west, a wise choice for sailing ships. From Teneriffe Vancouver proceeded in a generally southwest direction, past the Cape Verde Islands and across the Atlantic to within about 650 miles of the coast of Brazil. About midnight on May 27 the equator was crossed in 25° 15' west longitude, and after sailing almost due south for a fortnight, the ships swung round to a southeast course that took them back across the Atlantic to the tip of Africa. Becoming impatient once more with the slow sailing of the *Chatham*, Vancouver decided on June 28 to part company with her and hurry on to the Cape. The *Discovery's* superiority in sailing was probably less than Vancouver thought, since four days later the ships were still in sight of one another. And when the *Discovery* reached the Cape on July 9, it was to find (in Menzies' words) 'to our no small surprize [that] the Chatham in this small run got into Simon's Bay a day before us, thus verifying the scriptural proverb that "the race is not always to the Swift."'[2]

The stop at the Cape lasted five weeks, considerably longer than Vancouver intended. This was due in part to extensive repairs required by the *Discovery*, and to the slow delivery of provisions and stores, which had to be hauled from Cape Town, much of the way over a very bad road. As was the custom, the officers lived most of the time in Cape Town, where they were most hospitably received. Manby remarks that the Dutch had 'the greatest veneration for all Navigators employed on Discovery'[3] which ensured them 'a handsome reception'. References to Cook were frequent, and Bell met Col. Robert Gordon, to whom Captain King had given 'the double-barrel'd Gun that Cook had in his hand when he was kill'd' and who also possessed 'a piece of the Resolution which he has preserved tipp'd with Silver'.[4]

Menzies was able to make a number of botanical excursions and

---

[1] Gardner to Mrs George Clayton (his sister Dolly, mother of Robert Barrie) July 9 and July 23, 1791 (Gardner Papers; quoted by kind permission of Mr Tom L. Brock).

[2] Menzies, 28 June 1791. One of a number of entries in the available text of the journal that were obviously written after the event.

[3] Manby, Letters.   [4] Bell, July 1791.

reported enthusiastically to Banks. Although the country was 'apparently dreary' it was for him 'richer than any Garden, in the vast variety of its vegetable productions'.[1] Unfortunately his services were soon to be required in his alternate capacity as a surgeon. Shortly before the ships sailed on August 17, a Dutch ship arrived from Batavia with many of her crew suffering severely from dysentery, and the malady spread to the *Discovery* and *Chatham* and other ships in the harbour. Vancouver hastened to get away, in the expectation that fresh air would check the disease, but this proved to be a vain hope. Three or four men were ill when the *Discovery* sailed; the next day there were twelve men on the sick list. Every attention was paid to diet and cleanliness, but the epidemic was to cause one death and last many weeks. Cranstoun, surgeon of the *Discovery*, was an early victim, and Vancouver turned to Menzies with a request that he should attend the sick, which he agreed to do. Cranstoun never recovered his health, and although a year passed before the change was recognized officially, from this point onward Menzies in fact officiated as surgeon of the ship.

Vancouver had an explorer's mind, which abhorred a geographical vacuum; it was this desire to fill in some of the blanks and remove some of the uncertainties still existing in the map of the world that was taking him to 'the S.W. side of New Holland', ignorance of which he considered to be 'a real blot in geography'.[2] From the Cape of Good Hope he sailed almost directly eastward, the latitude both of the Cape and his landfall in New Holland being very close to 35° S. It was a course the Dutch had been following since the early years of the seventeenth century, when they discovered that winds and currents being what they were, much the quickest way to reach Java was to sail eastward until they neared the Australian coast, and then northward to their destination. Occasionally discovery had been added to this voyaging. In 1622 Cape Leeuwin, the southwest tip of the continent, was named for the ship from which it was first sighted, and in 1627 the *Golden Zeepaert*, having made her landfall much farther south than usual, traced the south coast eastward almost as far as Spencer Gulf. But Dutch curiosity, when not stimulated by commercial possibilities, was limited, and in the ensuing century and a half no one had ventured farther east. But maps appeared, based on Dutch exploration, that gave a reasonably accurate impression of the coastline of the whole western

[1] Menzies to Banks, 10 August 1791. Brabourne Papers, Mitchell Library, Sydney.
[2] Vancouver to Grenville, Cape of Good Hope, 9 August 1791. Quoted in George Godwin, *Vancouver: A Life* (London, 1930), p. 204.

half of Australia. Vancouver hoped to see as much of the south coast as possible, perhaps even fill in the gap between the *Golden Zeepaert*'s eastern limit and Van Diemen's Land (Tasmania), and ascertain whether the latter was part of the mainland or detached from it.

On the way from the Cape he planned to investigate shoals that were said to exist in a large area to the southeast, and to verify the location of St Paul and Amsterdam islands. Bad weather and poor visibility made the search for the shoals (which did not in fact exist) inconclusive, and he sailed between the two islands without sighting either. Strong westerly gales and high and irregular seas made progress slow and life in the heavily laden ships uncomfortable and sometimes hazardous. They approached New Holland cautiously, 'not choosing', in Vancouver's words, 'to make too free with a coast entirely unexplored'. In the daytime the ships probed for land; at night they retired to the safety of the open sea. Land finally came in sight on September 26, and displayed a range of cliffs that reminded many of the English coast near Falmouth and the Lizard, and prompted Vancouver to name the region New Cornwall. The ships moved slowly eastward, on the lookout for a harbour, and on the 28th made the major discovery of this part of their voyage, the spacious inlet that Vancouver named King George the Third's Sound, now King George Sound.

The next morning he took formal possession of the country and thereafter small parties set out from the ships each day to explore and survey the sound. They expected to meet natives, but none appeared. The three small villages they chanced upon, consisting of huts of the most primitive sort, were all deserted. Some fish weirs and a few crude spears and clubs were the only native work they saw. Both officers and midshipmen took considerable interest in this first new-found land; five of their logs include sketches of the sound, and several describe the visit in some detail. Menzies seems to have been the most adventurous of the explorers; he climbed a mountain in order to secure a better view of the sound and its surroundings, and was entranced by the number and variety of the plants and shrubs, many of which were in full bloom.[1]

It was here that Vancouver bestowed the first of the several hundred place names he was to leave on the map of the world. The general pattern set would be followed elsewhere. The first three names mentioned in the *Voyage of Discovery* are Cape Chatham (now Chatham Island), Cape Howe and Mount Gardner, all honoring

[1] Menzies, Sept. 30, Oct. 1, 4, 1791.

Admiralty officials or naval officers. Commemorative and descriptive names next appear: Eclipse Islands (commemorating an eclipse of the sun), Bald Head (descriptive of its 'smooth appearance'), Seal Island (much frequented by seals), and Michaelmas Island (named on Michaelmas Day) are typical. King George the Third's Sound was the first of many names honoring royal personages, the second being Princess Royal Harbour, the name given to one of the inner bays of the sound. It was commemorative as well, as it was bestowed on the Princess's birthday. New Cornwall (which is not mentioned in Vancouver's narrative and which never came into use) was the first to recall counties, towns and physical features in England, while categories yet to appear included the names of noble families, friends and relatives.

The practical purpose served by the call at King George Sound was to replenish the ships' supply of wood and water. This was accomplished in a week, but the ships were wind bound for another five days. Conditions improved on October 11 and they put to sea, only to meet poor visibility, and weather that hampered exploration and soon made it hazardous. They were nearing the great array of islands and reefs now known as the Archipelago of the Recherche, which even the modern mariner is strongly advised to avoid. Time was now becoming a consideration, and Vancouver realized that he must not take risks that might imperil the main purpose of his voyage. He sighted the southernmost of the islands in the archipelago, named it Termination Island, and 'with great reluctance' abandoned his 'favorite project of further examining the coast'.

From his first landfall to Termination Island the distance was about 325 miles, but east of King George Sound only parts of the coast were glimpsed. Menzies took a very modest view of what had been accomplished: 'We have indeed ascertained that the South West point which was named Cape Chatham,...is about two degrees & a half of Longitude more to the Eastward than it is laid down in our Charts. We have also settled the relative positions of the different head lands as far as we came & discovered a harbour, and these are all the geographical improvements which we can be said to have made in our visit to this part of New Holland'.[1]

Vancouver had decided to sail directly to Dusky Bay (now Dusky Sound) in New Zealand. He had spent six pleasant weeks there in 1773 with Cook, who had found it an excellent spot in which to secure wood and water, make voyage repairs to his ships, and refresh their crews.

[1] Menzies, 14 October 1791.

All thought of trying to ascertain whether or not Van Diemen's Land was an island had been abandoned; the *Discovery* and *Chatham* passed to the south of it. South West Cape was sighted on October 26, and South East Cape, the eastern extremity of the short south coast, dropped astern the following evening. The ships then crossed the Tasman Sea in the remarkably short time of six days and dropped anchor inside Five Finger Point, in Dusky Sound, on November 2.

Of the many bays in the sound Cook had recommended Facile Harbour as an excellent anchorage, but, cautious navigator that he was, Vancouver decided to examine it before taking the ships in. While he and Broughton and Whidbey were engaged on this mission a violent storm arose that for a time seriously imperiled the *Chatham*'s safety and compelled the *Discovery* to seek shelter in an alternative anchorage, Anchor Island Harbour. Johnstone, master of the *Chatham*, had watched these developments with great anxiety, and commented in his journal upon the importance of 'taking Shelter, and getting properly secured upon the very first arrival'[1] when entering unfamiliar waters. Later he noted the wisdom of arriving 'at low water, or at least with the early flood', as channels were then better defined, and if a ship should strike bottom, the rising tide would lessen the danger and help her to get afloat.[2]

As it happened, Anchor Island Harbour was found to be very well suited to meet Vancouver's needs. Wood, water and spruce beer (highly regarded as an antiscorbutic) were the prime requirements, and all could be met close at hand, as Menzies noted: 'abreast of the ship a fine run of fresh water was discovered with wood close to the shore sufficient to supply all our wants; there were likewise found large Trees of what has been called New Zealand Spruce, so that the whole business of wooding, watering brewing &c could be carried on here with great ease under the commanding officers eye from the ship'.[3] The *Chatham*, which had moved into Facile Harbour when the storm subsided, was equally well served, especially for water, for she found 'a run so commodious as to fill the Casks in the boat whilst she lay afloat, by fixing our hose to the Stream, which...fell into the harbour over an eminence, forming a Beautiful Cascade'.[4] Cook had found inhabitants in the sound, but Vancouver saw none, nor were any animals seen. But

---

[1] Johnstone, 6 November 1791.   [2] *Ibid.*, 19 November 1791.

[3] Menzies, 4 November 1791. Baker declared that the beer, made to Cook's recipe, was 'the best Beer of the Spruce kind I ever tasted.'

[4] Johnstone, 6 November 1791.

birds were very numerous and fish (in Mudge's phrase) were 'plenty beyond conception'. Here at last the ravages of the flux contracted at the Cape came to an end. When the *Discovery* left King George Sound twenty-two men were still suffering from dysentery; most of them were recovering by the time the ship reached Dusky Sound, and thanks to the rest and change of diet available there, only two were on the sick list at the end of the three weeks' stay. The *Chatham* had no men ill.

Cook had surveyed virtually the whole of Dusky Sound, and the accuracy of his work was impresssive. Johnstone commented that 'whenever my excursions led me to follow him in this maze of Islands; with others I was charmed with that degree of accuracy and exactness with which his plan exhibited each channel and place'.[1] The only spot Cook had left unexplored was the end of Breaksea Sound, which divides into Vancouver Arm and Broughton Arm, named after the officers who examined them. Cook's sketch of the sound was the basis for the map published as an inset on Vancouver's chart of S. W. New Holland, and it is interesting to note that the caption refers to 'additions and improvements' made by the *Discovery* and *Chatham*, but makes no claim to corrections.

The ships left Dusky Sound on November 22. That evening a storm arose that increased to a gale of great violence, and in the night the ships lost contact with one another. The next morning, Manby records, the *Discovery* 'in a short time...refused every movement of the Helm – in this critical moment, I was sent below and to my astonishment found seven feet of water in the hold'. At first it was feared that she had sprung a leak, but it was 'soon found that this immensity of Water had not proceeded from a leak in her bottom, but had forced its way through the tarpaulins at each Hatchway, as the Main Deck was three feet deep with Water'. Clogged pumps had caused the trouble; they were soon put to rights, and by evening the ship was clear of water. Meanwhile a greater danger had been encountered: the *Discovery* found herself amongst the uncharted reefs and islands that Vancouver appropriately named The Snares. Manby was convinced that 'had darkness continued two hours longer the Ship must [have] been inevitably dashed to pieces. We had now just reason to congratulate ourselves on the two preservations we had experienced in one Night.'[2]

As the *Chatham* failed to reappear, much anxiety was felt for her safety, lest she should have come to grief on The Snares, but all the

---

[1] Johnstone, 19 November 1791.   [2] Manby, Letters.

Discovery could do was to sail on to the appointed rendezvous in Matavai Bay, in Tahiti, and hope that she would be found there.

At daylight on December 22 land suddenly appeared; Vancouver had chanced upon Rapa Island, which he thought was called Oparo. Several hundred natives soon came off in single and double canoes, and though timid at first, they swarmed on board when a first venturesome visitor was seen to be well treated. Manby found their 'dexterity in thieving' amazing. Mudge described them as 'Thieving every thing that could be got at, or rather taking as a matter of Course whatever caught their attention, not having the smalest Idea of the Fraud'. They 'seemed to be perfectly unacquainted with every thing they saw, or heard, except Iron which caught their attention beyond description'; but they had a curious lack of understanding of the weight of large iron objects, and were enraged by their inability to make off with the armourer's anvil, the anchors and the ships guns. A further note by Mudge reveals that the *Discovery* carried a Newfoundland dog. The natives were afraid of it at first, but on seeing it 'fetch, and carry a Pocket Handkerchief, their gestures and Acclamations, were unbounded'.

Vancouver was intrigued by what appeared to be (and in fact were) forts or fortified villages that had been built on the ridges and peaks that are characteristic of the island. Only Mudge seems to have had no doubts about what they were; he described the island as being 'remarkable for its Hippahs, or Garrisons, having one on the summit of each Peak'.[1] His log includes a small profile that illustrates the island's extremely mountainous nature. Efforts were made to induce Vancouver to land, but the *Discovery* simply lay offshore for a few hours and then proceeded on her way.[2]

Meanwhile the *Chatham* had escaped The Snares and had also made a discovery – Chatham Island, east of New Zealand, which Broughton named in honour of the First Lord of the Admiralty, not after his ship, as is often assumed. Although the temper of the natives was uncertain, Broughton, Johnstone and others went on shore, and did their best to establish friendly relations with them. Displaying considerable courage, John Sheriff, a midshipman, went among them alone and unarmed,

---

[1] Mudge, 24 December 1791.

[2] Hewett notes that the fortifications 'were by some supposed to be Erected by the Bounty's people who also Imagined that this deterred Captn. Vancouver from running in and Anchoring As had they been found there he would have been under the necessity of Engaging and taking them.' For a description of the fortified villages and a photograph see Peter H. Buck, *Vikings of the Pacific* (Chicago, 1959), p. 183.

and although some efforts were made to detain him, Sheriff felt that this was due simply to curiosity. Later the natives became hostile, a clash occurred, shots were fired, and to the distress of Broughton and Johnstone one native was killed. In the course of the visit Broughton took formal possession of the island. All this occurred in what Broughton called Skirmish Bay, an appropriate name that has not survived.

The *Chatham* sailed on to Tahiti, where she anchored in Matavai Bay on December 27. She had once again outsailed the *Discovery*, which greatly worried Broughton in view of the latter's 'superiority in sailing, which had given us reason to believe her arrival would have preceded ours, at least a week'. To his relief, the *Discovery* appeared, safe and sound, on December 30.

This was Vancouver's fourth visit to Tahiti; he had been there with Cook in 1773, in 1774 and again in 1777. The island had a great reputation both as an idyllic spot and as a haven where ships could make voyage repairs and recruit their crews with fresh provisions. It could offer hogs, dogs and fowl and an abundance of fruit and vegetables – a most welcome change after the salt beef and other unsavory fare that made up the usual rations at sea. Manby noted a class distinction: 'The rich and Oppulent fare Sumptuously on Dogs and Hogs, the Lower classes live on Bread fruit and other Vegetables.'[1]

There was no such discrimination in the ships. Puget records that the day after the *Discovery* arrived they 'Served Fresh Pork to the Ships Company with Bread fruit Cocoa Nuts & Plantains, which we continued to do During our Stay & afterwards at Sea while it lasted.'[2]

Vancouver had intended to refit his ships at the Sandwich Islands, but soon decided instead to prolong his stay at Tahiti and have the work done there. Requirements varied from a careful examination of sails and rigging to the building of a replacement for the *Chatham*'s jolly boat, which had been swept away in a storm. Puget was put in charge of a shore establishment that Bell notes 'had the appearance of a small encampment – besides the Observatory and the Captain's Marquee, there was a Tent for the Officers and two large Tents for the people employ'd ashore, and for working in.'[3]

Few of the native chiefs Vancouver had known in 1777 were still

---

[1] Manby, Letters.

[2] Puget, 31 December 1791. (One of a number of entries that show that Puget's log is a fair copy, made some time after the event.)

[3] Bell, 2 January 1792.

alive. Much the most important of the survivors was the chief whom Cook had known as Otoo (Tu). Then regarded as rather a timid soul, in spite of his imposing physique, the fortunes of war, inheritance and marriage had since given him commanding authority over northern Tahiti and some of the nearby islands. He had also acquired a young son, who, in accordance with custom, had succeeded both to his name and authority, while he himself had been relegated to the status of regent and had adopted the name of Pomurrey (Pomare). He welcomed Vancouver warmly, and Vancouver devotes much of his narrative to an account of his relations with Pomurrey, his two brothers and his wives. Most of them lived on the ships at times, all received and gave gifts on a generous scale, and, to his intense gratification, Pomurrey was honored with salutes from the ships' guns when he came on board and went ashore. Vancouver found other former friends in Mahow (Mahau), chief of Morea, who was Pomurrey's brother-in-law, and Potatau, chief of the district of Punaauia, in western Tahiti. He quickly established relations with other chiefs. Here and elsewhere, as Bern Anderson points out, Vancouver displayed 'an uncanny faculty for sifting out the various ranks and relative importance of the native chiefs, and of treating each with the deference due to his rank and position'.[1] He had a genuine liking for Pomurrey, but he was also shrewd enough to know that a friendly chief was more likely to make an effort to keep the natives under control, and to ensure a steady flow of provisions to the ships.

Inevitably some problems arose between ship and shore. Following Cook's example, Vancouver had issued an order forbidding all trading by crew members until the needs of the ships had been met. It was a necessary order, intended to keep the barter value of trade goods at a reasonable level; and it is interesting to note that even while it was in force Pomurrey at times insisted that the prices Vancouver proposed to pay were too high. But it was naturally an unpopular order, and Vancouver's most severe and persistent critic, George Hewett, surgeon's mate in the *Discovery*, complained that when the ban was raised on January 15 there was little left to purchase. Even more unpopular was the restriction placed on shore leave. Only sick men (who were few in number) and those actually required for duty on shore were permitted to leave the ships. Perhaps, remembering the fracas at Teneriffe, Vancouver feared that quarrels with the natives would arise, but doubtless it was Bligh's experience that he had chiefly in mind. The

---

[1] Anderson, *Surveyor of the Sea*, p. 58.

delights of shore leave, which made the men anxious to remain in the islands, was recognized as having been the chief cause of the famous mutiny. Bell took the part of the seamen, pointing out 'how very anxious every person must be to get ashore – and what a relaxation it must be, after having been five weeks at Sea – and especially when at such a place as Otaheite.... Why should poor Sailors...be debarr'd those recreations which they see every Officer on board enjoy?'[1] The deprivation was all the more trying because sweltering weather made the atmosphere below decks stifling, and a heavy swell in the bay often caused the ships to roll prodigiously.

The Tahiti visit lasted almost four weeks. At first all went smoothly, but in the last fortnight complications arose. Mahow, the chief of Morea and brother-in-law of Pomurrey, had been critically ill when he was brought from the island to meet Vancouver, and on January 14 word was received that he had died. Various taboos were promptly imposed followed by elaborate funeral rites. Vancouver and Menzies were permitted to attend some of the ceremonies, which both describe in detail, but they were not allowed to gratify an eagerness to witness the embalming of the corpse – a desire that one suspects was motivated by simple curiosity as much as by a wish to add to scientific knowledge. 'Embalming' seems scarcely to have been the appropriate term, as Vancouver states that only three days after Mahow's death his body was 'in a very advanced state of putrefaction' and emitted 'extremely offensive exhalations'.

Within a day or two of Mahow's funeral three exasperating events threatened to destroy the good relations that Vancouver enjoyed with Pomurrey and other chiefs. One concerned axes, which Vancouver had lent to four of the chiefs to enable them to have wood cut for the ships. When he asked for their return, three of the chiefs complied at once; the fourth, Moerree, made a determined effort to retain one axe. Next came thefts of linen from the *Chatham*. All early visitors to Polynesia comment upon the thieving propensities of the natives, and petty thefts which had been overlooked, perhaps unwisely, had occurred during the first weeks of Vancouver's stay. The natives washed clothes for the officers, and as shirts were one of the things they most coveted, the temptation to steal eventually became too great to resist. Johnstone was the first to suffer, then Walker, the surgeon, lost half a dozen shirts. The climax came when a bag of Broughton's linen, containing upwards of a dozen shirts, was stolen – a serious loss, as it was impossible to replace

[1] Bell, 3 January 1792.

the garments. Lastly, Towereroo, the Hawaiian boy that Vancouver had been instructed to return to his native island of Molokai, absconded. He had become infatuated with the daughter of Poeno, chief of Matavai, and had decided that he wanted to live with her in Tahiti.

Vancouver's reaction to these happenings was immediate and violent. Moerree's behaviour was specially annoying because he had been on intimate terms with both Vancouver and Broughton. Vancouver let it be known that he proposed to burn Moerree's house, and when actual preparations to do so began, the missing axe was returned. Moerree himself kept out of sight until the ships had sailed. When Boba, a servant, was seized on suspicion of having played a part in the thefts of linen, Vancouver ordered a halter to be put round his neck, announced that he would be hanged if Broughton's shirts were not returned, and, according to Hewett, 'in a Passion snatched hold of the Halter himself and drew it so tight as nearly to deprive the Man of Life'. Next, as Menzies records, he let it be known that if the shirts 'were not brought back very soon, he would desolate the whole district & destroy all their Canoes'.[1] This threat and the harsh treatment of Boba alarmed the natives and resulted in a wholesale exodus; houses were stripped and deserted; canoes were spirited away. Even Pomurrey made off, and some time passed before relations and negotiations could be resumed. Pomurrey was able to convince Vancouver that the unfortunate Boba was innocent and he was released. It was suggested that the stolen linen had probably been taken to a part of the island in which Whytooa, one of Pomurrey's brothers, had much influence, and he was asked to assist in its recovery. He agreed, but did nothing; at a time when he was supposed to have left on this mission he was found at home, 'in soft dalliance with his wife'.[2] Vancouver was convinced that some of the chiefs had been privy to the desertion of Towereroo, who possessed some guns and a knowledge of firearms that they would have found very useful. Vancouver let it be known that unless Towereroo was returned, none of the gifts he had intended to distribute upon leaving would be presented, and he cancelled a fireworks display to which the natives were looking forward with keen anticipation. The missing shirts were never recovered, but on January 13 Pomurrey and his two brothers returned with Towereroo, accompanied by canoes laden with such a profusion of provisions that all of them could not be taken on board the ships. Vancouver thereupon relented to the extent of presenting the intended gifts to Pomurrey and

[1] Menzies, 20 January 1792.   [2] Vancouver, I, 132.

others, but not to Whytooa, nor did he provide the display of fireworks.

Vancouver's reaction seems to have been excessive. It recalls Cook's even more extreme outburst at Morea in 1777, when the theft of a goat caused him to burn houses and destroy canoes. The cause may well have been the same: fatigue, and nervous irritability resulting from the failing health from which we know Vancouver was beginning to suffer. Broughton, who was a particular friend of Whytooa, defended him and persuaded Vancouver to allow him to keep the going-away gifts that Broughton had given him. Bell thought Whytooa's failure to search for the linen was due to indolence, 'his whole time & thought being taken up in Eating & drinking &c.'.[1] Everyone except Vancouver seems to have wished that it had been possible to leave Towereroo in Tahiti, as they felt that his best chance of happiness would be there, but Vancouver took the view that he could not deviate from the order to convey him to the Sandwich Islands. He had a low opinion of Towereroo, and punished him for his attempt to desert by turning him out of the gunner's mess and leaving him to get along as best he could among the seamen.

Vancouver's narrative added little or nothing to general knowledge of Tahiti. It cannot be compared in this respect with the journals of Cook and several of his officers, nor with Bligh's journal.[2] Vancouver was aware of this, and pleaded that the shortness of his stay and 'various concurring circumstances' had afforded him little opportunity to gratify 'the inquiring mind... with much additional information.' The point has merit. His own stay lasted less than four weeks, whereas Cook, paying his third visit, had spent seven weeks in Tahiti in 1777, and a further ten weeks amongst the other islands in the group, or nearly four months in all. Bligh's visit in 1789 had lasted five months. But Vancouver and others did make one or two comments of interest. The mutiny on the *Bounty* led him to take a sharp look at the women, whose attractions were a principal cause of it. He was not impressed: 'I cannot avoid acknowledging how great was the disappointment I experienced, in consequence of the early impression I had received of their superior personal endowments.... The extreme deficiency of female beauty on

---

[1] Bell, 23 January 1792.

[2] Cook's own comment is of interest: 'So much, or rather too much, has been published of Otaheite and the neighbouring islands already that there is very little room for new remarks; I have however been able to collect some, that will tend to clear up former misstakes as well as give a little information.' – 8 December 1777. Cook, *Journals*, III, 253.

these islands makes it singuarly remarkable, that so large a proportion of the crew belonging to the Bounty, should have become so infatuated as to sacrifice their country, their honor, and their lives, to any female attachments at Otaheite.'[1] The implication that the women had seemed more beautiful in former times moved Hewett to comment that at the time of his first visit Vancouver 'was a Young Man but that not being now the Case the Ladies of course were not so Attractive'. Hewett had met some of the wives chosen by the mutineers; one he considered 'as pretty a little figure as I ever saw extremely lively Chatty and pleasing', while another was 'a very fine Woman noble in her manner Voice lofty (like Siddons)'. Manby's journal shows that the young men in the *Discovery* who were fortunate enough to be employed on shore were far from indifferent to the charms of the Tahitian girls.

Vancouver does not mention that most of the officers conformed to the Tahitian custom of adopting a *taio*, or friend. Bell described his experience: 'Whilst I was walking the Deck a man came alongside in a double Canoe, and getting out of her, he stopp'd me, began wrapping me up in fine Cloth till I was as large round the middle as a Beer But, he then order'd in a very large Hog & some Plantains, Cocoa Nuts &c. that were in his Canoe which he presented me with for "Tyo" (or friendship) he then insisted on changing names with me, which is the custom allways observed here, when the man professes himself your friend.' This was no momentary impulse on the part of the native; 'he wou'd frequently make two or three trips to the Ship in a day' and 'there was scarce a day that he did not come on board with some present or other'.[2] He 'render'd me many excellent Services, and deserved every return I could make him…he express'd his sorrow very strongly at our departure'.[3] Manby found his *taio* in a higher stratum of society. It will be recalled that Puget had been put in charge of the shore establishment; 'the Lieutenant Governorship', Manby relates, 'was given to me much to my satisfaction. I took up my residence in a snug tent during our stay and very soon got included in all the social customs practised by these generous people. The first step is to select a Chief who swears to be your friend, guide and protector during the stay, with this person you change names, and according to the term of Otahita he is called your Tio. One of the greatest Warriors Otahita produces was my declared Tio. I then assumed the name Toubaino and he that of Mappée the nearest they could come to my name.…This

[1] Vancouver, I, 147–8.   [2] Bell, January 1792.
[3] *Ibid.*

worthy fellow had a very excellent habitation near the Tents...His Wife, Daughter and female relations were at my Command. His House Hogs and everything belonging to him was at my disposal and a large Retinue of domesticks were subservient to my Nod – in short he made me Lord of all in return I give him a Matress in my Tent and made him welcome to what it produced.'[1] When the *Discovery* sailed 'My Tio importuned me to secret him in the Ship declaring he would not leave me   poor fellow it was impossible.'[2]

Vancouver recalled a passage inserted by Cook's editor in the official account of his third voyage expressing deep concern over the degree to which the natives had become dependent on the 'conveniences' brought to them by Europeans. Vancouver believed that these had 'made them regardless of their former tools and manufactures, which are now growing fast out of use, and, I may add, equally out of remembrance.'[3] This Hewett denied. His impression was that the natives 'had both Bone and Stone Tools exceedingly well made which they commonly used', but he added the interesting observation that 'great numbers were also made during our stay here...only to Sell [these] were bad enough.' Trade in souvenirs for tourists was already beginning in 1792.

The *Discovery* and *Chatham* left Tahiti on 24 January 1792, bound for the Sandwich Islands. Vancouver felt that at last, after nearly ten months, his voyage of discovery had really begun, 'having now for the first time pointed our vessels' heads towards the grand object of the expedition' – the islands and the Northwest Coast. He estimated the distance to Hawaii to be 'nearly 800 leagues'. Actually it was much more; Puget states that the *Discovery* logged 3895 miles on the passage. Vancouver intended to pay only a brief visit to the islands, as he was arriving later than he expected. He hoped that the storeship *Daedalus* would be awaiting him there, and he would replenish the ships' water supply.

The southern tip of Owhyhee (the island of Hawaii) was sighted on March 1, and two days later the ships paused off Karakakooa (Kealakekua) Bay. No landing was made, perhaps because for Vancouver it was a place of unhappy memory. For others it had a morbid fascination. Bell records that 'it gratified us not a little at seeing the memorable place where England lost one of the greatest Navigators

---

[1] Manby, Letters, 1 January 1792.   [2] *Ibid.*, 24 January 1792.
[3] Vancouver, I, 145.

of the Age, (Captain Cook) – we stood pretty near the Shore – and were pointed out the Spot where that horrid melancholy Massacre was committed.'[1]

His journal shows that Vancouver was already taking a keen interest in island affairs, but during this first brief visit he could gain only a very general impression of the political changes that had occurred since Cook's death. Kalanioupuu, who had then ruled over all Owhyhee, had died in 1782. Wars and power struggles followed, and Tamaahmaaha (Kamehameha), the late king's nephew, emerged finally as the most powerful chief in the 'Big Island'. Titeeree (Kahekili), in Cook's time in control of most of Maui, had since extended his rule to Oahu, and, through his younger brother Taio (Kaeo), to Kauai and Niihau. Vancouver saw neither Tamaahmaaha nor Titeeree, as a war between them was believed to be imminent and they were with their armies. He heard one version of these events from Tianna (Kaiana), an ambitious and aggressive chief who had travelled to China with Meares and after his return had thrown in his lot with Tamaahmaaha. He claimed to be his equal in status, but in reality was chief of the district of Puna, in eastern Owhyhee, which was part of Tamaahmaaha's sphere of influence. A more accurate account of the relations between Tamaahmaaha and Tianna was given by Kahowmotoo (Keeaumoku), father of Tamaahmaaha's queen and chief of Kona, the district in which Karakakooa Bay was situated.

The change that disturbed Vancouver most was the introduction of firearms. Guns and ammunition were becoming a favorite item of barter in the fur trade on the Northwest Coast, and many of the ships engaged in it visited the islands and discovered that they could dispose of arms to great advantage there. Menzies noted the change in attitude since his last visit in 1788: 'nothing was now held in greater estimation or more eagerly sought after than arms & powder by those very people who but a few years back shuddered at the report of a musquet, but which they now handle with a degree of ease & dexterity that equalld the most expert veteran.'[2] Vancouver was puzzled at first by the reluctance of the natives to provide provisions, but it soon became evident that this was due to his firm refusal to offer arms in exchange. The difficulty was overcome finally by the friendliness of some of the chiefs and by Vancouver's insistence that all the arms in his ships were the property of King George and could not be offered for sale.

Arms had both intensified ambitions and become essential for

[1] Bell, 4 March 1792. [2] Menzies, 3 March 1792.

military success. Tamaahmaaha and Titeeree were both eager to secure them. Colnett recorded with pride the way in which a timely gift of arms had countered the efforts of Manuel Quimper to gain good will in the islands for Spain when the two had chanced to meet in 1791 in Kailua Bay, some distance north of Karakakooa: 'By a little well timed liberality, I wiped out every impression of their superiority...and by a Present of a three Pound swivel, a few musquetes, and two or three Blunderbusses, I stood well with the great, and got well supplied with hogs, and other articles when they [the Spaniards] could not get an individual thing.... My supply of Powder came very apropos, they being at war with the other Isles.'[1] Tianna had become a chief of importance largely because he possessed arms which he had brought from China. Vancouver refers at length to the seizure of the small American schooner *Fair American*, and the massacre of her crew, early in 1790, by Tamaahmotoo (Kameeiamoku), chief of Kohala district. Although this was primarily an act of personal revenge for ill-treatment, the vessel itself and the guns she carried were important additions to his military strength. Tamaahmaaha disapproved strongly of the attack and took possession of the schooner, but it encouraged Tianna to contemplate attacks on much larger vessels. In 1791 he had visited the American trading ship *Hope* and her commander, Joseph Ingraham, had detected him making inquiries about 'the number of men, guns, and quantity of powder on board, etc.'[2] Vancouver was certain that in a similar way Tianna had looked over the *Discovery* with a view to seizing her, but had been discouraged by the size and discipline of her crew, which far surpassed that of trading ships.

Tianna had talked with Towereroo, the Hawaiian youth Vancouver had brought back to the islands, and (in Vancouver's words) the conversation 'had induced him to believe that the services of this lad might be of great importance to him'. He offered Towereroo 'a very handsome establishment of house, land, and other advantages'. Although he distrusted Tianna, Vancouver judged it best to accept the offer. Conditions on Molokai, Towereroo's native island, were very disturbed, and there seemed to be little prospect of settling him there satisfactorily. Vancouver makes it clear that the arrangement with Tianna was to some degree tentative; he would leave Towereroo with him 'for the present' and when he returned in the autumn 'might be

[1] F. W. Howay (ed.), *The Journal of Captain James Colnett* (Toronto, 1940), p. 220.
[2] Mark D. Kaplanoff (ed.), *Joseph Ingraham's Journal of the Brigantine Hope on a Voyage to the Northwest Coast of America* (Barre, Mass., 1971), p. 73.

enabled to form some judgment of his treatment.'[1] In this expectation Towereroo left some of his possessions in the ship for safekeeping. In spite of this provision, Vancouver's action met with severe criticism; some regarded it as a sequel to his insistence on carrying Towereroo away from Tahiti. Manby states that Towereroo 'with joy agreed to the plan, no doubt happy in the idea of parting with a set of Men who had treated him with the utmost barbarity by tearing him from the object of his affections.'[2] Bell wrote: 'Poor fellow, I pity'd him when I thought how much happier he wou'd have been had he been suffered to remain at Otaheite' and added that 'poor Towereroo was put ashore like a Convict to his place of transportation.'[3]

The *Discovery* soon moved on to Wahoo (Oahu); on March 7 she rounded Diamond Head and anchored in Waikiki Bay. But again the welcome was subdued, and as watering arrangements were unsatisfactory Vancouver sailed on to Whymea (Waimea) Bay, in Attowai (Kauai), where Cook had made his first landing in 1778. Here the work of the ship progressed satisfactorily, and although Kaeo was absent, Vancouver met his young son and heir and the regent who had been left in charge of affairs. British trading ships had made a considerable impression. Vancouver was pleased by the 'strong predilection and attachment which the young prince had conceived for the subjects of Great-Britain' and amused to find that he had assumed 'the title King George; not suffering his domestics to address him by any other name.'[4] For a day or two the atmosphere was pleasantly relaxed. Vancouver and Menzies explored the Waimea River valley, while Manby, a good shot, was followed by crowds when he went hunting and 'became of great consequence in the Eyes of the Natives from the destruction made among the Feather'd tribe.' He adds that 'the Indians made the best Spaniels ever hunted with, as they drove the Ducks from the Swamps and picked them up with delighted eagerness as they fell.'[5]

On March 11, when returning from a pleasant walk along the beach, Vancouver suddenly saw large fires burning on the hills. Assuming that they were hostile signs that presaged an attack, he became thoroughly alarmed, and his fears mounted as he received different explanations from different chiefs. Menzies and Johnstone did their best to reassure him, as both had seen similar fires on previous visits, and were convinced (in Johnstone's words) that they had been lighted 'to

---

[1] Vancouver, I, 156. [2] Manby, Letters, March 1792.
[3] Bell, 4 March 1792. [4] Vancouver, I, 185.
[5] Manby, Letters, March 1792.

consume the old and withered grass that the spring may produce a new growth more tender than the old which serves them for thatch to their houses'.[1] But Vancouver would not be reassured. Hewett states that he 'behaved like a Madman raged and swore which terrified the Indians'. Even allowing for Hewett's prejudice against Vancouver it is evident that this was another of the sudden outbursts of temper and tension to which he was becoming subject. His simple statement that he 'returned on board' avoids mention of a near fatal accident. Although a very heavy surf was running, he insisted on being taken back to the ship immediately. It was a foolhardy decision. The native canoe that was taking him out to the *Discovery*'s pinnace upset, and two of the midshipmen, who in true sailor fashion could not swim, nearly lost their lives. Vancouver chose to believe that this accident was a deliberate attempt on his own life, refused to re-enter the canoe, and swam through the surf to the waiting boat. The next evening, although conditions were still dangerous, he ordered Puget and others who were still on shore to embark forthwith, and there were more near drownings.

Thereafter matters improved. In the hasty return to the ships muskets and axes had been lost in the surf, while other items, including Manby's highly prized double-barrelled fowling piece, had had to be left on shore. The temptation to make off with such treasure trove must have been great, but Menzies relates that 'Every article was found in the same situation in which it was left, & even the most valuable articles that had been lost in the surf were at the instigation of the Chiefs recovered & laid with the rest & the whole delivered to the Officers in the most handsome manner.'[2] The following day the ships were visited first by the elderly regent and then by the young prince, who impressed Vancouver very favorably. As a parting gesture of good will Vancouver provided a display of fireworks to the delight and astonishment of the natives.

After a five-day stay the *Discovery* and *Chatham* left Attowai (Kauai) early on the morning of March 14, and later the same day they anchored off Onehow (Niihau). Yams, popular with ships because they would keep for two or three months at sea, were obtainable there in quantity. Johnstone states that the *Chatham* took about eight tons of them on board and the *Discovery* secured considerably more. This transaction completed, the ships sailed on March 16, bound for the Northwest Coast. Vancouver had nowhere received any tidings of the

[1] Johnstone, 11 March 1792.   [2] Menzies, 13 March 1792.

Daedalus, which he now expected would meet him later in the year at Nootka Sound.

First Survey Season

The voyage from the islands to the coast of North America lasted almost exactly a month. Baker states that land was sighted at 5 p.m. on April 18, ship's time; Vancouver, who uses civil time in his journal, gives the date as April 17. As he had made no adjustment for the fact that he had sailed eastward around the world (and would make none until he reached St Helena), by local time, which would be used by the Spaniards he was soon to meet, the date was April 16.

His landfall was near latitude 39° 20′ N, in the vicinity of Cape Cabrillo, about 115 miles north of San Francisco Bay. He would have preferred to begin his examination of the coast farther south, but judged it best to turn northward at once. He was behind his intended schedule, and he was anxious to see something of the Strait of Juan de Fuca before arriving at Nootka Sound. During daylight hours the ships endeavoured to keep land clearly in sight, while keeping a safe distance from it, a feat often made difficult by stormy weather and poor visibility. 'As we had now entered upon our Station, and the Survey of the Coast,' Bell explains, 'we were obliged to haul off at dark & spend the night in short boards [tacks], that we might take up the Land in the morning where we left off the Evening before.'[1]

The first prominent feature seen on the coast was Cape Mendocino. At first Vancouver associated Punta Garda, to the south, with the cape, but later he placed the name in the correct position on his chart. On April 22 the ships passed Trinidad Head, which Vancouver called Rocky Point, a name since moved to a lesser feature a little to the north. On April 23, St. George's Day, he named Point St. George, one of only three names he bestowed on features between his landfall and Cape Flattery that have been retained. Dragon Rocks, off Point St. George, and most appropriately named, are now St. George Reef. Cape Orford, in latitude 42° 50′ N, sighted on the 24th, has become Cape Blanco. The next day Vancouver reached a part of the coast that Cook had seen, where in latitude 43° 18′ N he saw what he was reasonably certain was Cook's Cape Gregory, known since 1850 as Cape Arago. The next afternoon he passed Cape Foulweather, off which he experienced the sort of weather that had prompted Cook to bestow the name. Vancouver's narrative reminds us that Cook saw very little of the

[1] Bell, 18 April 1792.

coast. After sighting these capes bad weather forced him out to sea and he did not regain the coast until he was in latitude 47° 05′ N. This glimpse of land lasted only one day, at the end of which he sighted Cape Flattery, in latitude 48° 23′ N. The cape is the southern entrance point of the Strait of Juan de Fuca, but poor visibility and approaching night prevented Cook from seeing the strait and led him to make his famous but unfortunate remark that there was not 'the least probability that iver any such thing exhisted.'[1]

South of Cape Blanco (Vancouver's Cape Orford) the ships had a first brief encounter with North American Indians.[2] Though opinions as to their cleanliness varied (Menzies described them as being 'of a copper colour but cleanly' while Manby, sometimes given to exaggeration, thought them 'filthy and stinking'), the general impression they made was favorable. They did not hesitate to bring their two canoes alongside the ships, were friendly and courteous and honest in their trading. Puget states that the items offered in barter included 'a Sea Otter Skin which was purchased'[3] – the expedition's first glimpse of the luxurious fur that had brought numbers of trading vessels to the Northwest Coast. This was the first of many purchases made by officers of the ships in the course of the survey, but Vancouver was careful not to compete with commercial vessels; he would permit no trading when any were near at hand.

At no great distance north of Cape Foulweather the ships came to the part of the coast that had been seen by Meares. The first important landmark was Cape Lookout, now Cape Meares, which was the southern limit of his exploration. The second was Cape Disappointment, on the north side of the entrance to the Columbia River.

Vancouver has been criticized many times for not paying more attention to the Columbia, and it is true that here and elsewhere he showed a curious indifference to rivers. He or his boat parties were at the mouths of the Fraser, Skeena, Nass and Stikine, but none of the four appears on his charts. Yet the various logs of the voyage show that in each instance, the Columbia included, the existence of a river was either assumed or strongly suspected. The failure to explore them is explained in part by Vancouver's instructions: 'it seems desirable', they read, 'that in order to avoid any unnecessary loss of time, you

---

[1] Cook, *Journals*, III, 294.

[2] They were Tututni Indians, who occupied the lower valley of the Rogue River, and the coast north and south of its mouth.

[3] Puget, 25 April 1792.

should not, and are therefore hereby required and directed not to pursue any inlet or river further than it shall appear to be navigable by vessels of such burden as might safely navigate the Pacific Ocean.' That Vancouver had passed on this directive to his officers, and that at least one of them obeyed it with reluctance, is shown by a remark by Puget, when he decided not to venture up the Skeena: 'the Channel could not be termed Navigable therefore we had no Business to pursue [it] but this would not have prevented its further Examination had it not absolutely been attended with very great Danger to the Boats'.[1] What deterred Vancouver himself was the never-ending line of mountains that paralleled the coast, which he assumed, quite correctly, would place a limit, if not to the rivers themselves, at least to the possibility that they might be navigated for any great distance by such a vessel as the *Discovery*. It is a pity that Broughton's exploration of the Columbia, made a few months later, stopped just short of the chasms and rapids that would have proven Vancouver's assumption to be correct; and it is significant also that Broughton found river depths and conditions such that he left the *Chatham*, small as she was, within a few miles of the mouth of the river and proceeded upstream in the ship's boats.

The Columbia had been noticed in 1775 by Bruno de Hezeta. Strong currents and the famous bar prevented him from entering, but he was so sure that he was off 'the mouth of some great river, or of some passage to another sea'[2] that he gave it a name, Río de San Roque. It was shown on his own chart and on at least nine other Spanish charts of later date, but Vancouver may have been more impressed by Meares' more recent experience, in 1788. Although 'a prodigious Easterly swell rolled on the shore' Meares attempted to enter, but the water shoaled alarmingly, breakers were seen, and 'from the mast-head, they were observed to extend across the bay. We therefore hauled out.' Meares went on to say that he could 'now with safety assert, that...no such river as that of Saint Roc exists, as laid down in the Spanish charts'.[3] But some of those in the *Discovery* and *Chatham* thought otherwise. Menzies noted that he could see 'from the Mast head the appearance of a river or inlet';[4] Baker noted that 'there appear'd to be a small opening which from the colour of the water I suppose to be a River';[5]

---

[1] Puget, 14 July 1793.

[2] Quoted by Warren Cook, *Flood Tide of Empire. Spain and the Pacific Northwest, 1543–1819* (New Haven, 1973), p. 78.

[3] John Meares, *Voyages Made in the Years 1788 and 1789, from China to the North West Coast of America* (London, 1790), pp. 167–8.

[4] Menzies, 27 April 1792.   [5] Baker, 28 April 1792.

and Bell wrote that 'there was every appearance of an opening there, but to us the Sea seem'd to break entirely across it'.[1] Vancouver himself went no further than to note that off the cape the sea 'changed from its natural, to river coloured water'.

Three factors undoubtedly influenced his decision to sail on without exploring the bay: he was anxious to avoid delay in beginning his survey of the very broken coast that he knew lay to the north; weather conditions promised to enable him to reach the Strait of Juan de Fuca quickly, and the breakers across the entrance made it clear that an attempt to enter might well result in serious damage to or even the loss of a ship. Manby's narrative, probably written shortly after the event, gives a fairer impression than Vancouver's own unfortunate remark that he did not consider 'this opening worthy of more attention'. On April 27, Manby wrote, 'we observed a considerable breach in the Land...we approached it, as near as safety would permit as a continued roll of tremendous breakers lay right across its entrance, it may prove [to be] a River and perhaps admissible at certain periods. We had it not in our power to loiter away any time on it at present, intending to inspect it farther on a future day.'[2]

North of Cape Disappointment Vancouver saw the other two features that still retain the names he gave them – Point Grenville and Destruction Island. The next morning, April 29, came his historic meeting with the Boston trader *Columbia*, commanded by Robert Gray – the first vessel the expedition had encountered in eight months. In both his text and his chart Meares had credited Gray with having in effect circumnavigated Vancouver Island, but when Puget and Menzies visited the *Columbia*, Gray, 'struck, with astonishment', explained that he had done no more than enter the Strait of Juan de Fuca, sail up it for about 17 leagues, and then leave it by the same opening by which he had entered. Gray also mentioned the Columbia River, which he had already tried once to enter, and it was clear that he intended to make a second attempt. Vancouver's comment was: 'if any inlet or river should be found, it must be a very intricate one, inaccessible to vessels of our burden, owing to the reefs and broken water...in its neighbourhood'.[3]

A few hours after this discussion with Gray the *Discovery* and *Chatham* entered the fabled Strait of Juan de Fuca. Hewett contends that until the last minute Vancouver, intensely loyal to Cook, doubted

---

[1] Bell, 27 April 1792.　　　　　　[2] Manby, Letters, 27 April 1792.
[3] Vancouver, I, 223.

its existence. The ships rounded Cape Flattery, but had difficulty in identifying it. Menzies, in the *Discovery*, wrote: 'We saw no point worthy of particular notice in the situation Capt Cook places Cape Flattery'.[1] In the *Chatham*, Johnstone 'did not decidedly observe any prominence, so as to be convicted which was the real Cape Flattery'.[2] Vancouver was being guided by the 'excellent sketch' of the entrance to the strait prepared in 1788 by Captain Duncan of the *Princess Royal*, on which Cape Flattery appears as Cape Classet. Duncan had made a substantial error in latitude, and until the identity of the two could be established, Vancouver adopted the latter name.

As he came up the coast Vancouver had been constantly on the watch for a harbour in which to refit his ships and replenish their stores of wood and water. He arrived in the Strait of Juan de Fuca 'thoroughly convinced' that he 'could not possibly have passed any safe navigable opening, harbour, or place of security for shipping on this coast, from cape Mendocino to the promontory of Classet'.[3] Though he had failed to notice several bays, including Coos Bay and Willipa Bay, both now busy ports, they were inconspicuous and in the then state of channels and bars it would have been extremely dangerous for a vessel the size of the *Discovery* to attempt to enter them. Later the *Daedalus* would venture into Grays Harbor, which Vancouver passed at night, but even there the bar was hazardous and it was not a convenient port in which to service and refit a ship. Having passed Cape Flattery, Vancouver's first priority was to find such a haven, and he found it in Port Discovery (now Discovery Bay), on the southern shore, about 70 miles east of the cape. There the ships anchored on May 2.

Vancouver's plan for his survey, which Anderson aptly characterized as being 'rendered infallible by its simplicity',[4] was to trace every foot of the continental shore. If a Northwest Passage existed, this would certainly reveal it. He was confident that he had carried such a survey from his landfall to Port Discovery. That harbour had been first reconnoitered by the ships' boats, and as the *Discovery* and *Chatham* would be delayed for some time in port, Vancouver determined to carry out a further reconnaissance by the same means. On May 7 the little flotilla, provisioned for five days, set out to trace the southern shore of the strait eastward. Menzies and Vancouver were in the *Discovery*'s

---

[1] Menzies, 29 April 1792.   [2] Johnstone, 29 April 1792.
[3] Vancouver, I, 224.
[4] Bern Anderson (ed.) 'Peter Puget's Journal of the Exploration of Puget Sound', *Pacific Northwest Quarterly* xxx (1939), p. 180n.

pinnace (which Vancouver often refers to as the yawl), Puget was in her launch, and Johnstone accompanied them in the *Chatham*'s cutter.

There were to be many such expeditions, but Vancouver seems to have had no such expectation at the time; he was simply anxious to get on with the survey and saw in the boats a means of doing so until such time as the ships were ready to move on. The experience of this first expedition was to be both typical and revealing. It showed that the coastline was as broken as the rough maps of the fur traders suggested, and that the survey would call for the examination of innumerable passages, bays and inlets. A few miles east of Port Discovery the boats came upon a deep opening leading to the south. Turning to investigate it, they were soon involved in unravelling the intricate system of waterways, extending nearly a hundred miles, that comprises Puget Sound. The continental shore first led Vancouver into Port Townsend and then, when the main channel divided, into Hood Canal, some 50 miles in length. Thanks in part to bad weather, more than the allotted five days were required to examine it and return to Port Discovery. When the ships were ready to move, Vancouver sent the *Chatham* to investigate the San Juan Islands, clearly visible to the north, while the *Discovery* sailed down the unexplored channel of Puget Sound as far as Restoration Point, opposite the future site of the city of Seattle. From there two boat expeditions, one headed by Puget and Whidbey and the other by Vancouver himself, pushed southward to trace the numerous passages and inlets into which the sound divides. Meanwhile the *Chatham*, having made a hasty survey of the islands, had joined the *Discovery* and had then been sent to investigate a large inlet branching off to the northeast. When Vancouver, Puget and Whidbey returned to the *Discovery* she joined the *Chatham* in what Vancouver later named Possession Sound. As the name suggests, he there took formal possession of the country. Still more boat expeditions were required to complete the tracing of the continental shore around the winding perimeter of Puget Sound. The task had taken an entire month, and as the ships left the sound through the same opening by which they had entered, it was evident that this great effort had advanced the survey northward by only a few miles.

In some respects it had been a chastening experience. The weather had been variable, and although those in the boats were frequently impressed with the beauty of the country, they more than once had to endure torrents of rain that soaked them and their belongings. Indians were met with from time to time, and although most of them responded to friendly advances, one encounter that nearly ended in bloodshed showed that constant vigilance was essential. Several of the parties continued exploring beyond the period for which they were provisioned, and they found it most difficult to secure additional food. Puget had occasion to be grateful that 'the People were not averse to eating Crows of which we could always procure plenty.'[1] Finally, it became clear that the survey of the coast would have to be carried out in great part by the boats; ships even as large as the little *Chatham*, let alone the *Discovery*, could not safely navigate the channels and inlets the expedition seemed certain to encounter. Many of them would be so narrow and hemmed in by mountains that wind conditions would be erratic, tides and currents strong, and water depths, even close to shore, often so great that ships could not anchor. Many times it would be found that the only way to moor the ships would be to tie them up to trees along the shore. All this Vancouver had taken into account while the survey of Puget Sound was still in progress. 'I became thoroughly convinced', his journal for May 25 reads, 'that our boats alone could enable us to acquire correct or satisfactory information respecting this broken country; and although the execution of such a service in open boats would necessarily be extremely laborious, and expose those so employed to numberless dangers and unpleasant situations, that might occasionally produce great fatigue, and protract their return to the ships; yet that mode was undoubtedly the most accurate, the most ready, and indeed the only one in our power to pursue for ascertaining the continental boundary.'[2]

As already mentioned, Vancouver depended heavily on Whidbey and Johnstone, navigating officers of the *Discovery* and *Chatham*, both of whom had had surveying experience, for the success of the boat expeditions. During the 1792 surveying season Puget was nominally in charge of most of them, but Whidbey accompanied him, and Vancouver had given him specific instructions to follow Whidbey's directions 'in such points as appertain to the Surveying of the shore &c.'[3] Puget described most of his expeditions in considerable detail in his journal, and Menzies, who accompanied both Whidbey and Johnstone on occasion, also described his experiences. The surviving volume of Johnstone's journal describes only the first expedition from Port Discovery, but Vancouver quotes or paraphrases many later

---

[1] Puget, 25 May 1792.　　　　　　　　　[2] Vancouver, I, 267.

[3] Puget quotes the text of one of Vancouver's orders, dated 6 June 1792, after his journal entry for May 20.

entries from it. Whidbey's journal has disappeared, but here again Vancouver frequently gives a description of an expedition that must have been derived from it.

Arrangements for the survey were soon reduced to an efficient routine. The *Discovery* and *Chatham* would take shelter in a suitable anchorage, preferably one where wood and water were available, where spruce beer could be brewed, and where the observatory could be set up on shore to check the longitude and the going rate of the chronometers. From this base one or two boat expeditions would be sent out to explore the adjacent parts of the continental shore. Each usually consisted of two boats, manned by an officer, a midshipman or two, some marines and rowing crews. The boats were armed with swivels, muskets, small arms and sporting guns. They were provisioned for a stated period, often ten days or a fortnight, and carried a surprising variety of trade goods to enable them to barter with the Indians and make gifts to them. They carried tents for the men and a marquee for the officers, but during the first season the boats themselves had no covering; this was remedied before the second season. Weather permitting, the working day began at 4 a.m. and often lasted until dusk or later. When possible, the boats landed for meals, but these stops were usually short. Cooking was done after the crews had come ashore for the night. Sometimes officers and men had to sleep in the boats, an ordeal they detested.

Mention has been made of the Indians. The last paragraph of Vancouver's instructions directed him 'to use every possible care to avoid disputes with the natives...[and] by a judicious distribution of the presents [provided]...and by all other means, to conciliate their friendship and confidence.' This was much more than a pious injunction. Vancouver made every effort to carry it into effect, and he was helped greatly in this endeavour by the generous quantity and great variety of trinkets and trade goods with which the ships had been supplied.

Apart from the brief encounter with a few of the Rogue River Indians on the Oregon coast, the first natives met with were the Makah Indians, whose villages were near Cape Flattery. They were Nootkan speaking, and Menzies and others who had been on the coast before were able to communicate with them. Farther east, in Port Discovery and Puget Sound, the Indians were Salish-speaking Clallam, whom no one could understand. Vancouver seems to have been curiously slow to grasp the fact that he would meet with a variety of languages as he worked his way up the coast. Menzies usually made an effort to learn at least a few words of each of them, and hit upon the expedient of persuading the Indians to count, in the hope that the numerals might provide a clue to the relationship of the newly encountered language with those that had gone before.

Most of the Indians displayed considerable eagerness to trade and a surprising willingness to part with bows, arrows, fishing gear, implements and garments that must have cost them a great deal of labour. The goods they accepted in return varied greatly. Some of the natives on the outer coast, who had encountered ships engaged in the maritime fur trade, were already shrewd and discriminating traders, hopeful of securing firearms. Those meeting Europeans for the first time, or less familiar with them, were interested in iron and copper and such items as mirrors, scissors, beads and buttons. On the whole relations were good, in Puget's opinion because barter was conducted 'with the Strictest honesty on both Sides – this however,' he adds, 'I greatly attribute to a proper treatment of these People on our Part, for we would never accept any Article till the Owner was satisfied with what was offered in Exchange.'[1]

It is greatly to the credit of Vancouver and his officers that in three seasons only one clash with the Indian occurred that involved bloodshed. The first of the few other occasions when it was narrowly averted occurred early on, in Carr Inlet, when Puget and Whidbey were exploring the southern part of Puget Sound. It was probably due to ignorance of the power of firearms; shots which had been fired earlier had been greeted with derision. Eight canoes finally approached in threatening fashion, and in a last effort to avoid a clash Puget ordered a swivel to be fired over their heads. This had the desired effect and the incident ended with a typical about-face in Indian attitude. One minute they were about to attack; the next they had unstrung their bows and were eager to offer their weapons for barter. Menzies remarks that 'they were readily purchased from them, as by this means we disarmed them in a more satisfactory manner.'[2] No doubt plunder had been the motive for the attack. With no understanding of the protection afforded by guns, the boats must have looked like easy prey not only on this but on many later occasions. The *Chatham*'s cutter and launch were respectively only 22 and 19 feet in length; the *Discovery*'s boats were probably only slightly longer. In Puget Sound the Indian canoes

[1] Puget, 9 June 1792. [2] Menzies, 21 May 1792.

were probably no larger, but on the northern coast the boat expeditions would meet dugouts twice and three times these lengths, manned by anything up to 50 men. It was difficult to conceal the trade goods carried in the open boats, and Puget noticed that 'a Great Display of various Articles' that the government had supplied so liberally often caused 'long Consultations among the Natives'. A transaction might be completed to their satisfaction, 'yet their Eyes were continually fixed on what remained in the Boats'. Puget did not 'mean to assert from this, that their Intentions were hostile, it might be Admiration or Curiosity and on the other Hand, we may equally suppose their Consultations were not held for any good Purpose but merely to possess by Strategem or Force what they found [they] could not by Trade'.[1] The price of safety was eternal caution, and Vancouver instructed his men to avoid landing if possible when Indians were present in considerable numbers.

Vancouver made no pretence to any expert knowledge about the Indians. When he left Port Discovery he admitted in his journal that intercourse with them had been so limited that he had been able to learn little about them. Later Puget confided to his journal that he, too, felt that his knowlege was scanty, nor, owing to their very imperfect knowledge of languages, and 'the very Short time we remain at any Place either in the Ships or Boats' did he think they would 'ever be well acquainted with their Manners and Customs.'[2] Thomas Manby, the midshipman, accompanied Puget on several of his boat excursions and evidently begged him to stop at the different villages they came upon, but Puget felt that the visits would have been so brief that they would not justify the risks involved. So far as the Indians in Puget Sound were concerned, Vancouver and others wrought better than they knew. Erna Gunther, the authority on the natives of the region, states that the 'combined observations' of Vancouver, Puget, Menzies and Bell 'provide rich detail about the Indians of this area.'[3] To these four, two other sources should be added – Manby's letters, and the collection of artifacts gathered by George Goodman Hewett, surgeon's mate of the *Discovery*. The various journals suggest that many of the officers probably bartered bows and arrows and other items as souvenirs, but most of them have disappeared. Hewett's collection, consisting of more

[1] Puget, 9 June 1792.
[2] *Ibid.*, 11 June 1792.
[3] Erna Gunther, *Indian Life on the Northwest Coast of North America as seen by the Early Explorers and Fur Traders during the Last Decades of the Eighteenth Century* (Chicago, 1972), p. 75.

than 150 items, fortunately found its way to the British Museum nearly a century after it was gathered. It comprises nearly 40 per cent. of the material included in Dr. Gunther's census of objects in European museums that were gathered on the Northwest Coast in the eighteenth century.[1]

After a short visit to Cypress Island, in the San Juan group, the *Discovery* and *Chatham* returned to the continental shore and found a highly satisfactory anchorage in Birch Bay, about four miles south of the 49th parallel, now the boundary between Canada and the United States. The marquee, tents and observatory were set up on shore, water was found nearby, and blacksmiths, carpenters and brewers were soon busy at their trades.

The next day, June 12, Vancouver, Puget and Manby set out on one of the most interesting and important of the boat expeditions. They headed north, while Whidbey was to leave the next day to head south, there to examine the part of the continental shore that had been bypassed owing to the detour through the San Juan Islands. Vancouver's expedition was notable on three counts: he passed the mouth of the Fraser River, which critics contend he should have discovered; he explored Burrard Inlet; and on returning to Birch Bay he found the Spanish survey ships *Sutil* and *Mexicana* anchored near Point Grey.

The estuary of the Fraser consists of a very low-lying delta that fans out to a width of nearly twenty miles, between Point Roberts and Point Grey. Today much of this delta has been diked and reclaimed, but in Vancouver's day most of it was flooded by the spring freshet, which would be at or near its height in mid-June. Under such conditions the river channels were difficult to see, and this problem was made much greater by the vast shoals – now known as Roberts Bank and Sturgeon Bank – that blanket the whole of the estuary. These would keep the ships' boats at least three or four miles from shore – indeed, Vancouver mentions seven or eight miles. Nevertheless his narrative and Puget's journal make it clear that they were aware that they were off the mouth of a considerable river. Vancouver states that 'two openings' were noted between Point Roberts and Point Grey and adds: 'These can only be navigable for canoes, as the shoal continues along the coast to the

---

[1] See C. H. Read, 'An Account of a Collection of Ethnographical Specimens formed during Vancouver's Voyage in the Pacific Ocean,' *Journal of the Anthropological Institute*, Nov. 1891, pp. 99–108. Hewett's collection includes items from Tahiti and the Sandwich Islands as well as the Northwest Coast. His own manuscript list came to the British Museum with the collection.

distance of seven or eight miles from the shore, on which were lodged, and especially before these openings, logs of wood, and stumps of trees innumerable.'[1] The 'two openings' were the main channels through the delta by which the Fraser reaches the sea, and it is asking a great deal to assume that Vancouver did not realize that the logs and stumps could only have reached the delta by being swept down to it by a large river in freshet. Puget's reference reads: 'Two Places...had much the Appearance of a large River, but the Shoals hitherto have prevented our having Communication with them.'[2] The surprising fact is that neither mentions the discoloured river water which the freshet pushes out into Georgia Strait, and which is usually separated from the sea water by a clearly defined line. In any event, Vancouver and Puget concluded, quite correctly, that there was no sign of a channel that would be navigable by such a vessel as the Discovery, and in accordance with his instructions, Vancouver moved on to the north.

Officially the entrance to Burrard Inlet, which is now synonymous with Vancouver Harbour, lies between Point Grey and Point Atkinson, four miles to the north. The inlet consists essentially of three parts: a broad outer anchorage (English Bay); an extensive inner harbour, beyond the First Narrows, whose shores are now occupied by the city of Vancouver and several satellite communities; and two arms into which the inlet divides at its eastern end, Port Moody and Indian Arm. Locally many people who refer to 'the inlet' mean the inner harbour, and some early maps similarly confine the name to the waters east of the First Narrows. This has a bearing upon the question as to who discovered Burrard Inlet, an achievement often popularly credited to Vancouver. At the time of his visit Vancouver had no inkling that the Spanish schooner Santa Saturnina, commanded by José Maria Narváez, had been in these waters in 1791 and had ventured into English Bay. Narváez therefore deserves to rank as the inlet's discoverer. But Vancouver was the first mariner to pass through the First Narrows and explore the inner harbour. This he did on June 13. Just inside the narrows he passed an Indian village (Homulchesun), and some fifty curious and friendly Indians followed the boats in canoes as they travelled eastward to a point where Vancouver probably could see the end of Port Moody. As dusk was approaching, he then turned back and spent the night on the south shore, opposite the entrance to Indian Arm. This he did not explore, as it seemed clear that it was of no great extent or importance. He expected to meet the Indians again the next morning as he left the

[1] Vancouver, I, 300.   [2] Puget, 12 June 1792.

inlet, but as he set off at the usual departure time of 4 a.m. and the boats moved briskly under sail, no contacts were made, although some of the natives were seen.

It is surprising that Vancouver's occasional comments on natural features and scenery do not include some comment on the inlet, where he had just explored one of the world's finest landlocked harbours. Perhaps he was impressed by the difficulty that sailing ships might experience in navigating the First Narrows. This problem did not arise seventy years later, when merchant ships began to frequent the inner harbour, for by that time steam tugs were available to tow them into port and out to sea.

As the boats had travelled north from Birch Bay, just before their visit to Burrard Inlet, Vancouver and Puget had come in sight of the main expanse of the Strait of Georgia – in Puget's words, they had 'a Clear & uninterrupted view to the NW.' Although Meares' story that Nootka was on the west side of a huge island around which Gray had sailed in the *Lady Washington* had been disproven by Gray's own denial, Indian reports seem to have bolstered the idea that such an inside passage might in fact exist. Puget shared this hope. 'This Prospect,' he wrote, 'was truly flattering, as we now began to have hopes of finding a passage through, instead of being obliged to return to Sea by Cape Flattery.' But there was 'still one great Obstacle to surmount before the Completion of our present Sanguine Expectations, that of a Change in the Flood Stream which still continues with its usual Rapidity from the Southward.'[1] A tide flowing from the north would be certain evidence of a connection with the ocean. That evidence was to be forthcoming a fortnight later.

From Burrard Inlet Vancouver and Puget continued up the continental shore, exploring first Howe Sound and then Jervis Inlet, and investigating the numerous bays and minor inlets encountered in their progress. Jervis Inlet, nearly 50 miles in length, was another of the many long, narrow waterways that Vancouver was to encounter that had the disconcerting characteristic of varying little in their width, thus making it impossible to gauge their length without following them to their ends. Its examination was marred by an unfortunate incident involving Manby. As they were about to leave the inlet Puget joined Vancouver in the pinnace, leaving Manby in charge of the launch. Daylight faded, the launch fell behind, and Manby did not see that Vancouver was not leaving the inlet by the same way he had entered it. Manby followed

[1] Puget, 12 June 1792.

the latter route, with the result that the boats became separated. Left without either compass or provisions, Manby had to find his way back to Birch Bay as best he could. His crew, he tells us, 'suffered every hardship fatigue and hunger could inflict', but he reached the *Discovery* before Vancouver, who arrived in a fury: 'his salutation I can never forget, and his language I will never forgive, unless he withdraws his words by a satisfactory apology.'[1] No doubt Vancouver was weary after a boat expedition that had travelled over 300 miles and had lasted 12 days instead of the week for which it had been provisioned; but this seems to have been another of the occasional outbursts to which Vancouver was becoming subject. He evidently held no grudge against Manby, for he appointed him master of the *Chatham* three months later. Manby was less forgiving. He states that he would have refused the appointment in England, 'but here rejoiced at it' as the transfer 'cleared me from a Man, I had such just reason to be displeased with.'[2]

On June 22, when returning to the *Discovery*, Vancouver was astonished to find two small Spanish schooners anchored near Point Grey. These were the *Sutil* and *Mexicana*, commanded respectively by Dionisio Galiano and Cayetano Valdés, frigate captains in the Spanish Navy, who in Vancouver's absence had already made contact with Broughton and Whidbey. Hitherto Vancouver had believed that he was the first explorer to have ventured any great distance into the Strait of Juan de Fuca, and he admits frankly that he 'experienced no small degree of mortification' when he learned that the mission of the schooners was to carry farther a survey that had already examined not only the full length of the strait, but had traced the eastern shore of the Strait of Georgia to a point some distance beyond Jervis Inlet. Perhaps he found some consolation in the fact that the Spaniards knew nothing of Puget Sound.

The presence of the schooners was the latest manifestation of Spain's increasing uneasiness about the security of her claims to the Northwest Coast. In April of 1789, eight months before it was known in Madrid that Martínez had seized several British ships at Nootka, a royal order had approved the establishment of a permanent fortified post in the sound. There was soon added to this a determination to survey as much as possible of the Northwest Coast. The Conde de Revilla Gigedo,[3] regarded by many as the ablest of all the viceroys of New Spain, was

---

[1] Manby, Letters, June 1792.   [2] *Ibid.*, September 1792.
[3] His full name, which needs to be given only as a matter of record, was Juan Vicente de Güemes Pacheco de Padilla Horcasitas y Aguayo, conde de Revilla Gigedo.

appointed to that office and directed to carry these policies into effect. As this would obviously require an increase in the naval forces based on San Blas, seven officers travelled to Mexico with the new viceroy. Senior amongst them was Juan Francisco de la Bodega y Quadra, who was to become both a political opponent and a personal friend of George Vancouver.

Quadra, as he is usually referred to in English documents of the time, was born of Spanish parents in Lima in 1743; he was thus Vancouver's senior by fourteen years. He received his naval training in Spain, and was one of an earlier contingent of officers who had been set to San Blas in 1774. The following year, as a young man of 32, he made the remarkable voyage to Alaskan waters in the 33-foot *Sonora* that proved his ability and won him both honour and promotion. After serving in the Naval Department at San Blas for a decade he attained the rank of captain in 1785 and was transferred to Spain. In 1789, when the exploration and defence of the Pacific Coast was being discussed, he was called as an expert witness, and his appointment to the command at San Blas followed. He had confidence in the new viceroy, and an extensive correspondence testifies to the trust and friendship that existed between them.

When Revilla Gigedo reached Mexico City he was greeted with the news of the seizures at Nootka. He realized that they were sure to strain relations with Great Britain, and might well raise the whole question of the future sovereignty of the Pacific Coast. Within a few weeks he reached three decision. First, he believed that Martínez had made a grave mistake when he had abandoned Nootka in October 1789, and that it must be reoccupied and strengthened as soon as possible. To accomplish this, on December 8 he instructed Quadra to send three ships north in January 1790 with the necessary men, arms and equipment. Secondly, as soon as Nootka was secure, work was to begin on a survey of the coast. 'These vessels,' the viceroy wrote, 'are to perfect, as information can be obtained, the knowledge of the coast and islands which are now laid down confusedly, or of those they may discover between the Puerto de San Lorenzo and the one named Principe Guillermo'[1] – that is, between Nootka Sound and Prince William Sound. Finally, the viceroy believed that the men and ships seized at Nootka should be released, but it is interesting to note that, as ships were in short supply on the San Blas station, he was not averse

[1] Quoted in H. R. Wagner, *Spanish Explorations in the Strait of Juan de Fuca* (Santa Ana, Calif., 1933), p. 11.

to making temporary use of them. Two of the three vessels he instructed Quadra to send north were Colnett's *Argonaut* and *Princess Royal* (which the Spaniards had renamed *Princesa Real*). In the event, Quadra held the *Argonaut* at San Blas, where she was handed over to Colnett, but the *Princesa Real* sailed for Nootka early in February, accompanied by the much larger *Concepción* and *San Carlos*. Francisco Eliza was in command of the expedition, and Salvador Fidalgo and Manuel Quimper captained the *San Carlos* and *Princesa Real*. All three had come from Spain with Quadra in 1789.

Nootka was found deserted, and as soon as its defences were in reasonably good condition Eliza turned to the matter of exploration. His own ship, the *Concepción*, he kept at Nootka as a guard ship, but on May 4 Fidalgo left in the *San Carlos* on an exploratory voyage that was to take him to Prince William Sound, Cook Inlet and Kodiak Island. Eliza had no instructions to investigate the Strait of Juan de Fuca, and he seems to have sent Quimper on this mission because the *Princesa Real* happened to be available. The intention was that she should be handed back to Colnett at Nootka, but as he did not appear, Eliza seized the opportunity to make further use of her. Quimper sailed for the strait on May 31, and, as his chart shows, carried out the first examination of both its shores for its entire length. The eastern end was explored by longboat, which passed the entrance to Puget Sound under the impression that it was nothing more than a bay, but entered Port Discovery, which was named Puerto de Quadra. Both Fidalgo and Quimper sailed back to San Blas without returning first to Nootka, and by coincidence both arrived on November 11.

Quadra was already busy with plans for further exploration in 1791. Eliza had remained at Nootka, and early in February Quadra sent him instructions for the coming season. But on March 12 Quadra received word of the signing of the Nootka Sound Convention, and a further communication was sent to Eliza the same day. Plans for the coming summer were somewhat modified, but the general objective remained the same: Quadra wanted nothing less than a detailed plan of the entire Northwest Coast from Mount St. Elias southward. It would be a monumental task, as Vancouver was to discover, but in a gallant effort to make at least a start on the survey Eliza sailed from Nootka on May 4 in the *San Carlos*, accompanied by the small schooner *Santa Saturnina*, which was Meares' *Northwest America* in rebuilt form. Contrary winds defeated Eliza's efforts to sail northward, and instead he turned south and examined Clayoquot Sound and Barkley Sound, and then headed for the Strait of Juan de Fuca. The significant discoveries of this expedition were made by José Maria Narváez, in the little *Santa Saturnina*. On July 1, while Eliza remained at Port Discovery, Narváez set out in the schooner, accompanied by a longboat, to push through the San Juan Islands and see what lay beyond them. He passed through Rosario Strait and then proceeded up the continental shore, which he traced as far as the north end of Texada Island. He then crossed to the east coast of Vancouver Island and followed it southward. His survey was not comparable to Vancouver's; bays and inlets were not investigated in the methodical way that became the routine proceeding for the British expedition; but he did conclude that a considerable river (the Fraser) must exist somewhere in the vicinity of Point Roberts and Point Grey, and he discovered the outer anchorage of Burrard Inlet. He carried the examination of the Strait of Georgia to the latitude of Nootka Sound, and his findings strengthened the hope that the strait continued on to the north and was linked in some way with the Pacific Ocean. Narváez hoped to explore Admiralty Inlet, the entrance to Puget Sound, but Eliza was anxious to get back to Nootka, where the *San Carlos* arrived on August 29. To his astonishment he learned that in his absence the great scientific expedition headed by Alejandro Malaspina had visited the Northwest Coast and had left Nootka to return to California only the previous day.

Malaspina had come north in accordance with instructions from Madrid that had reached him at Acapulco. They were prompted by an address delivered in Paris by Philippe Buache de Neuville, the French cartographer, before the Académie des Sciences in November 1790. Buache there declared his belief in the truth of a narrative written by one Lorenzo Ferrer Maldonado about 1609. Maldonado claimed that in the course of a voyage made in 1588 he had discovered the Strait of Anian, which he stated opened into the Pacific in latitude 60° N. When first published in 1788 his narrative had aroused little interest, but the endorsement of such a noted geographer as Buache gave it considerable importance. The Nootka Convention, signed only a month before Buache spoke, and the heightened interest in the Northwest Coast caused by the Nootka crisis, may have been another factor. The Malaspina expedition was then progressing slowly up the west coast of the Americas, and the Spanish Government decided to instruct him to depart from his intended itinerary and test the truth of Maldonado's claim.

Malaspina left Acapulco on 1 May 1791 and sailed directly to

Alaskan waters. On June 27 he entered Yakutat Bay, which touches the 60th parallel. A cleft in the mountains gave rise to high hopes that Maldonado's strait had been found precisely where he had said it was, but a search ended in what is still called Disenchantment Bay. After following the coast westward to the entrance to Prince William Sound, Malaspina turned south and on August 12 anchored in Nootka Sound, where he remained until the 28th. In a geographical sense his cruise had been largely an exercise in futility, but his scientific staff enabled his expedition to study the natives and natural history in a way that Vancouver was quite unable to do. At Yakutat Bay they assembled a remarkable collection of notes, drawings, paintings and artifacts descriptive of the Tlingit Indians, and a second important collection was made at Nootka.[1]

Malaspina's northern cruise had two results that were of immediate importance to Vancouver. First, Malaspina shared Quadra's conviction that an adequate survey of the Northwest Coast should be completed as soon as possible. To further it, he detached two capable young officers from his command to assist in carrying it out. They were Dionisio Alcalá Galiano and Cayetano Valdés, whom Vancouver would meet near Point Grey in June 1792. Secondly, Malaspina had intended to visit the Sandwich Islands and spend the summer of 1791 making a thorough examination of them, but the search for Maldonado's strait forced him to abandon this project. Had it been carried out, the course of events during Vancouver's later visits to the islands might have been quite different. Owing to this change in plans, the only Spanish visitor to the islands was Manuel Quimper, who spent some weeks there in March and April of 1791. As the *Princesa Real* (the former *Princess Royal*) had not been reclaimed by her owners in 1790, as expected, Quadra suggested that she should be sent to Manila and thence to China, there to be delivered to Colnett or his agents. En route she could call at the Sandwich Islands and secure some information about conditions and commerce there. While in Kailua Bay, in the island of Hawaii, whom should Quimper meet but Colnett himself in the *Argonaut*. The two nearly came to blows, but better relations were soon established.

From Galiano and Valdés Vancouver learned that Quadra had been appointed Spanish commissoner to carry out the terms of the Nootka

---

[1] Unfortunately Malaspina became involved in political scandal and fell into disfavour soon after his return to Spain. He was arrested and imprisoned, and as a result little was published about his expedition for almost a century. Many of the drawings and artifacts have only become available in recent years.

Sound Convention and that he was now awaiting him at Friendly Cove. The Galiano–Valdés expedition was proof that the impending settlement had not led to any curtailment of Spanish plans for exploration in 1792, and no doubt Vancouver heard that a second expedition was also in progress. Commanded by Jacinto Caamaño, it was to make a new survey of Bucareli Bay and then test the truth of Colnett's claim that he had discovered the fabled strait of Bartholomew de Fonte at about 53° N. If the strait existed, Spanish priority of discovery might well be important. Caamaño touched at many of the bays and inlets around the perimeter of Dixon Entrance, and then followed the mainland coast of Hecate Strait south to about 52° 30′ N. His conclusion was that Clarence Strait, extending northward from Dixon Entrance, was de Fonte's strait.[1]

Cordial relations were quickly established between Vancouver and the Spanish commanders, thanks in part to the happy chance that Galiano had some knowledge of English. No one in either of the British ships could speak Spanish; the thought that it might be advantageous for Vancouver to have a competent interpreter seems not to have occurred either to Grenville or the Admiralty.

Vancouver, who regarded the 130-ton *Chatham* as a poor thing, was shocked by the 46-ton *Sutil* and *Mexicana*, which he considered 'the most ill-calculated and unfit vessels that could possibly be imagined for such an expedition'.[2] But they were as large as many of the ocean-going ships of the day; the *Princess Royal*, which had sailed around the world, was of 50 tons. Vancouver had been instructed to cooperate with any Spanish vessels he met with, and it was arranged that the two expeditions should exchange information and, when practicable, cooperate in the survey. Vancouver showed Galiano his sketches of Burrard Inlet, Howe Sound and Jervis Inlet, and in return was shown a copy of Eliza's chart recording the Spanish discoveries in the Strait of Juan de Fuca and the Strait of Georgia. A small mystery surrounds the proposal that the survey should become a joint venture. Vancouver implies that it was the Spaniards that suggested this, and Menzies, basing his note on Vancouver's report, states that as they had been sent 'on the same service' they 'proposed a junction of the Vessels & Crews to facilitate an examination of these Streights.'[3] But in their diary of

[1] For Caamaño's journal and a facsimile of his map, showing his route and discoveries, see 'The Journal of Jacinto Caamaño', ed. by H. R. Wagner and W. A. Newcombe, *BCHQ* II (1938), pp. 189–222; 265–301.
[2] Vancouver, I, 313.   [3] Menzies, 23 June 1792.

the voyage Galiano and Valdés state that the suggestion came first from Vancouver and that later he 'renewed his argument...in such terms that not only were we obliged to agree but we comprehended that if we did not it would be discreditable, not only as far as we were concerned, but even for the public credit of the nation'. They foresaw difficulties because the British had better ships and equipment, but there could be compensations; they might gain some insight into British motives and techniques: 'en route we might discern their views relative to these countries and the true object of their explorations in them, gaining at the same time an idea of their methods of service and mode of working.'[1]

The four ships now moved north to Desolation Sound – a name that reflects Vancouver's opinion of the spectatular but rugged scenery of the Northwest Coast. From it both Vancouver and Galiano sent out boat expeditions, and some attempt seems to have been made to have them avoid duplication of effort. But this cooperation had limits. Vancouver was happy to see the Spaniards investigate islands or any coastline to the west, but he was unwilling to delegate the examination of any part of the continental shore. Toba Inlet proved to be the test case. As Puget set out to survey it he met Valdés, who reported that he had followed it to its end and found it closed. Puget describes the meeting in his journal: 'As I had no Orders from Captain Vancouver respecting the Spanish Survey in case of meeting their Boats; their Determination of this Inlet proved of no Service to us, for we were under the Necessity of following it up to its Source; We therefore took our Leave of Signior Valdez...& continued on with the Examination of this Inlet'.[2] Valdés protested to Vancouver, pointing out 'that the way to advance the surveys was to treat one another with perfect confidence and that he might reckon on this frankness on our side. Mr. Vancouver replied, however, that although he would always have the greatest confidence in our work, he did not think he would be free from responsibility if he did not see it all for himself, for he was expressly directed in his instructions to survey all the inlets on the coast from lat. 45° up to Cook's river.'[3]

While Puget and Whidbey had been surveying Toba Inlet and adjacent waters, Johnstone had been following the continental shore

[1] Quoted in Wagner, *Spanish Explorations*, p. 215.

[2] Puget, 29 June 1792.

[3] From Wagner's text of the *Viage de las goletas Sutil y Mexicana* (Madrid, 1802), translated by G. F. Barwick and amended by Wagner and by Capt Harold Grenfell, R.N.; in *Spanish Explorations*, p. 269.

farther north. Bute Inlet was a major discovery, but quite as important were the Arran Rapids, where the 'rapidity of the tide' caused Johnstone to conclude, quite correctly, 'that this narrow passage had communication with some very extensive inlet of the sea'.[1] Shortage of provisions forced him to return to the ships, but he left immediately on a further exploration that resulted in the discovery of Johnstone Strait and a clear view of Queen Charlotte Sound, which was obviously an arm of the ocean. To Johnstone therefore belongs the honour of having been the first European to establish the insularity of Vancouver Island. Meanwhile Puget had crossed to the east coast of the island, had rounded Cape Mudge and discovered the entrance to Discovery Passage. Here again strong evidence of a northern opening to the ocean was found: 'For the first time since our Entrance into the Streight [of Georgia],' Puget wrote in his journal, 'we perceived the Water flowing by the Shore & the Stream running at the Rate of five Knots from the Northward. This certainly was the most favorable prospect, we had had of finding a passage to the Northward for the Ships & most gladly did we pursue this Inlet'.[2]

Johnstone reported that it would be hazardous to attempt to take the *Discovery* and *Chatham* through the narrow channels on the route to the ocean that he had pioneered, but Puget believed that they could navigate Discovery Passage safely. Vancouver therefore chose the latter route. This resulted in the separation of the British and Spanish vessels, as Galiano, though warned repeatedly of its dangers, was determined to attempt Johnstone's routes with the aid of his survey, a copy of which was given to him. The parting was cordial; in their diary Galiano and Valdés wrote that it came 'after an intercourse, not only harmonious, but of the closest friendship. We dined together various times, sometimes in their vessels and sometimes in ours.'[3]

The British ships left Desolation Sound on the morning of July 13 and later in the day rounded Cape Mudge and anchored within the entrance to Discovery Passage. Here Puget had found Yaculta, the first Kwakiutl Indian village known to have been visited by Europeans. A week later, far up Johnstone Strait, Vancouver would visit a much larger Kwakiutl village at the mouth of the Nimpkish River. Vancouver and Menzies both seem to have had some difficulty in grasping the fact that, like the Clallam they had met in Puget Sound, the Kwakiutl were a nation quite distinct in identity and language from the Nootka – a

---

[1] Vancouver, I, 326.   [2] Puget, 5 July 1792.
[3] Wagner, *Spanish Explorations*, p. 217.

distinction somewhat blurred in this instance because, owing to social and trading contacts, some of the Kwakiutl had some knowledge of Nootkan.

When they left Yaculta the ships entered Seymour Narrows, the southern part of Discovery Passage, notorious for its swift tides and currents, which may attain a speed of 15 knots; but the *Discovery* and *Chatham* passed through with astonishing ease. Equally astonishing is the freedom from serious accidents that the ships had enjoyed and continued to enjoy as they worked their way up the coast with its innumerable reefs, rocks and shoals. This was due partly to cautious navigation and partly to the use of the ships' boats to carry out a major part of the coastal survey. Their good fortune was to desert them briefly after they had left Johnstone Strait and had entered the much broader waters of Queen Charlotte Sound, where fog added to their difficulties. On August 6 the *Discovery* struck a reef, was thrown on her side as the tide fell and escaped disaster by the narrowest of margins. Fortunately she righted herself and floated off when the tide rose, virtually undamaged. The next day the *Chatham* grounded, but her plight was less serious and once again no serious damage resulted.

Queen Charlotte Strait was perhaps the most dangerous area that Vancouver encountered in the whole of his voyage. A modern chart shows a perfect maze of islands, shoals, reefs and rocks. A number of openings have been plotted through them, but the main navigation channel is near the southwestern shore, far from the northern continental shore that Vancouver was following. By sheer chance, often groping their way in fog, the vessels eventually found this channel. Visibility had been so limited for several days that Vancouver afterwards looked upon this as the least reliable part of his whole survey, and it is hereabouts that one of the very few significant omissions is found on his chart. Deceived by the narrow channels on either side of Bramham Island that lead to them, he was unaware of the existence of Seymour Inlet, which runs inland for nearly 35 miles, and the shorter Belsize Inlet north of it.

Although he knew that Quadra was awaiting him, Vancouver was not anxious to arrive at Nootka Sound before the storeship *Daedalus*, as he had been informed that she would bring him further instructions to guide him in his negotiations with the Spanish commissioner. He decided therefore to delay his arrival and to make some further additions to his survey.

The ships sailed north to Fitz Hugh Sound, where on August 11 they anchored in Safety Cove, on the east side of Calvert Island. From there boat expeditions were sent northward and southward to examine the continental shore. Smith Sound, Rivers Inlet and finally Burke Channel were thus added to the chart. Johnstone's party, the last to complete its work, carried the survey far up Burke Channel to Menzies Point, in latitude 52° 18′ N. A seasonal change in the weather was one reason for calling a halt. Menzies, who was with Johnstone, noted that it had 'now become so cold wet & uncomfortable that the men were no longer able to endure the fatiguing hardships of distant excursions in open Boats exposed to the cold rigorous blasts of a high northern situation'. He went on to pay a notable tribute to the boat crews, who 'enduring at times the tormenting pangs of both hunger & thirst, yet on every occasion struggling who should be most forward in executing the orders of their superiors to accomplish the general interest of the Voyage.... And if we look back on the different winding Channels and Armlets which the Vessels & Boats traversed...it will readily be allowd that such an intricate & laborious examination could not have been accomplished in so short a time without the cooperating exertions of both Men & Officers whose greatest pleasure seemd to be in performing with alacrity & encountering the dangers & difficulties incidental to such service with...persevering intrepidity & manly steadiness'.[1]

On August 17 the British trading vessel *Venus* appeared off Safety Cove and brought word that the *Daedalus* had arrived at Nootka. She also brought the tragic news that Lieutenant Hergest, her commander, William Gooch, the astronomer who was coming to join the expedition, and a seaman had been killed by the natives when the ship called at the Sandwich Islands. Hergest was a particular friend of Vancouver's, and this added to his firm determination to see that the murderers were apprehended and executed when next he visited the islands. He decided to discontinue the survey immediately, and as soon as Johnstone's boat party returned, the ships left for Nootka Sound. They became separated in thick weather, and, true to form, the *Chatham* entered the sound on the morning of August 28 (August 27 by Spanish local time), a few hours before the *Discovery*.

Galiano and Valdés had progressed much more slowly on their survey than the British ships, and in spite of Vancouver's detour to the north they arrived at Nootka three days after him. By that narrow margin Vancouver gained the distinction of being the first to circumnavigate Vancouver Island. This applied only to himself, and not to

---

[1] Menzies, 18 August 1792.

his expedition, which had not yet travelled from Nootka Sound south to Cape Flattery. Vancouver had sailed from the cape to the sound with Cook in 1778. Galiano and Valdés were the first to sail around the island in one continuous voyage.

Vancouver and Quadra

The formalities called for by naval etiquette were scrupulously observed when the *Discovery* arrived in Friendly Cove. The British ship and the Spanish fort exchanged 13-gun salutes, and next morning, when Quadra visited the *Discovery* and *Chatham*, he was honored with a 13-gun salute as he boarded and left each vessel. Later in the day, at a dinner offered by Quadra, a toast drunk to the healths of the Kings of Great Britain and Spain was accompanied by a royal salute of 21 guns, which was followed by a 17-gun salute to the success of Vancouver's mission. Salutes were very much the order of the day, as the ships engaged in the fur trade were all armed and tended to conform to naval custom. 'Saluting,' Menzies wrote later, 'was so common among the Trading Vessels that visited the Cove that there was scarely a day past without puffings of this kind from some Vessel or other, & we too followed the example, & puffed it away as well as any of them, till at last we were become so scarce of ammunition to defend ourselves from the treacherous Indians, that we were obliged to get supplies of Powder from both the Spaniards & Traders before we left the Coast.'[1]

The extent of the Spanish establishment and the scene of activity it presented surprised Menzies, who accompanied Vancouver when he dined with Quadra. The governor's residence, substantial in size, was 'two story high, built of Planks with a Balcony in the front of the Upper Story after the manner of the Spanish Houses'. After dining, Menzies 'took a walk round the place & found several other Houses erected here by the Spaniards as Barracks, Store Houses & an Hospital... there were several spots fenced in, well cropped with the different European Garden stuffs, which grew here very luxuriantly.... There was a well-stocked poultry yard, & Goats Sheep & Black Cattle were feeding round the Village. Blacksmiths were seen busily engaged in one place & Carpenters in another, so that the different occupations of Building & repairing Vessels & Houses were at once going forward. In short,' he concludes, 'the Spaniards seem to go on here with greater activity

---

[1] Menzies, 2 October 1792. A few pages from the *Discovery*'s powder record have survived.

& industry than we are led to believe of them at any of their other remote infant Settlements.'[1]

A warm personal friendship developed quickly between Vancouver and Quadra, and this survived the serious differences over policy in which they were soon involved. Quadra had charm and an obvious sincerity that inspired liking and confidence. His hospitality had become proverbial; the officers of any vessel that entered the harbour were welcome at his table, which was graced by sterling silver and offered a menu the like of which few of the guests had enjoyed for many months. He was gifted with an ability to be hospitable and in a measure informal without prejudicing his position and authority. Warren Cook remarks that 'What Martínez had tried to accomplish with arguments and threats, Bodega [y Quadra] secured through helpfulness and generosity.'[2] Maquinna, the Indian chief from whom the Spaniards had secured the site of their establishment, was likewise welcome at Quadra's table, and Vancouver and others remarked upon the trust and good relations that existed between the Indians and the Spaniards. An unusual sense of peace and security prevailed at Nootka. In his own log Quadra noted what he rightly conceived to be the reason: 'I can perhaps flatter myself that treating these Indians as men ought to be treated, and not like individuals of inferior nature, I have lived in the very breast of tranquility.'[3] When, near the end of Vancouver's stay, a young boy from one of the Spanish ships was found murdered and mutilated, Quadra refused to take any drastic action against the Indian community as a whole, as the identity of the murderer had not been discovered. It is interesting to find that Vancouver's treatment of the Indians was akin to Quadra's. Mozino, the botanist, who was at Nootka at this time, wrote in his *Noticias de Nutka*: 'The English commandant was no less humane toward the Indians than the Spanish had been. Both left an example of goodness among them. "Cococoa [like] Quadra," they say, "Cococoa Vancouver," when they want to praise the good treatment of any of the captains who command the other ships.'[4]

Friendship, as noted, in no way interfered with Quadra's conduct of his negotiations with Vancouver, which were much more difficult and prolonged than Vancouver had anticipated. The relevant part of his original instructions has already been quoted: he was to meet at Nootka

[1] Menzies, 28 August 1792.
[2] Cook, *Flood Tide of Empire*, p. 360.
[3] Quoted in Cook, *Flood Tide of Empire*, p. 340.
[4] José Mariano Mozino, *Noticias de Nutka* (Toronto, 1970), p. 89. This edition translated and edited by Iris Higbie Wilson.

a Spanish official empowered to hand over to him 'the buildings and tracts of land, situated on the north-west coast...or on the islands adjacent thereto, of which the subjects of His Britannic Majesty were dispossessed about the month of April, 1789, by a Spanish officer.' And as the preparation of 'the particular specifications of the parts to be restored' still required 'some further time', these would be sent to him by the storeship, due to sail a few months later. To his dismay Vancouver found that the brief additional instructions brought to him by the *Daedalus* did not include any 'particular specifications'; they were simply accompanied by a copy of a letter from Count Florida Blanca, the Spanish first minister, to the governor at Nootka, directing him to put the representatives of the King of Great Britain 'into possession of the buildings and districts, or parcels of land, which were occupied by the subjects of that sovereign in April, 1789, as well in the port of Nootka...as in the other, said to be called Port Cox'. This mention of Port Cox, in Clayoquot Sound, was the only additional detail provided. One must assume that despite a long interrogation, the British officials had been unable to secure any description from Meares that they were prepared to endorse. Vancouver was thus left with only a very general conception of the properties he was expected to repossess, and with no directions whatever as to what he was to do with them after they had been handed over.

Quadra soon introduced a further matter which took Vancouver completely by surprise. Pitt had wanted the Nootka Convention to set a geographical limit to Spanish sovereignty on the Northwest Coast, but Florida Blanca succeeded in his efforts to have any provision of the kind omitted. However, once the convention was signed, Spain was faced with the fact that the entire coast from San Francisco (the most northerly Spanish post) and the most southerly Russian post (in Prince William Sound) was now open to all comers. Under these changed conditions the establishment at Nootka, which was expensive to maintain and was quite unsuitable as a site for a miliary post and mission on the Spanish model, had lost much of its value. Some retreat southward was desirable, but it should be to a strategically located new post that would be recognized internationally as marking the northern limit of Spanish territory. On Christmas Day 1790, just two months after the signing of the convention, a royal order suggested that this new fortified post should be built at the entrance to the Strait of Juan de Fuca, and that the boundary line should begin at the north point of entrance to the strait and run due north to 60° N. It was an ingenious proposal, for although it would require Spain to abandon all claim to the coast north of the strait, it would retain for her the vast territories in the interior of the continent, and would make the strait itself Spanish territorial waters. This latter point was important, for at the time little was known about the strait, and no one knew what passages and inlets might branch off from it, extending far into the interior and possibly even reaching the Atlantic.

Florida Blanca's letter ordering restitution of the 'buildings and lands' at Nootka was written on 12 May 1791, six weeks after Vancouver's departure from Falmouth. The same day a royal order directed that in addition to carrying out the transfer, the Spanish commissioner to be sent to Nootka should endeavor to secure British agreement to a boundary settlement. Word to this effect came to Quadra in a dispatch from Viceroy Revilla Gigedo dated 29 October 1791, and it explains the plans for exploration that he carried into effect in 1792. First, the season's major expedition, commanded by Galiano accompanied by Valdés, was to enter the Strait of Juan de Fuca and find out as much as possible about the Strait of Georgia, which Eliza had partly explored in 1791. Secondly, Salvador Fidalgo, sailing directly from San Blas, was to establish the post at the entrance of the strait that was intended to replace the establishment at Nootka. The site chosen was Núñez Gaona (Neah Bay), on the southern shore about five miles east of Cape Flattery. Quimper had discovered this bay, taken formal possession of it, and named it, in 1790. Thirdly, as we have seen, on the chance that the strait that de Fonte claimed to have discovered might exist, Jacinto Caamaño was to search for it at its presumed location at 53° N. Finally, Quadra himself was to proceed to Nootka and meet the British commissioner who was due to arrive in the course of the summer. Spanish expectations were clearly reflected in documents of the time which refer to Quadra's mission either as the *Expedición para la Entrega de Nootka* (Expedition for the Delivery of Nootka) or the *Expedición de Límites* (Boundary Expedition).

Quadra arrived in Nootka Sound at the end of April, one day after Vancouver had rounded Cape Flattery and entered the Strait of Juan de Fuca. He had expected Vancouver to come directly to Nootka, and the viceroy had instructed him to endeavour to detain him there, in the hope that Galiano would be the first to enter the strait.[1] This hope was not fulfilled; four months passed before Vancouver's ships anchored in Friendly Cove, and in the interval he had been the first to establish

[1] Wagner, *Spanish Explorations*, p. 50.

the insularity of Vancouver Island. But the delay in meeting Quadra was to be costly. As we have seen, Quadra came to the Northwest Coast prepared to give Vancouver possession of Nootka Sound, in accordance with the loosely worded provisions of the Nootka Sound Convention. Generally speaking, those provisions were based on the claims made by Meares in his famous memorial and his *Voyages to the North West Coast of America*. In the latter he had described a grant of land he had received from Maquinna, the chief of the Indians who had a village in Friendly Cove, and a substantial two-storey building he had erected upon it. Both were prominent on the list of properties of which Meares claimed to have been dispossessed by Martínez in 1789. Unfortunately for Vancouver, a number of navigators who had visited Nootka in 1788 and 1789 returned in the summer of 1792, and their accounts of what had transpired convinced Quadra that, apart from the seizure of his ships, which had already been released, Meares' claims for compensation were unfounded.

First to arrive, on June 11, was Francisco José Viana, a Portuguese, captain of the *Felice Adventurer*, who in 1788 and 1789 had been nominal captain of the *Iphigenia*, one of the ships owned by Meares and his associates. Questioned about the buildings Meares had erected at Friendly Cove, he replied: 'The house we had on shore was very small and made from a few boards got from the Indians, and when we sailed it was pulled to pieces: and when Dn. Joh Martinez entered the port of Nootka [in 1789], there was not the least remains of a house &ca.' On July 23 the famous *Columbia* arrived, commanded by Captain Robert Gray, who had been master of the *Lady Washington* in 1788 and 1789. On August 1 she was followed by the American trading ship *Hope*, commanded by Joseph Ingraham, who had been Gray's first mate in the *Lady Washington*. Manby believed that Quadra was strongly influenced by Ingraham's testimony, which he and Gray submitted jointly early in August. It confirmed Viana's statement and gave additional details: 'we observe your wish to be acquainted with what house or establishment, Captain Meares had at the time the Spaniards arrived here [in 1789]. We answer, in a word, *None*. On the arrival of the Columbia in the year 1788, there was a house, or rather a hut, consisting of rough posts, covered with boards made by the Indians; but this Capt: Douglas [supercargo of the *Iphigenia*] pulled to pieces, prior to his sailing for the Sandwich Islands, the same year. The boards he took on board the Iphigenia; the roof he gave to Capt: Kendrick [then commanding the *Columbia*], which was cut up and burnt as fire wood on board the Columbia: so that on the arrival of Dn. E: J: Martinez there was no vestige of any house remaining.' Gray and Ingraham also refuted Meares' statement that he had purchased land from Maquinna 'or any other Chief, we never heard of any, although we remained among these people nine months, and could converse with them perfectly well.' They added that Maquinna himself denied any such purchase.

The negotiations between Vancouver and Quadra lasted three weeks. They consisted of a dozen letters, interspersed by several personal discussions. Communication was at times difficult or slow, as neither government had provided its commissioner with an interpreter. Vancouver considered himself 'excessively fortunate in finding a young gentleman, by the name of [Thomas] Dobson, on board the Store-ship, who spoke and translated the Spanish language very accurately.'[1] His translations suggest that Vancouver exaggerated his abilities, but his presence was nevertheless a godsend. With future needs in mind, Vancouver transferred him to the *Discovery* as a midshipman early in September.

Vancouver's summaries of the letters and discussions are honest and accurate, but certain points emerged more clearly in retrospect than they did at the beginning. As regards the restoration of the 'buildings and tracts of land' that were to be restored to the British, Quadra stated his position in a letter written the day after Vancouver's arrival, and never deviated from it. He first pointed out that in 1789 it was 'known to all nations' that 'by solemn treaties; by discoveries; and by a possession immemorial' Spain owned the coast north of California. Martínez was therefore quite within his rights in preventing Meares from establishing a permanent post at Nootka Sound. He accepted the evidence of Viana, Gray, Ingraham and Maquinna and considered that Meares' claims for the loss of buildings and lands at Nootka were completely unfounded; no buildings had existed in 1789 and Meares had no title to land in Friendly Cove. 'Things thus established to their primitive state,' Quadra wrote, 'it is clear that Spain has nothing to deliver, nor the smallest damage to make good.'[2]

Despite this forthright statement, Vancouver seems to have been reassured for the moment by the next paragraph in Quadra's letter, in which he expressed a willingness to withdraw to a new post in the

---

[1] Vancouver's report to London, Nootka Sound, 26 September 1792. P.R.O., C.O. 5/187 f. 107.
[2] Quadra to Vancouver, 29 August 1792. *Ibid.*, f. 108.

Strait of Juan de Fuca and (in a badly translated passage) made first mention of the boundary proposal: 'far from thinking to continue in this port' Quadra was 'ready, without prejudice to our legitimate right, nor that of the Courts better instructed resolves, generously to cede to England the Houses, Offices, and gardens which has with so much labour been cultivated [at Nootka], and retire to Fuca;...[which] ought to be our last [i.e., most northerly] establishment, and there fix the dividing point'. North of Fuca the coast would be common ground for English and Spanish, conforming to the 5th article of the Nootka Convention, while the English would not 'pass to the South of Fuca.'[1]

Although years later, in his published journal, Vancouver printed the words 'without prejudice to the legitimate right of Spain' in italics, for the moment the offer to 'cede' the Spanish establishment seems to have deceived him. Quadra inquired who would be placed in charge of it, and Vancouver replied that he would be leaving Broughton and the *Chatham*. They toured the village together, inspected living quarters, gardens, livestock and store houses, and discussed which of the latter could best accommodate the surplus supplies from the *Daedalus*. 'Thus conceiving all matters firmly arranged,' Vancouver wrote later, 'I gave all necessary directions for the clearing of the Store Ship; which was immediately set about.'[2] But it soon became apparent that Quadra was yielding only occupancy; there was to be no question of any transfer of sovereignty, which was what Quadra had meant by 'our legitimate right'. Later he modified his position slightly. On September 11 he wrote: 'I comprehend the first article of the Convention only to extend to the delivery of the territories which in April 1789 were occupied by British subjects',[3] which he was willing to define as the small area on which Meares had built his hut in 1788. In reply, Vancouver spelled out his own conception of the properties to be restored:

What I understand to be the territories of which His Britannic Majesty's subjects were dispossessed of, and to be restored to them by the 1st. article of the convention and Count Floridablanca's letter, is this place [Nootka Sound] in toto, and Port Cox: of which, if it is not in your power to put me in full possession, I can have no idea of hoisting the British flag on the Spot you have pointed out in this cove, of but little more than a hundred yards in extent any way. If therefore that is your situation I must decline receiving any such restriction on the part of His Britannic Majesty: and so soon as His Britannic

---

[1] *Ibid.*   [2] *Ibid.*, f. 113.

[3] Quadra to Vancouver, 11 September 1792. *Ibid.*, f. 116.

Majesty's Vessels under my command are in readiness, I shall proceed to Sea, until I shall receive further directions from the British Court on this Subject.[1]

Quadra's rejoinder was brief: 'You say you are authorized to receive the whole:– I am not free to deliver in those terms.'[2] As the last sentence of Vancouver's statement indicates, the only solution was to refer the matter to the governments in London and Madrid and await instructions as to how to proceed.

Just as Quadra was leaving Nootka, and too late to add his evidence to their discussions, Vancouver learned that Robert Duffin, supercargo of a Portuguese trading ship that had entered the sound, had been at Friendly Cove with Meares in 1788. From him Vancouver obtained a sworn statement, which he describes in detail in his narrative, that flatly contradicted the testimony of Gray and Ingraham. Duffin asserted that Meares had indeed purchased from Maquinna and his brother Callicum 'the whole of the Land, that forms Friendly Cove', that he had erected a substantial house and various out buildings, and that the house had been in good condition when Meares left Nootka. Vancouver gives no indication of what degree of credence he gave to Duffin's account, but he sent a copy to the Admiralty and it aroused some interest in London.[3]

At the very beginning of the negotiations Vancouver had refused to be drawn into any discussions regarding the sovereign rights to the coast or the setting of a northern boundary to Spanish territory. In his first letter he so informed Quadra: 'I do not...conceive myself at all authorised to enter into any negotiation further than that which is contained in the substance of Count Floridablancas's letter, which authorises you to restore, and me to receive' the properties of which the British had been dispossessed in 1789.[4] Had discussions taken place it is certain that no agreement would have resulted, for Vancouver believed that Drake's discoveries in 1579 had given Great Britain a valid claim to the coast as far south as his landfall. Accordingly, when on June 4, in Possession Sound, he had taken formal possession 'of all the countries we had lately been employed in exploring', he defined them as 'the coast, from that part of New Albion, in the latitude of 39° 20′

[1] Vancouver to Quadra, 13 September 1792. *Ibid.*, f. 117.

[2] Quadra to Vancouver, 13 September 1792. *Ibid.*, f. 118.

[3] Duffin to Vancouver, Nootka, 21 September 1792. P.R.O., Adm 1/2628, ff. 640–641v. There is another copy, in which the text varies slightly, in C.O. 5/187, ff. 45–46v. For Vancouver's summary see his *Voyage*, I, 404–6.

[4] Vancouver to Quadra, 1 September 1792. P.R.O., CO. 5/187, f. lllv.

north...to the entrance of this sea, said to be the supposed Straits of Juan de Fuca; as likewise all the coast islands, &c. within the said straits...together with those situated in the interior sea we had discovered...[and which] I have honored with the name of The Gulph of Georgia'.[1] Whether Quadra ever became aware of this claim does not appear.

In spite of these differences, Vancouver dined almost daily with Quadra, and at the latter's suggestion they paid a visit to Maquinna, who was at his village near the head of Tahsis Inlet. Maquinna was highly pleased with this attention, which Quadra seems to have planned as a means of improving Maquinna's relations with the English. It was while they were on their way back to Friendly Cove that Quadra asked Vancouver to name some port or island after them both. Vancouver, 'conceiving no place more eligible than the place of our meeting' named the island he had just circumnavigated Quadra and Vancouver's Island, a compliment Quadra 'was excessively pleased with'.[2] Nearly a century later, when the island had long been British and the name had been shortened by usage to Vancouver Island, H. H. Bancroft, the historian, in a cynical mood and aided by hindsight, hazarded the guess that 'Both commanders were well aware that in thus giving so large a body of land their joint names, and so recording it in the text and on the maps of the expeditions of Vancouver and of Galiano and Valdés, one, and but one, would remain, and that would depend entirely as to which nation the territory fell.'[3]

Vancouver took prompt steps to inform the British Government about events at Nootka, and to ask for instructions as to his future course of action. Zachary Mudge, 1st lieutenant of the *Discovery*, sailed for China on September 30 in the Portuguese brig *Fenis and St. Joseph* on the first stage of a journey to London. He took with him a detailed narrative that included copies of the letters exchanged by Quadra and Vancouver and a rough sketch of the discoveries made to date by the expedition. To make the immediate problem clearer, Vancouver also sent a drawing of Friendly Cove by midshipman Henry Humphrys, showing the Spanish village and the site of Meares' building; this was later engraved and printed in the *Voyage of Discovery*.[4] In January

[1] Vancouver, I, 289.
[2] Vancouver's report to London, Nootka Sound, 26 September 1792. P.R.O., C.O. 5/187, f. 114.
[3] H. H. Bancroft, *History of British Columbia* (San Francisco, 1887), p. 29n.
[4] What appear to be the complete papers taken to London by Mudge are in P.R.O., C.O. 5/187, ff. 106–125. The drawing and chart are not foliated.

Broughton, commander of the *Chatham*, would be sent from Monterey on a similar mission.[1]

Vancouver was worried lest his refusal to accept any of Quadra's proposals might not meet with approval, and he sent with Broughton a private letter to Evan Nepean explaining and justifying his actions. He complained bitterly at not having received adequate instructions by the *Daedalus*; he had not received 'a single line either officially or privately' from Nepean or his office. As for the difference of opinion with Quadra, the latter had 'considered himself only authorised and directed to ceed that small pittance of rocks and sandy beach such being the only space in the Port of Nootka the English occupied in 1789'; 'this chasm', he contended, could not 'possibly be considered as the districts or parcels of Land &c intended to be ceeded to me on the part of His Britannic Majesty. No — there can be little doubt I should either [have] proven myself a most consumate fool or a traitor to have acceeded to any such cession without positive directions to that effect.' Finally, he explained that the contents of this letter were intended to be confidential 'excepting my conduct should fall under that sensure as to require such Vindication as is here pointed out.'[2]

It is convenient to note here the sequel to the impasse reached in the negotiations between Vancouver and Quadra.

Mudge arrived in London early in June 1793; Broughton followed in July. They found that France had declared war on England in February and had followed this with a declaration against Spain in March. Between the two declarations, on February 12, Britain and Spain had signed a Nootka Claims Convention, by which Spain agreed 'to pay as an indemnity to the parties interested in' the ship *Argonaut* (in other words to Meares and his associates) 'the amount of two hundred and ten thousand hard dollars in specie' as compensation for the seizures at Nootka and other losses incurred.

Now that the two countries were wartime allies it might have been expected that there would be little inclination to carry the matter further, but it was not lost sight of. The very day Mudge arrived, Lord Grenville, now Foreign Secretary, wrote to Henry Dundas, his

---

[1] Broughton took to London copies of the letters written by Vancouver and Quadra, the latter in both the original Spanish and in an English translation. He also took views and charts, many of which are now in the Hydrographic Department at Taunton. The copy of Vancouver's journal, from Falmouth to Nootka, is missing. For the Vancouver–Quadra correspondence see C.O. 5/187 ff. 89–101.

[2] Vancouver to Nepean, Monterey, 7 January 1793. P.R.O., C.O. 5/187, ff. 75–8.

successor as Secretary of State, that they 'must soon think of a communication to be made to Spain on the subject of Vancouvers late dispatch'. Two documents in the same file, a 26-page review and a brief scribbled memorandum, give glimpses of official thinking on the subject. Both are undated and unsigned, but they were certainly written at this time. The first includes a comment on the statements submitted by the trading ship captains regarding Meares' establishment in Friendly Cove:

In comparing the evidence respecting these houses, if that should be regarded as a material point, there can be little doubt in preferring the oath of one person [Duffin] to the simple asseveration of three, one of whom is a Portuguese, employed as a screen by the first adventurers, & now probably in the power of the Spanish Governor, and the other two Americans under obligations as they themselves confess both to Sr Quadra & Don Martinez.

This is followed by the shrewd remark that, in any event, the statements were irrelevant: 'the evidence such as it is, relates only to the dimensions of the house, and its existence after Meares departure, when the demolition of it contrary to his orders, could not affect any right which he had acquired by erecting and leaving behind him such a building.'[1]

Philip Stephens, Secretary of the Admiralty, whose handwriting makes the deciphering of the endorsements on many documents of the time difficult, was probably the author of the memorandum. As it is brief, very much to the point, and foreshadowed the general direction that the negotiations with Spain would take, it deserves to be quoted in full:

My Idea as to Nootka is as follows.

I think Capt Vancouver was very naturally induced from the nature of his instructions, and a Recollection of the original Ground of Quarrel to hesitate and ultimately to decline closing the Transaction on the terms suggested by the Spanish Commandant. I regret however that it was not closed on those terms, for We would have been in Possession and under those Circumstances would have been on a better footing for negotiating at home, than when the Spaniards are in possession, and when they may feel a Point of honour not to depart from the Ground agreed by their Commandant. All that We really are anxious about in this particular part of the Business is the Safety of our National honour which renders *a Restitution* necessary. The *Extent* of that Restitution is not of much moment, and in truth the only Evidence to which either Party can resort, will justify the claim of either side. The true State of

[1] P.R.O., C.O. 5/187, ff. 53–53v.

the fact appears to be that Mears never was in possession of more than the spot where the tent now stands in the Drawing made by Mr. Humphrys, and therefore in a *narrow* and literal sense *Restitution* is complied with by recovering that Spot, But we are justified in maintaining that the transaction cannot admit of so narrow a Construction, the Place being so small as not to admit of a divided Property. I think this last Circumstance may afford a good way of terminating the dispute, for instead of insisting *solely* upon our Right let us mix with it in our Statement the obvious Inconvenience of a Division, and by negotiating upon it in that Manner, I daresay Lord St Helens will find no great difficulty in persuading the Spanish Minister to make the Concession absolute which the Spanish Commandant at Nootka did not think himself at liberty to do. The Use of the Harbor must of course remain common to both Parties.[1]

Stephens and Vancouver were on friendly terms, and he shows understanding of the latter's dilemma. But it is clear that he considered that Vancouver's instructions would have permitted him to occupy Friendly Cove on the terms Quadra suggested, and that in his view this would have strengthened rather than compromised Britain's claim to possession. The criticism that Vancouver anticipated thus materialized, and Nepean added his letter of justification to the official file.

Lord St Helens was again charged with the task of reaching what it was hoped would be a final settlement with Spain. Broughton was sent to Madrid to give him the advantage of the advice of someone who had personal knowledge of the terrain. In November St Helens reported that he was still without an answer from the Spanish minister, and in December he notified London that he had received one but that it was 'highly unsatisfactory'. However, on 11 January 1794 he was able to sign the Convention for the Mutual Abandonment of Nootka, a compromise agreement that left national honours intact and made no mention of a northern limit to Spanish sovereignty. British and Spanish representatives were to meet at Nootka 'in the place, or near, where the buildings stood which were formerly occupied by the subjects of His Britannic Majesty'; the Spanish representative was to read a declaration restoring the 'buildings and districts of land' seized in 1789, and the British representative was to acknowledge their restoration; the British official would then 'unfurl the British flag over the land so restored in sign of possession'. And after these formalities 'the officials of the two Crowns' were to withdraw 'their people from the said port of Nootka'. As for the future, while the subjects of both

---

[1] *Ibid.*, ff. 81–84v.

nations were to be free to enter Nootka and erect temporary buildings there, it was agreed that neither would form any permanent settlement 'or claim any right of sovereignty there to the exclusion of the other' and that they would 'mutually aid each other...against any other nation which may attempt to establish there any sovereignty or dominion'.

Vancouver knew nothing of all this. No communication was sent to him after the signing of either convention; he heard of the settlement in November 1794, when he was at Monterey, homeward bound after completing his survey of the Northwest Coast. The Spanish Commandant there had received news of it from the Viceroy of New Spain. The highly unsatisfactory additional instructions dated 20 August 1791, brought to Vancouver by the *Daedalus*, were the only word he received from the Admiralty until his return to England in the autumn of 1795. His isolation in the interval was total.

The Columbia and California

Quadra sailed from Nootka on September 22. Vancouver was not able to follow until October 12. The delay was due initially to the necessity of reloading the stores that had been landed from the *Daedalus*, and later to bad weather. They had agreed upon a rendezvous at Monterey. At one time San Francisco had been proposed, as Vancouver intended to call there. This was in keeping with his instructions to ascertain 'with as much precision as possible, the number, extent and situation of any settlements' on the coast between 30° and 60° N. Quadra was probably unaware of this directive, but Vancouver's intention to call at various California harbours did not disturb him. Menzies notes that when the expedition arrived at San Francisco they found that the commandant had been 'particularly requested' by Quadra to supply 'every accommodation the Settlement afforded' if Vancouver should touch there.[1] Quadra seems to have seen no element of espionage or miliary threat in Vancouver's activities. This had been suggested already by his dispersal of the Spanish warships that had been assembled at Nootka. In anticipation of Vancouver's arrival these included the 36-gun frigate *Santa Gertrudis*, sent out from Spain, and the new brigantine *Activa*, carrying 12 guns, built at San Blas in the spring of the year. In May they joined the older 36-gun frigate *Concepción*, which had spent the winter at Nootka as a guard ship. But as the weeks passed and

[1] Menzies, 15 December 1792.

Vancouver failed to appear, the inroads that the crews of the two large ships were making on his supplies worried Quadra much more than any military threat from the *Discovery* and *Chatham*. In July he sent them both south. When Vancouver finally appeared only the *Activa* was in Friendly Cove.

On his way south Vancouver planned to investigate two of Robert Gray's discoveries – Grays Harbor and the Columbia River – both of which he had entered early in May, just after his meeting with Vancouver south of Cape Flattery. Grays Harbor was to be examined by the *Daedalus*, and Whidbey was transferred temporarily to her to conduct the survey. She managed to enter safely on October 18, though hampered by flood tides and a bar across the entrance. The survey proved to be a tedious task, but Whidbey was able to prepare a detailed chart. His verdict was that the port appeared 'to be of little importance in its present state'. Entrance was made hazardous by a shifting bar – water depths changed even between the time of their arrival and departure. There was a channel of sorts in the middle of the bay, but it was surrounded for the most part by wide shoals, many of which were dry at low water. Boats could reach the shore only in two or three places. Vancouver's account of the visit, obviously taken from Whidbey's journal, is the only one available, as the journal itself has disappeared.

The *Discovery* and *Chatham* arrived off the entrance to the Columbia on the 19th. There followed a terrifying battle with breakers and bars such as many other vessels were to experience in years to come. 'I must here acknowledge', Bell wrote in his journal, 'that...I never felt more alarmed & frightened in my life, never having been before in a situation where I conceived there was so much danger.'[1] The *Chatham* succeeded in entering but conditions appeared to be so hazardous that Vancouver decided, after a second attempt, not to take further risks with the *Discovery* and proceeded in her to San Francisco. The decision was a wise one, as no vessel as large as the *Discovery* had yet crossed the bar. The *Columbia* was of 212 tons, and the *Jenny* of Bristol, which the *Chatham* was surprised to find anchored in Baker Bay, was of only 78 tons.

Vancouver quotes or paraphrases Broughton's detailed description of his exploration of the Columbia, which is fortunate, as Broughton's original journal is not available. Bell provides the only other first-hand account. Broughton had a copy of Gray's rough sketch of the river,

---

[1] Bell, October 1792.

which shows that Gray did not venture farther than Grays Bay, about 20 miles from the entrance. Broughton's definition of a river required its water to be fresh, and Grays Bay is part of the Columbia's broad estuary, which Broughton looked upon as a salt-water bay. After finding a safe anchorage for the *Chatham*, he set out with the launch and cutter to explore the river proper, of which he evidently considered himself the discoverer. This was reached about 10 miles beyond Gray's final anchorage, where Bell notes 'we had, properly Speaking, only got to the mouth of the River, for at the bottom of the deep bay, we entered a tolerably Board River of Fresh Water'.[1]

The boats worked their way laboriously upstream against the current. They were provisioned for a week, and at the end of it Broughton estimated, very accurately, that they were 100 miles from the *Chatham*. He named Point Vancouver to mark the limit of his exploration, and at nearby Possession Point took formal possession of the country for King George the Third. Bell regretted that it was necessary to turn back, as he suspected the river '*might* communicate with some of the Lakes on the opposite side of the Continent' and be of interest to the Hudson's Bay Company[2] – an arresting remark, as within twenty years the Columbia would become a regular travel route for fur traders. Broughton seems to have had a contrary opinion. Manby, who had been left in command of the *Chatham*, notes that 'they' (presumably meaning Broughton) had 'every reason to believe another day or two would have brought them to its source'.[3] Broughton would have been astonished to learn that he had left over a thousand miles of the Columbia unexplored.

The Indians in the river valley were numerous; on occasion canoes carrying several hundred had been near the boats, but, in Bell's words, they had 'behaved with the utmost friendship and quietness'.[4] The bars and breakers at the Columbia's mouth continued to be the chief danger encountered. All the time that Broughton had been exploring the river the *Jenny* had waited in Baker Bay, watching for a moment when it seemed reasonably safe to put to sea. She was held for another four days after the *Chatham* joined her. This last delay was annoying, but it had its compensations: 'during this time,' Bell notes, 'our Sportsmen were very Successful'; geese were found in the marshy flats 'in astonishing numbers...many dozens were Shot, besides Ducks Snipes &c. in plenty. Mr. Manby was likewise so fortunate as to kill a very fine Fallow

[1] *Ibid.*
[2] *Ibid.*, November 1792.
[3] Manby, Letters, November 1792.
[4] Bell, November 1792.

deer, so that what with Venison, Wild Fowl & Salmon which the natives brought us in abundance, we contrived to live tolerably well'.[1] Improved weather on November 11 brought attention back to the serious business of leaving the river safely. Conditions seemed better than they actually were; the two ships crossed the bar successfully, but beyond it they met a 'tremendous Surf' that nearly overwhelmed them. On the way in the *Chatham* had lost her jolly boat, while in the estuary she had grounded and nearly suffered disaster, and on her way out her launch was stove in.

Broughton prepared a large chart of the river which he later took with him to London – the first to portray the lower Columbia with some accuracy and in considerable detail. It would be interesting to know if it was included in the copies of the expedition's charts that Vancouver gave to Quadra at Monterey, and, if so, whether Quadra's copy included the place-name Possession Point. For, as the act of possession performed there indicated, Quadra may have retained Nootka Sound and refused to give up any of what he deemed to be Spain's sovereign rights, but Vancouver's expedition likewise continued to recognize the British claim to New Albion.

At this point Vancouver gives some account of the voyage of the storeship *Daedalus*, which sailed from England late in August 1791 under the command of Lieutenant Richard Hergest and had come to the Northwest Coast by way of Cape Horn and the Sandwich Islands. To replenish her water supply Hergest steered for the southern group of the Marqueses, which Cook had visited on his second voyage, in 1774. On 22 March 1792 he anchored in Resolution Bay (Vaitahu Bay) in the island now called Tahu Ata. Within a few hours it was discovered that the *Daedalus* was on fire, caused by spontaneous combustion in stores that had been improperly stowed. Fortunately the blaze was extinguished before the ship herself suffered any damage. Later, from Monterey, Vancouver was to write to the Admiralty complaining bitterly that improper storage had not only caused a fire but had damaged or ruined substantial parts of the stores and provisions she had brought to Nootka. Slop-clothes, beds, hammocks, sails, wine, spirits and salt provisions had all suffered.[2] The only good thing about the fire was that it had not occurred at sea.

[1] *Ibid.*
[2] Vancouver to the Admiralty, at sea, 15 October 1792 (forwarded to London from Monterey). P.R.O., Adm 106/1434.

Sailing north from Tahu Ata Hergest encountered – and thought he was the first to discover – the seven islands that form the northern group of the Marqueses. Vancouver published in his *Voyage* a chart of the group prepared by William Gooch, the astronomer. Later it was learned that Joseph Ingraham, commander of the Boston brigantine *Hope*, had happened upon the islands in April 1791. He gave them American names (Washington, Adams, Lincoln, etc.), and 'claimed them as a new discovery, belonging to the United States of America'.[1] They were sometimes referred to as the Washington Islands, but the American claim to them was never made good. Unaware of all this, Hergest named them again. Later they became part of French Polynesia and received French names, which in turn have been displaced by those of native origin.

Tragedy overtook the *Daedalus* when she reached the island of Oahu, in the Sandwich Islands, where Hergest, Gooch and a seaman were murdered by the natives. Vancouver relates the circumstances in detail. The remarkable thing is that Hergest became the victim of precisely the sort of incident he had foreseen and worried about. He was serving in the *Resolution* when Cook was killed at Kealakekua Bay in 1778, and feared that trouble with the natives might occur again. In June 1791, when the *Daedalus* was preparing to sail for the Pacific, Philip Stephens, Secretary of the Admiralty, informed the Navy Board that Hergest was 'apprehensive of some danger from the Natives of the different Islands which he will be obliged to visit on account of the small number of Men aboard' and the Lords of the Admiralty directed the Board 'to allow one Mate & Five Seamen to the Daedalous [sic], in addition to those the Owners are obliged by Charter Party to provide for her'.[2] Nevertheless Hergest and Gooch, both unarmed, imprudently wandered away from the watering party on the beach, and when the latter became involved in a fracas that angered the natives, both were killed.

Gales soon assailed the *Discovery* as she moved south from the Columbia. Her voyage to San Francisco, a distance of less than 600 miles, took more than three weeks. It was an uncomfortable time for all on board, and Menzies records that at one point 'the ship Labored & pitchd so much that John Davies a Seaman was washed off the

---

[1] Quoted from 'An Account of a recent discovery of seven islands in the South Pacific, by Joseph Ingraham,' *Collections*, Massachusetts Historical Society, 1st series, II (1793) pp. 20–24. An editorial refers to the islands as Ingrahams Islands.

[2] Stephens to Navy Board, 14 June 1791. P.R.O., Adm 2/595, p. 355.

spritsail yard arm, but the Ship being immediately hove up in the wind & the Jolly Boat lowerd down from the Stern he was fortunately picked up alive'. Menzies adds an interesting comment: 'This man owed his life entirely to the manner in which we carried our Jolly Boat suspended to the Ship's Stern, for had she been to hoist out off the Booms, she would have been too late to save him. I think it therefore a good practice, which I believe is now become general in the East India Company's service of carrying a small Boat on the Ship's quarter, where it is lowerd down by a single tackle on the least emergency of this kind.'[1] This speaks well for Vancouver's concern for the lives of his crew, for it was not customary in the Royal Navy at the time, and he continued the arrangement even after it was found to involve considerable risk of damage to the boats. The *Chatham* lost two jolly boats, one in New Zealand waters and the other on the Columbia bar.

Early in the voyage symptoms of scurvy made an unwelcome appearance – the first of only two outbreaks reported on the long voyage. Vancouver had made strenuous efforts to ward off disease by ensuring good physical conditions on board. Weather permitting, the ships were kept dry and fumigated, and much emphasis was placed on cleanliness of the persons, bedding and clothes of the crew. Cook had instituted a three-watch system that reduced stress, and Vancouver may well have done the same. But the men had just experienced a most fatiguing summer, with long spells of duty in open boats; supplies of fresh provisions had been very limited, and gales and heavy rain were now keeping the ship damp and their clothing wet. Knowledge of vitamin C was still far in the future, and neither Cook nor Vancouver was aware that scurvy was caused by a deficiency of it. Nor were they aware that good physical conditions had contributed much more to the prevention of disease than their so-called antiscorbutics. Of the two in which they placed greatest faith, essence of malt contained no vitamin C whatever and sauerkraut contained very little. As long before as 1747 James Lind had proven that lemon juice, rich in vitamin C, was a certain cure for scurvy, but half a century passed, and Vancouver's great voyage was over, before the Admiralty finally ordered its general issue to the fleet in 1795. Banks had cured himself on Cook's first voyage by recourse to a private supply of lemon juice, but Cook himself seems to have been indifferent to it. But there was some realization of its value, for Cranstoun, surgeon of the *Discovery*, had included 42 bottles of 'Robs of Oranges & Lemons' in his list of articles required for the

[1] Menzies, 1 November 1792.

voyage.[1] Vancouver now turned to this supply. He notes that 'recourse was immediately had' not only to essence of malt, but also to 'inspissated juice of oranges and lemons, which from some removed the disorder, and checked its progress in others'.[2]

As Vancouver neared his April landfall, at about 39° N, he resumed his survey of the coast and did his best to carry it southward. The weather improved somewhat, but he was forced to leave some features, including Bodega Bay and Drakes Bay, for future examination. He sailed through the Golden Gate on the evening of November 14. Ships usually lay a short distance inside the entrance, where it was convenient to reach the presidio; but, as Menzies notes, although the *Discovery* was expected and a gun was fired in greeting, 'no Boat came off to shew us the proper Anchorage'.[3] She therefore continued along the southern shore and spent the night in Yerba Buena Bay, with the result that her first visitors in the morning were a Spanish sergeant and a Franciscan father from the mission, which was relatively close by.

The visit to San Francisco – the first made by a foreign vessel – lasted only ten days. The major work of overhauling the ships, taking on a capacity cargo of stores from the *Daedalus*, and preparing dispatches, letters and charts to be forwarded to England, would be done at Monterey. The call was made primarily in accordance with Vancouver's instructions to inform himself about the Spanish settlements north of 30°, and to secure fresh provisions and some rest and recreation for the crew of the *Discovery* as soon as possible.

Heamegildo Sal, the elderly acting commandant at the presidio, followed the instructions he had received from Quadra and did everything possible to make the stay of Vancouver and his officers a pleasant one. Dinners and entertainments were offered on shore by Sal and on the *Discovery* by Vancouver. Horses were provided whenever any of the officers wished to ride about the country. The highlight of the visit was an excursion to the Santa Clara Mission. Vancouver, Puget, Baker and Johnstone led the party, accompained by Orchard, clerk of the *Discovery*, and two midshipmen. Six armed guards ensured their safety, and they were followed by a cavalcade of 40 remounts. It was an interesting outing, but the sailors, quite unused to riding, suffered

[1] Cranstoun to Vancouver, 21 January 1791. P.R.O., Adm 1/2628, f. 598.
[2] Vancouver, I, 427. On the health of ships' crews and the scurvy problem at this time see Sir James Watt (Surgeon Vice-Admiral), 'Medical Aspects and Consequences of Cook's Voyages', in Robin Fisher and Hugh Johnston (eds.), *Captain James Cook and His Times* (Vancouver and London, 1979), pp. 129–157.
[3] Menzies, 14 November 1792.

acute discomfort because of a misunderstanding that had led them to believe that the distance was 18 miles, whereas in reality it was 18 leagues.

At San Francisco and later at Monterey the missions offered generous hospitality. Beef and mutton were plentiful, and the fathers could offer fresh fruits and vegetables from their gardens, which far surpassed those at the presidios. Vancouver's admiration for the Franciscans was unbounded and was shared by Menzies and others. As a rule there were only two or three missionaries at each mission and the calls on their time, patience and energy were endless. The military were interested in livestock, as the large herds of black cattle, sheep and horses testified, but their husbandry involved little labour. The missions devoted much more attention to agriculture, both for their own support and that of the populous Indian villages attached to them. The fathers hoped – in vain – that the example of these activities and their evident productiveness would encourage the Indians to cultivate crops on their own.

The *Chatham* arrived at San Francisco on November 22. She and the *Discovery* sailed on the 25th and arrived the next day at Monterey, where they found the *Daedalus* awaiting them. Vancouver's little squadron was thus together again, and it was possible to get on with the considerable tasks of refitting the ships, replenishing their stores and provisions from the cargo of the *Daedalus*, and preparing the latter for a voyage to Port Jackson. Vancouver himself was much occupied in the preparation of an extensive docket of dispatches, charts and drawings which were to be sent to London. He had decided that they should be taken thither by Broughton, who, he explains 'had been privy to the whole of my transactions with Senr. Quadra at Nootka; and whose abilities and observations would enable him, on his arrival in England, to satisfy the Board of Admiralty on many points of inquiry, for which it was impossible I could provide in my dispatches'.[1] At one time Vancouver intended to send Broughton home in the *Chatham*, but when Quadra agreed very readily to allow him to accompany him to San Blas and from thence to proceed to England by way of Mexico, the *Chatham* stayed with the *Discovery* – much to the disappointment of many of her crew, who had been looking forward to the delights of London.

The social life enjoyed at San Francisco was resumed at Monterey, where Quadra gave Vancouver and his officers a warm welcome. Dinners, entertainments, horse racing, riding and hunting were the

[1] Vancouver, II, 33.

order of the day. Outings on horseback were frequent, and Menzies noted that 'Whenever we went out in this manner Sr Quadra's Plate & Cooking Equipage &c travelled with us, so that we had always the luxury of dining off Silver, & on the best of every thing he could afford.'[1] A bull fight was held in the square of the presidio most evenings, a spectacle that Manby for one found barbarous and distressing. Vancouver gave a display of fireworks, the first seen by most of those who witnessed it.

At San Francisco Sal, following instructions from Quadra, had provided Vancouver with supplies but had declined any payment for them; 'he had been strictly enjoined by Senr. Quadra, on no pretence whatever to accept any pecuniary recompence from me', Vancouver states; 'as every thing of that nature would be settled by himself on our meeting at Monterrey'.[2] But at Monterey Quadra also refused to accept any payment. Vancouver could not insist, and made such return as he could by offering gifts of trade goods, wines and utensils to be distributed between the missions and the presidios. Later Vancouver learned that Quadra had made himself personally liable for the supplies provided for Vancouver's ships. Menzies understood that he had given 'the Governor of Monterrey Bonds to the amount of 1800 dollars for the refreshments which our Vessels received while we staid in California'.[3]

This extraordinarily generous treatment was evidently due to Quadra personally, and was probably made possible because Vancouver had chanced to arrive during an interregnum. Monterey was the seat of the government of Alta California, which for the moment was without a govenor. The previous incumbent had died and his successor had not yet arrived. In his absence José Dario Arguello, who had been commandant at San Francisco, had moved to Monterey. Nominally he was in charge, but although Quadra's official jurisdiction was limited to San Blas and the naval ships and establishments, it was clear that he had assumed control. Bell states that Quadra had in effect usurped Arguello's authority and taken temporary command of the province improperly; but he hastens to add that this usurpation 'sprung not from haughty ambition, or ostentatious pride, or from any motive that could throw the slightest taint on Mr. Quadra's character as a private Man, it was readily allowed that he err'd only from want of knowledge, and that his principal motive was the having it in his power by this means

---

[1] Menzies, 9 January 1793.   [2] Vancouver, II, 26.
[3] Menzies, 20 May 1793.

to behave to us in the generous hospitable manner in which he afterwards did, and which he could not have answered for in Lieut. Arguello had he suffered him to remain Commanding Officer.'[1] This comment is unjust to Arguello, who proved to be as friendly as Quadra himself. But it is interesting to speculate upon what might have happened if José Joaquin de Arrillaga, the new governor, had assumed office before Vancouver arrived. Arrillaga was prepared to observe very strictly the regulations intended to keep contacts with foreign vessels to a minimum and to prevent foreigners from gaining information about California and its defences. The fact that Vancouver's mission was in part a diplomatic one, and that he had shared details of his survey with Quadra were to Arrillaga matters of little moment. He was highly displeased when he arrived and heard of the freedom of movement that had been accorded the British officers, and Vancouver's reception was to be very different when he called again at San Francisco and Monterey in the autumn of 1793.

It has been charged that Vancouver 'cleverly parlayed his personal friendship with Bodega [y Quadra] into an inspection of the California ports and bases on the pretext of needing repairs and [on his later visits] awaiting further instructions' and was thus able to see 'at first hand that the garrisons were weak and the presidios defenseless.'[2] Certainly Vancouver describes the military establishments and the missions at some length, but there is little about his descriptions to suggest espionage. They simply record what one would expect an observant naval officer to notice. Menzies' journal includes a comparable account, from a somewhat different point of view, but he shared Vancouver's very favourable impression of California and its possibilities, and his surprise that Spain had made so slight an effort to develop and protect it. This Menzies ascribed to indolence, and cited the garrison at Monterey as an example. They cultivated only one small garden and he criticized 'their not rearing in a country like this where the Soil is so very productive, a sufficient quantity of Vegetables for their own consumption...but they live entirely on Garrison provision, & indulge in their native indolence.'[3]

The *Daedalus* was to sail to Port Jackson by way of the Marquesas, Tahiti and New Zealand. This would enable her to fulfil several

[1] Bell, November 1792.

[2] Michael E. Thurman, 'Juan Bodega y Quadra and the Spanish Retreat from Nootka 1790–1794', *Reflections of Western Historians: Papers of the 7th Annual Conference of the Western History Association...1967* (Tuscon, 1969), p. 61.

[3] Menzies, 8 December 1792.

missions, details of which Vancouver gave in his instructions to James Hanson, formerly lieutenant of the *Chatham*, who had succeeded the unfortunate Hergest as her agent and commander. Vancouver was anxious to provide the young colony in New South Wales with livestock, and Quadra generously made cattle and sheep available for this purpose. Hanson was to secure provender for them at the ports of call, in addition to replenishing his supplies of wood and water. Vancouver hoped he might be able to add hogs, goats and fowl at Tahiti. Also at Tahiti the *Daedalus* was to pick up 20 survivors of the ship *Mathilda* who had been stranded on the island since she had been lost on a shoal in February 1792. Finally, in New Zealand, Hanson was to use his 'best endeavours' to take 'one or two of the natives of that country versed in the operations necessary for the manufacture of the flax-plant', in the hope that they could instruct the settlers in Australia in the art of dressing and weaving flax, which grew luxuriantly on Norfolk Island.[1] At Port Jackson she was to secure stores and supplies sufficient to provision the *Discovery* and *Chatham* for a year and bring them to Nootka Sound, where a rendezvous was arranged for the autumn.[2]

The *Daedalus* sailed on 29 December 1792; the *Discovery* and *Chatham* did not get away until January 15, partly owing to the weather, and partly due to a fruitless search for two deserters from the *Chatham*. Three Spanish vessels sailed with them, one being the brig *Activa*, carrying Quadra and Broughton. British and Spanish parted company on the 18th. Menzies records that Quadra, Broughton 'and some of the Spanish Officers came and dind on board the Discovery, this was the parting dinner & consequently they did not leave us till a late hour; as soon as they went on board we bore up under the Brig's Stern, manned ship at midnight & gave them three cheers & then parted, we shaping our course S b W & they to the South eastward for San Blas.'[3] As it happened, Quadra had little more than a year to live, and he and Vancouver were not to meet again.

[1] By guile, Hanson was able to seize Hoodoo and Tokee, two young Maori chiefs, at Doubtless Bay, near the northern tip of New Zealand's North Island. 'One was a priest and the other a warrior, and on Norfolk Island they proved themselves inexperienced in the art of dressing and weaving flax. Even so, before they were repatriated, they taught the convicts to improve the quality and output of the cloth.' The episode had a happy ending. They were treated 'with great kindness' by Lieut. Gov. King and 'were returned to their home by the *Britannia* nine months later.' – Geoffrey Blainey, *The Tyranny of Distance* (Melbourne, 1966), p. 35.

[2] Vancouver to Hanson, Monterey, 29 December 1792. For the complete instructions see *Historical Records of New South Wales*, I, pt. 2 (Sydney, 1914), pp. 681–83.

[3] Menzies, 18 January 1793.

Hergest's death and the departure of Mudge and Broughton resulted in several promotions. Hanson, lieutenant of the *Chatham*, had been appointed to succeed Hergest as agent of the *Daedalus*. Puget had succeeded Mudge as 1st lieutenant of the *Discovery*, and when Broughton left for England Vancouver appointed him commander of the *Chatham*. He was given only acting rank, and Vancouver informed the Admiralty that he was to be in command during Broughton's absence, 'or until their Lordships' pleasure shall be known.' As this implies, Vancouver hoped that Broughton would return with 'further directions for the guidance' of his conduct. If Broughton came in another ship, Puget would be 'a very proper person to continue in the command of the Chatham.'[1] Broughton did return to the Pacific, but his ship did not sail from Plymouth until February 1795. By that time Vancouver had completed his survey and was far down the coast of South America on his way home. In November 1794, realizing that there was no likelihood of Broughton's return in time to participate further in the voyage, he had confirmed Puget in his appointment.

Two midshipmen benefitted by the promotions, Spelman Swain and – in spite of the incident at Birch Bay – Thomas Manby. Swaine served first as master of the *Chatham* and later became 3rd lieutenant of the *Discovery*. Manby succeeded Swaine as master of the *Chatham* and late in the voyage was appointed to an acting lieutenancy.

Hawaii: the Second Visit

Vancouver's account of the Sandwich Islands and the Sandwich islanders is much more lively and informative than his description of the Northwest Coast and its Indian inhabitants. It is obvious that he took a much greater personal interest in them. In keeping with the eighteenth century's preference for an orderly landscape, he found the spectacular scenery of the Northwest Coast dreary and inhospitable,[2] and his descriptions of the Indians give the impression of being something that was expected of him, rather than the result of any spontaneous interest. When his narrative is dealing with the coastal survey, the prime purpose of the expedition, it is only natural that it should receive most of the attention; but even so the contrast is striking.

[1] Vancouver to Stephens, Monterey, 13 Jan. 1793. P.R.O., Adm 1/2629, f. 49v.

[2] Galiano and Valdés shared this opinion: 'the lonely and barren abodes of the interior of this strait [Juan de Fuca] offer no attraction to the trading navigator.... The philosopher alone might perchance find in these regions material for contemplation, in view of a soil and of tribes of people as near to the primitive condition of the world as they are distant from European civilisation, which they neither appreciate nor desire.'

Several circumstances accounted for this. One was much better communication. Vancouver, Menzies and several of the officers evidently had a considerable knowledge of the Hawaiian language, and they had the additional advantage of contact with a number of white men, notably John Young and Isaac Davis, who had lived some time in the islands and were acquainted with the manners and customs of the natives. Intercourse was aided greatly by the fact that the same language was common to all the islands in the group. Equally important, Vancouver was able to pay repeated visits to a number of bays in Hawaii, Oahu and Kauai, and sometimes spent several weeks in one spot. By contrast, although he had a smattering of Nootkan, this was seldom of help to him elsewhere, as each important tribal group on the Northwest Coast had its own distinctive language. The ships were constantly on the move; Nootka Sound was the only place they visited more than once. The anchorages where they paused were not chosen for communication, but to serve the purposes of the survey. The only Indians seen were those who appeared out of curiosity, or who approached the ships or their boats with trade or plunder in mind.

Physical conditions were another important circumstance. The Hawaiian Islands are famous for their pleasant climate, and Vancouver took his ships there three times to enable his crews to enjoy some rest, recreation and the luxury of fresh provisions. Hawaiian villages were clean and pleasant places, and the food was appetizing. These were conditions that encouraged contact and friendship, whereas the Northwest Coast Indian villages were characterized by filth, stench and vermin, and except for fish and game, Europeans found most of the food of the Indians revolting.

Finally, Vancouver had become interested in the islands when he visited them with Cook, and when he returned to them he became much concerned about their internal affairs and political future. On the Northwest Coast, Maquinna was the only Indian chief with whom he seems to have established a personal relationship of any significance, but in the Sandwich Islands he came to know many of the chiefs relatively well. For the most important of them, Kamehameha, he had the highest regard, and a warm personal friendship developed between them.

In the course of the month-long voyage from Monterey to Hawaii Vancouver yielded once more to his explorer's instincts and seized the opportunity to search for the Los Majos islands. These were shown on old Spanish charts about 10° of longitude east of the island of Hawaii, but in the same latitude. Portlock and Dixon had searched for them unsuccessfully in 1786, and when the records of the La Pérouse expedition were published in 1797 they would show that he, too, searched for them the same year. Having conducted his own search with what Manby terms 'undiscribable caution' Vancouver was satisfied that no islands existed in the area indicated on the charts. But there was a further possibility: were the Los Majos Islands in reality the Sandwich Islands, wrongly located on the map due to the difficulty, only recently overcome, of ascertaining longitude with any accuracy? On the face of it this seemed unlikely, for although Spanish ships had long been sailing regularly between Mexico and Manila, the route they followed on their westward voyages took them far to the north of the Sandwich Islands, while their eastward route lay far south of them. Nevertheless it was conceivable that a ship badly off course could have stumbled on the islands, and strong currents, of which the Spaniards had little knowledge, could account for the discrepancy in longitude. Vancouver makes no mention of this possibility himself, no doubt because he would have been reluctant to admit that the Spaniards might have discovered the islands before Cook. But it is clear that the matter was discussed at length in his ships. Manby, master of the *Chatham*, later went so far as to contend that 'considering the very imperfect state Navigation was brought too, at so early a period, I assure myself the Sandwich Islands, is the Los Majos of the Spaniards'.[1] Menzies surmised that 'they may turn out to be the Sandwich Islands from their being placed in the same parallel of Latitude, & from the uncertain mode Navigators formerly had of ascertaining their Longitude'.[2] Anderson, who discussed the whole matter at some length and regarded the question as still an open one, points out that, quite independently, La Pérouse had come to the same conclusion.[3]

On February 12 the ships sighted Ka Lae, the southern tip of the island of Hawaii. There they separated. To further Vancouver's survey they were to circumnavigate the island and meet at Kealakekua Bay. The *Chatham* was to follow the western shore, while the *Discovery* took the much longer route up the east coast and around the northern point of Hawaii.

In addition to wintering in a pleasant climate, Vancouver had come to the islands with two objectives in mind, neither of which related to his instructions. One concerned their political future. He was imbued

---

[1] Manby, Letters, 8 March 1793.   [2] Menzies, 6 February 1793.
[3] Anderson, *Surveyor of the Sea*, p. 129.

with the hope that he might be able to promote their welfare by negotiating a peace agreement that would halt the inter-island fighting that had broken out repeatedly during the past decade. And without any official knowledge or approval, he cherished the hope that such an agreement might lead to a link of some kind with Great Britain. The other object was more immediate: he was determined to see that the natives responsible for the murder of his friend Hergest and Gooch, the astronomer, were punished for their crime. If he were to succeed in the first objective, he would have to negotiate with two ambitious chiefs who between them ruled the islands, and between whom wars had been frequent: Kamehameha (Tamaahmaaha), whose authority extended to all Hawaii, and Kahekili (Titeeree), who controlled Maui, Oahu, Kauai and sundry lesser islands. The murders would concern only Kahekili, as they had been committed on Oahu.

Vancouver had had no opportunity to meet either of these chiefs during his brief stay in the islands in 1792, but when the *Discovery* was proceeding down the west coast of Hawaii and paused at Kaiakekua Bay, north of Kealakekua Bay, he was surprised and pleased to find that Kamehameha had come there to meet him. He had a vague recollection of having seen him when he was with Cook, but both had changed greatly and matured in the interval. Vancouver, then a midshipman, was now an experienced naval officer; Kamehameha, merely the nephew of the ruling chief in 1778, was now undisputed ruler of Hawaii. Each immediately recognized the other as a person of consequence, and confidence quickly developed between them – a relationship encouraged by Vancouver's meticulous recognition of Kamehameha's rank.

In spite of Kamehameha's cordial welcome, which was followed by a spectacular state visit to the *Discovery* after she and the *Chatham* had arrived in Kealakekua Bay, Vancouver continued to be on his guard. Memories of Cook's death in the bay were still vivid. He had been disturbed by the insistent demands of the natives for guns, and by evidence of a traffic in arms carried on by the trading ships that were visiting the islands with some frequency. There was even a rumour, soon found to be false, that Kealakekua Bay itself was fortified. Kamehameha was as anxious as Vancouver to safeguard the ships, and they cooperated in arrangements for their protection. Only chiefs were allowed on board and only officers and men on duty were permitted to go ashore. A highly unpopular order stipulated that midshipmen could leave the ships only if accompanied by an officer. All private trading was banned, and Kamehameha himself undertook to see that the ships were supplied with hogs and vegetables, 'declaring [in Menzies' words] that as they belonged to King George they must not in his Dominions traffic for refreshments like other Vessels'.[1] For greater security, Vancouver had 'the Field pieces...got upon deck...& about forty stand of small arms were kept loaded under a sentinel's charge on the quarter deck'.[2]

To help ensure that all would go smoothly, Kamehameha ordered John Young and Isaac Davis, who had spent nearly three years in the islands, to watch over the welfare of the *Discovery* and *Chatham*. They performed admirably; Menzies acknowledged that they 'made themselves extremely useful...as they understood the Manners & Customs of the Inhabitants & their Language, one of them lived on board each Vessel, especially in the day time, & transacted all business of intercourse & trafic between us & the Natives, with such candour & fairness as entitled them to our approbation & regard & reflected much credit on their conduct.'[3] Both men were on the island as a result of the massacre of the crew of the small schooner *Fair American* off the coast of Kona in 1790, a tragedy Vancouver discusses at length. It was instigated by Kameeiamoku (Tamaahmotoo), chief of Kohala District, and Davis was the sole survivor. Young, boatswain of the trading ship *Eleanora*, was ashore at Kealakekua Bay at the time, and Kamehameha, fearing a reprisal, detained him to prevent word of the massacre from reaching the vessel. It seems probable that he knew that the *Fair American* had been commanded by a son of the captain of the *Eleanora*. Kamehameha deplored Kameeiamoku's savage act, took Davis and Young under his protection, presently gave them the status of chiefs, and was ably and loyally served by them for many years. Vancouver shared Kamehameha's abhorrence of the deed and its perpetrator, and it is a measure of the importance he attached to the negotiations for peace that he eventually received Kameeiamoku in order to include him in the last discussion of his proposals in 1794.

Vancouver spent much of his time during the fortnight the ships lay in Kealakekua Bay endeavouring to convince Kamehameha and other chiefs that peace would be in the best interest of all concerned. He evidently had a considerable knowledge of the recent history of the islands. He refers to the '11 years of war' they had suffered, meaning since 1782, when the death of Kalaniupuu, the old King of Hawaii,

---

[1] Menzies, 2 March 1793.   [2] *Ibid.*, 22 February 1793.
[3] *Ibid.*, 7 March 1793.

had been followed by wars between his heirs and successors. Hostilities had next broken out between Kamehameha and Kahekili, both of whom hoped to possess themselves of the other's territories. In 1790, when Kahekili was on Oahu and his brother Kaeo was on Kauai, Kamehameha seized the opportunity to invade and overrun Maui and Molokai. But the conquest proved to be temporary; Kahekili and Kaeo rallied their forces and not only regained the islands but ravaged part of the coast of Hawaii. The issue was decided for the moment in a major naval battle near Waipio Bay, on the north coast of Maui, in the spring of 1791. Vancouver believed firmly that the possession of arms encouraged the inter-island wars, and it is significant that at Waipio both fleets included double canoes carrying cannon and foreigners to man them. Young and Davis are said to have been in charge of Kamehameha's guns. Kamehameha was victorious, but the outcome was merely the restoration of the status quo; neither side retained any of its conquests. To Kamehameha and the other chiefs Vancouver seems to have spoken quite frankly. He relates that he deplored 'the continual state of warfare that had so long disgraced their islands; without any other motive that could be urged as an excuse for despoiling each other's lands, or destroying their fellow creatures, than a wild and inordinate ambition to possess themselves of each others territories, which experience had shewn them they were incapable of retaining after conquest.'[1]

Relative quiet had now reigned for the better part of two years, but this was due much more to exhaustion and a need to recoup forces than to any genuine desire for peace. Large standing armies on Hawaii and Maui faced one another across the Alenuihaha Channel, and neither side trusted the other sufficiently to withdraw them. Indeed, lack of confidence in the good faith of Kahekili proved to be a major obstacle that Vancouver was unable to remove, and later, when he reached Maui, he was to find that Kahekili and his chiefs were equally distrustful of Kamehameha. Instead of a peace agreement, Kamehameha and his chiefs would have much preferred to have enlisted Vancouver as an ally in a renewed war against Kahekili. In an effort to attract support they alleged that the murders of Hergest and Gooch, about which they knew he felt very strongly, had been ordered by Kahekili's brother and committed in his presence. For Vancouver a war could thus be one of personal revenge. With this proposal Vancouver would have nothing to do.

Probably because it was refused so flatly, Vancouver does not

[1] Vancouver, II, 155–6.

mention in his journal that he made a first attempt at this time to persuade Kamehameha to cede the island of Hawaii to Great Britain, a proposal he was to advance again with greater success the following year. Fortunately Menzies and Manby both noted the negotiations. Kamehameha had staged a sham battle for the benefit of Vancouver and his officers, and Vancouver had reciprocated with a fireworks display. 'As a great number of Chiefs & Natives were collected to see these entertainments,' Menzies writes, 'Captain Vancouver was very urgent with Tamaiha-maiha [Kamehameha] to take this opportunity of declaring himself & his Subjects together with the whole Island under the dominion of the King of Great Britain, but this he positively declined to do unless Captain Vancouver would promise to leave one of the Vessels behind at the Island to assist in defending him & his people from the inroads of their Enemies, which was certainly a very strong & reasonable argument.'[1] Manby records that Kamehameha demanded that Vancouver leave either a ship 'or a force with Guns...pointing out the imprudence of our accepting the Island without guarding it.' Kamehameha added that Kahekili might well launch his threatened invasion in Vancouver's absence, and he wondered whether it could be expected that the Hawaiians 'would fight with firmness for their Country, if they had imprudently given it away to those who would not protect it,' a reply that 'totally put a stop to any further proposals'.[2]

On March 8 the *Discovery* and *Chatham* sailed from Kealakekua Bay. Next morning they paused in Kawaihae Bay, where Vancouver left some remarks about his visit to Hawaii for the guidance of future visitors. He testified that Kamehameha, 'with the generality of the Chiefs, and the whole of the lower order of the People' had 'conducted themselves toward us with the strictest honesty, civility and friendly attention', but he warned that Kaiana and a few other chiefs were 'persons not much to be trusted' and roundly condemned Kameeiamoku, who had been responsible for the capture of the *Fair American* and the massacre of her crew. In an effort to discourage the arms traffic he pointed out that the people had supplied the ships 'with water, wood and all kinds of refreshments &ca. in the greatest perfection; for which they received neither arms or ammunition, but cheerfully and eagerly disposed of their commodities for other articles of Commerce, infinitely more useful and necessary to their comforts.'[3]

[1] Menzies, 4 March 1793.
[2] Manby, Letters, 7 March 1793.
[3] Quoted from the copy in the Public Archives of Hawaii. Puget copied the statement, which is dated 9 March 1793, into his log.

On the 10th the ships reached Maui, where they first anchored in Maalaea Bay. There they were met by Kamohomoho, a younger brother of Kahekili, who conducted them to the Lahaina anchorage at the north end of the island, where they remained for a week. Vancouver was soon visited by Kahekili and his brother Kaeo, with whom he shared authority in the leeward islands. It was Vancouver's first meeting with Kahekili, but somewhat to his surprise Kaeo greeted him as an old friend whom he had met at the time of Cook's visit, and as proof of this produced a lock of Vancouver's hair that he had treasured as a memento of the occasion. Kaeo was also well and favorably known to Menzies, who had met him when the *Prince of Wales* was at Kauai, and who remembered him as 'a great favourite both with the Officers and Crew for his kind attention & friendly behaviour towards them'.[1] These past contacts helped to establish cordial relations, and Vancouver soon was able to introduce his 'favorite object' of a peace agreement with Kamehameha. Provisions were scarce in Maui, and he pointed out the ruinous results of the last invasion, when fields and irrigation ditches had been destroyed and livestock that could not be carried away had been killed. He was listened to with attention, but a familiar difficulty soon appeared: Kahekili and his chiefs had no faith in the integrity of the chiefs of Hawaii. Nevertheless, at the conclusion of long discussions Kaeo asked Vancouver to take him to Hawaii when he returned to the islands, and he would endeavour to negotiate personally with Kamehameha. Meanwhile this offer was to be conveyed to Kamehameha in a letter that Vancouver left to be forwarded to him.

The matter of the murders was dealt with expeditiously. Vancouver's first purpose was to judge whether Kahekili himself had been involved in the crimes; a story had gone the rounds that he and Kaeo had been insulted by Ingraham, commander of the *Hope*, and that Kahekili in reprisal had ordered the execution of the first white man to fall into their hands. Hergest was said to have been the victim.[2] Vancouver soon satisfied himself that this story was false and that neither Kahekili nor Kaeo was in any way implicated. They both assured him that Hergest and Gooch had done nothing to provoke nor justify the assault, and Kahekili's strong disapproval of it had been shown by the fact that three of the men involved in it had been executed. But Kahekili admitted that three or possibly four men who were believed to have been involved were still at large, and Vancouver insisted that steps be taken

[1] Menzies, 16 March 1793.   [2] Puget, 13 March 1793.

to see that they, too, were punished. Kahekili agreed, and it was arranged that his brother Kamohomoho should accompany the *Discovery* to Oahu and see that efforts were made to apprehend them. Undoubtedly Vancouver was motivated to some extent by a desire to revenge the death of a friend, but he was convinced that if retribution were not exacted the prestige and safety of all whites who came to the islands would be in jeopardy. In his own words, it was essential that it should be made clear to the islanders 'that no distance in time would in future secure any from detection, or prevent the punishment which such crimes demand.'[1]

The morning the *Discovery* sailed from Lahaina one of the sudden outbursts of temper to which Vancouver was becoming subject threatened to endanger his good relations with Kahekili. Vancouver simply records that Kahekili left the ship 'in a very sudden manner' and that Kaeo assured him that 'such was his common practice of retiring';[2] but Menzies tells a different story. A piece of ribbon had been stolen, and Vancouver 'in endeavouring to recover this trifle put himself into such a passion & threatened the Chiefs with such menacing threats that he terrified some of them out of the ship with great precipitation; The King [Kahekili] in particular came running into my Cabin before I knew any thing of the business & instantly jumping into his Canoe through the port hole, paddled hastily to the shore & we saw no more of him. Taio [Kaeo] who was not so easily frightened & who was among the last that left us, was the first who told me the cause of Taiteree's [Kahekili's] sudden departure as he came into my cabin soon after to get his last present. Excepting this little fracas which I was sorry should happen for so trifling a circumstance at the time we were leaving them we enjoyd the utmost tranquility during our stay' – the results, in Menzies' opinion, of the wise policy of allowing only chiefs to board the ships.[3]

At Lahaina the *Discovery* and *Chatham* temporarily parted company. When leaving Nootka Sound in October the *Chatham* had scraped some rocks, and at Lahaina it was possible to have her hull examined by native divers. Their 'dexterity and skill' surprised Manby. 'Two of them went down at the same instant and with a piece of line exactly measured the defective part, bringing up word that all the False keel abaft the Main Chains was entirely torn off, the Gripe a good deal shatter'd and much plank, and Copper beat off different parts of her.'[4] These reports

[1] Vancouver, II, 179.
[2] *Ibid.*, 199.
[3] Menzies, 18 March 1793.
[4] Manby, Letters, 16 March 1793.

alarmed Manby, but Puget concluded rightly that the hull itself was still sound. As the range of the tides at the Sandwich Islands was too small to make it practicable to beach the *Chatham*, Vancouver ordered Puget to proceed at once to Nootka Sound and make the necessary repairs there.

Vancouver did not forget that he had been instructed to employ himself 'very diligently in the examination and survey' of the islands, and he seized every opportunity to examine parts of them that had not yet been visited. Before heading for Nootka, the *Chatham* was to sail along the north coast of Molokai. Puget dutifully noted details of the survey in his journal, but his general impression was summed up in a single sentence: 'I never witnessed so Barren and desolate an appearance as the North Side of this Island afforded.'[1] When the *Discovery* moved on from Maui to Oahu she sailed along the south shore, thus completing the examination of the island. Vancouver's impressions were mixed. The eastern part of the coast 'presented not only a rich but a romantic prospect' but the western part had 'a dreary aspect'.[2]

The *Discovery* anchored off Waikiki on March 20. She sailed again on the 24th, but in this brief interval Vancouver had seen three men seized, tried, condemned and executed for the murders of Hergest and Gooch. The executions, which Vancouver wisely insisted should be carried out by one of the native chiefs, were preceded by a trial of sorts — an enquiry would be a better description — in which Vancouver heard and then reviewed carefully what evidence was available. He describes the whole procedure in detail, and only a few points need be mentioned here.

It became clear that the murders had been due in great part to Hergest's own rashness. Vancouver had the benefit of the first-hand account of Kapaeiku, a young native who had gone ashore with Hergest from the *Daedalus*. Kapaeiku stated that he had urged Hergest not to land, as no chief was present who could restrain the crowd in case of need, but Hergest disregarded his advice, both then and when he advised him not to walk to the village, where the murders occurred. The evidence given to Vancouver was largely circumstantial, but he felt that the guilt of the prisoner accused of having killed Hergest was reasonably certain. That of the other two men seemed less so. Kapaeiku had tried to defend Hergest, had seen him killed, and stated that the murderer was living not far away. He went ashore with native chiefs

---

[1] Puget, 17 March 1793.   [2] Vancouver, II, 202.

to assist in his apprehension, but to Vancouver's annoyance became fearful that the prisoner's friends and relatives would kill him, and avoided returning to the *Discovery* to identify him in Vancouver's presence. This made the chief witnesses James Coleman, an American sailor living on Oahu, who testified that the prisoner was the man Kapaeiku had pointed out to him as Hergest's murderer, and Thomas Dobson, formerly a midshipman on the *Daedalus*, who identified him as a native who had behaved in an insolent fashion alongside the ship and had paddled hastily to shore just before Hergest and Gooch disembarked. This evidence, and statements by the chiefs, finally convinced Vancouver, but doubts about the justice of the convictions still linger. The supposition is that in order to placate Vancouver the chiefs simply picked up three men at random and brought them to the ship,[1] ostensibly to trade their pearls. Doubts are based in part on the fact that the men boarded the *Discovery* voluntarily. Hewett, the never-failing critic of Vancouver, contends that it was well known that he was determined to see those implicated in the murders punished, and, this being so, it was inconceivable that guilty men would have come to the ship of their own free will. On the other hand, Vancouver mentions specifically that the matter 'had been conducted by the chiefs with the most profound secrecy', and there had been little time for word of the intended arrests to spread. The *Discovery* arrived about three o'clock in the afternoon, and the three men came on board the next morning.

From Waikiki Vancouver set sail for Kauai, proceeding first along the south coast of Oahu, where Whidbey was able to make a pioneer survey of Pearl Harbor. Vancouver had hoped to examine the north coast of Kauai, but contrary winds prevented the *Discovery* from weathering the north-east point of the island, and he was to be frustrated again when he attempted later to approach the coast from the west. His business at Kauai was limited to renewing his acquaintance with the regent and young prince he had met the previous year, and to settling two young Hawaiian girls that he had brought from Nootka. Niihau, which had been their home, had suffered so devastating a drought that Vancouver judged it best to find a home for them in Kauai,

---

[1] Broughton was informed by Kamehameha when he visited Oahu in Feb. 1796, that 'the men who were executed alongside the Discovery had not committed those murders, but were unfortunate beings whom the chief selected to satisfy Captain Vancouver.' W. R. Broughton, *A Voyage of Discovery to the North Pacific Ocean* (London, 1804), p. 42. But Kamehameha was not on Oahu in 1792, when the murders occurred, and his is hearsay evidence.

and this he was able to do. Only one day was spent in Waimea Bay. The Ship's water supply was replenished, but here as at Maui and Oahu hogs and provisions were very scarce. Nothing was to be expected at Niihau, but before leaving for Nootka, Vancouver sailed sufficiently close to it to ascertain that Cook was right in believing that Lehua Island, off its northern end, was detached from it.

Second Survey Season

Contrary winds and cold, stormy weather made the *Discovery*'s voyage to the Northwest Coast long and tedious. A leak developed in her bow that caused some anxiety and necessitated almost continuous baling with buckets or manning of the pumps. Hope of making repairs probably influenced Vancouver's decision to put into Trinidad Bay, which he had intended to examine later as part of his survey of the Californian and Mexican coasts. Land was sighted near Cape Mendocino on April 26, and the *Discovery* anchored in the bay on May 2. The ship was in need of wood and water, both of which proved to be readily available, and although the visit lasted only three days, Whidbey completed a sketch of the harbour. The natives met with, some sixty in number, seem to have caught Vancouver's interest, as he describes them in some detail.

After this respite the *Discovery* struggled on northward, again in the face of contrary winds. The leak continued to be troublesome, but the cause was at last discovered – some of the caulking in the rabbeting at the bow had been washed out – and a smooth sea made temporary repairs possible. Nootka was reached on May 20, where Vancouver learned that the *Chatham* had sailed just two days before. On the 15th Puget had opened sealed orders instructing him to sail north and resume the coastal survey alone if the *Discovery* had not arrived by that date.

Vancouver devotes only two paragraphs to the *Chatham*'s visit to Nootka, but it deserves more extended notice. There is, for instance, a story behind his statement (inaccurate, as will appear) that Puget 'put into Porto Buena Esperanza, to wait more favorable weather'. Puget had sighted the coast of Vancouver Island on April 7, after a fast passage of 22 days from Maui. His landfall was north of Nootka, and as a gale was brewing he consulted a chart given to him by Quadra and sought shelter in what he thought was Bahia de Buena Esperanza (now Esperanza Inlet). Tahsis Inlet runs south from the eastern end of this inlet to Nootka Sound, and Puget decided to follow this sheltered inside passage to Friendly Cove. But in reality he had entered Nuchatlitz Inlet, south of Esperanza Inlet, which was not shown on the Spanish chart. This ends in a closed basin connected with the main inlet by an extremely narrow channel through which the tides rush with great velocity. When Puget set out (as he thought) for Tahsis Inlet, the *Chatham* was in dire peril for a few moments as she was caught by the tide and swept through the narrows, her yard arms scraping the trees as she went. After several attempts she succeeded in getting back through the narrows at slack water, but other tribulations awaited her. By the time improving weather enabled her to leave for Nootka she had lost one anchor, which she had the good fortune to retrieve, and lost another that she was unable to recover. Part of Puget's graphic account of this adventure is quoted elsewhere. Friendly Cove was reached finally on April 15.

Salvador Fidalgo, who had arrived at Nootka a few days before Vancouver's ships had sailed in October 1792, was still in command of the Spanish post. He and his garrison had endured a miserable winter. Rain had been almost incessant; dampness had destroyed their flour; two-thirds of the crew of the guard ship *Princesa* had developed scurvy and some of them had died. Provisions from the *Chatham* helped restore the survivors to health. Manby remarks that 'every Spaniard with a Grateful Heart, acknowledged us their deliverers from the jaws of Death'.[1] Unfortunately a malady of some sort soon disabled many of the *Chatham*'s seamen for a time, but Fidalgo was happy to provide assistance that made it possible for the work of repairing her to go forward. Damage to her keel could only be repaired if she were careened, and this was accomplished with Spanish tackle and the assistance of the *Princesa*. As the *Chatham* had to be emptied, Fidalgo assigned store rooms on shore, accommodated her officers in his own quarters, and insisted that they remain even after the ship was again serviceable.

Manby's letters give many interesting details of the sojourn at Nootka and include one of the earliest first-hand descriptions of inter-tribal trading on the Northwest Coast. While the *Chatham* was undergoing repairs Tatoosh, chief of the Indians living at the entrance to the Strait of Juan de Fuca, arrived in Nootka Sound with 'Canoes of immense size' laden with 'small white shells' (presumably dentalia) which he proceeded to exchange for sea otter, bear, wolf and other skins. This transaction concluded, Maquinna, the chief at Friendly

[1] Manby, Letters, April 1793.

Cove, 'almost immediately fitted out five Canoes and sent them under the charge of his Brother, to Trade part of his new acquired Wealth with other Tribes that lay far to the Northward.' Maquinna explained, with the aid of a rough sketch, that the canoes would be hauled ashore at the head of the inlet and carried through the woods for ten days to inland waterways, where the Indians 'would eagerly give Skins for a small portion of these Shells'. Manby envisaged them moving on eastward 'as a continual chain of barter, exists between Tribe and Tribe, through this amazing track [sic] of Country, which in time, will no doubt, find their way to our factories in Canada, or the back settlements of Hudsons bay'.[1]

Manby gives pleasant glimpses of Fidalgo, one occasioned by the language difficulty: 'One of his domesticks speaks a little English, therefore stands Interpreter but when this Man is not at hand, curious scenes, repeatedly ensue as our Conversation is generally carried on, by a few words, of all Languages – & Signs – Altho the Noo[t]ka Lingo forms the greatest part. Some times we understand each other – At other times not. The honest Don, slaps his forehead, sh[r]ugs his Shoulders, and exclaims: Diable What a pity; what a misfortune; it is that so many Languages should prevail in this little World....I dare say the Inhabitants of the moon are more sensible and adopt one general dialect.' Manby characterizes Fidalgo as 'An intelligent Man. A Man of learning science and great abilities, his Mouth would never open, but most likely I should acquire knowledge.'[2] Certainly he set out to make himself agreeable to the officers of the *Chatham* and later to those of the *Discovery*. On the eve of the *Chatham*'s departure he offered a 'sumptuous farewell Dinner', gave the ship 'All the Greens from his Garden' and a supply of pigs. Maquinna, too, was generous; his parting gift was 'no less than six Bucks, and a remarkable fine Doe.'[3]

Manby refers to Fidalgo as 'this provident, and benevolent Spaniard' and Vancouver had much the same impression. But while outwardly friendly and genuinely grateful for the timely assistance Puget had given him, it is evident that he viewed the presence and activities of the Vancouver expedition with deep suspicion. As will appear, this feeling was shared by other Spanish officers in New Spain; even Quadra seems to have had his doubts. In July, after he had been relieved at Nootka and had returned to San Francisco, Fidalgo wrote to Viceroy Revilla Gigedo warning him of danger from the arms of Vancouver's ships

[1] *Ibid.*, 10 May 1793.   [2] *Ibid.*, May 1793.
[3] *Ibid.*

and relaying the fantastic rumour that he might attack Monterey or San Diego.[1] No wonder the welcome that Vancouver would receive in California in the autumn would be somewhat less than cordial.

The *Discovery*'s stay in Friendly Cove was limited to three days, as Vancouver was most anxious to join the *Chatham*. But this was sufficiently long for him to notice the new fortifications that Fidalgo had built on San Miguel Island, adjacent to the cove. The old fort had been dismantled by Quadra, who took its guns to San Blas. Vancouver dismissed the new construction as being primarily a make-work project: Fidalgo had 'very justly considered employment as essentially necessary to the preservation of his people's health'.[2] Bell considered that its eleven 9-pounders 'cou'd only annoy Vessels of small force' and that it was probably built 'in consequence of the order to warn foreigners [except the British] coming on this coast'.[3] But Menzies looked upon it as evidence that Spain expected to retain possession of Nootka Sound.

The *Discovery* found the *Chatham* in a cove at the entrance of Burke Channel, and the two ships moved some distance up the inlet to a better anchorage in Restoration Bay. Vancouver had expected to have five months available for his survey, but the long 52-day passage from the Sandwich Islands had reduced the time available to four months. The routine that had proven satisfactory in 1792 was followed again in 1793. A suitable anchorage was found for the ships, ideally one where wood and water were available, where spruce beer could be brewed, and where the observatory could be erected on shore. Seven anchorages were used progressively in the course of the season. The most satisfactory was probably Salmon Cove, in Observatory Inlet, where the only disappointment was the salmon, which were incredibly plentiful but of poor quality. The worst was near Work Island, in Princess Royal Channel. Manby, who had to stand by the *Chatham*, found it dreary in the extreme: there was 'a constant torrent of Rain – Neither Fish or Fowl, could be procured, or even a Nettle top gather'd to eat, with our salt Beef'.[4] Bell remarks that 'from its inhospitable qualities [it] obtained the name of Starve-Gut Cove'.[5]

From these anchorages the boat expeditions left to examine the maze of islands and inlets in detail. During the winter welcome improvements

---

[1] Fidalgo to Revilla Gigedo, San Francisco, 20 July 1793. Cited in Cook, *Flood Tide of Empire*, p. 407.
[2] Vancouver, II, 253.   [3] Bell, May 1793.
[4] Manby, Letters, June 1793.   [5] Bell, 29 June 1793.

had been made in the boats themselves. Each was now equipped with an awning, and (in Menzies' words) each 'had likewise a small Tent furnished with a thick painted [waterproof] floor cloth sufficient to shelter the whole Boats Crew comfortably at night or in bad weather. And all their provisions & spare clothes were snugly packd up in painted Canvas bags secure from any harm.'[1] By Vancouver's order those serving in the boats were 'supplied with an additional quantity of wheat and portable soup, sufficient to afford them two hot meals every day', and the officer in charge was provided with extra spirits which he could issue at his discretion.[2] Fish, game and greens were picked up along the way whenever possible and at times unusual items were included in the menus. On the eve of June 4, the King's birthday, Johnstone returned to the *Chatham* with some bear's meat. Manby recounts that this 'enabl'd us, to provide a sumptuous feast to Celebrate...[we] partook of Bear Steaks, stewd Eagle, and roasted Muscles, with as much glee as a City Alderman attacks his Venison'.[3]

Vancouver took personal charge of only two of the boat expeditions in 1793 – evidence of his failing health. Whidbey or Johnstone commanded the others. In the course of his first expedition, one of those sent out from Restoration Bay, Vancouver examined most of Fisher Channel, the full extent of Dean Channel, and Return Channel. His descriptions of his own expeditions are more detailed and lively than those commanded by others, which is to be regretted, as neither Whidbey's journal nor Johnstone's for this period has survived. Vancouver records their movements and discoveries conscientiously, but his accounts tend to resemble sailing directions in a pilot book. For the most part he found the coast cold, wet and dreary; the scenery rarely aroused his interest or admiration. One small exception occurred in Cascade Inlet, which branches off from Dean Channel. Vancouver named it after the waterfalls along its sides, and he was moved to remark that 'They were extremely grand, and by much the largest and most tremendous of any we had ever beheld.'[4]

Elcho Harbour, a lesser inlet a few miles farther down Dean Channel, is of historical interest because two major explorers – Vancouver travelling by sea and Alexander Mackenzie by land – both visited it within a few weeks of one another. Vancouver camped at its entrance on the night of June 4; Mackenzie's party passed the night of July 21 on a large rock near the entrance. In the morning, Mackenzie relates,

---

[1] Menzies, 29 May 1793.
[2] Vancouver, II, 261.
[3] Manby, Letters, June 1793.
[4] Vancouver, II, 268.

he 'mixed up some vermilion in melted grease, and inscribed, in large characters, on the South-East face of the rock...this brief memorial – "Alexander Mackenzie, from Canada, by land, the twenty-second of July, one thousand seven hundred and ninety-three."'[1] It marked the completion of the first crossing of North America north of Mexico. It was also the conclusion of a search, made by the North West Company, for an overland route from the Atlantic to the Pacific that was analogous to the search for a waterway connecting the two that was part of the mission upon which Vancouver was engaged.

The only Indians Vancouver mentions having met anywhere near Elcho Harbour were friendly. He accepted their invitation to visit their village, in a cove near the entrance to Cascade Inlet. By contrast, Mackenzie found the Indians in Dean Channel bold and inclined to be hostile. In a puzzling passage he records that one of them 'made me understand, with an air of insolence, that a large canoe had lately been in this bay, with people in her like me, and that one of them, whom he called *Macubah*, had fired on him and his friends, and that *Bensins* had struck him with the flat part of his sword.' Later other Indians repeated 'that *Macubah* had been there, and left his ship behind a point of land in the channel, South-West from us; from whence he had come to their village in boats, which these people represented by imitating our manner of rowing'.[2] *Macubah* would seem to be unmistakeably a reference to Vancouver, but a suggestion that by *Bensins* the Indians meant Menzies is ruled out because he was not with Vancouver's party. Nor is there any record or suggestion of any clash with the Indians of the kind described. It is conceivable that boats from a trading vessel paid an unrecorded visit to the inlet, as Mackenzie noted that the Indians used the English words 'No, no' when refusing an offer made for an otter skin, and he was convinced that on another occasion he owed his life to the fact that 'they knew the effect of fire-arms'.[3]

Vancouver's second boat expedition was made two months later, from the Salmon Cove anchorage in Observatory Inlet. It was the longest of the season, both in time and in distance travelled. His first expedition had lasted ten days; the boats were absent 23 days on the second, although they had been provisioned for only a fortnight. Vancouver explored Observatory Inlet, Portland Canal and Pearse Canal, then swung to the north and circumnavigated Revilla Gigedo

[1] W. Kaye Lamb (ed.), *The Journals and Letters of Sir Alexander Mackenzie* (Cambridge, 1970), p. 378. (Hakluyt Society Extra Series No. 41).
[2] *Ibid.*, p. 377.　　　　　　　　　　　　　　[3] *Ibid.*, p. 381.

137

Island. The excursion almost ended fatally, for while following the western shore of the island southward the party had to fend off much the most dangerous Indian attack that the survey was to experience. Vancouver admits freely that it was made possible by carelessness or over confidence; he and Whidbey and Johnstone had been so successful in their efforts to establish good relations with the Indians they encountered that their 'apprehensions of any molestation from them were totally done away.'[1] He had gone ashore to make the routine observations essential for the survey and was not unduly alarmed by the way the Indians crowded about him. He succeeded in getting away in the pinnace, but the Indians quickly surrounded it in their canoes and it became apparent that they were bent on mischief or plunder. Guns were snatched from the boat and Vancouver's plight soon became critical. Puget, in the launch, was too far astern to afford protection, and Vancouver's problem became one of fending off disaster until Puget could come to his support. This he succeeded in doing. Reluctantly he then gave the order to fire, and the Indians broke off the attack at once and made for the land. Various estimates were made of the casualties they suffered; Puget thought that eight or ten were killed. Vancouver was determined to punish them by destroying their canoes, but when he found that two of the seamen had been wounded he changed his mind. Fortunately Menzies was with the party and could give them proper medical attention. Three place names – Traitors Cove, Escape Point and Betton Island (named after one of the wounded men) – commemorate the attack.

This clash was with Tlingit Indians, an aggressive tribe who occupied the coast of Alaska all the way from Pearse Canal and Portland Canal to Mount St Elias. It was their custom to have an old woman of high rank in the stern of their war canoes, and Vancouver relates that whenever they seemed to hesitate in the attack they were urged on 'by the vociferous efforts' of these old vixens. The Tlingit were the fourth major tribe the expedition had met since the survey had been resumed in May, each of which occupied a well-defined area. The first anchorage in Restoration Bay, in Burke Channel, had been in Kwakiutl territory. These Indians had been encountered first the previous season at their village adjacent to Cape Mudge. That was the southern point of their territory, which included both the Vancouver Island and mainland sides of Discovery Passage, Johnstone Strait and Queen Charlotte Sound, and the coast thence northward almost to the Skeena River, including

[1] Vancouver, II, 365.

adjacent islands and inlets. Dean Channel and Burke Channel were partial exceptions. Their lower reaches were occupied by the Bella Bella Indians, a subdivision of the Kwakiutl (some of whom Vancouver and Mackenzie had met in the vicinity of Elcho Harbour), but the upper reaches of Dean Channel and North and South Bentinck Arm, into which Burke Channel divides, were the home of the Bella Coola. They were a distinct, compact, isolated tribe, kinsmen of the Salish, who lived to the south. The Skeena River was a stronghold of the Tsimshian, whose territory ran northward to Observatory Inlet and the Nass River, and thus occupied an area between the Kwakiutl and the Tlingit.

As already remarked, the descriptions of the Indians given by Vancouver, Puget and others are usually short, primarily because contacts were often brief and the language barrier prevented any communication of much consequence. Only striking or curious points are commented upon. The ceremonial arrival of chiefs, who would circle the ships in their canoes, singing or chanting, seems always to have aroused comment. The Nootka Indians are usually the standard of comparison; houses, for instances, were either like or unlike those with which Vancouver and others had become familiar in Nootka Sound. Johnstone was much interested in the houses of the Bella Coola, and the Bella Bella village perched on top of a large rock in Johnson Channel aroused considerable interest. Everyone was surprised by the great size of the beams and planks in many of the dwellings. Clothing or lack of it was often commented upon. Trading vessels frequently exchanged clothing for furs, and in addition to jackets and trousers, colourful military tunics and other garish items were palmed off on the natives. Bell notes that one man who visited the *Chatham* 'seemed ready dressed to play the Ghost in Hamlet, having on a compleat suit of Stage Armour'.[1] Nothing aroused more interest (and repulsion) than the large lip ornaments, known as labrets, worn by many of the Indian women on the northern coast. In their youth a cut had been made in their lower lip, the full width of the mouth, and this was gradually stretched until it could accommodate an oval-shaped wooden labret that might be more than three inches long and an inch and a half wide. Vancouver characterized them as 'hideous appendages...and an instance of human absurdity, that would scarcely be credited without ocular proof'.[2] Manby, who had a weakness for the ladies, and who declared that elsewhere 'No other fault could be found with the Heavenly sex than a want of cleanliness' (which soap and water soon

[1] Bell, September 1793.   [2] Vancouver, II, 280.

cured when occasion required), reacted to the labrets 'with disgust and abhorrence....Nor did I conceive it possible till that instant, that Women lovely Women, in any shape, could assume a loathsome appearance, but so it is.'[1]

Many of the dozen expeditions commanded by Whidbey and Johnstone were just as trying and tedious as those undertaken by Vancouver, and one of Johnstone's first ventures was marked by tragedy. He had traced Mathieson Inlet northward and the party stopped for breakfast in a small inlet at its head. As a welcome supplement to the rations brought from the ships the party gathered and ate mussels, as they had done frequently without ill effect. On this occasion, however, Barrie, the midshipman in charge of the small cutter, and three of his crew developed acute food poisoning and one of the men, John Carter, died within a few hours. It was the only casualty suffered during the three surveying seasons. Vancouver at once forbade the eating of mussels – an understandable but unnecessary move, as the danger seems to be confined to a small area, now appropriately marked by the names Mussel Inlet, Carter Bay and Poison Cove.

Vancouver's relative indifference to rivers has been noted. Early in July Whidbey reconnoitred the mouth of the Skeena and later the same month Johnstone entered Nass Bay, at the mouth of the Nass. They were obliged to report that the estuaries were both very shallow, and much encumbered with shoals and rocks. Mindful of his instructions, Vancouver dismissed them as unimportant. They were 'too insignificant to be dignified by the name of rivers and in truth scarcely deserve the appellation of rivulets'. Again ignoring the Fraser, he expressed surprise that they were the only ones 'that had yet been discovered north of the river Columbia'.[2] What Whidbey and Johnstone thought of this we do not know, but there were some who wished the rivers could have been examined more thoroughly. Puget regretted that he could not explore the Skeena, and Menzies was considerably disturbed by the failure to probe the estuary of the Nass. He recalled the Indian tale of an opening 'called Nass' that was said to be the starting point of a far journey, and speculated that the river 'might issue from or communicate with some interior Lake extending to a considerable distance inland'. It 'might in the end turn out of the greatest utility to the commercial interest of our Colonies on the opposite side, by directing the adventurous & persevering views of the Canadian and

[1] Manby, Letters, June 1793.   [2] Vancouver, II, 373.

Hudson's Bay Traders to a part of the Coast where their laudable endeavours would most likely succeed in penetrating across by an interior chain of Lakes & Rivers, & by that means might be enabled to draw yearly from this Coast the greatest part of its rich & valuable Furs'.[1] It is interesting that he should have expressed this view at precisely the time when Alexander Mackenzie was pioneering just such a route across the continent in the interests of the Canadian fur trade.

The last weeks of the 1793 season were an unfortunate time for Johnstone. He made two errors of omission for which, under the circumstances, he can scarcely be blamed, but which were to take considerable time and effort to correct the following year. On August 28, having traced the continental shore through Ernest Sound and Eastern Passage, he reached the head of Sumner Strait, one of Alaska's major waterways. Its north-eastern corner is a mass of shoals and mud flats that Johnstone found it impracticable to cross. This prevented him from learning that the shoals lay in the wide, shallow estuary of the Stikine River, which thus went unrecorded. It also prevented him from seeing that the northern coast of Sumner Strait was not unbroken, as he thought, and that the continental shore ran on to the north, following a narrow water link between the strait and the head of another major waterway, Frederick Sound. Thus when Johnstone skirted the shallows and turned westward, he was following the coast of a large archipelago that need not have been examined. And a fortnight later he compounded the error by failing to notice the entrance to Keku Strait, which provides another link between Sumner Strait and Frederick Sound about 40 miles to the west.

Sumner Strait is L-shaped, and tracing what was thought to be the continental shore along its northern and western shores was the final activity of the surveying season. The *Discovery* and *Chatham* had moved north, and had found a completely sheltered last anchorage in a cove adjacent to the point where the strait swings to the south. As a violent storm sprang up soon after that might well have endangered them, Vancouver named it Port Protection. Whidbey headed the last boat expedition, which carried the survey to the western point at the entrance to Sumner Strait. As Vancouver considered that his survey had now disposed once and for all of the claims of Juan de Fuca and Bartholomew de Fonte, he named the point Cape Decision.

He was far from happy with the progress he had made. Perhaps the state of his health was making him impatient. Frequently he had been

[1] Menzies, August, 1793.

disappointed and exasperated by the great amount of time and energy that had to be expended in examining what seemed to be an endless series of channels and inlets. On his own 23-day expedition the boats had travelled over 700 miles, but they had done so 'without having advanced our primary object of tracing the continental boundary more than 20 leagues [northward] from the station of the ships [in Observatory Inlet].'[1] During the whole season he had followed the continental shore from about 52° north latitude to about 56° 30', a distance in a direct line of about 315 miles. He took some comfort from the hope 'that, in all probability, we had overcome the most arduous part of our task, and that our future researches would be attended with less disappointment and fatigue'.[2]

The ships left Port Protection on September 21, bound for Nootka Sound. Instead of sailing south in Hecate Strait, between the Queen Charlotte Islands and the mainland, Vancouver had decided to head out into the Pacific and sail down the west coast of the Islands, which 'had been reported to have been very erroneously delineated in the charts already published'.[3] For guidance he turned chiefly to the chart published in his *Voyage* by George Dixon, who had visited the islands in 1787. Other charts he consulted included that of Jacinto Caamaño, recording his visit to the islands and the adjacent coast in 1792, and a number of small charts by Charles Duncan, which had been published by Dalrymple. He found none of them very satisfactory, and complained that the Spanish chart in particular bore little resemblance to the coast as he saw it. Nevertheless, if Dixon, Duncan or Caamaño had given a name to a feature that he could identify with fair certainty, in most instances Vancouver adopted it for his own chart.

Vancouver's visit to Nootka was brief. The ships arrived on October 5 and sailed on the 8th, as soon as they had replenished their stores of wood and water and had cut a number of spars.

Spain's interest in Nootka was obviously declining. Although trading vessels had reported that during the summer Spanish ships had come as far north as the Strait of Juan de Fuca, Ramón Saavedra, the commandant at Nootka, had received no communication from Mexico since the *Discovery* had called there in May. Menzies noted that the Spanish ships were said to be engaged on a survey of the coast from the strait southward. As he considered this to be a duplication of the survey made the previous year by Vancouver, of which Quadra had

[1] Vancouver, II, 371.   [2] *Ibid.*, p. 418.
[3] *Ibid.*, p. 421.

been given a copy, he added the comment: 'hence it would appear that they put as little trust in our examination as we put in theirs'.[1]

More lay behind the Spanish expedition than this suggests, for it had been the result of a thorough reconsideration of Spanish strategy on the Northwest Coast. Viceroy Revilla Gigedo had always been concerned about the heavy expenditure incurred for northern exploration and the maintenance of the establishment at Nootka. He considered this particularly objectionable and probably pointless in view of the freedom of movement that had been granted to British ships by the convention of 1790. He feared that the British were interpreting the convention as granting them liberty to settle in any unoccupied area north of the existing presidios and missions in California. When a new minister took charge of colonial affairs in Madrid, Revilla Gigedo seized the opportunity to submit a comprehensive review of the problems Spain faced on the coast. His conclusions were that Spain should discontinue northern exploration and should withdraw from Nootka; that the northern boundary of Spanish territory should be fixed at the Strait of Juan de Fuca, as he had advocated previously; and that efforts should concentrate on protecting California by learning as much as possible about the coast from the strait southward, and, if need be, by establishing posts north of San Francisco.[2]

Two expeditions resulted from these deliberations. One was the coastal survey that Menzies had heard about at Nootka; the other was intended to found a post at Bodega Bay. In the course of his consultations Revilla Gigedo had asked Galiano and Valdés and others for their views on further northern exploration. Galiano favoured its continuance but Valdés and others were opposed. Valdés, who had been much impressed by Vancouver's ships and equipment, contended that it was unnecessary. Vancouver would be extending his survey northward, and (in the words of Wagner's paraphrase) 'the talents of his officers, their methods and resources, warranted the belief that they would accomplish this task with skill'.[3] The latter opinion prevailed, and it may be noted that it was evidently assumed that Vancouver would again make copies of his charts available, as he had done in 1792.

The Bodega Bay project was prompted by a growing suspicion that

[1] Menzies, 5 October 1793.

[2] Revilla Gigedo to Manual de Godoy, 12 April 1793. Summarized by Warren Cook in *Flood Tide of Empire*, pp. 403–4.

[3] H. R. Wagner, *The Cartography of the Northwest Coast of America to the Year 1800* (Berkeley, 1937), I, p. 237.

the British might be planning to settle in the bay, which is less than 50 miles north of San Francisco. Vancouver himself seems to have been partly responsible for this: Warren Cook states that in conversation with Quadra the latter gained the impression 'that Britain entertained a special interest in possessing a port close to the northernmost Alta California settlement'[1] (an impression that would have been intensified had it been known that as he sailed southward Vancouver ordered the *Chatham* to examine Bodega Bay). To counter this threat the *Sutil*, commanded by Juan Batista Matutu, had been sent to the bay in July to establish a post there. The *Aranzazú* followed with men and supplies, but her deep draught prevented her from entering and the project was abandoned. The coastal survey fared somewhat better. Eliza in the *Activa* turned back about latitude 44°, but the little *Mexicana*, commanded by Martínez y Zayas, struggled on and reached the Strait of Juan de Fuca late in July. Revilla Gigedo had placed considerable stress on the importance of exploring the Columbia River, as he had it in mind to found a settlement at its mouth. The *Mexicana* entered the river, but having advanced a few miles she ran aground on a shoal. Indians in war canoes gathered, and she made no attempt to probe further. On her way south she called at Bodega Bay, found no settlement had been established there, and moved on to San Francisco, where she arrived on September 17. So ended what proved to be the last Spanish exploring expedition to the Northwest Coast.

As the *Discovery* and *Chatham* sailed south from Nootka their crews were anticipating a friendly welcome at San Francisco and Monterey, and an opportunity to enjoy some rest and recreation on shore. Vancouver had written to the Viceroy, thanking him for the hospitality accorded the previous year, and in May, at Friendly Cove, he had received a reply conveying 'the most flattering assurances of every support and assistance that the kingdoms of New Spain were capable of bestowing.'[2] But the welcome he was to receive was anything but friendly. José Joaquin de Arrillaga, who was deeply suspicious of the British and would have preferred to close the ports to all foreign ships, had arrived at Monterey to assume control of Alta California. His suspicions had been increased in July, when Fidalgo arrived from Nootka bringing rumours that Vancouver might attack Monterey or San Diego. Fidalgo reported the rumours to the Viceroy, and doubtless to Arrillaga's satisfaction he received orders in September to be on his guard lest British ships should arrive. He sent copies to the commandants

[1] Cook, *Flood Tide of Empire*, p. 406.   [2] Vancouver, II, 253.

of the various presidios [1] and supplemented them with details of drastic restrictions that he directed them to impose on any vessels that might arrive.

Heamegildo Sal, who had been so helpful and friendly at the time of Vancouver's previous visit, was still commandant at San Francisco. Reluctant to inform Vancouver of the restrictions Arrillaga had ordered him to enforce, he paid his first visit to the *Discovery* almost surreptitiously, late at night. Menzies records that it 'did not appear to be any wise ceremonious on the contrary it was frank & friendly in him to take so early an opportunity in paying his respects & renew his friendship, for he did not then give the least hint of the restrictions that were to take place'.[2] He preferred to break the unpleasant news in writing, which he did in two letters received by Vancouver the next morning. The restrictions, which Vancouver describes in detail, were indeed drastic, even humiliating. His relatively temperate reaction to them surprised and displeased many. Bell, for example, considered that Vancouver 'condescended to act below his dignity and consequence as Commander of a British Man of War'.[3] But the reason is clear. It was obvious that Sal, a good friend, was not responsible for the restrictions, and Vancouver preferred to cut short his visit to San Francisco and proceed to Monterey, where he could confront Arrillaga.

Amongst the petty restrictions, Vancouver had been denied permission to ride to the nearby mission, but Menzies notes that the Franciscan fathers visited the *Discovery* 'to pay their respects & condole with us in our restraints', and that they 'sent on board a supply of Vegetables such as Greens Radishes Pumpkins Water Melons & a parcel of hazel nuts, together with a basket of pears & peaches of the produce of Sta. Clara'.[4] In addition the ships were able to secure beef and mutton. The denial of shore leave had been a bitter disappointment to the midshipmen, but Bell observed that the fresh provisions 'in great measure consoled some of them, who were fonder of their Bellies than the Amusement of Riding, Walking, Shooting &c.' But others held a contrary opinion, that Bell himself shared: 'I would cheerfully & willingly have dispensed with the Beef and Greens for the enjoyments of Riding & Shooting after being Cooped up in a little uncomfortable Brigg [the *Chatham*] for so long a time.'[5]

---

[1] Arrillaga to the presidio commandants, 23 September 1793. Cited in Cook, *Flood Tide of Empire*, p. 407n.

[2] Menzies, 21 October 1793.

[3] Bell, October 1793.

[4] Menzies, 23 October 1793.

[5] Bell, October 1793.

There is no doubt that Arrillaga was genuinely alarmed by the weakness of the Spanish defences on the coast, and by the fact that Vancouver had become aware of how weak they were. The state of affairs in Europe contributed further to his uneasiness. The latest advices, dated in February, had brought word that the King of France had been beheaded and that war with France was imminent. When the *Chatham* arrived at San Francisco Puget noticed at once that 'every body appeared active in putting the Settlement in a State of Defence', and that 'Distrust appeared to reign predominant in every thing respecting us.'[1] Menzies saw 'eight long brass four pounders...& a considerable quantity of Shot' lying on the beach, 'so that if we might judge from appearances & the great preparations now going forward, they seem to have taken some alarm at the defenceless state of this settlement, for in our former visit we only observd one Cannon in the whole place & that simply lashd to a log of wood'. Work was in progress on a 10-gun battery on a nearby eminence, '& a more suitable situation could not be fixd on, as it perfectly commanded the [harbour] entrance'.[2] In the prevailing atmosphere Vancouver was moved to note that the site of the battery 'was commanded in return by a hill at no great distance to the south-eastward',[3] and Puget outlined in his journal ways and means by which he considered the new battery could be silenced or captured.[4]

The ships sailed from San Francisco on October 24. The next morning, to Vancouver's relief and satisfaction, they met the *Daedalus*, which had returned from New South Wales with much needed stores and provisions. When notes were compared, it was found that she had narrowly missed meeting the *Discovery* off Nootka Sound, where she had been sighted but not recognized.

The distance to Monterey was no more than 80 miles, but thanks to adverse weather the *Discovery* spent a week on the way. Contact was lost with the *Chatham* in fog and, true to form, she outdistanced her consorts when sailing alone and was anchored in the harbour when the *Discovery* and *Daedalus* arrived on November 1.

Vancouver fared no better at Monterey than at San Francisco. To begin with Arrillaga was formally courteous, but he then insisted on negotiations in writing, and on strict observance of the restrictions Vancouver had already encountered. Amongst other things he inquired the nature of Vancouver's mission. To this Vancouver sent a compre-

---

[1] Puget, 21 October 1793.
[3] Vancouver, II, 500.
[2] Menzies, 21 October 1793.
[4] Puget, 21 October 1793.

hensive reply, the key points of which Menzies summarized in his journal. Vancouver 'remonstrated against the illiberality of these restrictions particularly in our situation who were King's Vessels & employ'd on a public service of which the Spaniards by their being put in possession of all the Surveys & discoveries on the Coast had an opportunity to reap the earliest advantage he therefore demanded such mitigations of these restraints as would enable us to carry on our operations in refitting the Vessels in this Port'.[1] But Arrillaga was unyielding, and Vancouver at last reacted in a way that must have given satisfaction to Bell and others. In a dispatch to the Admiralty he reported that 'the whole tenor' of Arrillaga's reply 'though in some measure offering to alleviate our necessities, was in such a sneering, forbidding and ungracious stile, I considered it far too degrading and humiliating to the character and situation in which I am placed to accept such offers, but under circumstances of the greatest distress and necessity; which fortunately not being our situation, at half past ten at night, on the 5th of November, with a light wind, in company with the Chatham and Daedalus, we sailed out of Monterrey Bay'.[2] Bell adds the interesting details that Vancouver had determined not to wait upon Arrillaga, 'nor to Salute the Fort... [and] orders were also given not to hoist our Colours, nor in any way to pay any respect to the Port whilst we were so unhandsomely treated'.[3]

Vancouver had let it be known that he intended to visit San Diego. Arrillaga at once objected and observed that such a visit would be pleasing neither to the Viceroy nor to the Court of Spain. He indicated further that it would be useless, as the same restrictions that Vancouver had met in San Francisco and Monterey would also apply there. But Vancouver would not be deterred, and the southern cruise proved to be a pleasant one.

The first port of call was Santa Barbara, where Vancouver was surprised and pleased to receive a cordial welcome from the commandant, Felipe de Goycoechea, who assured him 'that every refreshment the country could afford was perfectly at our command'.[4] Here at last the 'young gentlemen' could indulge in riding and shooting, though Vancouver set limits to their activities for fear they might give offence. As usual, he made friends with the fathers at the mission, whose

---

[1] Menzies, 5 November 1793.
[2] Vancouver to Stephens, San Diego, 6 December 1793. P.R.O., Adm 1/2629, ff. 82–88, for the complete text.
[3] Bell, November 1793.   [4] Vancouver, II, 451.

buildings and gardens impressed him greatly. Father Vicente, one of the missionaries stationed at Buena Ventura, happened to be at Santa Barbara and Vancouver carried him home in the *Discovery*, which gave him an opportunity to pay a visit to the mission there.

The ships reached San Diego on November 27. The commandant, Antonio Grajero, had recently succeeded José Zuniga, who had not yet left to assume his new post. Both gave Vancouver a cordial welcome. Later Vancouver reported to the Admiralty that Grajero told him that when he was leaving San Blas 'Quadra informed him that he might expect us to visit this port in the course of the winter, strictly requesting, in such case, that he would shew us every civility and attention in his power, and whatever expence &c. might accrue on that account he would be answerable for'.[1] But just four days before Vancouver arrived Grajero had received orders from Arrillaga to impose the restrictions that had been enforced at San Francisco and Monterey. These specifically forbade the unloading of the *Daedalus* and limited shore transactions to the securing of wood and water. All Grajero could do was to be as generous as he dared in the provision of refreshments.

Vancouver's chief motive for visiting San Diego had been the hope that some word from London might be awaiting him there. Arrillaga had sought to discourage him by saying that any dispatches would be forwarded in the first instance to him, but Vancouver was nevertheless greatly disappointed when he learned that Grajero had received nothing. Vancouver then asked Grajero if he would forward progress reports and charts that he was anxious to send to the Admiralty. This Grajero agreed to do, and Vancouver and his staff spent a busy few days drafting dispatches and copying surveys. An extra copy of the chart was made for Quadra. Along with it Vancouver sent Quadra a private communication describing the treatment he had received from Arrillaga. But this protest can have had no effect; Quadra was already gravely ill, had left his post at San Blas, and had only a few months to live.

The ships sailed from San Diego on December 9 and headed south to fulfil Vancouver's intention to complete his survey of the coast to 30° north latitude. For guidance he used a chart given to him by Quadra. The Spaniards regarded it as the best available of the region, but Quadra had warned Vancouver against its 'incorrectness...as he did not know on what authority the coast southward of Monterey had

[1] Vancouver to Stephens, San Diego, 6 December 1793. P.R.O., Adm 1/2629, f. 39.

been laid down'.[1] The warning was timely, for Vancouver found it highly inaccurate. This had one interesting result. When Vancouver observed prominent features that seemed to have no place or name on the Spanish chart, he seized the opportunity to name them after Spaniards in California who had been friendly and helpful. Dume, Vicente, Fermin, Lasuen and Felipe points were all named after Franciscan fathers, and all but the last of these names has survived. Sal, Arguello, Grajero and Zuniga points were named after commandants; only the first two names survive. Significantly, there was no Point Arrillaga.

Vancouver later informed the Admiralty that he had traced the coast to 'the latitude of 29° 54′ North'. The actual southern limit was probably the present Punta Baja, in 29° 56′. It is clear that he considered 30° as being the southern limit of New Albion as discovered by Drake, but he seems not to have gone so far as to think that a British claim to sovereignty could be extended to coincide. The survey had been an astonishing achievement. In two relatively short seasons he had carried it from 30° to beyond 56°, a distance of over 1700 miles, to which the convolutions of the coastline and the expeditions in boats had added thousands more.

Vancouver concludes his account of his visit to California by giving his impressions of the state and prospects of New Spain. He mentions first how carefully he tried to avoid giving any cause for suspicion or friction by not showing 'too great curiosity' about such sensitive matters as military establishments. But he and his officers between them learned a good deal about what was then virtually an unknown land, so far as the outside world was concerned. This ignorance had been in effect New Spain's first line of defence on the coast, and it was being broached by the presence of ships attracted by the maritime fur trade. From the military point of view Vancouver was struck 'by the defenceless state of what the Spaniards consider as their fortresses and strongholds. Should the ambition of any civilized nation tempt it to seize on these unsupported ports, they could not make the least resistance'. Economically, he was surprised by the failure to make any attempt to develop the resources of the country, although the large herds of black cattle and the flourishing gardens at the missions hinted at its possibilities. In sum, he was impressed with how little Spain had gained in return for the money and effort that had been expended on

[1] Vancouver, II, 485.

California, and this gave rise to a puzzling question: 'why such an extent of territory should have been thus subjugated, and after all the expence and labour that has been bestowed upon its colonization turned to no account whatever, is a mystery in the science of state policy not easily to be explained.'[1]

Hawaii: the Last Visit

Vancouver had a variety of objectives in view as his three ships headed for the Sandwich Islands. Some were of a routine nature. The ships themselves were badly in need of a refit; the provisions and stores that the *Daedalus* had brought from New South Wales had not yet been transferred to the *Discovery* and *Chatham*; and the crews were looking forward to the rest and refreshment that had been denied them in California, except briefly at Santa Barbara. But there were also matters of broader import. The survey of the islands was still incomplete; Vancouver was anxious to see if there was any possibility of following up the negotiations for peace between Hawaii and Maui that he had initiated the previous year; and he was hopeful that he might be able to persuade Kamehameha to cede the island of Hawaii to Great Britain.

The ships left San Diego on 14 December 1793 and sighted Hawaii 24 days later, on 8 January 1794. Vancouver went first to Hilo Bay, where he had agreed to meet Kamehameha. It was the king's favorite part of the island, and he had described the bay as comparing favorably with Kealakekua Bay as an anchorage. Strong north winds that swept it and a quick survey by Whidbey showed that it was quite unsuitable for Vancouver's purposes, and he decided to proceed to Kealakekua at once. Kamehameha had boarded the *Discovery*, and, no doubt with memories of Cook's death in mind, Vancouver was determined that he should accompany him, as his presence would ensure good behaviour of the natives. Kamehameha demurred, pointing out that a taboo was in effect and that he could not leave without the consent of the priests. Vancouver insisted and Kamehameha finally yielded; emissaries were sent ashore to settle matters with the priests. Vancouver states that Kamehameha had been won over by 'a sort of artifice' – the contention that his reluctance was due to unfriendliness, a charge he felt deeply. But Bell contends that Vancouver turned the rivalry between Hawaii and Maui to account and told Kamehameha that 'if he did not accompany him round, he would instantly quit the Island,

[1] *Ibid.*, p. 501.

and proceed to Mowee, where all the presents intended for him should be given to Titeree [Kahekili]; this Stagger'd him, and he then consented to go'.[1]

Six very satisfactory weeks were spent at Kealakekua Bay. As a precautionary measure, communication between the ships and the shore was strictly controlled. The portable observatory was set up near the morai, with Whidbey in charge, but except for working parties shore leave was again restricted. Kamehameha undertook to see that the ships' water casks were filled and that they were generously supplied with hogs and fresh provisions. To avoid misunderstandings with the natives, a chief was assigned to remain in each vessel, and in addition John Young was again assigned to the *Discovery* and Isaac Davis to the *Chatham*. Vancouver found it 'impossible to avoid making a comparison between our reception and treatment here, from these untaught children of nature' and that offered by 'the educated civilized governor of New Albion and California'.[2] He later informed the Admiralty that the unloading of the *Daedalus* and 'refitting the rigging, and every other necessary service the Vessels required' had been 'effected with the greatest ease and pleasantry; highly indebted to the civil, honest and friendly behavior of the whole of the inhabitants of this Island'.[3] Although the stores brought by the *Daedalus* were less than Vancouver expected, when they had been received the *Discovery* was provisioned for eighteen months and the *Chatham* for fifteen months. Vancouver was somewhat concerned that the ships might run out of supplies before the survey of the Northwest Coast was completed, but he decided not to ask for any further provisions from Port Jackson.

Unloaded at last, the *Daedalus* sailed for New South Wales on February 9. By her Vancouver sent a progress report to the Admiralty, but this took nearly two years to reach London and did not arrive until some months after Vancouver himself had returned. The *Daedalus* also carried three midshipmen who were being discharged and sent back to England by way of Port Jackson: the Hon. Thomas Pitt (who was not aware as yet that he had succeeded his father as Baron Camelford) and Thomas Clarke from the *Discovery*, and Augustus Boyd Grant from the *Chatham*. Pitt had long been a thorn in Vancouver's flesh. As early as January 1793 he had noted in a postscript to a letter to Evan Nepean that his conduct had been 'too bad for me to represent in any one

[1] Bell, January 1794.
[2] Vancouver, III, 11.
[3] Vancouver to Stephens, Hawaii, 8 February 1794. P.R.O., Adm 1/2629, f. 35v.

respect.'[1] But he was highly connected, and his dismissal was to have unhappy consequences for Vancouver, as will be described later.

With the *Daedalus* away and work on his own ships progressing satisfactorily, Vancouver could devote much of his attention to discussions with Kamehameha regarding the cession of Hawaii to Great Britain. He was convinced that the importance of the Sandwich Islands was bound to increase as commerce in the North Pacific grew, and that Great Britain would benefit from possession of them. He refers in his narrative to 'the priority of claim that England had' to the islands, meaning their discovery by Cook in 1778. But the Nootka controversy had shown that something more than discovery was necessary to perfect a title, and he was hopeful that a 'voluntary resignation' to Great Britain 'would be the means of establishing an incontrovertible right and of preventing any altercation with other states hereafter.'[2] Nor would the benefits be all one-sided. Kamehameha, for his part, was much disturbed by the violence from which the natives had suffered at the hands of foreigners and by the way in which they had been cheated and exploited by unscrupulous traders. What troubled him most was their inability to defend themselves against armed Europeans. It was clearly desirable that they should seek a powerful friend, and of the nations whose ships were frequenting the islands, Great Britain seemed to him to be much the most desirable ally.

Undoubtedly this preference was due in great part to his personal friendship with Vancouver. The United States would have been the obvious alternative, but he had no comparable relationship with any American. A subtler reason may have been the fact that Great Britain was a monarchy. Being a king himself, Kamehameha had no difficulty in visualizing King George both as a person and as a ruling sovereign. In 1793 he had given Vancouver a magnificent feather cloak, which had been worn by no one but himself, with a strict injunction that it was to be given to King George and that no one else was to wear it before the presentation. Nor was the role of the *Discovery* unimportant. She was a very big ship by Kamehameha's standards, and her guns and large well disciplined crew gave an impression of authority and power far superior to that given by trading vessels. No other man-of-war had visited the island of Hawaii since Cook's day.

Kamehameha was early convinced of the wisdom of reaching an agreement with Vancouver, but it was necessary to gain the support

[1] Vancouver to Nepean, Monterey, 7 January 1793, P.R.O., C.O. 5/187, f. 78.
[2] Vancouver, III, 31.

of the six district chiefs. This presented a problem, as Vancouver was at odds with two of them. Keaweaheulu, chief of the district of Kau, was in disgrace because a cartridge box stolen from the *Discovery* had been found in his house. This offence was relatively easy to forgive. Much more serious was the case of Kameeiamoku, of Kohala district. Vancouver had always refused to meet him because he had been responsible for the capture of the schooner *Fair American* and the massacre of all but one of her crew, but in view of the importance of the proposed cession Vancouver finally agreed to include him in the discussions. This was a diplomatic move, and the result, he tells us, of a determination 'by an act of oblivion in my mind, to efface all former injuries and offences.'[1] It enabled him to meet five of the six district chiefs, but some of his officers were outraged by the decision. To Bell, Kameeiamoku was 'a Pirate, and a murderer, suffered to commit these acts with impunity...Surely Captain Vancouver's lenity has in this instance been carried to too great a length'.[2] Menzies agreed: 'We cannot defend the policy of thus countenancing either the acquaintance or friendship of such a notorious villain'.[3]

The cession was finally agreed to and signed at what Bell terms a 'grand council', held in the cabin of the *Discovery* on the evening of February 25. The Hawaiians present were Kamehameha, the five district chiefs, and the king's brother and cousin. Britain was represented by Vancouver, Baker, Whidbey, Swaine and Menzies. Bell gives such a circumstantial account of the proceedings that it seems almost certain that he was present as well. His account of Kamehameha's opening remarks to the chiefs is interesting: 'Being all seated in the Cabbin His Majesty rose up, and in a Speech of some length, acquainted his Chiefs, that such had been the friendly intercourse, that had subsisted between him, and his good, faithful Brother King George, and such had been his liberality in the munificent presents made for the good of the Island through Captain Vancouver whom he considered as the Agent or representative of the said brother, and well knowing the political advantages that may be looked for to arise from a junction with so powerful a King, he hoped he should have their approbation to give up the Island of Owhyee to his said Brother, and acknowledge themselves his true and lawful subjects. On the question being put, it was agreed to without a negative.'[4]

A record of the cession was left in the form of two copper plates,

---

[1] Vancouver, III, 33.   [2] Bell, February 1794.
[3] Menzies, 21 February 1794.   [4] Bell, February 1794.

one of which was to be erected in a conspicuous spot at Kealakekua Bay, and the other at the king's residence at Hilo. Vancouver quotes the inscription, which stated that 'the principal chiefs of the island' had 'unanimously ceded the said island of Owhyee to His Britannic Majesty, and acknowledged themselves to be subjects of Great Britain'.[1] But it is extremely doubtful that Kamehameha and the chiefs understood the meaning of the word 'cede' and the surrender of sovereignty that it implied. It is amply clear that what they sought and what they thought they would receive was protection, and that they were thinking in terms of a protectorate, not annexation. And it seems equally clear that Vancouver must have given some undertaking that protection would be provided, or they would not have agreed to the cession. The previous year, when Vancouver first suggested it, Menzies noted (in a passage already quoted) that Kamehameha had 'positively declined' to entertain it 'unless Captain Vancouver would promise to leave one of the Vessels behind at the Island to assist in defending him and his people', which Menzies felt was 'certainly a very strong & reasonable argument.' There is no reason to suppose that he felt differently in 1794. In marginal notes in his copy of the *Voyage*, Hewett contends that in earlier discussions Vancouver had promised that a force of 500 men would be sent to the island, and he states that at the time of the cession Kamehameha asked Vancouver to give his word that 'a Ship and sold[iers] to live on shore' would be provided, 'as it was fair if they [beca]me subjects of G [Brit]ain they should be protected by K. George and not left to [mer]ely protect themselves.'

It was probably the existence of the 36-foot schooner *Britannia* that tipped the scales in favour of cession. Her construction was just beginning when Vancouver arrived in Kealakekua Bay, but, to Kamehameha's considerable distress, little had been accomplished because no experienced shipbuilders were available. Vancouver promptly offered the services of his carpenters. By the time he left, the schooner was all but completed. Kamehameha had guns with which to arm her, and Vancouver provided the equipment necessary to outfit her. None of the other chiefs in the islands would have a vessel equal to her. Menzies relates that, as the discussion of the cession proposal was nearing its end, Keaweaheulu (whom he calls Cavahero) 'earnestly asked what advantages were they to gain by this cession of the Island. Would the King of Britain fight their battles & defend their plantations? Would he leave a Vessel at the Island to guard their Coast from

[1] Vancouver, III, 57.

invasion? or would he give them arms & ammunition to defend themselves & their property? if he would do either of these he said he should readily give his consent.... A desultory conversation then took place...in which it was urged by the King & others, that the Boat which our Carpenters had built for them, when equipped and riggd with the Cordage & Canvas that had been given to them from both Vessels, would be the means of defending the Island & overawing their enemies from further attack. They then came to a general agreement to cede the Island'.[1]

The most puzzling aspect of the cession is that Vancouver never mentioned it in any known letter to the Admiralty or the Foreign Secretary. Nor is there any evidence that it was known to the general public until the publication of the *Voyage of Discovery* in 1798. As late as 1824, when Kamehameha II was visiting England, the Admiralty, when briefing the Foreign Office, informed it that 'The details of this transaction and Captain Vancouver's reason for accepting the cession are to be found in the third volume of his voyage.'

The failure of the British Government to act in the matter is much less difficult to understand. By the time Vancouver returned to England the country had been at war with France for two years, and with one brief respite war would be the order of the day thereafter for two decades. In this context the Sandwich Islands would seem very distant and insignificant – certainly not a problem demanding early attention. Yet in spite of this neglect, the conception of a British connection survived in the islands – a fact still commemorated by the inclusion of the Union Jack in the Hawaiian state flag. Some sense of obligation grew up in England, and after the conclusion of the Napoleonic wars it was decided to honour what was evidently regarded as an undertaking given by Vancouver to provide a ship for the defence of the islands. Kamehameha died in 1819, but the schooner *Prince Regent* was built in New South Wales, armed with six guns, and delivered to his son, Kamehameha II at Honolulu on 1 May 1822.[2] The young king, for his part, was anxious to continue a connection with Britain, and in a letter of thanks addressed to King George IV he informed him that 'The whole of these islands having been conquered by my father, I have succeeded to the government of them, and beg leave to place them all under the protection of your most excellent Majesty'.[3] The

---

[1] Menzies, 26 February 1794.
[2] Unfortunately she was wrecked on the east coast of Oahu only a few months later.
[3] Quoted in Kuykendall, *The Hawaiian Kingdom 1778–1854* (Honolulu, 1938), p. 76.

following year he decided to fulfil a cherished ambition and visit England. He and his queen, with their entourage, arrived in May 1824. They seem to have come unannounced, but were received by the government with respect and courtesy. Canning, the Foreign Secretary, gave a reception in their honour. An audience with King George was arranged, but before it was to take place both Kamehameha and his queen were stricken with measles, and both died in July, within a few days of one another. Their bodies were carried back to Honolulu in the frigate *Blonde*.

With the death of Kamehameha, leadership of the Hawaiian delegation was assumed by Governor Boki, of the island of Oahu. On September 11, shortly before the departure of the *Blonde*, Boki was received in audience by King George, with Canning present.[1] In his authoritative history, *The Hawaiian Kingdom, 1778–1854*, Ralph Kuykendall quotes what he regards as the best account of the discussion of the future status of the islands:

The King then asked Boki what was the business on which you and your King came to this country?...

Then Boki declared to him the reason of our sailing to Great Britain. We have come to confirm the words which Kamehameha I gave in charge to Vancouver thus – 'Go back and tell King George to watch over me and my whole Kingdom. I acknowledge him as my landlord and myself as tenant (or him as superior and I inferior). Should the foreigners of any other nation come to take possession of my lands, then let him help me.'...

And when King George had heard he thus said to Boki, 'I have heard these words, I will attend to the evils from without. The evils within your Kingdom it is not for me to regard; they are with yourselves. Return and say to the King, to Kaahumanu and Kalaimoku, I will watch over your country, I will not take possession of it for mine, but I will watch over it, lest evils should come from others to the Kingdom. I therefore will watch over him agreeably to those ancient words.'[2]

One of the Englishmen at the audience testified later that 'George the 4 did promise (in my presence) the Islands his protection.'[3] At the time the cession was signed in 1794 Vancouver had made it clear that no

[1] The King disliked Canning heartily, and the original audience for Kamehameha cannot have been easy to arrange. The King 'was still talking of Canning in similar terms to Wellington in May 1824....."Think of that damned fellow wanting me to have the King and Queen of the Sandwich Islands to dinner," he expostulated the next month, "as if I would sit at table with such a pair of damned cannibals."' The Duke of Wellington and Francis Bamford (eds.), *The Journal of Mrs. Arbuthnot* (London, 1850), I, p. 319.

[2] Quoted in Kuykendall, *The Hawaiian Kingdom*, p. 79. Kekuanaoa was the author of the statement.   [3] *Ibid.*, p. 79.

interference with the religion, customs or internal government of the country was intended, and this was confirmed in King George's statement.

A curious later episode should be mentioned. Forty-nine years to the day after Vancouver secured the cession of Hawaii, on 25 February 1843, the Sandwich Islands briefly became a British possession. In January Rear Admiral Richard Thomas, commander-in-chief Pacific, had received reports and heard rumours that prompted him to send H.M.S. *Carysfort*, commanded by Lord George Paulet, to Honolulu. The reports alleged that the British consul and other British nationals were being unfairly treated by the Hawaiian authorities; the rumours suggested that France and perhaps the United States intended to take over the islands. The *Carysfort* arrived off Honolulu on February 18, and in an excellent example of gunboat diplomacy, Paulet compelled Kamehameha III to sign a provisional cession on the 25th. As soon as Admiral Thomas heard of Paulet's unauthorized actions he sailed for Honolulu, where he arrived on July 26. He negotiated an agreement with the King that guaranteed the rights and privileges of British subjects, and on the 31st the independence of the islands was restored. Thomas Square in Honolulu commemorates the act of restoration.[1]

Vancouver had been successful in negotiating the cession, but the discussions at the time made it quite clear that there was no prospect of attaining his second objective – a peace agreement between Kamehameha and Kahekili. Kamehameha and his chiefs were just as determined as ever to conquer Maui and the other islands to the west at the first opportunity. Menzies noted that Kamanawa, the district chief who did not attend the discussions, had 'remained in his district to take care of the arms & ammunition that were stored up in the royal residence at Aheedo [Hilo], that place being at this time the principal repository for the most valuable warlike stores of every kind that had been collected from the different Vessels that visited the Island.'[2] Vancouver himself records that Keeaumoku, chief of Kona, recalled the attacks that had been made from Maui and proposed 'that when a force for their protection should be obtained from England, the first object of its employment ought to be the conquest of Mowee'.[3] Menzies elaborates: Keeaumoku 'an old warrior got up & said, that he agreed to cede the Island, but trusted that by so doing they should not be hindered from weilding [*sic*] their Spears against their enemies.

---

[1] For a good account of Paulet's intervention see *ibid.*, pp. 213–21.
[2] Menzies, 21 February 1794.   [3] Vancouver, III, 55.

He said that Taiteree [Kahekili] King of the other Islands had at different times made four descents on Owhyee, & that they had as yet made only one descent on his territories, he therefore urgd the justice of making three descents more, to be even with him, & when the event of these three descents were accomplished he should then rest satisfied'. [1] Vancouver concluded reluctantly that the only possible chance of any success in peace negotiations would lie in a series of personal visitations in which he himself would move back and forth between Hawaii and Maui. His prime commitment to the completion of the coastal survey made this impossible.

He would have been shocked had he known how quickly the whole governing structure of the islands was to change. Within little more than a year Kahekili, his son Kalanikupule, his brother Kaeo and Kamehameha's supposed friend Kaiana were all dead, and Kamehameha had extended his kingdom to Maui, Lanai, Molokai and Oahu.

The chain of events was touched off by the death of King Kahekili, only a few months after Vancouver left the islands. Control of his kingdom, the most important parts of which were Maui and Oahu, then passed to his son and brother. In a matter of months friction developed between them, and the ultimate result was a pitched battle in December on the shores of Pearl Harbor in which Kalanikupule triumphed and Kaeo was killed.

Shortly before this battle three trading ships, all of which Vancouver had encountered several times, arrived at Waikiki – the *Lady Washington*, commanded by Kendrick, and the *Jackal* and *Prince Lee Boo* under Brown and Gordon. Kalanikupule had received assistance from them, but his victory was to prove fatal to all three captains. Kendrick was killed accidentally in mid-December by a salute fired from the *Jackal*. Kalanikupule, his ambition mounting, came to the conclusion that possession of the *Jackal* and *Prince Lee Boo* should enable him to defeat Kamehameha. On 1 January 1795 he succeeded in seizing both ships, and their captains were killed. On January 12 the ships sailed to attack Hawaii, but their crews managed to regain possession of them, and, with singular forbearance, they put Kalanikupule and his queen ashore unmolested.

Kamehameha now took to the warpath, swept through Maui and Molokai and moved on to Oahu. There Kaiana justified the doubts that Vancouver and others had had about him (Puget characterized him as 'a dangerous and deceitful Character')[2] and deserted to the enemy.

The devastating last battle of the campaign took place in the spring or summer of 1795, in the Nuuanu valley, northwest of Honolulu. Kaiana was killed; Kalanikupule escaped but was captured later and sacrificed to the war god. Kamehameha was anxious to complete his conquest by occupying Kauai and Niihau, but to reach them he would have had to ferry his forces across the wide and often rough waters of Kauai Channel. It was not until 1810 that he gained control of them by reaching an agreement with Kaumualii (Tamooerrie), who as a boy had charmed Vancouver at Kauai in 1792, and who agreed to accept the status of a tributary kingdom.

Ruthless in war, Kamehameha was an enlightened and constructive ruler in time of peace. There seems to be general agreement that the unification of the islands that he brought about was much to their benefit, and that Vancouver's peace efforts, although thoroughly well intentioned, could not have produced more than a temporary settlement.

But to revert to Vancouver's voyage: relations with the natives had become so friendly that toward the end of the stay at Kealakekua Bay restrictions on shore leave were relaxed somewhat. Menzies had never considered himself bound by them to the same extent as others, and he had made arrangements with Kamehameha that enabled him to make two extensive excursions inland. He was anxious to examine the flora and to combine botanizing with mountain climbing. Kamehameha assigned a chief to safeguard and guide him and provided a numerous train of bearers. The first party left the ships on January 16; it included Swaine, Heddington, and one or two other midshipmen. Its objective was Hualalai (8,269 feet), which they were the first Europeans to climb. Heddington drew the sketch of the crater that was engraved and published in the *Voyage of Discovery*.[1] The second expedition was considerably more ambitious. Menzies was anxious to scale Mauna Loa (13,680 feet), one of the two highest peaks on Hawaii. Heddington was again with him, but was forced to turn back at the 11,000-foot level. Menzies, Baker, McKenzie (a midshipman) and a native reached the top on February 16. It was probably the first time Mauna Loa had been climbed, as the natives had shown great reluctance to venture beyond the snow line. Vancouver accords these notable expeditions only brief mention, but they are described at considerable length in Menzies' own journal.

---

[1] It is there titled 'The Crater on the Summit of Mount Worroray Owhyee', the version of the name used by Vancouver.

The *Discovery* and *Chatham* left Kealakekua Bay on February 26. Kamehameha was anxious to postpone his final parting with Vancouver as long as possible, and travelled in the *Discovery* as far as Kawaihae Bay. With him were his queen and a number of retainers; others endeavoured to keep up with the ship in canoes. There is ample evidence that a remarkable relationship had grown up between Vancouver and the King. Vancouver had been able to persuade Kamehameha to ignore a taboo; he had intervened in a delicate domestic crisis and had brought about a reconciliation between Kamehameha and his favorite queen; he had been permitted to participate in religious rites at a morai. Kamehameha had personally watched over Vancouver and his ships, and the generosity with which he had met their every need is reflected in a dozen logs and journals.

Vancouver records that as a parting gift Kamehameha presented 'near an hundred hogs of the largest size, and as great a quantity of vegetables as both vessels could well dispose of'.[1] Unfortunately, at the last moment, some unrecorded circumstance must have aroused the irritability to which Vancouver was becoming subject, and caused him to mar their farewells by the refusal of what would seem to have been a very modest request. Menzies relates that Kamehameha 'askd Capt Vancouver at parting, to add to his other presents as much red cloth as would make him a *Maro*, a thing in great estimation at this time amongst the Chiefs, & would not require above half a yard of cloth; this was refused him, from what motives we know not, & he left the ship apparently in a huff. On his way to the shore he went with the Queen & John Young to take leave of his friends on board the *Chatham*, where he complained of Capt Vancouvers stinginess, & told the story in a manner that induced the Commander of the Vessel [Puget] to present him with the last piece of red cloth he had. The refusal of a trifle of this kind, on such an occasion, cannot be viewed in a favorable light, when we reflect on the boundless generosity of this worthy prince towards us, his zeal and perseverance in our favor, his studious care at all times to preserve a good understanding between us & his people, his ready compliance to all our requests, his hospitality & kind protection to all those whose duty or desire of recreation, led them to traverse the country'.[2]

Vancouver spent his last fortnight in the islands filling the three gaps that still remained in his survey of them. From Hawaii he sailed north to Maui and examined its northern coast. In Kahului Bay he heard that

[1] Vancouver, III, 64.　　　　　　[2] Menzies, 1 March 1794.

a few days before an explosion had killed several chiefs and had destroyed the greater part of Kahekili's supply of gunpowder – news that would have gladdened the heart of Kamehameha. He then moved on to Molokai, where he had some hope of meeting Kaeo, but a taboo was in force and a meeting could not be arranged. From Molokai Vancouver proceeded to Oahu, where he traced the eastern coast to Kahuku Point, its northern extremity, rounded it, and sailed on to Waimea Bay. There he expected to find Kahekili, but he had gone to Waikiki, and as all hope of concluding a peace agreement with Kamehameha had vanished, Vancouver was not disposed to take the time to follow him. His next stop was at the familiar anchorage in the other Waimea Bay, in Kauai. The *Chatham* had been detached, with orders to endeavour to weather Kauai's northeast point and survey its northern shore, and this she succeeded in doing. The survey of the islands was thus complete, and it only remained to call at Niihau, in the hope of securing a supply of yams. But the drought encountered there the previous year had continued and few were available – at least on the open market. Hewett contends that this was 'partly in consequence of having a Chief on Board to assist in buying' and that he 'bought many in the Morning when no chief was stirring and even then they were hidden in the canoes till they were certain of having an opportunity of selling them undiscovered.' The chief who acted as middleman evidently exacted a toll that the natives were reluctant to pay.

The ships left Niihau on March 14. Vancouver was anxious to locate Bird Island (Nihoa); Menzies had been with Colnett in the *Prince of Wales* when he discovered it in 1788. The little island was found on the 15th, and the ships then swung round to the north and headed for the Northwest Coast.

Third Survey Season

Instead of resuming his survey at Cape Decision, the point to which he had carried it in 1793, Vancouver had decided to proceed first to Cook's River (as it was still presumed to be). From there he would move eastward to Prince William Sound, and then complete his tracing of the continental shore by following it southward.

Two considerations lay behind this decision. First, if the survey were to be made from north to south, it was only sensible to have it begin at the most northerly feature he was expected to investigate. He had been instructed to carry the survey to the 60th parallel, and this ran through the known portion of Cook's River. Secondly, if no passage had been discovered south of it, Vancouver had been instructed to devote special attention to the river. The Admiralty believed that there was 'the greatest probability' that it rose in lakes known to the traders of the Hudson's Bay and North West companies, and that it might become a travel route of considerable commercial importance. Although he had not yet examined the whole of the coast, one gathers that by this time Vancouver had little or no expectation that a passage to the Atlantic would be found. As a consequence, as he tells us, the examination of Cook's River 'appeared to me to be the most important, and I did not doubt would prove the most laborious part of our task in the ensuing campaign'.[1]

In a measure, Vancouver was now entering upon known ground. Hitherto he had been forced to feel his way; existing maps had offered little in the way of reliable guidance. But he had been with Cook in 1778, when he made his landfall near Cape Edgecumbe, had sailed north along the coast, and had entered Prince William Sound and Cook's River. Vancouver had with him copies of the narratives and maps of traders and others who had since visited the region, notably those of Meares, Portlock and Dixon. Both Johnstone and Menzies had been with Colnett when the *Prince of Wales* entered Prince William Sound in 1788. Fidalgo's explorations in the sound and Cook's River in 1790 were recorded on the map of the Pacific Coast prepared by Quadra in 1791, a copy of which he had given to Vancouver. Although all these charts were incomplete and frequently inaccurate, they did indicate the general shape of Prince William Sound and much of the detail of Cook's River. All indicated that south of the sound Vancouver could look forward to a long stretch of virtually unbroken coast, extending at least as far as Cross Sound, that could be surveyed with relative ease and speed.

The *Discovery* and *Chatham* lost contact soon after they passed Bird Island, and although once in close proximity to one another, they were not to meet again for the better part of two months. Chirikof Island, sighted on April 3, was the first land seen from the *Discovery*. Sailing on northwestward, she passed the Trinity Islands and the east coast of Kodiak and Afognak islands. At this time Vancouver was still uncertain whether or not Kodiak was part of the mainland, but before he left Alaskan waters he had become convinced of its insularity, and it appears as an island on his chart.

[1] Vancouver, III, 80.

He entered Cook's River on April 12, and, once again, the *Chatham*
had arrived two days before the *Discovery*. Severe weather caused her
to seek shelter in Port Chatham, behind Cape Elizabeth, at the entrance
to the inlet, where she remained for about a fortnight, taking on wood
and water and making voyage repairs. Unaware of her presence, the
Discovery continued on up Cook's River and soon encountered the
hazards that were characteristic of it. These included extensive shoals,
many of them strewn with large boulders, mud flats, strong swift-
flowing tides with an amazing diurnal range of as much as 33 feet, and,
at the time Vancouver entered it, great quantities of ice released by
the spring breakup. He had been anxious to begin his survey as early
as possible, but in these high latitudes spring came later than he
anticipated. Cook had not been bothered by ice, but he had come to
the inlet seven weeks later in the year. Vancouver might have noted
that in the first week of May 1787 Dixon had found the *Nootka*, the
ship in which Meares had wintered in Prince William Sound, 'still fast
in the ice'.[1] The problem became more serious as the *Discovery* moved
north, and for a time she was menaced by large chunks that were carried
to and fro by the tides. Some struck her hull with great violence, and
for a time it was too dangerous to use the boats, which both isolated
her from the shore and delayed the progress of the survey. Possibly
the worst hazard was the danger that the floes might sever the anchor
cables. Both the *Discovery* and the *Chatham* lost an anchor while they
were in the inlet.

Vancouver was about to disprove Cook's belief that in 1778 he had
explored the estuary of a major river rather than an inlet, and it is
worthwhile to note the steps by which Cook had reached that opinion.
He entered the inlet on May 20 because he had some hope that it might
be part of a passage leading northwards to the Arctic. But that hope
was slight and was soon abandoned. On the 26th, when no more than
well within the entrance, he wrote that the mountains and the terrain
in general 'had every...appearance of being part of a great Continent,
so that I was fully persuaided that we should find no passage by this
inlet.'[2] Cook's mission was to find a passage, and he himself seems to
have been ready to turn back at this point. The Arctic summer is short;
he had been instructed to search for a passage north of 65°, and he was
anxious to reach that latitude as soon as possible. Nevertheless he
proceeded up the inlet and explains that his 'persevering in it was more
to satisfy other people than to confirm my own opinion'.[3] It was on

---

[1] George Dixon, *A Voyage Round the World* (London, 1789), p. 155.
[2] Cook, *Journals*, III, 361.   [3] *Ibid.*

May 30, when near the narrows between the East Foreland and the West Foreland, that the increasing freshness of the water at low tide convinced him 'that we were in a large River and Not a Strait that would communicate with the Northern Seas. But as we had proceeded so far I was desirous of having stronger proofs and therefore weighed with the next flood and plyed higher up or rather drove up with the tide'.[1] By June 1, when he had reached the point at which the inlet divides into two arms, he felt that he 'had many other & but too evident proofs of being in a great River'.[2] Most uncharacteristically, he was then satisfied with a very cursory examination of the two arms, both of which he assumed to be rivers, and advanced the opinion that it was 'but reasonable to suppose that both these branches are Navigable much farther than we examined them; and that by means of this River and its several branc[h]es a very extensive inland communication lies open'.[3]

Cook looked upon the whole episode as virtually a waste of time. On June 6, the day the *Resolution* left the inlet, he wrote in his log: 'It is now sixteen days since we came in sight of the land before us, which time has been spent to very little purpose...nothing but a triffling point in Geography has been determined, and a River discovered that probably opens a very extensive communication with the Inland parts'.[4] This latter suggestion – and it was little more – was to have consequences that Cook cannot have anticipated. It was seized upon by the 'theoretical navigators' whom Vancouver despised, caused Peter Pond to jump to the conclusion that Cook's River was the outlet of the Mackenzie River (and to alter his map accordingly), roused the interest of the British Government, and was thus in part responsible for Vancouver's own presence in the inlet.

As soon as ice conditions permitted, Vancouver prepared to put Cook's theory to the test. On April 28 Whidbey left with two boats to explore the eastern arm that Cook had named Turnagain River. Only two days were required to prove (in Vancouver's words) that it was 'no longer intitled to the name of a river' and it appears on his chart as Turnagain Arm. Having been provisioned for ten days, Whidbey then headed down the inlet and examined both its shores as far as East Foreland and West Foreland. He returned to the *Discovery* on May 4 and on the 6th Vancouver, Baker and Menzies set out to explore the main or northern branch. Before the day was out they had come within

---

[1] *Ibid.*, p. 364. [2] *Ibid.*, p. 365.
[3] *Ibid.*, p. 367. [4] *Ibid.*, p. 368n.

sight of its termination, and Vancouver decided henceforth to substitute the name Cook's Inlet for Cook's River. In his journal, somewhat indirectly, he expressed regret that 'the great and first discoverer of it' had not 'dedicated one day more to its further examination'.[1] Menzies was prompted to make the most explicit criticism of Cook found in any of the logs and journals: 'we cannot well reconcile Capt Cook's account of this part of the Coast to his usual precision & accuracy, as he states that they tracd the river as high as the Latitude of 61° 30' North, without seeing the least appearance of its source, yet we found its termination a few miles short of that Latitude'.[2] An implied criticism lay behind Vancouver's remark that 'it was not possible to avoid a certain degree of mortification from the reflection, that our opinions respecting the extent to which these waters were likely to lead, had been extremely erroneous'.[3] He took comfort from the fact that the time taken by the exploration of the supposed river had been relatively short, and this made it much more likely that his survey of the continental shore could be completed in 1794.

On the evening of May 6 two guns were heard from the *Discovery* and next morning the *Chatham* was seen nearby, lying at anchor. She had left Port Chatham on April 29, and in accordance with his instructions Puget had crossed the inlet and sailed northward along its western shore. Both ships had been visited by parties of natives, some of them accompanied by one or several Russians, and Puget had accepted an invitation to visit a Russian post near the North Foreland. At this time two rival companies were competing energetically for furs in the region, and this was one of two establishments in the inlet belonging to the Lebedev-Lastochkin Company; the other was farther south, on the eastern shore, at the mouth of the Kenai River. Puget's chief impressions were of friendliness and filth. The buildings were primitive, of creature comforts there were none, and food and clothing were on a par with those of the natives. No effort had been made to dispose of waste or garbage, and Puget and his companions discovered that the spring thaw had produced a stench that they found unbearable. Later, when the *Chatham* joined the *Discovery* and the two ships came down the inlet, Vancouver and Menzies visited the companion post at the Kenai River. Here, as at the North Foreland, the welcome was friendly but conditions were so unsavoury that they cut short their stay.

Vancouver knew of a third Russian post in the inlet, near its entrance

[1] Vancouver, III, 125.   [2] Menzies, 6 May, 1794.
[3] Vancouver, III, 126.

in a cove close to Port Graham. This was owned by the rival
Shelikof-Golikov interests. Since 1790 their operations had been
managed by Aleksander Baranof, from headquarters on Kodiak Island.
Able and energetic, Baranof was a rising star, and when the Russian-
American Company, which united Russian fur-trading interests, came
into existence in 1799, he would become its manager and in effect
governor of Alaska. Russians from the Port Graham post thrice assured
Vancouver that Baranof was anxious to meet him and would be
arriving soon, but each time he failed to keep the rendezvous.
Vancouver was particularly anxious to see him because he understood
that he would be accompanied by an English-speaking interpreter. Why
the Admiralty failed to provide either Cook or Vancouver with an
interpreter, when both were expected to have dealings with the
Russians, is a mystery. Some small assistance may have been given by
the boatswain of the *Chatham*. Menzies states that he 'could speak
Russian tolerably well' but adds that 'he had great difficulty to make
out the dialect spoke by these people, & very often found it
impracticable'.[1]

Both in Cook Inlet and later in Prince William Sound the expedition
found the natives friendly and inoffensive. At one point when exploring
the sound Johnstone and his boat crews found themselves camping for
the night near ten Russians and in what seemed to them uncomfortably
close proximity to some 250 natives. Johnstone was distinctly uneasy,
but judged that if the Russians had no fears all should be well. The
tribes to which the natives belonged cannot be identified. Beaglehole
remarks that Prince William Sound 'has been dotted with a shifting
pattern of Eskimo, Tlingit and Athapascan villages. It is not now
possible to assign each group met by Cook to its certain category,
because there was an extensive mingling of material culture.'[2] The same
is true of Vancouver. Identification is complicated further because the
Russians brought natives to the Alaskan mainland from the Aleutians
and even from Asia. Hewett states that most of the Indians he saw with
the Russians were from Unalaska and Kamchatka, and he ascribes their
fidelity and submissiveness to the fact that their houses and women were
being held at home as hostages. Menzies adds a confirming detail. When
he met a group that visited the *Discovery* in Port Chalmers he 'found
that one of them was a Russian, another was a native of Oonamak
[Unimak] near Onnalaska & the rest were Kodiak Indians'.[3]

---

[1] Menzies, 7 June 1794.   [2] Cook, *Journals*, III, 344n.
[3] Menzies, 5 June 1794.

Whatever the precise cause may have been, the natives evidently handed over their entire catch of furs to the Russians. In 1778, while in Cook Inlet, some years before the Russians became active there, Cook shrewdly remarked that he was convinced that 'they were never amongst these people, nor carry on any commerce with them, for if they did they would hardly be cloathed in such valuable skins as those of the Sea beaver [the sea otter]; the Russians would find some means or other to get them all from them'.[1] That is precisely what had happened by the time of Vancouver's visit, when he found that their clothing 'chiefly consisted of garments made from the skins of birds or quadrupeds, of not the least value'.[2]

From the Russians Vancouver had learned that a portage no more than a dozen miles in length linked Turnagain Arm, in Cook Inlet, with Passage Canal, in Prince William Sound. The Kenai Peninsula, which forms most of the eastern shore of the inlet and much of the western shore of the sound was thus almost an island, connected to the mainland by this narrow isthmus. As no opening of interest to Vancouver could be south of it, this made it unneccessary for him to examine the peninsula's south coast in any detail. At one time he had thought of visiting the post and shipyard that Baranof's company had established in what is now Resurrection Bay, as he was anxious to examine the *Discovery*'s bottom and make sure that she had not sustained serious damage in her several groundings in Cook Inlet. But she had come through rough weather without showing any indication that her hull was not sound, and Vancouver decided to press on to Port Chalmers, near the north end of Montague Island, in Prince William Sound. This would be a convenient base from which to pursue the examination of the continental shore. In addition to wood and water, spars would be readily available there – an important matter since the *Discovery*'s foreyard had been carried away in a sudden violent squall, and her bowsprit was rotten. Sails and rigging had also suffered and something in the nature of a minor refit was called for.

Vancouver would be satisfied with nothing less than a survey of the entire perimeter of Prince William Sound. To accomplish this, two boat expeditions set out on May 26. Whidbey and Johnstone were again in command. Whidbey was instructed to proceed first to the southwest point of entrance, soon to be named Cape Puget. From there he was to begin an examination of the western and northern shores of the sound, and the eastern shore as far south as Snug Corner Cove, the

---

[1] Cook, *Journals*, III, 371.   [2] Vancouver, III, 151.

sheltered anchorage that Cook had found for his ships. This cove was to be the starting point of Johnstone's part of the survey. From it he was to work his way down the eastern shore to the ocean, and having reached the Pacific, Vancouver expected him to continue on and examine the coast as far as Kayak Island and Cape Suckling.

In great part Whidbey was venturing into unknown territory, and he charted it with his usual competence. A few days after leaving the *Discovery* he was forced to return in order to bring an injured seaman back to the ship, but otherwise, except for delays and discomfort due to bad weather, all went well. In the course of the expedition he had his first experience with an avalanche, when one thundered down within a hundred yards of the spot where he and his crews were encamped during a storm, and he met with numerous huge glaciers, which filled the ends of most of the inlets he examined. Johnstone was to some extent on familiar ground, as he had been in the sound with Colnett in 1788, and the charts of Cook and several of the traders gave him a fair indication of the geography of the eastern shore. But it had never been examined in detail, and this Johnstone did in meticulous fashion. This first part of his survey ended in Orca Inlet, and it was here that he spent the anxious night with several hundred natives close by. The inlet ends in a broad opening to the ocean between Point Whitshed and Hinchinbrook Island, and as soon as he reached it Johnstone realized that it would be impracticable to continue the survey down the coast, where his boats would be exposed to the open ocean. Faced with a maze of shoals and a tremendous surf he decided that he must change his plans, especially as he had already been away from the ships for ten days, the period for which the boats had been provisioned.

Johnstone was reluctant to retrace his course up Orca Inlet, and was hopeful that the land on its northern shore (Hawkins Island) might be separated from Hinchinbrook Island by an opening of some sort. If so, it would provide a much shorter route back to Port Chalmers. Hawkins Island Cutoff fulfilled his hopes, and he proceeded along the northern coast of Hinchinbrook Island to its western extremity, now appropriately named Johnstone Point. There he turned south in order to visit Port Etches, so named by Portlock in 1787 in honour of the Etches family, part owners of both his own ship and Johnstone's *Prince of Wales*. There in 1793 the Lededev-Lastochkin Company had established the important post known as the Konstantin and Elena fort. The

Russians were friendly, but once again lack of knowledge of their language prevented any very meaningful communication.

Johnstone returned to Port Chalmers on June 8. Three days later the *Chatham* sailed with instructions to carry out the survey of the coast beyond Hinchinbrook Island that he had been unable to undertake in open boats. Johnstone had not been expected to venture further than Cape Suckling, but the *Chatham* was to push on to Port Mulgrave, in Yakutat Bay, where the *Discovery* expected to join her.

Whidbey did not get back to the *Discovery* until June 15. His survey had been a gruelling task: he estimated that his boats had travelled about 420 miles. He had found Prince William Sound strangely devoid of inhabitants; only about a dozen natives had been encountered. By the time he returned the *Discovery* was almost ready to sail, and she got away on the 17th. In most respects Port Chalmers had proven to be a satisfactory anchorage, but access to it was hazardous. As she left it, the *Discovery* impaled herself on a rock, fortunately without suffering any material damage. Her foreyard and bowsprit had been replaced, sails and rigging repaired, and supplies of wood and water replenished. Fish, game and greens had all been scarce, but Vancouver considered that the spruce beer brewed 'far exceeded in excellence any we had before made upon the coast.'[1]

At first winds were weak and fluctuating. On the 19th the *Discovery* was still off Hinchinbrook Island and, Menzies notes, 'as we were not likely to get out soon, rather than drift backwards & forwards with the tides, we bore up...& stood into Port Etches'.[2] It was a brief involuntary 24-hour visit, but the welcome was friendly and it gave Vancouver an opportunity to see the Russian post.

The voyage eastward and then southward proved to be tedious. As the *Chatham* would have examined the coast, Vancouver expected to reach Yakutat Bay relatively quickly, but instead he was a fortnight on the way. Time and the ship, in Vancouver's phrase, were 'uninterestingly employed' and in his journal this caused him to turn to comment in place of chronicle. Surprisingly, his chief topic was the deficiencies in Cook's account of his exploration of Prince William Sound and the adjacent coasts. Only a single observation for latitude and longitude was recorded, nor was there 'any topographical description of the coast, nor of the rocks and islands that lie off from it'. This 'would argue an inattention to nautical occurrences' which

---

[1] Vancouver, III, 197. [2] Menzies, 19 June 1794.

Vancouver believed was 'no where else to be met with in the works of that justly renowned and most celebrated navigator'.[1] He placed the blame on Cook's editor and 'errors of the press', but Beaglehole has shown that details of the kind Vancouver expected to find are not found in Cook's papers. Cook was impatient to move on to the north and the 65th parallel at which he had been instructed to begin his search for a passage; convinced that none opened into Prince William Sound, he attached little importance to its examination.

The *Chatham* fired a gun when the *Discovery* was sighted off Yakutat Bay, and Manby came out in a native canoe to guide her into Port Mulgrave, where the *Chatham* lay at anchor. But the canoe deserted him, and wind conditions made it impracticable for the *Discovery* to enter. Manby perforce had to remain on board and proceed with her to Cross Sound, the next rendezvous. The only incident of interest on the way was a meeting with the schooner *Jackal*, which Vancouver had last seen in June 1793 in Dixon Entrance, when she was serving as tender to the *Butterworth*, commanded by Captain Brown. In the interval the *Butterworth* had left for England and Brown had transferred to the *Jackal*. He intended to accompany the *Discovery* to Cross Sound, but the ships lost contact and he decided to pay a visit to Port Mulgrave, where he found the *Chatham*.

Despite 'nine tedious days' spent in covering the 40 leagues between Cape Suckling and Yakutat Bay, the *Chatham* had had a much more interesting experience than the *Discovery*. Unfortunately no extensive first-hand account of it is known to exist. Puget, Johnstone, Manby and Bell were all on board, but their highly informative journals all end before the *Chatham* returned to the Northwest Coast. Happily both Vancouver and Menzies describe the cruise in some detail. Vancouver seems to have secured most of his information from Puget, while Menzies frequently cites Manby as his source.

Nothing on the coast called for detailed examination until the *Chatham* arrived off Controller Bay and Kayak Island, with Cape Suckling just beyond. The bay is largely a great expanse of mud flats, with shallows in the centre, while Kayak Island lies in a bed of shoals, with rocks along its shores that reach a climax in Pinnacle Rock, at its southern tip. Puget did what exploring was prudent in the *Chatham* and then sent a midshipman in one of the boats to sound the channel between Kayak Island and the mainland. He decided that it was too hazardous to attempt to take the *Chatham* through it, and in any event

[1] Vancouver, III, 194.

the midshipman had been able to trace the continental shore, making the transit unnecessary.

Yakutat Bay was reached on June 26, and the next three days were spent exploring it. Puget first traced its western shore as far as the narrows opposite Point Latouche. He then sent a boat to investigate the bay beyond the narrows. At first sight this appeared to be an opening of some interest, but it was found to be blocked by the Hubbard Glacier and now bears the appropriate name of Disenchantment Bay. The *Chatham* then came down the eastern shore, felt her way through the tangle of islands northeast of Port Mulgrave, and found a safe anchorage in the port itself on the 29th.

When off Point Manby, at the entrance to Yakutat Bay, Puget had been surprised to hear gunfire. Presently the *Chatham* was visited by five Kodiak Indians. The next day Puget discovered that they were part of a huge party of some 900 Kodiak natives, employed by Baranof's company to hunt sea otters. Nine or ten Russians accompanied them, chief of whom turned out to be Egon Purtov, whom Puget had met in Cook Inlet. From this party Puget and Manby learned something of the way in which the Russians were conducting the fur trade along the coast east of Prince William Sound. Vancouver remarks that they seemed to have no wish to have any 'commercial intercourse' with the natives of the region. They had little in the way of trade goods and depended solely upon their Kodiak hunters. 'Mr. Portoff,' Menzies writes, 'sends the Kodiak hunters out to Sea in parties of from 10 to 20 Canoes in different directions & they never fail to return daily with fish & a number of Sea Otters which they skin for the Russians & use the carcases stewd for their own feeding.'[1] Vancouver adds an interesting detail, which indicates that the hunters expected to carry on a supplementary traffic on their own. Their stock in trade included 'bows, arrows, darts, spears, fish-gigs, whale-gut shirts, and specimens of their very neat and curious needle-work'. And though so far from home, they had come 'well provided, in expectation of finding a profitable market before they returned'. They were quick to realize the possibilities of a souvenir trade, and those not engaged in hunting 'seemed to be industriously employed in making such articles of curiosity as found the most ready market amongst their English friends'.[2]

Understandably the Russians were not popular with the natives in

[1] Menzies, 2 July 1794.
[2] Vancouver, III, 233.

171

Yakutat Bay and elsewhere on the coast. In Menzies' words, they conceived them 'as intruders in their territories, draining their shores & coasts of Seals Otter & Fish on which their subsistence chiefly Depends, & that too without making the least return for their depredations.'[1] Clashes between hunters and natives appear to have been frequent; one such had occurred before Purtov came to Yakutat Bay. A Russian had been murdered, six natives had been killed in retaliation, and Purtov was holding a native chief captive. The Kodiak hunters were so numerous that the Yakutat Bay natives had abandoned their village when they arrived, but some soon returned. As many as a hundred appeared finally. This alarmed Purtov, who had little faith in his hunters as a fighting force, and he moved them to an encampment on Point Turner, opposite the *Chatham*'s anchorage, where her guns could afford some protection. Purtov announced his intention of leaving the bay as soon as the *Chatham* sailed, but the day before she left the *Jackal* appeared. In effect she took over the role of guard ship, and the Russians and their hunters stayed on until the end of her short visit.

Before Puget sailed, Purtov had entered into conversations with the natives, using the captive chief as an emissary. Friendly relations of a sort were established, but the natives soon broke the peace by capturing six Kodiak Indians, whereupon Purtov in turn seized seventeen natives and held them hostage. Captain Brown of the *Jackal* was appealed to, and with his support an exchange of prisoners was arranged. Brown, Menzies tells us, was soon busy 'collecting Furs from the Natives, for though the Russian party had been there before Mr Brown & remaind during his stay, the animosities which subsisted between them & the Natives precluded their having any chance of rivalship in trade, nor had they indeed proper articles to purchase any furs were they even upon the best of terms with them, their sole dependence being on the success of their Kodiak hunter[s] as already noticd'.[2]

That success was considerable. Purtov had secured nearly 2000 pelts during this stay in Yakutat Bay. This result caught Baranof's attention and he decided to build a post there, instead of on Kayak Island, as was first intended. He himself visited the bay in August 1795 and left an advance party of 30 men. The following August he returned and construction of a fort began. Baranof is said to have established more friendly relations with the natives, but the history of Russian contacts with them is not a happy one.

The *Discovery* entered Cross Sound on July 7 and found a sheltered

[1] Menzies, 24 July 1794.   [2] Ibid., 26 July 1794.

and convenient anchorage off George Island, in the bay that Vancouver named Port Althorp. The *Chatham* joined her there the next day. The extent of the coast that remained unexplored was now relatively limited (Cross Sound is only about 150 miles north of Cape Decision, where work had ended in 1793), but it was a safe assumption that the sound would lead to an array of interior waterways that would make the tracing of the continental shore a considerable task.

Vancouver lost no time in getting the survey under way. On July 10 Whidbey, accompanied by Menzies and Le Mesurier, a midshipman, left the ships with three boats, provisioned for a fortnight. Vancouver explains that he sent three boats instead of the usual two 'To guard as much as possible against accidents'.[1] He had always worried about the boat expeditions, especially when, as happened frequently, they failed to return within the period for which they were provisioned. He seems to have worried more as the great survey neared completion. As Whidbey, Johnstone and the rest had survived so many perils, he became particularly anxious that nothing should happen to them or their crews in these final weeks. This greater anxiety may have been in part a reflection of the state of his own health, upon which he makes one of his rare comments. Since the ships had returned to the coast it had been 'too indifferent' to allow him to take 'any share in the several distant boat excursions'. A few days after Whidbey left he decided to attempt a survey of some of the nearby islands, 'but by noon...a most violent indisposition' forced him to return.[2]

Whidbey found that at least in the first stages of his survey ice would be a major hazard. The survey began at Cape Spencer, the northern point of entrance to Cross Sound, and followed the north (or continental) shore, where the ice was particularly troublesome. Taylor Bay, the first opening investigated, was found to be blocked by the vast Brady Glacier. The first night, spent in Dundas Bay, was an anxious one. Menzies writes that looking eastward 'the arm appeared as far as we could see...strewd over with vast quantities of ice floating backwards and forwards with the Tides & currents, many huge pieces of which grounded at low water in the bay that kept us in continued anxiety & alarm for the safety of the boats & the utmost vigilance became necessary to prevent their being damaged or carried adrift by the ice, notwithstanding which the Chatham's Cutter was actually tore from her grapnel, & owing to the darkness of the night, was some distance adrift before she was observd'.[3]

[1] Vancouver, III, 214. [2] *Ibid.*, 238, 239.
[3] Menzies, 11 July 1794.

The next large opening was the entrance to Glacier Bay, and the extent to which ice conditions have changed since 1794 is indicated by the small attention devoted to it. Together with Icy Passage to the east, it is described as 'two large open bays, which were terminated by compact solid mountains of ice, rising perpendicularly from the water's edge'. Today Ice Passage is free of year-round ice and the ice has retreated up Glacier Bay for the astonishing distance of more than 60 miles. The ice is thought to have attained its maximum extent about 1750, and would already have retreated some distance at the time of Vancouver's visit.

On July 13 the boats reached a veritable meeting of the waters – the point at which Icy Strait, which they were following, meets with Lynn Canal, extending northward, and Chatham Strait, the most extensive of all the Alaskan inland passages, to the south. Here Whidbey paused to make observations, and the brief stop was memorable on two counts. First, Menzies and others 'observd that the tide of flood came from the Southward [up Chatham Strait] & went rapidly into the arm we came from [Icy Strait], which made it pretty evident that the southern branch communicated with the sea'. Secondly, the boat crews were able for once to vary the diet of ships' salt provisions upon which they had been living for some time past. Some of the party shot plovers and sea pies. Menzies describes the sequel: 'Here we dressd our game & found no difficulty in procuring plenty of salubrious greens to relish them, for the beaches every where here produced abundance of wild orach, which in our situation was conceived equal to the best spinnage. Some Natives that came in a Canoe brought us also some fish, so that with these additional luxuries, we made a very hearty meal, nor did any of us seem to regret the want of regular cooking or high season sauces, in short no one who has not tried to can conceive the high relish which these excursions give to the most homely fair.'[1]

Whidbey now turned north, to follow the continental shore up the western side of Lynn Canal. The boat crews found the going tedious and tiring. Strong head winds made progress slow, and like a number of other inlets the expedition had examined, the canal varied little in width and seemed to continue on interminably. 'This', Menzies notes, 'put almost every one in a bad humour at the extent & direction it was likely to carry us.'[2] He himself was an exception, as he found compensation in the interesting new plants he came across from time to time along the way.

Few Indians were encountered until the boats reached the head of

<hr>

[1] Menzies, 13 July 1794.　　　　　　[2] *Ibid.*, 14 July 1794.

the canal and entered Chilkat Inlet, where Chilkat Indians (a branch of the Tlingit) were met in some numbers. They appeared to be friendly, but not long after Whidbey started back down Lynn Canal, tracing its eastern shore, a near clash occurred that recalled the attack mounted by the Indians in Behm Canal. Only one chief in a large canoe, who treated the boats to an astonishing display of song and dance, had been seen in the evening, but dawn revealed that other canoes had arrived in the night. Presently at least a hundred Indians had assembled. In addition to native weapons, some had muskets and seemed quite able and prepared to use them. For a few minutes, as in the Behm Canal, the situation was critical. Menzies, who was in the pinnace with Whidbey, explains that the crew had passed the night in her, and that she 'was still in such confusion on account of our sleeping in her, that we could not readily get at all our fire arms.' The Indian chief boldly brought his canoe alongside and jumped into the pinnace, bent on plundering or capturing her, but the crew forced him out, prevented others from following him, and fended off the canoe. The boats, Menzies relates, were soon 'in perfect readiness to resist any attack' and the reaction of the Indians was characteristic. Having failed to secure what they wanted by force, they hoped to secure it by trade: 'they declind any further attempts towards plundering us, and now sollicited in a more peaceable manner with furs & sea otter skins in their hands to come alongside to barter with us, but their apparent treacherous behaviour rendered this inadvisable, & none of them were afterwards sufferd to come near any of the boats'.[1] After following hopefully for some miles, they gave up and withdrew.

The eastern shore of Lynn Canal led Whidbey not to Chatham Strait, as no doubt he anticipated, but into the northern end of Stephens Passage, which is separated from Chatham Strait first by a peninsula and then by the great bulk of Admiralty Island. Here Whidbey again encountered Indians whose movements and actions were alike unfriendly. Harassed by them as night was falling, he turned back, under the mistaken impression that he had glimpsed the end of Stephens Passage. As on several previous occasions, a right-angle turn had made it appear that a waterway extended no farther. To keep clear of the Indians Whidbey kept his crews rowing all night and returned to Lynn Canal by way of Saginaw Passage. There is a hint of disapproval in Vancouver's action in naming the northern tip of Admiralty Island, where Lynn Canal and Saginaw Passage meet, Point Retreat.

Whidbey next entered Chatham Strait, which offered a broad

[1] Menzies, 17 July 1794.

175

opening southward, unobstructed as far as the eye could see. He followed the western side of Admiralty Island, which, because of his mistake in thinking that Stephens Passage, on its eastern side, was no more than a closed bay, he assumed to be the continuation of the continental shore. The only incident of note was a further encounter with a large party of Indians. At first it seemed that trouble might be brewing, but it soon became evident that their chief interest was in trading. Vancouver records that they had sea otter skins 'in great abundance, and many were thrown into the boats, for which they thankfully received any trifling article of wearing apparel',[1] which they preferred to copper and iron, once in great demand. Whidbey had not progressed far before the ebb and flow of the tides confirmed that Chatham Strait led to the ocean. By the time he reached the southern point of Admiralty Island, which Vancouver later named Point Gardner, in honour of his patron, he had a clear view of the Pacific between Cape Decision and Cape Ommaney. For a moment, with Cape Decision in sight, it appeared that the survey of the continental shore had been completed, but it was then discovered that Point Gardner was the meeting place of Chatham Strait and Frederick Sound, a wide inlet stretching far to the northeast. As the boat crews were weary and running short of provisions, the sound was clearly far too extensive to make an immediate examination practicable, and Whidbey decided to return to the ships and report.

The day they arrived – July 26 – the *Jackal* entered Cross Sound. Her commander, William Brown, who was to be killed in the Sandwich Islands a few months later, deserves more attention than he has received. The two major errors made during Vancouver's survey of the continental shore of what is now British Columbia and Alaska were Johnstone's failure to detect and pass through Dry Strait, which links the upper waters of Sumner Strait with Frederick Sound, and Whidbey's failure to pursue the exploration of Stephens Passage, which runs southward to Frederick Sound. The continental shore is so close to Dry Strait that it can be seen across the small intervening islands, and beyond the strait it runs on northward to form the eastern shore first of Frederick Sound and then of Stephens Passage. Vancouver's laborious examination of the many islands lying west of these waterways added much of interest to his charts, but was thus a waste of time and effort from the point of view of the main purpose of his survey. Brown in the little *Jackal* was about to correct both errors.

[1] Vancouver, III, 257.

Menzies tells the story in one of several passages in his journal that indicate that the text that has come down to us was amended some time after the events described. The *Discovery* and *Chatham* left their Cross Sound anchorage on July 28. In the entry for that date Menzies writes that the *Jackal* was then 'preparing to proceed to visit the inland tribes of Indians we had discovered in our boat expedition, with expectations from our reports of procuring a good collection of furs.... In the prosecution of this object we afterwards understood that Mr Brown carried his Vessel to the northward [in Lynn Canal] as far as the boats had penetrated, where he was very civilly treated by those very Indians whose conduct appeared to us so suspicious, & in going to the Southward he discovered a clear navigable passage for his Vessel by the Channel [Stephens Passage] we had too hastily quitted on the evening of the 18th, by which he continued his route, passing through another passage [Dry Strait], that had escaped the vigilance of our boat examinations, upwards of 20 leagues inland from Cape Decision, which last year was supposd to be the Continent, but which he provd to the contrary: And,' Menzies adds, 'this instance will clearly shew, that where the examination is so difficult & intricate, however carefully performed, it can have no pretentions to infallability.'[1]

Whidbey's discovery that Chatham Strait led southward to the Pacific meant that the land mass between it and the ocean was composed of islands. Two large islands, Chichagof and Baranof, comprise most of the area, but the very much smaller Kruzof Island, off the west coast of Baranof Island, is historically interesting because its principal features are Cape Edgecumbe and Mount Edgecumbe, the first prominent features on the Alaskan coast noted and named by Cook in 1778. Vancouver called the group King George the Third's Archipelago, but the name did not survive for long.

He decided to take the *Discovery* and *Chatham* south and to seek an anchorage near Cape Ommaney (the southern tip of Baranof Island) at the entrance to Chatham Strait. From there boat expeditions would be able to fill in the gap that still remained in his chart of the continental shore. Menzies considered that 'the interior navigation' by way of Chatham Strait 'excepting close to Cross Sound appeared very eligible',[2] but Vancouver preferred an ocean passage that would enable him to survey the exterior coast. Bad weather and poor visibility made this difficult, as the numerous islands and rocks strewn along the shore made it essential to keep a safe distance from land, but nevertheless his

[1] Menzies, 28 July 1794.   [2] *Ibid.*, 23 July 1794.

chart is a very fair representation of the coast. The ships left Cross Sound on July 29, and rounded Cape Ommaney two days later. A few miles up the western shore of Chatham Strait, on Baranof Island, they found the well sheltered harbour that Vancouver would later name Port Conclusion.

Whidbey and Johnstone were again in command of the boat expeditions. Their instructions assumed that the continental shore had been traced from the south as far as Cape Decision, and from the north as far as Point Gardner. The task remaining was to explore the ramifications of Frederick Sound, the major opening to the east between these two points. Whidbey was to proceed to Point Gardner, at the entrance to the sound, and follow its northern shore. Johnstone was to go first to Cape Decision and having traced the coast northward to the entrance of Frederick Sound, would follow its southern shore eastward. When the two expeditions met, the immense task of tracing the continental shore from 30° to beyond 60° north latitude would have been completed.

Whidbey traced the northern shore of the sound to its junction with Stephens Passage, then followed the passage all the way to the right-angle bend that he had mistaken for its termination when he had entered it after examining Lynn Canal. He recognized his surroundings, but continued on as far as Point Retreat. Just as his exploration of Chatham Strait had revealed that the large land mass west of it consisted of islands, so his exploration of Stephens Passage now showed that the extensive land mass west of it was also insular – in this instance one very large island that Vancouver would name Admiralty Island. The eastern side of Stephens Passage was thus shown to be the continental shore, and Whidbey set about tracing its intricacies southward. Miserable weather put him in no mood to appreciate scenery, and Vancouver notes that he reported that the vicinity of the famous Taku Glacier, in Taku Inlet, 'exhibited as dreary and inhospitable an aspect as the imagination can possibly suggest.'[1] There were few bays or inlets to detain him long, and he was soon back at the junction of Stephens Passage and Frederick Sound.

From Chatham Strait to Stephens Passage the general direction of the sound is northeast; beyond its meeting with the passage it swings to the southeast. Whidbey turned into it, clinging to the continental shore, and followed it to the termination of the sound in the shallows and mud flats off the northern mouth of the Stikine River. Two

[1] Vancouver, III, 278.

islands – Dry Island and Farm Island – masked his view of the larger shallows off the river's southern mouth. These were the shallows that, the previous year, had prevented Johnstone from discovering Dry Strait, the narrow channel between Frederick Sound and Sumner Strait. Coming from the north, Whidbey evidently saw the strait, but, in Vancouver's words, 'as it was considered not to be navigable' he 'was anxious to lose no time in the further extension of his researches.'[1] Brown in the *Jackal* would navigate the strait, and Vancouver would learn of this when he and Brown met for a last time at Nootka Sound. Meanwhile Whidbey began tracing the other side of Frederick Sound, under the impression that it was a continuation of the continental shore.

Whidbey had two encounters with Indians that threatened to develop into serious clashes. The first was at the head of Stephens Passage, where he evidently met natives belonging to the same villages that had caused him to turn back on his earlier exploring expedition. A warning shot, intended to keep them at a distance, was ignored, but when a second shot was aimed at and struck one of their canoes, they turned away at once. The next evening, when returning down Stephens Passage, those in the boats (to quote Menzies) 'heard the most hideous lamentations & yellings that can possibly be conceived' from which they conjectured that some of the Indians 'had been either killd or badly wounded by the shot fird at the Canoe'. Whidbey 'regretted that such a measure was then necessary in order to get rid of them'.[2] The second incident was more serious and the Indians involved were clearly bent on mischief. It occurred in Frederick Sound, when the boats were about half way back to the junction of the sound and Stephens Passage. As before, a canoe approached and ignored a warning shot, but withdrew at once when a second shot was fired directly at the canoe. Whidbey and his crews had landed in a cove to dine, but he became uneasy, suspecting that an attack of some kind was imminent, and moved his men back to the boats. They were no more than clear of the land when Indians burst out of the woods in an attempt to surprise and overwhelm them. This was to be the last hostile move by Indians against Vancouver's men, and it is interesting to note that in some respects it resembled the first one, when Puget and his boat crews were threatened when exploring Puget Sound.

Shortly after this incident Whidbey was delighted to meet Johnstone's boats. They had travelled a much shorter distance over a more difficult route. After tracing the heavily indented coast between Cape Decision

---

[1] *Ibid.*, p. 281.   [2] Menzies, 19 August 1794.

and the entrance to Frederick Sound, Johnstone had entered the sound and had soon turned to investigate Keku Strait. A relatively wide bay at its entrance, much of which is encumbered with islands and reefs, leads to a narrow and intricate channel leading southward. Having worked his way through it, Johnstone discovered that the bay into which it emptied was a part of Sumner Strait that he had attempted to survey in September 1793, but had been forced to turn back by the multitude of rocks and shoals that characterize it. Once again the discovery of a passage had shown that land to the west of it was an island, and the outer perimeter of what is now Kuiu Island was thus shown to be no part of the continental shore.

After a tedious trip back through the strait Johnstone resumed his examination of the south shore of Frederick Sound, and little of interest occurred before he met Whidbey. This meeting took place on August 16 and the next day, in accordance with his instructions, Whidbey took formal possession of the country. This was done with as much pomp and ceremony as circumstances permitted: colours were displayed and volleys fired. The two parties had met on the birthday of Frederick, Duke of York, hence Vancouver's decision to bestow the name Prince Frederick's Sound, since shortened to Frederick Sound.

Except for one brief break, the weather at Port Conclusion had been unsettled and wet, but work on preparing the ships for the long voyage homeward had proceeded apace. The crews were kept busy securing wood and water, brewing spruce beer, repairing sails and rigging, caulking decks, and cutting spars and timbers for lumber. In spite of the weather Menzies with various companions explored the nearby countryside. 'Their object,' he writes, 'was amusement & recreation, mine was examining the produce of the country, & as the woods here were interspersed with small Lakes clear spots & Savannas, they afforded a fine scope for my pursuit.'[1]

As usual, Vancouver had worried about the safety of the boats and Menzies soon shared his anxiety. They had been provisioned for a fortnight, but Vancouver had expected that they would accomplish their missions in about ten days. As time passed beyond this period he became extremely concerned. Remembering Whidbey's recent encounters with unfriendly Indians he was severely critical of the fur traders who had made firearms available to them so freely. This, he notes, 'has not only given the natives a degree of confidence that renders them bold and importunate, but the dread which they once

[1] Menzies, 5 August 1794.

entertained for musketry is greatly lessened by their becoming so familiar with them.' They 'are daily becoming formidable, especially to the parties in our small boats.' This 'gave us but too much reason to be apprehensive that we had at length hazarded our little boats, with the small force they were able to take for their defence, once too often.'[1] It is interesting to note that because of the growing power of the Indians he doubted if it would have been practicable to carry out the survey at any later date; 'the means we possessed to repel their attacks, would, in all probability, have been insufficient for our protection, had it been our lot to have tried the experiment one year later.'[2]

His one source of comfort was his faith in his officers and seamen: 'it is a tribute that is justly due to the meritorious exertions of those under my command, that I should again acknowledge the great consolation I derived on all painful occasions like this, by having the most implicit confidence in the discretion and abilities of my officers, and the exertions and ready obedience of my people.'[3] He had his reward on the 17th day, when all four boats returned together, their crews wet and weary but happy in the realization that the great survey had been completed. Menzies describes the occasion and pays tribute to all who had been engaged in its execution. The appearance of the boats 'instantly changed our alarms & gloomy reflections to a sudden glow of joy that brightened every countenance for...it was to our minds a presumptive proof that they had finishd the laborious & intricate examination of this coast, & when they reached the Vessels & confirmd our conjecture of this desirable event, our feelings may be more easily conceived than describd, a mutual exchange of three congratulating cheers from the crews of each Vessel expressd the cordial satisfaction they all felt on this joyous occasion, in having thus put an end so successfully to a tedious & laborious enterprise for the completion of which an uncommon zeal had actuated every individual to the most unwearied & persevering exertions, under all the circumstances of hardships & laborious toils of dangers & difficulties to which the nature of the service unavoidably exposd them they on all occasions performd their duty with alacrity & cheerfulness, & with a manly perseverance that contributed in the highest degree to attain the great object in view.'[4]

In his narrative Vancouver summed up his accomplishment with merited satisfaction. He was confident that his survey would 'remove

---

[1] Vancouver, III, 271.   [2] *Ibid.*, p. 284.
[3] *Ibid.*, p. 271.   [4] Menzies, 19 August 1794.

every doubt, and set aside every opinion of a *north-west passage*, or any water communication navigable for shipping, existing between the North Pacific, and the interior of the American continent within the limits of our researches.'[1] Oddly enough, when reporting to Stephens at the Admiralty from Nootka early in September he made no direct reference to the non-existence of a passage. He simply asked Stephens to inform 'my Lords Commissioners of the Admiralty, that it is with the greatest satisfaction I am at length able to inform them of our having finally traced and determined the Continental boundary of N.W. America from the latitude of 29° 54 North and longitude 244° 33 E^t North-Westward; through all the various turnings and windings, so far as its different inlets have been found safely navigable for our boats, to Cape Douglas [in Cook Inlet].' Then follows the sentence that by implication denies the existence of a passage: 'During this investigation we have never been able to penetrate beyond the barrier of the lofty mountains, which, covered with eternal frost and snow, extend nearly in a connected chain, along the western border of the continent I believe, to its utmost Northern limits; though in some instances considerably farther removed from the ocean than in others.'[2]

Weather delayed the departure of the *Discovery* and *Chatham* from Port Conclusion until August 24, and their passage south to Nootka Sound was marred by storms, adverse winds, fog and the loss of a valued seaman. When they anchored in Friendly Cove on September 2, Vancouver found there two Spanish officers well known to him – Ramón Saavedra, commanding the *San Carlos*, who had been on garrison duty at Nootka since the spring of 1793, and Salvador Fidalgo, who had just arrived from San Blas in the *Princesa*. To his sorrow, Vancouver learned that Quadra, whom he had hoped to meet again, had died in March. His successor as commandant at San Blas and as Spanish commissioner for Nootka, Brigadier José Manuel de Alava, had come north in the *Princesa*. He and Vancouver were soon on friendly terms; both were anxious to conclude the negotiations about Nootka that Quadra had begun in 1792, but neither had received the necessary instructions from their respective governments. Alava was so confident that word would arrive shortly from Madrid that he had ordered a vessel to be kept in readiness at San Blas to bring dispatches to Nootka with the least possible delay. He and Vancouver agreed that

---

[1] Vancouver, III, 295.
[2] Vancouver to Stephens, Nootka Sound, 8 September 1794. P.R.O., Adm 1/2629, f. 56.

they would wait at Friendly Cove until October 15, in the expectation
that instructions would be received by that date.

Some of the period of waiting could be put to good use. The
refitting of the *Discovery* and *Chatham* begun at Port Conclusion
continued. The Spaniards were helpful in many ways; as on several
other occasions, Spanish caulkers were employed. The observatory was
set up on shore and the task of correcting the surveys and compiling
charts proceeded apace. Vancouver personally soon had time on his
hands, and he suggested to Alava that they should repeat the expedition
he had made with Quadra in 1792 and visit Chief Maquinna, who
was again at his winter village near the head of Tahsis Inlet. The party,
which travelled in four boats, numbered 56. Maquinna was greatly
pleased and impressed. Menzies, Puget and Swaine accompanied
Vancouver, and both he and Menzies describe the visit in considerable
detail.

The delay at Nootka disappointed Vancouver's crews. Writing to
Banks, Menzies noted that they had arrived 'all in perfect health, &
in high Spirits, with the Idea of returning home but we are now
detained, God knows how long, till the arrival of a Vessel which is
expected from St. Blas with the determination of the two Courts
relative to this port'.[1] Unknown to Menzies, Vancouver feared that
a much longer delay was possible. In his view, it was essential that a
settlement about Nootka should be reached before he could sail for
England. He ended a letter to Stephens at the Admiralty by pointing
out 'that in failure of receiving any instructions from their Lordships,
for the execution of my commission respecting these territories, I
consider myself as bound to remain in these seas; in which case, the
Chatham will be dispatched in due time to China, in order to procure
the necessary supplies that may be required.'[2] Vancouver soon became
weary of waiting; early in October, writing to his friend and London
agent, James Sykes, he remarked that he was 'once more entrap'd in
this infernal Ocean, and am totally at a loss to say when I shall be able
to quit it'.[3]

No communications having been received by October 15, Vancouver
left Nootka immediately, bound for Monterey. Alava, who was to join
him there, sailed the following day in the *Princesa*. As Nootka was not

---

[1] Menzies to Banks, Nootka, 8 September 1794. Brabourne Papers, Mitchell Library, Sydney.

[2] Vancouver to Stephens, Nootka, 8 September 1794. P.R.O., Adm 1/2629, f. 58.

[3] Vancouver to Sykes, Nootka, 3 October 1794. Vancouver City Archives.

being evacuated, Saavedra was left to spend another monotonous and uncomfortable winter at the little settlement in Friendly Cove. At this point nothing went according to plan for Vancouver. The *Discovery* and *Chatham* became separated in fog shortly after sailing, and the *Discovery* in particular encountered trying conditions most of the way to California. These culminated in a most violent storm that opened seams and flooded the gun room. Vancouver had intended to visit 'the bay of Sir Francis Drake', but wind and weather prevented this. At Monterey he found the *Chatham* awaiting him; as Menzies remarks, she 'as usual had got the start of us.'[1]

Almost the first item of business transacted at Monterey concerned the men who had deserted there in January 1793, when Vancouver was paying his first visit to California. All had been apprehended and held in custody by the Spaniards. They included the *Chatham*'s armourer, one of her marines, and three men from the *Daedalus*. Of the latter three, Vancouver would accept only Thomas Smith, a convict who had stowed away in the *Daedalus* at Port Jackson. The others he rejected, as he explained later in England, on two grounds: they were not British subjects, and as the *Daedalus* was a merchant ship he had no jurisdiction over her crew. Vancouver was presented with a bill for the maintenance of the five, but this he declined to pay because he had no funds that he was authorized to expend for such a purpose. He made it clear, however, that he was ready to recommend payment to the Admiralty when he returned to England. This seemed at the time to be agreeable to the Spanish governor, but Vancouver was to hear more of the matter later.

Puget reported that the obnoxious Arrillaga had departed, and that José Dario Arguello was acting commandant, pending the arrival of Don Diego de Borica, the new governor. The reception accorded them had been most friendly; 'they were sufferd to take the recreations of the shore without the least restraint & were supplied with refreshments in the same liberal manner as on their first visit [in 1792].'[2] Vancouver had learned from Alava that the letter he had written to Quadra protesting against the treatment he had received in 1793 had been forwarded to the Viceroy, whose 'very humane and liberal intentions'[3] towards the expedition were once again prevailing. Arguello, Menzies records, 'assured us that he was instructed by the Viceroy to supply us with every kind of refreshment the country afforded, & not only

---

[1] Menzies, 6 November 1794.   [2] *Ibid.*
[3] Vancouver, III, 316.

us, but English Vessels in general visiting the Port'.[1] These arrangements were confirmed at once by Borica when he arrived and assumed office as governor on November 11.

Vancouver confesses that he 'could not help feeling very great disappointment, anxiety and concern' when he found that no word from London was awaiting him at Monterey. However, he was not 'totally destitute of hope, that some letters might have arrived at St. Diego',[2] and unlikely as this seemed, Arguello obligingly sent a special courier south on the chance that something might have been received there. He would return empty handed, but on November 11, while he was still absent, an express arrived from Mexico City bringing Alava his long-awaited instructions regarding the settlement of the Nootka controversy.

He was to carry into effect the provisions of the 'Convention for the mutual abandonment of Nootka' that Britain and Spain had signed in Madrid on 11 January 1794. This directed that British and Spanish commissioners were to meet at Nootka 'in the place, or near, where the buildings stood which were formerly occupied by the subjects of His Britannic Majesty'. There the Spanish commissioner was to read a declaration restoring 'the buildings and districts of land...of which the subjects of His Britannic Majesty were dispossessed by a Spanish officer toward the month of April 1789'. A counter declaration, to be read by the British commissioner, would acknowledge the restoration. Thereupon, the convention continued, 'the British official shall unfurl the British flag over the land so restored in sign of possession. And...after these formalities the officials of the two Crowns shall withdraw, respectively, their people from the said port of Nootka.'

Thus Meares' buildings and lands, real and imaginary, had a last field day. As they were to be abandoned, Spain no longer saw any point in objecting to the grandiose description of them, which was quoted almost verbatim from the original convention of 1790, the accuracy of which had been challenged so determinedly by Quadra.

For Vancouver there was news of a sort. He records in his narrative that 'the Spanish minister's letter set forth, that this business was not to be carried into execution by me, as a fresh commission had been issued for this purpose by the Court of London.' One senses that this was somewhat of a blow to Vancouver's pride, and that he was glad to learn later (as indicated by a marginal note added to his text) that the 'fresh commission' had in fact been intended in the first instance

---

[1] Menzies, 7 November 1794.   [2] Vancouver, III, 327.

for himself, and for the special commissioner only in his absence. Unaware of this, and, as he states, 'relying on the authenticity of the intelligence I had derived from Sen.ʳ Alava, I did not long hesitate, but determined on making the best of my way towards England, by the way of cape Horn'.[1]

One or two items of business required attention before he could set sail. One was the mundane task of replenishing the water supplies of the two ships. This was a slow and tedious task, as the nearest source was some distance from the harbour. Vancouver wished to stay at Monterey sufficiently long to rest his crews, some of whom, contrary to Menzies' blithe report to Banks from Nootka, were not in the best of health. Menzies himself notes in his journal that there were 'some sick and convalescents on board' and that he 'recommended to the Captain that they should be landed for their more speedy recovery, which was complied with'. A tent was erected on shore to serve as a temporary hospital.[2] Vancouver was somewhat apprehensive that his ships might come to grief on the last stage of their long voyage, and to guard against the loss of the data they had gathered he was anxious to forward dispatches and duplicates of his surveys to the Admiralty. This considerable task was increased when, following Quadra's example, Alava asked for copies of the surveys 'for the use and information of the Spanish court'. Finally, for some reason not stated, doubts had arisen in Vancouver's mind as to whether the dispatches and charts he had sent to London the previous year had been received, and he decided to send duplicates of them as well.

A fortnight was required to compile all these items, but on November 24 those destined for London were entrusted to an express that was leaving Monterey for Mexico City. Upon the advice of Borica and others they were addressed to the new Viceroy, the Marqués de Branciforte, with the request that he forward them to London. What became of them thereafter remains a mystery; there is no indication that they ever reached London. Nor did Banks receive a letter that Menzies wrote to him from Monterey, which presumably was sent by the same courier. There would seem to be only two likely explanations: they were either lost in transit or sequestered by the Spanish authorities in Mexico City.

If Vancouver had been aware of the terms of the 'fresh commission' he might well have chosen to await its arrival. This would not have entailed a long delay. The substitute British commissioner, Lieut.

[1] *Ibid.*, p. 332.   [2] Menzies, 11 November 1794.

Thomas Pearce of the Marines, who seems to have been chosen for the mission largely because he spoke Spanish, arrived in Mexico City on November 30, two days before the *Discovery* and *Chatham* sailed from Monterey. He travelled on to San Blas and left for Nootka in the *Activa* on 13 January 1795. Alava joined the ship at Monterey. No doubt the war that Britain was waging in Europe accounted for the contrast in the two delegations that landed in Friendly Cove on March 16: on the one hand, a Spanish Brigadier accompanied by naval and military forces, and on the other a lone British lieutenant without so much as a batman.

Alava immediately ordered Saavedra to prepare to evacuate Nootka, a measure that included dismantling the fortifications, loading the ordnance on the ships, and demolishing the buildings in the little settlement. Pearce protested, as he felt he was entitled to take possession of something more than a heap of rubble. Letters passed back and forth between Alava and himself, but during the exchanges the work of demolition went on steadily and was carried to completion. Alava had not been impressed by Pearce. Later he reported to the Viceroy that he 'possessed very little firmness of character.'[1] By March 28 everything of value had been put on board the *Activa* and *San Carlos* and that morning the official ceremony of restoration took place.

Before leaving the sound Alava distributed gifts to the Indian chiefs. Pearce reported later to the Duke of Portland, the Home Secretary, that he had informed the chiefs that 'His Majesty had determined to take them under his protection – with this Account they all seemed much pleased, observing that the English had ever been their good Friends'. And he added: 'The British Colours I have committed to the Charge of Maqueena, or Maw-queena, the most powerful Chief, with directions to Hoist them whenever a vessel appeared in sight; this mark of confidence gratified him very much.'[2] Pearce did not mention that Alava had very generously allowed him to distribute some of the gifts given to the chiefs, as he himself had nothing to offer except the flag.[3]

By the time the *Discovery* and *Chatham* were ready to leave Monterey Vancouver had to recognize that 'all expectation of Mr.

---

[1] Alava to Branciforte, San Blas, 23 April 1795. Quoted in Christon I. Archer, 'Retreat from the North: Spain's Withdrawal from Nootka Sound, 1793–1795'. *B.C. Studies*, no. 37, Spring 1968, p. 33.

[2] J. Forsyth, 'Documents connected with the final settlement of the Nootka Dispute', British Columbia Historical Assn., *Second Annual Report and Proceedings* (Victoria, B.C., 1924) p. 35.

[3] Archer, 'Retreat from the North', *B.C. Studies*, n. 37, Spring 1978, p. 34.

Broughton's return and of his resuming command of the Chatham' was at an end.[1] On 26 November 1794 he therefore confirmed Puget in the command he had held in an acting capacity for nearly two years. But Vancouver had been right in thinking that the Admiralty would probably send Broughton back to the Pacific, and only a series of delays, due to a combination of minor accidents and wartime conditions, prevented him from arriving in time to meet Vancouver. Broughton was preparing to sail when Pearce left England, and this explains Pearce's displeasure at the destruction of the buildings at Friendly Cove. He himself had no force available to take possession of them, but he believed that Broughton's arrival was probably imminent. How he expected to reconcile even a temporary British occupation of Nootka with the terms of the convention that called for its immediate mutual abandonment by Spain and Britain is unexplained.

The Admiralty had lost little time in arranging for Broughton's return to the Pacific. He had arrived in England in July 1793, and less than three months later, on October 3, he was promoted to post rank and appointed to command the *Providence*, 420 tons, then lying at Woolwich.[2] Later Zachary Mudge, the other messenger that Vancouver had sent to London, joined her as 1st lieutenant. To begin with it was assumed that Broughton would sail in time to rejoin Vancouver on the Northwest Coast. One evidence of this is that on the last day of the year the Admiralty instructed him to receive on board John Crosley, an astronomer, who (in his own words) had been appointed by the Board of Longitude 'to succeed the late Mr. William Gooch and make use of the Instruments carried out by him on board the *Daedalus* and left on board H.M.S. *Discovery*, Captain Vancouver.'[3] But long delays ensued. When Broughton received his final orders on 2 October 1794 – a year less a day since the *Providence* had been commissioned – she had progressed no farther than Spithead. Broughton records that his orders 'were, that I should survey the southern coast of the south-west part of South America, upon the idea that Captain Vancouver, who had similar orders, would not be able to fulfil them.'[4] He was to proceed

---

[1] Vancouver, III, 336.

[2] Like Broughton, the *Providence* was making her second visit to the Pacific. She had been purchased for Bligh's second voyage to Tahiti, when he succeeded in taking breadfruit trees to Jamaica, the mission that had been aborted by the famous mutiny on the *Bounty*.

[3] John Crosley to Dr Nevil Maskelyne, n.d. [1798]. Quoted in Alan Reid, 'Broughton's Schooner', *Mariner's Mirror*, LXIV (1978), p. 243. Also Broughton to the Board of Longitude, Macao, 1 April 1797. *Ibid.*, p. 242.

[4] Broughton, *Voyage of Discovery to the North Pacific Ocean*, p. 64.

to the Northwest Coast by way of Port Jackson, Tahiti and the Sandwich Islands. Later in October the *Providence* moved on to Plymouth Sound, where a vast convoy of over 400 sail, which she was to accompany on the first part of her voyage, was assembling. A long spell of bad weather caused further months of delay, and the convoy did not put to sea until 15 February 1795.

Thirteen months later, in March 1796, after a leisurely voyage, Broughton arrived off Nootka Sound. He had learned from an English brig encountered off the island of Hawaii that Vancouver had sailed for home, and he approached Friendly Cove with some caution. An officer sent to reconnoitre reported 'that the spot on which the Spanish settlement formerly stood was now occupied by an Indian village.' Later Maquinna[1] gave Broughton letters from Pearce and Alava that confirmed Vancouver's departure and that the Spaniards 'had delivered up the port of Nootka, &c....agreeably to the mode of restitution settled between the two Courts.'[2]

Maintaining his leisurely pace, Broughton tarried in Nootka Sound for more than two months, until May 21. The *Providence* was badly in need of repairs and he decided that these should be carried out at Marvinas Bay, farther up the sound, rather than in Friendly Cove. This was an anchorage long used by the Americans, and he was joined by the brig *Lady Washington*, which Vancouver had met several times, both on the coast and in the Sandwich Islands. She was also in need of extensive repairs, and the crews of the two ships assisted one another.

Southbound for Monterey the *Providence* – the last ship of the Royal Navy to visit the Northwest Coast for seventeen years – somewhere passed the *Sutil*, the last Spanish naval vessel to visit Nootka Sound. The Marqués de Branciforte, Viceroy of New Spain, had decided that an occasional Spanish presence on the coast was required to protect Spain's interest, and he proposed to send a ship north every six months to keep a watch on foreign encroachments. The voyage of the *Sutil* was intended to be the first of the series. As things turned out, it proved to be the last as well.[3]

[1] The name 'Maquinna' was borne by a succession of chiefs, and there is some question as to whether this was the same Maquinna with whom Meares and Vancouver had had dealings. For a fuller discussion see p. 661.

[2] Broughton, *Voyage of Discovery to the North Pacific Ocean*, p. 50.

[3] Archer, 'Retreat from the North', *B.C. Studies*, no.37, Spring 1978, p. 35. The *Sutil* arrived at Nootka on June 16 and sailed for Monterey on the 22nd. The voyage from San Blas had lasted three months, and five or six of her crew of nine were ill when she arrived. Her commander, Don José Tovar, was able to recruit five replacements from the American

The *Providence* arrived at Monterey on June 6. Instead of the friendly welcome he expected, Broughton was given a chilly reception very like that Arrillaga had extended to Vancouver in the autumn of 1793. He acknowledges that his ship was 'most amply supplied with excellent fresh beef, mutton, vegetables, and milk' but the governor's attitude was one of suspicion:

The Governor, Signor Don Diego Borica, a colonel of cavalry in the Spanish army, was absent on our first arrival; but he returned two days after, when I requested of him to erect a tent for the astronomer, for settling the rates of the watches, which he refused to grant, saying, that his orders were to relieve our absolute want of necessaries, but in no other instance were they allowed to assist us. We were prevented either from riding or walking into the country; nor did we receive the least civility or attention from any officer in the settlement. There was no intercourse between us scarcely: they did not visit our ship, or we intrude on their society. So unsocial was their conduct, that I thought myself justified in not saluting the fort in our sailing, though it was evident that they expected the compliment, from the preparations they made there.[1]

Friendliness had been confined to the missionaries, who incurred Borica's displeasure because of it. Broughton notes that he 'received one present of a bullock with vegetables, from the Fathers at the mission of St. Carmelo; but the rigid conduct of the Governor prevented them from sending any more. They were the same hospitable priests whom I met in 1792.'[2]

Borica's attitude was undoubtedly due to a marked deterioration in the relations between Spain and Great Britain of which Broughton knew nothing. The war with France, her traditional ally, had not gone well for Spain. Northern provinces had been overrun, and the Spaniards were moving toward an accommodation with the French. As early as March 1795, when Pearce and Alava were nearing Nootka Sound, Madrid had warned the Viceroy of New Spain that a break with Britain

trading ship *Otter*, which arrived opportunely from Australia on June 19. Thomas Muir, the Scottish radical, who had been transported to Botany Bay, had escaped in the *Otter* and he travelled to Monterey in the *Sutil*. Governor Borica gave him a cordial welcome, but the Viceroy was suspicious and the Spaniards soon changed their tune. Tribulations were to mark the last years of Muir's short life. Tovar was tried and dismissed from his ship for having taken Muir on board. See Marjorie Masson and J. F. Jameson, 'The Odyssey of Thomas Muir', *American Historical Review* xxix (1923–24), pp. 57–61.

[1] Broughton, *Voyage of Discovery to the North Pacific Ocean*, p. 35. Documents in the Archivo General de Mexico reveal that Broughton brought astronomical instruments worth £250 from London that were intended for Quadra, but the latter had died more than two years before he arrived. Masson and Jameson, 'Odyssey of Thomas Muir', p. 58n.   [2] *Ibid.*, p. 62.

was probably imminent. A treaty signed in July provided for a French withdrawal from the occupied provinces in return for the cession of eastern Hispaniola (now Haiti). It seemed obvious that a formal alliance would follow. All this was known to Borica. A few weeks after Broughton sailed from Monterey the expected alliance was signed, and early in October 1796 Spain declared war on Britain.

The Homeward Voyage

Vancouver's homeward voyage began in earnest with his departure on 2 December 1794 from Monterey, the last port he expected to visit for some months to come. Unfortunately details and comments regarding it, other than those given in his own narrative, are scanty. Menzies' journal ends in March 1795, and the logs that continue beyond that date, although for the most part meticulously kept, are concerned almost entirely with the movements and business of the ships.

Vancouver was expected to survey the southern part of the west coast of South America, but the supplementary instructions he had received by the *Daedalus* had given him most positive orders to keep clear of the Spanish settlements south of 30° N, the southern limit of his coastal survey. He was 'to take the utmost care...on no account whatever to touch at any port on the continent of America' south of that latitude or north of 44° S, the point at which his South American survey was intended to begin. But as he sailed southward Vancouver, ever the explorer, wished to ascertain or verify the correct positions of a number of islands and other features.

The first of these was the island of Guadaloupe, which was sighted on December 8. The ships then swung back towards the coast, as Vancouver was particularly anxious to check the position of Cabo San Lucas, the southern tip of the Baja California peninsula. Its location had been ascertained accurately in 1769, by a French expedition sent thither to observe the transit of Venus, and it would thus give Vancouver an opportunity to test the accuracy of his own observations and hence the accuracy of his charts. He was justly gratified by the result; he had placed the cape within less than a mile of its true position. From this, as he modestly states, he 'had now great reason to presume, that the position of the western coast of America between cape St. Lucas in California, and cape Douglas in Cook's Inlet, as heretofore stated by me, would be found tolerably correct.'[1]

Vancouver next headed for the Tres Marias Islands, off the Mexican

[1] Vancouver, III, 345.

coast, partly from a desire to establish their position, but also in the hope that he could there replenish the ships' supply of water. But it was the dry season of an exceptionally dry year, and when Whidbey and Manby went ashore on Isla Maria Magdalena they found nothing but dry water courses. Vancouver continued to keep fairly close to the the continent as far as Cape Corrientes, south of the islands, but there he took his final departure from the North American coastline and headed for the supposed positions of Cocos Island and the Galapagos. The positions assigned to them by earlier navigators varied considerably, and Vancouver soon discovered the reason – strong currents carried his ships as much as 50 miles in 24 hours. As Menzies noted in his journal, 'such are the fluctuating directions & strength of the currents in this part of the Ocean, that no reliance can be placed on the Longitude of any Land settled by the dead reckoning'[1] – and it was upon this that early calculations had perforce to be based. Fortunately Vancouver could check his own position by lunar observations and his chrono-meters, but he found himself groping for the islands under most unpleasant conditions. The ships met with light variable winds and calms; their progress, in Vancouver's words, was 'tardy and irksome beyond all description.'[2] For nearly a month they advanced, on the average, no more than 40 miles a day – a rate that exasperated their crews, impatient as they were to get back to England. For six weeks after the ships left Monterey no rain fell and they endured what Menzies considered to be 'the most parching & oppressive heat we ever experienced at sea.'[3] Water reserves ran low, and at the end of December Vancouver found it necessary to reduce the daily ration allowed to the *Discovery*'s crew. Some compensation was found in an astonishing abundance of fresh food. Turtles were plentiful, the sea teemed with fish, and some of the beef, mutton and poultry secured at Monterey was still available. These provisions and an extra allowance of grog helped to make the expedition's fourth Christmas a truly festive occasion.

Cocos Island finally hove in sight on January 20, but owing to light winds and strong currents it was the 23rd before the *Discovery* and *Chatham* anchored in Chatham Bay. Four days were sufficient to supply the ships' needs as wood, water and coconuts were all plentiful. The island had been visited by buccaneers and sighted by Anson, but as little was known about it, Vancouver gave as detailed a description as the

---

[1] Menzies, 4 February 1795.   [2] Vancouver, III, 354.
[3] Menzies, 15 January 1795.

limited time available permitted. A message was found recording the visit of James Colnett, in the whaler *Rattler*, in July 1793. Whidbey, accompanied by Puget and Menzies, circled the island in an effort to prepare a sketch of it, but the weather was so bad that Menzies notes that 'under such circumstances a regular survey...could not be attained.'[1] Whidbey duly produced a sketch, but it reflected the difficult conditions under which it had been compiled. Unlike his usual careful work, it was crude and highly inaccurate, and compared very badly with the much more professional chart drawn by Colnett and reproduced in his *Voyage*, published, like Vancouver's, in 1798.

From Cocos Island the ships sailed slowly southward. The intention was that they should rendezvous at Islas Juan Fernandez, to replenish their wood and water. On the way Vancouver hoped he might encounter the Galapagos Islands and determine their position. Any expectation of doing so seemed to have vanished when they stumbled upon two small islands that proved to be the northernmost of the group. Sailing on southward the ships passed down the western shore of Albemarle (Isabela) much the largest of the Galapagos, and Narborough (Fernandina) Island, which lies so close to it that for a time Vancouver thought they were one. The islands, volcanic in origin, are forbidding in appearance. Menzies considered them 'the most dreary barren and desolate country I ever beheld',[2] while Baker described Albemarle as being 'nothing but a large Cinder, without any sign of Verdure or Vegetation.'[3] But when Whidbey and Menzies landed at the northern end of Albemarle, like many later visitors they were astonished to find it teeming with life and populated by a curious blend of tropical and polar beasts and birds: 'with Seals & Penguins in vast abundance, whilst the surface of the adjacent sea...swarmed with large Lizards swimming about in different directions & basking at their ease'.[4] They saw none of the famous giant tortoises, from which the islands derived their name, as they lived high up in the vegetation on the slopes of the volcanoes. Nor did Menzies become aware of the unique nature of the islands. Each, in Jacques Cousteau's phrase, 'seems to be a closed universe' in which animals have evolved over the centuries without outside contacts.

The Galapagos were left behind on February 10. Within a week Vancouver had become so impatient with the poor sailing of the *Chatham* that he decided to part company with her and hurry on to Juan Fernandez, where he ordered Puget to join him. Puget was usually

---

[1] Menzies, 24 January 1795.   [2] *Ibid.*, 7 February 1795.
[3] Baker, 8 February 1795.   [4] Menzies, 7 February 1795.

on good terms with Vancouver, but he resented a criticism of the *Chatham*'s station-keeping that was appended to this order – 'a Sort of Complaint or animadversion on our conduct in not strictly following the motions of the Discovery since our quitting Monterey'. Only the day before Puget had remarked in the privacy of his rough journal upon the 'amazing Distance of the Discovery from the Chatham at most times in fresh Breezes', adding that 'her Superiority of Sailing gives her the Choice of that Distance.' This made it difficult to maintain contact, especially at night, and Puget had 'often wondered that a separation did not take Place.' Vancouver seems to have been strangely reluctant to recognize the *Chatham*'s difficulties. She was left with no guide except the movements of the *Discovery*; 'no signal [was] made for a [change of] Course'.[1]

At first the *Discovery*, now sailing alone, made good progress; Vancouver described it as 'not only expeditious, but very pleasant.'[2] But two misfortunes awaited her. The first occurred on March 8, when she encountered heavy squalls. In the worst of these, as Vancouver later reported to the Admiralty, it was discovered that the head of the mainmast was 'so badly sprung, about eight feet below the hounds, that with every security which was possible to be given at sea, we were only able to carry on it the Mizen-top-mast and Mizen-top-sail, and even these with much caution'.[3] The ship's rate of sailing was considerably reduced and as a consequence the much-maligned *Chatham* was sighted astern on March 19 and joined company the next morning.

Meanwhile, on March 14, Menzies had informed Vancouver that some of the crew had contracted scurvy. This Vancouver found 'inexplicable', a reaction that reflects the lack of knowledge that still existed about the cause, prevention and cure of the disease. The outbreak puzzled him because, as he explains, 'there had not been the slightest abatement or relaxation of the [preventive] measures I had adopted at the commencement of our voyage'.[4] These in great part followed the example set by his idol Cook, who was widely credited with having introduced health measures that prevented the fearful death tolls from scurvy that had been characteristic of long sea voyages for centuries. Cook recognized that good general health was the basic essential, and

---

[1] Puget, rough journal, 14 and 15 February 1795. B.L., Add MS 17550, ff. 25v, 26.
[2] Vancouver, III, 391
[3] Vancouver to Stephens, Valparaiso, 28 April 1795. P.R.O., Adm 1/2629, f. 91v.
[4] Vancouver, III, 393–4.

to promote this he attached great importance to the cleanliness of the crew's persons, bedding and quarters, to the provision of warm, dry clothing, and to the avoidance of undue fatigue. He had noted in a report to the Admiralty submitted after his second voyage that the *Resolution* (in which Vancouver served) had been 'kept clean betwixt decks and aird with fires or Smoaked with gunpowder mix'd with Water, or Vinegar...once or twice a week'.[1] A similar routine was followed in the *Discovery* and *Chatham*. Johnstone's log records that at one stage of the voyage the *Chatham* was 'Wash'd & smoak'd below' eleven times in a single month.[2]

Like Cook, Vancouver realized that if scurvy were to be avoided the salt beef, salt pork, salt fat, ship's biscuit and dried pease and beans that were the chief ingredients of the forbidding naval rations of the day had to be supplemented by antiscorbutics. When his ships were at sea, Cook placed great store by 'wort' (essence) of malt and sauerkraut. The former, he informed the Admiralty, was 'without doubt one of ye best Antiscorbutic Sea Medicines yet found out', while the latter could 'never be enough recommend[ed]' as it was 'not only a Wholesome Vegitable diat but high Antiscorbutic'.[3] We know today that essence of malt has no antiscorbutic value whatever and that sauerkraut has very little; but Vancouver shared fully Cook's faith in them. Much more important was what Beaglehole has well termed Cook's 'unremitting insistence on fresh food at every conceivable opportunity, fish, flesh and fowl...anything, as long as it was fresh'.[4] And Cook was prepared to set an example by eating whatever was available, whether or not it was palatable. The master's mate of the *Resolution* recalled that 'scarc[e]ly any thing Came wrong to him that was Green'.[5] It was to his care of the general health of his men and his insistence upon securing fresh provisions at every possible opportunity that his success in reducing the toll of scurvy was really due.

To Vancouver's evident relief what seemed to be a convincing explanation of the outbreak in the *Discovery* soon presented itself. The ship's cook confessed that, contrary to Vancouver's 'positive injunctions and orders' (in which Vancouver was again following Cook's example) he had given 'skimmings of the boiling salted meat' to the crew. The cook's honesty in confessing appealed to Vancouver and he inflicted

---

[1] Cook to the Admiralty, 1 August [?] 1775. Cook, *Journals*, II, 954.
[2] Johnstone, May and June 1792.
[3] Cook to the Admiralty, 1 August [?] 1775. Cook, *Journals*, II, 954.
[4] Beaglehole, *Life of Cook*, p. 704.   [5] Quoted in *ibid.*, p. 705.

no punishment. Perhaps for this reason he appears to have treated the matter as confidential at the time, as Hewett, surgeon's mate, states in one of the marginal notes in his copy of the *Voyage of Discovery* that he had never heard of any such confession. He adds the interesting details that 'the fat taken of[f] the Copper' was 'a perquisite of the Cooks' and that 'Several of the Gents on Board as [well] as myself & messmates bought this fat of the Cook...[to] eat it as Butter to our Bread'. And he makes the further comment: 'Seamen in long Voyages have few luxuries and the [fat] ought not to be curtailed but upon the most positive Proo[f] of its being pernicious which is not the case with fat taken f[rom] an Iron Boiler.' As he agreed that fat from a copper boiler was 'highly pernicious' one can assume that the so-called 'coppers' in the *Discovery* were iron vessels. Even Vancouver evinced some sympathy for the crew; he remarked upon 'the great insipidity of peas and beans alone, without the aid of butter, or other qualifying material' and admitted that it was 'not much to be wondered at that a deviation from restrictive rules in those respects should have taken place'.[1]

The skimmings from boiled salt meat may have been unhealthy, but they were not the cause of the scurvy, which is now known to be the result of a lack of vitamin C. The body's reserve 'pool' of the vitamin will last about 40 days if not replenished, and it may be noted that the outbreak in the *Discovery* occurred about 46 days after she left Cocos Island, the last source of fresh provisions. The supplies secured there were very limited, and Vancouver seems to have had a slight feeling of guilt on that account. In a report to Stephens he made no mention of scurvy, but remarked that Cocos Island had afforded 'some trivial refreshments in cocoa-nuts, fish, &c.; but, from the excellent state of health the crew of the two vessels then enjoyed, those things but little attracted our attention'.[2] Although he was acting surgeon of the *Discovery*, Menzies makes no mention of scurvy in his journal, the surviving portion of which ends a few days after he reported the outbreak to Vancouver. He refers to it briefly in two letters to Banks, but that is all. On medical matters generally his narrative is singularly uninformative. It was intended for Banks and others interested in natural history and in strange peoples and places. Presumably he kept medical notes in a surgeon's book, but nothing of the kind is known to have survived.

[1] Vancouver, III, 395.
[2] Vancouver to Stephens, Valparaiso, 28 April 1795. P.R.O., Adm 1/2629, f. 90v.

By the time the *Chatham* rejoined the *Discovery* Vancouver had decided that he would have to seek a port of refuge. Winter storms were sure to be encountered near Cape Horn, and this would be highly hazardous unless proper repairs were made to the *Discovery*'s mainmast. Vancouver's instructions, which ordered him 'on no account whatever' to touch at any Spanish port south of 30° N latitude, provided for an exception in the event of an accident endangering 'immediate safety'; but he took steps nevertheless to protect himself against possible future criticism. He had always considered his instructions to be secret, but on this occasion he made an exception. Puget was summoned from the *Chatham* and Vancouver consulted him and his own lieutenants about the course he ought to pursue. Valparaiso was relatively near at hand, and the decision to proceed thither was unanimous. No doubt the scurvy outbreak stressed further the necessity of this decision. The disease was spreading in the *Discovery* and it had broken out in the *Chatham* as well. To continue on a voyage that would last several months without taking steps to curb it would have been simple folly. At Valparaiso, where the ships anchored on March 26, Vancouver put the crews of both ships on a diet that included fresh beef and greens, new soft bread, apples, grapes and onions, and the men were soon restored to health.

Foreign ships were not very welcome at this time in Spanish American ports, but Vancouver was most fortunate in the officials he met. He found that the Governor of Valparaiso, Don Louis Alava, was a brother of Brigadier José Manual Alava, whom he had known as Spanish commissioner at Nootka. Alava was most friendly, but explained that before work could proceed on Vancouver's ships he would have to send a messenger to the capital, Santiago, and secure the approval of Don Ambrosio O'Higgins, Governor and Captain General of Chili. The latter not only ordered that every assistance should be given to Vancouver, but invited him to pay him a visit. Both he and Alava were evidently aware of the nature of Vancouver's expedition and knew no doubt that its surveys were being shared with Spain. And it is likely that O'Higgins, Irish born but immersed in South America for many years, welcomed the prospect of meeting with an interesting group of English-speaking naval officers.

It is somewhat surprising that Vancouver accepted the President's invitation. During the past year he had complained repeatedly about his health; as recently as the call at Cocos Island he had described himself as being 'in a feeble and debilitated state'. As the trip to

Santiago promised to be strenuous, one must assume that some improvement had taken place. The distance was about 90 miles, to be traversed on horseback. A new road was under construction, but only the sections close to Valparaiso and Santiago had been completed. The old road, much of which had still to be followed, was not much more than a beaten track, and new and old alike resorted to switchbacks to climb lofty hills and mountainsides.

O'Higgins instructed Alava to provide whatever riding horses, pack animals, provisions and equipment would be required for the journey and sent two Irish-born dragoons to act as guides and escort. Vancouver delayed his departure until the work of refitting the *Discovery* and *Chatham* was going forward satisfactorily. He was dismayed to find that the *Discovery*'s mainmast was in even worse condition than had been realized, and to learn that no spar sufficiently large to replace it was available. The only alternative was to patch up the original as well as circumstances permitted. On 1 April 1795, a few days after the ships reached Valparaiso, the crews celebrated the fourth anniversary of their departure from Falmouth, and it was not surprising that after such a lapse of time much of the rigging was found to be rotten and many of the sails in poor condition. A more thorough refit than was first anticipated was clearly necessary, and before Vancouver set out for Santiago, accompanied by Puget, Baker, Johnstone, Swaine and Menzies, carpenters, caulkers, sail-makers, coopers and armourers were hard at work on the two ships.

At the time of his death Vancouver had prepared the text of the printed *Voyage* as far as his arrival at Valparaiso. His brother John then completed it, basing the narrative on Vancouver's journals. He explains that there was one gap: 'The notes which he made on his journey from the port of Valparaiso to his arrival at St. Jago de Chili...were unfortunately lost; and I am indebted to Captain Puget for having assisted me with his observations on that occasion.'[1] The surviving fragment of Puget's account, now in the British Library,[2] ends when the party was about 15 miles from Santiago. It is in Puget's handwriting, but is in the first person, as if written by Vancouver himself. John Vancouver followed it closely in substance and sometimes in phraseology, but he added details that must have come from other sources.

What John Vancouver terms the 'numerous cavalcade' left Valparaiso on April 3 and reached Santiago on the 5th. Vancouver (or Puget) was astonished by the 'wretched little hovels, or huts, made principally

---

[1] Vancouver, I, xxxi. [2] B.L., Add MS. 17552.

of mud' that made up the small villages along the way. Those in which he spent the night, sleeping on an earthern floor, were found to be infested with vermin. Foreigners were a rarity; crowds gathered wherever the party stopped to eat or sleep. Vancouver had hoped to enter Santiago quietly and without fanfare, as he and his companions were very conscious of the shabbiness of their uniforms, threadbare after four years at sea, but O'Higgins had arranged otherwise, and they rode into the capital on elaborately caparisoned steeds.

They were warmly welcomed and handsomely entertained, not only by the Governor, but by the Bishop and leading officials and citizens. Vancouver evidently realized that the privilege of his visit was one sparingly accorded, and his account of his journey and sojourn in Santiago, as presented by his brother, runs to more than 15,000 words. The fact that years had passed since he had seen a community of comparable size no doubt stimulated his interest. He describes the city, the palaces of the Governor and Bishop, and the large new mint and cathedral that were under construction; gives glimpses of social life and comments on the character of the government, even going so far as to quote representative ordinances. He admired O'Higgins and notes some of the things he had accomplished for Chili, but here as elsewhere in New Spain he was struck by the indolence of the native population, and, on a more personal note, by the general lack of cleanliness. Dust and dirt were not confined to the primitive huts he had seen along the road from the coast. The floors of the apartments assigned to him and his officers in the palace were so covered with filth 'that it would rather have required a shovel than a brush for its removal'.[1]

When Vancouver left Valparaiso he thought it would take about a fortnight to complete the refitting in progress on the *Discovery* and *Chatham* and he intended to be back by the time the ships were preparing to put to sea. He returned on April 16, and was happy to find that her refurbished mainmast had been brought on board the *Discovery* the previous day. He explained in a letter to Stephens how its frailties had been dealt with: 'we had fortunately on board two stout fishes, with which, and by shortening the mast about three feet and turning it end for end, in order to bring the most defective part below the lower deck, we have added every security to the mast our situation is capable of affording'. Unfortunately a new problem immediately came to light. The mainmast was being rigged the day of Vancouver's return, and it was then discovered that the main-yard

---

[1] Vancouver, III, 428.

was rotten in the middle and badly sprung. As was the case with the mainmast, no spar of sufficient size to replace it was available, and again it was necessary to resort to makeshift measures: 'the only means we had to remedy that defect', Vancouver told Stephens, 'was by making a temporary yard out of a spare main-topmast, and the yard arms of the decaying yard'[1] – an uncomfortable compromise that resulted in a substitute main-yard consisting of three pieces. Fashioning it took time, and it was not ready for rigging until April 27. Vancouver spent the interval learning something about the trade, commerce and defences of Valparaiso. Here, as in California, he was puzzled and surprised by the weakness of the fortifications: 'It appeared to us to be very extraordinary, that, under the existing circumstances of Europe, and during a war between Spain and France, the fortifications of Valparaiso should remain in such a neglected, ruinous, and defenceless state, and that no measures should either be resorted to, or appear to be in contemplation, for putting them into a more respectable condition'.[2]

The weakened state of the masts, yards, rigging and sails of his ships resulted in two major changes in Vancouver's plans. First, he decided to take on sufficient stores and provisions at Valparaiso to enable him to return to England by way of St Helena, instead of calling at the Cape of Good Hope as had been intended. Secondly, with great regret, he concluded that he could not attempt to make the survey of the South American west coast south of 44° S that was contemplated in his instructions. It is doubtful, indeed, if this had ever been a practicable project; certainly it was not one that could be tacked on at the end of a voyage of exploration that had already lasted more than four years. The coast in question rivals those of British Columbia and Alaska in complexity; like them it is a mass of islands and inlets. By the time the ships finally sailed on May 6 they had spent six weeks at Valparaiso, and it is likely that any further lengthy delay in their homeward passage would have resulted in serious morale problems. Officers and men alike were weary, impatient and eager to return to England.

Vancouver's report to Stephens was dated April 28. It was his last effort to communicate with the Admiralty. In it he refers to his own arrival in England, which he assumes 'cannot be long after this letter makes its appearance'; but Stephens did not receive the letter until

[1] Vancouver to Stephens, Valparaiso, 28 April 1795. For the complete text of this interesting report see P.R.O., Adm 1/2629, ff. 91–4.
[2] Vancouver, III, 458.

December 26, eight months after it was written and three months after Vancouver himself had returned to London. Menzies fared better as a correspondent. When the *Discovery* arrived at Valparaiso she found there the South Sea whaler *Lightning*, hailing from Bristol, which was on the point of sailing for London. Menzies immediately wrote to Banks and gave the letter to her captain. Banks received it on June 30, in the remarkably short time of three months. What Menzies described as 'nearly a copy', dated April 28, was sent with Vancouver's letter and no doubt suffered a similar delay.

Little need be said about the two-month passage of the *Discovery* and *Chatham* from Valparaiso to St Helena. As they approached and rounded Cape Horn the weather was fully as bad as Vancouver had anticipated. Violent squalls were frequent and took their toll of the ships' worn sails and rigging. Matters improved greatly as they sailed northward in the Atlantic. As they were favored with clear weather, when they approached the supposed location of Isla Grande, alleged to have been discovered by Antoine La Roche in 1674 but not seen since, Vancouver kept a sharp lookout, but saw nothing. As usual, he complained about the poor sailing of the *Chatham*; even under reduced canvas the *Discovery* easily outdistanced her. After losing sight of her several times the *Discovery* finally lost all contact with her on June 9. But, again as usual, the *Chatham* made better progress when she was not obliged to follow the *Discovery*'s sailing pattern, and when the latter was about to enter St Helena Bay on the morning of July 3, the *Chatham* was sighted in the offing.

By European reckoning the date was July 2, as the *Discovery*, sailing eastward, had gained a day when she circled the globe. Vancouver had chosen to ignore this when dealing with the Spaniards on the west coast of America, but he recognized that he should now 'subscribe to the estimation of time, as understood by Europeans and the rest of the civilized world, to which we were now fast approaching'.[1] The change took effect at noon on July 6 (ship's time), which became noon on July 5.

The Admiralty was anxious to control the release of information about Vancouver's explorations, and Vancouver had been instructed to enjoin not only his officers but 'the whole crew, not to divulge where they have been until they have permission so to do'. Menzies took some liberties in his letters to Banks, but for the most part the order was strictly observed. 'I am sorry my worthy friend', Manby wrote to

---

[1] Vancouver, III, 475.

Captain Barlow, 'that I am not at liberty to make known our past Transactions of the Voyage or what will be our future route, as the Lords of the Admiralty have commanded silence on that subject, which must be attended too, especially by us, who expect to reap Promotion from the voyage.'[1] Vancouver applied the restriction even to his own personal correspondence. When he wrote to his brother John from Nootka in September 1794, just after he had completed the monumental coastal survey, the temptation to give some inkling of his accomplishment must have been very great, but he explained that he could only discuss his 'transactions' officially: 'You must therefore my dearest Van be content in being informed of my wellfare thus far'.[2]

The Admiralty had also instructed Vancouver to 'demand' that those on board surrender all 'log-books, journals, drawings, &c. they may have kept'. He was to do this 'before you leave the sloop' – which surely meant the end of the voyage. But, knowing that at St Helena 'opportunities would frequently occur...to communicate with our friends in England', Vancouver decided that the Admiralty order should be read publicly and enforced before arrival there. As a result, none of the surviving logs of the *Discovery* extends beyond 2 July 1795. There is one exception for the *Chatham*: Henry Humphrys, her Master, seems to have retained his log, or in any event continued it to chronicle the unexpected assignment that took her to Brazil – of which more later.

The only log kept in the *Discovery* that was not surrendered was that of Archibald Menzies. He was serving in a dual capacity – as botanist, in the interests of the Royal collections, under instructions from Banks and the Home Secretary, and as surgeon of the ship. He considered that his journals were being kept in his capacity of botanist, and that the only part of his records subject to Vancouver's authority was the surgeon's sick-book. He had foreseen that Vancouver would demand his journals, and in his letters to Banks from Valparaiso stated that when he did so he would 'seal up mine & address them to you'.[3] In the event he asked instead for permission to retain them (in Vancouver's words) 'for their more perfect completion', and to this Vancouver agreed. But a clash of wills on the matter was merely postponed.

The very day that Vancouver arrived at St Helena he was caught up in a sequence of events arising from the state of affairs in Europe.

---

[1] Manby to Barlow, Monterey, 9 January 1793. Special Collections, Library of the University of British Columbia.

[2] Vancouver to John Vancouver, Nootka, 8 September 1794. Yale University Library.

[3] Menzies to Banks, Valparaiso, 26 March 1795. Brabourne Papers, Mitchell Library, Sydney.

France had subjugated Holland, and hostilities broke out between Holland and Great Britain. The East India Company became fearful that the French might gain control of the Dutch colony at the Cape of Good Hope, and early in January 1795 its chairman proposed to the Secretary of War that the British should prepare to take possession of it. He stressed its importance – 'whoever is Master of the Cape will be able to protect, or annoy, our ships out and home' – and the suggestion was acted upon. On April 3 a naval force commanded by Vice-Admiral Elphinstone sailed for the Cape. Six weeks later a fleet of transports, carrying 3000 troops commanded by General Clarke, sailed for São Salvador, Brazil, there to await orders and an escort. Elphinstone had taken with him the armed East Indiaman *Arniston*, and on his way to the Cape he detached her to St Helena, to which she brought news of the planned assault on the Cape. The same day that Vancouver arrived a ship approaching St Helena was found to be the Dutch East Indiaman *Macassar*, which had left the Cape before it was known that war had broken out between Holland and Great Britain. In his narrative Vancouver simply states that he 'sent an officer on board...and took possession of her as a prize',[1] but others besides himself were involved. Colonel Robert Brooke, the Governor of St Helena, writing to Elphinstone a few days after the event, stated that the *Macassar* was 'seized on by my order' and credited Vancouver with merely having 'assisted me with his advice in conducting the business'.[2] The *Arniston* also claimed to have had a share in the capture, and later Elphinstone, as naval commander-in-chief of the area, contended that he was entitled to a share of any prize money that might be awarded. As we shall see, the matter involved Vancouver in a long wrangle that ended only a few months before his death.

He was glad to find that the *Discovery*'s makeshift main-yard could be replaced with a sound spar at St Helena, and various other defects were made good, including the ever-recurring leak in the bow. Those on board the *Chatham* had had an exceedingly uncomfortable time when she was rounding Cape Horn; Vancouver comments upon the violence of her motion, which caused her decks and sides to leak. She had to be kept battened down much of the time, which, Puget reported, kept her 'comparatively speaking, almost under water during the greater part of the passage'.[3] The health of her crew suffered, but they

---

[1] Vancouver, III, 473.
[2] Brooke to Elphinstone, St Helena, 9 July 1795. W. G. Perrin (ed.), *The Keith Papers*, vol. I (London, 1927), p. 325. (Navy Records Society)   [3] Vancouver, III, 474.

recovered quickly, and the ship herself did not require any extensive repairs.

On July 7 H.M.S. *Sphynx* (24 guns) put in an overnight appearance. She was hurrying to São Salvador with dispatches from Elphinstone to General Clarke, without the support of whose troops little could be accomplished at the Cape. On the 11th she was followed by the merchantman *Orpheus*, with a letter for Colonel Brooke, duplicates of the dispatches to Clarke, and others to be forwarded to London. Brooke reported the sequel to Elphistone: 'On receipt of the letter I consulted Captain Vancouver, and it was agreed that for fear of accidents the Chatham should proceed after the Sphynx, without it being known here where she was going to, and that Captain Vancouver himself should proceed to England with your despatches.'[1] The *Chatham* immediately prepared for sea and sailed for Brazil on the 12th. There Vancouver hoped that Puget would be able to join a convoy that he could accompany to England.

Meanwhile the *Arniston* was readying to sail for the Cape, taking 400 troops and such arms and supplies as could be mustered at St Helena. To these Vancouver contributed a number of items that were no longer needed in the *Discovery*. He explained to Elphinstone that as Brooke had informed him of 'the great embarrassment your expedition is under for want of light artillery and camp stores, I have taken the liberty... to supply four three pound field pieces with their furniture complete and a tolerable assortment of ammunition, together with a marquee, three or four small tents, three cases of axes, one of pick-axes, and some shovels; and though I cannot possibly be flattered that so trivial an augmentation is likely to be of any importance to the grand object you are about to undertake, yet secluded as we have been from serving our country in a miliary capacity during this critical and anxious war, I shall experience the greatest satisfaction should those things in the smallest degree tend to facilitate your operations.'[2]

Although he had been glad to be of assistance, Vancouver had some doubts about the propriety of his actions. In a second letter to Elphinstone he remarked that owing to the 'confidence and consultations' of Governor Brooke he had been 'induced to take probably a more active part in the military operations going forward in this island than the spirit of my commission and the orders I am under may contain; however, on maturely considering the pressing circumstances

[1] Brooke to Elphinstone, 12 July 1795. *Keith Papers*, I, p. 333.
[2] Vancouver to Elphinstone, St Helena, 10 July 1795. *Ibid.*, pp. 328–9.

of your important expedition, I have conceived such a mode of proceeding as an indispensable point of duty'.[1] No doubt he was thinking about his own passage to England. The captain of the *Orpheus* had informed him (wrongly, as he discovered later) that the French National Assembly had granted the *Discovery* and *Chatham* a safe conduct. His actions in assisting the capture of the *Macassar* and supplying arms to Elphinstone were hardly consistent with this privilege.

As he was approaching St Helena Vancouver had been disappointed to see a convoy leaving. He would have liked to have joined it and to have proceeded to England under its protection, but the condition of his ships made an immediate departure impracticable. He had now to decide whether to take the risk of sailing unescorted, or to suffer a delay of uncertain length until another convoy appeared. But first the *Macassar* required his attention. She was carrying a valuable cargo, but needed repairs before she would be sufficiently seaworthy to undertake the voyage to England. Vancouver had seconded Johnstone from the *Chatham* to take command of her, and he now transferred seventeen able seamen from the *Discovery* to give Johnstone the nucleus of an experienced and reliable crew. These matters having been attended to, he decided to chance a lone sailing. The *Discovery's* new main-yard was brought on board and rigged on July 15, and she sailed the next evening.

Vancouver had learned that the convoy he had sighted consisted of twenty-four East Indiamen and a number of Dutch prizes, escorted by H.M.S. *Sceptre* (64 guns), commanded by Captain William Essington. As some of the prizes were in very poor condition he knew that it would be travelling slowly, and he was hopeful that he might be able to overtake it. This he succeeded in doing on August 21. The convoy plodded on, for the most part in pleasant weather, keeping well to the westward, where it would be less likely to encounter a French squadron. The west coast of Ireland was sighted on September 12. The next day Essington led his charges into the Shannon, where all were moored safely, and where they were to await a stronger escort before proceeding to England.

Vancouver left immediately to report to the Admiralty in London, taking with him 'such books, papers and charts as had been previously selected as being essential to the illustration of the services' he had performed. Baker assumed command of the *Discovery*. It was an emotional moment for Vancouver, since it meant breaking ties with

---

[1] Vancouver to Elphinstone, St Helena, 13 July 1795. *Ibid.*, p. 330.

the officers and crewmen with whom he had shared perils, hardships and successes for nearly four years and a half, and leaving the ship in which they had lived and had been intimately associated over that long period. At the conclusion of the longest of all exploring and surveying expeditions he confessed to having three causes for satisfaction: he had brought safely home a remarkably high proportion – unprecedented in voyages of the kind – of the men who had sailed with him; he had spent several years in contact with native peoples, and his relations with them had been marred only once by a fatal clash of real consequence; and so far as the primary purpose of his voyage was concrned, he was confident that he had proven that no 'navigable communication between the waters of the Pacific and Atlantic oceans' existed within the limits of his survey.

Baker brought the *Discovery* into the Thames on October 20. Vancouver visited her at Longreach a day or two later, and she soon moved upriver to Deptford Yard. Late in the month she was joined there by the *Chatham*.

Some details of the *Chatham*'s voyage after she parted company with the *Discovery* at St Helena are given in Puget's rough journal and in the concise log kept by her master, Henry Humphrys. She had left St Helena on July 12 and arrived at São Salvador on the 27th. It had been an uncomfortable passage. Puget remarks upon 'the weakened state of my people' and notes that while the ship was at São Salvador 'the Ship's Company were Supplied with Oranges (4 each Man a Day) from the Representation of Mr. Walker Surgeon, as the Scurvy had once more made its appearance on Jos^h Patten Marine. I therefore purchased 3000 which cost four Pounds Sterling to be bought – which were served out according to the Proportion I have mentioned as Several of the People were complaining of Sore Gums and other Symptoms of Scurvy.' Beef was 'absolutely so bad...it was not worth bringing off' and mutton was 'wretched' but the ship was well supplied with 'Sallad Greens, Yams, Oranges, Pine Apples, Limes and other Fruits and Vegetables'.[1]

Humphrys records that at São Salvador the *Chatham* found the *Sphynx* and the thirteen transports, carrying General Clark and his troops, that the *Sphynx* was to escort to the Cape. They sailed almost immediately, but on the 30th, just as the *Chatham* was preparing to leave for England, the *Sphynx* limped back to port, having lost her foremast and suffered other substantial damage in a collision. Her commander, Captain Brisac, 'found himself under the necessity of

[1] B.L., Add. MS 17,548, f. 110.

detaining us (being ready for Sea) in order to get from us Iron, Nails & Steel & for the convenience of our Forge, two Sailmakers & our Carpenter.' Later, presumably to avoid further detention, the forge and two of the *Chatham*'s crew were transferred to the *Sphynx*. The *Chatham* sailed on August 19, cheering the *Sphynx* as she left the harbour.[1]

Her voyage homeward was not without incident. Puget's rough log reveals that disaster was narrowly averted on September 18, as she was nearing the Tropic of Cancer: 'About 1 We had a most fortunate escape from Fire. The paper of a Cartridge, flew after the discharge of One of the Musquits amongst some loose powder to which it immediately communicated amidst near three Hundred Ball Cartridges that had been put there for Safety. James Robertson who was at the Helm, however had the presence of Mind to snatch up a four pound Cartridge, to which the fire had Caught & to throw it Overboard, after which it was immediately smothered.'[2] Except for some difficulties caused by the worn condition of her sails the *Chatham*'s voyage was otherwise uneventful. She 'Saw the land of Old England' on October 16 and arrived at Plymouth the next day.

Two brief notes will serve to conclude this chronicle. The transports that the *Sphynx* had been obliged to leave without an escort reached the Cape safely and arrived just in time to enable Elphinstone and Clark to secure the capitulation of the Cape Colony on September 16. And the *Macassar*, shepherded by Johnstone, reached England safely on November 22.

[1] P.R.O., Adm. 55/26, ff. 286–305. The *Chatham* recruited one seaman in Brazil and, by order of Captain Brisac, carried five men to England as supernumeraries.

[2] B.L., Add. MS 17,551, f. 108.

III

AFTERMATH

Unfinished Business

THE high quality and magnitude of Vancouver's accomplishment as a marine surveyor have been widely recognized. Only when compared with his model and hero, Captain Cook, has he been found wanting. In his *Memoirs of Hydrography* Commander Dawson paid him this tribute: 'If Vancouver had not quite the varied talents and enterprise of Cook, the enormous amount of work compassed by him, show that at least he was as indefatigable....A vast extent of most intricate coast was by him delineated in the most faithful manner.'[1] Beaglehole characterized his great voyage as being 'celebrated for its detailed examination...of a coast so remarkably complicated that Vancouver's systematic and painstaking survey ranks with the most distinguished work of the kind ever done.'[2] Even William Laird Clowes, who would go no further than to grant that Vancouver possessed 'considerable ability and resolution' conceded that he was 'a good sailor and an accomplished surveyor'. But he went on to contend that 'some other qualifications for command were wanting. He was austere and unsympathetic. The corporal punishments on board the *Discovery* were excessive, and some of the Midshipmen were treated with harshness and even cruelty.'[3]

Before examining the bases for these and other charges it is significant to note that Vancouver's immediate preoccupation, after he rejoined the *Discovery* at Longreach, was the future welfare of her complement. His first letter to Evan Nepean, who had recently succeeded Stephens as Secretary of the Admiralty, was a plea entered on behalf of Matthew Brown, a deserter from H.M.S. *Alfred* who had given himself up to Vancouver at Nootka in September 1794: 'His conduct since coming on board this ship having been such as to merit my approbation, and being also a very good seaman, I am induced to

[1] L. S. Dawson, *Memoirs of Hydrography, 1750–1805* (Eastbourne, 1885), p. 17.
[2] J. C. Beaglehole, *The Exploration of the Pacific* (3rd ed., London, 1966), p. 322.
[3] W. Laird Clowes, *The Royal Navy: A History* (London, 1901), IV, 145.

intercede with their Lordships on his behalf; and hope their Lordships will approve of what I have done in bearing him as part of the Discovery's complement.'[1] The approval Vancouver sought was given promptly. Two days later he wrote again to Nepean, this time on behalf of seven men from the *Discovery* who had been ordered by the senior officer commanding at Shannon to join the East Indiaman *Burbridge*. When the latter arrived at Longreach it was learned that they had been impressed from her at the Downs.[2] Whether Vancouver's intercession was successful or not does not appear.

He next turned his attention to the future of his junior officers and midshipmen. Swaine and Manby had sailed as midshipmen, but as both had served their time at sea and passed their examinations before they left England, Vancouver had appointed them to lieutenancies in the *Discovery* as vacancies occurred. He now wrote to the Admiralty, describing them as 'two very active, diligent, and deserving officers', and asking that they be granted seniority as lieutenants from the dates of their appointments to the *Discovery*. This plea the Admiralty rejected, explaining that it was 'contrary to official practice to confirm vacancies of this description' and Swaine and Manby had to be content with new commissions dated 27 October 1795, the day the Admiralty received Vancouver's submission.[3]

In the same letter Vancouver listed three masters' mates (Barrie, Sykes and Stewart) and three midshipmen (Ballard, Harris and the Hon. Charles Stuart) who 'had served their time but had not yet passed their examinations and whose diligent and attentive behavior during the late Voyage merits my warmest recommendation to their Lordships favor and protection'. In a postscript he added the name of Humphrys, from the *Chatham*. All seven received their commissions within a month. Vancouver's commendation and, no doubt, a word in the right quarters from Vice-Admiral Sir Alan Gardner on behalf of his two nephews, Barrie and Humphrys, smoothed the way. 'When we appear'd before the great men to pass our examination', Barrie wrote to his mother, 'they tould us they thought it would be presumption in them to ask us any questions so they pass'd us bye wishing us all a speedy promotion.'[4] Meanwhile Vancouver had asked that all midshipmen in the *Discovery* should be exempted from a general order instructing him

---

[1] Vancouver to Nepean, 21 October 1795. P.R.O., Adm 1/2629, f. 51.
[2] *Ibid.*, 23 October 1795, f. 102.
[3] *Ibid.*, 26 October 1795, f. 131.
[4] Barrie to Mrs George Clayton (his mother), 6 November 1795. Barrie MSS, Perkins Library, Duke University.

to discharge her company into H.M.S. *Caroline*, and this was agreed to. It is interesting to find that he asked that two seamen who had 'attended me during the voyage and have been considered my servants' should be included in the exemption.[1]

These submissions do not seem to be in keeping with the austere, unsympathetic, harsh and cruel character pictured by Clowes, and we must next examine some of the evidence upon which his and other unfavorable judgments have been based.

The charges of Vancouver's most severe and unrelenting critic, George Goodman Hewett, surgeon's mate in the *Discovery*, were probably known only to a few, as they were recorded in the privacy of marginal notes scattered through the pages of his copy of the *Voyage of Discovery*. One of his first contentions is that Vancouver's reputation was such that he could not recruit an efficient crew: 'For this Voyage Capt. Roberts had collected as fine a Crew as ever sailed from England but when the Command was given to Capt. V none of those men woud enter and the Discovery notwithstanding the Admiralty Orders that none but able Seamen should be taken in her was obliged to be sent out with a ragged Complement of Fishermens Boys and other Fresh water Sailors as Vans. Character for Passion & Tyranny was well known among the good Seamen of the Navy.' Certainly there were some troublesome characters in the ship, but this indictment is grossly unfair to the crew as a whole, who obviously performed well. Vancouver, Puget, Menzies and Bell all had high praise for the men who manned the small boats that surveyed the coastal inlets. The tribute paid to them by Puget at the end of the second surveying season is particularly striking: 'It is impossible silently to pass over so hard and Labourious an Undertaking as the Duty of the Boats, without [noting] that indefatigable exertion and Attention that has on all Occasions been paid by the Officers under whose Direction they were conducted and also the Seamen who performed the Labourious task of the Oar. At this they frequently laboured from Morning till Night & allways performed that Duty with alacrity, not even a Murmur was heard. Necessity obliged us frequently to pull till Eleven at Night, which Still made no difference in the Hour of Departure.'[2]

Vancouver can rightly be described as passionate by nature if by this it is meant that he was subject to sudden and irrational outbursts of temper and violence. A few days after he joined the *Discovery* at

[1] Vancouver to Nepean, 27 October 1795. P.R.O., Adm 1/2629, f. 113.
[2] Puget, 19 September 1793.

Longreach in 1791 young Robert Barrie remarked in a letter to his mother that 'Cp^t Vancouver is in my opinion a verry good fellow but verry passionate'.[1] Instances, among others, have been cited in which he nearly strangled a native in Tahiti and so frightened visiting friendly chiefs in the Sandwich Islands that they fled the ship in terror. Even Broughton, commanding the *Chatham*, did not escape the rough edge of Vancouver's tongue. Exasperated by her poor sailing and by her apparent failure to respond to signals to put on more sail, Vancouver sent for Broughton and (in Hewett's words) 'in a most violent Passion reprimanded him for it'. Such outbursts seem to have been of short duration, and Vancouver seldom bore a grudge.

This shortness of temper was in all probability due to the state of Vancouver's health, which caused some concern even before the expedition sailed. From Falmouth, at the end of March 1791, he had assured Nepean that it had 'wonderfully improved', but in May he suffered a serious relapse. Banks states that Menzies 'Savd Vancouvers Life by putting him upon a nutritive diet when he thought himself within a few days of his dissolution by having adhered to a shore one this was soon after the ship left Teneriff.'[2] Menzies attended Vancouver throughout the voyage, but his journal throws no light on the nature of his illness. The only specific mention of an ailment is Barrie's remark at Monterey, in January 1793, that 'Capt. V. has had a fit of the gout but is got better'.[3] By 1794 ill-health was limiting his activities; early in 1795 he confessed to being 'in a very feeble and debilitated state'. His brother John used virtually the same phrase to describe his health after he returned to England, and Vancouver was to die in May 1798, a month before his 41st birthday.

The cause of Vancouver's death has long been a matter of discussion. Godwin tended to agree with a suggestion that he had contracted tuberculosis. Admiral Anderson thought that he was probably a victim of Graves's disease.[4] These were mere guesses, as neither biographer had any medical qualification. Recently Surgeon Vice-Admiral Sir James Watt has carefully reviewed all available evidence bearing upon Vancouver's health and behaviour and he is confident that he suffered

[1] Barrie to Mrs George Clayton, Longreach, 15 January 1791. Barrie MSS, Perkins Library, Duke University.

[2] Memo. by Banks, n.p., n.d. Probably 1796. Brabourne Papers, Mitchell Library, Sydney.

[3] Barrie to Mrs George Clayton, Monterey, 1 January 1793. Barrier MSS, Perkins Library, Duke University.

[4] Anderson, *Surveyor of the Sea*, p. 67.

from myxoedema (thyroid deficiency), with or without an associated Addison's disease. His physical symptoms, irritability and appearance all confirm this conclusion.

It seems clear that the *Discovery* was not a happy ship. Vancouver was respected for his abilities and accomplishments, but he was not liked. Manby's comment in a private letter to a friend written in January 1793 is revealing: 'Good health continues in our little squadron, though I am sorry to add not that good fellowship which ought to subsist with adventurers traversing these distance Seas, owing the conduct of our Commander in Chief who is grown Haughty Proud and Insolent, which has kept himself and Officers in a continual state of wrangling during the whole of the Voyage.'[1] Vancouver's ways were frequently arbitrary and rigid, though sometimes from the best of motives. In the first chapter of his narrative, when explaining the measures taken to safeguard the health of the crew, he explains that he 'had ever considered fire the most likely and efficacious means to keep up a constant circulation of fresh and pure air throughout the ship; in the fore part of every day good fires were burning between decks, and in the well'.[2] The difficulty was that Vancouver insisted that the fires be lit regardless of conditions. Banks notes that Menzies 'remonstrated severely against V.'s Practises particularly against the inhumanity of Smoking between decks while men in Fevers were laying there in their Hammocks & at last Prevaild'.[3] Hewett records incidents that suggest vindictiveness: 'All hands have been kept on Deck in bad Weather and although the Wind was fair yet have been kept Tacking the Ship merely to satisfy the Caprice of Captain Vancouver who swore there was a general neglect of Duty throughout the Ship and as they would not Work when there was Occasion they should when there was not.' In the course of the second visit of the ships to the Sandwich Islands what Bell describes as 'some trivial inattention of duty on the part of one or two of the midshipmen' prompted Vancouver not only to forbid any midshipman to go ashore except on duty, but to prohibit visiting between the vessels as well. 'An order so strange and unaccountable', Bell notes, 'created no little surprise and astonishment... and was at once justly conceived as harsh and unhandsome.' He continues: 'before I close this subject I cannot

---

[1] Manby to Barlow, 9 January 1793. Special Collections, Library of the Univeristy of British Columbia.

[2] Vancouver, I. 7.

[3] Memo. by Banks, n.p., n.d. Brabourne Papers, Mitchell Library, Sydney.

help observing that Captn. Vancouver has rendered himself universally obnoxious by his orders not only in the present instance to the Young Gentlemen but at various times to all ranks of Officers in the two Vessels under his command'.[1]

Midshipmen seem to have suffered particularly from the captain's displeasure, as, indeed, they did in many ships of the time. Bell, clerk of the *Chatham*, refers to 'my friends, the poor Kick'd about, abused, despised Midshipmen (of the Discovery) for whom it is conceived that nothing can be bad enough, neither Language or treatment'.[2] Hewett states that all of them refused to dine with Vancouver except Sykes, who was the son of Vancouver's London agent. Amongst them was the Hon. Thomas Pitt, son and heir of the first Baron Camelford. The *Discovery* was his second ship; the first had been the ill-fated *Guardian*, which when bound for New South Wales crashed into an iceberg not long after leaving the Cape of Good Hope. Though she was awash below decks, the survivors who stayed with the ship managed to bring her back to the Cape, where the wreck still lay when the *Discovery* called at False Bay. Vancouver's first impression of Pitt was favourable, but he was an active, hot-tempered, undisciplined youth and they were soon at loggerheads. In Janaury 1793 Vancouver remarked upon his bad conduct in a letter to Nepean, and by February of the following year he was unwilling to put up with him any longer and discharged him into the storeship *Daedalus*, which would take him to New South Wales, whence he could find his way home to England. Not a word about Pitt's misdemeanours or punishments appears in any of the available logs or journals, but there is evidence that he spent some days in irons and was flogged three times. Mast-heading was the punishment most often meted out to midshipmen, but flogging was not without precedent. Pitt was whipped in the relative privacy of the cabin, but 'in the Presence of all the midshipmen who were summond on the occasion'.[3]

In justice to Vancouver it must be noted that the corporal punishment of midshipmen was not confined to the *Discovery*. In the *Chatham* Augustus Boyd Grant proved to be a thorn in Puget's side. He, too, was sent home in the *Daedalus*, and when she sailed Puget described Grant's behaviour in his rough journal. Grant had been 'punished on many occasions & corporal punishment had no effect'. He had been 'excluded from the Society of Gentlemen, subsisted on [the]

---

[1] Bell, 28 February 1793.   [2] *Ibid.*

[3] Memo. by Banks, n.p., n.d. Brabourne Papers, Mitchell Library, Sydney.

humanity of one of the foremast people with whom he lived, & whose habits he had contracted in a most shamefull Manner. Threat of Admonition had no Effect on his feeling for [he was] lost to all [sense] of Disgrace, Respect or Reformation...After being tried in the Messes of the Gentlemen & by the Gunner – he was reduced to the Necessity of living with the Boatswain & Ship's Cook – there he soon grew troublesome & was even discharged from their Society he then persuaded the Gunroom Cook a Marine to admit him to their Mess, with these however he soon quarelled – & from that time he subsisted on the Generosity of the ship's Company. Mr. Grant had frequently requested I would allow him to quit the Chatham & he having on this occasion pointed out his particular disagreeable Situation, in a letter & begging leave to return home induced me to comply with his [request].'[1]

Hewett states that three midshipmen were flogged. Presumably the third was Thomas Clarke, of the *Discovery*, who was sent home in the *Daedalus* along with Pitt and Grant. But Pitt is the important figure; nothing more is heard of the other two.

To flog a midshipman was socially questionable, but to flog the son of a peer was to court disaster, and to flog this particular one was sheer folly. For Thomas Pitt was closely related to William Pitt, the Prime Minister, and John Pitt, Earl of Chatham, the First Lord of the Admiralty. When Vancouver returned to England it was to find that Thomas had succeeded his father as Baron Camelford and that his sister, Anne, had married Lord Grenville, the Foreign Secretary. Thomas arrived home in the summer of 1796 vowing vengeance, and from these circumstances arose the notorious 'Camelford affair' that was to cause Vancouver much distress and anxiety.

The midshipmen in the *Discovery* included another son of a peer, the Hon. Charles Stuart, son of the Earl of Bute. His relations with Vancouver and his reaction to the flogging of Pitt are described by Banks. Stuart 'soon fell into a Quarrell with the Capt & never would or did make it up he always refused to dine with him & once only when they got tipsey together on the Kings birthday was at all familiar with him. He then took a Razer from his waistcoat pocket & shewing it to V. said if Sir you ever flog me I will not survive the disgrace I have this Ready to cut my throat with – Mr. S experienced much inconvenience from the Captain's Revenge from the beginning of the

---

[1] B.L., Add. MS 17,548. Puget's rough journal, January 1794–September 1795, p. 8. Words have been supplied as the original has been damaged.

Quarrell he was often sent to the mast head as a punishment for trifling or supposd offences & kept there an unreasonable time but his Spirit never gave way he did his duty to the utmost of his Ability & bore the injustice he receivd patiently.'[1]

As already noted, when Vancouver returned to England he did everything in his power to secure promotions for his midshipmen. But his treatment of them raises the whole question of punishments in the *Discovery*, which Clowes condemned as excessive. Certainly they were much more numerous and severe than those inflicted on Cook's *Resolution*. Cook was usually mindful of the official instructions that limited the punishment for summary offences to a dozen lashes. Beaglehole notes that a sentence of 24 lashes was the most severe punishment meted out on his second voyage.[2] But discipline had become harsher during the unpopular American Revolutionary War and Peter Kemp, after examining a large number of ships' logs concluded that it was 'doubtful whether one captain in a hundred ever thought to obey the official instruction...Too often the sentence for quite minor misdemeanors was three or four dozen, and sometimes as much as six.'[3] So it was in the *Discovery*. Sentences of 24 lashes were frequent and penalties of 36 and even 48 lashes were not uncommon. There is no complete record of punishments in the ship; none of the logs records them consistently, and there are periods in which none is recorded, perhaps by Vancouver's order. At least 60 of the *Discovery*'s complement of 100 were flogged in the course of the voyage, some of them several times. As in most ships of the period, the most frequent offences were drunkenness, neglect of duty, insolence, fighting and theft. The usual penalty for fighting was 48 lashes; theft of any consequence was punished by as many as 60 or 72. The distinction of being the most frequent offender rests with George Rebold, an armourer recruited at the Cape, who was flogged at least ten times, usually for insolence and neglect of duty. The most severe punishment recorded, 144 lashes inflicted in two sessions, was for desertion. Kemp suggests that there would probably have been about 20 floggings a year in a frigate with a crew of 480.[4] In the ten-month period from February to November 1792, when punishments seem to have been recorded fairly systematically, they numbered 45 in the *Discovery*. Due allowance

---

[1] Memo. by Banks. Brabourne Papers, Mitchell Library, Sydney.

[2] Cook, *Journals*, II, 393n.

[3] Peter Kemp, *The British Sailor: A social history of the lower deck* (London, 1970), p. 185.   [4] *Ibid.*, p. 153.

must be made for the tedium of a long voyage, when breaks in routine were infrequent and shore leave and opportunities for recreation were very limited.

Discipline was almost as strict in the *Chatham* as it was in the *Discovery*. The incomplete entries in the logs show that punishments in her were proportionately as numerous, but less severe in the early stages of the voyage. Her complement was only 45, but 21 floggings are recorded in a nine-month period in 1792. While Broughton was in command relatively few exceeded the official limit of 12 lashes, but after Puget took over, early in 1793, they became fewer but more severe; 24 lashes seem to have become the routine penalty. The *Chatham* was evidently plagued with a small knot of trouble makers, as more than a third of all the recorded punishments were inflicted on three seamen.

Vancouver, like Cook, was purser of his ship. In that capacity he had charge of the ship's provisions, and on an expedition such as his, far from normal sources of supply, he purchased supplies along the way. He controlled the great variety of items that had been provided to enable the expedition to make gifts to native peoples and to trade with them. He also sold items from the 'slops' – the store of clothing from which the crew could buy coats, shirts, trousers, blankets and many other items. All of these transactions offered opportunities for manipulation and gain. The honesty of pursers was proverbially open to question, and the ever-critical Hewett extended the suspicion to Vancouver. He charged that 'avarice' was his 'ruling passion' and cites instances in which he claimed the crew had suffered as a consequence. Beef that had been salted down at Monterey soon spoiled, but to conserve the ship's sea stores Hewett contends that 'putrid provisions' were 'served by the Month together although there was good in the Ship only to fill the Pursers Pocket'.

When the *Discovery* reached the Northwest Coast furs offered further possibilities of profit. One of the most notable instances of trading mentioned in the journals occurred in July 1792 at the large Kwakiutl village in Queen Charlotte Strait. Hewett would have us believe that Vancouver there purchased furs on his own account and paid for them with 'Articles which were sent by Government to present to the Indians.' Manby, still smarting under the undeserved reprimand he had received from Vancouver the previous month, elaborates the charge and extends it to others: 'upwards of one hundred Canoes came off, and a vast quantity of all kinds of skins were purchased, those people who were intrusted with the various articles sent out by Government, made to their disgrace an amazing harvest – Bales of Cloath and blankets were sold with a lavish hand for Skins'.[1] Vancouver makes no attempt to conceal either the extent or nature of the trading. He relates that 'Sea-otter skins were the chief objects of our people's traffic, who purchased nearly two hundred in the course of the day.' He goes on to note that copper sheets and blue cloth were the items chiefly in demand by the Indians, and Menzies confirms his account in all essential particulars.[2] Nothing is said about the ownership or disposition of the furs, but Hewett contends that Vancouver sent two large shipments of skins to China, one from Nootka and the other later from the Sandwich Islands.

On the Northwest Coast, as in Tahiti and the Sandwich Islands, trade spread quickly from provisions to artifacts and souvenirs. Many instances are recorded in which the Indians showed a surprising willingness to part with bows, arrows and other items that must have cost them much labour. This trade had been anticipated. Barrie, for one, had equipped himself with some 'Beads & Nails' with which to barter.[3] From Nootka, towards the end of his first visit there, he informed his mother that he had 'made a pretty good collection of curiosities & such things as I could Purchase from the Indians.'[4] Later he added that he had 'got a few very verry fine sea otter skins'.[5] But some of those on board acquired such large collections that they could not possibly have been paid for with the relatively small quantity of trade goods they may have found it possible to bring with them. The assumption is that some arrangement – official or under the counter – gave them access to the ship's stores. As it happens, this applies particularly to Vancouver's two critics, Hewett and Manby. Hewett's own manuscript catalogue of his highly important collection, which was to find its way to the British Museum a century later, lists hundreds of items. And the long notice of Manby in Marshall's *British Naval Biography* refers to 'the innumerable curiosities collected by Captain Manby on his voyage around the world' and to the 'valuable furs of rare animals, procured on the N.W. coast of America'.[6]

---

[1] Manby, Letters, July 1792.   [2] Vancouver, I, 348; Menzies, 20 July 1792.

[3] Barrie to Mrs George Clayton, Longreach, 3 January 1791. Barrie MSS, Perkins Library, Duke University.

[4] *Ibid.*, Nootka Sound, 14 September 1792.

[5] *Ibid.*, Nootka Sound, 27 September 1792.

[6] John Marshall, *Royal Naval Biography* (London, 1823), II, 208. Marshall states that the furs and many other items were presented to the Princess of Wales.

Vancouver's arrogant ways and violent temper resulted in two clashes that prompted him to ask for courts martial. One was with Menzies. Banks had arranged that he should have a servant assigned to him to assist in his botanizing activities. In particular, he was to watch over the small cold frame on the quarter deck in which Menzies was endeavouring to bring back live examples of rare plants for the Royal Botanic Gardens at Kew. On July 28, after the *Discovery* had left St Helena, Menzies discovered that without any warning Vancouver had assigned his servant to duty with one of the watches, and that many of the delicate plants in the frame, which had been left uncovered, had been ruined by a downpour of rain. His disappointment and exasperation at this loss, coming as it did in the final weeks of the voyage, can be appreciated. Naturally, Menzies entered a vigorous protest. In a report to Nepean, Vancouver declared that he had 'behaved to me on the quarter-deck, with great contempt and disrespect', accused him of 'insolent and unbecoming behavior', and stated that 'his positive refusal to retract the harsh and improper expressions he made use of' compelled him to prefer a charge and ask for a court martial.[1] Menzies gave his version of the quarrel in a letter to Banks. He contended that 'coolly & without either *Insolence* or *contempt*' he had complained to the captain, who 'immediately flew in a rage, and his passionate behaviour and abusive language... prevented any further explanation – and I was put under Arrest, because I would not retract my expression, while my grievance still remained unredressed.'[2]

Antagonism between the two heightened when Menzies refused to surrender his journal, a step he had postponed at St Helena. He reiterated that the journal related to his activities as botanist and that Vancouver was concerned only with his duties as surgeon of the *Discovery*; 'in that capacity' he informed the captain, 'I kept no other Journals than the Sick-book, which is ready to be delivered up if you think it necessary.'[3] Once again the contestants stated their divergent views to Nepean and Banks, and Banks gave firm support to Menzies. In a letter to Nepean he pointed out that Menzies' servant was attending plants which had been 'brought a vast distance with unwearied attention & diligence' and that 'flesh & blood' could not be expected to 'see their whole hopes destroyed without uttering some complaint.'[4]

[1] Vancouver to Nepean, 13 September 1795. P.R.O., Adm 1/2629, ff. 62–3.

[2] Menzies to Banks, 14 September 1795. Royal Botanic Gardens, Kew.

[3] Menzies to Vancouver, 12 September 1795. P.R.O., Adm 1/2629, f. 99.

[4] Banks to Nepean, 1 October 1795. Draft in Brabourne Papers, Mitchell Library, Sydney.

As for the journals, Banks considered that Menzies had been 'wholly under my orders' and asked that they should be 'sent up to the board or delivered immediately to me'. By late October cooler tempers prevailed, and on the 24th Vancouver sent a brief note to Nepean informing him that Menzies had 'made an ample apology' and asking that his application for a court martial be withdrawn.[1] In the long run the only significant result was probably some increase in Banks' prejudice against Vancouver.

The second court martial arose from an incident that had taken place as long before as March 1792. The accused was Henry Phillips, carpenter of the *Discovery*. Just after the ship left the Sandwich Islands, bound for the Northwest Coast, a squall carried away the foretopgallant yard. Phillips prepared a replacement, but (in Puget's words) 'not finishing it agreeable to Capt. Vancouvers particular directions...was in the afternoon confined prisoner in his Cabin'.[2] In his report to the Admiralty Vancouver stated that 'having occasion to find fault with him for disobeying my orders' Phillips had 'behaved to me with so much insolence, contempt and disrespect' that he was sending him home in the *Daedalus* 'to be tried by a Court Martial...whenever circumstances may admit thereof'.[3] As it turned out, circumstances did not admit for three years and eight months, during which Phillips languished as a prisoner. The court martial finally took place at the Nore on 17 November 1795. Vancouver appeared, and as witnesses brought with him Puget, Barrie and Ballard. Phillips, evidently well advised, had submitted a dignified statement in his own defence that concluded as follows: 'if by any part of my conduct I have innocently offended against the Rules of the Service I humbly presume to hope Your Honors will consider it a want of experience this being the first time of my having had the Honor of serving in the Navy the discipline of which I had not been acquainted with or accustom'd to, neither did I conceive that I should have been treated with such language.'[4] The verdict of the court must have infuriated Vancouver. It found 'that the charges of general inattention to the Duties of his Employment and neglect of the Stores committed to his charge were not proved and that the charge of disobedience of Captain Vancouver's Orders on the 19th of March 1792 was not proved' but that the charge of 'Contemptuous and

---

[1] Vancouver to Nepean, 24 October 1795. P.R.O., Adm 1/2629, f. 104.
[2] Puget, 19 March 1792.
[3] Vancouver to Stephens, Monterey, 29 December 1792. P.R.O., Adm 1/2628, f. 642.
[4] Dated at the Navy Office, 29 March 1794. Adm 1/5333.

disrespectful behaviour' was proved, and for this Phillips was to be 'broke' as carpenter of the *Discovery* and reduced to serve for the remainder of the war then in progress in whatever ship or ships the Commander in Chief at the Nore should designate.[1]

The *Discovery* had been paid off on November 3, and the following day Vancouver went on half pay. Her officers and those of the *Chatham* were soon widely scattered. Those with whom Vancouver maintained some contact included Baker, who prepared the charts that were engraved for publication with the *Voyage of Discovery*, and Puget. Menzies states that Whidbey was 'the chief confident of C. Vancouver most part of the Voyage',[2] and this arose naturally from their long association, which dated back to their service together in the West Indies. Four days after the *Discovery* was paid off Vancouver wrote to the Navy Board praising 'the most signal services' Whidbey had rendered 'not only in the immediate line of his profession [as master], but likewise by his attention to practical Astronomy and Marine Surveying', and asking that he be promoted to Master Attendant.[3]

A few oddments of unfinished business relating to the voyage remained. Vancouver had 'judged it necessary at certain times...that the seamen employed in the boats on distant service, should be indulged with an extra allowance of spirits' and he asked that 'the quantity so issued, being twenty gallons' should be allowed on his account at the Victualling Office.[4] He next asked for credit at the Navy Slop-Office for 'sundry slop-clothes' that he had given to British seamen in the Sandwich Islands, whose continued presence there he considered would be helpful to later British visitors.[5] Both requests were granted.

At the end of the year, in an effort to improve his health, Vancouver went to Bristol Hot Springs. There, on 5 January 1796, to his 'great surprise and astonishment', he heard from Nepean that a strongly worded complaint had been lodged against him by the Spanish Ambassador. This accused him of having refused to pay the costs incurred by the deserters from the *Chatham* and *Daedalus* who had been held in custody by the Spaniards in California. In reply, Vancouver explained his predicament at Monterey: 'I did not know under what

[1] Minutes of Court Martial, 17 November 1795. Adm 1/5333.
[2] Menzies to Banks, 21 October 1796. Royal Botanic Gardens, Kew.
[3] Vancouver to the Navy Board, 7 November 1795. P.R.O., Adm 106/1434. Vancouver was told that his recommendation should have been directed to the Board of Admiralty. Presumably he did so, as Whidbey served as a Master Attendant for many years.
[4] Vancouver to Nepean, 17 December 1795. Adm 1/2629, f. 127.
[5] Vancouver to Nepean, 19 December 1795. *Ibid.*, f. 129.

head to charge them or on whom to give drafts for the money, nor
had I a sufficient sum by me to liquidate the debt, nor did I conceive
I was authorized to do so, even if I had possessed the means'. He
proposed therefore to refer the matter to the Admiralty as soon as he
returned to England, and this had seemed quite agreeable to Governor
Borica and General Alava. Some failure of communication had
evidently occurred, as Vancouver insisted that he had forwarded details
of the transaction 'at three different periods for their Lordships
information.'[1] Nepean acted promptly; on January 9 he informed the
Foreign Secretary that the Navy Board had been instructed to pay the
charges whenever a demand was received from the agent of the Spanish
Government.[2]

This was very much a tempest in a teapot. Vancouver recalled that
Borica and Alava had 'conceived the subject matter in question but
of trivial import', and in his journal he notes that the sum involved
was only $325.50.[3]

In a personal letter to Nepean Vancouver remarked that he was 'in
sufficient health to repair to Town' if necessary, but otherwise he
intended 'to take advantage of the salubrious air, and waters of this
place, for about a fortnight longer; by which time I hope to establish
the foundation of a perfect cure.'[4] Sometime in the next few weeks
he decided to move to Petersham, an attractive village adjoining
Richmond Park, where he could live quietly but still be close to
London. There he was to spend the remaining years of his life.

From Petersham on March 4 Vancouver wrote to the Board of
Longitude, pointing out that owing to the murder of William Gooch,
who was to have joined him at Nootka in 1792, he had in effect acted
as astronomer of his expedition. He described the various observations
he had carried out, submitted the books in which they had been
recorded, and hoped that they would meet with the Board's approval.
He hoped further that his services might be considered worthy of some
pecuniary recompence, and suggested that the case of Captains Cook
and King might provide a precedent.[5] His letter was addressed to the
celebrated astronomer William Wales, then Secretary of the Board.
Wales had sailed with Cook on his second voyage and had assisted in

[1] Vancouver to Nepean, Bristol, 6 January 1796. Adm 1/2629, ff. 303, 306–7.
[2] Nepean to Geo. Hammond, 9 January 1796. Quoted in Godwin, *Vancouver: A Life*, p. 278.
[3] Vancouver, III, 333.
[4] Vancouver to Nepean, Bristol, 6 January 1796. Adm 1/2629, f. 303v.
[5] Vancouver to Wales, 4 March 1796. Archives, Board of Longitude.

the training of the midshipmen, of whom Vancouver was one. The deferential, even diffident tone of the letter suggests that even after twenty years Vancouver still stood in some awe of him.

The Board instructed Wales to ascertain what had been done 'in similar Cases' and on June 11 he reported that 'the only cases he could find, at all resembling Vancouvers, were those of Captain Cook and Captain King'. But there had been an essential difference, as Cook and King had been 'under an engagement' with the Board before they sailed. As this had not been the case with Vancouver, the Board 'did not perceive how they could do anything in the Business.'[1] The books recording his observations were returned to Vancouver (and later disappeared, along with the rest of his papers), and there is no evidence that the Board even commended him for his labours.

There was an interesting sequel to this exchange. Early in 1797 the Admiralty received a petition from Whidbey 'praying to be paid for having acted in the capacity of Astronomer' during the *Discovery*'s voyage. On February 25 Nepean sent a copy to Wales 'to be laid before the Board of Longitude for their consideration in respect to the compensation desired by Mr. Whidbey'.[2] Vancouver had had to wait three months for his verdict; Whidbey's case was dealt with within a week. The minute reads in part: 'the Astronomer Royal having informed the Board that he had inspected the observations, and that the Gentlemen concerned in making them had shewn great industry, and made a variety of useful ones...the board were of opinion that the Gentlemen who made the observations are, on account of this extra-service, beyond their regular duty, entitled to some compensation, such as the Lords Commissioners of the Admiralty may think fit'.[3]

An entry in the Admiralty Abstracts records that the Navy Board was directed 'to pay Mr Whidbey...as Astronomer on Capt Vancouver's voyage at the rate of £200 p^r Annum for 327 days',[4] or a few shillings less than £180. Oddly enough, this entry is dated February 15, or ten days before the Lords of the Admiralty referred

---

[1] Minutes, Board of Longitude, March 5 and 11 June 1796. Cook noted the arrangement with the Board in his journal on 11 June 1776: 'Received on board several Astronomical & Nautical Instruments which the Board of Longitude intrusted to me and Mr King my second Lieutenant, we having engaged to that board to make all necessary Astronomical and Nautical observations that should accrue and to supply the place of an Astronomer which was intended to be sent out in the Ship.' Cook, *Journals*, II, 4.

[2] Nepean to Wales, 25 February 1797. Adm 2/789, p. 395.

[3] Minutes, Board of Longitude, 4 March 1797.

[4] P.R.O., Adm 12/74 (1797).

Whidbey's case to the Board of Longitude, which implies that they were simply seeking evidence to bolster a decision already made. The repeated reference to 'the Gentlemen' concerned in the observations suggests that there may have been some question of a grant to Vancouver as well as to Whidbey, but no record of any payment to Vancouver has yet come to light.

At this time Vancouver was desperately short of money, and any compensation received from the Board would have been most welcome. He was in debt, was being pressed by his creditors, and was being assisted by advances from James Sykes, his London agent. He had served as commander of his expedition from 16 December 1790 to 3 November 1795 – only six weeks short of five years – but had as yet received none of his back pay from the Navy. The reason for the long delay does not appear. At last in October 1797, two years after the return of the expedition, the Admiralty proposed to pay him at the rate of six shillings and sixpence per day for the time spent on the voyage. As he had served as purser of the *Discovery* as well as her commander, Vancouver asked that the rate be increased to eight shillings. Searching for a precedent, the Admiralty found that under similar circumstances Captain Bligh had been paid eight shillings, and it was therefore allowed to Vancouver. Even so the financial return for his services as commander of a long and strenuous expedition was anything but princely; the sum due at the eight-shilling rate was a little more than seven hundred pounds.

Vancouver had also encountered exasperating delays in securing payment of his share of the prize money arising from the seizure of the Dutch East Indiaman *Macassar* at St Helena. The case had been referred to the Admiralty Prize Court early in 1796, and in the weeks that followed Vancouver found that there were two other claimants, Governor Brooke of St Helena and Campbell Marjoribanks, captain of the East Indiaman *Arniston*, which was in harbour at the time of the seizure. On April 2 Vancouver submitted a memorial to the Treasury in which he supported his claim and described the capture. When the *Macassar* was sighted, 'being the Commanding Naval Officer of the Island of St. Helena', he and Governor Brooke concerted measures for the defence of the roadstead and the ships therein. It was decided that it would be best to let the *Macassar* enter harbour before attempting to board her, and when she did so 'two of the Discovery's Boats were dispatched', one commanded by Baker and the other by Swaine, 'who took possession of the Macassa [*sic*] & secured her in the Roadstead.'[1] From the beginning Brooke, who broadened his claim to include the St Helena garrison, had claimed that the *Macassar* had been seized by his orders, and he had so informed Admiral Elphinstone a few days after the capture.[2] Vancouver does not appear to have disputed Brooke's claim, but the only assistance from him that he acknowledged was 'a Guard of Soldiers to act as Centinels on board' the prize to prevent any tampering with her valuable cargo. It was the claim from the *Arniston* that roused Vancouver's ire. Though heavily armed, she was 'not sufficiently manned to make Use of near the Force she possessed' and Vancouver and Brooke had agreed that 'a certain proportion' of the officers and crews of Vancouver's ships should be sent to her in case the *Macassar*, which carried 34 guns, should resist seizure.[3] Vancouver felt so strongly about the matter that he sent a personal letter to Lord Chatham, First Lord of the Admiralty, in which he contended that 'the only assistance afforded by the Arniston, was the lending of a boat to carry out an anchor (after my Officers and people were in possession of the Ship) or some trivial business of that nature.' He explained that he was appealing to the First Lord because the claim of the *Arniston*, owned by the powerful East India Company, was being 'strongly supported by some person or persons high in Office', whereas he himself was feeling bereft of influential friends: 'as it were insulated, from all connections with persons of consequence; (probably occasioned in a great measure from the constant, remote, and distant services, in which my whole life has been engaged)'. He had 'no friend in power' on whom he could call to assist and support his cause.[4]

The rival claims were referred to the King's Advocate for consideration, and his report was submitted on June 27. His decision was that half 'the proceeds of the Ship and her Cargo' should be granted to the Crown and the other half divided equally between the three claimants – Vancouver and his crews, Governor Brooke and the St Helena garrison, and the captain and crew of the *Arniston*.[5]

If the Privy Council had approved this distribution fairly promptly the matter would have been settled, but action was still pending in

[1] Vancouver's memorial to the Treasury, 2 April 1796. Chatham Papers, P.R.O. 30/185.

[2] Brooke to Elphinstone, 9 July 1795. *Keith Papers*, I, p. 324.

[3] Vancouver's memorial. Chatham Papers, P.R.O. 30/185.

[4] Vancouver to Lord Chatham, 7 April 1796. Chatham Papers, P.R.O. 30/185.

[5] The report is enclosed in J. Heseltine, Doctors' Commons, to the Treasury, 30 June 1796. P.R.O., T.1/768, No. 2618.

January 1797 when Admiral Elphinstone returned to England. He promptly entered a claim for a share of the prize money and stated his case in memorials to the King and the Treasury. In brief, he contended that he had received instructions 'touching the Coast of Africa, Saint Helena, and the Indian Seas' under which he 'took charge of, and exercised the Chief Authority over all Your Majestys Ships and Vessels in those parts, and at those places.' He contended that this authority extended to Vancouver's ships as soon as they entered this area of command, within which 'the established law and invariable custom appropriates to a Commander in Chief a defined share in all captures.'[1] Vancouver disputed this argument in a letter to Nepean. He pointed out that he had just arrived at St Helena when the *Macassar* was sighted, and that he was 'so far from being under the orders of Sir Geo. K. Elphinstone...or any other Commanding or Superior Officer' that it was not until after the capture that he had 'sufficient leisure to acquire such information respecting who were the different commanding officers and the situation of affairs in Europe.'[2]

Elphinstone's claim delayed a settlement but did not change the awards. On 22 November 1797 the Privy Council approved the distribution proposed by the King's Advocate.[3] Just when the prize money was actually paid does not appear. In January 1798 Vancouver told his agent, James Sykes, who had been assisting him with advances, that it afforded him 'some satisfaction to find there is at length a probability of our shortly touching the cash'. He added that he expected his share of the prize money 'not only to discharge the whole of my debts, but also such little matters as I have become answerable for others...which will place me *most completely on velvet* – excepting the incurring expenses of the publication [of the *Voyage of Discovery*]; which will I trust at no very remote period be by itself most amply reimbursed.'[4] Late in February Barrie noted that his agent had not yet heard 'when the Macassars prize money will be paid',[5] but it was probably distributed before Vancouver's death in May. His estate was proved at £5,000,[6] and in his will, signed late in April, Vancouver states

[1] Elphinstone's Memorial to the King, received 16 January 1797. P.R.O., T./1, 779. His memorial to the Treasury is in the same file.

[2] Vancouver to Nepean, 9 February 1797. Quoted in Godwin, *Vancouver: A Life*, p. 144.

[3] For the decision see P.R.O., T.1/768, ff. 230–34v.

[4] Vancouver to Sykes, 11 January 1798. *Washington Historical Quarterly* XVII (1926), p. 125. The original letter was then in the collection of Mrs William Pitt Trimble, of Seattle.

[5] Barrie to Mrs George Clayton, 26 February 1798. Barrie MSS., Perkins Library, Duke University.   [6] Godwin, *Vancouver: A Life* (1930), p. 164.

that the bulk of his property was 'about to be engaged in the purchase and improvement of Ealing Manor in Berks'[1] – a transaction unlikely to have been undertaken unless his debts had been discharged.

The only available estimate of the monetary value of the *Macassar*'s cargo appears in a letter written by Barrie when the *Discovery* arrived in the Shannon. He stated that she carried 'a very rich cargo of Spices &c valu'd at the lowest market in holland at 90,000 £ besides a deal of money on board the amount of which we are ignorant of.'[2]

The Voyage; the 'Camelford affair'

Vancouver devoted the last two years of his life to the preparation of the detailed account of his great expedition that is reprinted in the pages that follow. Half a million words in length, it is a revised version of his own journal, the original of which has unfortunately disappeared, supplemented by additional data secured from journals, logs, charts and sketches by others who accompanied him on the voyage.

The beginning of this massive project is described in a letter from Vancouver to Nepean, dated 25 March 1796:

It having been communicated to me that it is the wish of the Lords Commissioners of the Admiralty, that I should prepare for Publick information, the result of the labours of the Voyage I had lately the honor of executing in His Majestys Sloop Discovery accompanied by the Chatham Armed Tender; and my journals, with most of my Charts and Drawings having been deliverd up to me for that particular purpose; I am to request you will be pleased to move their Lordships, that directions are given for such remaining Drawings & Charts as were constructed on Board the Discovery & Chatham, during the said voyage; now lodged in Mr. Dalrymples Office; should be deliverd to me for the purpose aforesaid; and as I am given to understand that in the instances of Captains Cook & King, the Government defrayed certain expences of the Publications; I humbly solicit Their Lordships indulgence to grant to me the same advantages, as likewise that they would communicate their pleasure, as to the particular persons they would please to employ, about the Drawings, Engravings &c; or whether they will approve of my fixing on such Artists of known abilities as are necessary to execute that part of the work in question.[3]

Alexander Dalrymple, a tireless compiler, collector and publisher of

[1] The will is dated 28 April 1798.

[2] Barrie to Mrs George Clayton, 12 September 1795. Barrie MSS., Perkins Library, Duke University.

[3] P.R.O., Adm 1/2629, ff. 310–310v.

charts, had served for years as hydrographer of the East India Company, and had been appointed to the newly created post of Hydrographer of the Navy only a month before the *Discovery* arrived in the Shannon.

On March 31, Nepean replied as follows:

Having laid before my Lords Comm^s of the Admiralty your Letter of the 25th instant relative to your publishing an account of the Voyage lately executed by you, I am commanded by their Lordships to acquaint you that they mean to give every reasonable advantage to you which they can, consistently with a due attention to the Claims of other Persons employed during the Voyage, and will immediately fix upon the Charts & Views which their Lordships are of opinion ought to be annexed to the Work. In the mean time their Lordships have given directions for the delivery of the Journals etc., now in Mr. Dalrymple's possession.[1]

No doubt Vancouver received the charts and journals, but Nepean's letter evidently failed to reach him. If it had arrived, he would doubtless have assumed that Nepean's reference to 'the Claims of other Persons' referred to Menzies, for reports had reached him that Menzies was to share in the publication relating to his voyage. In the same letter to Lord Chatham that dealt with the *Macassar* prize money he lodged a protest: 'I find it is the intention of the Admiralty, that the observations made by Mr Menzies, on the various subjects of the Natural History of the different Country we visited, should in some way be connected with my account of the Voyage; and that under such considerations Mr Menzies is to be benefited by a proportion of the profits that may result from the sale of the work'. He went on to point out that the voyage had involved him in heavy expence, and, smarting from the fact that his own pay was still in arrears (and would be for another 18 months) went on to contend that Menzies had no right to any recompence for the use of his papers: his pay 'during the Voyage was much more than double mine which together with his expenses, has been paid him since his return; and hence it is natural to conclude; since he has been so amply paid by Government that the results of his employment are the entire property of Government and totally at their own disposal.'[2]

Doubtless this proposal was inspired by Banks, the person of influence who was most interested in Menzies. No more seems to have been heard of it, but it may be noted that as late as January 1798 Menzies was writing to Banks thanking him for his 'friendly admonitions &

---

[1] P.R.O., Adm 2/784, p. 114.
[2] Vancouver to Lord Chatham, 7 April 1796. Chatham Papers, P.R.O., 30/185.

solicitations respecting the finishing of my Journal before Captain Vancouver's is published' which, Menzies assured him, 'is what I most ardently wish'.[1]

No reply from Lord Chatham has come to light, and for several months Vancouver received no word from the Admiralty about financial and other arrangements for the printing of his journal. Finally, in July 1796, 'understanding verbally' that it was 'their Lordships wish to be informed as to the expence and persons capable of being employed in providing the Plates that are to represent the Charts and Views of head lands and Islands, that are necessary to accompany the account I am preparing' he wrote to Nepean regarding the financing of the publication and submitted tentative estimates from a number of engravers. He went on to mention that he understood that 'a sum of about three Thousand Pounds, was granted by Government in aid of the publication of Captain Cooks last Voyage' and mentioned circumstances that made him feel entitled to comparable assistance. He reminded Nepean, as he had already reminded Lord Chatham, that the voyage had involved him in considerable personal expense, and that he had received none of the money due him from the Government since December 1790. He was 'hoping through their Lordships generous aid, to be enabled to lay out a sufficient sum of money on the publication in question to render it a more finished work than my own private finances will allow.'[2]

In his reply Nepean informed Vancouver that he was 'at liberty to employ proper People to Engrave the Charts & Views of Headlands' and 'upon each Plate being completed' their Lordships would 'order the Expence thereof to be defrayed.' He added that their Lordships would 'hereafter decide upon the Views which are to be engraved.'[3] Nepean made no mention of any further financial assistance, and payment for the engravings proved to be the only subsidy Vancouver was to be granted.

By the summer of 1797 he was receiving plates and proofs from engravers and was forwarding their bills to Nepean for payment. The Admiralty appears to have mislaid the original list of charts and views approved for reproduction, but fortunately a duplicate that Nepean asked for in February 1798, when the project was well along, has survived. 'Ten folio plates of Charts' and 'Six Folio plates containing

[1] Menzies to Banks, 3 January 1798. Brabourne Papers, Mitchell Library, Sydney.
[2] Vancouver to Nepean, 4 July 1796. P.R.O., Adm 1/2629, ff. 313–15.
[3] Nepean to Vancouver, 28 July 1796. P.R.O., Adm 2/785, p. 516.

Views of Head Lands Islands &c' were engraved for the folio atlas that was to accompany the three quarto volumes of text, and the latter would include eighteen plates – seventeen views and the small chart of Hergest's Islands. It is interesting to note that Vancouver at this time was not sure that he had received approval for the view of the Spanish village at Nootka Sound, which is now the best-known and most frequently copied of all the thirty-four plates. The engravings, most of which had been paid for by the time Vancouver sent the duplicate list, are priced individually, and having allowed £15 for titling, he estimated the total cost would be £1038/15/-. This he described as the 'Total expense to Government for the publication of the Said Voyage.'[1]

Vancouver was able to commission some of the best-known and most competent engravers of the day. James Heath was Historical Engraver to three kings – George III, George IV and William IV. James Fittler, Marine Engraver to George III, engraved views of many famous naval engagements, including the Battle of the Nile and Lord Howe's famous victory on the 'Glorious First of June'. John Landseer, father of the painter, Sir Edwin Landseer, had gained a reputation of his own as an engraver. Benjamin Thomas Pouncy was one of the busiest and most accomplished engravers of the time. These four engraved all the views in the three volumes of text, and Fittler and Pouncy also engraved the six folio plates of views. With the exception of one plate contributed by Samuel John Neele, who was highly regarded as a book illustrator, the folio charts were the work of less well-known figures. Thomas Foot and John Warner each engraved four plates; the tenth was the work of one B. Baker.

Vancouver's narrative has a special interest because, unlike those of such well-known travellers as John Meares, James Colnett and Alexander Mackenzie, it was not rewritten for publication by a ghost writer. It is a straightforward revision of the journal he kept during the expedition, and it is evident that the printed text follows it very closely. Occasionally, when describing events in which he did not take part himself, he quotes from or paraphrases the reports or journals of other members of the expedition, including Broughton, Johnstone, Puget and Whidbey. All but a hundred of the nearly fifteen hundred pages in the first (quarto) edition were either in type or ready for the printer when Vancouver died. This carried the narrative as far as the arrival of the ships at Valparaiso late in March 1795. Vancouver's

[1] Vancouver to Nepean, 15 February 1798. P.R.O., Adm 1/2630, ff. 38–40A.

brother John, who had been assisting him,[1] completed the text. He judged rightly that the only matters of major interest that remained to be dealt with were the transactions at Valparaiso and the visit of Vancouver and some of his officers to Santiago. Vancouver's notes describing the journey inland to Santiago were missing, and Puget, who had accompanied Vancouver, provided a substitute. He drafted his account in the first person, and this has led to the mistaken assumption that the copy now in the British Library, although in Puget's handwriting, was written by Vancouver himself. The description of Santiago may well be longer than Vancouver himself would have printed, but John made much more drastic cuts in the account of the voyage from Valparaiso to the Shannon than he would probably have approved. John explained his reason for doing so quite frankly: 'as no new incidents occurred in this part of the voyage, and as the insertion of log-book minutes, over a space which is now so frequently traversed, cannot either be useful or entertaining', he had 'endeavoured to compress that portion of the journal into as few pages as possible.' But throughout he 'strictly adhered to the rough documents before me',[2] and the uniformity of style between the earlier chapters and those he prepared for the printer bears this out. Even the shortening of the final chapter, describing the voyage from Valparaiso, was accomplished by excision, not by rewriting. The two most notable passages – the description of Vancouver's emotion when the cutter in which he had travelled innumerable times during the voyage was accidently destroyed, and the concluding paragraph – could only have been written by Vancouver himself.

Little is known about John Vancouver's early career. He and his brother Charles, who was also to become involved in Captain Vancouver's affairs, were both baptized on the same day – 11 No-

[1] The extent to which John Vancouver participated in the preparation of the text of the printed *Voyage* is uncertain. On 14 May 1798, two days after Captain Vancouver's death, in referring to the *Voyage* in a letter to the Earl of Dundonald, John stated that he hoped he would soon be able 'to regain my spirits so as to go on, and complete the arduous task on which I have been now more than two years fully and constantly employed'. John may have exaggerated somewhat, but Vancouver could not have prepared the text for the printer without considerable assistance, both clerical and editorial, as it must have been drafted at an average rate of 700 words or more per day. But the text seems to indicate nevertheless that Vancouver was in full control of the narrative until the final days of his last illness. For the letter to Dundonald see John Sugden (ed.), 'The Death of Captain George Vancouver', *Mariner's Mirror* LXVII (1981), 84. The signature of the writer is there given as 'C. Vancouver' but examination of the original, in the Scottish Record Office, shows that this should read 'J. Vancouver'.

[2] Vancouver, I, xxxii.

vember 1756 – but this may or may not indicate that they were twins.[1] John is said to have served for a time as Deputy Collector of Customs at King's Lynn, a post his father had held from 1748 to 1770. John was living in King's Lynn in 1788. Ties between him and his explorer brother were evidently very close. Vancouver ended a personal note written to him in September 1794 with the words: 'I am My Dearest Van Unalterably your ever affectionate & Sincere friend and Brother'. In the same note, doubtless to spare his brother anxiety, he made an ambiguous reference to 'good health' that could have referred to the health of the crew rather than his own, which was anything but good.[2] In 1796 John published *An enquiry into the causes and production of poverty and the state of the poor*. This caught the attention of Jeremy Bentham, whose copy, with a few manuscript notes, is in the British Library. By March 1797 he was at Petersham. Writing that month to his agent, Vancouver notes in a postscript that 'As writing is exceedingly pernicious to my present indisposition my brother who is here has been good enough to write this letter for me.'[3] But Vancouver's letters to Nepean continued to be in his own hand. The last in the Admiralty file is dated 29 March 1798, only six weeks before his death.

Vancouver was no more than well started on the task of preparing his journal for publication when the quiet of his life at Petersham was shattered by the return to England of young Thomas Pitt, now the second Baron Camelford. More than two years had passed since Vancouver had dismissed him from the *Discovery* at the Sandwich Islands and put him on board the *Daedalus*, bound for New South Wales. The adventures he met with thereafter are described in the biography entitled *The Half-Mad Lord*, by Nikolai Tolstoy. Throughout them he nursed twin ambitions: a consuming determination to revenge himself upon Vancouver for the unjust and humiliating treatment he considered he had received in the *Discovery*, and a comparable determination to secure the promotion in the Navy to which he felt his abilities entitled him.

Only two descriptions of the punishments inflicted on Camelford, and the misdeeds that occasioned them, are known. One is an account by Whidbey, quoted in a letter from Menzies to Banks; the other is

---

[1] George Vancouver was not baptized until he was nearly four years old, and the double baptism may have been just a matter of family convenience.

[2] Vancouver to John Vancouver, Nootka, 8 September 1794. Yale University Library.

[3] Vancouver to Sykes, 15 March 1797. Godwin, *Vancouver: A Life*, p. 284.

in a memorandum by Banks himself.[1] Camelford was a tall, strongly built youth, high spirited and attractive in many ways, but given to pranks, proud and intolerant of authority. His whole career, which was to end in a totally unnecessary duel, was tainted by temper and violence. No doubt he had aroused Vancouver's displeasure long before the expedition reached Tahiti, but it was there that the first flogging occurred. Vancouver's ruling that midshipmen would be permitted on shore only if on duty was highly unpopular, and to this he had added a ban on all contacts with women. Iron was much sought after by the natives, and Camelford was detected offering a girl some iron in return for her favours. Later in the voyage, when 'Romping with another of the midshipmen on the Quarter deck' he broke the glass in the binnacle. The cause of the third flogging is not known. In addition, he was charged with sleeping on his watch, and was kept in irons for ten days or a fortnight. During the first flogging Mudge, first lieutenant of the *Discovery*, attempted to intervene. Banks notes that Camelford had been put in his care by his parents, and Tolstoy adds that Mudge 'owed much to the patronage of the Camelford family'.[2] After the first 12 of the 24 lashes Mudge told Camelford 'that provided he would promise to behave better in future he would ask the Capt to Remit the remainder of the Punishment', but Camelford refused to be 'begged off'.[3]

From New South Wales, where he left the *Daedalus*, Camelford had contrived to get to China. There he took ship for India. His ship called at Malacca early in December 1794, where he was delighted to find the British frigate *Resistance*. Her commander, Captain Edward Pakenham, added Camelford to his ship's company, and the two agreed so well that only three weeks later, to Camelford's vast satisfaction, Pakenham promoted him to acting lieutenant. The year that followed was the happiest and most successful of his naval career. He and Pakenham became firm friends and Pakenham sent glowing reports of him to his mother, Lord Grenville and the Admiralty. But Camelford became restless; no further promotion was in prospect and his score with Vancouver remained unsettled. On 24 November 1795 he left the *Resistance*, which was once more at Malacca, and set out for England.

He was nine months on the way. In the course of them he was

[1] Menzies to Banks, 21 October 1796. Royal Botanic Gardens, Kew. Memorandum by Banks, n.p., n.d., Brabourne Papers, Mitchell Library, Sydney.

[2] Nikolai Tolstoy, *The Half-Mad Lord. Thomas Pitt 2nd Baron Camelford* (London, 1978), p. 22.   [3] Banks memo.

shipwrecked on the coast of Ceylon, tramped through the northern wilds of that island with a British secret agent, and sailed from Madras to Suez in an East India Company frigate. Early in June 1796, at Cattaro (Kotor), on the Dalmatian coast, he was quarantined for 40 days because he came from Alexandria, where the plague was prevalent. Still obsessed by his two ambitions, he there wrote to his mother, imploring her to secure his promotion to post captain, and sent an insulting letter to Vancouver, challenging him to a duel. Vancouver was directed to meet him at Hamburg on August 5 and a draft was enclosed to meet his expenses.

Neither letter achieved its purpose. Encouraged by Pakenham's favourable reports, Grenville, who was both Camelford's guardian and his brother-in-law, had already raised the question of his promotion with Lord Spencer, who had succeeded Lord Chatham as First Lord of the Admiralty. The first step would be confirmation of the rank of lieutenant, to which Pakenham had appointed him in an acting capacity. This, Lord Spencer pointed out, would be contrary to the rules of the service, and there was the further point that Camelford had not passed the necessary examination. Instead of early advancement to the rank of captain, that he craved, Camelford was thus faced with reverting, if only temporarily, to that of a mere midshipman.

The result of the letter to Vancouver was equally unsatisfactory. To begin with, it did not reach Petersham until August 17, a fortnight after the appointed rendezvous in Hamburg. What happened thereafter is detailed in Articles of Misdemeanor later submitted by Vancouver to the High Court of Chancery. He had replied to Camelford, at his London address, stating the position to which he held throughout the dispute. He 'did not feel himself at all in the situation in which his Lordship laboured to place him', did not consider himself 'called upon in a private capacity to answer for his Public conduct in the exercise of his official duty', and expressed his willingness 'to submit the Examination of his conduct...to any flag officer of His Majestys Navy.'[1] Camelford returned to London on September 1. Grenville, aware that trouble was brewing, had hoped to intervene, but Camelford, enraged by Vancouver's reply, went directly to Petersham, confronted Vancouver and demanded personal satisfaction. His language on this

---

[1] 'Articles of Misdemeanor exhibited in his Majestys High Court of Chancery by George Vancouver Esquire against the Right Honorable Thomas Lord Camelford...' [September 1796]. Cotes Papers, National Library of Wales.

and later occasions was anything but temperate; Vancouver recalled that he declared that he 'had thirsted' for his blood, 'and that the Idea had kept him alive or used words to that purport and effect'.

Vancouver immediately consulted friends, including Grenville; all supported his position and the proposal to refer the matter to a flag officer. What Grenville thought of the events in the *Discovery* we do not know, but he was eminently fair in his attitude to Vancouver. Thus encouraged, Vancouver wrote to Camelford on September 7, reiterating his position. His letter was delivered personally by his brother Charles, who was treated to a display of temper and abuse. Camelford declared that he would insult Vancouver publicly in a coffee house and thus force him to fight a duel; if he declined to do so, he 'would drive him from the Service wou'd compel him to resign his Commission and would finally wherever he should meet him box it out and try which was the better Man.' In a letter written to Vancouver the next day he endeavoured to provoke him and referred to him as a poltroon. Vancouver was now thoroughly alarmed; Camelford was obviously bent on mischief, and the outcome of a physical encounter between a powerfully built young man and a much older man in poor health was only too predictable. Recourse to the law was clearly essential: 'for the preservation of his Life and person' which he believed 'to be in the utmost danger from the said Thomas Lord Camelford' Vancouver asked the Court to require Camelford to find sureties for keeping the peace.[1]

Some uncertainty as to procedure now occurred, because a peer of the realm was involved. It was decided finally on September 20 that the matter must be referred to the Lord Chancellor, Lord Lough-borough. The next morning, accompanied by his brother Charles, Vancouver left their lodgings in Bond Street to go to the residence of the Lord Chancellor in Bedford Square. When they turned into Conduit Street they sighted Camelford across the way, and the encounter that was to become the subject of a famous caricature entitled 'The Caneing in Conduit Street' followed. Camelford immediately crossed the street, intent on attacking Vancouver. Charles managed to ward off his blows and evidently returned them with considerable effect. Camelford then made a second attack, which Vancouver himself fended off with a stick he carried in his hand. In spite of his youth and strength Camelford may well have got the worst of it. In an affidavit sworn to by Charles six months later, after another meeting with

---

[1] All quotations are from the 'Articles of Misdemeanour'.

Camelford, he quoted the latter as saying that he (Charles) had 'given him a damned hideing in Conduit Street, that his arm and shoulder were still black and blue from the blows he had received'.[1]

After this interruption the brothers kept their appointment with the Lord Chancellor, who asked Camelford to come to his home the next morning. 'So wild was his appearance', Tolstoy states, 'the Lady Loughborough persuaded a friend to remain outside the door to come if necessary to her husband's aid.'[2] But Camelford would listen to someone whose rank he respected; he became calmer, and the Lord Chancellor required him to provide sureties of £10,000 to keep the peace for a year. Grenville provided a quarter of the sum. There the matter might have ended had not the London *Herald* described the encounter in terms prejudicial to Vancouver. No names were mentioned, but all the town knew who had been involved. Charles felt that the charge must be refuted and his rejoinder appeared in the *Morning Chronicle* on September 24. It is of interest because it quotes or paraphrases Vancouver's initial response to Camelford, written on August 18. Vancouver then 'observed...that in whatever respect his Lordship might consider himself as an injured man, it was solely and alone to be ascribed to his own misconduct, and that the personal inconveniences he had incurred were (though with the greatest reluctance, imposed by his commanding officer) *indispensibly necessary to the maintenance of discipline and good order on board the Discovery*'. Enraged, Camelford protested at once to the Lord Chancellor, contending that 'the facts therein stated' were 'false and framed with much art and low cunning' and that he owed it to his character to refute them.[3] Loughborough replied that he was 'extremely sorry' that the letter had been published, noting that it was 'the more improper as the Gentleman whose name appears to it knew in what manner Your Lordship was engaged to take no step in this Business'.[4]

A little is now known about Charles Vancouver, hitherto a man of mystery. His chief interests were agriculture in the English counties and colonization in America. The first of his several sojourns in the United States was probably made before 1785, for in that year a 48-page

---

[1] Affidavit of Charles Vancouver, 5 May 1797. Cotes Papers, National Library of Wales.

[2] Tolstoy, *The Half-Mad Lord*, pp. 33–4.

[3] Camelford to the Lord Chancellor, 23 September 1796. Cotes Papers, National Library of Wales.

[4] The Lord Chancellor to Camelford, n.d. Draft in the Cotes Papers, National Library of Wales.

prospectus for an ambitious four-volume work entitled *A general compendium; or, Abstract of chemical, experimental, and natural philosophy* was published in Philadelphia. The complete work never appeared. Charles was back in England by the time Mudge arrived from Nootka with dispatches and letters from Captain Vancouver in June 1793, and it is interesting to find that he proposed to become involved in the settlement of his brother's difficulties with the Spaniards. In July Charles' friend John Tiott gave him a letter of introduction to Thomas Martyn, the botanist, who in turn proposed to introduce Charles to Sir Joseph Banks. Tiott's letter read in part:

Difficulties have occurred at Nootka Sound, which prevents a final settlement of the Dispute; & probably Government will find it necessary to send some persons there to settle those disputes. This gentleman is very enterprising & has great abilities. He has been some years endeavouring to establish a Colony in the back parts of America, and has overcome innumerable difficulties; but some unfortunate circumstances in this country have disconcerted all his hopes. He has taken up the Idea of penetrating to Nootka thro America by going to Quebec & from thence...to the boatable waters of the River Origen, or Oragan, or River of the West, which discharges itself into the Pacific Ocean a little to the Southward of King George's or Nootka Sound.'

Tiott hoped that Banks might 'recommend him to Government under whose auspices he would be very happy to engage in the undertaking.'[1]

This was a remarkable proposal, for no European had as yet crossed North America north of Mexico. But, as it happened, it was made just as the feat was about to be accomplished. Five days after Tiott wrote to Martyn, Alexander Mackenzie reached tidewater at the mouth of the Bella Coola River, thus completing his celebrated journey across the continent.

Charles now turned to his other interests, and in 1794 the Board of Agriculture published his *General view of the agriculture in the County of Cambridge*. A volume on the county of Essex followed in 1795, and other studies would appear after the turn of the century.

Charles Vancouver's letter in the *Chronicle* probably promoted the publication of the savagely satirical caricature by James Gillray depicting 'The Caneing in Conduit Street'. One of the several inscriptions reads: 'Chas Rearcover, Letter to be published after the parties are bound to keep the Peace'. Captain Vancouver appears as a gross, cowardly figure, crying 'Murder', with a long paper hanging

---

[1] John Tiott to Thomas Martyn, 14 July 1796. Richard H. Dillon, 'Charles Vancouver's plan', *Pacific Northwest Quarterly* XLI (1950), p. 356.

Plate 7. John Vancouver.

Plate 8. 'The Caneing in Conduit Street.' Caricature by James Gillray.

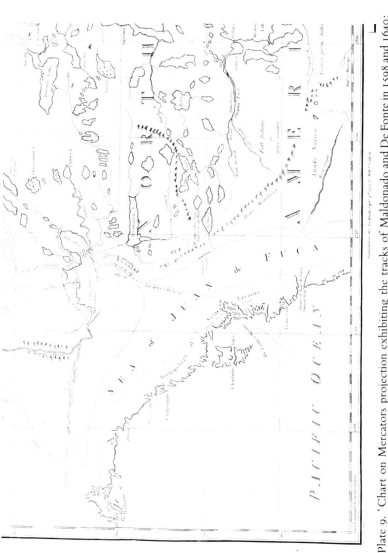

Plate 9. 'Chart on Mercators projection exhibiting the tracks of Maldonado and De Fonte in 1598 and 1640; compared with the modern discoveries.' From Goldson's *Observations*, 1793.

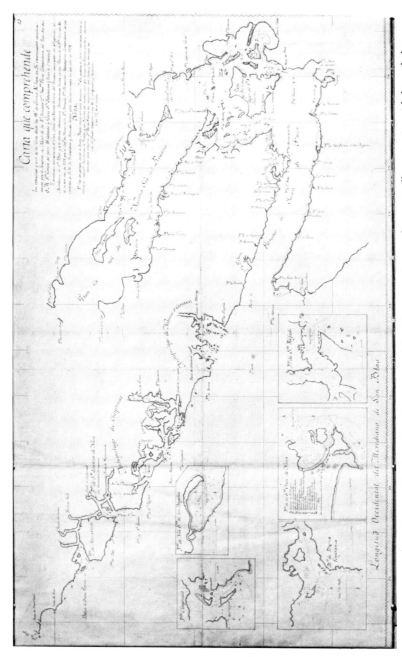

Plate 10. Map compiled at Nootka, after the return of the Eliza expedition of 1791. It illustrates Spanish knowledge of Juan de Fuca Strait and Georgia Strait at the time of Vancouver's arrival in 1792.

from his sword bearing the note: 'List of those disgraced during the Voyage – put under Arrest all the Ship's Crew – Put in Irons every Gentleman on board – Broke every man of Honor & Spirit – Promoted Spies &c.' He is trampling under foot the motto: 'Every Officer is the Guardian of his own Honor'. There are two references to other events on the voyage. A fur warehouse in the background displays 'Fine Black Otter Skins' and Vancouver has over his shoulders a feather cloak labelled 'The Present from the King of Owyhee to George III forgot to be deliverd.' (Why the presentation of the gift of Kamehameha was delayed we do not know, but it was finally presented to the King by the Duke of Portland in 1797.)

Random references indicate that the clash with Camelford was soon followed by a charge that a mutiny had occurred on the *Discovery*. A memorial to this effect was evidently submitted, but by whom and to whom does not appear. Writing from Portsmouth late in November 1796 Barrie told his mother that 'as the late affair is much talk'd over here, and as *we* are unjustly charged with *mutiny* (from what spring I know not) I have wrote to Mr. Vancouver for a written acquittal of such a charge as to myself.' And he added: 'I fear this discovery business will never be made up without a Public investigation of the affair which will be very disagreeable.'[1] Vancouver replied promptly with a generous tribute to Barrie's 'conduct and behaviour' whilst under his command.[2] Sykes, Vancouver's agent, evidently considered an inquiry 'an impossibility' but Vancouver thought otherwise. 'If the investigation is to stand over until I can attend personally to it,' he wrote to Sykes in March 1797 in a letter that reflects both his state of mind and state of health, 'most likely the whole business will be settled long ere that period arrive, as although I am undoubtedly in a recovering state it will be some months before I shall be able to venture a visit to London.' Sykes urged him to make his health the first consideration, but Vancouver replied that 'the ascertaining & refuting the *falsehood* in Question is an *indispensable duty*, which I owe to all those, whom at the time I had the honor to command.' He had not seen the memorial in which the charge had been made, and as he thought Sykes should be able to 'gain a sight of the paper in Question' he begged him to do so.[3]

---

[1] Barrie to Mrs George Clayton, 21 November 1796. Barrie MSS, Perkins Library, Duke University.

[2] Vancouver to Barrie, 20 November 1796. *Ibid.*

[3] Vancouver to Sykes, 15 March 1797. Godwin, *Vancouver: A Life*, p. 284.

No court of inquiry was ever convened. The state of Vancouver's health, which became worse rather than better, Camelford's absence in the West Indies, and his conduct there, doubtless all contributed to the decision.

The day before Captain Vancouver wrote to Sykes Charles Vancouver found himself again embroiled with Camelford. After the Conduit Street encounter Camelford had sent him a challenge, but as he was aware that Camelford had been required to find sureties to keep the peace for a year he had not responded. On 14 March 1797, while Charles was in the Piccadilly shop of Jesse Ramsden, the instrument maker, he was sighted by Camelford, who entered at once and demanded if he would meet him as soon as the year expired. Charles declined to give an immediate answer, whereupon Camelford, in the course of a long tirade, intimated 'that it was in vain for him or his Brother . . . to attempt any Palliatives for that revenge he was determined to have by some means or other'.[1]

Fortunately Camelford and Charles were soon a safe distance apart. Camelford joined a ship bound for the West Indies and Charles sailed for America. Charles returned to Europe in the autumn, but went first to Holland, where he tried unsuccessfully to sell some of his American property.[2] From Holland, on September 28, the day Camelford's sureties expired, Charles wrote to him, proposing, if he still insisted on a duel, that they should meet on Ham Common. He received no reply, as Camelford was out of the country, but later his letter fell into the hands of Camelford's mother. Greatly alarmed, she appealed to the Lord Chancellor, and the upshot was that Charles was required to provide sureties to keep the peace. He was unable to raise the sum required, and early in 1798 retired to Holland.

About the time that Camelford encountered Charles in Piccadilly he had at last been promoted to lieutenant. The formalities revealed that Captain Vancouver was not the only one who had been critical of his behaviour. Captain Edward Riou, who had commanded the *Guardian* when she met disaster, refused to sign the certificate for his promotion 'as during the time he was under my Command his

[1] Affidavit of Charles Vancouver, 5 May 1797. Cotes Papers, National Library of Wales. This was prepared for Captain Vancouver in case some statement of the kind was required during his absence in America. Charles was convinced of its substantial accuracy, 'from having made written minutes thereof within a few days after the same occurred.'

[2] There were also more personal reasons for the visit. He was in close touch with the van Coeverden family, now established in Vollenhove, on the Zuider Zee, and would marry Louise Josephine van Coeverden the following year.

Conduct was such as not to entitle him to it.'[1] Camelford seems always to have aroused strong feelings of either like or dislike and when, early in August 1797, he joined the *Vengeance*, a 74 attached to the squadron based on St Kitts, he quickly won the warm approval and even affection of her captain. No doubt it was his recommendation that prompted the Admiral commanding to give Camelford the acting rank of master and commander and appoint him to the sloop *Favorite*, whose captain had been taken ill. Camelford's naval career seemed at last to be set fair, but near disaster was in the offing. His arrogance, bad temper and propensity for violence soon ruined his prospects. His biographer remarks that he 'acted at this time in a violent and eccentric manner more appropriate to the Spanish Main a century earlier.'[2] Due to a blunder, his ship fired on a British fortification; a man was killed when his press gang attempted to seize seamen in a merchantman; and finally he shot and killed Lieut. Charles Peterson, for alleged mutiny. Personal differences contributed to this tragedy. Camelford and Peterson disliked one another cordially, and Peterson, who stood higher on the seniority list than Camelford, resented having to take orders from him to such a point that he was driven to refuse to obey them.

The opinion was widely held that Camelford was deranged. *The Times* commented that 'this is the best apology that can be made for his conduct in many instances.'[3] In the five years of life that remained to him Camelford was to continue to display the eccentricity and outbursts of violence that had characterized his naval career. But he was not without attractive qualities and friends who appreciated them. One of them was Robert Barrie, who had been a fellow midshipman in the *Discovery* for nearly three years, and whose letters to his mother contain interesting references to Camelford. Though he and Camelford were having a temporary disagreement at the time, he was quick to come to his defence after the Conduit Street encounter: 'I well know him to have a good heart and his true character is very different to that the world gives him he has only one fault and that a very common one he is a wild young man and tho he sometimes might act imprudently his conduct never merited the ignominious punishment he received [in the *Discovery*].'[4] Some time after Camelford's virtual dismissal from the Navy he wrote: 'be not alarmed at my intimacy with him, I have

[1] Quoted in Tolstoy, *The Half-Mad Lord*, p. 16, quoting P.R.O., Adm 1/2400.
[2] *Ibid.*, p. 46.
[3] Quoted *ibid.*, p. 77.
[4] Barrie to Mrs George Clayton, 12 October 1796. Barrie, MSS., Perkins Library, Duke University.

known him nearly ten years & his eccentricities aside I know not a more brave, generous, or Friendly fellow'.[1] Later Barrie probably became Camelford's best friend, and there is general agreement that if he had been available to reason with him before his duel with another good friend, Captain Thomas Best, in March 1804, the fatal encounter would have been avoided.

Thanks to Camelford and the press, the last year and a half of Vancouver's life was a trying time for him and his brothers. When Charles proposed to meet Camelford on Ham Common, he explained that he did so 'rather than subject my character to a renewal of those foul, false, and scandalous aspersions with which the public papers teemed' at the time of the Conduit Street encounter.[2] The Gillray caricature aroused widespread mirth and came near to making Vancouver a laughing stock. It will be recalled that a few months before its appearance he had remarked in his letter to Lord Chatham that he felt 'as it were insulated, from all connections with persons of consequence', and the public clash with Camelford accentuated that feeling. But he must have been aware that he had one friend at court. Throughout the whole affair Lord Grenville, in spite of being the 'person of consequence' closest to Camelford, made every effort to prevent violence and to keep the protagonists apart.

All through this troubled time Vancouver toiled at the task of preparing *The Voyage of Discovery* for the press. The text he wrote himself, but others provided the illustrations and charts. With the exception of the well-known view of the *Discovery* on the rocks in Queen Charlotte Sound, the original of which was by Lieut. Zachary Mudge, all the views published were from sketches by three of the midshipmen – John Sykes, Henry Humphrys and Thomas Heddington. Vancouver had a considerable collection from which to choose. Broughton had brought 27 sketches by Sykes and a dozen by Humphrys with him from Monterey. Hewett states that 'Many of the Young Gentlemen were not only able but in the course of the Voyage did take a great many Views &c but destroyed them all when they understood their Drawings must be given up and Published for the Emolument of Vancouver who had behaved in a most outrageous and Illiberal manner to most of them.' This is an exaggeration. Sykes handed over 90 drawings just

[1] *Ibid.*, 30 September 1800.
[2] Charles Vancouver to Camelford, 28 September 1797. Cotes Papers, National Library of Wales.

before the *Discovery* reached St Helena, and at some stage Heddington 'lodged' a collection in the Hydrographic Office. The sketches selected for publication were redrawn for the engravers by William Alexander, later the first Keeper of Prints and Drawings in the British Museum.

For help with the charts Vancouver turned to Joseph Baker, upon whom he had depended heavily throughout the voyage. Mudge and Broughton, the couriers Vancouver sent to London, both took with them charts showing what had been accomplished during the first surveying season. Only a small preliminary sketch was available when Mudge left Nootka in September 1792,[1] but Broughton, leaving Monterey three months later, was able to take two much larger and more detailed charts.[2] One of the latter was the first to include data from Spanish sources. Its elaborate title includes the note: 'The parts of the Coast [coloured] red, are copied from Spanish Charts constructed by the Officers under the orders of Sen.^{res} Quadra and Malaspina.' The Spanish contribution consisted of virtually the whole of the coast of Vancouver Island, with the exception of the east coast from a point a little south of Cape Mudge to the Nimpkish River; this Vancouver had examined himself. Vancouver's acknowledgement was a well deserved courtesy, but it also gave notice that he was accepting responsibility only for the continental shore, which his own ships and boats had traced in detail. It is interesting to find that while the delineation of that shore on this early chart differs only in very minor respects from that on plate 5 in the folio atlas, the Spanish contribution was revised drastically, not always for the better. This is particularly true of the part of the chart depicting Nootka Sound and the adjacent coastlines. The sound itself is shown much more accurately and in greater detail on the 1792 manuscript map than on the engraving, while Esperanza Inlet, north of the sound, is shown on the earlier chart but is omitted altogether on the later version. Vancouver distrusted Spanish maps, often with good reason, but it is difficult to account for these particular changes, as he was personally familiar with Nootka Sound and certainly knew of the existence of Esperanza Inlet. From the first Vancouver had entrusted the compilation of the expedition's master charts to Baker, but he cannot be blamed for these inaccuracies; the map title states that both charts were prepared by him 'under the immediate inspection' of Captain Vancouver.

Three times in the later stages of the voyage Vancouver sent charts

---

[1] Now in P.R.O., C.O. 5/187.
[2] Now in the Hydrographic Department at Taunton.

to London recording the progress of the survey, but none of them is now available. Some have disappeared; others were lost in transit. The final versions of his charts for the Admiralty were prepared during the homeward passage. At Monterey Baker had been appointed first lieutenant of the *Discovery*, and drafting them became his chief responsibility. Barrie notes that thereafter he had 'for the most part of the voyage the Charge of the 1st Lieuts watch, he being employ'd about the Charts &c.'[1] Baker's assistant was midshipman Edward Roberts, who had been strongly recommended to Vancouver by William Wales, and who fulfilled Vancouver's expectation that he would 'be of great use both as a draughtsman, and a calculator.'[2]

In the folio atlas the titles of the seven sectional charts of the North American coast and the chart of the Sandwich Islands all state that they were prepared by Baker under the 'immediate inspection' of Captain Vancouver. The chart depicting the coast as a whole is similarly ascribed to Edward Roberts (in back pocket). The phrase somehow suggests a certain reluctance on Vancouver's part to give credit to others. This suspicion is heightened by a proof copy of the engraved version of the chart of the Sandwich Islands in the map library of the Hydrographic Department at Taunton. On the proof Baker's name appears in larger capital letters than Vancouver's. In the final engraving the order of magnitude has been reversed. The lack of any acknowledgement to Broughton is surprising. His name is not mentioned on the first plate in the atlas, devoted to the expedition's discoveries in the southern hemisphere, although it was based largely on sketches by him.

The publication date on all ten of the plates is 1 May 1798, eleven days before Vancouver's death. The precise date when *A Voyage of Discovery* was published does not appear, but it was probably late in August or early in September. It was soon noticed that Broughton's important detailed survey of the Columbia River was represented in the atlas only by a small-scale outline on plate 5. To make good this omission it was engraved and published by Aaron Arrowsmith on 1 November 1798. For some reason he reverted to the name by which the river had been known previously and entitled the engraving *Plan of the River Oregan from an Actual Survey*. Its appearance cannot have been due to any action on Broughton's part, as he did not return to England, after the loss of the *Providence*, until February 1799.

---

[1] Barrie to Mrs George Clayton, 12 September 1795. Barrie MSS, Perkins Library, Duke University.

[2] Vancouver to Stephens, 17 April 1791. P.R.O., Adm 1/2628, f. 607.

Publication of the *Voyage* had been greatly delayed by Vancouver's failing health. As early as the summer of 1796 Barrie, to whom Vancouver had promised a copy, thought that it 'must come out very soon'.[1] But various postponements followed. 'I have heard that Vancouver's Voyage is to come out in May,' Barrie wrote to his mother in March 1798, 'but he has put it off so often that there is no saying it will be so.'[2] Of the notices that greeted its appearance two are of considerable interest. The lengthy summary and comment in the recently founded *Naval Chronicle* gave it almost fulsome praise: 'We have not of late years perused any voyage so well composed, and throughout arranged in so judicious and able a manner, as the valuable one that has been presented to the public in these volumes. Both in point of composition and ability, it must always rank high among those works which are considered as naval classics by professional men. At the head of these the relation of Lord Anson's Voyage has long been placed: and we think, with due submission to the opinion of others, the present one by Vancouver deserves in point of literary merit to be held in equal estimation.'[3]

Barrie did not receive the complimentary copy he expected,[4] but he was able to examine a set briefly early in October. He gave his impressions in a letter to his mother: 'I have seen it and from the partial skim I had over it it appears to me to be written in very plain language & to abound with too Much tautology [technology?] to be pleasant reading to any but a nautical person – but I am now reading the voyage of Perouse which is told in the most elegant language and all his misfortunes of which he had many are most pathetically related – but it is not fair to draw a comparison between Vancouver who was a mere sailor & Perouse who was himself a man of education & besides assisted by several men of science. Vancouver however I hear from those who have read it is pretty correct his Charts are excellent perhaps indeed without doubt the best in the world – of the drawings I am no judge.'[5]

---

[1] Barrie to Mrs George Clayton, 1 August 1796. Barrie MSS, Perkins Library, Duke University.

[2] *Ibid.*, 13 March 1798.

[3] *Naval Chronicle*, 1 (1799), 221.

[4] 'I know if Capt Vancouver was alive he would have given me a Copy yet as he never actually promis'd me one I dont see that consistent with Propriety I can ask it of his Brother. The Lieuts. of each ship have copies – but I (tho frequently doing Lieuts duty) was only a Midshipman – and not one of that class have been presented with a Book.' The price per copy was 6 gns. Barrie to Mrs George Clayton, 3 October 1798. The original letter is in the collection of Mr Tom L. Brock, who very kindly provided a facsimile copy.

[5] *Ibid.*

Six months later his opinion was much less favorable: 'I have read Vancouver's Voyage,' he wrote in May 1799, 'and even tho. I accompanied him I think it is one of the most tedious books I ever read.'[1]

The truth lies somewhere between Barrie and the *Chronicle*. The narrative is the plain unvarnished tale that Vancouver's own introduction warns the reader to expect, without 'elegance of diction' or 'purity of style' but giving an honest and straightforward account of the expedition and its accomplishments. The voyage is described in the same detailed and conscientious way in which Vancouver's ships and boats carried out their survey. As remarked previously, at times the text resembles official sailing directions, but this is intentional; text and charts were designed to be both a description of exploration and a navigational aid for mariners sailing the waters surveyed. John Vancouver's remark that he had omitted 'log-book minutes' from the account of the homeward voyage from Valparaiso suggests that this was a concept with which he had little sympathy. But, as Vancouver explains, the purpose of the expedition was 'to obtain useful knowledge' and he considered it his duty to convey that knowledge 'in a way calculated to *instruct*, even though it should fail to *entertain*.'[2] Unfortunately in one respect John Vancouver found it impracticable to complete the work as his brother had planned it. There are a good many descriptions of native peoples and natural history scattered through the volumes, but Vancouver had something further in mind. He 'had made many curious observations' which he intended to bring together in one or more supplementary chapters, but the notes were so fragmentary that John could not attempt to draft a text. But he did add a few notes made by Vancouver after his return to England, notably an account of his conversations with Captain Colnett.[3]

The second review of special interest appeared in the *Annual Register* for 1799. The length of the article – 20 pages – was an acknowledgement of the importance of the expedition, but Vancouver would have found its concluding paragraphs exasperating. His claim to have proven that no entrance to a passage through the continent existed within the limits of his survey was questioned, and his failure to investigate the Columbia River when it was first sighted returned to haunt him. The initial statement reads: 'The labours of this voyage have much lessened

[1] Barrie to Mrs George Clayton, 8 May 1799. Barrie MSS, Perkins Library, Duke University.
[2] Vancouver, I, xxix.   [3] *Ibid.*, xxxi.

the grounds of reasonable hope that any navigable water communication exists, between the Atlantic and Pacific oceans, through the continent of America – but that they are, "as conclusive as possible," will not, by many, be readily admitted. Whatever contempt may be shewn for closet discoveries, they have certainly some support, while there remain openings without any ascertained termination, for the indulgence of speculative fancies concerning a N.W. passage. It may likewise be argued that, as the river Columbia and Port des Français [Lituya Bay] were passed by Captain Vancouver, if not without being noticed, without being thought worthy of examination, so might other openings equally have escaped observation'. And the review concluded: 'On the whole, we must be allowed to repeat, that the prospect is considerably lessened, but, that it is by no means yet proved, that a N.W. passage does not exist.'[1]

Some years were to pass before it was realized that the wide-ranging travels of fur traders, and in particular the expeditions of Samuel Hearne and Alexander Mackenzie, both of whom had reached the Arctic Ocean, had shown that Vancouver was correct, and that no navigable water communication could exist south of the Arctic itself.

Vancouver's narrative aroused considerable interest abroad; within three years versions of it had been published in four languages. A handsome French edition consisting, like the original, of three quarto volumes and a folio atlas, was published in Paris in 1799 (an VIII). It was followed by two versions in German and editions in Danish and Swedish, all in two volumes. John Vancouver decided to publish a new English edition, and this appeared in six octavo volumes in 1801. The copper plates from which the folio atlas was printed had been stolen (a pointless theft, as no use seems ever to have been made of them), and revised and reduced versions of the charts on two folding sheets were substituted. All the illustrations in the quarto volumes were retained, but the views in the atlas were omitted. The example this set was again followed promptly by the French; an octavo edition in six volumes (five of text and an atlas volume) was published in Paris within a year. Demand seems to have been brisk, as it was soon reprinted. Much later, in 1827–38, a Russian version in six volumes was published in St Petersburg (Leningrad). It is surprising that no Spanish translation appeared. The only part of the *Voyage* translated seems to have been the account of Vancouver's visit to Santiago. In 1902, more than a century after the event, a translation was published in that city.

[1] *Annual Register*, 1799, pp. 495–6.

The text of John Vancouver's octavo edition has been followed in the present reprint. He described it as 'A new edition, with corrections', but in addition to correcting the numerous misprints in the first edition he made a number of minor revisions. Dates are run into the text instead of appearing as marginal notes, which makes it easier to follow the narrative. Punctuation was revised and a host of superfluous commas were eliminated. Spelling was made more uniform, and the names of the days and the months were made to begin with a capital letter. Numbers are dealt with more consistently. Occasionally John Vancouver revised the wording; instances of any interest or significance are indicated in the footnotes. These changes, though unimportant in substance, make the narrative more attractive to the modern reader without impairing the character or integrity of Captain Vancouver's text. One less fortunate change, rarely noticed, has caused some confusion in place names.[1] For some unknown reason John decided to substitute 'channel' for 'canal' in the descriptions of waterways on the Northwest Coast. In a good many instances Vancouver's original terminology has been retained: Hood Canal, Portland Canal and Lynn Canal are examples. In others, 'channel' has won out, as in Burke Channel, Dean Channel and Grenville Channel. In still others neither is now used and 'inlet' has been substituted, as in Burrard Inlet, Jervis Inlet and Bute Inlet. The changes were made only in the text; they did not extend to the new engraving of the chart of the coast, which followed the nomenclature of Vancouver's original.

An astonishing proportion of the 388 place names bestowed during the voyage have survived, either in original or modified form. They are easily identified, as they are printed in small capitals in the text of both editions. Except for the names given by Broughton along the Columbia River, few of which are now in use, nine out of ten of Vancouver's names still apply. All fifteen of those mentioned in his description of the survey of the southwest coast of Australia are still current. Relatively few place names are mentioned in the original logs and journals, and it is usually impossible to ascertain when individual names were decided upon. Some were obviously bestowed at the time the features were sighted or explored; Mount Baker and Puget Sound

---

[1] To cite an example: 'It is a curious fact that Vancouver named many places "channels" in his journal, but wrote them down as "canals" on his excellent charts. This was the case with Hood's Canal.' E. S. Meany, *Vancouver's Discovery of Puget Sound* (New York, 1907; Portland, Ore., 1942), p. 110. Entries in the place-name lists in Wagner's *Cartography of the Northwest Coast of America* show that he, too, was unaware of the changes John Vancouver had made in the second edition.

are examples. The manuscript chart prepared by Baker and sent to London at the end of 1792 includes about half the names mentioned in Vancouver's account of the year's work. No doubt the same was true of the charts of the surveys carried out in 1793 and 1794, neither of which is now available. Additional names were added when Baker prepared the final versions of the charts on the homeward voyage from Monterey. Thus in his description of the survey of Behm Canal, carried out in August 1793, Vancouver states that he named Point Higgins and nearby Vallenar Point after Senor Higgins de Vallenar, president of Chili, with whom he had no dealings until his visit to Santiago in April 1795. The ever-critical Hewett seizes upon this discrepancy, which is of interest only because it shows that place names were added to the narrative and charts until late in the day.

Place names commemorating Vancouver have played a significant part in making him and his achievements better known. Three were to be of special importance: Vancouver Island, Fort Vancouver and the city of Vancouver, British Columbia. Vancouver has been accused of vanity in naming so large a feature as the island after himself. His dispatch to the Admiralty, written at the time, shows that it was bestowed following a request by Quadra that Vancouver 'would name some port or Island after us both, in commemoration of our meeting and the friendly intercourse that on that occasion had taken place; ... and conceiving no place more eligible than the place of our meeting, I have therefore named this land...The Island of Quadra and Vancouver'.[1] Thereafter it was the most prominent name on maps of the coast, and appeared on most British, French and Spanish maps of the period. But as Spanish interest in the region dwindled, so did Quadra's name. The Hudson's Bay Company played a major part in the transition; by 1824 'Vancouvers Island' had become the usual designation in its correspondence. By that time the United States was challenging British claims on the Northwest Coast, and in 1825, when the company established a new trading post on the Columbia River, Governor George Simpson christened it Fort Vancouver: 'The object of naming it after that distinguished navigator is to identify our claim to the Soil and Trade with his discovery of the River and Coast on behalf of G^t Britain.'[2] Fort Vancouver soon became the regional headquarters of

---

[1] Vancouver's 'Narrative of my proceedings...', Nootka, 26 September 1792. P.R.O., C.O. 5/187, f. 114.

[2] Frederick Merk (ed.), *Fur Trade and Empire. George Simpson's Journal...1824–1825* (Cambridge, Mass., 1931), p. 124. Entry for 19 March 1825.

the company and so continued until the Oregon boundary settlement placed it in American territory. The city of Vancouver, Washington, has grown up around its site. Vancouver Island soon became a widely known geographical feature, and the founding of the Colony of Vancouver Island in 1849 gave the name final and offical status. In 1884 W. C. Van Horne, then general manager of the Canadian Pacific Railway, decided to take advantage of the fact. The railway's trans-continental line was nearing completion and a name was required for the city-to-be on Burrard Inlet that would be its western terminus. He chose the name Vancouver because it was already associated in the public mind with the nearby island, and would therefore have the highly desirable effect of 'approximately locating the point at once'.[1] A sizeable community, harbinger of the great city and seaport of the future, had already sprung up by the time it was incorporated in 1886.

Through the years Vancouver's name has been given to a number of lesser features on or near the Northwest Coast, and to one prominent peak, Mount Vancouver (15,700 ft.), on the Yukon–Alaska boundary. The mountain, and nearby Mount Cook, were named by W. H. Dall of the United States Coast and Geodetic Survey in 1874. In Western Australia Cape Vancouver, Vancouver Rock and the Vancouver Peninsula commemorate his discovery of King George Sound, and in New Zealand Vancouver Arm, in Dusky Sound, recalls his survey there. Staten Island, off the coast of Tierra del Fuego, northeast of Cape Horn, would seem to be an unlikely place to be associated with Vancouver, but he was there with Cook on New Year's Day 1774, and bays on the northern and southern shores have been named Port Cook and Port Vancouver.

Captain Vancouver's will was signed on 28 April 1798.[2] He died on May 12 and on the 18th was buried in the churchyard of St Peter's, Petersham. His grave is marked by a plain headstone with the simple inscription: 'Captain George Vancouver | Died in the Year 1798 | Aged 40.' In 1840 the church vestry passed a resolution 'That it be suggested to the Hudson Bay Company that it would be a proper mark of respect to the memory of Captain Vancouver of the Royal Navy if a plain Monument Tablet were erected to him in Petersham Church.' The company agreed and the tablet was provided in 1841. Since 1929 a wreath from the Mayor and Council of the City of Vancouver has been placed on the grave each May.

[1] Van Horne to A. Ross, 21 November 1884. Archives, Canadian Pacific Limited, Montreal.
[2] For the text of the brief will see the appendix.

A word or two should be said about the later careers of John and Charles Vancouver. At the time of Captain Vancouver's death, John was living at Sutton, in Suffolk. In 1801, the year the second edition of the *Voyage* appeared, he was appointed agent to the Earl of Warwick. The Sutton property was sold and he moved to Tachbrook House, which belonged to the Warwick estate. He carried out his duties with such injudicious enterprise and energy that he involved the Earl in financial difficulties, and they parted company in 1804. Years later, in 1825, John published a memoir 'exhibiting the unmerited causes' of the 'reprobation and obloquy' that had befallen him.[1] In his later years he lived in London, where he died about the end of 1828. His will, dated 11 December, was proven on 3 February 1829. As already noted, Charles married Louise Josephine van Coeverden in 1799 at Vollenhove, in Holland, and after visiting John and other relatives in England he and his wife sailed for America. They spent several months in Philadelphia, then the capital of the United States, and were widely entertained. Mrs Vancouver was presented officially to Mrs Adams, wife of the President. The next two years were spent in Kentucky, after which the Vancouvers returned to Philadelphia for the winter of 1802–3. They were back in England in the autumn of 1803 and visited John at Warwick before travelling on to Vollenhove.[2] Charles evidently returned to England, as over the period 1808–13 he published surveys of agriculture in the counties of Devon, Hampshire and Huntingdon. He is said to have died in Virginia in 1815.

The later careers of the men who served in the *Discovery* and *Chatham* are of considerable interest. All the officers and midshipmen were living at the time of Vancouver's death, but two of them were not to survive for long. In October 1799 young Henry Humpheys died of smallpox, much to the grief of his cousin, Robert Barrie. Humphrys' career ended under a cloud, as the previous year a court martial had found him guilty of disrespect to his captain, and had ordered him dismissed from his ship and put at the bottom of the list of lieutenants. In January 1800 Commander James Hanson, who had sailed with the expedition as lieutenant of the *Chatham* and had been transferred to the *Daedalus*, was drowned in the sinking of his command, the sloop *Brazen*. By that

---

[1] *A Memoir exhibiting the unmerited causes of reprobation and obloquy which befel an Unfortunate Individual, resulting from his sincere attachment & zealous desire of improving the estates and meliorating the concerns of the Late Earl of Warwick* (Stratford-on-Avon, 1825).

[2] Details from a summary of the diary of Louise Vancouver, provided by Mr Adrien Mansvelt.

time mortality amongst the crewmen had been very high. Vancouver noted in 1796 that when the ships returned their crews 'were immediately turned over into other Ships of War and sent on Service',[1] and war and disease quickly took their toll. Writing to his mother at the time of Humphrys' death, Barrie remarked: 'He completes the 20th of the Discoverys who have died in their beds since we came home, 19 have been killed in action – & several Wounded in short one way or another we are almost all done up.'[2]

So far as the officers and midshipmen were concerned, he was unduly depressed. Most of them, himself included, were to survive a good many years – several to old age. Seven were to attain flag rank, but none of them was commissioned in time to have a command afloat. First of the seven was Puget, who was promoted to captain in 1797 and who twice commanded the famous 'fighting Temeraire'. He had considerable gifts as a strategist, which were demonstrated in 1804 by a detailed plan to attack the French fleet bottled up in Brest, and in 1805 by a proposal to capture the island of Ushant, off Brest, which provided the French with a valuable lookout from which to observe the movements of the British blockading squadron. These were followed in 1806 by plans to seize Valparaiso, which he remembered well from his visit there in the Chatham in 1795. These projects were admired but never carried out, but in 1807, at the second battle of Copenhagen, Puget commanded the attack by an in-shore squadron of cutters, brigs and bomb ketches that resulted in the capitulation of the city and the capture of the Danish fleet. His last service was as Commissioner of the Navy at Madras, in 1810–18, where he brought about a notable reduction in costs and corruption and superintended the removal of the naval headquarters to a new dockyard at Trincomalee, in Ceylon. Having risen to the top of the seniority list of captains, Puget was promoted to Rear Admiral in 1821. The Indian climate had ruined his health and he had retired to Bath, where he died the following year.[3]

The paths of Vancouver's officers crossed from time to time. Puget was to have been succeeded by James Johnstone, his lieutenant in the Chatham, who had been serving as Commissioner at Bombay, but

---

[1] Vancouver's memorial to the Treasury, 2 April 1796. P.R.O. 30/185.

[2] Barrie to Mrs George Clayton, 2 November 1799. Barrie MSS, Perkins Library, Duke University.

[3] For a full account of Puget's career see Robert C. Wing and Gordon Newell, Peter Puget (Seattle, 1979).

Johnstone's health had suffered to such an extent that he was unable to take up his new post. He and Puget returned to England together. Puget kept in touch with Joseph Baker; they were neighbours for a time and each named a son after the other. Baker was promoted to captain in 1809 and saw considerable action in the Baltic as commander of the frigate *Tartar*. She was wrecked on Anholt Island in August 1811, and although Baker was acquitted by a court martial, this seems to have ended his sea service. He was later in charge of a prisoners of war camp near Bristol. He died in 1817. Two of his sons attained high rank in the services: Admiral James Vashon Baker and General Sir William Baker. Captain Casper J. Baker, a son of the Admiral, renewed the family's association with the Northwest Coast in 1903–4, when he commanded the cruiser *Flora* on the Pacific Station. [1]

Broughton and Mudge were last mentioned as having sailed from Monterey in the *Providence* in June 1796. Having assumed (incorrectly as it transpired) that Vancouver had surveyed the southern part of the west coast of South America, Broughton asked his officers what they considered would be the most useful service the *Providence* could perform. All agreed that Broughton should endeavour to fill in the last blank on the map of the North Pacific by examining the coast of Asia from Chusan, in about 30° N to the shallows in the Straits of Tartary (now Tatarski Strait) in about 52° N. The *Providence* plodded across the Pacific by way of the Sandwich Islands (where two of her crew were killed by the natives) and sighted the Japanese coast in September. She visited a harbour at the south end of Hokkaido Island, and after cruising northward along its shore sailed southward to Macao, where she arrived in December. Broughton – quite rightly, as it proved – was very conscious of the dangers facing a lone ship in strange waters, and at Macao he purchased an 87-ton schooner to accompany the *Providence* on her survey. It was long thought that this schooner had been built at Tahiti by men from the *Bounty* who hoped to sail in her to Batavia, but it is now known that she was the *Prince William Henry*, which had spent several seasons trading for furs on the Northwest Coast. [2] She had paid her first visit to Nootka in October 1792, just as Vancouver was about to leave for California.

The two ships left Macao in April 1797 on what was expected to be Broughton's main surveying expedition, but in May the *Providence*

<hr/>

[1] John T. Walbran, *British Columbia Coast Names* (Ottawa 1909; new facsimile edition, Vancouver, 1971), p. 29.

[2] Alan Reid, 'Broughton's Schooner', *The Mariner's Mirror* LXIV (1978), pp. 241–44.

was wrecked on a reef east of Formosa (Taiwan). Natives at a nearby island assisted the survivors, and the schooner, overcrowded to a degree, carried them back to Macao. Nothing daunted, Broughton there discharged most of his crew (including Mudge) and late in June set out in the *Prince William Henry* to prosecute his survey. He succeeded in reaching his northern objective, and from it traced the Asiatic coastline southward to the south point of Korea. He then crossed the wide entrance to the Yellow Sea and charted the harbour of Chusan in 30° N, thus completing a survey that was no mean achievement. In 1804 Broughton published an account of his expedition entitled *A Voyage of Discovery in the North Pacific Ocean*, but it makes tedious reading, as it is devoted in great part to the 'log-book minutes' to which John Vancouver objected in his brother's narrative.

The high point in Broughton's career came in 1807, with his appointment as captain and commodore in the East Indies. Unfortunately his service there was not to end happily. In 1809 he set out from Malacca to make an attack on Java, but was considered to have been unduly cautious in carrying it out. The following year Rear Admiral Stopford joined the squadron and took command. Furious at being superseded, Broughton accused him of 'behaving in a cruel, oppressive, and fraudulent manner unbecoming the character of an officer, in depriving me of the command of the squadron'. He applied for a court martial, but it was not granted. When serving with Vancouver, Broughton had been well regarded, but at this time he was not popular. Lord Minto wrote in a private letter: 'The little commodore's brief hour of authority came to an end, to the great relief of all in the fleet and army.'[1] He returned to England in 1812, commanded a ship or two in home waters, and in 1819 became a Colonel of Marines. He died in Florence in 1821.

Mudge's later years were very different. He returned to England from Macao in May 1798, the month of Vancouver's death, and found that he had been promoted to commander the previous November. In 1800 he advanced to post captain. Two years later he took command of the frigate *Blanche* in the West Indies, and in 1805, when carrying dispatches intended for Nelson from Jamaica to the Barbados his ship was captured and sunk by a French squadron. Mudge was acquitted in the subsequent court martial. His last command was the 74-gun *Valiant*, in 1814–15. He lived on for 38 years thereafter. In 1830 seniority brought him flag rank; he advanced to Vice-Admiral in 1841 and to Admiral in 1849. He died in 1852 at the age of 82.

[1] Walbran, *British Columbia Coast Names*, p. 66.

Plate 12. Vancouver's grave in the churchyard of St Peter's Church, Petersham.

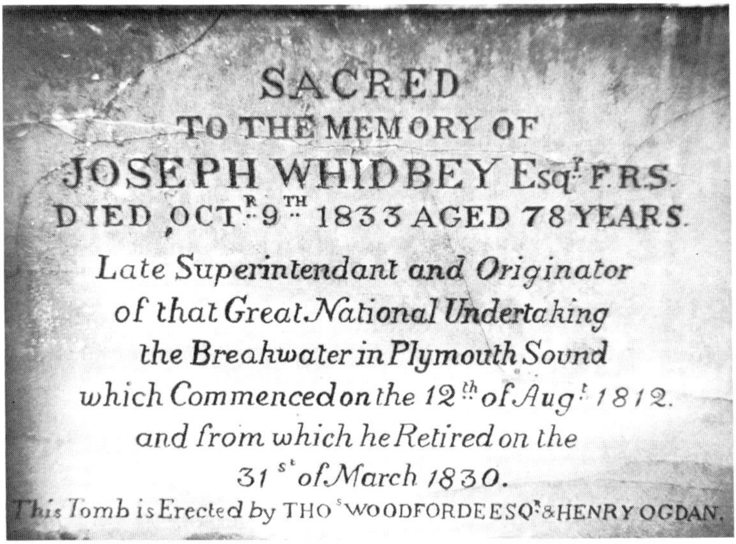

SACRED
TO THE MEMORY OF
JOSEPH WHIDBEY Esq.r F.R.S.
DIED OCT.r 9 TH 1833 AGED 78 YEARS.
Late Superintendant and Originator
of that Great National Undertaking
the Breakwater in Plymouth Sound
which Commenced on the 12 th of Aug.t 1812.
and from which he Retired on the
31 st of March 1830.
This Tomb is Erected by THO.s WOODFORDE ESQ.r & HENRY OGDAN.

Plate 13. Tombstone of Joseph Whidbey in Taunton, Somerset.

Plate 14. Plaque to Peter Puget, on his tombstone at Woolley, near Bath, where he spent the last three years of his life.

Of the midshipmen, Manby and Barrie seem to have had the most interesting careers. Late in 1796 Manby was given command of the 44-gun *Charon*, which was soon engaged in convoy duty, and he accomplished the extraordinary feat of escorting 4758 vessels from the Downs to Ireland without the loss of a single ship. It was intended that Lord Camelford should succeed Manby in command of the *Charon*, but one of his wild adventures prevented this. Promoted to post captain, Manby next commanded the *Le Bourdelais*, in which Barrie served as one of his lieutenants. Some years later, when in command of the *L'Africaine* in the West Indies, Manby had a distressing experience when his ship was carrying sick servicemen home to England. Yellow fever became rampant, nearly a third of those on board died, and Manby himself nearly succumbed. In 1808 rumours were afloat that two French frigates were bound for Davis Strait to destroy the Greenland fishery, and Manby was sent in the *Thalia* to investigate. The service record he compiled for the Admiralty bears the note: 'Gave up command of the Thalia [in March 1809] in consequence of ill health, from the effect of Yellow fever and the cold of Greenland.' He retired to an estate in Norfolk, was promoted to Rear Admiral in 1825, and died in 1834.[1]

Before joining Manby in the *Le Bourdelais* in 1800, Robert Barrie had spent five rather unhappy years in Sir Alan Gardner's flagships *Queen* and *Royal Sovereign*; he did not feel that his uncle was taking any very active interest in his advancement. His first command was the *Calypso* in 1801, and he was advanced to post rank in 1802. The next dozen years were marked by periods of great activity. He was appointed to the *Pomone* (38 guns) in 1806, and the next year she was engaged in an action off Brest that resulted in the capture of 14 brigs and the destruction of three others. Barrie himself considered that his greatest exploit was an attack on Sagone Bay, Corsica, in May 1811, in which the *Pomone* and two other ships silenced the batteries and sank the two French warships and an armed merchantman that were in harbour. This action was depicted in a series of three prints, published in London in 1812. The *Pomone* was wrecked later in the year, but a court martial attached no blame to Barrie. Some time after war broke out with the United States he was appointed to the *Dragon*, a 74, and from September 1813 until May 1814 he was commodore commanding the highly important blockade of the Chesapeake. He summarized his

[1] Manby's career is described in one of the longest notices in John Marshall, *Royal Naval Biography*, vol. 1 (London, 1823), pp. 199–212. The service record is in P.R.O., Adm 9/2 no. 99.

activities in a letter to his mother: 'My squad took upwards of eighty-five vessels. But I had so few ships under my orders that I would not weaken the crews by sending the Prizes into Port. Therefore they were all destroyed except about sixteen.'[1] (This had the unfortunate result of greatly decreasing his prize money.) In a later action a frigate was destroyed and over twenty other vessels captured or sunk. He was engaged in operations on the Georgia coast when peace was declared. From 1819 until 1834 Barrie was Senior Naval Officer in Canada and Commissioner for the naval dockyard at Kingston. He was knighted when he retired, and advanced to K.C.B. in 1840. He had attained flag rank in 1837, and died in 1841.

The other three midshipmen to attain flag rank were Spelman Swaine, Volant Vashon Ballard and John Sykes. In June 1802 Lord St Vincent gave Swaine command of the sloop *Raven*, in the Mediterranean, and he performed a service in her of which he was immensely proud. He added a note to his service record to recall that he 'led Lord Nelson's Fleet through the Straits of Bonificio on which occasion was complimented by Lord Nelson it being the first ship of that magnitude that had gone thro!'.[2] Like many of Vancouver's officers and midshipman, Swaine suffered shipwreck. The *Raven* was lost off the coast of Sicily in 1804, and in 1815 he lost another ship, the *Statira*, which came to grief on the rocks off Cuba. For the last fourteen years of his life he served as magistrate and chief bailiff of the Isle of Ely. He was promoted to Rear Admiral in 1846, at the ripe age of 77, and died in 1852.

Few details are available about Ballard's carrer. He was promoted to post captain in 1798, and seems to have spent his most active years in command of the *Blonde*. In 1807 she captured seven privateers within a period of a few weeks and added two French frigates to her score in 1809–10. Ballard was promoted to Rear Admiral in 1825 and died at Bath in 1832.

John Sykes, son of the London Navy Agent, was promoted to commander in 1800 and to post captain in 1806. He held a long series of sea appointments until 1837, but seems to have encountered little in the way of action or excitement. He retired with the rank of Rear Admiral in 1838, and lived on for twenty years to receive promotions to Vice-Admiral in 1848 and to Admiral in 1858. He died in the latter

---

[1] Barrie to Mrs George Clayton, 22 April 1814. The original letter is in the collection of Mr Tom L. Brock, who supplied other data for this paragraph, and who is preparing a life of Sir Robert Barrie.   [2] P.R.O., Adm 9/56 no. 3918.

year, and as his age was entered in the *Discovery*'s muster roll as 19 when Vancouver sailed, presumably he was 87 years old.

He was the longest-lived of the officer-midshipman group, but not the last survivor. That distinction belongs to Thomas Heddington, who, aged 15 when the expedition sailed, had been its youngest member. He was promoted to commander in 1806, but never advanced beyond that rank. His name last appears in the *Navy List* for March 1860, and it may be assumed that he died later in the year, at the age of 84.

Midshipman John Stewart is a person of some interest. He was a nephew of Rear Admiral Stewart, and writing from Nootka in September 1792 Vancouver informed the admiral that John 'had conducted himself with the greatest propriety and made himself excessively useful in attending to most of the important pursuits of our expedition.'[1] Stewart was also related to Admiral Elphinstone (later Viscount Keith), and from St Helena Vancouver assured him that young Stewart was 'a very excellent officer and deserving of every attention in case you should be inclined to wish his joining your squadron after our return to England'.[2] The *Naval Chronicle*, in a lengthy biographical notice, states that Keith did indeed patronize him 'in a conspicuous manner, and placed him in situations where his great abilities might appear'.[3] But before Keith entered the picture Stewart had encountered adventure. The *Arab*, the first ship to which he was appointed after his return, was wrecked in November 1795, and he was imprisoned by the French for a time before being exchanged. In 1797 he was with Keith in the *Queen Charlotte*, and when the ship burned in 1800 he was prominent in the rescue efforts. He was promoted to post captain in 1801, but died only ten years later at the early age of 37.

James Johnstone and Joseph Whidbey, who had carried out much of the detailed surveying for the Vancouver expedition, had very different later careers. Johnstone had been promoted to acting lieutenant of the *Chatham*, and he was confirmed in that rank after his return to England. In 1798 he joined the *Sans Pareil*, bound for the West Indies, flying the flag of Admiral Lord Hugh Seymour. Archibald Menzies, who had served with Johnstone on the Halifax Station as early as 1783, was once again a shipmate. Johnstone was promoted to commander in

[1] Vancouver to Admiral Stewart, September 1792. Scottish Record Office, Seaforth Papers, GD 46 17/6.

[2] Vancouver to Elphinstone, 10 July 1795. *Keith Papers*, 1, p. 329.

[3] *Naval Chronicle* XXVIII (1812), p. 4. The 'Memoir of the Public Services of the late Captain John Stewart, R.N.' runs to 47 pages.

1802 and to post captain in 1806. In 1808 he was appointed to the *Leopard*, based on Cape Town, and in 1810 moved to the *Scipion*, flagship of Rear Admiral Stopford. He may well have witnessed the humiliation of Broughton, who had been the first commander of the *Chatham*, when Stopford superseded him as commander of his squadron after the much criticized attack on Java. Johnstone was Commissioner of the Navy at Bombay from 1811 to 1817, and it was intended that he should then succeed Puget at Madras, but, as already noted, his health had failed and he was forced to return to England.

Whidbey, master of the *Discovery*, was recommended for promotion to master attendant by Vancouver, and the promotion followed. In 1806, when Master Attendant at Woolwich Dockyard, he was instructed to go to Plymouth with John Rennie, the famous civil engineer, and, with the master attendant there, to survey the harbour with a view to the building of a breakwater that would protect the entrance to Plymouth Sound. The plan proposed in their report was adopted, and when construction began in 1812, Whidbey was appointed resident superintendent. He held the position until ill health forced him to resign in 1830. He died at Taunton, Devon, in 1833. The breakwater, a mile in length, was completed in 1841.

Menzies' spell of duty in the *Sans Pareil* was his last in the Royal Navy. He then came ashore for good, qualified as a Doctor of Medicine at the University of Aberdeen, and established a medical practice in London. There he lived quietly until his death in 1842 at the age of 87. Menzies gives the impression of being a gentle soul, but one ready to endure hardships and physical risks in the pursuit of knowledge pertaining to natural history, native peoples, or any other matter that he considered interesting or significant.

Vancouver annoyed and even exasperated Menzies at times, but he respected his ability, integrity and complete devotion to duty. Indeed, Vancouver could wish for no better epitaph than the tribute Menzies paid him when he recalled the voyage in his 80th year: 'What days those were – a fine group of officers – all gone now – a credit to the Captain – he chose them all, except me; Baker and Whidbey; yes, and Johnstone – they became Captains too – Mudge and Puget – Admirals both of them. Those books that Vancouver wrote – strange that he could put so much of himself into the printed page. He was a great Captain.'[1]

[1] Quoted in Frank Turnbull, 'Vancouver and Menzies, or Medicine on the Quarter-deck', *Bulletin* of the Vancouver Medical Association, April 1954 (offprint), p. 11. This was the Osler lecture, delivered on 2 March 1954.

SOURCES

THE *Voyage of Discovery* is clearly a revised version of George Vancouver's own journals, but unfortunately the originals have disappeared. Vancouver lodged them with the Admiralty at the conclusion of the expedition, but they were given back to him when it was arranged that he should prepare them for publication. After his death they must have come into the possession of his brother John, but they were never returned to the Admiralty.

Vancouver's personal papers have also disappeared. Writing to Evan Nepean on 15 February 1798, he stated that a list of plates about which Nepean was inquiring was 'with other papers at a friends house in Berkshire', but the friend was not identified. A few papers are said to have been in the possession of the Peppercorne family, descendants of John Vancouver, who were living in Jersey, but these were destroyed in a fire during the German occupation. Mrs Caroline Bundy, granddaughter of Eliza Peppercorne (née McArthur), who was in turn a granddaughter of John Vancouver, has a miniature of him and a small desk once owned by Captain Vancouver.

Three logs that Vancouver kept as a lieutenant are in the National Maritime Museum. A fragmentary log records some of his service in the *Martin* (Adm L/M/16B. 9 Dec. 1781–16 May 1782); his short log of the *Fame* is complete (Adm L/F/115. 17 May 1782–3 July 1783), but that of the *Europa* only begins when he became her 2nd lieutenant (Adm L/E/155. 24 Nov. 1787–23 Nov. 1788).

Vancouver's letters to the Secretary of the Admiralty, including dispatches written while his expedition was in progress, are in P.R.O., Adm 1/2628–30. His report on his negotiations with Quadra and other correspondence are in P.R.O., C.O. 5/187. Some letters regarding the outfitting of the ships are found in the Navy Board Records (P.R.O., Adm 106), particularly in the Deptford Yard letter books. The location of various individual letters and documents scattered through other official files and in private collections is indicated in the footnotes when reference is made to them.

Logs and journals

In October 1795 Vancouver sent 16 logs from the *Discovery* to the Admiralty. Twelve of these are now available; those kept by Robert Barrie, Edward Harris, the Hon. Charles Stuart and Joseph Whidbey are missing. The latter is probably the most serious loss, judging by paraphrases and references to it in Vancouver's narrative. Whidbey was master of the *Discovery* throughout the voyage and participated in many of the most important boat expeditions.

In addition to the dozen logs on Vancouver's list we have part of an anonymous log kept in the *Discovery* and the log of Zachary Mudge, her 1st lieutenant, who left her in September 1792 to proceed to England with dispatches. There was considerable movement between the two ships. Spelman Swaine and Thomas Manby, whose logs are on Vancouver's list, both served as master of the *Chatham*, Swaine for a few weeks and Manby for two years. Peter Puget, originally 2nd lieutenant of the *Discovery*, took command of the *Chatham* in September 1792, and late in the voyage Henry Humphrys left the *Discovery* to become master of the *Chatham*. James Scott, a midshipman, served in the *Chatham* for most of the voyage, but moved to the *Discovery* for nearly four months near its end. There are three logs that relate exclusively to the *Chatham*, but none is known that was kept by either Broughton, her first commander, or Hanson, his lieutenant. In all there are thus twenty official logs, varying greatly in length and character, that record movements and activities of the expedition.

By great good fortune two interesting and highly informative private journals are available, and by further good fortune one was kept in each of the ships. The writer of a third private journal, unfortunately incomplete, moved from one ship to the other.

It will be convenient first to describe these three private journals and to note two brief logs that were kept in the *Discovery* in 1790 before Vancouver assumed command of her in mid-December.

Menzies, Archibald, botanist and surgeon. Private journal kept in the *Discovery*, primarily for the information of Sir Joseph Banks and the Royal Botanic Gardens at Kew.

B.L., Add. MS 32641. Dec. 1790–16 Feb. 1794. National Library of Australia, MS 155. 21 Feb. 1794–18 Mar. 1795.

Both manuscripts are in Menzies' own handwriting. A fair copy, several passages show that it was copied some time after the events described. Presumably the original, now missing, continued until the end of the voyage in September 1795.

A detailed and highly informative journal, running in all to 550 folios. It can be supplemented by papers in a number of collections, notably the following: Banks Papers in the Brabourne Papers, Mitchell Library, Sydney, which include letters from Menzies to Banks written during the voyage, and other papers relating to the expedition and Menzies' part in it; Banks Papers in the Sutro Library, San Francisco; the records of the Royal Botanic Gardens, which include a file of letters from Menzies, mostly written before or during the voyage. The Menzies family presented a small but interesting collection of papers to the Provincial Archives of British Columbia which includes Menzies' own copy of his instructions, signed by Banks.

Bell, Edward, clerk of the *Chatham.* Alexander Turnbull Library, Wellington, New Zealand. 1 Jan. 1791–26 Feb. 1794. The MS is in two volumes, and presumably there was originally a third volume, now missing.

A most interesting private journal, kept 'at the request of my friends on leaving home'. It is unsigned, but it has long been assumed that Bell was the author. What appears to be proof is found in an entry dated 23 Feb. 1793, at Kaelekakua Bay, where Vancouver had just issued an order 'forbidding all persons except Officers to go on shore but on duty.' Bell continued: 'However as I did not conceive that my situation [as clerk] in the Ship brought me under these Tyrannical Laws, more than Mr. Orchard [clerk of the *Discovery*] who I observed was a *free man.* I attended not to the order, nor did Mr P[uget, commander of the *Chatham*] extend it to me.'

Manby, Thomas, served successively as midshipman in the *Discovery,* master of the *Chatham,* and 3rd lieutenant of the *Discovery.* William Robertson Coe Collection, Yale University Library. 18 Feb. 1791–22 June 1793. Recently the Oregon Historical Society acquired another copy, in which spelling and punctuation frequently differ from the Yale copy, but the text is otherwise identical. Neither transcript is in Manby's own handwriting.

A private journal written in letter-like instalments, most of them dated. It breaks off in mid-sentence, and the continuation has disappeared. It was intended for Manby's friend John Lees, of Dublin, whom he warns 'not to expect philosophical transaction and observation, or the works of Nature unfolded like a Naturalist, but the scribble of a plain blunt Seaman to his Dearest Friend'. It is in fact an interesting and perceptive account of the earlier part of the voyage. The journal must have been kept secretly, as Manby retained possession of it. He also kept an official log, noted below, which was duly surrendered to Vancouver and forwarded to the Admiralty.

The two brief logs kept in the *Discovery* in 1790 before Vancouver was commissioned to command the expedition are the following:

Whidbey, Joseph. P.R.O., Adm 52/2262. 1 Jan.–20 May 1790.
There are two versions. The first (ff. 1–10) ends on May 19, and bears a certificate, signed by Roberts, stating that Whidbey had served as master under

his command 'from the 1st Day of January 1790 to the 19th Day of May 1790.' The somewhat shorter version (ff. 11–22) is signed by Whidbey.

Anonymous. P.R.O., Adm 53/403. 16 June to 14 Dec. 1790.

Kept while the *Discovery* was serving as a receiving ship during the Nootka Sound crisis and for a month or two after the work of outfitting her for an exploring expedition had been resumed. By December Roberts was again in command and Whidbey had returned to his post as master. The final entry reads: 'at 9 am Mr. Widbey [*sic*] the Master went to the Pay Office in London with the Ship Company Paid her off and put the Ship out of Commission.' The following day Vancouver was appointed to succeed Roberts as her commander.

Official logs

These are noted in alphabetical order. All twenty are in the Public Record Office. Some in effect become journals when the ships are in harbour. The most notable example of this is Puget's log, which includes extensive accounts of many of the anchorages visited and of most of the boat excursions in which he participated. Many of the logs kept by midshipmen are routine in character and confined almost entirely to ship's business. The wording of many entries is so similar that it appears to have been derived from a single source. The middies were obligated to keep logs, and may have agreed among themselves upon the wording, or perhaps taken it from the ship's log.

Eight of the logs end on 1 or 2 July 1795, when the *Discovery* was approaching St Helena and Vancouver took possession of all logs. Seven of the twenty bear the note 'Recd. 25th Octr. 1802', but the significance of the date is not known.

Additional logs certainly existed and have disappeared. In commenting on the loss of the third volume of Anderson's journal of Cook's third voyage, Beaglehole remarks: 'It may have been lost with other records of the voyage at Deptford before the transfer of the Admiralty collections thence to the custody of the Public Record Office in 1841.' Records of Vancouver's expedition may have suffered a like fate.

Anonymous. Adm 51/4534 pt. 4. *Discovery*, 3 Mar. 1791–8 May 1792. Possibly the first part of the missing log kept by the Hon. Charles Stuart, who joined the ship at Portsmouth on 3 Mar. 1791.

Baker, Joseph, successively 3rd, 2nd and 1st lieutenant of the *Discovery*. Adm 55/32. 22 Dec. 1790–27 Nov. 1792. Adm. 55/33. 28 Nov. 1792–1 July 1795. The longest of the logs kept by officers, running in all to 455 folios. Many 'observations' about the places visited. 2 charts and 7 views, all in the first part.

Ballard, Volant Vachon, midshipman. Adm 55/29. *Discovery*, 1 Mar. 1791–2

July 1795. Served as the ship's clerk 1 Dec. 1792–1 Dec. 1794. A concise, carefully kept log, much of which is now illegible.

Browne, John Aisley, midshipman. Adm 51/4533 pt. 53. *Discovery,* 1 Jan. 1791–26 Mar. 1795. Complete but concise. Like Ballard's log, is in many places almost impossible to read.

Dobson, Thomas, midshipman. Adm 51/4534 pt. 7. *Discovery,* 15 Mar. 1794–2 Dec. 1794. Titled 'No. 2'. Adm 51/4534 pt. 8. *Discovery,* 2 Dec. 1794–1 July 1795. Titled 'No. 3'. The first part is missing.

Heddington, Thomas, midshipman. Adm 55/15. *Chatham,* 1 Feb. 1791–13 Jan. 1793. Adm 55/16. *Chatham,* 14 Jan. 1793–2 July 1795. A note at the end of the latter, dated 4 July 1795 'Off St. Helena', states that it is the log of the *Chatham* 'From the Time of Lieutenant Pugets taking the Command to the Time of the Delivery of our Log Books.' Heddington drew many sketches in the course of the expedition but there are none in his log. A careful chronicle.

Humphrys, Henry, midshipman in the *Discovery* and master of the *Chatham.* Adm 55/26. *Discovery,* 16 Dec. 1790–27 Nov. 1794. *Chatham,* 27 Nov. 1794–Oct. 17, 1795. A carefully written fair copy. Humphrys evidently retained possession of his log (or a copy of it), as it continues until the end of the voyage. Like Heddington, he drew many sketches and there are 13 views and 3 surveys in his log.

Johnstone, James, master and later lieutenant of the *Chatham.* Adm 53/335. *Chatham,* 2 Jan. 1791–20 May 1792. A carefully written fair copy; interesting and informative. Vancouver quotes or paraphrases descriptions from later parts, but unfortunately only this first part (179 folios) has survived. Includes one view and five surveys.

McKenzie, George Charles, midshipman. Adm 51/4534 pt. 5. *Discovery,* 26 Nov. 1791–11 Dec. 1792. Adm 51/4534 pt. 6. 12 Dec. 1792–25 Feb. 1794. Consists in all of only 82 folios. In journal rather than log format.

Manby, Thomas, master's mate of the *Discovery,* master of the *Chatham* and 3rd lieutenant of the *Discovery.* Adm 53/403 ff. 187–245. *Discovery,* 16 Dec. 1790–5 June 1792; ff. 252–57. 6 June–26 Sept. 1792. Adm 51/2251. *Chatham,* 27 Sept. 1792–8 Oct. 1794. Adm 53/403 ff. 246–51. *Chatham,* 9 Oct.–25 Nov. 1794; ff. 257–300. *Discovery,* 2 Dec. 1794–2 July 1795. Manby's original log, frequently expanded into a journal when the ship was in harbour. Six surveys.

Mudge, Zachary, 1st lieutenant of the *Discovery.* Adm 51/4533 pt. 52. 4 Jan. 1791–1 Oct. 1792. A few descriptive notes. Two views. Mudge drew the view of the *Discovery* on the rocks that was engraved and published in the *Voyage.* The last entry reads in part: 'sailed the Portuguese Brig with Mr Mudge for his passage to China on dispatches.'

Orchard, Henry Masterman, clerk and midshipman in the *Discovery.* Adm 55/31. *Discovery,* 1 Dec. 1792–30 Nov. 1794. The log kept by Orchard during the two years when Vancouver, for reasons unknown, changed his status from clerk to midshipman.

Pigot, Robert, midshipman. Adm 55/30. *Discovery,* 7 Jan. 1791–7 Jan. 1795. Adm 51/4534 pt. 9, *Discovery,* 8 Jan.–2 July 1795. Four views.

Puget, Peter, 2nd and 1st lieutenant of the *Discovery*; commander of the *Chatham*. Adm 55/27. *Discovery*, 4 Jan. 1791–14 Jan. 1793. Adm 55/17. *Chatham*, 13 Jan. 1793–6 Feb. 1794. Four views. A fair copy, but in Puget's own handwriting throughout. The most interesting and valuable of all the officials logs, and in great part a journal. A personal and often outspoken account. Presumably there was a third volume, now missing. As noted below, Puget's rough logs are in the British Library.

Roberts, Edward, midshipman. Adm 51/4534 pt. 1. *Discovery*, 19 Feb. 1791–11 Feb. 1792. Titled 'Book 1st'. Adm. 51/4534 pt. 2. 31 Mar. 1793–12 Apr. 1794. Titled 'Book 3rd'. Originally in four books, of which only the first and third have survived. Some interesting notes and comments.

Scott, James Woodward, midshipman. Adm 51/4534 pt. 3. *Chatham*, 3 Mar.–17 Aug. 1791. Adm 55/14. *Chatham*, 18 Aug. 1791–7 Oct. 1793; *Discovery*, 8 Oct. 1793–19 Feb. 1794; *Chatham*, 20 Feb. 1794–29 May 1795.

Sherriff, John, master's mate. Adm 53/334. *Chatham*, 18 Aug. 1791–6 June 1795. Seven views and eight surveys. An interesting, informative log, with many descriptive entries in journal form. Many parts are now difficult or impossible to read.

Stewart, John, midshipman in *Discovery*. Adm 51/4533 pt. 54. 1 Jan.–11 July 1791. Adm 55/28. 12 July 1791–28 July 1794. Adm 51/4533 pt. 55. 29 July 1794–2 July 1795. Three surveys. Expands into a concise journal when the ship was in harbour.

Swaine, Spelman, master's mate in *Discovery*, briefly master of the *Chatham*, 3rd lieutenant of *Discovery*. Adm 51/4532 pt. 1. *Discovery*, 18 Dec. 1790–30 Aug. 1792. *Chatham*, 31 Aug.–26 Sept. 1792. Adm 51/4532 pt. 2. *Discovery*, 27 Sept. 1792–2 July 1795.

Sykes, John, midshipman. Adm 55/25. *Discovery*, 18 Dec. 1790–28 Feb. 1795. Sykes drew many sketches during the voyage but there are none in his log. Neatly kept but not very informative.

Other manuscript sources

Home Office Records
P.R.O., H.O. 28/61. Correspondence with the Admiralty
Includes draft dispatches outlining the plan to establish a settlement on the Northwest Coast and papers relating to John Meares, his memorial, and the Nootka Sound crisis.

P.R.O., H.O. 42/18. George III correspondence
Items relating to arrangements for Vancouver's expedition, including communications between Banks and Grenville regarding Menzies, his instructions, and the instructions given to Vancouver regarding him.

Admiralty 9/2. Returns of Officers' Services
Adm 9/2 consists of memoranda tabulating their services, provided in 1817 and subsequent years by naval officers. They include returns from Broughton, Mudge, Puget, Johnstone, Manby, Swaine and Barrie. A further return by Mudge is in Adm 196/5 no. 378.

Puget, Peter. 'Papers relating to the voyage of the *Discovery* and *Chatham*, 1790–1795.' Presented to the British Museum by Puget's son, Capt. W. D. Puget, R.N., in 1848.

B.L., Add. MS 17542–44. Rough logs, 1 Jan. 1791–25 Jan. 1793. Add. MS 17548. Rough log 15 Jan. 1794–Sept. 1795. There is an additional log for the period 18 Aug.–16 Oct. 1791 in Add. MS 17548.

Add. MS 17545 and 17550–51 contain notes in both log and journal form. Add MS 17552 includes the originals or copies of orders issued to Broughton or Puget by Vancouver regarding the treatment of native peoples, restrictions on shore leave, arrangements for rendezvous, etc., and the surviving part of the description of the overland journey from Valparaiso to Santiago prepared by Puget for John Vancouver.

Cotes Papers, National Library of Wales
Extracts relating to Lord Camelford's quarrel with Vancouver and the threatened duel, first with Vancouver and later with his brother Charles, 1796–98. The papers include the affidavits sworn to by Vancouver and his brother.

Barrie, Robert. Barrie MSS, Perkins Library, Duke University, Durham, North Carolina. These include a long series of letters, almost all addressed to his mother, Mrs George Clayton. Those of interest in the present context were written between 1790 and 1804. Barrie became a close friend of Thomas Pitt, second Baron Camelford, and most of the later letters relate to him.

Additional Barrie letters are in the possession of Mr Tom L. Brock, of Victoria, B.C., who most kindly provided photocopies.

The Barrie Papers in the Massey Library at the Royal Military College, Kingston, Ontario, contain no references to his years with Vancouver.

Hewett, George Goodman. Comments on page margins and on interleaved pages in his copy of the quarto edition of the *Voyage of Discovery*, now in the Provincial Archives of British Columbia. Unfortunately before the Archives acquired the volumes they were rebound and trimmed so heavily that parts of many of the marginal notes were cut off. Hewett's comments are useful and interesting but should be used with some caution, as most of them are highly critical of Vancouver.

Drawings

Vancouver makes no direct reference to the lack of an official artist for his expedition, but a remark in his introduction to the *Voyage* suggests that he had been somewhat concerned about the matter: 'It was with infinite satisfaction that I saw, amongst the officers and young gentlemen of the quarter-deck, some who, with little instruction, would soon be enabled to construct charts, take plans of bays and harbours, draw landscapes, and make faithful representations of the several headlands, coasts and countries, which we might discover'. Mudge's drawing of the *Discovery* on the rocks, engraved for publication in the *Voyage*, and a very similar sketch by Baker in his log, show that some of the officers had considerable artistic ability, but the bulk of the drawings that have so far come to light, in one form or another, were the work of three midshipmen, John Sykes, Henry Humphrys and Thomas Heddington.

Lieut. Cdr. A. C. F. David, of the Hydrographic Department of the Ministry of Defence, at Taunton, Somerset, is endeavouring to locate and list all drawings and engravings that stemmed from the Vancouver expedition, and his catalogue includes not far short of 300 items. This total includes the 58 views engraved for the first edition of the *Voyage* (17 on plates in the text and 41 in the folio atlas). Of this number 31 were taken from original drawings by Sykes, nine from sketches by Humphrys (including the well-known view of the Spanish village in Friendly Cove), and Heddington contributed 13. Commander David notes that the artists 'confined themselves almost entirely to drawings of landscapes and headlands' – in other words, to aids to navigation. 'There is a total lack of botanical drawings, and drawings of the natives and their artifacts, where they appear, are on a small scale. It is in these fields that the absence of an official artist is felt. . . . From a seaman's point of view the three amateur artists achieved all that was required. Indeed a number of their views are still used to illustrate Admiralty Sailing Directions.'

Nine of the official logs contain a total of 45 views. Neither Sykes nor Heddington included any drawings in their logs, but Humphrys included 13. Almost all the other original drawings are in two repositories, the Hydrographic Department at Taunton and the Robert B. Honeyman Collection in the Bancroft Library of the University of California, at Berkeley. There are 117 drawings at Taunton and 65 at Berkeley. Sykes is the major contributor to both collections; two thirds of the items in each are either original drawings by him or copies of his drawings. Humphrys is much less well represented by 17 drawings at Taunton and only seven at Berkeley, and there are no drawings by Heddington in either place. The Taunton collection includes many views that were undoubtedly executed during the voyage, but, with two possible exceptions, all those at Berkeley were drawn at a later date. With those two exceptions, all were drawn on paper watermarked 1797. Of the 65 views, all but 14 are copies of drawings held at Taunton. The absence of any views by Heddington suggests that the copies may have been made after 1808, as in October of that year Heddington asked the Admiralty to return the views and surveys he had deposited when the expedition returned, and the Admiralty did so. Whether or not his drawings are still in existence is not known.

Random items are found in widely separated collections. Humphrys' original drawing of the Spanish village in Friendly Cove is in the P.R.O. (C.O. 5/187); a sheet of four drawings of King George Sound and the coast of SW Australia, which appear to be good copies of originals by Humphrys, are in vol. CXVI of the King's Topographical Collection in the British Library. What would appear to be Mudge's original drawing of the *Discovery* on the rocks is in the Dixson Library, in Sydney, Australia. In 1814 Heddington published two of his views of the island of Hawaii in the form of handsome aquatint engravings by M. Dubourg. There are sets in the Bernice P. Bishop Museum in Honolulu and the National Library of Australia. The Library of the University of British Columbia, in Vancouver, has a fine enlargement of Humphrys' view of Friendly Cove ($84 \times 25\frac{1}{2}$ cms) which Commander David thinks is probably the work of a Spanish copyist.

Surveys

Commander David's search has extended to surveys and charts, manuscript and engraved, as well as views.

Original surveys are relatively few in number; less than 60 have come to light. Five of the official logs (those of Baker, Johnstone, Humphrys, Sherriff and Stewart) contain a total of 21 surveys. All five have a survey of King George Sound, the expedition's first discovery, and Johnstone adds a sketch of the SW coast of Australia. There are three surveys of Anchor Island Harbour, the *Discovery*'s anchorage in Dusky Bay, and Johnstone sketched both The Snares and the part of the coast of Chatham Island that could be seen from the *Chatham*. A rough outline by Stewart of the coast of Oahu east and west of the Waikiki Bay anchorage is the only original survey of any part of the Sandwich Islands, which is surprising in view of the relatively long periods the ships spent amongst them. Only eight of the surveys in the logs depict features on the Northwest Coast.

There are some 30 manuscript surveys at Taunton and five in the Colonial Office records at the P.R.O. The most interesting and historically important of these are the charts that Vancouver sent to London after the 1792 surveying season. The preliminary versions taken by Mudge are at the Public Record Office in C.O. 5/187; the much more detailed and elaborate charts sent with Broughton are in the Hydrographic Department. Baker's charts of the Northwest Coast and Broughton's own survey of the Columbia River are outstanding. The latter was not included in the atlas published with the *Voyage*, but it was engraved and issued by Arrowsmith in 1798, shortly after the *Voyage* appeared. The engraving exists in two later states, dated 1831 and 1840. There is a copy of the former at Taunton and of the latter in the collections of the Oregon Historical Society, in Portland.

Other items of special interest at Taunton include 11 rough surveys by Johnstone (one of the SW coast of Australia, three of the Northwest Coast and seven of the Galapagos Islands). There is a similar survey of Burke Channel, unsigned but certainly by Johnstone, in C.O. 5/187. A few items relating to the voyage of the *Daedalus* have been found. The Hydrographic Department has two rough surveys of the Marquesas Islands, evidently drawn during her visit there. A rough journal and other papers of William Gooch, the ill-fated astronomer who was a passenger in the *Daedalus*, include 'A Plan of the Harbour of Port Praya in the Island of St Jago' (Praia, capital of the Cape Verde Islands, on the island of Sao Tiago), and four drawings, one of a three-masted ship, presumably the *Daedalus*.

Heddington asked that his surveys (18 in number) as well as drawings should be returned by the Admiralty in 1808, and like the views they have disappeared. The Hydrographer of the day, when agreeing to their return, referred to them in somewhat disparaging terms, stating that they appeared 'to be nothing more than copies taken from a General Survey of the North West Coast of America carried on under the direction & command of the late Captain Vancouver'.

What appears to be the compilation chart for plate 5 of the folio atlas, depicting the Northwest Coast from 45° 30' N to 52° 15' N is in the Public Record Office map collection (C.O. 700 British Columbia

No. 1). At Taunton there is an incomplete proof of the engraved chart of the Sandwich Islands (plate 16 in the folio atlas).

A few copies of a variant of the quarto edition of the *Voyage* exist in which there are no plates in the three volumes of text; all views and charts are gathered together in the folio atlas. Presumably these were advance copies, prepared for special presentation. The British Library has two complete sets (one from the library of Sir Joseph Banks), a third is in a private collection in the United States and a fourth in the library of the University of British Columbia. The British Library has a third copy of the atlas only (from the library of King George III), and there is another in the Naval Historical Library. Stanford University has the three volumes of text but lacks the atlas. At the Washington State Historical Society in Tacoma Commander David saw a further variant of the atlas. This consists of 'pulls from the plates in various states of engraving...Some of the plates have 3 states, some 2 and others [including all the charts] only the final printed version.'

Editions of the 'Voyage of Discovery'

A Voyage of Discovery to the North Pacific Ocean, and Round the World: in which the Coast of North-west America has been carefully examined and accurately surveyed. Undertaken by His Majesty's Command, Principally with a view to ascertain the existence of any Navigable Communication between the North Pacific and North Atlantic Oceans; and performed in the years 1790, 1791, 1792, 1793, 1794 and 1795, in the Discovery sloop of war, and armed tender Chatham, under the command of Captain George Vancouver. London, Printed for G. G. and J. Robinson, 1798. 3 vols. and folio atlas.
   Facsimile reprint. Amsterdam, N. Israel; New York, da Capo Press, 1967. (Bibliotheca Australiana, nos. 30–32.)
A Voyage to the North Pacific Ocean, and Round the World;...performed in the years 1790, 1791, 1792, 1793, 1794, and 1795...under the command of Captain George Vancouver. A new edition, with corrections. London, Printed for John Stockdale, 1801. 6 vols.
Voyage de découvertes, à l'océan Pacifique du Nord, et autour du monde; dans lequel la côte nord-ouest de l'Amérique a été soigneusement reconnue et exactement reveleée:...exécuté...par le capitaine George Vancouver. Tr. d l'anglais. Paris, Imprimerie de la République, An VIII [1799]. 3 vols. and folio atlas.
Voyage de découvertes, à l'océan Pacifique du Nord, et autour du monde... exécuté...par le capitaine George Vancouver; tr. de l'anglais par P. F. Henry.... Paris, Imprimerie de Didot Jeune, An X [1801]. 5 vols. and atlas. Reprinted in 1802.
Georg Vancouvers Reisen nach dem nördlichen Theile der Südsee während der jahre

1790 bis 1795. And dem Englischen übersetzt und mit Anmerkungen begleitet von Joh. Friedr. Wilh. Herbst...Berlin, In der Vossischen Buchhandlung, 1799–1800. 2 vols. (*Magazin von merkwurdigen neuen Reisebeschreibungen*, vols. 18–19.)

Georg Vancouvers Opdagelses reise i de nordlige dele af sydhavet og lang med de vestlige kyster af Amerika fra 1790 til 1795. Oversat af Br. Juul. Kjøbenhavn, Trykt paa A. Soldins Forlag hos B. Brünnich, 1799–1802. 2 vols.

En Upptächts-Resa till Norra Stilla Hafvet och kring jordklotet, att Pä Kongl Engelsk Befallning och omkostnad i Synner het forska efter nägot segelbart sammanhang imellan Norra Stilla och Norra Atlantiske Haven, förättad ahren 1790, 1791, 1792, 1793, 1794, 1795, under commando af George Vancouver; Ifran Engelskan i Sammandrag utgifven af Anders Sparrman. Stockholm, Anders Zetterberg, 1800–1801. 2 vols.

[Vancouver, George,] *Puteshestvie v sievernuiu chast Tikhago Okeana, i vokurk sveta sovershennoe v 1790, 1791, 1792, 1793, 1794 i 1795 godahk, perefod s Angliskago. Izdano osh Gosudarsshvennago Admiralsheiskago Departamenska.* Sankpeterburg, V. Morskoi Tipografii, 1827–1838. 6 vols.

Vancouver, George, *Voyage à l'océan Pacifique du Nord et autour du monde*....Paris, Lecointe, 1833. 6 vols. (*Nouvelle bibliothèque des voyages, ou choix des voyages les plus intéressants*, vols. 84–89.) [The 6th volume carries the narrative only as far as chapter VIII of Book IV (one chapter short of the end of vol. 2 of the 1798 edition). The only copy available for examination, in the Special Collections of the Library of the University of British Columbia, provides no clue as to whether or not additional volumes were published which completed the edition.]

Several of the editions published on the continent were abridgements. Other publications derived from the *Voyage of Discovery* included the following:

Vancouver, George, *Entdeckungsreise in den nördlichen Gewässern der Südsee, und langst des westlichen Küsten von Amerika, von 1790 bis 1795. Aus dem Englischen von M. C. Sprengel.* Halle, in der Rengerschen Buchhandlung, 1799. 308 pp.

Voyage à l'Océan-Pacifique du nord et autour du monde, de 1790 à 1795...Paris et Amsterdam, chez J. E. Gabriel Dufour, 1807. 222 pp. An abridgement written for children.

and Broughton, W. R., *A Narrative or Journal of A Voyage to the North Pacific Ocean, and Round the World, performed...by Capt. George Vancouver, and Lieutenant Broughton.* London, Printed for J. Lee, 1802. 80 pp. Ferguson describes it as 'A rare chapbook account of the Voyage'.

Viaje á Valparaiso l Santiago de Jorje Vancouver.... Traducido por Nicola Peña M. de la edición francesa del año VIII (1799). Santiago de Chile, Impr. Mejia, 1902. xxiv, 104 pp.

Abridged versions or summaries were included in various collections of voyages, including the following:

'Voyage Round the World, in 1790, 1791, 1792, 1793, 1794, and 1795.' *A General Collection of Voyages and Travels*. Vol. 12, London, 1813, pp. 117–392.

'Voyage of Discovery of the North Pacific Ocean, and Round the World.' *The World: or The Present State of the Universe*. Vol. I, London, 1806, pp. [345]–496.

A

VOYAGE OF DISCOVERY

TO THE

NORTH PACIFIC OCEAN,

AND

ROUND THE WORLD;

IN WHICH THE COAST OF NORTH-WEST AMERICA HAS BEEN CAREFULLY
EXAMINED AND ACCURATELY SURVEYED.

Undertaken by HIS MAJESTY's Command,

PRINCIPALLY WITH A VIEW TO ASCERTAIN THE EXISTENCE OF ANY
NAVIGABLE COMMUNICATION BETWEEN THE

North Pacific and North Atlantic Oceans;

AND PERFORMED IN THE YEARS

1790, 1791, 1792, 1793, 1794, and 1795,

IN THE

DISCOVERY SLOOP OF WAR, AND ARMED TENDER CHATHAM,

UNDER THE COMMAND OF

CAPTAIN GEORGE VANCOUVER.

IN THREE VOLUMES.

VOL. I.

LONDON:
PRINTED FOR G. G. AND J. ROBINSON, PATERNOSTER-ROW;
AND J. EDWARDS, PALL-MALL.

1798.

Plate 15. Title-page of vol. I of the 1798 edition of *A Voyage of Discovery*.

TO

THE KING.

SIR,

YOUR MAJESTY having been been graciously pleased to permit my late brother, CAPTAIN GEORGE VANCOUVER, to present to YOUR MAJESTY the narrative of his labours, during the execution of your commands in the Pacific Ocean, I presume to hope that, since it has pleased the Divine Providence to withdraw him from YOUR MAJESTY's Service, and from the society of his Friends, before he could avail himself of that condescension, YOUR MAJESTY will, with the same benignity, vouchsafe to accept it from my hands, in discharge of the melancholy duty which has devolved upon me by that unfortunate event.

I cannot but indulge the hope, that the following pages will prove to YOUR MAJESTY, that CAPTAIN VANCOUVER was not undeserving the honour of the trust reposed in him; and that he has fulfilled the object of his commission from YOUR MAJESTY with diligence and fidelity.

Under the auspices of YOUR MAJESTY, the late indefatigable CAPTAIN COOK had already shewn that a Southern Continent did not exist, and had ascertained the important fact of the near approximation of the Northern Shores of Asia to those of America. To those great discoveries, the exertions of CAPTAIN VANCOUVER will, I trust, be found to have added the complete certainty that, within the limits of his researches on the Continental Shore of North West America, NO INTERNAL SEA, OR OTHER NAVIGABLE COMMUNICATION whatever exists, uniting the Pacific and Atlantic Oceans.

I have the honour to be,
SIR,
With the most profound respect,
YOUR MAJESTY's
Most faithful and devoted
Subject and Servant,
JOHN VANCOUVER.

INTRODUCTION.

In contemplating the rapid progress of improvement in the sciences, and the general diffusion of knowledge since the commencement of the eighteenth century, we are unavoidably led to observe, with admiration, that active spirit of discovery by means of which the remotest regions of the earth have been explored; a friendly communication opened with their inhabitants; and various commodities, of a most valuable nature, contributing either to relieve their necessities, or augment their comforts, introduced among the less-enlightened part of our species. A mutual intercourse has been also established, in many instances, on the solid basis of a reciprocity of benefits; and the productive labour of the civilized world has found new markets for the disposal of its manufactures. Nor has the balance of trade been wholly against the people of the newly-discovered countries; for, whilst some have been enabled to supply their visitors with an abundance of food, and the most valuable refreshments, in exchange for iron, copper, useful implements, and articles of ornament; the industry of others has been stimulated to procure the skins of animals, and other articles of a commercial nature; which they have found to be eagerly sought for by the traders who now resort to their shores from Europe, Asia, and the eastern side of North America.

The great naval powers of Europe, inspired with a desire not only of acquiring, but also of communicating, knowledge, had extended their researches, in the 16th and 17th centuries, as far into the Pacific Ocean as their limited information of the geography of the earth, at that time, enabled them to penetrate. Some few attempts had also been made by this country towards the conclusion of each of those centuries; but it was not until the year 1764 that Great Britain, benefiting by the experience of former enterprizes, laid the foundation for that vast accession of geographical knowledge which she has since obtained, by the persevering spirit of her successive distinguished circumnavigators.[1]

By the introduction of nautical astronomy into marine education, we are taught to sail on the hypothenuse, instead of traversing two sides of a triangle, which was the usage in earlier times; by this means, the circuitous course of all voyages from place to place is considerably shortened; and it is now become

[1] The exploring expedition commanded by Commodore the Hon. John Byron, which sailed in June 1764, is regarded as the first important manifestation of the revival of British interest in the Pacific, following the successful conclusion of the Seven Years War. See R. E. Gallagher (ed.), *Commodore Byron's Journal of his Circumnavigation, 1764–6* (Cambridge, The Hakluyt Society, 1964).

evident, that sea officers of the most common-rate abilities, who will take the trouble of making themselves acquainted with the principles of this science, will, on all suitable occasions, with proper and correct instruments, be enabled to acquire a knowledge of their situation in the Atlantic, Indian, or Pacific Oceans, with a degree of accuracy sufficient to steer on a meridional or diagonal line, to any known spot; provided it be sufficiently conspicuous to be visible at any distance from five to ten leagues.

This great improvement, by which the most remote parts of the terrestrial globe are brought so easily within our reach, would nevertheless have been comparatively of little utility, had not those happy means been discovered, for preserving the lives and health of the officers and seamen engaged in such distant and perilous undertakings; which were so successfully practised by Captain Cook, the first great discoverer of this salutary system, in all his latter voyages round the globe. But in none have the effects of his wise regulations, regimen, and discipline, been more manifest, than in the course of the expedition of which the following pages are designed to treat. To an unremitting attention, not only to food, cleanliness, ventilation, and an early administration of antiseptic provisions and medicines, but also to prevent, as much as possible, the chance of indisposition, by prohibiting individuals from carelessly exposing themselves to the influence of climate, or unhealthy indulgences in times of relaxation, and by relieving them from fatigue and the inclemency of the weather the moment the nature of their duty would permit them to retire; is to be ascribed the preservation of the health and lives of seafaring people on long voyages. Instead of vessels returning from parts, by no means very remote, with the loss of one half, and sometimes two-thirds of their crews, in consequence of scorbutic and other contagious disorders; instances are now not wanting of laborious services having been performed in the most distant regions, in which, after an absence of more than three or four years, during which time the vessels had been subjected to all the vicissitudes of climate, from the scorching heat of the torrid zone to the freezing blasts of the arctic or antarctic circles, the crews have returned in perfect health, and consisting nearly of every individual they had carried out; whilst those who unfortunately had not survived, either from accident or disease, did not exceed in number the mortality that might reasonably have been expected, during the same period of time, in the most healthy situations of this country. To these valuable improvements, Great Britain is, at this time, in a great measure indebted, for her present exalted station amongst the nations of the earth; and it should seem, that the reign of George the Third had been reserved by the Great Disposer of all things, for the glorious task of establishing the grand key-stone to that expansive arch, over which the arts and sciences should pass to the furthermost corners of the earth, for the instruction and happiness of the most lowly children of nature. Advantages so highly beneficial to the untutored parts of the human race, and so extremely important to that large proportion of the subjects of this empire who are brought up to the sea service, deserve to be justly appreciated; and it becomes of very little importance to the bulk of society, whose enlightened humanity teaches them to entertain a lively regard for the welfare and interest of those who engage in such adventurous undertakings for the advancement of science, or for the extension of commerce, what may be the animadversions or sarcasms of those few unenlightened minds that may peevishly demand, 'what beneficial consequences, if any, have followed, or are likely to flow, to the discoverers, or to the discovered, to the common interests of humanity, or to the increase of useful knowledge, from all our boasted attempts to explore the distant recesses of the globe?' The learned editor,* who has so justly anticipated this injudicious remark, has, in his very comprehensive introduction to Captain Cook's last Voyage, from whence the above quotation is extracted, given to the public, not only a complete and satisfactory answer to that question, but has treated every other part of the subject of Discovery so ably, as to render any further observations on former voyages of this description totally unnecessary, for the purpose of bringing the reader acquainted with what had been accomplished, previously to my being honored with his Majesty's commands to follow up the labours of that illustrious navigator Captain James Cook; to whose steady, uniform, and indefatigable attention[1] to the several objects on which the success of his enterprizes ultimately depended, the world is indebted for such eminent and important benefits.

Those benefits did not long remain unnoticed by the commercial part of the British nation. Remote and distant voyages being now no longer objects of terror, enterprizes were projected, and carried into execution, for the purpose of establishing new and lucrative branches of commerce between North West America and China; and parts of the coast of the former that had not been minutely examined by Captain Cook, became now the general resort of the persons thus engaged.

Unprovided as these adventurers were with proper astronomical and nautical instruments, and having their views directed almost intirely to the object of their employers, they had neither the means, nor the leisure, that were indispensably requisite for amassing any certain geographical information. This became evident, from the accounts of their several voyages given to the public; in which, notwithstanding that they positively contradicted each other, as well in geographical and nautical facts as in those of a commercial nature, they yet agreed in filling up the blanks in the charts of Captain Cook with extensive islands, and a coast apparently much broken by numberless *inlets*, which they had left almost intirely unexplored.

The charts accompanying the accounts of their voyages, representing the

* Dr. Douglas, now Bishop of Salisbury.
[1] The first edition reads: 'steady, uniform, indefatigable, and undiverted attention'. This is the first of a considerable number of minor verbal changes made by John Vancouver in the second edition. Only those that seem to have some interest or significance have been noted.

North West coast of America to be so much broken by the waters of the Pacific Ocean, gave encouragement once more to hypotheses; and the favorite opinion that had slept since the publication of Captain Cook's last voyage, of a north-eastern communication between the waters of the Pacific and Atlantic Oceans, was again roused from its state of slumber, and brought forward with renovated vigour. Once more the Archipelago of St. Lazarus was called forth into being, and its existence almost assumed, upon the authority of a Spanish admiral named De Fonte, De Fonta, or De Fuentes; and of a Mr. Nicholas Shapely, from Boston in America, who was stated to have penetrated through this archipelago, by sailing through a mediterranean sea on the coast of North West America, within a few leagues of the oceanic shores of that archipelago; where he is said to have met the Admiral.[1] The straits said to have been navigated by Juan De Fuca were also brought forward in support of this opinion;[2] and, although the existence or extent of these discoveries remained still to be proved by an authenticated survey of the countries which had been thus stated to have been seen and passed through, yet the enthusiasm of modern *closet philosophy*, eager to revenge itself for the refutation of its former fallacious speculations, ventured to accuse Captain Cook of "hastily exploding" its systems; and, ranking him amongst *the pursuers of peltry*, dared even to drag him forward in support of its visionary conjectures.

With what reason, or with what justice such animadversions have been cast upon one, who, unhappily for the world, does not survive to enforce his own judicious opinions founded as they were on the solid principles of experience, and of ocular demonstration, uninfluenced by any prejudice, and unbiassed by any pre-conceived theory or hypothesis; it is not my province to decide: let it suffice to say, that the labours of that distinguished character will remain a monument of his pre-eminent abilities, and dispassionate investigation of the truth, as long as science shall be respected in the civilized world; or as long as succeeding travellers, who shall unite in bearing testimony to the profundity of his judgment, shall continue to obtain credit with the public.

Although the ardour of the present age, to discover and delineate the true geography of the earth, had been rewarded with uncommon and unexpected success, particularly by the persevering exertions of this great man, yet all was not completed; and though, subsequent to his last visit to the coast of North-West America, no expedition had been projected by Government, for

---

[1] For the text of de Fonte's narrative and a commentary see H. R. Wagner, 'Apocryphal Voyages to the Northwest Coast of America', in *Proceedings of the American Antiquarian Society*, new series XLI (1931), 190–218.

[2] On de Fuca's alleged discovery of a strait in 1592 see Wagner, 'Apocryphal Voyages', pp. 184–90. The present strait, about a degree N of the position given by de Fuca, was entered by Captain C. W. Barkley in the trading ship *Imperial Eagle* in July 1787. His wife noted that he 'immediately recognized' it as the strait discovered by de Fuca and named it after him. See W. Kaye Lamb, 'The Mystery of Mrs Barkley's Diary', *BCHQ*, VI (1942), 43.

the purpose of acquiring a more exact knowledge of that extensive and interesting country; yet a voyage was planned by His Majesty for exploring some of the southern regions; and in the autumn of the year 1789, directions were given for carrying it into effect.

Captain Henry Roberts, of known and tried abilities, who had served under Captain Cook during his two last voyages,[1] and whose attention to the scientific part of his profession had afforded that great navigator frequent opportunities of naming him with much respect, was called upon to take charge of, and to command, the proposed expedition.

At that period, I had just returned from a station at Jamaica, under the command of Commodore (now Vice-Admiral) Sir Alan Gardner, who mentioned me to Lord Chatham and the Board of Admiralty; and I was solicited to accompany Captain Roberts as his second. In this proposal I acquiesced, and found myself very pleasantly situated, in being thus connected with a fellow-traveller for whose abilities I bore the greatest respect, and in whose friendship and good opinion I was proud to possess a place. And as we had sailed together with Captain Cook on his voyage towards the south pole, and as both had afterwards accompanied him with Captain Clerke in the Discovery during his last voyage,[2] I had no doubt that we were engaged in an expedition, which would prove no less interesting to my friend than agreeable to my wishes.

A ship, proper for the service under contemplation, was ordered to be provided. In the yard of Messrs. Randall and Brent, on the banks of the Thames, a vessel of 340 tons burthen was nearly finished; and as she would require but few alterations to make her in every respect fit for the purpose, she was purchased; and, on her being launched, was named the Discovery.

The first day of the year 1790 the Discovery was commissioned by Captain Roberts; some of the other officers were also appointed, and the ship was conducted to His Majesty's dock-yard at Deptford, where she was put into a state of equipment; which was ordered to be executed with all the dispatch that the nature of the service required.

For some time previous to this period the Spaniards, roused by the successful efforts of the British nation to obtain a more extended knowledge of the earth, had not only ventured to visit some of the newly-discovered islands in the tropical regions of the Pacific Ocean, but had also, in the year 1775, with a spirit somewhat analogous to that which prompted their first discovery of America, extended their researches to the northward, along the coast of North-West America.[3] But this undertaking did not seem to have reached

[1] As an A.B. on the second voyage and as master's mate on the third. Roberts drew the charts that were engraved for the published account of the third voyage.

[2] Vancouver's memory was at fault. They had been shipmates in the *Resolution* on Cook's second voyage, but on the third Roberts served in the *Resolution* while Vancouver was in the *Discovery*.

[3] The first Spanish voyage to the Northwest Coast, commanded by Juan Pérez, was in 1774. The second, in 1775, was made by two ships commanded by Bruno de Hezeta and Juan Francisco de la Bodega y Quadra.

beyond the acquirement of a very superficial knowledge of the shores; and though these were found to be extremely broken, and divided by the waters of the Pacific, yet it does not appear that any measures were pursued by them for ascertaining the extent to which those waters penetrated into the interior of the American continent.

This apparent indifference in exploring new countries, ought not, however, to be attributed to a deficiency in skill, or to a want of spirit for enterprize, in the commander* of that expedition; because there is great reason to believe, that the extreme caution which has so long and so rigidly governed the court of Madrid, to prevent, as much as possible, not only their American, but likewise their Indian, establishments from being visited by any Europeans, (unless they were subjects of the crown of Spain, and liable to a military tribunal) had greatly conspired, with other considerations of a political nature, to repress that desire of adding to the fund of geographical knowledge, which has so eminently distinguished this country. And hence it is not extraordinary, that the discovery of a north-western navigable communication between the Atlantic and Pacific Oceans, should not have been considered as an object much to be desired by the Spanish court. Since that expedition, however, the Spaniards seem to have considered their former national character as in some measure at stake; and they have certainly become more acquainted than they were with the extensive countries immediately adjoining to their immense empire in the new world; yet the measures that they adopted in order to obtain that information, were executed in so defective a manner, that all the important questions to geography still remained undecided, and in the same state of uncertainty.

Towards the end of April, the Discovery was, in most respects, in a condition to proceed down the river, when intelligence was received that the Spaniards had committed depredations on different branches of the British commerce on the coast of North-West America, and that they had seized on the English vessels and factories in Nootka sound. This intelligence gave rise to disputes between the courts of London and Madrid, which wore the threatening appearance of being terminated by no other means than those of reprizal. In consequence of this an armament took place, and the further pacific equipment of the Discovery was suspended; her stores and provisions were returned to the respective offices, and her officers and men were engaged in more active service. On this occasion I resumed my profession under my highly-esteemed friend, Sir Alan Gardner, then captain of the Courageux, where I remained until the 17th of the November following; when I was ordered to repair to town for the purpose of attending to the commands of the Board of Admiralty.

The uncommon celerity, and unparalleled dispatch, which attended the equipment of one of the noblest fleets that Great Britain ever saw, had probably its due influence upon the court of Madrid, for, in the Spanish convention,[1] which was consequent on that armament, restitution was offered

---

* Sen.ʳ Quadra.   [1] The Nootka Sound Convention of 28 October 1790.

to this country for the captures and aggressions made by the subjects of His Catholic Majesty; together with an acknowledgment of an equal right with Spain to the exercise and prosecution of all commercial undertakings in those seas, reputed before to belong only to the Spanish crown. The extensive branches of the fisheries, and the fur trade to China, being considered as objects of very material importance to this country, it was deemed expedient, that an officer should be sent to Nootka to receive back, in form, a restitution of the territories on which the Spaniards had seized, and also to make an accurate survey of the coast, from the 30th degree of north latitude north-westward toward Cook's river; and further, to obtain every possible information that could be collected respecting the natural and political state of that country.

The outline of this intended expedition was communicated to me, and I had the honor of being appointed to the command of it. At this juncture it appeared to be of importance, that all possible exertion should be made in its equipment; and as the Discovery, which had been selected on the former occasion, was now rigged, some of her stores provided, and she herself considered, in most respects, as a vessel well calculated for the voyage under contemplation, she was accordingly directed to be got ready for that service; and the Chatham armed tender, of 135 tons burthen, built at Dover, having been destined to accompany the Discovery on the former occasion, was ordered to be equipped to attend on the voyage now to be undertaken, and was sent to Woolwich to receive such necessary repairs and alterations as were deemed requisite.

The Discovery was copper-fastened, sheathed with plank, and coppered over; the Chatham only sheathed with copper. The former mounted ten four-pounders, and ten swivels; the latter, four three-pounders and six swivels. The following list will exhibit the establishment of the officers and men in the two vessels.

An Account of the Number of Officers and Men on board the Discovery Sloop of War, in December, 1790.

OFFICERS.				NO.	NAMES
Captain	-	-	-	1	George Vancouver.
Lieutentants -	-	-	3		Zachariah Mudge, Peter Puget, Joseph Baker,
Master	-	-	-	1	Joseph Whidbey.
Boatswain	-	-	-	1	
Carpenter	-	-	-	1	
Gunner	-	-	-	1	
Surgeon	-	-	-	1	
Midshipmen-	-	-	6		
Master's mates	-	-	3		
Boatswain's mates -	-	3			
Carpenter's mates -	-	3			
Gunner's mates	-	-	2		
Surgeon's mates	-	-	2		
Carpenter's crew	-	-	4		
Master at arms	-	-	1		
Corporal	-	-	-	1	
Sail-maker	-	-	-	1	
Sail-maker's mate -	-	1			
Armourer	-	-	-	1	
Cook -	-	-	-	1	
Cook's mate	-	-	1		
Clerk -	-	-	-	1	
Quartermasters	-	-	6		
Able Seamen	-	-	38		
Sergeant	-	-	-	1	
Corporal	-	-	-	1	Marines.
Privates	-	-	-	14	

Total   100[1]

[1] This was her authorized complement. Only 80 men had actually been mustered by the end of December.

An Account of the Number of Officers and Men on board the Chatham armed Tender, in December, 1790.

OFFICERS.				NO.	NAMES.
Commander	-	-	-	1	Lieut. W. R. Broughton.
Lieutenant	-	-	-	1	James Hanson.
Master	-	-	-	1	James Johnstone.
Boatswain	-	-	-	1	
Carpenter	-	-	-	1	
Gunner	-	-	-	1	
Surgeon	-	-	-	1	
Midshipmen	-	-	-	4	
Master's mates	-	-	-	2	
Boatswain's mates	-	-	-	2	
Carpenter's mates	-	-	-	2	
Gunner's mates	-	-	-	2	
Surgeon's mate	-	-	-	1	
Sail-maker	-	-	-	1	
Armourer	-	-	-	1	
Clerk	-	-	-	1	
Quartermasters	-	-	-	4	
Able Seamen	-	-	-	10	
Sergeant	-	-	-	1	} Marines.
Privates	-	-	-	7	

Total   45[1]

[1] The *Chatham*'s authorized complement. The mustering of her crew did not begin until the first days of January 1791.

I had great reason to be satisfied with these arrangements; the second and third lieutenants, and the master of the Discovery, whom I had the honor of being allowed to name for this service, had all served some years with me, under the command of Sir Alan Gardner, both at home and in the West-Indies; the other officers were men of known character, possessing good abilities, and excellent dispositions, which their subsequent conduct and zeal, exhibited on all occasions, sufficiently demonstrated.

In the former equipment of the Discovery, Captain Roberts and myself had undertaken to make all such astronomical and nautical observations, as the circumstances occurring in the voyage might demand. This task now devolved upon me alone; but with the assistance of Mr. Whidbey, I entertained little doubt of accomplishing the proposed object, at least in an useful manner; for which purpose we were supplied by the Navy Board with such an assortment of instruments as I considered to be necessary.

It was with infinite satisfaction that I saw, amongst the officers and young gentlemen of the quarter-deck, some who, with little instruction, would soon be enabled to construct charts, take plans of bays and harbours, draw landscapes, and make faithful representations[1] of the several head-lands, coasts, and countries, which we might discover; thus, by the united efforts of our little community, the whole of our proceedings, and the information we might obtain in the course of the voyage, would be rendered profitable to those who might succeed us in traversing the remote parts of the globe that we were destined to explore, without the assistance of professional persons, as astronomers or draftsmen.

Botany, however, was an object of scientific inquiry with which no one of us was much acquainted; but as, in expeditions of a similar nature, the most valuable opportunities had been afforded for adding to the general stock of botanical information, Mr. Archibald Menzies, a surgeon in the royal navy, who had before visited the Pacific Ocean in one of the vessels employed in the fur trade,[2] was appointed for the specific purpose of making such researches; and had, doubtless, given sufficient proof of his abilities, to qualify him for the station it was intended he should fill. For the purpose of preserving such new or uncommon plants as he might deem worthy of a place amongst His Majesty's very valuable collection of exotics at Kew, a glazed frame was erected on the after part of the quarter-deck, for the reception of those he might have an opportunity of collecting.

The Board of Admiralty, greatly attentive to our personal comforts, gave directions that the Discovery and Chatham should each be supplied with all such articles as might be considered in any way likely to become necessary, during the execution of the long and arduous service in which we were about to engage. Our stores, from the naval arsenals, were ordered to be selected

---

[1] 'portraits' in the first edition. Profiles and sketches of coastal features are meant.
[2] The *Prince of Wales*, Captain James Colnett, which had traded on the Northwest Coast in 1787 and 1788.

of the very best sorts, and to be made with materials of the best quality. In addition to the ordinary establishment, we were supplied with a large assortment of seines and other useful fishing tackle of various kinds. The provisions were furnished at the victualling-office with the greatest care, all of which proved to be excellent, and manifested the judgment which had been exercised in the selection and preparation of the several articles. To these were added a large proportion of sour-krout, portable soup,[1] wheat instead of the usual supply of oatmeal for breakfast, the essense of malt and spruce, malt, hops, dried yeast, flour, and seed mustard; which may all be considered as articles of food. Those of a medicinal nature, with which we were amply supplied, were Dr. James's powders,[2] vitriolic elixir; the rob of lemons and oranges,[3] in such quantities and proportions as the surgeon thought requisite,[4] together with an augmentation to the usual allowance, amounting to a hundred weight, of the best peruvian bark.[5]

To render our visits as acceptable as possible to the inhabitants of the islands or continent in the Pacific Ocean, and to establish on a firm basis a friendly intercourse with the several tribes with which we might occasionally meet, Lord Grenville directed that a liberal assortment of various European commodities, both of a useful and ornamental nature, should be sent on board from the Secretary of State's office. From the Board of Ordnance the vessels were supplied with every thing necessary for our defence, and amongst other articles were four well-contrived three-pound field pieces, for the protection of our little encampment against any hostile attempts of the native Indians, amongst whom we should necessarily have frequent occasion to reside on shore; and for the amusement and entertainment of such as were peaceably and friendly disposed towards us, we were furnished with a most excellent assortment of well-prepared fireworks. So that nothing seemed to have been forgotten, or omitted, that might render our equipment as complete as the nature of the service we were about to execute could be considered to demand. But as I have hitherto only pointed out in general terms the outline of the intended expedition; the various objects it proposed to embrace, and the end it was expected to answer, will be more clearly perceived by the perusal of the instructions under which I was to sail, and by which I was to govern my conduct; and the reader will be thereby enabled to form a judgment, how

[1] Portable soup 'was invented by a Mrs. Dubois, and consisted of vegetables, mixed with liver, kidney, heart, and other less desirable portions of the ox, boiled to a pulp. This was allowed to cool and harden and then cut into slabs.' – Peter Kemp, *The British Sailor* (London. 1970), p. 119. Kemp notes that it was 'thought to be a deterrent against the scurvy, but in fact had no anti-scorbutic properties at all'.

[2] A popular non-febrile remedy prepared by a Dr Robert James (1703–76).

[3] The juice of the fruit, reduced to a syrup by boiling, and preserved with sugar.

[4] On 21 January 1791 Vancouver sent Stephens a letter from Cranstoun, surgeon of the *Discovery*, asking for 1,500 pounds of portable soup, 30 bottles of James's fever powders, 36 bottles of elixir of vitriol and 42 bottles of robs of oranges and lemons. – P.R.O., Adm 1/2628, f. 598.

[5] The bark of the cinchona tree, from which quinine is procured.

far His Majesty's commands, during this voyage, have been properly carried into execution.

'By the Commissioners for executing the office of Lord High Admiral of Great Britain and Ireland, &c.[1]

'The KING having judged it expedient, that an expedition should be immediately undertaken for acquiring a more complete knowledge, than has yet been obtained, of the north-west coast of America; and, the sloop you command, together with the Chatham armed tender (the Lieutenant commanding which, has been directed to follow your orders) having been equipped for that service; you are, in pursuance of His Majesty's pleasure, signified to us by Lord Grenville, one of his principal Secretaries of State, hereby required and directed to proceed, without loss of time, with the said sloop and tender, to the Sandwich islands in the North Pacific Ocean, where you are to remain during the next winter; employing yourself very diligently in the examination and survey of the said islands: and, as soon as the weather shall be favorable (which may be expected to be in February, or at latest in March, 1792), you are to repair to the north-west coast of America, for the purpose of acquiring a more complete knowledge of it, as above mentioned.

'It having been agreed, by the late convention between His Majesty and the Catholic King, (a printed copy of which you will receive herewith) that the buildings and tracts of land, situated on the north-west coast above mentioned, or on islands adjacent thereto, of which the subjects of His Britannic Majesty were dispossessed about the month of April, 1789, by a Spanish officer, shall be restored to the said British subjects, the court of Spain has agreed to send orders for that purpose to its officers in that part of the world; but as the particular specification of the parts to be restored may still require some further time, it is intended that the King's orders, for this purpose, shall be sent out to the Sandwich islands, by a vessel to be employed to carry thither a further store of provisions for the sloop and armed tender above mentioned, which it is meant shall sail from this country in time to reach those islands in the course of next winter.

'If, therefore, in consequence of the arrangement to be made with the court of Spain, it should hereafter be determined that you should proceed, in the first instance, to Nootka, or elsewhere, in order to receive, from the Spanish officers, such lands or buildings as are to be restored to the British subjects; orders to that effect will be sent out by the vessel above mentioned. But if no such orders should be received by you previous to the end of January, 1792, you are not to wait for them at the Sandwich islands, but to proceed in such course as you may judge most expedient for the examination of the coast above mentioned, comprized between latitude 60° north and 30° north.

'In which examination the principal objects which you are to keep in view are,

'1st, The acquiring accurate information with respect to the nature and

---

[1] Known as the Board of Admiralty.

extent of any water-communication which may tend, in any considerable degree, to facilitate an intercourse for the purposes of commerce, between the north-west coast, and the country upon the opposite side of the continent, which are inhabited or occupied by His Majesty's subjects.

'2dly, The ascertaining, with as much precision as possible, the number, extent, and situation of any settlements which have been made within the limits above mentioned, by any European nation, and the time when such settlement was first made.

'With respect to the first object, it would be of great importance if it should be found that, by means of any considerable inlets of the sea, or even of large rivers communicating with the lakes in the interior of the continent, such an intercourse, as hath been already mentioned, could be established; it will therefore be necessary, for the purpose of ascertaining this point, that the survey should be so conducted, as not only to ascertain the general line of the sea coast, but also the direction and extent of all such considerable inlets, whether made by arms of the sea, or by the mouths of large rivers, as may be likely to lead to, or facilitate, such communication as is above described.

'This being the principal object of the examination, so far as relates to that part of the subject, it necessarily follows, that a considerable degree of discretion must be left, and is therefore left to you, as to the means of executing the service which His Majesty has in view; but, as far as any general instructions can here be given on the subject, it seems desirable that, in order to avoid any unnecessary loss of time, you should not, and are therefore hereby required and directed not to pursue any inlet or river further than it shall appear to be navigable by vessels of such burden as might safely navigate the Pacific Ocean: but, as the navigation of such inlets or rivers, to the extent here stated, may possibly require that you should proceed up them further than it might be safe for the sloop you command to go, you are, in such case, to take the command of the armed tender in person, at all such times, and in such situations as you shall judge it necessary and expedient.

'The particular course of the survey must depend on the different circumstances which may arise in the execution of a service of this nature; it is, however, proper that you should, and you are therefore hereby required and directed to pay a particular attention to the examination of the supposed straits of Juan de Fuca, said to be situated between 48° and 49° north latitude, and to lead to an opening through which the sloop Washington is reported to have passed in 1789, and to have come out again to the northward of Nootka. The discovery of a near communication between any such sea or strait, and any river running into, or from the lake of the woods, would be particularly useful.

'If you should fail of discovering any such inlet, as is above mentioned, to the southward of Cook's river, there is the greatest probability that it will be found that the said river rises in some of the lakes already known to the Canadian traders, and to the servants of the Hudson's bay company; which point it would, in that case, be material to ascertain; and you are, therefore, to endeavour to ascertain accordingly, with as much precision as the circumstances existing at the time may allow: but the discovery of any similar communication more to the southward (should any such exist) would be much more advantageous for the purposes of commerce, and should, therefore, be preferably attended to, and you are, therefore, to give it a preferable attention accordingly.

'With respect to the second object above mentioned, it is probable that more particular instructions will be given you by the vessel to be sent to the Sandwich islands as aforesaid; but, if not, you are to be particularly careful in the execution of that, and every other part of the service with which you are entrusted, to avoid, with the utmost caution, the giving any ground of jealousy or complaint to the subjects of His Catholic Majesty; and, if you shall fall in with any Spanish ships employed on any service similar to that which is hereby committed to you, you are to afford to the officer commanding such ships every possible degree of assistance and information, and to offer to him, that you, and he, should make to each other, reciprocally, a free and unreserved communication of all plans and charts of discoveries made by you and him in your respective voyages.

'If, in the course of any part of this service, you, or the officers or the people under your command, should meet with the subjects or vessels of any other power or state, you and they are to treat them in the most friendly manner, and to be careful not to do any thing which may give occasion to any interruption of that peace which now happily subsists between His Majesty and all other powers.

'The whole of the survey above mentioned (if carried on with a view to the objects before stated, without too minute and particular an examination of the detail of the different parts of the coast laid down by it) may, as it is understood, probably be completed in the summers of 1792 and 1793; and, in the intermediate winter, it will be proper for you to repair, and you are hereby required and directed to repair accordingly, to the Sandwich islands; and, during your stay there, you are to endeavour to complete any part which may be unfinished of your examination of those islands.

'After the conclusion of your survey in the summer of 1793, you are, if the state and circumstances of the sloop and tender under your command will admit of it, to return to England by Cape Horn, (for which the season will then probably be favorable;) repairing to Spithead, where you are to remain until you receive further order; and sending to our secretary an account of your arrival and proceedings.

'It seems doubtful, at present, how far the time may admit of your making any particular examination of the western coast of South America; but, if it should be practicable, you are to begin such examination from the south point of the island of Chiloe, which is in about 44° south latitude; and you are, in that case, to direct your attention to ascertaining what is the most southern

Spanish settlement on that coast, and what harbours there are south of that settlement.

'In the execution of every part of this service, it is very material that you should use, and you are therefore hereby strictly charged to use every possble care to avoid disputes with the natives of any of the parts where you may touch, and to be particularly attentive to endeavour, by a judicious distribution of the presents, (which have been put on board the sloop and tender under your command, by order of Lord Grenville) and by all other means, to conciliate their friendship and confidence. Given under our hands the 8th of March, 1791.'

CHATHAM.

RD. HOPKINS.

HOOD.

J. T. TOWNSEND.

'*To George Vancouver, Esq. Commander of His Majesty's Sloop the Discovery, at Falmouth.*'

'By command of their Lordships,

PH. STEPHENS.'

ADDITIONAL INSTRUCTIONS.

'By the Commissioners for executing the office of Lord High Admiral of Great Britain and Ireland, &c.

'Lieutenant Hergest, commanding the Dædalus transport, (by whom you will receive this) being directed to put himself under your command, and to follow your orders for his further proceedings; you are hereby required and directed, to take him, and the said transport, under your command accordingly; receiving from her the provisions and stores intended for the use of the sloop you command, and the Chatham armed tender, or such part thereof as the said ship and tender shall be able to stow.

'And whereas you will receive herewith a duplicate of a letter from Count Florida Blanca,[1] to the Spanish officer commanding at Nootka, (together with a translation thereof) signifying His Catholic Majesty's orders to cause such officer as may be appointed on the part of His Britannic Majesty, *to be put in possession of the buildings, and districts, or parcels of lands therein described, which were occupied by His Majesty's subjects in the month of April, 1789, agreeable to the first article of the late convention,* (a copy of which has been sent to you) and to deliver up any persons in the service of British subjects who may have been detained in those parts; in case, therefore, you shall receive this at Nootka, you are to deliver to the Spanish officer, commanding at that port, the above-mentioned letter from Count Florida Blanca, and to receive from him,

---

[1] First Minister of Spain, 1776–92.

conformably thereto, on the part of His Britannic Majesty, possession of the buildings and districts, and parcels of land, of which His Majesty's subjects were possessed at the above-mentioned period.

'In case, however, this shall not find you at Nootka, when Lieutenant Hergest arrives there, but be delivered to you at the Sandwich islands, or elsewhere, and the said lieutenant shall not have then carried into execution the service above-mentioned, (which in the event of his not falling in with you he is directed to do) you are immediately to proceed to Nootka, and to carry that service into execution as above directed, taking the said lieutenant and transport with you if you shall judge it necessary. But as they are intended afterwards to proceed to New South Wales, to be employed there, under the orders of commodore Phillip,[1] you are not to detain them at Nootka, the Sandwich islands, or elsewhere, longer than may be absolutely necessary, but to direct Lieutenant Hergest to repair with the said transport to port Jackson, with such live stock, and other refreshments, as may be likely to be of use in the settlements there; and to touch at New Zealand in his way, from whence he is to use his best endeavours to take with him one or two flax-dressers, in order that the new settlers at port Jackson may, if possible, be properly instructed in the management of that valuable plant.

'Previous, however, to your dispatching him to port Jackson, you are to consider whether, in case of your not being able to take on board the whole of the transport's cargo, any future supply of the articles of which it is composed, will be necessary to enable you to continue your intended survey; and, if so, you are to be careful to send notice thereof to Commodore Phillip, who will have directions, on the receipt of your application, to re-dispatch the transport, or to send such other vessel to you with the remainder of those supplies (as well as any others he may be able to furnish) to such rendezvous as you shall appoint.

'And whereas Mr. Dundas[2] has transmitted to us a sketch of the coast of North America, extending from Nootka down to the latitude of 47° 30″, including the inlet or gulf of Juan de Fuca;[3] and as from the declarations which have lately been made, there appears to be the strongest disposition on the part of the Spanish court, that every assistance and information should be given to His Britannic Majesty's officers employed on that coast, with a view to the enabling them to carry their orders into execution; we send you the said sketch herewith, for your information and use, and do hereby require and direct you to do every thing in your power to cultivate a good understanding with the officers and subjects of His Catholic Majesty who may fall in your way, in order that you may reap the good effects of this disposition of the Spanish court.

---

[1] Captain (later Vice-Admiral) Arthur Phillip, first Governor of New South Wales.

[2] Henry Dundas (later Viscount Melville), who succeeded Grenville as Home Secretary in June 1791.

[3] Presumably the map covering this precise area prepared by López de Haro in 1790.

'You are to take the utmost care in your power, on no account whatever, to touch at any port on the continent of America, to the southward of the latitude of 30° north, nor to the north of that part of South America, where, on your return home, you are directed to commence your intended survey; unless, from any accident, you shall find it absolutely necessary, for your immediate safety, to take shelter there: and, in case of such an event, to continue there no longer than your necessities require, in order that any complaint on the part of Spain on this point may, if possible, be prevented.

'If, during your continuance on the American coast, you should meet with any of the Chinese who were employed by Mr. Meares and his associates, or any of His Majesty's subjects, who may have been in captivity, you are to receive them on board the sloop you command, and to accommodate them in the best manner you may be able, until such time as opportunities may be found of sending them to the different places to which they may be desirous of being conveyed; victualling them during their continuance on board, in the same manner as the other persons on board the said sloop are victualled. Given under our hands the 20th of August, 1791.'

CHATHAM.
J. T. TOWNSHEND.
A. GARDNER.

'To George Vancouver, Esq. Commander of His Majesty's Sloop the Discovery. By command of their Lordships,
PH. STEPHENS.'

LETTER

FROM COUNT FLORIDA BLANCA.

(Translated from the Spanish.)

'In conformity to the first article of the convention of 28th October, 1790, between our court and that of London, (printed copies of which you will have already received, and of which another copy is here inclosed, in case the first have not come to hand) you will give directions that His Britannic Majesty's officer, who will deliver this letter, shall immediately be put in possession of the buildings and districts, or parcels of land, which were occupied by the subjects of that sovereign in April, 1789, as well in the port of Nootka, or of Saint Lawrence, as in the other, said to be called port Cox,[1] and to be situated about sixteen leagues distant from the former to the southward; and that such parcels or districts of land, of which the English subjects were dispossessed, be restored to the said officer, in case the Spaniards should not have given them up.

'You will also give orders, that if any individual in the service of British subjects, whether a Chinese, or of any other nation, should have been carried away and detained in those parts, such person shall be immediately delivered up to the above-mentioned officer.

'I also communicate all this to the viceroy of New Spain by His Majesty's command, and by the royal command I charge you with the most punctual and precise execution of this order.

'May God preserve you many years.

(Signed)
THE COUNT FLORIDA BLANCA.'

ARANJUEZ, 12*th May*, 1791.

'*To the Governor or Commander of the port at Saint Lawrence.*'

---

[1] The Spanish name for Nootka was Puerto de San Lorenzo de Nuca. Port Cox was to the S, in Clayoquot Sound.

'By the Commissioners for executing the office of Lord High Admiral of Great Britain and Ireland, &c.[1]

'IN addition to former orders, you are hereby required and directed, by all proper conveyances, to send to our secretary, for our information, accounts of your proceedings, and copies of the surveys and drawings you shall have made; and, upon your arrival in England, you are immediately to repair to this office, in order to lay before us a full account of your proceedings in the whole course of your voyage; taking care, before you leave the sloop, to demand from the officers, and petty-officers, the log-books, journals, drawings, &c. they may have kept, and to seal them up for our inspection; and enjoining them, and the whole crew, not to divulge where they have been until they shall have permission so to do: and you are to direct the lieutenant commanding the Chatham armed tender to do the same, with respect to the officers, petty-officers, and crew of that tender. Given under our hands the 10th of August, 1791.

CHATHAM.
J. T. TOWNSHEND.
A. GARDNER.'

'To George Vancouver, Esq. Commander of His Majesty's Sloop the Discovery. By command of their Lordships,
PH. STEPHENS.'

Amongst other objects demanding my attention, whilst engaged in carrying these orders into execution, no opportunity was neglected to remove, as far as I was capable, all such errors as had crept into the science of navigation, and to establish in their place, such facts as would tend to facilitate the grand object of finding the longitude at sea; which now seems to be brought nearly to a certainty, by pursuing the lunar method, assisted by a good chronometer. On this, as well as some other subjects, it is highly probable, that great prolixity and repetition will be found in the following pages; it will, however, readily appear to the candid perusers of this voyage, that, as the primary design of the undertaking was to obtain useful knowledge, so it became an indispensable duty, on my part, to use my utmost exertions and abilities in doing justice to the original intention; by detailing the information that arose in the execution of it, in a way calculated to *instruct*, even though it should fail to *entertain*. And when the writer alleges, that from the age of thirteen, his whole life, to the commencement of this expedition, (fifteen months only excepted) has been devoted to constant employment in His Majesty's naval service, he

---

[1] This order was sent to Vancouver at his own suggestion. In a letter to Stephen written from Falmouth on 20 March 1791, he had pointed out that he had found nothing in his instructions 'respecting the delivering up the Journals, Charts, Observations, &c. &c. of the Officers, ships company & persons on Board at the conclusion of the expedition'. – Adm 1/2628, f. 613.

feels, and with all possible humility, that he has some claims to the indulgence of a generous public; who, under such circumstances, will not expect to find elegance of diction, purity of style, or unexceptionable grammatical accuracy: but will be satisfied with 'a plain unvarnished' relation, given with a rigid attention to the truth of such transactions and circumstances as appeared to be worthy of being recorded by a naval officer, whose greatest pride is to deserve the appellation of being zealous in the service of his king and country.

ADVERTISEMENT

FROM THE EDITOR.

As a considerable delay has necessarily taken place in the publication of this work, in consequence of the decease of the late Captain Vancouver, it becomes of absolute necessity to give an accurate account of the state of the work at the period when his last fatal indisposition rendered him incapable of attending any more to business; lest the melancholy event which has retarded its completion should tend to affect its authenticity in the public opinion.

The five first volumes, excepting the introduction, and as far as page 43 of the sixth and last volume, were printed;[1] and Captain Vancouver had fisnished a laborious examination of the impression, and had compared it with the engraved charts and headlands of his discoveries, from the commencement of his survey in the year 1791, to the conclusion of it at the port of Valparaiso, on his return to England in the year 1795. He had also prepared the introduction, and a further part of the journal as far as page 408 of the last volume.[2] The whole, therefore, of the important part of the work, which comprehends his geographical discoveries and improvements, is now presented to the public, exactly as it would have been had Captain Vancouver been still living. The notes which he had made on his journey from the port of Valparaiso to his arrival at St. Jago de Chili, the capital of that kingdom, were unfortunately lost; and I am indebted to Captain Puget for having assisted me with his observations on that occasion.[3]

Ever since Captain Vancouver's last return to England, his health had been in a very debilitated state, and his constitution was evidently so much impaired by the arduous services in which, from his earliest youth, he had been constantly engaged,* that his friends dared to indulge but little hope that he

---

[1] In the first edition: 'as far as page 288 of the third and last volume'.

[2] John Vancouver failed to revise this reference, which refers to the first edition. Captain Vancouver prepared the text as far as the entry for 28 March 1795, which ends on page 246 of the sixth and last volume of the second edition.

[3] The surviving part of Puget's manuscript is in B.L., Add. MS. 17552.

* The late Captain Vancouver was appointed to the Resolution by Captain Cook in the autumn of the year 1771, and on his return from that voyage round the world, he undertook to assist in the outfit and equipment of the Discovery, destined to accompany Captain Cook on his last voyage to the North pole, which was concluded in October, 1780. On the 9th of December following he was made a lieutenant into the Martin sloop; in this vessel he continued until he was removed into the Fame, one of Lord Rodney's

would continue many years amongst them. Notwithstanding that it pleased the Divine Providence to spare his life until he had been able to revise and complete the account of the geographical part of his late Voyage of Discovery, a circumstance which must ever be regarded as most fortunate by all the friends of science, and especially by those professional persons who may hereafter be likely to follow him, through the intricate labyrinth which he had so minutely explored; yet it will ever be a consideration of much regret, that he did not survive to perfect the narrative of his labours. He had made many curious observations on the natural history of the several countries he had visited, and on the manners, customs, laws and religion, of the various people with whom he had met, or amongst whom he had occasionally resided; but had been induced to postpone these miscellaneous matters, lest the regular diary of the voyage should be interrupted by the introduction of such desultory observations. These he had intended to present in the form of a supplementary or concluding chapter, but was prevented by the unfortunate event of his illness.

Most of the papers, which contain these interesting particulars, are too concise and too unconnected for me to attempt any arrangement of them, or to submit them to the reader without hazarding Captain Vancouver's judgment as an observer, or his reputation as a narrator, rigidly devoted to the truth. But as some of the notes, which he made upon the spot, are of too valuable a nature to be intirely lost, I shall venture to subjoin them to the History of the Voyage, as nearly as possible in his own words, without attempting any such arrangement of them, as might tend to diminish their authenticity, or bring into doubt that scrupulous veracity from which Captain Vancouver never departed.

The whole narrative of the Voyage of Discovery having been brought to its conclusion at Valparaiso, by Captain Vancouver himself, there only remains for me to add, that in preparing for the press the small remainder of his journal, comprehending the passage round Cape Horn to St. Helena, and from thence to England, I have strictly adhered to the rough documents before me; but as no new incidents occurred in this part of the voyage, and as the insertion of log-book minutes, over a space which is now so frequently traversed, cannot either be useful or entertaining. I have endeavoured to compress this portion of the journal into as few pages as possible.

In performing this painful task, I have had severe and ample cause to lament the melancholy office to which I have been compelled, by the death of him

---

fleet in the West-Indies, where he remained until the middle of the year 1783. In the year 1784 he was appointed to, and sailed in the Europa to Jamaica, on which station he continued until her return to England in September 1789. On the 1st of January 1790, he was appointed to the Discovery, but soon afterwards was removed to the Courageux: here he remained until December, 1790, when he was made master and commander, and appointed to the Discovery. In August, 1794, he was, without solicitation, promoted to the rank of post-captain, and was paid off on the conclusion of his last voyage in November, 1795. After this period he was constantly employed, until within a few weeks of his decease, in May, 1798, in preparing the following journal for publication.

whose early departure from this life has deprived His Majesty of an active and able officer, truth and science of a steady supporter, society of an uniformly valuable member, and in addition to the feelings of many who live to regret the loss of a sincere friend, I have to deplore that of a most affectionate brother.

JOHN VANCOUVER.

(Second Edition)

ADVERTISEMENT.

THE Publisher finds it necessary only to state, for the information of the Purchasers of this new Edition, that the copper-plates of the charts contained in the folio volume, which accompanied the first Edition, were all stolen, and may therefore be considered as irrecoverably lost.

The whole of the Views, except the headlands*, are retained. The general chart, and that of the New Discoveries, &c. are re-engraved, and will, it is conceived, completely satisfy the majority of his Readers.

It must, however, be observed, that the other charts are indispensably necessary for such as may hereafter navigate those seas. This Edition has received throughout the requisite corrections of the Editor, JOHN VANCOUVER, Esq.

No work has maintained a higher character in the public estimation than this Voyage, and the expence of the quarto Edition could alone have prevented its being universally read.

The loss of the Plates, has, of course, greatly enhanced the value of the few Copies of the original Edition, which were not at that time sold. They may, however, be had until Christmas next, with the folio volume of charts at Twelve Guineas; but should any then remain they will be advanced to Fifteen Guineas.

PICCADILLY,
26th October, 1801.

* These are six in number, and may be had, price Seven Shillings.

CONTENTS

BOOK THE FIRST.

CHAPTER V.

CHAPTER VI.

CHAPTER VII.

BOOK THE SECOND.

VISIT THE SANDWICH ISLANDS; PROCEED TO SURVEY THE COAST OF NEW ALBION; PASS THROUGH AN INLAND NAVIGATION; TRANSACTIONS AT NOOTKA; ARRIVE AT PORT ST. FRANCISCO.

CHAPTER I.

CHAPTER IX.

CHAPTER X.

CHAPTER XI.

BOOK THE THIRD.

Transactions at two Spanish settlements in New Albion; examination of Columbia river; occurrences on board the Dædalus; second visit to the Sandwich islands.

CHAPTER I.

CHAPTER II.

CHAPTER III.

CHAPTER IV.

CHAPTER V.

CHAPTER VI.

CHAPTER VII.

CHAPTER VIII.

BOOK THE FOURTH.

SECOND VISIT TO THE NORTH; SURVEY OF THE AMERICAN COAST FROM FITZHUGH'S SOUND TO CAPE DECISION; AND FROM MONTERREY TO THE SOUTHERN EXTENT OF OUR INTENDED INVESTIGATION.

CHAPTER VI.

CHAPTER VII.

CHAPTER VIII.

CHAPTER IX.

BOOK THE FIFTH.

THIRD VISIT TO THE SANDWICH ISLANDS—CONCLUDE THE SURVEY OF THE COAST OF NORTH-WEST AMERICA.

CHAPTER I.

CHAPTER II.

CHAPTER III.

CHAPTER IV.

CHAPTER V.

CHAPTER VI.

CHAPTER VII.

CHAPTER VIII.

CHAPTER IX.

CHAPTER X.

BOOK THE SIXTH.

PASSAGE TO THE SOUTHWARD ALONG THE WESTERN COAST OF AMERICA; DOUBLE CAPE HORN; TOUCH AT ST. HELENA; ARRIVE IN ENGLAND.

CHAPTER I.

CHAPTER II.

CHAPTER III.

CHAPTER IV.

CHAPTER V.

CHAPTER VI.

A

VOYAGE

TO THE

NORTH PACIFIC OCEAN,

AND

ROUND THE WORLD.

———◦◦———

BOOK THE FIRST.

TRANSACTIONS FROM THE COMMENCEMENT OF THE
EXPEDITION, UNTIL OUR DEPARTURE FROM OTAHEITE.

CHAPTER I.

Equipment of the DISCOVERY *and the* CHATHAM—*Departure from Falmouth—Visit
and Transactions at Teneriffe—Occurrences and Observations during the Passage
to the Cape of Good Hope—Transactions there, and departure thence.*

ON the 15th of December, 1790, I had the honor of receiving my commission
as commander of His Majesty's sloop the Discovery, then lying at Deptford,

where, the next morning, Thursday the 16th, I joined her, and began entering men.

Lieutenant William Robert Broughton having been selected as a proper officer to command the Chatham, he was accordingly appointed;[1] but the repairs she demanded prevented her equipment keeping pace with that of the Discovery; which in most respects being completed by Thursday the 6th of January, 1791, the sails were bent, and the ship got in readiness to proceed down the river. With a favorable wind on the following day, Friday the 7th, we sailed, and anchored in Long Reach about five in the evening. Although this trial of the ship may appear very insignificant, yet as she had never been under sail, it was not made without some anxiety. The construction of her upper works, for the sake of adding to the comfort of the accommodations, differing materially from the general fashion, produced an unsightly appearance, and gave rise to various opinions unfavorable to her qualities as a seaboat; for which reason it was natural to pay the minutest attention to her steering and other properties when in motion; and we obtained in the course of this short trip, the pleasing prospect of her proving handy, and in all other respects a very comfortable vessel. Various necessary occupations detained us in Long Reach until Wednesday the 26th, when, having taken on board all our ordnance stores, and such things as were wanted from Deptford dock yard, we proceeded down the river on our way to Portsmouth. My orders for this purpose were accompanied by another, to receive on board and convey to his native country, *Towereroo*, an Indian,[2] from one of the Sandwich Islands, who had been brought from thence by some of the north-west American traders, in July, 1789. This man had lived, whilst in England, in great obscurity, and did not seem in the least to have benefited by his residence in this country.[3]

---

[1] Broughton received his appointment on 28 December and joined the *Chatham* on 1 January 1791.

[2] Like Cook, Vancouver used the word 'Indian' when referring to the natives of the Pacific Islands as well as to those of North America.

[3] Spelling of the name varies, as Hawaiian was still an unwritten language. The modern spelling is Kualelo. Menzies tells his story in some detail. The boy, a native of Molokai, joined the British sloop *Princess Royal*, commanded by Charles Duncan, in January 1788. He was then only 11 or 12 year old. In the autumn, when the vessel returned to the islands after a trading cruise on the Northwest Coast, Towerero begged to be taken to Britain. Duncan consented, and he travelled to China in the *Princess Royal*. There he joined the *Prince of Wales*, in which Menzies was serving as surgeon. The ship arrived in England in July 1789. 'Toworero spent the first Winter & Spring down at Plymouth under the care and tuition of Mr. James Johnstone who commanded the Prince of Wales from China & was soon after appointed to superintend a division of Ships in Ordinary at that Port. This gentleman's first object was to have him inoculated for the small Pox which he underwent with little inconvenience, & then he was sent to a public school in the neighbourhood where great pains was taken to learn him to read and write. The first he seems could not be accomplished, for though he soon acquired a thorough knowledge & pretty exact pronunciation of the simple letters of our Alphabet, yet no power of art could carry him a step farther & get him to join or mingle these different sounds together in

Unfavorable winds prevented our reaching the Downs until Sunday the 30th; where they still continued, and, being attended with very boisterous weather, detained us until Thursday the 3d of February; when, with a strong gale from the northward, we proceeded down channel. About noon we passed the South Foreland, and had the misfortune to lose John Brown,[1] who fell overboard and was drowned. He was one of the carpenter's mates, an exceedingly good man, and very much regretted. About noon on Saturday the 5th, we anchored at Spithead, where Rear-Admiral Goodall's flag was flying on board His Majesty's ship Vanguard, in company with twelve sail of the line and several frigates.

Some defects in the ship's head were already evident, as the bumkins and a considerable part of the head were now washed away.[2] These repairs, with such other duties as were necessary, I gave orders to have executed; and my presence being required in London, I repaired thither; where I remained until Sunday the 27th, when I returned to Portsmouth, with orders to proceed to Falmouth.

On former voyages of this description, it had been customary to pay the officers and ship's company the wages that had become due whilst they had been employed in the equipment of the vessels, which in general had occupied six months or upwards; enabling them by such means more effectually to provide themselves with those comforts which such long and remote services ever demand. But as a similar payment to the crews of the Discovery and Chatham, (whose complements were now complete) for the short time they had been in pay, would have been of little assistance; the Lords of the Admiralty, at my solicitation, had the goodness to grant them three months pay in advance; which was accordingly received free of all deductions.

I have already mentioned that the Navy Board had supplied me with an

the formation of a word. But in writing he made greater progress, that is, he soon acquired a habit of copying whatever was placed before him with great exactness in the same manner he would do a drawing or a picture; indeed to the art of Drawing in general he appeard most partial, & would no doubt in a short time make great proficiency with the aid of a little instruction, but in this uncultivated state of his mind he seemd fondest of those rude pictures called Caricatures & frequently amused himself in taking off even his friends in imitation of these pieces.

'The next summer he accompanied Mr. Duncan to Hudsons Bay, where that Gentleman was sent to examine the Great Inlets & make discoveries on the interior navigation of that Country, but from reasons best known to the [Hudson's Bay] Company's servants abroad he was not duly equippd to enter on his plans of Operation, so he was obligd to return again to London contrary to expectation the following Autumn when Toowerero remaind with his Patron till he embarkd on board the Discovery.' – Menzies, 4 March 1792. Toworero and a boy from the island of Niihau, who also arrived in the Prince of Wales, were the first Hawaiians seen in England. Toworero's patron was the same James Johnstone who joined the Chatham as master.

[1] Thomas Brown, according to the muster roll. He was a native of Glasgow, aged 26.

[2] This was to be a recurring problem, as Vancouver's letters to the Admiralty from Teneriffe and the Cape of Good Hope, and later entries in his journal show.

assortment of mathematical instruments; and the Board of Longitude, in compliance with the wishes of the Admiralty, provided in addition two chronometers; one made by the late eminent Mr. Kendall, (the excellence of which had been manifested on board the Discovery during Captain Cook's last voyage, and which had lately been cleaned and put into order by its very worthy and ingenious maker, a short time before his decease;)[1] the other lately made by Mr. Arnold.[2] These had both been deposited at the observatory of the Portsmouth academy, for the purpose of finding their respective errors, and for ascertaining their rate of going. The former was delivered to me, with such observations as had been made to that effect; whence it appeared to be fast of mean time at Greenwich, on Tuesday the 1st of March at noon, $1'$ $30''$ $18'''$, and to be gaining on mean time at the rate of $6''$ $12'''$ per day. The latter was directed to be put on board the Chatham, which vessel had now arrived from the river.

Having completely finished our business with the dock-yard on the evening of Thursday the 3d, we dropped down to St. Helen's, and the next morning, Friday the 4th, proceeded down channel, leaving the Chatham behind, not as yet quite ready to accompany us; in our way we stopped at Guernsey,[3] and on Saturday the 12th arrived at Falmouth, where I was to wait the arrival of the Chatham, and to receive my final instructions for the prosecution of the voyage. An Admiralty messenger presented me with the latter on Sunday the 20th; but the Chatham did not arrive until the 31st, when Lieutenant Broughton, who had orders to put himself under my command, received such signals and instructions as were necessary on this occasion. He informed me, that they had experienced a very boisterous passage from Spithead, and that the Chatham had proved so very crank, as, in some instances, to occasion considerable alarm.[4] The length of time I had already waited for her arrival rendered this intelligence very unpleasant; as, demanding immediate attention, it would cause further delay, which I much wished to avoid; especially as a favorable gale for clearing the channel now prevailed. The apprehension of further detention by contrary winds, should we lose the present opportunity by breaking up the Chatham's hold for the reception of more ballast, induced me to resort to another expedient, that of lending her all our shot, which when stowed amidships as low down as possible, and every weight removed from

---

[1] This was the chronometer known as K3, completed in 1774. Larcum Kendall, its maker, died in 1790. The chronometer is now in the National Maritime Museum, Greenwich, on permanent loan from the Hydrographer of the Navy.

[2] John Arnold's no. 82, which was carried in the Chatham.

[3] The Chatham also visited Guernsey. 'Our business here was only to supply ourselves with a Private Stock of Spirits, Wine, Tea, &c.' – Bell, 19 March. Spirits and wine purchased there were duty free.

[4] 'It blew as heavy a Gale of wind as the oldest Seaman on board ever remembered, and we were really in a critical situation.' At Spithead the Discovery 'was glad to see us – it having been reported that we were lost'. – Bell, 26 and 27 February.

above, we flattered ourselves would be the means of affording a temporary relief to this inconvenience.[1]

A gentle breeze from the N.E. at day dawn on Friday the 1st of April, enabled us to sail out of Carrack road, in company with the Chatham; and at midnight we took a long farewell of our native shores. The Lizard lights bore by compass N.N.W. ½W. about eight leagues distant; and the wind being in the western quarter, we stood to the southward. Towards the morning of Saturday the 2d, on the wind's shifting to the south, we stood to the westward, clear of the English channel; with minds, it may easily be conceived, not intirely free from serious and contemplative reflections. The remote and barbarous regions, which were now destined, for some years, to be our transitory places of abode, were not likely to afford us any means of communicating with our native soil, our families, our friends or favorites, whom we were now leaving far behind; and to augment these painful reflections, His Majesty's proclamation had arrived at Falmouth, the evening prior to our departure, offering bounties for manning the fleet;[2] several sail of the line were put into commission, and flag officers appointed to different commands: these were circumstances similar to those under which, in August, 1776, I had sailed from England in the Discovery, commanded by Captain Clerke, on a voyage which in its object nearly resembled the expedition we were now about to undertake.[3] This very unexpected armament could not be regarded without causing various opinions in those who, from day to day, would have opportunities of noticing the several measures inclining to war or peace; but to us, destined, as it were, to a long and remote exile, and precluded, for an indefinite period of time, from all chance of becoming acquainted with its result, it was the source of inexpressible solicitude, and our feelings on the occasion may be better conceived than described.

Having no particular route to the Pacific Ocean pointed out in my instructions, and being left at perfect liberty to pursue that which appeared the most eligible, I did not hesitate to prefer the passage by way of the Cape of Good Hope, intending to visit the Madeiras, for the purpose of procuring wine and refreshments. Our course was accordingly so directed against winds very unfavorable to our wishes. At noon on Sunday the 3d we reached the latitude 48° 48' north, longitude by the chronometer 6° 55' west; where the cloudy weather preventing our making the necessary observations on the sun eclipsed, produced no small degree of concern; as with the late improvement

[1] While at Woolwich the Chatham had taken on 8 tons of iron ballast, but four days later, 'As it was conceived that the Vessel would be sufficiently deep without the Iron Ballast – it was relanded in the yard.' – Johnstone, 22 January. At Spithead she received from the Discovery '550 Four Pounders, round Shot & 112 Four Pounder, Case Shot.' – Heddington, 1 April.
[2] The proclamation called for a fleet mobilization to support Pitt's intervention in the Russo-Turkish War.
[3] The reference is to Cook's third voyage. The War of American Independence was in progress when it sailed.

of applying deep magnifying powers to the telescopes of sextants, the observations on solar eclipses are rendered very easy to be made at sea; and although we were not fortunate enough on this occasion to procure such, at the interesting periods of the eclipse, as would have put this improvement fully to the test, yet it was evident that these observations to persons not much accustomed to astronomical pursuits would be rendered plain and easy, by the reflected image of the sun being brought down to the horizon; so that the beginning and the end of the eclipse would be ascertained by the help of these deep magnifying telescopes with great precision; and probably it may not be unworthy the attention of the Board of Longitude to contrive, and cause such calculations to be published, as would tend to render these observations generally useful in the various parts of the globe, without the tedious process of calculating eclipses. The wind, continuing in the southern quarter, rendered our progress slow; the weather, however, being clear, afforded us employment in taking some good lunar observations; which, reduced to the noon of Tuesday the 12th, gave the mean result of four sets, taken by me, 12° 24′ west longitude; four sets taken by Mr. Whidbey, 12° 30′; the chronometer at the same time shewing 12° 9′; and as I considered the latter to be nearest the truth, the lunar observations appeared to be 15′ to 21′ too far to the westward. The longitude, by dead reckoning, 13° 22′, and the latitude 44° 22′ north. The error in reckoning amounting almost to a degree, seemed most likely to have been occasioned by our not having made sufficient allowance for the variation of the compass on our first sailing, as, instead of allowing from 22° to 25°, which was what we esteemed the variation, our observations for ascertaining this fact, when the ship was sufficiently steady, shewed the variation to be 28° and 29½° westwardly. These opportunities, however, had not occurred so frequently as I could have wished, owing to a constant irregular swell that had accompanied us since leaving the land, and caused so much motion and pitching, that the whole head railings, bumkins, &c. were again washed away.

On Saturday the 16th, in latitude 42° 34′ north, longitude 12° 31′ west, the variation of the compass, by the mean result of six sets of observations taken by three compasses differing from 25° 57′ to 27° 35′, was observed to be 26° 29′ westwardly. The current was found to set in a direction E.N.E. at the rate of a quarter of a mile per hour. The whole of the day being perfectly calm, with remarkably fine weather, induced me to embrace the opportunity of unbending all our sails which wanted alteration, and to bend an entire new suit; these I caused to be soaked overboard for some hours, that the sea water might dissolve the size used in making the canvass, and by that means act as a preventive against the mildew in hot rainy weather. This process might probably be found useful in the operation of bleaching.

On our departure from England, I did not intend using any antiseptic provisions, until the refreshments which we might be enabled to procure at the Madeiras should be exhausted; but light baffling winds, together with the crank situation and bad sailing of the Chatham,[1] having so retarded our progress, that, by Thursday the 21st, we were advanced no further than the latitude of 35° 7′ north, longitude 14° 40′ west: sour krout and portable broth had, for some days, been served on board each of the vessels; the store-rooms had been cleared, cleaned, and washed with vinegar, and the ship had been smoked with gunpowder mixed with vinegar. As I had ever considered fire the most likely and efficacious means to keep up a constant circulation of fresh and pure air throughout a ship; in the fore part of every day good fires were burning between decks, and in the well. Both decks were kept clean, and as dry as possible, and notwithstanding the weather was hot, and the smoke and heat thence arising was considered as inconvenient and disagreeable, yet I was confident that a due attention to this particular, and not washing too frequently below, were indispensable precautions, and would be productive of the most salubrious and happy effects in preserving the health and lives of our people. These preventive measures becoming the standing orders of the Discovery, it will be unnecessary hereafter to repeat that they were regularly enforced, as they were observed throughout the voyage with the strictest attention. It may not, however, on this subject, be improper to remark that, if instead of biscuit, seamen were provided with fresh soft bread, which can easily be made very good at sea, and a large proportion of wholesome water, where the nature of the services will admit of such a supply, they would add greatly to the preservation of that most valuable of all blessings, health.

The evening of Saturday the 23d, being remarkably fine and serene, brought us in sight of the island of Porto Sancto, bearing by compass S.W.½W. 20 leagues distant; the next afternoon we passed its meridian, when the chronometer shewing its longitude to be 16° 24′ 15‴,[2] varying only one minute to the westward of the true longitude of that island, proved it was going very well. As Madeira was our object, every effort was exerted to gain Funchal Road, until the evening of Monday the 25th, when the wind becoming excessively variable, and the weather gloomy and unsettled, that station seemed ineligible for executing the service of which the Chatham stood in need; namely, the breaking up her hold, for the purpose of receiving a large portion of ballast. Considering therefore the roadstead of Sta Cruz as better calculated for this business, we proceeded towards Teneriffe. The wind which had been generally from the west, veered round by the north, as we advanced to the southward, and settled in the N.E. trade, accompanied with fine pleasant weather, which, on Tuesday the 26th, in latitude 30° 54′ north, afforded me an opportunity of obtaining several sets of lunar distances with the different

[1] The *Chatham's* poor sailing qualities – which Vancouver described as being 'so contrary to what every person expected' – were to be a constant source of annoyance and inconvenience. The logs record countless signals ordering her to put on more sail, and *Discovery* was frequently obliged to shorten sail in order to keep her in company. In spite of this, when sailing independently she was to show a disconcerting ability to reach a rendezvous before the *Discovery*.

[2] The longitude of Vila de Porto Santo is now given as 16° 20′ W.

sextants in the ship. These were twelve in number, of the following eminent makers in London, (viz.) Ramsden, Dollond, Troughton, Adams, and Gilbert, though the greater number were made by Mr. Ramsden. They all agreed exceedingly well together, and their mean result shewed the longitude to be 16° 21′ 32″; the chronometer made the longitude 16° 31′ 15″ west; and as there could be no doubt of the latter being nearest the truth, the result of the lunar observations, by the several sextants, appeared to be 9′ 43″ too far to the eastward. On the other side of the moon, my lunar observations were 15′ to the west of the true, or nearly the true, longitude, as was proved on our making the Madeiras. This evinces the accuracy with which these observations are in general capable of being made with good instruments, and by a careful observer.

In the morning of Thursday the 28th, the peak of Teneriffe was seen bearing by compass S.W. about sixteen leagues distant; and , in the evening, as we approached the roadstead of Sᵗᵃ Cruz, we were met by the master attendant, who placed the ship in what, he said, he conceived the best birth in the roadstead, and the Chatham in our immediate neighbourhood.

When the ship was secured, an officer was sent to inform the governor of our arrival, and to solicit his permission to take on board such wine, and refreshments as we required; but having understood that he had waved a return of salute to some of His Majesty's ships that had lately visited Teneriffe; I did not choose to risk a refusal, however polite, to comply with this compliment.[1] The officer was civilly received, and the contractor was, the next morning, directed to supply the different articles of which we stood in need.

Accompanied by Mr. Broughton, Mr. Menzies, and some of the other officers, on Friday the 29th, in the forenoon, I waited on his Excellency Senʳ Don Antonio Guitierres, the governor general of the Canaries, who then resided in the city of Sᵗᵃ Cruz. His excellency received us with the politeness usual on these occasions, and assured us of his readiness to afford us every assistance; but apologized that the poverty of the country prevented his inviting us to his table. Attended by the same party, on Sunday, the 1st of May, I visited the city of Lagoona,[2] and after satisfying our curiosity with its external appearance, we returned to Sᵗᵃ Cruz, and dined with Mr. Rhoney, an Irish gentleman, to whose hospitality we were greatly indebted.[3] Had we

[1] Vancouver omits the explanation: 'Captⁿ Vancouver as is customary asked him [the Governor], if we saluted, whether he wou'd not return the same number of Guns; he politely thank'd him, but declined the compliment as the quantity of Powder they had, was so small, they could not afford to answer salutes.' – Bell, April 1791.

[2] Laguna. The town was in a sad state: 'depopulation was so great, that in every Streit the Grass was growing half a foot high'. – Bell, April 1791.

[3] Vancouver makes no mention of a near fatal fracas that occurred when he returned from Laguna. Bell describes it in his private journal, and Menzies describes it both in his journal and in a letter written four days after the event: 'Being a holy-day [Sunday 1 May] a number of Men from both Vessels were permitted to take the recreation of the Shore. Capt. Vancouver with a party of officers rode to see the City of Laguna about two Leagues off, and returned to Santa Cruz to dinner; In the afternoon the Midshipman who went

not fortunately met with him immediately on our landing, we should have been much inconvenienced, as there did not appear another person on the island who was inclinable to offer us shelter from the scorching rays of the sun, or to afford us the smallest refreshment.

We had the mortification, this morning, of finding the small bower cable cut through nearly in the middle, which seemed to have been occasioned by an anchor lying at the bottom. The loss of an anchor in a situation where no other could be procured, was a matter of serious concern; no pains were spared to regain it until the afternoon of Thursday the 5th, when all our exertions proved ineffectual; and being apprehensive that other lost anchors might be in its vicinity, we weighed, went further out, and again anchored in 30 fathoms water on a soft dark oozy bottom intermixed with small white shells, having the northernmost church steeple in a line with the centre of the jetty, bearing by compass N. 48 W. and the southernmost fort S. 71 W. about three quarters of a mile from the town. This anchorage appeared to be far preferable to our former situation, being nearly as convenient for the landing place, without the hazard of damaging the cables by anchors which small vessels might have lost nearer in shore; and which is the only danger to be apprehended here, as the bottom is good holding ground, and, to all appearance, perfectly free from rocks.

The surf that had beaten with great violence on the shores for some days past, and for sheltering against which the pier of Sta Cruz is but ill contrived, had much retarded the Chatham's business of taking on board shingle ballast,[1] and prevented the completion of that object until late on Saturday night the 7th, when we put to sea, and directed our course to the southward.

on shore for the liberty-men had a scuffle with the Chatham's people on the wharf which induced the Spanish Sentinels to interpose and one of them had his Musket renched out of his hands by one of our Marines, upon which he immediately ran to alarm the guard, at this time Capt. V— & some of the officers came down to the water side and were endeavouring to get the people into the boat, when the Spanish guards arrived, accompanied by a numerous mob, & began to knock down our men & officers without distinction. Capt. V— was thrown from the wharf into the sea & luckily taken up by our boat without being much hurt, the attack then became so general that the Hble. Mr. Pit & some others jumped into the Sea and swam to the boat to save their lives. Mr. Baker, 3rd Lieutenant of the Discovery, who was indeed the only Officer armed & in full uniform, & had never shown the least sign to draw upon them was knocked in the head in several places & wounded. Many of the Men were likewise bruised & wounded in several places, but none I believe dangerously.... That the quarrel originated with our people is, I think, pretty evident from every information I can collect, but that the Spanish Guard acted very unbecoming Soldiers will not, I think require much examination.' – Menzies to Banks, Teneriffe, 5 May 1791. Banks Papers, Mitchell Library. Whidbey 'had a miraculous escape of his life, for being near the wall two Soldiers run at him with charg'd Bayonets, which he most luckily avoided by stepping a little on one side, and the Bayonets went against the Wall with so much force as to break them.' – Bell, May. Vancouver sent a letter of remonstrance to the Governor, who in reply expressed regret, stated that disciplinary action was being taken, but contended that the British sailors had caused the quarrel.

[1] The *Chatham* took on about 23 tons of ballast. This consisted of 'Beach Stones which were very suitable being a fine clean pebbly Stone free from all sand'. – Johnstone, 29 April.

The ballast which the Chatham had now taken on board certainly prevented her being so very crank, but it did not seem to have contributed to her sailing, as the Discovery still preserved a great superiority in that respect.

Not having supposed we should have been so long detained at Teneriffe, I took no steps for making astronomical observations on shore; those taken on board shewed the longitude by the chronometer to be 16° 17′ 5″, only 50″ to the westward of the true longitude, as laid down in the requisite tables:[1] the latitude by our observations was 28° 28′ 38″, and the variation, by the mean result of all our cards and compasses, was 16° 38′, differing from 15° 58′ to 17° 17′ westwardly.

For the information of those who may be induced to visit Teneriffe at this season of the year with the hope of procuring refreshments, I must remark, that we found the wine, water, and beef exceedingly good, and were induced to take some days supply of the latter to sea; but fruit, vegetables, poultry, and all kinds of live stock were very indifferent, and most extravagantly expensive.

Towards noon of Sunday the 8th, we lost sight of the Canaries. The trade wind blew a pleasant gale, the sea was smooth, and the weather, being fine, enabled us to make some excellent lunar observations; those I took shewed the longitude to be 16° 52′ 36″; those taken by Mr. Whidbey 16° 52′ 30″; and the chronometer shewed 16° 47′ 45″. The latitude, at this time, was 27° 5′ north; and the variation, by three compasses differing from 15° 10′ to 18° 51′, was 17° 33′ 40″ westwardly.

Our course from the Canaries was directed to the westward of the cape de Verd Islands, which we gained sight of and passed on the forenoon of Saturday the 14th. The N.W. extremity of the island of St. Antonio appeared, by our observations, to be situated in 17° 10′ north latitude, and 25° 3′ 22″ west longitude;[2] the variation of the compass 12° 32′ 15″ westwardly. The fresh beef that we had brought from Teneriffe being exhausted, on Wednesday the 18th, portable broth and sour krout were again served to the ships' crews; at this time we had reached the latitude of 9° 35′ north, longitude 23° 27′ west, when the weather, which had been pleasant and attended with a fresh gale from the N.E. very materially altered: the wind slackened and veered round to the north, and the atmosphere, though not cloudy, was encumbered with a bright haze nearly approaching to a fog, but without the least dampness or humidity. Through this medium the heavenly bodies were sufficiently visible whilst terrestrial objects were only discernible at small distances. This very singular appearance continued a few days until Saturday the 21st, when, in latitude 6° 20′ north, and longitude 22° 40′ west, the northerly breeze died away, the dense atmosphere disappeared, and they were succeeded by calm, cloudy, hot weather, the thermometer standing from 80° to 83°, attended with some heavy showers of rain and gusts of wind in various directions, though

---

[1] The position of Santa Cruz de Tenerife is lat. 28° 27′ N, long. 16° 14′ W.
[2] Santo Antão is meant, in lat. 17° 05′ N, long. 25° 10′ W.

generally from the eastern quarter between N.E. and south. Our progress, with this kind of weather, was slow until Tuesday the 24th, when, in latitude 4° 25′ north, longitude 21° 36′ west, we seemed to have passed the line of those unpleasant and frequently unhealthy regions. The steadiness of the gentle gale, and the serenity of the weather indicated our having reached the S.E. trade winds; these conjectures were soon established by the wind gradually increasing, so that, about midnight on Friday the 27th, we crossed the equator in 25° 15′ west longitude.[1] The variation to this point had gradually, though not very regularly, decreased to about 9° westwardly; and the lunar observations, lately taken, had corresponded within a few minutes with the longitude shewn by the chronometer.

Crossing the equator so far to the westward has been frequently objected to, as being liable to entangle ships with the coast of Brazil. I am, however, of a different opinion, and conceive many advantages are derived by thus crossing the line; such as, pursuing a track destitute of those calms and heavy rains, which are ever attendant on a more eastwardly route. By every information I have been enabled to collect, it does not appear that much is to be gained in point of distance by crossing the equator in a more eastwardly longitude; since it seems that vessels which have pursued their southerly course to cross the line under the 10th, 15th, or 20th meridian of west longitude, have, by the trade wind blowing there in a more southerly direction, been driven equally as far west, to the 25th, 26th, and 27th degrees of west longitude before they have been enabled to gain the variable winds, without the benefit of a constant breeze and fair weather, which with the very little interruption between the 21st and 24th, was experienced during this passage.

From the equator, with a brisk trade wind, we steered with a full sail and flowing sheet; which by the 1st of June brought us to the latitude of 7° 52′ south, longitude 29° 7′ west; whence we ceased stretching further to the westward, and made a good course a few degrees to the eastward of south; so that on Thursday the 9th we had reached the latitude of 19° 47′ south, longitude 27° 27′ west, approaching to the parallel of the islands Trinadada and Martin Vas. The wind now permitted our steering well to the eastward of south; but lest an error should have existed in our longitude, or in that of those islands, I directed the Chatham to increase her distance from us by holding a south course, for the purpose of gaining a view of that land; by sun-set we were in the latitude of 20° 9′ south, the parallel of those islands,

---

[1] '…the usual ceremonies of Shaving, Ducking &c. those who had not before cross'd it were performed by Neptune & his Gang;…as a little Grog exempted those who chose to pay the fine from undergoing the unpleasant operation, several of the Young Gentlemen paid this fine, and the Gods got so very merry, that one of them tired of being out of his element jump'd overboard, – at that time the Vessel was going very quick through the Water with Studding Sails & Royals set, the Ship was instantly hove up into the wind, but the man had caught hold of a Rope, which fortunately was towing under the Chains – before this was effected – and he was thus providentially saved.' – Bell, 27 May. This incident occurred in the Chatham.

but saw nothing of them. The longitude of the former is stated to be 28° 50′, that of the latter 28° 34′ west;[1] allowing their longitude, and that of the ship, to have been accurately ascertained, we passed them at the distance of 24 and 19 leagues.

On Sunday the 12th we crossed the southern tropic in 25° 18′ west longitude; the variation of the compass had now gradually decreased to 4° 30′ westwardly, and having lately taken many very good lunar distances of the sun and stars on different sides of the moon, I assumed their mean result as the true longitude, or nearly so; by which, the observations for the longitude, according to the chronometer, appeared to be 14′ 25″ too far to the eastward; whence it should appear, that it was not gaining quite so much as had been allowed in consequence of its rate, as ascertained at Portsmouth. After crossing the tropic of Capricorn,[2] the wind became very variable, as well in point of strength as in direction, so that on Tuesday the 28th we had only advanced to the latitude of 31° 56′ south, longitude 4° 18′ west.

The weather was in general very pleasant: and the Chatham, to our great mortification, continued to sail equally slow in light as in fresh gales, which materially affected the progress of our voyage; the object of which was of such a nature that it would allow of no opportunity of being passed by, that, with propriety, could be embraced for the advancement of geography and navigation; and as Captain Cook's chart of the Sandwich islands presented little field for any improvement that could occupy the several winters we were likely to pass in their vicinity, I resolved in our way to the Pacific Ocean to visit the S.W. part of New Holland,[3] and endeavour to acquire some information of that unknown, though interesting country. Having much business to perform at the Cape of Good Hope in the carpenter's department, it became expedient, for the carrying into execution the whole of my plan, that no time should be lost; particularly as our passage from England had already exceeded the limits of my expectations. These reasons induced me to make the best of our way in the Discovery to the Cape of Good Hope, and should the Chatham be able to keep up with us, she was directed so to do; if otherways, Mr. Broughton was provided with sufficient instructions.

The wind was light and variable, until Friday, July the 1st, in latitude 33° 54′ south, longitude 58′ 40″ west, it blew a fine gale from the N.N.E. attended with pleasant weather; the Chatham until this evening remained in sight, but in the morning was not within the limits of our horizon. As we approached the African shore the weather became very unsettled, with sudden transitions from calms to heavy gales, attended with much thunder, lightning, and a heavy swell from the westward and S.W. One of these gales, on Tuesday the 5th,

[1] The latitude of both islands is 20° 30′ S; longitude of Trinidade is 29° 20′; of Martin Vas 28° 52′. They are about 650 miles E of the coast of Brazil.

[2] Misprinted 'tropic of Cancer' in the first edition.

[3] The name Australia, which was to supersede New Holland, appeared in print as early as 1793, but its general adoption seems to have stemmed from a recommendation by Matthew Flinders in *A Voyage to Terra Australis*, published in 1814.

reduced us for a few hours to our courses. The wind became southwardly with pleasant weather on Thursday the 7th, when a strange sail was descried to the N.E. holding a course, as if intending to pass the Cape, and some of us thinking the sea was discoloured, we tried for soundings, but found no bottom with 140 fathoms of line. After passing the 27° of south latitude, many oceanic birds were our constant companions, consisting of three kinds of albatrosses, the quebrantahuessos,[1] pintadoes, the sooty, the black, and small blue petrels, with some few other small birds of the same tribe; amongst which were but few of the storm petrel, which in these regions are generally numerous. Most of these, by the 7th, had disappeared, and, in their place, were seen the blue petrel of the larger sort, though comparatively in small numbers; at noon the observed latitude was 35° 13' south, longitude 14° east. The wind blew a strong gale from W.S.W. in the afternoon of Friday the 8th, when judging the Cape of Good Hope to bear from us N. 66 E. true, distant 18 leagues, we experienced, for the space of about seven miles, a most extraordinary agitation in the sea, to be compared only to a large cauldron of boiling water; this was supposed to be the effect of two contending currents, and for that reason I did not try soundings. I was also particularly anxious to gain sight of the land, which, in the event of the chronometer proving correct, there was great probability of doing before dark; but not seeing it we stood on till ten in the evening, when, by our lunar observations, supposing the Cape land to be about eight leagues distant, we hauled to the wind, and plied in order to preserve our then situation until the morning of Saturday the 9th. At day light the Cape was in sight, bearing east by compass, eight leagues distant. This instance will, I trust, be not the only one I shall be able to adduce, to prove the utility of the lunar method of finding the longitude, and the very great importance that such information must be of to every sea officer.

At this season of the year, the boisterous weather and the prevailing winds from the N.W. rendering Table Bay not only excessively unpleasant but insecure, our course was directed to False Bay. At noon, the observed latitude was 34° 26' south, the Cape of Good Hope then bearing E.N.E. five or six miles distant. This promontory, and the dangerous rocks that lie in its neighbourhood, we passed, and stood into False Bay, where in the evening, the weather falling calm, we anchored in 40 fathoms water; the Cape bearing west by compass, ten miles distant; Simon's Bay N.N.W. and the False Cape S.E.; in this situation the chronometer shewed the longitude to be 18° 52' 45", making an error, or variation in its rate of going, as ascertained at Portsmouth, of 18' 30" equal to 1' 14" of time since the first day of March; which will, without doubt, be received and considered as being very correct; it also corresponded with my observations, and what on that subject I had noticed on the 12th of June.

Our passage through the Atlantic Ocean being thus accomplished, it

---

[1] Quebrante huesos (Spanish); the giant petrel.

becomes requisite, in compliance with the method proposed in the introduction for correcting the errors of navigation, to have some retrospect to this passage, especially since passing the Cape de Verd islands.

From the island of St. Antonio, until we had crossed the latitude of cape St. Augustine,[1] we were materially affected by currents; and between the latitude of 6° north and the equator, strong riplings were conspicuous on the surface of the sea. These currents, contrary to the general opinion, seem to possess no regularity, as we found ourselves, day after day, driven in directions very contrary to our expectations from the impulse we had experienced on the former day, and by no means attended with that periodical uniformity, pointed out by Mr. Nicholson in his lately revised and corrected Indian directory, published in the year 1787.[2] On the contrary, instead of the currents at this season of the year, agreeably to his hypothesis, setting to the northward, the most prevailing stream we experienced set to the south, and more in a south-eastern than a south-western direction. This very able mariner, still wedded to formerly adopted opinions, strongly recommends the variation of the compass as a means for ascertaining the longitude at sea:[3] yet, had we been no better provided, we might have searched for the Cape of Good Hope agreeably with his propositions, to little effect: for when we were in latitude 35° 7′ south, with 20° 16′ west variation, we had only reached the longitude of 6° 30′ east; and again, when in latitude 35° 22′ south, with 22° 7′ west variation, we had only advanced to the longitude of 11° 25′ east, instead of being, according to Mr. Nicholson's hypothesis, in the first instance nearly under the meridian of the cape of Good Hope, and in the second, under that of cape Aguilas;[4] and it was not until we had near 26° of west variation, that we approached the meridian of the Cape of Good Hope. The observations for the variation were made with the greatest care and attention; and though

[1] Cabo de S. Agostinho, in the easternmost part of Brazil.

[2] William Herbert, *A new directory for the East Indies...the whole (originally begun and carried on from the most approved charts and plans by W. Herbert, W. Nichelson and others) much approved and augmented by Samuel Dunn*. 6th ed. (London, 1787). For Cook's account of his encounter with the currents in the South Atlantic see his *Journals*, III, 21–2.

[3] Presumably Vancouver was referring to *The Navigator's Assistant* by William Nicholson (London, 1784). The relevant passage reads: 'The variation of the compass affords a method of determining the longitude. For, in the Southern part of the Atlantic, and in a considerable part both of the Pacific and Indian oceans, the quantity of the variation changes very fast in running upon a parallel. If, therefore, a ship be in a known latitude, and the variation of the compass be found by observation, it will be easy to determine the longitude, provided the observer be furnished with a chart or table of the longitudes corresponding with given quantities of latitude and variation. It is a valuable property of this method, that it gives the longitude the most accurately in those parts of the world where ships sailing from Europe are most particularly in need of it. The principal impediment to its use, is the want of a chart or table, which, on account of the change which the variation suffers in time at any given place, ought to be frequently renewed, from sea journals, at public expence.' p. 108. Cook had no faith in Nicholson's theory: 'That the variation may be found to [such] a degree of accuracy...as to determine the longitude within a degree or sixty miles I do absolutely deny.' *Journals*, III, 23n.

[4] Cape Agulhas, the S extremity of Africa, SE of the Cape of Good Hope.

generally considered as very correct, they differed from one to three, and sometimes four degrees, not only when made by different compasses placed in different situations on board, and the ship on different tacks, but by the same compass in the same situation, made at moderate intervals of time; the difference in the results of such observations, at the same time, not preserving the least degree of uniformity. Hence the assertion amounts nearly to an absurdity, which states, 'that with 20° to 20° 10', or 20° 30' westwardly variation, you will be certain' of such and such longitude; and it is greatly to be apprehended, that navigators who rely on such means for ascertaining their situation in the ocean, will render themselves liable to errors that may be attended with the most fatal consequences. Other methods are, I trust, in a fair train for accomplishing this desirable object; and I yet hope to see the period arrive, when every sea-faring person capable of using a quadrant, will, on due instruction, be enabled by lunar observations to determine his longitude at sea. It has been already observed, that such information may be acquired with ease, and without laborious study or tedious application; this was further warranted by our example on board the Discovery; where, on our departure from England, Mr. Whidbey and myself could be considered as the only proficients in this branch of science; but now, amongst the officers and gentlemen of the quarter deck, there were several capable of ascertaining their situation in the ocean, with every degree of accuracy necessary for all the important purposes of navigation.

With a light southwardly breeze in the morning of Sunday the 10th, we weighed anchor, and with the assistance of our boats a-head, towing the ship, we reached Simon's bay at about seven in the evening, where we anchored in twelve fathoms water; False cape bearing by compass in a line with the south point of the bay, S. 37 E. Noah's ark, S. 51 E. the Roman rocks, S. 86 E. and the flag-staff on the battery, S. 89 W. about a quarter of a mile from the shore.

The day before a brig was seen in shore of us, which was supposed to be the Chatham; but as the private signal was not acknowledged by her, we concluded ourselves mistaken. Our first conjectures, however, proved to be right, as Mr. Broughton now informed me the signal had escaped their attention. Since we had separated, the Discovery had outsailed her consort only the night's run; the Chatham not having hauled her wind or shortened sail on Friday night, she was the next morning within the same distance of the land as the Discovery. Nothing had occurred during this separation worthy of notice. I was made excessively happy to understand from Mr. Broughton, that the officers and crew of the Chatham, like those of the Discovery, were in general very healthy. Beside the Chatham, we found here His Majesty's ship the Gorgon;[1] the Warren Hastings, and Earl Fitzwilliam Indiamen from

---

[1] An interesting meeting of the ships, as the intention had been that the *Gorgon* should accompany the *Discovery* to the Northwest coast if the plan to establish a settlement there, proposed early in 1790, had been carried out.

Bengal; two port Jackson transports from China bound home; three with convicts bound to port Jackson; two American, and some Dutch and Danish merchant ships; the total amounting to seventeen sail in the bay.

In the morning of Monday the 11th, an officer was sent on shore to acquaint the resident commandant of the port, Mr. Brandt,[1] of our arrival, and to request his permission to procure such refreshments and stores as our wants now demanded, and to erect our observatory and such tents on shore as might be requisite for carrying into execution the necessary refitment of the vessels; with all which Mr. Brandt very politely complied; and, on the return of the officer, the garrison was saluted with eleven guns; which compliment being equally returned, attended by Mr. Broughton and some of the officers, I waited on Mr. Brandt, who received us with the greatest politeness and hospitality, the well known characteristics of that gentleman. Having, on a former occasion, benefited by his good offices in the excellency of the supplies provided for the Resolution and Discovery,[2] I concerted measures with him, on the present, for the like purpose. Mr. Brandt undertook, in conjunction with Mr. De Wit, of Cape Town,[3] to see all our necessities provided for with the best of the several commodities the country afforded. The Discovery's bowsprit, being found infinitely too weak, was taken out in order to be strengthened by one of the fishes we had on board; the whole of the head railing, having been washed away, was to be replaced,[4] the vessels wanting caulking fore and aft; the rigging, overhauling; casks to be set up for receiving provisions and water; the sails repairing, and several materially altering; the powder airing; and the skids and booms raising, for the better enabling of the people to work upon deck; the ship proving sufficiently stiff to admit of such accommodation. Artificers were hired to assist our own in these several duties; which being in a state of forwardness by the 14th, Mr. Broughton and myself paid our respects to Mr. Rhenias, the acting governor at Cape Town,[5] with the further view of inspecting the stores and provisions, the major part of which were to come from thence. Four of our seamen, whose constitutions seemed unequal to the service in which they had engaged, and whom I had now an opportunity of replacing, were sent on

---

[1] Christoffel Brand (1738–1815), merchant and official Resident at Simons Bay, known over a long period for his hospitality and helpfulness. Officers of British ships were often guests in his home; Cook stayed with him in 1772 and again in 1775. Brand sent Banks, whom he met in 1772, collections of plants and animals. He was born in Cape Town; a grandson was President of the Orange Free State.

[2] Late in 1776, when the ships were outward bound on Cook's third voyage, they spent some weeks in Table Bay.

[3] Probably Peter John (or Pieter Johannes) de Wit, at this time one of the contractors who supplied provisions to visiting ships.

[4] A report submitted to Vancouver on 17 July by Henry Phillips, carpenter of the Discovery, lists the many repairs needed and includes the item: 'Seats of ease, all to be new, the old being washed away.' – Adm. 1/2628, f. 634.

[5] Johan Isaac Rhenius, acting Governor of the Cape of Good Hope from 24 June 1791 to 3 July 1792.

board the Warren Hastings; and, with her, on Monday the 18th, sailed for England.[1]

All our stores and provisions being forwarded from Cape Town by Friday the 5th of August, we took leave of the governor and our Cape friends, from whom we had experienced the most attentive civility; and having completed such observations as were wanted, the observatory with the instruments were, on Tuesday the 9th, sent on board.

By Thursday the 11th, all our transactions were finished with the shore; having obtained for each vessel a supply of provisions, which completed our stock for eighteen months at full allowance, and a due proportion of stores for the like period. I took on board also seven ewes and six rams;[2] an assortment of garden seeds, vine cuttings, and other plants that were likely to grow, and prove valuable acquisitions to our friends in the South-Sea islands. As I intended putting to sea the next day, we were busily employed in preparing the ship for that purpose, which, on the morning of Friday the 12th, we attempted; but the wind shifting to the S.S.E. permitted our taking only a more outside birth for the better convenience of sailing when the wind should prove more favorable.

It is customary at the Cape of Good Hope for so many of the officers as can conveniently be spared to take up their residence on shore. In this respect I had conformed to old practices, but was excessively mortified, at my return on board, to find that several of our people had, within a few days, become indisposed with a dysentery, which at first seemed of little importance, but had now put on a very serious appearance; and some of the patients were extremely ill. The cause of this unfortunate malady it was hard to ascertain: the crew had not been subject to inebriety; their provisions had been of the best quality, and most wholesome nature; and every precaution had been taken to prevent their sleeping on deck, or exposing themselves to the dew or night air. No neglect of the salutary measures generally observed, or individual indiscretion of any sort seemed to have produced this lamentable visitation, whose contagious influence suffered no one to escape unattacked; although

---

[1] Swaine states that the four men were 'Invalided by Scurvey'. – 17 July. Further crew changes became necessary later: 'The ill state of health of the Boatswain of the Discovery [Thomas Keld] having made it necessary to send him on shore to sick quarters, and not being sufficiently recovered to proceed the Voyage, I have appointed the Boatswain of the Chatham [William House] to Act in his room, and have given an order to one of the Boatswain's mates in the Discovery (Jno Noot) to Act as Boatswain of the Chatham.' – Vancouver to Stephens, 12 August 1791. Adm. 1/2628, f. 636. The 'Run List' of the Discovery shows that two seamen deserted at the Cape. A master's mate in the Chatham had to be invalided ashore and a seaman was discharged. The seven vacancies in the two ships were 'fill'd up by some Men, got out of the Transports & India Ships' in port. – Bell, July.

[2] Though loaded to her utmost capacity, the Chatham also managed to take on a few animals: 'Our decks at this time was as much lumbered as they had been at any one period of the passage. . . . The Launch was filled with Eighteen Sheep we had taken in here.' – Johnstone, 13 August.

myself and officers did not feel its effects so violently as they were experienced by the people. The same disorder had not only appeared on board the Chatham, and the transports bound to port Jackson, but on shore; and at length it was attributed to a large Dutch ship lately arrived from Batavia, from which many men had been sent on shore to the hospital very ill, and dying with that and other infectious disorders. The surgeon of the Discovery was seized in a very sudden and singular manner, and reduced to an extreme state of delirium, without any other symptoms which indicated fever.[1]

To persons, situated as we were, on the eve of quitting the civilized world, and destitute of all help and resources, but such as we carried with us, such a calamity was of the most serious and distressing nature; and was not only severely felt at the moment, but tended to destroy the good effects we had every reason to expect from the very excellent and abundant supply of refreshments the Cape had afforded. I now became excessively anxious to get to sea,[2] lest the Batavian ship should communicate any other disorder, or a worse species of that with which we were already attacked. This earnest desire, a S.E. wind and calms prevented our accomplishing until Wednesday the 17th, when, about noon, a light breeze springing up from the N.W. we sailed, in company with the Chatham, out of Simon's Bay, and saluted the garrison with eleven guns, which were equally returned.

Few of our transactions, whilst at our last station, appeared worthy of recording excepting the occurrences at the observatory, where I did not think any observations were at all necessary for ascertaining the longitude; as that must have been accurately determined long ago by persons of greater information and superior abilities. The latitude; the rate and error of the chronometer; and the variation and dip of the magnetic needle, were the principal objects that occupied our attention. The former would not have attracted much of my notice, had it not appeared by the first day's observations, that a very material difference existed between the latitude shewn by my observations, and the latitude of Simon's Bay as stated by Captain King in the 3d vol. of Cook's Voyage to the Northern Hemisphere, where, in page 484, it is said that 'the latitude of anchorage place in Simon's Bay is, by observation, 34° 20' south.' This, however, is most probably an error of the press, since, immediately afterwards, we find the Cape point is said to be in 34° 23' south; which point is at least 12 or 13 miles to the southward of Simon's Bay. Our observatory was situated near the south point of this bay, and its

[1] Alexander Purvis Cranstoun. He did not regain his health and was invalided home a year later.

[2] Puget shared this anxiety, but for a different reason. To him the Cape was attractive only because it offered an opportunity to repair and provision the ships: 'Both Vessels were put in a thorough State of Repair, all Deficiencies of Provisions were filled up, as this most likely would be our last European Port for some years.... I have only to say I never left a Place with so little Regret as I did the Dutch Society & their Settlement altogether – all that can be said of it, is its excellence in affording Refreshments, which it does in very great Abundance.' – Puget, 17 August.

latitude, deduced from 26 meridional altitudes of the sun and stars, was 34° 11′ 40″,[1] this, on allowing the distance to the Cape point, will be nearly found to agree with its latitude; which was further confirmed by our observations on passing it the day we entered False Bay.

By the first observations, made on shore, the chronometer shewed the longitude to be 18° 39′ 45″, which was 17′ 45″ to the eastward of the truth, and corresponded with what has been stated before, that it was not gaining at the rate we had allowed: further observations, however, demonstrated that, although it might have been gaining less during the passage, it was now evidently gaining on its Portsmouth rate, and was found on the 8th of August at noon, to be fast of mean time at Greenwich, 17′ 49″ 6‴, and gaining on mean time at the rate of 9″ 28‴ per day. Mr. Arnold's chronometer was found to have gone but indifferently on board the Chatham; and, at the observatory, it was fast of mean time at Greenwich 1ʰ 18′ 48″ 6‴, and gaining on mean time at the rate of 16″ 11‴ 8⁗ per day. The variation of the magnetic needle, taken at the observatory by our different compasses and cards, in twenty sets of azimuths, varied from 24° 3′ to 27° 48′; the mean result being 25° 40′ west variation.

The vertical inclination of the south point of the magnetic needle was observed to be

Marked end	North, face East,	48° 30′
Ditto	North, face West,	48 20
Ditto	South, face East,	48 40
Ditto	South, face West,	48 30

Mean inclination of the south point of the dipping needle	48 30

N.B. The longitude throughout the voyage, and until our arrival at St. Helena, on our return to Europe, will be reckoned eastward.

The latitude inserted in the following chapters, and until the 13th of February, 1792, when it will be otherwise distinguished, is to be received, and considered as south latitude.

The positive or relative situations of all coasts, capes, promontories, islands, rocks, sands, breakers, bays, ports, &c. &c. will hereafter be stated as *true, or by the world*; and those *bearings* which will be taken from any local situation, whether on board the vessels, or in the boats, will be inserted according to compass, and be so expressed.

[1] The position of Simons Bay is now given as lat. 34° 12′ S, long. 18° 26′ E.

CHAPTER II.

Departure from False Bay—Death of Neil Coil by the Flux—Proceed towards the Coast of New Holland—Discover King George the Third's Sound—Transactions there—Leave King George the Third's Sound—Departure from the Southwest Coast of New Holland.

THE nature of our voyage rendering every precaution necessary to prevent, as far as was possible, a separation of the vessels, Mr. Broughton, in case of parting company, was provided with a list of rendezvous; and, the better to insure our rejoining, I now deemed it expedient that he should be furnished with a copy of my instructions, and the route I intended to pursue; together with ample directions, that, in the event of a total separation, he might be enabled to carry the objects of the expedition into execution.[1]

Although our stay at the Cape had far exceeded my expectations, yet I did not abandon the design of visiting the S.W. part of New Holland. The season would probably be too far advanced for acquiring so much information as I could have wished, yet there still remained a fair prospect of obtaining some intelligence, which would render the task less difficult to those, whose particular object it might hereafter be to explore that country.[2] I therefore on sailing out of False Bay, appointed our next rendezvous off, what in the

[1] Vancouver's letter to Broughton shows that he regarded his instructions as personal and secret, to be revealed only in an emergency. The last rendezvous appointed was Waimea Bay, in Kauai; if the *Discovery* had not joined the *Chatham* there by 10 February 1792, Broughton was 'to proceed, in the execution of my instructions for the Survey of the North West Coast of America, a Copy of which you will herewith receive, sealed. But which are not however to be opened until... [there is] not the smallest possibility of my joining you that season.' – 16 August 1791. B.L., Add. MS 17552.

[2] Shortly before he left Simons Bay Vancouver wrote to Grenville, expressed regret that he had not had a chance to receive his 'final opinion' on the proposed New Holland survey, and outlined his plans: 'it is my intention to fall in with the S.W. Cape of New Holland, and should I find the shores capable of being navigated without much hazard, to range its coast and determine whether it and Van Dieman's Land are joined, which from information at present extant appears somewhat doubtful'. – Vancouver to Grenville, 9 August 1791. Quoted in George Godwin, *Vancouver, a Life* (London, 1930), p. 204. To Broughton he wrote: 'in case of any such discovery, I shall touch at Port Jackson to inform Governor Phillips thereof. But in case no passage exists, I shall proceed round Van Dieman's land to a Port towards the North East part of Maria's Islands... intending there to complete our wood and water.' – 16 August 1791. B.L., Add. MS 17552.

charts is called Lyon's Land,[1] in about the 35th degree of south latitude—in case of separation to cruise there two days; and, not meeting with the Discovery, then to proceed agreeably to other instructions.

The Albemarle, Admiral Barrington, and Britannia transports bound to port Jackson, followed us out of the bay: of these ships, as well as of the African coast, we took leave in the evening, and directed our course to the southward. During the night, the wind veered to the N.W. and blew so hard a gale that we were obliged to double reef the topsails and take in the foresail, as the Chatham was a great distance astern; and not being in sight at day-break, we hauled to the wind: about seven she was seen to the westward, and, having joined company, we steered to the S.S.E. together. The N.W. wind gradually increased, attended with violent squalls and heavy rain, until Saturday the 20th, when it became a perfect storm, obliging us to strike the top gallant masts, and reducing us to the foresail, which we were necessitated to carry, though under great apprehension of its being blown to pieces, in order that we might reach a more temperate region. The sea ran excessively high, and the wind in violent flurries raised the spray into a kind of fog, or mist, which at intervals was quite salt, when not mixed with the showers of rain, which were frequent, and very heavy: in one of these we again lost sight of the Chatham, and seeing nothing of her on its clearing away, the foresail was furled, and the ship brought to, under the storm staysails. In this situation, the Discovery proved much easier and drier than we had reason to expect, as she was now extremely deep with stores and provisions. At this time, we were visited by many albatrosses, and an innumerable variety of birds of the petrel tribe. About noon on Sunday the 21st our consort was again in sight, and on her joining company, we resumed our course to the S.E. under the foresail. This very boisterous weather, accompanied with much thunder and lightning, continued with intermissions sufficient only to tempt our spreading some additional canvas, (which was scarcely unfurled before it was again necessary to take it in) until Monday the 22d; when it so far moderated as to permit the close reefed topsails to be kept set. In the afternoon, we passed the Albemarle and Admiral Barrington. The sight of these vessels was very grateful to our feelings, particularly of the latter, which we had understood was an old debilitated ship, for whose safety during the late violent stormy weather we had been greatly apprehensive. The wind, in the morning of Tuesday the 23d, being moderate, the top-gallant, and studding-sails were set; the weather, however, was unsettled, with showers of hail and rain; and a heavy irregular swell rolled at the same time from the northward and south west. In the intervals of fine weather, I got some lunar observations which shewed the longitude at noon to be 31° 55'; the chronometer by the Portsmouth rate 31° 29'; by the Cape rate 31° 42'; the latitude 39° 8'. Many whales were now

[1] Meaning the area in the general vicinity of Cape Leeuwin, the SW extremity of Australia. It was discovered in 1622 by the Dutch ship *Leeuwin* (Lioness), and first appeared on the map as 'Land van de Leeuwin'.

playing about the ship, but a less number of oceanic birds attended us than usual.

The weather being tolerably fair on Wednesday the 24th, enabled me to make some further lunar observations. The mean result of these, and those taken the preceding day *brought forward by the chronometer*, shewed the longitude at noon to be 34° 13'. By this expression is to be understood the space east or west, which the ship may have passed over in the interval of time between the taking one set of lunar observations and that of another; the extent of which space is ascertained, not according to the vague mode of the ship's run, as appears by the log, but from the distance shewn by the chronometer; whereby the result of many observations made in different situations are reduced to any one particular point. The chronometer at this time, by the Portsmouth rate, shewed 33° 50', by the Cape rate 34° 5', the latitude 39° 28', and the longitude by account 36° 17'. The weather continued very changeable; but the wind being gentle in the northern quarter afforded an opportunity of sending on board the Chatham, whence we understood that, in consequence of a violent sea having stove in the midship stern window on the morning of the 20th, it had been necessary to bring to until that damage was repaired.[1]

The wind freshened, attended with frequent squalls, on Friday the 26th; when, having reached latitude 39° 45', longitude 37° 53', we were able for the first time since our departure from the Cape to observe the variation; which, by the mean result of two compasses, differing from 32° 53' to 35° 5', was found to be 32° 59' westwardly. In the space we were now approaching, namely, between the meridians of 38° 33' and 43° 47' east longitude, and the parallels of 34° 24', and 38° 20' south latitude, seven different shoals are said to exist. To acquire some information respecting a circumstance so interesting to navigation, I had held this southwardly course; but the very stormy weather we had lately contended with, and the appearance of its again returning, rendered a search for these shoals not altogether prudent. To attempt the examination of the whole space I considered as not more necessary than discreet; but since in the event of their existence, it was highly probable they would be found connected, I was induced to shape a course so as to fall in with the south-easternmost, said to lie in latitude 38° 20', longitude 43° 43', which had been reported to have been seen by several Dutch vessels.[2] On

---

[1] The accident had been much more alarming than this brief mention suggests. Johnstone records that the *Chatham* 'Ship'd a great deal of water at the Breach' before it could be secured. A distress signal was hoisted but the *Discovery* failed to see it, 'but continued on, until she lost sight of us...so that had the accident proved as fatal as first Alarm Suggested we could not have received any relief from that quarter'. – Johnstone, 20 and 21 August.

[2] One of the reports probably concerned the existence of the Slot Van Capelle, a shoal reported in 1748 by a Dutch ship of that name in lat. 36° 24' S, long. 41° 20' E. Although its existence was never confirmed, it remained on charts until recently. In 1963 Walters Shoals, in the Madagascar Plateau, S of the island, were discovered by the South African surveying ship *Natal* and named after her commander. They are located a little to the N

Sunday the 28th, in latitude 38° 56′, longitude 42° 30′, the wind at W.S.W. increasing with great violence obliged me to desist from this enquiry, and for our own safety, in the event of these shoals having existence, to hawl to the S.E. The gale soon became a storm, attended with heavy squalls, hail, rain, and a most tremendous sea from the westward and S.W. which made it necessary to strike the top-gallant masts, and reduced us to the foresail; which, with great apprehension of losing it, we were obliged to carry in order to pass clear of the space assigned to these hidden dangers.[1] It is, however, worthy of remark, that, notwithstanding our course was directed so wide of the allotted spot, we certainly passed it at no great distance in the night, as by our observations the next day, Monday the 29th, instead of making fourteen miles southing, which the reckoning gave, we found ourselves twelve miles to the north of the latitude we were in the preceding day, the longitude 45° 4′. Whether this difference is to be ascribed to any current produced by the interruption these shoals may give to the oceanic waters, when pressed eastwardly by the prevailing westwardly winds, or to the bad steerage of the ship, cannot be positively determined; but as the Chatham steered precisely the same course, the inference seems rather favorable to our having been influenced by a current occasioned probably by the existence of such shoals. On the violence of the storm abating, we made sail and resumed our eastwardly course, intending to pass in sight of the islands of St. Paul and Amsterdam. During the gale we were visited by a great number of the various kinds of oceanic birds; yet these by no means seemed to indicate the vicinity of land or shoals, since they are constantly met with throughout the southern ocean.

The weather that succeeded this storm being delightfully pleasant, attended with a smooth sea, and a gentle gale between the north and N.E. made me regret that we had not experienced this favorable change somewhat earlier, as it would probably have enabled us to have acquired some satisfactory information as to the existence of the shoals in question; but having now no

of the area outlined by Vancouver in lat. 33° 12′ S, long. 43° 49′ E. The minimum depth of water found was 10 fathoms.

[1] The storm was even more uncomfortable for those in the smaller Chatham: 'This Stormy weather was felt peculiarly hard by us as our Decks were most inconveniently crowded with Casks, and so much top Weight made her rowl prodigiously, and kept her buried to such a degree in the Water, that the Decks were afloat fore & aft. The Officer's live Stock, consisting of Sheep, Goats, Hogs, Poultry, &c. to a considerable number were (the greatest part of them) kill'd by the severity of the wind, and rainy weather, and the violent motion of the Vessel which was indeed very unpleasant, and fatal likewise to no inconsiderable quantity of Glass & Crockery ware, some of which had been purchased at a very dear rate at the Cape of Good Hope.' – Bell, August. The Discovery also had bad moments: 'In one of these squalls in the night time we were taken aback, & what rendered our situation somewhat critical the light in the binnacle was extinguished, so that the man at the helm was obliged to steer at random.' – Menzies, 26 August. Puget notes that at one time 'The Lightning was so vivid & fierce that it deprived me of Sight for the space of ten minutes.' – 28 August.

leisure for this inquiry, I was obliged to rest contented with having exerted our fruitless endeavours in the attempt, and embraced this valuable opportunity of getting ourselves and ship clean, dry, and comfortable; which since our leaving the land had been very ill effected.

The flux still continued amongst us, and some of our patients were yet very much indisposed; we however were in hopes that the present fair weather would soon restore to us the blessings of health. Some good observations were procured in the course of this day, Tuesday the 30th, and of the preceding day with our different compasses: those taken on the 31st differed from 30° 45' to 35° 45'; and those on Thursday the first of September from 30° 58' to 35° 7'; the mean result of seven sets of azimuths was 32° 47' westwardly variation; the latitude at noon 38° 19', and the longitude 51° 21'. We were not long indulged with a continuance of the fine weather: the wind gradually veered to the N.W. and westward, and increased to a fresh gale; which, however, did not reduce us below the top-sails; although the weather bore a very threatening appearance; the sky was obscured with dark gloomy clouds, from which some rain fell; yet the sea was smooth, and the weather altogether was infinitely more pleasant than we had lately experienced.

At noon on Sunday the 4th, in latitude 38° 6', longitude 61° 36', the first seal we had seen since our departure from the Cape amused itself in playing about the ship for some time; but our companions, the oceanic birds, had not lately been very numerous; these visitors were mostly pintadoes, and other small birds of the petrel tribe.

Four sets of lunar observations were obtained on Monday the 5th, which shewed the longitude to be 64° 14' 40"; the chronometer by the Portsmouth rate 63° 46', and by the Cape rate 64° 10', the latitude 37° 52'. The variation on Wednesday the 7th, in latitude 38° 15' and longitude 69° 33', was observed to be 25° 52' westwardly. The same gloomy weather continued with a fresh gale at N.N.W. In the night we had the misfortune to lose Neil Coil,[1] one of the marines, who fell a sacrifice to the baneful effects of the flux caught at the Cape, which attacked him with much greater violence than any other person on board. He was an exceedingly good man; his loss was sensibly felt, and much regretted. In addition to this calamity, disasters of the same nature seemed not likely to terminate: another of our people, who had suffered very severely by this dreadful contagion, but who was so much recovered as to be nearly equal to his duty, was so affected by this poor fellow's dissolution, that he relapsed with very unfavorable symptoms. Our convalescents were still numerous; and the work of death having commenced, we knew not where it might end, or where we could recruit the strength which we might thus lose; our whole complement being scarcely equal, when in the highest health, to the service we had to perform.[2] One reflection was, however, highly

[1] The name is given as Neil Coyle in the muster roll.

[2] In a note dated 10 September, the day after Coyle's death, but obviously written later, Menzies records that 'As the Surgeons [Cranstoun's] own state of health at this time did

satisfactory; that, in point of comfort, and professional assistance, no one thing within our power to supply, had been omitted for the present relief of the distress, or for the prevention of any melancholy consequences in future; and we trusted, with the Divine blessing, and a steady adherence to the conduct, which we had observed, finally to subdue and extirpate this dreadful malady.

In the evening of Thursday the 8th I took some lunar distances with the star Antares, which, with those taken on the 5th, shewed the longitude by their mean result, to be 73° 44′; the chronometer by the Portsmouth rate 73° 1′, and by the Cape rate 73° 27′; the latitude 38° 45′, and the variation 23° 36′ westwardly.

The next evening, agreeably to our reckoning, we were passing between the islands of St. Paul and Amsterdam, distant from the latter about five or six leagues. The weather was thick and rainy, yet I continued to hope that a favorable interval would enable us to see one or both of these islands, having steered this eastwardly course with a wish to correct an error that appears in Captain Cook's charts of the southern hemisphere. In these the island of St. Paul is laid down in the latitude of 37° 50′, corresponding with the situation assigned to it in the requisite tables; and to the north of this island, in about the latitude of 36° 40′ is placed another called the island of Amsterdam: now the island which Mr. Cox in the Mercury[1] stopped at, and called Amsterdam, is in sight of and situated 17 leagues to the *south* of the island of St. Paul. Captain Bligh, in the Bounty, also saw the same island, and allots to it nearly the same situation as does Mr. Cox. For these reasons, if there be an island to the north of St. Paul, in latitude 36° 40′, there must be three instead of two of these islands,[2] which I believe has never been understood to be the fact. The weather, however, precluded my forming a just opinion as to this point, which I fully intended to ascertain, could we have seen either of the islands; but the rain and haze continuing to obscure every object at the distance of two leagues, we perceived no indication of the vicinity of land, notwithstanding the immense number of whales and seals which are said to frequent these islands. Of the latter we did not see any, and of the former but one; which was the only whale we had observed since that mentioned on the 23d of last month. From hence towards the coast of New Holland, our course was directed between the tracks of Dampier and M. Marion, over a space, I believe, hitherto

not permit him to attend much to that of others, Captain Vancouver in this situation requested me to take charge of the sick for him, which I readily complied with, & we were fortunate enough in not meeting with any more losses & in getting clear of the disease entirely in six or seven weeks time.' – 10 September.

[1] The British brig *Mercury*, 152 tons, commanded by John Henry Cox, visited Amsterdam Island at the end of May 1789 and sighted St. Paul Island on 1 June. For an account of her voyage, in the course of which she visited Tahiti, Hawaii and Unalaska, see George Mortimer, *Observations and Remarks made during a Voyage...in the brig Mercury* (Dublin, 1791). She made several visits to the Northwest Coast as the *Gustavus III*, flying Swedish colours.

[2] There are only two islands. The position of Amsterdam Island is lat. 37° 50′ S, and that of St. Paul Island is 38° 41′ S. The long. of both is 77° 33′ E.

unfrequented.[1] In this route, assisted by a fine gale between north and W.N.W. we made great progress, so that our observed latitude on Sunday the 18th was 36° 49', longitude 103° 48': for some days past we had experienced a very heavy swell from the S.W. though the wind prevailed from the northward.

The situation of that part of New Holland for which we were now steering, being ill defined, and a probability existing that banks might extend a considerable distance into the ocean, we tried, but gained no soundings with 180 fathoms of line. On Monday the 19th, in latitude 36° 45', longitude 105° 47', the variation was observed to be 14° 10' westwardly. The wind at N.N.E. attended with heavy squalls and rain, increased with such violence, as to oblige us to strike the top-gallant masts, and to furl the top-sails. The pintado birds that, for some days past, had nearly disappeared, again visited the ship, accompanied by a great variety of the petrel tribe, with some albatrosses; and it now seemed evident, that the appearance of these inhabitants of the ocean, was increased in point of numbers and in variety, in proportion to the violence of the wind; as in moderate weather few only were visible. We continued to try for soundings at certain intervals, but did not reach bottom at the depth of 180 fathoms. The wind at W.S.W. blew a strong gale, and the night of Tuesday the 20th being dark and squally, we hauled to the wind, and plied; lest the land, which is represented as very low, or shoals, might be nearer than we expected; at day-break we again resumed our eastwardly course, observing every night the like precautions.

In the morning of Friday the 23d, conceiving that the land could not be at any great distance, and that the coast might lie to the north of the course we were steering, the Chatham's signal was made to look out on the larboard beam. The wind from the westward blew a strong gale, accompanied with a very heavy sea;[2] but the sky being clear, permitted me to obtain some good lunar observations, which, with those taken on the 21st, shewed the longitude at noon to be 114° 14'; the chronometer, by the Portsmouth rate 113° 32', by the Cape rate 113° 55', the latitude 35° 7'. Soon after mid-day, the wind at W.S.W. increased to a very heavy gale; and not choosing, under such circumstances, to make too free with a coast entirely unexplored; we hauled the wind to the southward, under the foresail and storm staysails. Towards sun-set, land was said to be seen from the mast-head to the E.N.E. and, although this was not absolutely certain, yet it was extremely probable, as we had passed several leagues over the space assigned to Lyon's Land in most of the maps. A press of sail was now carried in order to keep to the windward,

---

[1] In 1699 Dampier sailed E and somewhat to the N from the Cape of Good Hope, and reached the coast of Australia far to the N of Vancouver's landfall. Marion du Fresne, in 1772, sailed SE to Crozet Island, and thence eastward to Tasmania; Cook followed a very similar course in 1776. Vancouver's landfall was almost due E of the Cape.

[2] 'We had now an exceeding rough sea which frequently broke over the Ship, one of these about ten at night was so boisterous that it nearly washed some of the people off the quarter deck, & even wrenched the man at the wheel from his station into the lee scuppers.' – Menzies, 23 September.

having no bottom at the depth of 120 fathoms; in consequence of which, and a very heavy sea, the larboard side of the head, with the bumkin, &c. was entirely torn away. On the gale's moderating the next morning, Saturday the 24th, we stood to the north, in quest of the land; but some of the officers conceiving they saw land to the S.E. we hauled our wind again in that direction until noon, in latitude 35° 28', longitude 115° 10', when, being disappointed, we again stood to the north, under double reefed topsails, until eight in the evening: we then tacked to spend the night, which bore a very threatening appearance, over a space we were already acquainted with, and found bottom at 70 fathoms depth, composed of white sand, and broken shells; the latitude at this time was 34° 51', the longitude 115° 12'. The very gloomy appearance of the night rendered our carrying a press of sail indispensably necessary to preserve an offing, as the soundings strongly indicated the land not to be distant. During the night we did not reach the bottom with 100 fathoms of line; and the morning of Sunday the 25th, evinced our conjectures respecting the weather not to be ill founded; as, about four o'clock, the slings of the main yard were carried away; to replace which, we were compelled to furl all the sails on the main-mast; but, before this could be accomplished, the increased violence of the storm obliged us to take in all our canvas but the foresail, to strike the top gallant-masts, and to get in the jib-boom and sprit-sail yard. In this situation we continued until towards sun-set, when having no bottom with 110 fathoms of line, we stood to the N.W. under close-reefed topsails, in the full assurance of meeting the land in that direction. In the course of the night, the gale gradually abated, and in the forenoon of the next day, Monday the 26th, the wind becoming perfectly calm, an opportunity was afforded us of repairing the many damages which our rigging had sustained in the late boisterous weather. At noon the observed latitude was 35° 23', the longitude 115° 52'; in this situation, soundings could not be gained at the depth of 220 fathoms. In the afternoon a light breeze sprang up, from the northward, with which we steered to the north-eastward, and soon discovered land from the mast-head, bearing by compass from N.E. to N. 27 E. It seemed of a moderate height, resembling in appearance the land in the British Channel,[1] and was supposed to be about ten or twelve leagues distant – No soundings with 120 fathoms of line. The wind veering to the N.W. enabled us to steer for the land, and having neared it about three leagues, it was seen from the deck bearing from N. 7 E. to N. 73 E. by compass; at which time, bottom was found at the depth of 65 fathoms, composed of coarse sand, and broken coral. The depth of water had, at eight in the evening, gradually decreased to 50 fathoms; when, having advanced about four miles nearer, we tacked and plied in order to preserve our situation with the land until morning.

By the result of our soundings during the night, 70 fathoms would seem

[1] The first land sighted was the cliffs along the coast some miles W of Chatham Island. Menzies noted that it bore 'a striking resemblance to the land about Falmouth and the Lizard.'

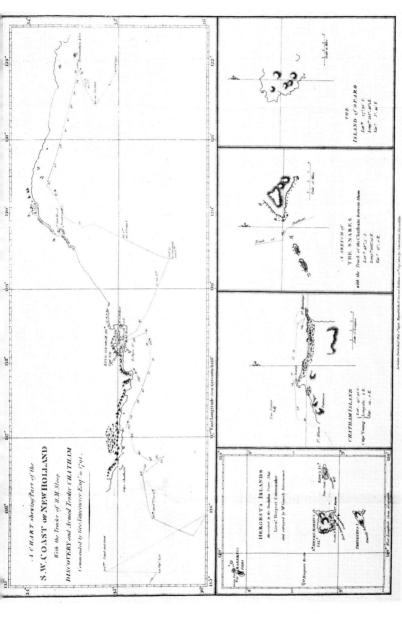

Plate 16. Reduced facsimile of Vancouver's chart of the S.W. Coast of New Holland.

A DESERTED INDIAN VILLAGE in KING GEORGE III Sound, New Holland.

Plate 17. 'A deserted Indian Village in King George III. Sound, New Holland.'

to be the edge of a bank about nine leagues from the shore,[1] consisting of fine sand, and broken shells, corresponding with the soundings we had found on the 24th; for had that depth of water been nearer in shore, we could hardly have avoided seeing the land before dark on that evening.

At the dawning of day on the 27th, we made all sail for the land, having a gentle gale from the N.W. with a smooth sea and pleasant weather. The depth of water, as we proceeded, gradually decreased to 24 fathoms, with a bottom of coral, coarse sand, and shells; about nine we were well in with the land, and bore away along the coast, keeping within a league or two of the shore; which by the compass stretched from N. 44 W. to N. 81 E. and appeared nearly straight and compact, consisting of steep rocky cliffs to the water's edge, interspersed with, here and there, some small open sandy bays, and a few islets and rocks, which extended near a mile from the main. The westernmost land now in sight (being the northernmost seen the preceding night) is remarkable for its high cliffs, falling perpendicularly into the sea; and if it be detached, which is by no means certain, is about a league in circuit. It forms a conspicuous promontory, to which I gave the name of CAPE CHATHAM; in honor of that noble earl, who presided at the Board of Admiralty on our departure from England. The land to the westward takes a direction from cape Chatham N. 59 W. and the land to the eastward S. 81 E. This Cape, by our observations is situated in latitude 35° 3′, and in 116° 35′ 30″ of longitude.[2]

The flux still continued to affect the health of some in both vessels; and although the patients were daily assisted with fresh provisions, and might be considered in a state of recovery, yet they remained in a very debilitated and reduced condition. In the hope that a little recreation, from change of scene and what the soil of this country might afford, would prove salutary to their enfeebled constitutions, I determined to put into the first port we should be so fortunate as to discover; and, that an eligible situation might not escape our vigilance, we ranged the coast within three or four miles of its shores, which are of moderate elevation, and may in general be deemed steep and bold. The verdure on all the projecting points is removed to a considerable height on the rocks, whose naked bases sufficiently prove how excessively they are beaten by a turbulent ocean. The country, immediately along the sea side, consists of a range of dreary hills, producing little herbage, of a brownish green hue, from a soil that seems principally composed of white sand, through which protrude large masses of white rock of various sizes and forms: these singular protuberances on the summits of many of the hills, strongly resembled the

[1] This surmise was correct. The edge of the continental shelf is about 25 miles offshore. Depths at the edge vary from about 55 to 100 fathoms; in some places these plunge abruptly to 400 fathoms or more just beyond the edge.

[2] As Vancouver suspected, the promontory was on an island and his Cape Chatham is now Chatham Island. Its position is lat. 35° 02′ S, long. 116° 30′ E. The cape was named for John Pitt, second Earl of Chatham, First Lord of the Admiralty from July 1788 to December 1794.

remains of lofty edifices in ruin. The interior country afforded a more agreeable appearance, being pleasantly interspersed with hills and dales, and covered with lofty forest trees of considerable magnitude, which our glasses plainly distinguished; though we could no where perceive any smoke or other indication of the country being inhabited. Towards noon, the Chatham made the signal for having discovered a port to the northward; into which they were directed to lead; but finding it only a shallow bay, we soon bore away along the coast. Our observed latitude was 35° 8', longitude 117° 6' 30". In this situation, the coast, by compass, extended from N. 68 W. to S. 83 E. the nearest shore bearing N. 6 W. about a league distant; in the morning the variation of our surveying compass was observed to be 6° 30' westwardly. The coast we passed along in the afternoon differed little from that noticed in the morning, but the inland country was not sufficiently elevated to be seen beyond the hills near the sea side. At six in the eveming, a small detached islet bore, by compass, S. 87 E. the easternmost part of the main in sight N. 86 E. a projecting point whence extends westward a long range of white cliffs N. 76 E. the nearest shore N. 24 E. distant five miles; and the westernmost land in sight, the same which formed the eastern extreme at noon, N. 45 W. The wind was very gentle with alternate calms, and the weather, during the night, was mild and pleasant. In the morning of Wednesday the 28th, we found our progress had been very slow along the coast, although our distance from the shore had increased, with soundings from 40 to 50 fathoms. We had again an opportunity of observing the sun eclipsed, but were not so fortunate as to notice its commencement, or greatest obscuration; the end was however observed by Mr. Whidbey to be at 19ʰ 43' 53", and by myself 19ʰ 43' 46" apparent time; this was ascertained by our sextant telescope, as recommended on a former occasion. I much regretted that we had not gained a port on this coast, where, on shore, we might have compared such observations with the results from better instruments, which would have tended to establish the utility of the process. The latitude at this juncture was 35° 25'. It was now proved, that the white cliffs seen the preceding night, formed the southernmost point of this part of the coast, which I distinguished by the name of CAPE HOWE, in honor of that noble earl. It is situated in latitude 35° 17', longitude 117° 52'.[1] The small detached islet lies from cape Howe S. 68 E. distant three leagues. The land considered on Tuesday night as the easternmost part of the main now appeared to be an island, beyond which were seen a high rocky bluff point, and a high mountain forming the easternmost land in sight. A light breeze from the N.N.W. permitted us to draw in with the coast; which at noon bore by compass from N. 50 W. to N. 37 E. the high mountain N.

---

[1] The true position of the cape is lat. 35° 08' S. long. 117° 36' E. It was renamed West Cape Howe by Flinders in 1801 to avoid confusion with Cape Howe on the SE coast of Australia, named by Cook in 1770. Howe was Admiral commanding the Channel Fleet assembled in 1790 when it seemed likely that the Nootka controversy would result in war with Spain; it included the *Courageux*, in which Vancouver served.

35 E. to the eastward of which, a round hummock, seemingly detached N. 52 E. the land appearing like an island from N. 16 W. to N. 24 W. was now seen to comprehend a cluster of barren rocky isles, which being the nearest land was about ten miles distant; and the high rocky bluff point N. 8 E. In this situation, the observed latitude was 35° 22′, longitude 118° 16′; which was eight miles further south, and eleven miles further east than the log shewed. Many whales were playing about the ship during the morning. The high mountain conspicuously remarkable for its superior elevation above the neighbouring hills, I distinguished, after my highly esteemed friend Sir Alan Gardner,[1] by the name of MOUNT GARDNER; and the barren rocky cluster of isles, by the name of ECLIPSE ISLANDS.[2] The weather was pleasant; and aided by a gentle breeze, a port, round the high rocky bluff point, soon presented itself, into which the Chatham was directed to lead, and, by four, was sufficiently advanced to determine on its eligibility. The weather by this time had become thick and rainy, with much thunder and lightning; but as the soundings continued regular, we stood into the port, and passed the high rocky bluff point in thirty fathoms water; directing our course close along its shore, which is a high and nearly perpendicular cliff; the sounding suddenly shoaled to twelve fathoms, and gradually decreased afterwards, until abreast of the second white sandy beach; where we anchored in six fathoms water, having a clear bottom of fine white sand.

A continuation of the thick weather prevented our seeing about us until the morning of Thursday the 29th; which being delightfully serene and pleasant, discovered our situation to be very snug and secure in a spacious sound, open 13° of the compass only to the sea. The high rocky bluff point forming the S.W. extremity of the sound, which, from its smooth appearance, and being destitute of verdure, obtained the name BALD-HEAD, bore by compass S. 85 E.; a high rocky island in the entrance, which, from its beaten appearance by its opposition to the sea, and S.W. wind, obtained the name of BREAK-SEA ISLAND, from N. 82 E. to N. 69 E.; Mount Gardner, N. 70 E.; another high island named MICHAELMAS ISLAND, N. 62 E.; a small high island called SEAL ISLAND,[3] being a great resort of those animals, north; a low flat rock, S. 75 W.; and to the N.W. was an extensive white sandy beach; which promising success to the seine, a boat was dispatched with Lieutenant Puget on a fishing

---

[1] After the expedition left England Gardner (later Admiral Lord Gardner) became a lord of the Admiralty, and he signed Vancouver's supplementary instructions in August 1791.

[2] Named to commemorate the eclipse of the sun witnessed on 28 September.

[3] These four names, all bestowed on 29 September, Michaelmas Day, have been retained, but the first two are now spelled Bald Head and Breaksea Island. Michaelmas Island and Breaksea Island are named Inner Entry Island and Outer Entry Island on the manuscript sketch map in Johnstone's log. Menzies states that Bald Head originally 'obtained the name of Cape Princess Royal it being discovered on [29 September] her Royal highnesses birth day.' – 11 October. Presumably the name was changed to Bald Head when Vancouver decided to name Princess Royal Harbour after the princess.

party. After breakfast, accompanied by Mr. Broughton in the Chatham's cutter, Mr. Menzies, Mr. Whidbey, and myself, proceeded in the yawl, first to attend the success of the fishermen, and then to examine if the sound would afford a more eligible situation than that which we now occupied. The seine was hauled on the third sandy beach from Bald-Head with little success. A stream of fresh water drained there through the beach, which, although nearly of the colour of brandy, was exceedingly well tasted; by this stream was a clump of trees, sufficient to answer our present want of fuel. At the borders of this clump was found the most miserable human habitation my eyes ever beheld, which had not long been deserted by its proprietor, as on its top was lying a fresh skin of a fish, commonly called leather jacket, and by its side was the excrement of some carnivorous animal, apparently a dog. The shape of the dwelling was that of half a beehive, or a hive vertically divided into two equal parts, one of which formed the hut, in height about three feet, and in diameter about four feet and an half; it was however constructed with some degree of uniformity, with slight twigs of no greater substance than those used for large baker's baskets: the horizontal and vertical twigs formed intervals from four to six inches square, and the latter sticking a few inches into the earth, were its security, and fixed it to the ground. This kind of basket hut was covered with the bark of trees, and small green boughs; its back was opposed to the N.W. whence we concluded those to be the most prevailing winds; just within its front, which was open the whole of its diameter, a fire had been made, but excepting the skin of the fish before-mentioned, there were neither bones, shells, nor other indication on what its poor inhabitant had subsisted. The reflections which naturally arose on seeing so miserable a contrivance for shelter against the inclemency of seasons, were humiliating in the highest degree; as they suggested, in the strongest manner, the lowly condition of some of our fellow creatures, rendered yet more pitiable by the apparent solitude and the melancholy aspect of the surrounding country, which presented little less than famine and distress.

The shores consisted either of steep naked rocks, or a milk-white barren sand, beyond which dreary boundary the surface of the ground seemed covered by a deadly green herbage, with here and there a few groveling shrubs or dwarf trees scattered at a great distance from each other. This very unfavorable appearance may not, however, originate from the general sterility of the soil, since it was evident, so far as we traversed the sides of the hills, that the vegetation had recently undergone the action of fire; the largest of the trees had been burnt, though slightly; every shrub had some of its branches completely charred; and the plants lying close to the ground had not escaped without injury. Thus entertaining no very high opinion of the country, but in the hope of meeting with some of the wretched inhabitants, we proceeded along the shores of the sound, to the northward, to a high rocky point, that obtained the name of POINT POSSESSION;[1] and, on reaching its summit, we

[1] Now Possession Point.

gained an excellent view of the sound in all directions. When on board, we had supposed that the sound branched into three arms, but it now became evident that there were only two. One, immediately behind this point, which is also its southern point of entrance, extended in a circular form, about a league across, bounded by a country much resembling that before described, though producing more trees, and with verdure of a livelier hue, and approaching nearer to the water's edge. The other, lying about three miles to the N.E. seemed almost as spacious, though its entrance appeared very narrow. The surrounding country in its neighbourhood presented a far more fertile and pleasing aspect. Nearly in the centre of that harbour was an island covered with the most beautiful herbage,[1] and instead of the naked rocks and barren sands that compose the coast of the sound, the cliffs which bounded these shores seemed to be of a reddish clay, and the general texture or character of the soil appeared to be more favourable to the vegetable kingdom, as from the summits of the hills to the water side was seen a stately and luxuriant forest.

The necessary observations being made at this station, the British colours were displayed, and having drank His Majesty's health, accompanied by the usual formalities on such occasions, we took possession of the country from the land we saw north-westward of Cape Chatham, so far as we might explore its coasts, in the name of His present Majesty, for him and for his heirs and successors. This port, the first which we had discovered, I honored with the name of KING GEORGE THE THIRD'S SOUND,[2] and this day being the anniversary of Her Royal Highness Princess Charlotte Augusta Matilda's birth, the harbour behind Point Possession I called PRINCESS ROYAL HARBOUR;[3] which with the sound formed Point Possession into a peninsula, united to the main by a very narrow barren sandy beach.[4] Here although we could not discover the least trace of its having at any time been the resort of the natives, yet in every part where we strayed, were seen the same effects of fire on all the vegetable productions.

The ceremony of taking possession being finished, we found a passage, narrow and shoal for some distance, into the north-eastern harbour; where a bar was found to extend across its entrance, on which there was only three fathoms water. Within the harbour, the deep water seemed to occupy some space to the N.E. and N.W.; but the day was too far advanced, to permit

---

[1] Green Island: 'about the Centre of the Harbor is a Small Island covered with exceeding fine verdure from which it obtained the name of Green Island.' – Manby, Letters, October.

[2] Since shortened to King George Sound. Puget notes that Vancouver called 'the Sound King George the Thirds & the Coast New Cornwall.' – 30 September. Vancouver makes no mention of the latter name, which he later applied to part of the Northwest Coast, but neither there nor in Australia has the name survived.

[3] Charlotte (1766–1828) was the eldest daughter of George III. The city of Albany has grown up on the N side of Princess Royal Harbour.

[4] On the E side of the peninsula was 'a small Island which had obtained the name of Curlew Island...' – Menzies, 4 October. It is so named on the sketch of the sound in Johnstone's log. It is now Mistaken Island.

our making any particular examination. The verdant island covered with luxuriant grass and other vegetables, terminated the extent of our researches; and as the situation of the vessels seemed as convenient as any other for procuring what the sound might afford, I determined to return on board, and lose no time in availing myself of the benefits it presented. In our way out of this harbour, the boats grounded on a bank we had not before perceived; this was covered with oysters of a most delicious flavour, on which we sumptuously regaled; and, loading in about half an hour, the boats for our friends on board, we commemorated the discovery by calling it OYSTER HARBOUR.[1]

In the morning of Friday the 30th, we began cutting wood and providing water, which sufficiently employed all our healthy men; whilst those who were still indisposed were directed to amuse themselves on shore. Finding it practicable to place the ship much nearer to the spot whence the wood and water were procured, the next day, Saturday the 1st of October, she was removed,[2] and, by Sunday the 2d, we had made such progress, that the yawl could be spared for the further examination of the sound. In her I proceeded to Princess Royal harbour, where, near a rocky cliff, on the S.W. side, was found a small shallow stream of excellent water. On tracing its meanders through a copse it brought us to a deserted village of the natives, amidst the trees, on nearly a level spot of ground, consisting of about two dozen miserable huts mostly of the same fashion and dimensions, with that before described, though no one of them seemed so recently erected. This village had probably been the residence of what may in this country be esteemed a considerable tribe; and the construction of it afforded us an opportunity of concluding, that however humble the state of their existence might be, they were not destitute of distinctions. Two or three huts were larger, and differed in shape from the rest, as if a couple were fixed close to the side of each other; but the parts which in that case would have cause a separation, were removed, and the edges joined close together, as described in the plate,[3] leaving the whole of their fronts open, and increasing their diameter about one third more than the rest. Yet were they not an inch loftier, nor were they of greater extent from the front to the back than the single one before-mentioned. Fires had been made in the fronts of all, but not recently; and, excepting some branches of trees that seemed to have been lately broken down, there were not any signs of this place having been visited for some time; and although we were very industrious to ascertain the food on which the inhabitants of this village

[1] Three features in this region were later named for Vancouver: Vancouver Peninsula, between King George Sound and Princess Royal Harbour, the tip of which Vancouver named Possession Point; Vancouver Rock, about 2 miles SW of Bald Head, and Cape Vancouver, on an islet off the promontory on which Mount Gardner rises.

[2] Two anchorages are shown on Vancouver's chart of the sound. The ships rounded Bald Head and first anchored on the S shore about 2 miles to the W. The second anchorage was a mile or more to the NW, off the point at the S end of Frenchman Bay.

[3] Opposite p. 54 in the first edition; p. 174 in the second.

subsisted, we still remained in ignorance of it; as neither shells, bones, nor any other relicts, which might serve as indications, could be found, notwithstanding this place had the appearance of a principal resort; for besides the habitations already mentioned, which were in pretty good repair, there were many others in different states of decay. This spot was intersected with several small streams of water, yet the same marks of fire were evident on all the vegetable kingdom; although none of the huts seemed to have been affected by it, which led me to suppose that this general fire was of a less recent date than at first I had imagined. In one of the larger huts, probably the residence of a chief, towards which were several paths leading in different directions, some beads, nails, knives, looking glasses, and medals, were deposited as tokens of our friendly disposition, and to induce any of the natives, who might, unperceived by us, have been in the neighbourhood, to favour us with a visit. Having gratified our curiosity, though at the expence of our feelings, in contemplating these very wretched and humiliating efforts of human ingenuity, we returned on board,[1] and having by the morning of Tuesday the 4th, replenished our water,[2] and taken on board a supply of firewood, Messrs. Puget and Whidbey went to Oyster harbour, with three boats, for the purpose of hauling the seine, and obtaining a quantity of those shell fish, previously to our proceeding the following morning to sea. In this part of our plan, however, we were disappointed, as the wind which had blown a steady moderate breeze from the N.W. towards the evening blew a strong gale from the S.E. with a heavy swell, and prevented the return of the boats; at the same time that the cloudiness of the weather precluded me from making those lunar observations, for the sole purpose of obtaining which I had remained on board.

The gale moderating the next morning, Wednesday the 5th, the boats returned, not having been very successful with the seine, but bringing a sufficient supply of oysters not only for our convalescents, but for the affording also of two or three excellent meals for all hands. As the S.E. wind and a heavy sea in the offing prevented our departure, Mr. Broughton was employed in examining the eastern side of the sound from Oyster Harbour to Mount Gardner: this was found nearly a straight and compact shore, on which Mr. Broughton landed in several places, where the same effects of fire were evident, although there were not any traces of the natives or of their habitations to be discovered.

The like causes of detension still operating, on Friday the 7th, a party was made for the further examination of Oyster Harbour, and by a little excursion into the country on that side to acquire some information of its natural

---

[1] Mudge adds one detail: 'The only thing [in the way of weapons] found were a few Spears about Three Foot and a half long and point'd at the End.' – 11 October.

[2] 'Completed our Water to 36 tons.' – Mudge, 7 October. Earlier Puget had noted that in order to procure the water, 'from the Looseness of the Sand we were obliged to sink a Puncheon as a Well.' – 30 September.

productions, and, if possible also, of the natives. After examining the channel as we proceeded to the upper part of the harbour, our attention was directed to several large black swans in very stately attitudes swimming on the water, and, when flying, discovering the under parts of their wings and breast to be white: this is all the description we were enabled to give of them, since they were excessively shy, and we were indifferent marksmen. In the northern corner of the harbour, we landed near a rivulet navigable only for canoes and small boats. It meandered in a northern direction between the hills, which, opening to the east and west, presented a spacious plain with forest trees occupying the banks of the rivulet, and the sides of the hills, even to their very summits. We proceeded about a league by the side of the rivulet, which flowed through so dead a flat, that its motion was scarcely perceptible, and continued to be brackish, although in its passage it received several other smaller streams of most excellent water. In it were an abundance of very fine fish, and on its banks were many black swans, ducks, curlews, and other wild fowl.[1] On the sides of this stream, as well as on the shores in Oyster Harbour, were seen the remains of several fish wears, about eight or nine inches high, evidently the sorry contrivance of the wretched inhabitants of the country: some of these were constructed with loose stones, others with sticks and stumps of wood; but none of them were likely to be of much utility at this season, as several were placed nearly at, and others above, what now seemed the high water mark; but we supposed at times, when the rain or other cause should extend the rivulet beyond its present bounds, which in width did not exceed thirty yards, and in depth four or five feet, these humble contrivances might arrest some small fish.[2] Great bodies of water evidently pass down this stream at certain seasons, as appeared by the river's occupying from two to three hundred yards on each side the rivulet, the soil of which was composed of sea sand and broken shells, and was destitute of any vegetable production. This space when overflowed must, from its winding course, form a most beautiful sheet of water. The wears for the taking fish, and steps made in the bark for

[1] Mudge comments in some detail on the wild life: 'A dead Cangaroo was the only Quadrupe[d] I met with...Birds they have a great variety, though not very numerous, such as Eagles, Pellicans, Hawkes, Swans, Owls and a number of smaller ones. The Oceanicks are chiefly Ducks, Shags, Pengins, Gulls, the Black, the Spotted Curlew – with a vast number of the Petrel Tribe. Fish are in great abundance Although we were unfortunate in being able to procure but very few – Leather Jackets, Parrot Fish, Jacks, and a sort of Mullet. Mackerell and various rock Fish. Mussells, Oysters, and Limpets were in the greatest plenty.' – 11 October.

[2] 'we saw some rude fish wares which did not bespeak much ingenuity in the contrivers. They consisted of a row of small boughs of Trees stuck close together in the sand about two or three feet & kept close at the top by cross sticks along both sides fastened together with small withes & along their bottoms some stones sand & gravel was raised up behind to prevent the fish escaping.' – Menzies, 2 October. 'The Tide rises over them & on its ebb, deposits the fish, that happen to be within its circumference; such is the simple & as it appears the only means they have of catching them.' – Baker, 11 October. The natives had neither nets nor hooks and lines, but Baker could not know that they were expert at spearing fish in shallow water.

the purpose of ascending some of the largest trees, though both excessively rude, were undoubtedly the effects of manual labour, and, with the huts, formed the only indications of the country being inhabited that we were able to discern. There were no paths in the woods, nor were any smokes to be seen over the extensive country we beheld, which fully satisfied us that any further search for the natives would be fruitless; and therefore we returned by a different route to the boats. In our way we saw the remains of two similar huts. Near these was an ant's nest much of the same shape and magnitude, though finished in a very superior style and manner, and shewing how very humble is the state of human existence, when unassisted by civil society, and undirected by the sciences. Having eaten our salt beef we proceeded homewards, much mortified that the many wild fowl we had seen had escaped our vigilance; but that we might not return empty handed, we stopped at one of the oyster banks, where, in about half an hour, we loaded our boat, and returned on board about nine o'clock in the evening. The bank on which we found them in greatest plenty and the best flavoured, is that which extends from the north or low point of the entrance towards the little verdant island. The wind blew a strong gale from the E.S.E. and a very heavy sea ran without the sound; but the vessels within rode perfectly quiet. This sort of weather, with much rain, continued until Monday the 10th, when we entertained hopes of getting to sea, as the wind veered to the south; but soon again resuming its former direction, attended by the heavy sea in the offing, we remained at anchor until the next day, Tuesday the 11th; which being more favorable to our purpose, though the wind was still adverse, we weighed, and turned out of the sound. About four in the afternoon we regained the ocean; but the wind at E.N.E. prevented our steering along the coast, and obliged us to stand to the south-eastward. Whilst we were getting under weigh, I caused to be deposited at the hut near the watering place some beads, knives, looking-glasses, and other trinkets, as a compensation to its solitary owner, should he ever return, for the wood we had cut down, and deprived him of: and to commemorate our visit, near the stump of one of the trees we had felled, in a pile of stones raised for the purpose of attracting the attention of any European, was left a bottle sealed up, containing a parchment on which were inscribed the names of the vessels, and of the commanders; with the name given to the sound, and the date of our arrival and departure. Another bottle, containing a similar memorandum, was likewise deposited on the top of Seal Island, with a staff erected to conduct any visitor to it, on which was affixed a medal of the year 1789. Those who may meet with the staff will most probably discover the bottle hidden near it. This precaution was here taken, on a presumption that Seal Island was entirely out of the reach of the inhabitants, which might not be the case where the first bottle was secreted.[1]

---

[1] Hewett, surgeon's mate in the *Discovery*, always highly critical of Vancouver, pours scorn on this opinion in a marginal note in his copy of the published *Voyage*: 'it is the greatest Absurdity to suppose this Island is out of the reach of the Natives when it is in

At sun-set the Eclipse Islands by compass bore N. 74 W. Bald-head N. 45 W. Mount Gardner N. 13 E. the hummock mentioned on the 28th, now evidently an island,[1] from N. 56 E. to N. 51 E. and the easternmost part of the main land in sight N. 42 E. whence the coast appeared to take a sharp turn to the northward. As we stood to the S.E. the wind gradually veered to the north, which, by day light of Tuesday the 11th,[2] led us out of sight of the coast; but as in the forenoon it was calm and the atmosphere very clear,[3] Mount Gardner was seen bearing N.W. 18 leagues distant. In this situation we had much swell from the eastward; and soundings could not be gained at the depth of 200 fathoms. The observed latitude was 35° 37', longitude 119° 24', which was 2' to the south, and 16' to the east, of what the log shewed. The wind was light and variable until the evening, when it settled in a steady breeze at S.W.; the swell from the east, and E.S.E. still continuing, indicated the land in that direction to be at some distance. Our unexpected detention by the late eastwardly winds, and the advanced season, conspired greatly against prosecuting researches on this coast; I determined, however, not to abandon that favorite object, provided the task should not prove too dangerous, and intricate; or that the direction of the coast should not lead us too far out of our way; as, in respect of the former, I acted without any authority in the investigation; and, in respect of the latter, our time would not now admit of sufficient leisure to persevere in the pursuit. Under these considerations our course was directed to the N.E. during the night, in hopes of passing within sight of the land lying to the eastward of Mount Gardner, so as to connect our survey. Not gaining bottom with 110 to 140 fathoms of line; and there being at day-break of Thursday the 13th no appearance of the coast, we steered north, which soon brought us within sight of land to the N.W. making like three islands; but on a nearer approach, the two westernmost were evidently connected by a low isthmus to the main land: but the connecting of the northernmost being uncertain, it obtained the name of DOUBTFUL ISLAND.[4]

the Sound where the Water is generally smooth and near the Shore of the Main Land from which any one might Swim or float himself upon a Log of Wood.' Seal Island is about a mile and a half from the shore. The natives living along the S coast from the Murray River, in Southern Australia, to King George Sound, in Western Australia, had neither canoes nor floats, but some of them at least could swim.   [1] Bald Island.

[2] In both the first and second editions the date is given incorrectly as Tuesday the 18th, and other dates to the end of the chapter are similarly a week in error. All have been corrected.

[3] The sea was so calm and the ships were making so little progress that Menzies and Broughton went off in a boat, in hopes of shooting a petrel that Menzies was anxious to collect. In their absence a shark was caught and hauled on board the Discovery. 'I regretted much not being on board to examine it,' Menzies wrote, 'more particularly as it had 42 young ones alive in its belly – which on being set at liberty were able to swim about with agility, each of them were about 11 inches long, & proves that this species which appeared to be Squalus glaucus is very prolific.' – 12 October.

[4] The name now applies to the four Doubtful Islands, lying E of Hood Point. Doubtful Island Bay is N of them.

From the westernmost land seen this morning, to the easternmost land seen on Tuesday evening, is a space of 14 leagues, stretching S. 58 W. and N. 58 E. in which no land was seen. The depth of water was at this time 30 fathoms; the bottom coarse sand, with broken shells and coral. The weather was delightfully pleasant; and, with a gentle gale at S.W. we steered along the coast, which now took a direction N. 55 E. our distance from the shore from two to four leagues. Doubtful Island, and the shores to the S.W. of it, nearly resembled the rest of the coast; but to the N.E. the coast presented a very different prospect being composed of high detached clusters of craggy mountains, on a base of low and to all appearance level land, well wooded, particularly to the N.W. of Doubtful Island, where the land falls back to a considerable distance, forming either a deep well-sheltered bay, or a low flat country. At noon, a high bluff point, extending from the northernmost cluster of mountains, the easternmost land then in sight, bore by compass N. 24 E. the most western and conspicuous cluster of apparently disunited mountains N. 67 W. about nine leagues distant; and the east point of Doubtful Island, the westernmost land at that time visible, S. 73 W. This land forms a remarkable point on the coast, and is in latitude 34° 23′, longitude 119° 49′; which, after Admiral Lord Hood, I distinguished by the name of POINT HOOD.[1] In this situation, our observed latitude was 34° 18′, longitude 120° 14′; being 13′ more to the north, and 6′ more to the east, than appeared by the log. Soon after mid-day, low land was descried, stretching out from the high bluff point, which we found situated not immediately on the shore, but some distance inland, whence a very low country extends to the sea coast, which takes a direction S. 70 E. Breakers in two detached places were discovered at this time lying at some distance from the land; the nearest of these about one o'clock, bore by compass N.E. four miles distant; the other, visible only from the mast-head, appeared to lie from the former E. by N. two leagues distant. At this time the depth of water was 35 fathoms; and as the wind blew directly on the shore, and the main land, though not more than four leagues off, was not sufficiently high to be distinctly seen from the deck; we hauled our tacks on board, and stood to the S.E. increasing our distance very slowly. At six in the evening, the nearest land was a rocky island, about two miles in circuit, which bore by compass N. 13 E. eight miles distant; and from the mast-head, the flat low coast was visible as far as E.N.E.; at nine the depth of water had gradually increased to forty fathoms. Considering our present as the most prudent tack to remain upon until we should meet shoals, or other impediments, I directed the Chatham to lead and sound; our depth gradually increased to 54 fathoms, and the coast in the morning of Friday the 14th was in sight from N.E. to east. The wind blew a light breeze from the S.S.E. with which we steered for the land until about nine, when we tacked in 60 fathoms. The land in sight, at that time, from the mast-head bore by

---

[1] The position of Hood Point is now given as lat. 34° 23′ S (which agrees with Vancouver's figure), long. 119° 34′ E.

compass from N.N.W. to E. by N. each extremity five or six leagues distant; all this was supposed to be the main, though between north and E.N.E. the land appeared somewhat broken, occasioned perhaps by some of its parts being elevated a little above the rest of the shore, off which breakers were seen to lie at some distance; and the land, which in the morning bore east, and now bore by compass N. 87 E. eight miles distant, was evidently a rocky island about a league in circuit, much resembling that which we passed the preceding evening. It proved the termination of our researches on this coast, and thence obtained the name of TERMINATION ISLAND; on it the sea broke with much violence, and between it and the main was a small low islet. The great depth of water indicated that the bank of soundings which we had hitherto found extending along the coast, terminated also on its approach to this island, as we had no where found so great a depth of water at this small distance from the shore; which, on being increased a few miles only, put the ship intirely out of soundings. At noon, the observed latitude was 34° 34′, longitude 121° 52′; twenty-two miles further east, and four further north than shewn by the log. In this situation the main land from the mast-head was seen bearing by compass N.N.W. to E.N.E. ½ E.; and Termination Island, situated in latitude 34° 32′, longitude 122° 8½′;[1] N. 84 E. Between the easternmost part of the main, seen the preceding evening, and the westernmost seen this morning, is a space of ten leagues, which we passed in the night without observing land; yet, from the regularity of the soundings, there can be little doubt of its being one continued coast, and that the course by us made good S. 76 E. is nearly parallel to its direction. The whole of this low country presented a dreary aspect, destitute of wood, or herbage, and interspersed with white and brown patches, occasioned, most probably, by the different colours of sand or rock, of which it is composed. We here noticed more coast and oceanic birds, than we had seen on any other part of the shores: as, besides gannets, and two or three different sorts of tern; albatrosses, and petrels, particularly the black and sooty, were in great abundance. The weather continued very fine, with a light variable breeze in the eastern quarter, which drew us, not only out of sight, and some distance from the coast, but prevented our making much progress in the direction, in which it seemed to bend, until Sunday the 16th, when the wind, settling in the western board, we steered to the E.N.E. in hopes of falling in with the land; and in the event of its taking a more northerly direction, the Chatham was ordered to look out three leagues on the larboard beam. At noon, the observed latitude was 35° 30′, the longitude 122° 40′. At this time, the wind suddenly shifted to the southward, and was accompanied by a very heavy swell in that direction, which strongly indicating the approach of boisterous weather, the Chatham's signal was made to join, and our course was directed E.S.E.; not daring under all the circumstances of our situation, to run the risk of encountering bad weather

---

[1] Termination Island is in lat. 34° 28′ S, long. 122° 00′ E.

on an unexplored coast, that presented to us so many dangers.[1] Besides, as the lowness of the shores which we had lately seen, and the distant shoals that we had found extending from them, would exact particular caution as we proceeded, more time would necessarily be required in the prosecution of such an inquiry, than the main object of our voyage would at present allow. I was therefore compelled to relinquish, with great reluctance, the favorite project of further examining the coast of this unknown though interesting country; and, directing our route over an hitherto untraversed part of these seas, we proceeded without further delay towards the Pacific Ocean.

[1] The dangers were even greater than Vancouver suspected, as his ships were nearing the Archipelago of the Recherche, consisting of a great number of islands and reefs scattered along the coast for more than 100 miles and in places extending 30 or 40 miles offshore. Even today mariners are advised to avoid the area whenever possible.

CHAPTER III.

Remarks on the Country and Productions on Part of the South-west Coast of New Holland—Extraordinary Devastation by Fire—Astronomical and nautical Observations.

ALTHOUGH the considerations adverted to in the foregoing chapter, rendered it impracticable to explore the S.W. coast of New Holland to the extent my wishes first led me to imagine, and prevented our ascertaining its boundary and connection with, or separation from, Van Dieman's land; yet the information we have acquired, will open a field to those whose duty it may hereafter be to perform that task; by shewing, that its S.W. part may be approached with the greatest safety, as its shores are bold with regular soundings to the distance of eight or nine leagues, and by the discovery of the very excellent harbour in King George the Third's Sound. Considering therefore its situation and conveniences as likely to become of material importance to those whose pursuits may induce them to navigate this and the Pacific Ocean, it may not be uninteresting to detail, in a more particular manner, the circumstances that occurred during our visit to a country hitherto so little known to Europeans.

Our survey comprehended an extent of 110 leagues, in which space we saw no other haven or place of security for shipping than the sound before mentioned; notwithstanding the opinion of Dampier,[1] who had considered the whole of the western part of New Holland as consisting of a cluster of islands. He was undoubtedly a judicious observer, of very superior talents; and, it is most likely, formed his opinion from the many islands which he found composing the exterior coast of the N.W. part of this extensive country. However just may be his conclusions as to that part of New Holland, they certainly do not apply to its south western side, as no very material separation, either by rivers, or arms of the sea, was discovered in the neighbourhood of our survey. Had such breaks in the coast existed, and had they escaped our observation, it is highly probable we should have met in the sea, or seen driven

---

[1] William Dampier, buccaneer and explorer, the first Englishman to visit Australia, landed in King Sound, on the NW coast, in 1688. His explorations were confined to that region, to which he paid a second and longer visit in the summer of 1699. His account of his travels attracted wide attention. See John Masefield (ed.), *Dampier's Voyages*, 2 vols. (London, 1936).

on its shores, drift wood and other productions of the interior country. The very deep colour also of the several streams of water may possibly be occasioned by the quality of the soil through which they flow; whence it may be inferred that, if any considerable inland waters had their source far in the country, or if any great body descended from its shores, the sea along the coast would in some measure have been discoloured; but neither of these evidences existed, for on our approach to the land, there was no previous appearance to indicate its vicinity. This opinion was further corroborated on inspecting the habitations and places of the natives' resort; where not the least remains of canoes, or other circumstances presented itself, which could convey the most distant idea of these people having ever trusted themselves on the water;[1] a circumstance which it is reasonable to suppose would sometimes have happened, had their country been insulated, or their travelling been interrupted by large rivers or arms of the sea; especially as all appearances favored the conjecture of their being by no means a stationary people. There was great reason, however, to conclude, that the country was well supplied with fresh water; as wherever we chanced to land, we easily procured that valuable article, not only where the soil was of considerable depth, but from streamlets issuing out of the solid rocks. This seemed to be the case even on the most elevated land, which caused a very singular appearance when the sun shone in certain directions on those mountains whose surfaces were destitute of soil; for on these, made humid by the continual oozing of the water, a bright glare was produced that gave them the resemblance of hills covered with snow.

Our researches afforded little matter worthy of notice excepting such as appertained to King George the Third's Sound. This port has its entrance in latitude 35° 5', longitude 118° 17'.[2] It is easily known on approaching it from the westward, as it is the first opening in the coast that presents any appearance like an harbour, eastward of Cape Chatham. The Eclipse Islands being the only detached *land* that can be so regarded, are an excellent guide to the sound, having, between them and Bald-head, some rocks on which the sea breaks with great violence. The port is safe, and easy of access any where between its outer points of entrance, Bald-head, and Mount Gardner, lying N. 62 E. and S. 62 W. 11 miles distant from each other. Mount Gardner is not less conspicuous and useful in pointing out the sound from the eastern quarter, than in its being rendered very remarkable by its handsome shape, and its rocky, and almost uninterrupted polished surface to its summit. Its base may be said rather to form the eastern extent of the coast, than the opposite point of the sound, there being within it a projection which more properly forms

<hr/>

[1] Vancouver's conclusion was correct. As already noted, the natives had no boats of any kind.

[2] By the 'entrance' Vancouver seems to have meant the opening between Bald Head and Breaksea Island. The lat. given is correct, but the long. is about 118° 02' E.

the N.E. point of the sound, lying from Bald-head N. 30 E. about five miles distant.[1] Between these latter points are Michaelmas, and Break Sea islands, each about a league in circuit, one mile apart, nearly equidistant between the two points, and affording to all appearance good channels on every side. The water suddenly decreases in its depth from 30 to 12 fathoms; the latter depth uniformly continuing across from point to point, I should conceive, must be an additional means of preventing any very heavy sea from rolling into the sound; which, in the most exposed place of anchorage convenient to the shore, is only open from E. by N. to S.E. by E. Between these limits are situated the two islands above-mentioned, whence the sound extends W. by N. about two leagues to Point Possession, and from our anchorage to Oyster Harbour, north about the same distance, with regular soundings in mid-channel of 12 to 15, and 10 to 6 fathoms close to the shore, excepting near Seal island, where there is a hole of 21 fathoms. The Discovery and Chatham were moored in a situation, not only very convenient as to communication with the shore, but I believe, in perfect security as it respected the element: for although the sea broke sometimes with such violence on Break Sea Island, that the surf ranged to its elevated summit, during a continuance of the boisterous weather; yet it did not occasion us the least inconvenience. A more eligible situation if required in the sound might very probably be met with above the flat rock,[2] as vessels would be there more completely land-locked; and a convenient sandy cove, easily to be discovered in that neighbourhood, is furnished with a stream of excellent fresh water,[3] which though to all appearance not better in quality than the water we received on board, was yet more pleasing to the eye, not being of so deep a colour.

Princess Royal Harbour admits of a passage into it about a quarter of a mile wide; nearest to the northern shore the depth is five or six fathoms, but on the southern, not more than $2\frac{1}{2}$ and three fathoms water; occasioned by banks of coral rock which are very conspicuous, and, not being liable to any of the violent agitations of the sea, are by no means dangerous. Within the points of entrance, the depth is regularly from four to seven fathoms, and the bottom clear, good holding ground. This depth, though occupying part only of the harbour, yet affords a sufficient space for several vessels to ride in safety.

Oyster Harbour is rendered admissible alone for vessels of a middle size, by the shallowness of the water on the bar, extending from shore to shore, on which we found 17 feet water only, although the depth increased from five to seven fathoms on each side. The deep water within the harbour did not seem of any great extent. In both these harbours the communication with the country is rendered unpleasant by the shallow depth of water in most places extending to a great distance from the shore. This inconveniency could easily

[1] Herald Point. Vancouver's view is now the accepted one; the entrance to the sound is taken as being between Bald Head and Herald Point.
[2] Flat Rock, a small island on the S shore of the sound.
[3] John Vancouver has here revised an awkward wording in the first edition.

be remedied, should it ever be an object so to do, by wharfs; although it is
not unlikely that on a more minute inspection the necessity for such a measure
would cease to appear.

In navigating the sound, we did not observe any danger that was not
sufficiently conspicuous to be avoided; circumstances however did not admit
of our acquiring that satisfactory information respecting Princess Royal and
Oyster harbours which fall into it, that could have been wished; yet so far
as relates to the sound, the annexed sketch will I believe be found to contain
no very material error.[1]

The appearance of this country along the coasts, resembles, in most respects,
that of Africa about the Cape of Good Hope. The surface seemed to be chiefly
composed of sand mixed with decayed vegetables, varying exceedingly in point
of richness; and although bearing a great similarity, yet indicating a soil
superior in quality to that in the immediate neighbourhood of Cape Town.
The principal component part of this country appeared to be coral; and it
would seem that its elevation above the ocean is of modern date, not only
from the shores, and the bank which extends along the coast being, generally
speaking, composed of coral, as was evident by our lead never descending to
the bottom without bringing up coral on its return; but by coral being found
on the highest hills we ascended; particularly on the summit of Bald-Head,
which is sufficiently above the level of the sea to be seen at 12 or 14 leagues
distance.[2] Here the coral was entirely in its original state; particularly in one
level spot, comprehending about eight acres, which produced not the least
herbage on the white sand that occupied this space; through which the
branches of coral protruded, and were found standing exactly like those seen
in the beds of coral beneath the surface of the sea, with ramifications of
different sizes, some not half an inch, others four or five inches in circumference.
In these fields of coral (if the term field be allowable) of which there were
several, sea shells were in great abundance, some nearly in a perfect state still
adhering to the coral, others in different stages of decay. The coral was friable
in various degrees; the extremities of the branches, some of which were nearly
four feet above the sand, were easily reduced to powder, whilst those close
to, or under the surface, required some small force to break them from the
rocky foundation from whence they appeared to spring. I have seen coral in
many places at a considerable distance from the sea; but in no other instance
have I seen it so elevated, and in such a state of perfection.

In the lower lands we frequently met with extensive tracts occupied by a
kind of okerish[3] swampy peat, or moorish soil of a very dark brown colour,
forming as it were a crust, which shook and trembled when walked upon;
with water oozing through, or running over the surface, in all directions.

---

[1] 'A survey of King George III.d Sound' is an inset on Vancouver's chart of 'part of
the S.W. Coast of New Holland'.

[2] Bald Head is 401 feet high.

[3] From 'oker', obsolete form of 'ochre'.

Through this soil most of the streams take their course, and it is to their impregnation in the passage, that the general high colour of the water is to be attributed.[1] These swamps were not always confined to low and level spots, but were found on the acclivity of the higher lands; and where these did not occupy the sides of the hills, the soil was deep, and appeared infinitely more productive than the surface of the plains; especially that through which the rivulet in Oyster Harbour has been mentioned to flow. In that plain we found, at irregular intervals, just beneath the surface, a substratum of an apparently imperfect chalk, or a rich white marle, seemingly formed of the same decayed shells, with which the course of the river abounded. These strata, about eight or ten yards broad, run perpendicularly to the rivulet; their depth we had not leisure to examine, although there seemed little doubt of finding this substance in sufficient abundance for the purposes of manure, should the cultivation of this country ever be in contemplation. The general structure of it seems very favorable to such an attempt, as the mountains are neither steep nor numerous; nor do the rising grounds form such hills as bid defiance to the plough; while they produce that sort of diversity which is grateful to the eye, and not unpleasant to the traveller.

This chalky earth was also found in the neighbourhood of a moorish soil; and, on a more minute examination, seemed much to resemble an earth described in Cronstadt's Mineralogy at the bottom of his note (γ) page 21.[2] It did not shew any signs of effervescence with acids, nor did it burn into lime; but, like the earth alluded to, contains a number of small transparent crystals. These were visible without a microscope; and as, on applying the blow pipe, vitrification took place, it might probably be usefully appropriated in making a sort of porcelain.

The stones we found were chiefly of coral, with a few black and brown pebbles, slate, quartz, two or three sorts of granite, with some sand stones, but none seeming to possess any metallic quality.

The climate, if a judgment may be formed by so short a visit, seemed delightful: for though we contended with some boisterous weather on our approach to the coast, nothing less ought reasonably to have been expected at the season of the vernal equinox, and breaking up of the winter. The gales we experienced in King George the Third's Sound, were not of such violence as to put vessels at sea past their top-sails; although whilst the S.W. wind continued a most violent sea broke with incredible fury on the exterior shores. This however can easily be imagined, when the extensive uninterrupted range which the wind in that direction has over the Indian ocean is taken into

---

[1] Menzies commented on the water: 'as it appeard of a dark brown tinge, somewhat like a strong infusion of Bohea tea, suspicions were at first entertaind of its salubrity, but on examining the marsh & black mould through which it oozed, I was convincd that these were sufficient to tinge it without giving it any noxious quality, and my opinion being askd concerning it I freely declard it' – 30 September.

[2] The reference is to Axel Fredrik Cronsted, *An Essay towards a System of Mineralogy* (London, 1770; 2d edition 1772).

consideration: during the continuance of this wind the atmosphere was tolerably clear, though the air was keen. Farenheit's thermometer, at the time of year answering to the beginning of April in the northern hemisphere, stood at 53°; but at all other times during our stay, varied between 58° and 64°, and the barometer from 29^{in} 90 to 30^{in} 50. Slight colds were caught by the crew, which ought rather to be imputed to their own want of care than to the climate, as on getting to sea the parties soon recovered. Our convalescents in the flux received much benefit, though their health could not yet be considered as thoroughly re-established. These circumstances induced an opinion, that the climate and soil bade fair to be capable of producing all the essentials, and many of the luxuries of life; although on the subject of agricultural improvement, I felt myself as unqualified to determine, as to enumerate scientifically the several trees, shrubs, and plants with which the country abounds. Of the two latter there appeared a great variety, and I believe afforded to Mr. Menzies much entertainment and employment. Amongst the most remarkable was the gum plant, found every where in great abundance, and answering, in all its characters, to the description and representation of that plant found at port Jackson, as mentioned in Philips's voyage.[1] Wild celery was found in quantities sufficient for our pea-soup, and daily to supply the people by way of sauce to their salted meat: this with samphire were the only eatable vegetables we procured. Other plants were numerous, and afforded a great variety of beautiful flowers. The shrubs also were abundant, and of many species; but neither these nor the trees grew so closely together as materially to incommode travelling, even in the neighbourhood of Oyster harbour, where the country is very well wooded; and as the branches of the trees do not approach within several feet of the ground, an extensive view is admitted in every direction. The forest trees seemed of four different sorts. The most common much resembled the holly,[2] but these were not of the larger sort; that which I took to be the gum tree of New South Wales, by its foliage and its producing a considerable quantity of gum, seemed to be a hard, ponderous, close-grained wood: of this description the larger trees seemed chiefly to consist; one of these measured nine feet four inches in girth, and was of a proportionable height.[3] Those from which our fuel was procured were of the myrtle tribe, not unlike the pimento of the West Indies,[4] in shape, appearance, and aromatic flavor of the foliage; and in the hard and close texture of the wood, which makes an excellent and pleasant fire, burning cheerfully yet consuming slow; whilst, from the smoke, a very spicy agreeable

[1] *The Voyage of Governor Phillip to Botany Bay with an Account of the Establishment of the Colonies of Port Jackson & Norfolk Island* (London, 1789). The gum tree is described on pp. 59–60. 'I met here with the Gum Plant of Botany Bay, *Metrosidera...*' – Menzies, 29 September.
[2] The holly-leaved Banksia, a small to medium-sized evergreen.
[3] Menzies visited 'a thick wood chiefly composed of the *Eucalyptus obliqua...* The thickest of these trees did not exceed 9 or 10 feet in the circumference of their stems'. – 7 October.   [4] The Jamaican pepper tree.

fragrance is exhaled. These do not, in general, grow to large timbers; but there is another species much resembling them, with rather broader leaves, and possessing like them an aromatic flavor, which grow to a considerable size. These, with a species not unlike the silver tree of the Cape of Good Hope,[1] were the trees that were found generally to compose the forest.

For the benefit of those who may visit the country hereafter, some vine-cuttings and watercresses were planted on the island in Oyster Harbour, and at the place from whence we procured our fuel; and an assortment of garden seeds, with some almonds, orange, lemon and pumkin seeds were sown. The whole being the produce of Africa, I should have entertained little doubt of their success, had it not been, that there was much to apprehend in their being over-run by the natural productions of the country.

Of the animal kingdom, so far as relates to the tenants of the earth, little information was derived. The only quadruped seen was one dead kangaroo; the dung, however, of these or some other animals feeding on vegetables, was almost every where met with, and frequently so fresh as to indicate that the animal could not be far removed.

Of the birds that live in or resort to the woods, the vulture may be said to be the most common, as we saw several of this species, or at least, birds that were so considered. Hawks of the falcon tribe, with several others of that genus; a bird much resembling the English crow, parrots, paroquets, and a variety of small birds, some of which sung very melodiously, were those which attracted our attention the most; but all were so excessively wild and watchful, that few specimens could be procured. Of the water fowl, the black swan seemed as numerous as any other species of aquatic birds in the neighbourhood of Oyster Harbour, but they were seen in no other place. There was also black and white pelicans of a large sort, seen at a distance; and though ducks were in great numbers, we were very unsuccessful in taking them. A very peculiar one was shot, of a darkish grey plumage, with a bag like that of a lizard hanging under its throat; which smelt so intolerably of musk that it scented nearly the whole ship.[2] There was also many gray curlews, and sea-pies;[3] of the latter we procured a few, which were excellent eating. The aquatic birds before enumerated, with shags, the common gull, two or three sorts of tern, and a few small penguins of a blueish colour, included the whole of the feathered tribe in the vicinity of the shores.

With the productions of the sea, we were not much more acquainted; which is rather to be attributed to our want of skill as fishermen than to its want of bounty. Some of the few fish we caught were very excellent, particularly of the larger sort; one much resembling the snook,[4] and another the calipevar

---

[1] *Leucadendron argentum*, a tree with silvery lancelate leaves, native to Cape Colony. OED.

[2] The musk duck. Puget states that it 'was so highly scented with Musk that it was disagreeable to approach it, within three Yards.' – October.

[3] Oyster-catchers.

[4] Presumably the snook barracuda.

of Jamaica,[1] both of high flavor; as was a kind of fish not unlike, nor inferior in quality to, the English red mullet. These, with the common white mullet, rock fish, mackerel, herrings, and a variety of small fish, were those we procured, though not in any abundance.

Whilst on the coast, whales and seals were frequently playing about the ship; of the latter, we saw about a score at one time on Seal island. The little trouble these animals took to avoid us, indicated their not being accustomed to such visitors. The throat and belly of these seals, which were of a large sort, were nearly white; between the head and shoulders, the neck rises in a kind of crest, which, with the back, was of a light brown colour; their hair was exceedingly coarse; the carcase very poor, and afforded little blubber; which, however, may be imputable to the season.

Reptiles and noxious animals seemed by no means to be numerous, as only two or three yellow, and bronze-coloured snakes were seen, which were good eating;[2] these, with a few lizards of the common sort, and some about eight or nine inches long of a thick clumsy make, dark colour, and altogether excessively ugly, were what composed that race of animals. Some beautiful beetles, common flies, and muskitoes, were occasionally met with, but not in such numbers as to produce inconvenience.

It would now remain to say something of the human species, the inhabitants of this country; but as we were not so fortunate to procure an interview with any one of them, all that can be advanced on this subject must be founded on conjecture or nearly so, and consequently very liable to error; it may, however, not be unacceptable to state such circumstances as, on the spot, occurred to our observation.

The natives appeared to be a wandering people, who sometimes made their excursions individually, at other times in considerable parties; this was apparent by their habitations being found single and alone, as well as composing tolerably large villages.

Besides the village I visited, Mr. Broughton discovered another about two miles distant from it, of nearly the same magnitude; but it appeared to be of a much later date; as all the huts had been recently built, and seemed to have been very lately inhabited. It was situated in a swamp, which might probably have been preferred to a higher and firmer land for the convenience of water. One or two huts of a larger size were here also observed; the rest were precisely of the same description with those in our neighbourhood. The larger trees in the vicinity of both villages had been hollowed out by fire, sufficiently to afford the shelter these people seemed to require. Upon stones

[1] Calipeva; the West Indian mullet.

[2] Bell gives further details: 'I went with a party of Gentlemen a little way into the Country but met with nothing remarkable except a very large Snake about Six feet & a half long. we found him asleep – and shot him – and afterwards at our dinner which we took on shore Skinn'd the Snake & eat part of him. it was a very handsome one, and we saw marks of many more in the Sand.' – 3 October. Menzies describes a snake 'about eight feet long'. – 10 October.

placed in the inside of these hollow trees fires had been made, which proved that they had been used as habitations, either for the inferior of the party, which would argue a further degree of subordination amongst them, or for those who were too indolent to build themselves the wattled huts before described. No one species of furniture or utensil was discovered in any of the houses; the only implements seen, were pieces of sticks intended as spears, rudely wrought, and the operation of manual labour upon them but slightly discernible. The bark was stripped off, and the thickest end, after having been burnt in the fire, was scraped and reduced to a blunted point, on one of which some blood was found still adhering.[1]

Destitute (as they seemed) of the means, and totally ignorant of every mode of embarkation, it is not likely that they place much dependence on marine productions for their subsistence; yet it was evident from the wears on the shores, and from the mouths of the brooks near the villages being stopped up, that they sometimes resort to the rivulets and to the sea for provisions. On this account, it was considered rather extraordinary, that the bones of the fishes on which they had fed were no where to be found; and this led to a supposition that those which their endeavours enabled them to procure were very small. It appeared still more extraordinary that, since they drew a certain proportion of their food from the sea, they should not have discovered so excellent a part of its produce as oysters and clams; notwithstanding that the latter show themselves on the beaches over which they must frequently walk; and that the former at low water require only wading half-leg deep on the shoals that extend from the main land to gather in a few minutes a day's subsistence. Neither did it appear that they had any knowledge of these, the limpets, nor any other shell fish found amongst the rocks; or if they had, for some reason not easily to be imagined, they certainly made no use of them; otherwise their shells in all human probability would have been seen near the places of their resort. Hence it may naturally be inferred, that the land principally supplies their wants, or hunger would long since have conducted them to such excellent resources. This opinion is supported by the extreme shyness of the feathered creation, and the wildness of the quadrupeds, whose footing, and the other signs of their being at no great distance without our obtaining any sight of them, sufficiently proved that they were constantly pursued. This circumstance may furnish a probable conjecture on the cause

---

[1] Hewett, always happy to disparage Vancouver, explains the origin of the blood stain: 'I was of this Party and I doubt not this was told to Captn. Vancouver by the Gunner [Collett] who without considering the probability of the Spear having fresh wet Blood upon it from having been used lately by the Indians and in a state of alarm called to every one to cock their Pieces the Blood however came from the finger of a Midshipman [John Nicholas] who had just cut it with a piece of Flag or Reed.' Puget describes the spears in more detail: 'The only Weapons we found were, a Stick rudely polished sharpened at one End about nine or Ten Feet long & ¾ of an Inch in Diameter, the other a piece of Wood bearing some Resemblance to a large Knife having an Handle & a Blade Tapered away at the Edge & pointed at the end.' – October.

of the very extraordinary devastation by fire, which the vegetable productions had suffered throughout the whole country we had traversed. Fire is frequently resorted to by rude nations, either for the purpose of encouraging a sweeter growth of herbage in their hunting grounds, or as toils for taking the wild animals, of which they are in pursuit.[1] When the forest is set on fire for such purposes in a dry season, its ravages may become very extensive; and the inflamable quality of the gum plant, which is here in great abundance, may operate to promote that general havock which we observed in the vegetable kingdom.

The destructive operations of fire were, however, evident in places where the gum-plant was not found for a considerable distance; and, positively speaking, in our excursion on shore, we did not see a spot that produced any vegetables, which had not visibly felt its effects. Where the country was well wooded, the loftiest timbers had the topmost of their branches burned; yet none seemed totally destroyed by it; and where the luxuriance of the soil had obliterated its baneful appearance amongst the growing shrubs and plants, the ground, on examination, was found strewed over with the remains of branches and stumps that had been partially consumed by fire. Had this conflagration been occasioned, as some of us supposed, by repeated storms of violent lightning and thunder, it is reasonable to imagine we should have seen the forest trees much torn and shattered to pieces; which in no instance was observed.

As nothing further occurred worthy any particular notice, I shall conclude my remarks on this country by stating the astronomical and nautical observations that were made for ascertaining its situation, and for other purposes of navigation.

The latitude of the situation of the ships in King George the Third's Sound, deduced from nine meridional altitudes of the sun, taken by four different observers and quadrants, all nearly agreeing together, gave their mean result –   35° 5′ 30″ south.

The longitude deduced from the mean result of 25 sets of lunar distances of the sun and stars, taken before our arrival; eight sets taken whilst at anchor in the sound; and 52 sets taken after our departure,

---

[1] Vancouver was right in assuming that the fires were set deliberately and he was the first to suggest that one purpose was to encourage 'a sweeter growth of herbage' (in modern terms, pasture management). Fire was also used systematically by the natives in the summer season to procure game by surrounding an area and then setting fire to the grass and underbrush. See the study by Sylvia J. Hallam, *Fire and Hearth* (Canberra, 1975). Burning, she tells us, was 'a deliberately regulated activity co-ordinated into the pattern of seasonal and diurnal movements and of men's and women's activities.' – p. 34. Menzies developed an interesting theory, based on the supposition that the natives used the gum from trees as food: 'we seldom met with these [eucalyptus] trees or the other gum plants any where about the Sound without observing their stems burnt or scorched with fire, on purpose no doubt of causing a quicker exudation of these concretions by means of heat.' – 7 October.

and reduced to our station there; making in the whole 85 sets, each set containing six observed distances, and equal to 510 observations, gave –   118° 14′ 13″ east.

Kendall's chronometer, allowing the Portsmouth rate, on our arrival shewed –   117 46 0

Allowing the Cape rate   118 23 0

Arnold's chronometer, on board the Chatham, allowing the Cape rate –   117 38 30[1]

By the daily observations made at anchor, Kendall's chronometer appeared to have altered its rate as settled at the Cape of Good Hope, and seemed to be going nearer to its original Portsmouth rate. The result of a fortnight's observations proved it to be gaining at the rate of 6″ per day; and admitting the longitude to be right as ascertained by our observations, it was, at noon on the 9th of October, fast of mean time at Greenwich, 26′ 14″: and as it was manifest on our arrival and during our residence at the Cape, that Kendall's chronometer was gaining materially on its Portsmouth rate, I have, in reducing the observations taken prior to our arrival in King George the Third's Sound, adopted a mean rate, which I trust will render the result of the several observations liable to little error.

The variation of the magnetic needle on board, whilst at anchor, by two compasses, differed from 3° 55′ to 7° 11″. The mean result of 12 sets shewed 5° 20′ westwardly variation.

The vertical inclination of the South point of the magnetic needle, marked end North, face East   -   65° 49′

Marked end North face West   -   -   -   63

Marked end South face East   -   -   -   65 28

Marked end South face West   -   -   -   65 20

Mean vertical inclination of the South point of the marine dipping needle   -   -   -   -   64 54

Our observations with regard to the tides were rather indecisive, as their fluctuation in the sound seemed to be greatly influenced by the force and direction of the wind; our last visit, however, to Oyster Harbour afforded an opportunity of noticing that the rise and fall appeared on that day to be about four feet, and that it was high water 3ʰ 42′ after the moon passed the meridian. Whilst on the coast the vessels were constantly found to be further advanced, than what the run of the log intimated; but whether this was occasioned by errors in this practice, or by a current continually pressing eastward along the coast, we had no positive means of discovering; though, from our conclusions at the time, the latter should seem to be the case, as the log was not only used with much circumspection, but the line was frequently remeasured, and always found according to its due proportions.

[1] The correct long. was probably about 117° 57′ E.

CHAPTER IV.

Passage from the south-west Coast of New Holland—Pass Van Dieman's Land—
Arrival in Dusky Bay, New Zealand—Violent Storms—Leave Dusky Bay—
A violent Storm—Much Water found in the Ship—Part Company with the
Chatham—Discover the Snares—Proceed towards Otaheite—Arrive and join
the Chatham there.

OUR apprehensions of approaching boisterous weather, proved in the sequel
to have been ill founded; for notwithstanding the S.W. swell on the 17th
greatly increased, a gentle gale continued to attend us, chiefly from the western
quarter, with pleasant weather. With this we steered to the S.E. and without
the occurrence of any intervening circumstance worth relating,[1] made such
progress, that on Wednesday the 26th we had sight of Van Dieman's Land,
bearing by compass E.N.E. 10 or 12 leagues distant. Soundings at this time
could not be gained at the depth of 80 fathoms. During this passage few oceanic
birds had been seen; a continual and heavy swell had rolled between the south
and west, and we experienced the same sort of influence in our reckoning as
on the coast of New Holland, in finding the ship every day further advanced
than we expected.[2] A continuance of fine weather allowed several lunar
observations to be taken, which were directed to the purpose of ascertaining
the longitude of our last station. The breeze from the S.E. was very light,
and it was not until late in the day that the land could be plainly distinguished.
At seven o'clock in the evening we tacked and stood to the S.W.; the
Mewstone[3] bearing by compass S. 88 E.;[4] the easternmost part of the main
land in sight N. 82½ E. the south-west cape[5] being the nearest land N.E. three

---

[1] The *Chatham* had one small adventure. On 'the Night of the 23rd being in bed I was
awakened by a violent shock as if the Vessel had struck upon a Rock and on enquiry found
it was a large Whale we had struck.' – Bell, October.

[2] 'since our departure from King George 3rd Sound the Ship has been regularly set
6 or 7 Miles to the East & as much to the South, more than the Log will give.' – Baker,
27 October. The ships were under the influence of the Southern Ocean Current.

[3] The most southerly island of the Maatsuyker group, so named by Furneaux because
of a resemblance to the Mewstone at Plymouth.

[4] The courses and bearings given in this sentence are inaccurate and confusing and differ
from those recorded in several of the logs. Those kept by Baker and Puget show that the
text at this point should read: 'tacked and stood to the S.E.; the Mewstone bearing by
compass N. 88 E.'

[5] The South Cape is meant – a puzzling mistake, as several of the logs show that the
present South West Cape, the SW extremity of Tasmania, was correctly identified by that

or four leagues distant; land appearing like an island, N. 11 W. and the westernmost part of the main land N. 5 W. This land lies from the south-west cape N. 16 W. about nine leagues distant: between these points the coast seemed to be much broken, with some small islands lying a few miles from the shore. It was nearly calm during the night, and although within three or four leagues of the land, soundings could not be gained at the depth of 130 fathoms.

In the morning of Thursday the 27th we steered along the coast, with a fine breeze from N.N.W.; and about eight, under the meridian of the south-west cape,[1] the chronometer gave the longitude by the

last rate	-	-	-	-	-	-	-	-	146° 27' 0"
By the Cape rate	-	-	-	-	-	147	7	15
By the Portsmouth rate	-	-	-	-	146	8

The former, places the south-west cape 20' further east than the longitude assigned to it by Captain Cook. The chronometer placed the Swilly rock which we passed in the evening, according to the last rate, in longitude - - - - 147° 23' 30"[2]

According to the Cape rate   148   3   45

Portsmouth rate   147   2

By the last rate the chronometer was $17\frac{1}{2}'$ to the east of Captain Cook's longitude of this rock, and made the mean difference of the longitude of this coast, 18' 45" to the eastward of Captain Cook's calculations; whence it would appear, that either the chronometer had acquired that error since our departure from King George the Third's Sound, or that we had placed that port a few miles too far to the eastward. The nearest land at six in the evening, was the south cape of Van Dieman's,[3] which bore by compass N. 24 W. 6 or 7 leagues distant. Having now a fine gale at N.N.E. we took two reefs in the top-sails; shaped a course for Dusky Bay in New Zealand;[4] and by signal to the Chatham appointed Facile Harbour in that bay as the next place of rendezvous.[5]

name by other observers. The coast to which Vancouver refers in the next sentence runs W from South Cape, not from South West Cape, as he implies.

[1] Log entries show that the present South West Cape is meant; its long. is variously given as 145° 59' E and 146° 03' E.

[2] The correct position is long. 147° 13' E. The island, in lat. 43° 52' S, is the southernmost point of Australia. It was discovered in 1642 by Tasman, who named it Pedra Brancka after an island on the coast of China that he thought it resembled. Cook refers to it as Swilly Island. It is now generally referred to as Pedra Blanca.

[3] South East Cape is meant.

[4] Now Dusky Sound; discovered and named by Cook in March 1770.

[5] The change of plan was a disappointment to the ships' crews. 'This news was very unwelcome to us, who had flatter'd ourselves, (and not without some reason) that it was not improbable but we might go to Botany Bay – as it was no great deal out of our way; and a desire to see that place, which may in a few years be a flourishing Colony, was but

The dysentery, though nearly subdued on board both vessels, had left those who had been afflicted with it in a very feeble and reduced state; and not knowing of any place so easily within our reach, where such excellent refreshments could be procured with so much facility, together with timber for planks, spars, tent poles, &c. &c. of which we stood in great need, I was induced to make choice of Dusky Bay, notwithstanding the inconvenience it labours under from the great depth of water, and want of anchorage in its entrance.

A favorable wind, attended in general with tolerably fine weather, varied between the N. and W. and afterwards between the W. and S. with fresh gales, until Wednesday the 2d of November; when about nine in the forenoon we were brought within sight of the coast of New Zealand, bearing by compass E.N.E. 12 or 14 leagues distant. We stood for the land, making all sail with a fresh breeze at S.W.; but the weather was so exceedingly hazy, that it was one o'clock in the afternoon[1] before it was plainly distinguished; when Five Finger Point[2] was seen bearing by compass N. E. 7 leagues distant, and the west cape E. by N. ½ N. The wind in the evening veered round to the N.N.W. and being light, with alternate calms, the boats were hoisted out to tow; by which means, and with the additional assistance of a heavy swell rolling up Dusky Bay, we anchored about nine that evening in 40 fathoms soft bottom, in the arm leading into Facile Harbour. Five Finger Point by compass bore S. 38 W.; the west point of Parrot Island N. 35 E.; and the nearest shore W.N.W. half a mile distant. About eleven the Chatham anchored, and, though within us, was in 60 fathoms water.

Although in the year 1773 I had visited Dusky Bay with Captain Cook in the Resolution, I had never been in Facile Harbour;[3] for this reason I deemed it expedient, previous to moving the vessels, to examine and determine on a situation there most convenient for our several employments. On this occasion I was accompanied by Mr. Broughton and Mr. Whidbey. Having made our choice, we were greatly alarmed on our return by the report of two guns; but as the wind had much increased since our departure from the ships, we were not long at a loss how to account for this signal, and concluded that one or both of the vessels had driven from their anchorage.

We were no sooner clear of the islands than our conjectures were in part

natural.' – Bell, 25 October. Manby thought that weather conditions determined the decision: 'Capt. Vancouver originally intended to Wood and Water at Maria's Islands which lay a little to the Northward of Van Diemans Land, but the Wind for the last day or two had been baffling, settling in the NW we bore away for new Zealand.' – Letters, October.

[1] Misprinted 'forenoon' in the second edition.

[2] 'The north point of this bay...is very remarkable there being off it five high peaked rocks standing up like the four fingers and thum of a mans hand on which account I have named it *Point five fingers*.' – Cook, *Journals*, I, 264.

[3] Cook was in Dusky Sound from 26 March to 11 May 1773, but for almost the whole of this time the *Resolution* was anchored in Pickersgill Harbour, on the S side of the sound. Facile Harbour is on the NE shore.

confirmed. The Chatham was stationary, but the Discovery was moving; and by the time we reached her, about one o'clock, she was nearly abreast of Five Finger Point. We found that, on the ship's driving, a second anchor had been resorted to; but the depth of water being upwards of 70 fathoms, she was not brought up; that anchor was again at the bows, and the other nearly up; so that we were shortly enabled to set the sails; and, having a strong gale at the N.N.W. though attended with heavy squalls, I was not without hopes of reaching our destination in Facile Harbour before dusk. But about five, a very violent gust of wind carried away the strap of the fore-topsail sheet block; the staysail sheets and haulyards gave way; and the fore-topmast staysail split: the gale seemed to be increasing, and as we were in too narrow a channel to repair these damages before we should have lost all the distance we had gained, it was exceedingly fortunate that we had Anchor Island Harbour to leeward of us, for which we immediately steered; and running in by the western entrance, anchored at the mouth of the cove in 26 fathoms, soft muddy bottom; and after veering to half a cable, our stern was in 13 fathoms water, about 40 yards from the island that lies at the bottom of the cove. The ship was steadied by hawsers, from the bows to the points of the cove, and from the quarters to the trees on each side. The gale increased during the night; and it became necessary to strike the lower yards and top-gallant masts. Our apprehensions for the safety of the Chatham were not relieved until, by rowing over to the Petrel Islands[1] the next forenoon, Friday the 4th, and by walking across the land, we had the happiness to see her ride in perfect safety; but as she was directly to windward, and the gale continued to increase, Mr. Broughton was unable to get on board. Satisfied with the security of her station, we returned to the Discovery, when the violence of the gale from the N.W. obliged us to strike the topmasts, it not being in our power to veer more cable, or allow the ship to drive, without her being on the rocks astern; of which, even with these precautions, we entertained some fears; although in a situation perfectly land locked, and the weather shores not more than five cables length distant. The violence of the gale still continuing, the small bower anchor was dropped under foot. In the evening the wind moderated a little, which seemed to be for the sole purpose of acquiring and returning with new vigor, as, by two on Saturday morning the 5th, the gale increased to so violent a storm, as to oblige us to lower the top-masts close down to the cap, and to get our yards and top-gallant masts fore and aft on the deck. From five o'clock until eight, it blew a perfect hurricane, attended with torrents of rain. We were happily in a very snug, secure little harbour, yet the sea beat with such unremitting violence against the rocks immediately astern of us, that had either the anchor or cable given way, little else but inevitable destruction must have followed. Our anxiety was infinitely increased by our solicitude for the welfare of the Chatham; but as the storm with us at N.W. by W. was directly from off the high land under which she rode, we comforted ourselves with

---

[1] These islands shelter the bay that forms Anchor Island Harbour.

the hope she might not experience its fury to the degree it affected us. About nine a most tremendous gust caused the ship to roll excessively; this was immediately followed by a flash of lightning, and a heavy crash of thunder, which broke up the storm; and in the space of half an hour, the weather might be considered, comparatively speaking, as fair and pleasant. Mr. Broughton immediately repaired to the Chatham, and had the inexpressible pleasure of finding that she had rode out the gale in a manner far beyond all expectation. At her station the storm had blown from the N.N.E. directly down the arm in which she was at anchor; the sea broke intirely over her, though it had not a fetch of three miles, and in a channel not three quarters of a mile wide; yet with her yards and topmasts close lowered, and two anchors down, she rode out this heavy storm in perfect security.[1] Mr. Broughton lost no time in getting under weigh, and worked into Facile Harbour; to which place, notwithstanding our having been obliged to seek shelter here, it was my intention to have gone; but as we were now completely dismantled, and finding that from these shores all our wants could be conveniently supplied, I determined to remain quiet,[2] and to set about the several repairs we required with all possible dispatch. Parties were immediately employed on the different services of cutting wood for fuel, timber for spars and planks; brewing spruce beer; repairing the sails and rigging, casks, &c. &c. which necessary and essential duties engaged every person on board. A small boat with four men, daily employed in fishing, never returned without an abundance of excellent fish for present use, and a supply for every one who chose to salt them for future occasions. The N.W. gale did not intirely abandon us, it again blew with considerable violence on Sunday the 6th, after which it moderated, and the weather became settled, serene and pleasant, particularly when the wind, which was generally the case, had its direction from the south or western quarters; by which means our several duties were executed pleasantly and with great ease.

By Sunday the 13th, these necessary operations were in such a state of forwardness, as to allow a large party of officers and gentlemen in two boats, accompanied by Mr. Broughton in the Chatham's cutter, to attend me on an excursion over this spacious bay, with the hope of becoming acquainted with some of the inhabitants; and if circumstances permitted, to explore the upper part of the northern arm,[3] which by Capt. Cook was called, 'NO BODY KNOWS WHAT,' and the only part he did not thoroughly examine.

On Monday the 14th we found the arm in which Captain Cook places

---

[1] It was a more anxious time for those in the *Chatham* than this description suggests: 'All this day and night it blew dreadfully – and we expected every minute either to part our Cables or drive – but tho' the Squalls were as hard as many on board ever remember'd to have seen, we had but very little Sea with them.' – Bell, November.

[2] The separation of the ships was not popular with some of those on board: 'the distance precluded any intercourse between the young Gentlemen of the Vessels and in this dreary place their Society would have added much to each other's Comforts.' – Bell, November.

[3] Breaksea Sound.

Apparent Island,[1] to be divided into two branches, leaving that land a peninsula joined to the main land, by a very high, though narrow ridge of mountains. The perpendicular height, and very extraordinary shape, of the rocky part fronting the arm, render it a most singular and majestic promontory. Mr. Broughton undertook the right hand, or southern branch, which he found winding, first in a direction nearly N.E. by E. about $3\frac{1}{2}$ miles; then E.S.E. about half a league; and there, in a northern direction, terminating in a small cove. The northern arm we found to run nearly straight about N.E. for five miles, then turning round to the northward, for half a league further, and ending in a small cove with very shallow water, in a north western direction. The heads of these arms, in conformity with Captain Cook's name of their entrance, I have called SOME BODY KNOWS WHAT.[2] We were exceedingly fortunate in having most delightful weather for these examinations, and returned on board in the afternoon of Tuesday the 15th,[3] though not without some disappointment that, after three days excursion, and landing in many places, particularly in Cascade and Indian coves, which were formerly the resort of the natives, we no where found any traces of them, or any circumstance that in the least indicated the country being at present inhabited; if one or two miserable huts be excepted, which the officers of the Chatham met with in the neighbourhood of Facile Harbour, but which had not the appearance of having been lately occupied.[4] Pleasant weather still continuing, on Wednesay the 16th I took a survey of Anchor Island Harbour. It appeared to be perfectly secure, and may be found convenient, when accident may prevent vessels getting into Facile Harbour. It has two entrances; that to the north of the Petrel Islands is a fair and clear channel, though of great depth; its general soundings being from 33 to 38 fathoms; in the narrowest part it is about a cable's length wide, and, I believe, free from any danger; as the shores are steep, without any sunken rocks or shoals, excepting within the passage close under the south side of large Petrel Island, where they are

---

[1] This was not an island, but the promontory at the end of the peninsula that separates the two arms into which Breaksea Sound divides, and which Vancouver and Broughton were about to explore. It is now called Chatham Point.

[2] The two arms are now named Vancouver Arm and Broughton Arm after the officers who explored them.

[3] Despite the delightful weather, the expedition ended with an ordeal for the crew of the *Chatham's* cutter. Johnstone described the return to the ship: 'The evening falling moderate facilitated our passage over to the Chatham which some time before we had doubts of being able to accomplish that night against the wind which then blew pretty stiff, and the weariness of the boats crew which from four days incessant rowing they had become so feeble as to be scarcely able with their utmost exertions to keep the boats stem to the Sea. However by favour of the wind going down we arrived on board about Sunset.' – 14 November. Menzies describes the expedition in some detail, 12–15 November.

[4] Cook had seen several families of natives in Dusky Sound in 1773, and Menzies wondered if his gifts to them might have been the cause of their disappearance 'by affording a pretext for war to a more powerful tribe, ambitious to posess the riches he left them ...' – 21 November.

discoverable by the weeds growing upon them, and are quite out of the way of its navigation. The other passage is to the southward of the Petrel Islands; and as, in all probability, a strong northerly wind would alone induce any person to make choice of this in preference to Facile harbour, the S.W. point of large Petrel Island should be kept close on board, (which may be safely done) in order to weather the rock that appears above water in the middle of the harbour, and to avoid a sunken one of which there is not the least indication, and on which there is no greater depth than twelve feet at low water. Between this sunken rock, and the point from off which it lies about three quarters of a cable's length, and nearly in the direction to what I have called ENTRY ISLAND, are sixteen fathoms. Keeping the rock in the harbour, which is always visible, in a line with what I have called NORTH ENTRY ISLAND,[1] will be sufficient direction, to pass within the above-mentioned point and the sunken rock. This, however, with some other particulars, is better illustrated by the annexed sketch; which, with one of Facile Harbour taken by Mr. Broughton, I have subjoined to a copy of Captain Cook's most excellent chart of this port, with such trifling additions as in the course of our observations we have been able to make:[2] and on this head, I shall only further remark, that Anchor Island harbour, although a very safe and secure port, is not a very convenient one to get to sea from, owing to its narrow limits, great depth of water, and the above sunken rock which we discovered in its western entrance.

Most of our business with the shore being finished, our rigging overhauled, sails bent, and the ship ready for sea, with very fine weather and a gentle breeze from S.S.E., on the morning of Friday the 18th we sailed out of the cove. The Chatham was not yet in readiness to depart; in order, however, that we might be conveniently stationed to proceed together when circumstances should admit, I intended to place the ship abreast of Facile Harbour; but the breeze failing, and the tide setting us towards the islands that lie from it, we were obliged to anchor sooner than I wished in 38 fathoms soft bottom. Five Finger Point by compass bore S. 40 W.; west point of Anchor Island S. 12 W. and the south point of Parrot Island[3] N. 53 W. a quarter of a mile distant. The day was nearly calm, but the next morning brought with it a fresh breeze from the southward. The Chatham having completed her business, stood out into the roadstead, which obtained the name of TEMPEST ROAD,[4] from the storm she there rode out on our arrival: but not seeing any probability of getting to sea, she returned into Facile Harbour. The gale increased towards noon, but in the evening the weather became delightfully pleasant.

[1] The small island SW of the Petrel Islands is now called Entry Island, but there is now no North Entry Island.

[2] The two sketches, together with one of Pickersgill Harbour and the revised version of Cook's chart, are all insets on Vancouver's chart of the SW coast of New Holland. Menzies records that when the survey of the two arms at the end of Breaksea Sound was completed 'we drank a cheerful glass to the memory of Capt. Cook'. – 14 November.

[3] The name has been retained.

[4] Unfortunately this attractive name has not survived.

On the morning of Sunday the 20th, about seven o'clock, a fresh breeze from the S.W. set in, accompanied by an unusually heavy swell, which giving us reason to apprehend some violence from the wind in that direction, we weighed, ran into Facile Harbour, and anchored abreast of the passage leading out through Parrot and Pigeon islands,[1] in 38 fathoms soft bottom. This passage, though not exceeding a cable's length in width, we found to be a very excellent one, with soundings from nine to five fathoms close to the shores. These soundings are on a ridge from island to island, as the water deepened to upwards of 30 fathoms immediately on either side. The Chatham was at anchor near us, and both vessels were conveniently stationed for proceeding to sea on a favorable opportunity presenting itself. The wind continued to blow very strong from the S.W. and brought with it a surf which broke very heavily on the shores in the bay; yet the vessels rode perfectly quiet. On Monday the 21st, the sky became intirely obscured, with dark gloomy weather,[2] and the wind became variable with much rain. The next morning was perfectly calm, and although it did not rain, the heavy atmosphere continued. We were now employed in completing our stock of water, and in procuring wood, spruce, or rather a species of cypress, and the tea plant, for brewing at sea.[3] Towards noon, a breeze springing up from the N.W. both vessels sailed out of Dusky Bay. A very heavy swell rolled from the S.W. and westward; but having a fresh breeze, by four o'clock Five Finger Point bore N. by E. a league distant.

Thus we quitted Dusky Bay, greatly indebted to its most excellent refreshments, and the salubrity of its air. The good effects of a plentiful supply of fish, and spruce beer, were evident in the appearance of every individual in our little society. The health of our convalescents was perfectly re-established, and excepting one with a chronic complaint, and two wounded by cuts in their legs, we had not a man on the surgeon's list; though, on the most trifling occasion of indisposition, no person was ever permitted to attend his duty. Some wild fowl were procured,[4] though they were by no means found in

[1] The two islands on the S side of Facile Harbour. Pigeon Island is wrongly spelled 'Pidgeon' Island on Vancouver's chart of the harbour.

[2] The first edition reads: 'the former serenity gave place to dark gloomy weather'.

[3] The 'spruce...or cypress' was the rimu, and the tea plant the manuka. Cook recorded his experience of brewing at Dusky Sound: 'I have already made mention of our brewing Beer which we at first made with a decoction of the leaves of the spruce tree mixed with Inspissated juce of Wort and Mellasses but finding that the decoction of Spruce alone made the Beer to astringent we mixed with it an equal quantity of the Tea plant which partly destroyed the Astringency of the other and made the Beer exceeding Palatable and esteemed by every one on board.' – Journals, II, 137. He went on to describe the brewing process in some detail. 'Our Spruce Beer,' Bell noted, 'which was made after the directions given by Capn. Cook prov'd excellent and was served out to the Ship's Company in lieu of Spirits.' – November. Baker considered it 'the best Beer of the Spruce kind I ever tasted.' – 22 November.

[4] Some of the hunting methods were unusual: 'the way we managed with the Parrots was by first endeavouring only to wound one, whose noise soon brought numbers to the spot; – had we had more ammunition we might have shot a hundred Parrots in a very little time.' – Bell, November.

The ISLAND of OPARO in Lat.^{de} 27°.36' S.th Long.^{de} 219° E.^t or 141° W.^t Variety.. Isolena.. 7 Miles

Plate 18. 'The Island of Oparo [now Rapa Island].'

The entrance of *PORT CHATHAM COOK'S INLET in Lat.ᵈᵉ 59°1'N.ᵗʰ Long.ᵗᵘᵈᵉ 209°3'E bour'from N.50°E to N.24°E the 4 Mile Var.ᵗⁿ 25°15'E.*

T.Boddington

Plate 19. 'The entrance of Port Chatham Cook's Inlet.'

such numbers as when the Resolution was here in the year 1773, owing, in all probability, to the difference of the season; to which, possibly, is to be ascribed, our being unable to ascertain whether the geese then left here had propagated.

Captain Cook's very excellent description of this place precludes any material additions;[1] and leaves me, as a transitory visitor, little else than the power of confirming his judicious remarks and opinions. One circumstance, however, may not be unworthy of notice. Mr. Menzies here found the true winter's bark; exactly the same plant as that found at Tierra del Fuego; but which escaped the observation of Captain Cook and our botanical gentlemen in 1773: of this, with the antarctic birch, flax, and one or two other plants, we took specimens on board, though the period of our reaching England seemed too distant to entertain hopes of their continuing alive.[2] Captain Cook's recommendation of Facile Harbour to vessels bound to the southward, is highly judicious, as it is in all respects a safe, commodious, and convenient station; capable of supplying every article that can be expected from this country, without going out of sight of the vessel: and it is rendered still more eligible, by our having found so good an outlet with northerly or N.W. winds, between Pigeon and Parrot islands; as, in consequence of the high land drawing those winds directly down the harbour, the western entrance will be found less convenient. No time should be lost on arriving in this bay, to seek security in some of its harbours: which, as Captain Cook very truly observes, 'are numerous, safe, and convenient.'[3] For although the weather we experienced after the storm on our arrival, may justly be considered as delightful summer weather, yet it cannot be denied that the northerly winds blow with incredible fury; and as they always take the direction of the arms of the bay, they cause in them, though they are very narrow, a considerable sea, which, in addition to their great depth of water, render such anchoring

[1] Vancouver does not mention the sand flies that Cook had found 'so troublesome that they exceed every thing of the kind I ever met with.' – *Journals*, II, 136. Bell commented: 'we [did not] see any living thing on shore except the Birds and a small Sand fly but this annoy'd us more than perhaps fifty animals wou'd for no sooner did we set our feet on shore that [sic] we were cover'd with those Flys, and their Sting is as painful as that of a Musquitto, and made us Scratch as if we had got the itch – indeed one of my Legs became so much swell'd by this means, that I was forced to apply a poultice to it and was lame for two or three days.' – November.

[2] 'I...was not a little pleasd to meet with pretty large trees of the *Wintera aromatica*...' 'I brought with me live plants...which were planted in the frame on the quarter deck.' – Menzies, 9 and 17 November. He had had good hunting in Dusky Sound; earlier he 'made an excursion into the woods & met with a vast variety of Ferns & Mosses I had never before seen. These are two tribes of plants of which I am particularly fond, therefore no one can conceive the pleasure I enjoyed unless placed under similar circumstances. I returned on board in the afternoon loaded with my treasures...' – 4 November.

[3] Cook's actual words in his journal are: 'The worst that attends it [Dusky Sound] is the depth of Water which is too great to admit of anchorage except in the Coves or Harbours and near the shores and even in many places this last is not to be done, the anchoring places are however numerous enough and equally safe and commodious.' – *Journals*, II, 131.

places neither pleasant nor secure. I should not, however, suppose these storms to be very frequent, for two reasons. First, during our stay here, from the 26th of March until the 11th of May in the year 1773, which may be considered as comprehending part of the winter season, we had no gale of wind comparable in point of violence to that which we had lately experienced. This was my fifth visit to New Zealand[1] and its neighbourhood; and although I have certainly seen much boisterous and tempestuous weather, I never before contended with so violent a storm. Secondly, the mountains in Anchor Island, Resolution Island, and all those of moderate height round the Bay (the land of Five Finger Point alone excepted), which on our arrival were perfectly free from snow, were after the storm covered with it a considerable way down. Were such falls of snow to happen frequently, it is natural to conclude that vegetation would be severely checked, and that its productions would not have been found to flourish, as they certainly do in a most luxuriant manner. A few days fine weather soon removed the greater part of the snow; and that which remained on the high, distant, barren mountains, which for some days past had been entirely free from clouds, was observed to be greatly diminished.

I shall conclude our transactions in Dusky Bay, by noticing the few astronomical and nautical observations that were made in Anchor Island Harbour.

The badness of the weather on our first arrival, and the short time I purposed to remain, made me conclude that the erection of the observatory on shore would be to little purpose. The latitude of the harbour was found to be one minute south of Captain Cook's calculation, or 45° 45′ 36″.[2] His determination is, however, most likely to be correct, as mine was deduced from one day's observation only, with an artificial horizon; and, having agreed so nearly, any further investigation I deemed unnecessary.

The mean result of ten sets of altitudes taken between the 9th and 16th of November, for ascertaining the longitude of the chronometer, and to form some judgment as to its rate of going, were as follows, viz.

By the Portsmouth rate it placed Anchor Island Harbour in longitude	166° 42′ 23″
By the Cape rate	167° 55′ 12″
By King George the Third's Sound rate	167° 7′ 40″
The true longitude as assigned to that place by Captain Cook	166° 15′ 54″
Makes the Portsmouth rate east of the truth	26′ 29″
Cape rate ditto	1° 39′ 18″

---

[1] On Cook's second voyage, on which he served in the *Resolution*, Vancouver had visited Dusky Sound in March–May 1773 and Queen Charlotte Sound in November 1773 and again in October 1774. In the *Discovery*, on the third voyage, he was in Queen Charlotte Sound in February 1777. This was his fifth visit to New Zealand, but only his second to Dusky Sound.

[2] The position of Anchor Island is lat. 45° 46′ S, long. 166° 31′ E.

King George the Third's Sound ditto   51' 46"
Mr. Arnold's watch on board the Chatham gave the
longitude of Facile Harbour, according to the Cape
rate   165° 48' 52"[1]

Esteeming the true longitude of Anchor Island harbour to be 166° 15' 54",
the chronometer was fast of mean time at Greenwich on the 16th at noon
26' 34"; whence it appeared, that it had gone nearly at mean time since leaving
King George the Third's Sound, and that its having differed from Captain
Cook's assigned longitude of Van Dieman's land was occasioned by its not
having gained at the rate we allowed, and of course the longitude of King
George the Third's Sound was not wrong. By the result of our observations
here, it gained on an average about 3" per day, which error I shall allow, until
a better opportunity of ascertaining its rate may offer.

The variation of the magnetic needle, observed on shore by three different
compasses in 18 sets of azimuths, varied from 11° 17' to 17° 26', the mean
result of which was 14° 55' 45" east variation. The vertical inclination of the
south point of the magnetic needle on board was found to be—

Marked end	North, face East,	70° 3'
Ditto	North, face West,	69 8
Ditto	South, face East,	70 5
Ditto	South, face West,	69 35

Mean inclination of the south point of the dipping
needle   69 43

As we increased our distance from the land, the N.W. wind increased also.
A swell at this time coming very heavily from the S.W. made me apprehensive
the wind would shift round, and blow hard in that direction. The state of
the mercury in the barometer, the gloominess of the weather, and every other
appearance of the evening, indicated more wind from the S.W. than would
be pleasant to be caught in on this dreary coast: we therefore steered south
under as much sail as we could carry, and made the necessary signals to the
Chatham for the like purpose. Our lofty canvass was, however, spread a very
short time before it blew so hard a gale, that we were under the necessity
of close reefing the topsails, getting down the top-gallant yards, and striking
the masts. The night was extremely dark; which, by ten, prevented our seeing
the Chatham. The wind was now at N.N.W. very happily not on the shore,
as by three in the morning of Wednesday the 23d its increased violence obliged
us to furl the topsails. At this moment we were alarmed by finding six feet
water in the hold, which the ship felt excessively. labouring much by being
pressed down forward with that weight of water. This very unpleasant
circumstance obliged us to scud directly before the wind and sea, for the
purpose of freeing the ship; when, by receiving much water in the waste, the
casks of beer and water stowed upon deck, broke from their securities and
were stove to pieces The cause of so much water in the hold, at first a matter

---

[1] Facile Harbour is in lat. 45° 42' S, long. 166° 34' E.

of great surprize, was soon accounted for. The hand pumps had been, and were still, choaked; which induced the carpenter to believe, that because they discharged no water there was none in the ship.[1] This, in all probability had governed his examination all the latter part of the time we had been in port, and produced an accumulation that might have been attended with the most serious consequences, had not one of the quarter-masters heard in the tier, the water rushing about in the hold. The hand pumps were soon in order; and, to relieve the ship as soon as possible, the cross piece of the bits was unshipped, the launch got forward, and with the chain pumps the vessel by seven o'clock was made perfectly dry. The gale had now increased to a most furious storm, nearly equal to that we had experienced in Dusky Bay. The torrents of rain which fell, mixing with the sea raised by the violent flurries of the wind, kept us so much in darkness that we could not perceive any thing at the distance of an hundred yards in any direction; nor were we able to resume our southwardly course; the wind and sea obliging us to steer S.S.E. or right before the storm. We had not seen the Chatham since eleven o'clock the preceding evening, but concluding she would stand on if able to pursue a southwardly course, I did not wish to bring to for her; particularly, as the wind was such as would soon set us clear of the coast of New Zealand which was doubtless a very desirable object.

Towards nine in the forenoon of Thursday the 24th the storm began to abate; at ten the wind veered round to the W.S.W.; the rain ceased, and the atmosphere became clear, but the Chatham was not to be discovered in any direction. There was, however, great probability of her being to windward; and as I was still apprehensive of a S.W. gale before we should be clear of this coast, I determined to lose no time in getting far enough to the southward to enable us to sail round the land and the Traps with such a wind. As Matavai bay in Otaheite[2] was the next appointed rendezvous, I concluded Mr. Broughton would do the same, and make the best of his way with the Chatham to that port. The mainsail and close-reefed topsails (all the sail the ship would bear) were now set, and keeping the wind on the beam, we steered S.S.E.; when about eleven o'clock, to our great astonishment, land was

---

[1] Manby gives additional details. In the midst of the storm the *Discovery* 'refused every movement of the Helm – in this critical moment, I was sent below and to my astonishment found seven feet water in the hold, this unwelcome report roused every man to his exertions.' When it was found that the pumps were reducing the water level 'it was likewise soon found that this immensity of Water had not proceeded from a leak in her bottom, but had forced its way through the tarpaulins at each Hatchway, as the Main Deck was three feet deep with Water. between each Gun we had Puncheons of Spruce Beer and Water the whole of them broke adrift and were working from side to side until they were stove. it was some time before this was affected, as they threaten'd destruction to any that approached them.' – Letters, 23 November.

[2] Tahiti, discovered by Wallis in 1767. 'From the two words, *o Tahiti*, signifying "it is Tahiti", which a native would have said in responding to the question, "What land is this?" these explorers made a natural mistake in writing the name of the island "Otaheiti"...' – Teuira Henry, *Ancient Tahiti* (Honolulu, 1928), 11.

discovered, bearing east four or five leagues distant. We knew of no land nearer than the south cape of New Zealand; and, by the courses we had steered there was scarcely a possibility of our being within less than 18 or 20 leagues of the Cape: but being flattered with the prospect of a meridional observation for the latitude, our decision was postponed until that should be ascertained. Noon brought us nearer the land, which by compass bore from N.E. by E. to E.N.E. at the distance of three or four leagues only. By a tolerably good observation in latitude 48° 5' it was clearly proved, that this land could not, from its situation, be any part of New Zealand, as it was nearly three fourths of a degree to the southward of the most southern promontary of that country. Our longitude by the chronometer, was at this time 166° 4'; which situation was 18' more south, and 13' more east, than the log gave. The weather, though very hazy, being something clearer than before noon, we beheld, as we passed this land at the distance of two or three leagues, the sea breaking upon its shores with great violence, and discovered it to be composed of a cluster of seven craggy islands, extending about six miles in a direction N. 70 E. and S. 70 W. They appeared destitute of verdure, and it is more than probable they never produce any. The largest, which is the northeasternmost, I should suppose to be in extent equal to all the rest; it is about three leagues in circuit, sufficiently elevated to be seen in clear weather eight or nine leagues off, and is situated in latitude 48° 3', longitude 166° 20'.[1] The latitude was ascertained by three sextants which nearly agreed; and the longitude reduced by the chronometer from Dusky Bay, by three sets of altitudes in the afternoon; viz. one set before we passed its meridian; another under it; the third after we had passed it. As these severally corresponded within a mere trifle, when reduced to the same point, I should presume that the longitude above stated is not likely to be materially incorrect. It was matter of some surprize how these islands could have escaped the attention of Captain Cook; but on laying them down in his chart of New Zealand, I found his tracks had not at any time reached within at least ten leagues of them. From the south cape they bear S. 40 E. 19 leagues, and from the southernmost part of the Traps S. 62½ W. 20 leagues distant. These islands, or rather rocks, for they appeared perfectly steril, I have named, on account of their situation, and the sort of weather there is great reason to expect in their vicinity, THE SNARES; as being very likely to draw the unguarded mariner into alarming difficulties.[2] At four o'clock in the afternoon, the Snares bore by compass N. 30 W. five or six

[1] The position of the Snares is given as lat. 48° 01' S, long. 166° 35' E.
[2] Vancouver undoubtedly had a Cook precedent in mind when choosing the name. On 9 March 1770 Cook discovered a ledge of rock and others soon came in sight: 'as we pass'd these rocks in the night at no great distance and discover'd the others close under our lee at day light it is apparent that we had a very fortunate escape. I have named them the *Traps* because they lay as such to catch unwary strangers.' —*Journals*, I, 261. 'As these were now considered a new discovery, they were called the *Snares*, a name sufficiently applicable to their lurking situation & appearance, & will we hope induce any vessel bound this way to give them a good birth.' – Menzies, 23 November.

leagues distant. At day-light the next morning, Friday the 25th, we hauled to the N.E. By noon, the gale had sufficiently moderated to admit the spreading of all our canvass; at noon the observed latitude was 48° 18', longitude 169° 33'. I cannot avoid here mentioning the concern I felt in beholding the last of our sheep thrown overboard; the race of animals of the brute creation on board the Discovery, had certainly been very ill fated; out of thirty sheep taken on board at Portsmouth, no more than two came to the table, the rest died before we reached the equator; nor were we much more fortunate in the like number of wethers received at the Cape; two thirds of these, with seven ewes and six rams, intended as presents to our friends in the South Sea islands, were at this time dead; notwithstanding they were all taken on board in exceedingly high condition, and had neither wanted care, plenty of wholesome food, nor good lodging.[1]

With a pleasant favorable gale; sometimes in the N.W. but chiefly from the S.W. quarter, and with tolerably fine weather, we stood to the E.N.E.; and made such progress, that by noon on the 8th of December we had reached the latitude of 37° 27', longitude 207° 14'. The wind veered round to the north with a moderate breeze, attended by dark gloomy weather and some rain. On Saturday the 10th we were surrounded by a very thick fog, which, with much rain at intervals, continued until Tuesday the 13th; when having a fine breeze at S.S.W. the fog cleared away, but it still remained very cloudy. We were however enabled to ascertain our situation for the first time since the 8th, to be in latitude 36° 13', longitude 214° 33', varying since that day 53' more to the north, and 28' more to the east, than was shewn by the log. We stood to the north, under all the sail we could spread, but were not suffered long to pursue this course. In the latitude of 31° 43', longitude 214° 11', at noon on Thursday the 15th the wind veered round, and settled between the N.E. and N.N.E. obliging us to ply with a moderate breeze to the northward; in doing which so little was gained, that on Saturday the 17th we had only reached the latitude of 31° 8', longitude 214° 34'. The wind now blew a fresh gale from the north, the topsails were reefed, the weather was very dark, gloomy, and excessively sultry, with continued lightning and thunder at some distance, until the morning, when the wind died away, and in its stead, extremely vivid forked lightning, with incessant peals of thunder, accompanied by torrents of rain, attended us, without intermission, until noon of Sunday the 18th. The thunder and lightning then ceased, but the rain still continued; and, contrary to our expectation, the wind resumed its N.N.E. direction, and blew so hard as to make the striking our top-gallant yards necessary. A remarkably smooth sea, with heavy, damp, close, cloudy weather, and little

---

[1] Hewett charges that 'The Sheep were in the Long Boat where they were Constantly wet.' Johnstone notes that when the *Chatham* left False Bay 'The Launch was filled with eighteen Sheep we had taken in here.' Most of them soon perished in stormy weather. – Johnstone, 21 August and 2 September. Open boats on deck would not seem to be described properly as 'good lodging'.

alteration in the wind, attended us until Tuesday the 20th; it then moderated, and the top-gallant sails were spread.

Since the 17th we had not obtained any correct observations; but, by our reckoning, the latitude at noon was 30° 17', longitude 215° 22'. Although the wind from the north and N.N.E. was attended with sudden and violent flurries, yet the sea continued smooth, which indicated, that land, probably of some extent, existed not very far distant in that direction. After noon, we stood to the eastward about four leagues: when, suddenly, a very heavy swell was met from N.N.E. which was soon followed by such an increase of wind from that quarter, as reduced us to our close-reefed topsails. This gale, which proved the breaking up of the northerly wind, was of short duration: in the evening it moderated, and veered round by the east to the S.S.W. We made all sail to the north by west; but it was not until the wind became a very fresh breeze, that we were enabled to steer that course against the northerly swell, which drove the ship astern. This evening there were several small white tern hovering about the ship, seemingly with great inclination to alight on board. On the morning of Wednesday the 21st, the head sea had for the most part subsided, and the wind seemed to have settled in the southern quarter: and blowing a gentle breeze with very pleasant weather, enabled me to obtain six sets of lunar distances, whose mean result reduced to noon gave the longitude 215° 22' 45". The chronometer, by the last rate shewed 215° 16' 45", the latitude was 29° 15'; which was, at this time, 6' further north than we expected.

We continued our route to the northward; which, with a gentle gale at S.S.E. and pleasant weather, brought us, by day-light on Thursday the 22d, in sight of land, bearing by compass N.E. ½ N. At first it appeared like three small high islands, the easternmost much resembling a vessel under sail. This land being at a considerable distance from the tracks of former navigators, I steered for it, in order to be satisfied of its extent, productions, and other circumstances worthy observation, In the forenoon, eight sets of lunar distances were obtained: which, as before, nearly corresponding with each other, gave, by their mean result, when reduced to noon, 215° 42' 40", these, with those taken the preceding day, comprehending 14 sets of distances, gave 215° 39'. The latitude, by several sextants, was determined to be 27° 54'.

Since seeing the land in the morning, we had run eleven leagues; and had approached it sufficiently near to perceive, that all we had at first seen was united. It now bore, by compass, from N. 29 E. to N. 43 E. about five leagues distant, with a small island lying off its eastern side N. 45 E.

Assisted by a gentle S.E. gale, with fine pleasant weather, at three in the afternoon we were within about a league of the shore; yet no bottom was to be gained at the depth of 180 fathoms. Several canoes came off to the ship, and all means were used to invite them on board. They declined our entreaties, but seemed very solicitous that we should accept their invitations to land: which they signified by waving their paddles towards the coast, and by desiring us, in the language of the Great South-Sea nation, to go nearer to the shore. We bore away with that intent, but soon again brought to, on observing that two or three canoes were paddling in great haste towards the ship. After some persuasion, four men in one of the canoes came near enough to receive some presents, which seemed to please them exceedingly; and though their countrymen appeared to rebuke them for their rashness, the example was shortly followed by several others. It was not, however, without shewing every demonstration of friendship, that any could be prevailed upon to come on board, until at length, the man who had brought about this intercourse seemed determined to establish it, by complying with our desires. On his entering the ship, he trembled and was much agitated; apprehension, astonishment, and admiration, equally appearing at the same instant; and though, on his being made welcome after the usual fashion,[1] and presented with a small iron adz, his countenance became more serene and cheerful, yet he still appeared in a state of great anxiety. He soon communicated his reception and treatment to his surrounding countrymen; and we shortly had as many visitors as it was pleasant to entertain. They all seemed perfectly well acquainted with the uses to which they could apply iron, and how to estimate its value amongst themselves; as also the manner in which it was regarded by Europeans. They made no scruple, even with some force, to take articles of iron out of our hands;[2] and, in lieu of them, with great courtesy and address presented, in return, some few fish, fishing-hooks, lines, and other trifles, which they seemed to wish should be accepted as presents, and not received in exchange.[3] Looking-glasses, beads, and other trinkets of little importance, at first attracted their attention, and were gladly accepted; but no sooner did they discover that articles made of iron were common amongst us, than they refused all other presents, and wanted to barter every other gift for iron. I could not prevail on any of them to accept a few medals.

Their visit seemed prompted only by curiosity,[4] as they were completely

[1] 'One man after much intreaty came on board [and was] embraced agreeable to the fashion of the Society Island by touching noses with the Captain.' – Manby, Letters, 22 December.

[2] 'The belaying pins on the quarter deck, the hook & eyes about the guns & rigging & every thing about the Forge particularly attracted their roving eyes & hands which incessantly moved about with the utmost rapidity. One of them seeing an Anchor laying on the forecastle attempted to take it up with the same strength he would apply to a piece of timber of an equal bulk & appeared much surprized when he could not move it.' – Menzies, 22 December. They were attracted to 'the Iron ringbolts attempting to tear them out of the Deck and Sides. others tried to carry the Guns from their carriages while others dragg'd at the Anchors with the utmost fury, expressing their rage they could not move them.... For dexterity in thieving, few can equal them, however concealing the Stolen Articles put their abilities to the test being destitute of any kind of Cloathing.' – Manby, Letters, 22 December.

[3] 'They had not the least Idea of Barter. Whatever you ask'd them for, they gave with cheerfulness. At the same time, Thieving every thing that could be got at'. – Mudge, December 24.

[4] Hewett noted that 'They opened our Shirt bosoms to see if any Women were among us.'

unarmed, and brought with them (except the few fish, &c.)[1] neither articles of food, nor manufacture. A few spears, and a club or two, were seen in one or two of the canoes only; two or three indifferent slings for stones were also noticed; with which they parted without the least reluctance.

We lay to until five o'clock in the hope of obtaining the name of this island, or of any other which might exist in its neighbourhood. These people were evidently of the Great South-Sea nation; speaking, with some little difference of dialect, the same language; and resembling the Friendly islanders, more than the inhabitants of any other country. On this occasion, *Towereroo* the Sandwich islander was of little assistance; having been taken at an early period from home, and having been long absent, he had so much forgotten his mother tongue, as to be scarcely able to understand the language of these people better than ourselves. Two or three of them remained on board nearly an hour; but so unfixed and unsteady was their attention, which wandered from object to object, that it was impossible to gain from them any information. Their answers to almost every question were in the affirmative; and our enquiries as to the name of their island, &c. were continually interrupted by incessant invitations to go on shore. At length, I had reason to believe the name of the island was Oparo;[2] and that of their chief *Korie*. Although I could not positively determine that these names were correctly ascertained, yet as there was a probability of their being so, I distinguished the island by the name of OPARO, until it might be found more properly entitled to another. By six in the evening, we had nearly seen round the island, which is of little extent; and not choosing to lose the advantage of a fine southwardly wind, we proceeded to the N.N.W. under all the sail we could spread.

As it was not my intention to stop at Oparo, no delay was occasioned by examining for anchorage, which probably may be found on both sides of its N.W. point. To the southward of that point is a small bay with a stony beach, through which there was the appearance of a considerable stream of water falling into the sea. The shores in most parts were so perfectly smooth, that landing might have been effected without the least difficulty. Round to the north of that point is another small bay, in which are a small islet and some rocks; behind these, the shore may be approached with great ease at any time. Indeed, there was not any part of the island which appeared to have been acted upon by heavy violent surfs, as the verdure in many places reached to the water's edge. The south extremity of the island appeared in some points of view to form a right angle, without the least interruption in the sides; about half a mile to the south-east is a small detached islet; the shores are interspersed with sandy beaches; its greatest extent, which is in a N. 18 W. and S. 18 E. direction, is about six miles and a half, and it may possibly be about eighteen miles in circuit. This island is situated in the latitude of 27° 36′; and, by our lunar observations of the two preceding days reduced to its centre by the

---

[1] The words in parentheses were added in the second edition.
[2] Now Rapa Island

chronometer, is in longitude★ 215° 58′ 28″;[1] the mean of the variation was 5° 40′ eastwardly.

Its principal character is a cluster of high craggy mountains, forming in several places, most romantic pinnacles, with perpendicular cliffs nearly from their summits to the sea; the vacancies between the mountains would more probably be termed chasms than vallies, in which there was no great appearance of plenty, fertility or cultivation; they were chiefly clothed with shrubs and dwarf trees. Neither the plantain,[2] nor other spontaneous vegetable productions common to the inhabited tropical islands, presented themselves. The tops of six of the highest hills bore the appearance of fortified places, resembling redoubts; having a sort of block house, in the shape of an English glass house, in the centre of each, with rows of pallisadoes a considerable way down the sides of the hills, nearly at equal distances. These, overhanging, seemed intended for advanced works, and apparently capable of defending the citadal by a few against a numerous host of assailants. On all of them we noticed people, as if on duty, constantly moving about.[3] What we considered as block houses, from their great similarity in appearance to that sort of building, were sufficiently large to lodge a considerable number of persons, and were the only habitations we saw. Yet from the number of canoes that in so short a time assembled around us, it is natural to conclude that the inhabitants are very frequently afloat, and to infer from this circumstance that the shores, and not those fortified hills which appeared to be in the center of the island, would be preferred for their general residence. We saw about thirty double and single canoes, though most of them were of the double sort: the single canoes were supported by an outrigger on one side, and all built much after the fashion of the Society Islands, without having their very high sterns, though the sterns of some of these were considerably elevated; and their bows were not without some little ornament. They were very neatly constructed, though the narrowest canoes I ever saw. When it is considered that the builders of them are nearly destitute of iron, and possessed of very few implements of that valuable metal; and when the miserable tools they have generally recourse to for such operations are regarded, the mind is filled with admiration at their ingenuity, and persevering industry. The island did not appear to afford any large timber; the broadest planks of which the canoes were made, not

★ Vide Astronomical observations at Otaheite.

[1] Rapa Island is in lat. 27° 35′ S, long. 144° 25′ W (215° 35′ E). A sketch of the part of its coastline seen by Vancouver is an inset on his chart of the SW coast of New Holland.

[2] Misprinted 'plantation' in the second edition.

[3] Vancouver's surmise was correct. For a description of the fortified villages and a photograph see Peter H. Buck, *Vikings of the Pacific* (Chicago, 1959), p. 183. Hewett made them an excuse to retail a derogatory remark about Vancouver. He states that the fortifications 'were by some supposed to be Erected by the Bounty's people [the mutineers] who also Imagined that this deterred Captn. Vancouver from running in and Anchoring As had they been found there he would have been under the necessity of Engaging and taking them but the greater probability is that they were like the Hippahs of New Zealand and Erected by the Natives.'

exceeding twelve inches, confirmed us in this opinion, as they were probably cut out of the largest trees. Some of the stoutest double canoes accommodated from twenty-five to thirty men, of whom, on a moderate computation, three hundred were supposed to have been seen near the ship. These were all adults, and apparently none exceeding a middle-age; so that the total number of inhabitants on the island can hardly be estimated at less than fifteen hundred. In this respect it must be considered prolific, notwithstanding its uncultivated appearance. The natives, however, appeared to be exceedingly well fed, of middling stature, extremely well made; and in general, their countenances were open, cheerful, and strongly marked with indications of hospitality. They were all, to a man, very solicitous that some of us should accompany them to the shore; and those who last quitted the ship, endeavoured with all their powers of persuasion, and some efforts of compulsion, to effect their purpose. On their departure they took hold of the hand of every one near them, with a view to get them into their canoe. They all had their hair cut short; and, excepting a wreath made of a broad long-leaved green plant, worn by some about the waist, they were intirely without clothing. Although the custom of tatowing prevails so generally with all the islanders of this ocean, these people were destitute of any such marks.

Independent of the protection their fortified retreats may afford, it did not appear that they were subject to much hostility, as scarcely any scars from wounds or other marks of violence were observed on their bodies. Their elevated fortified places (for certainly they had every appearance of being such) led some of us to conjecture, that they were frequently annoyed by troublesome neighbours from some other islands not far distant. But, as the canoes we saw were not even furnished with sails,[1] nor had any appearance of having been ever equipped for an expedition beyond their own coast, it may reasonably be inferred, that they were not accustomed to voyages of any length. Yet, on the other hand, when the small extent of their island is taken into consideration, it is hard to reconcile that it is not the fear of foreign enemies, but the apprehension of domestic insurrection, that has induced the laborious construction of their fortified retreats; and as to the S.E. of this island there is an extensive space in the ocean hitherto but little frequented; it is not improbable that some islands may exist there, the inhabitants of which may occasionally make unfriendly visits to these people.

Leaving Oparo, we had pleasant weather with a gentle breeze from the S.E. At eight in the morning of Friday the 23d, the island was still visible from the deck, bearing by compass S.S.E. ½ E. at the distance of 18 leagues. The breeze between E. and S.E. carried us rapidly to the N.N.W. and brought us on the evening of Sunday the 25th into the vicinity of some low islands discovered by Captain Carteret, and named the Duke of Gloucester's islands. The evening was dark and gloomy, and not choosing to pass the spot assigned to them in the night, we continued to make short trips under our top-sails,

[1] Menzies states that they 'had also double canoes with Sails'. – December 22.

until daylight; after which we again resumed our course. Our latitude at noon of Monday the 26th was 19° 58', longitude 211° 46', which was 9' further south, and 23' further west, than was shewn by the log. At about 1° 33' to the west of the situation of the Duke of Gloucester's islands according to Captain Carteret, we passed their latitude,[1] without seeing any appearance of land. Having now a fresh gale at east, we entertained the pleasing hope of reaching Otaheite the next day; this flattering prospect was of short duration. Towards the evening, the wind veered to the N.E. and its violence obliged us to close reef the top-sails. The gale was attended with very heavy squalls, and a torrent of rain continued almost without intermission until the evening of Wednesday the 28th, when it ceased, and the wind still at N.E. became moderate. By standing on to the N.N.W. day-light the next morning, Thursday the 29th, presented us with a view of Matavai,[2] or Osnaburgh island, at the distance of seven or eight leagues, bearing by compass N.E. by E. Our course was immediately shaped for Otaheite, the south point of which was visible by eleven o'clock, bearing by compass S. 70 W. eight or nine leagues distant. The wind coming to the north prevented our reaching Matavai Bay, and obliged us to ply to windward during the night. In the morning of Friday the 30th, with a gentle breeze from the N.E. we stood for Matavai under all the sail we could spread. About eight o'clock, a canoe came alongside with two pigs and some vegetables; a present from a sister of Otoo, residing in that part of the island of which we were then abreast. The natives informed me that we had been expected, and that they had been looking out for us two days, in consequence of information they said they had received from an English vessel, then at anchor in Matavai Bay; and their description of her being perfectly intelligible, I did not hesitate to believe it was the Chatham, of which we shortly experienced the happiness of being convinced. Mr. Broughton soon visited us, and brought with him an early and acceptable supply of the excellent productions of this fertile country. About ten, we anchored in Matavai Bay.[3] Our mutual gratulations on meeting were extremely heightened, by receiving and communicating the happy tidings, that every individual composing the society of each vessel was in a most perfect state of health.[4] Mr. Broughton had, since his arrival, received repeated marks of friendship and attention from the good people of the island. Having deemed it expedient to establish the following regulations on board the Discovery, I delivered a copy of them to Mr. Broughton, and directed that the rules might be strictly observed, and attended to on board the Chatham;[5] after which,

[1] lat. 20° 40' S.
[2] 'Matavai' was written in error for 'Maitea', now spelled Mehetia.
[3] This was Vancouver's fourth visit to Tahiti. He had been there with Cook on his second voyage in August 1773 and April 1774, and again with Cook on his third voyage in August 1777.
[4] 'Except the Surgeon', as Hewett (surgeon's mate) rightly notes. The health of Cranstoun, surgeon of the Discovery, continued to show no improvement.
[5] 'Which Orders,' Hewett states, 'were taken no Notice of by Mr. Broughton.' But Hewett was in the Discovery and Bell, clerk of the Chatham, comments that 'These

Mr. Broughton presented me with a narrative of his proceedings during the time of our separation.

RULES and ORDERS for the guidance and conduct of all persons in, or belonging to His Majesty's Sloop Discovery and Chatham tender; enjoined to be most strictly observed in all intercourse with the natives of the several South-Sea islands.[1]

The principal, and indeed sole design, of the Discovery and Chatham calling at the islands in the Pacific Ocean, being to acquire such refreshments as those islands may be found to afford; and as these refreshments are to be purchased with articles which Europeans esteem of little value;— if each individual be permitted to make such bargains as he may think proper, not only the value of these articles will soon be reduced in the estimation of the Indians, but, until a proper and good understanding be established between the natives of the different islands, and ourselves, it may subject us to such disturbances as may be attended with the most fatal consequences. And as a due proportion of time will be allowed before the vessels depart from any island, (circumstances admitting thereof) for the providing such articles of curiosity, &c. as any person may be inclined and able to purchase:

It is, First, strictly enjoined, that no officer, seaman, or other person, in such commerce with the Indians, do give such articles of value, for any article of curiosity, as may tend hereafter to depreciate the value of iron, beads, &c. &c.

Secondly, That every fair means be used to cultivate a friendship with the different Indians, and on all occasions to treat them with every degree of kindness and humanity.

Thirdly, As proper persons will be appointed by the respective commanders to trade with the natives, for the necessary provisions and refreshments; it is strictly enjoined that no officer, seaman, or other person, excepting him or them so appointed, do on any pretence, presume to trade, or offer to trade, for any article whatever, until permission shall have been granted for so doing.

Fourthly, Every person employed on shore, on any duty whatever, is strictly to attend to the same: and if it should appear that by neglect, any of the arms, working tools, boats furniture, or other matters committed to the charge of one or more persons, be lost, or suffered to be stolen, the full value of the same will be charged against his, or their wages, and he or they will likewise suffer such other punishment, as the nature of the offence may deserve; and as the additional pay, and the emoluments of the artificers, serving in His Majesty's navy, is for their encouragement, and the diligent performance of their duty in their respective trades or occupations, and for providing themselves with the requisite working tools, all such implements or tools

regulations were but proper, and they were found to be strictly attended to.' – December 30.

[1] Vancouver's *Rules and Orders* were very similar to those issued by Cook under like circumstances. For the text of the *Rules* Cook issued when approaching Tahiti in April 1769, see the *Journals*, I, 75–76.

belonging to the several artificers of the two vessels, are by their respective owners to be carefully preserved, that they may be always able to perform the duties of their respective departments; and should any one be hardy enough to fail in his obedience to this order, he shall be disrated from his employment during the continuance of the voyage, and suffer such other punishment as the crime may deserve.

Lastly, The same penalty will be inflicted on every person, who shall be found to embezzle, or be concerned in embezzling, or offering to trade with, any part of the ships or boats stores, furniture, &c. &c. be these of what nature soever.

Given on board His Majesty's Sloop Discovery, at sea, the 25th of December, 1791.

(Signed)
GEORGE VANCOUVER.

CHAPTER V.

Mr. Broughton's Narrative, from the Time of his Separation, to his being joined by the Discovery at Otaheite; with some Account of Chatham Island, and other Islands discovered on his Passage.

THE wood we had received in Facile Harbour, (on Tuesday the 22d of November) with the spruce-beer and water upon deck, had brought the vessel so much by the head, that, together with the high sea now running, obliged us to deviate from our southwardly course and keep before the storm, which raged with great violence; and notwithstanding every precaution a wave struck our stern, about six o'clock on Wednesday morning, washed away the jolly boat, and sat us all afloat upon deck.[1] Having, about nine, run by estimation to the south of the Traps, to prevent our shipping so much water, I brought to, under a reefed trysail, and fore staysail. By noon, the gale had considerably abated, the sea subsided, and the horizon became tolerably clear; but the Discovery was not to be seen in any direction. After duly weighing all circumstances since the commencement of the gale, our separation from the Discovery appeared now complete; and the chance of our meeting again until our arrival at our next rendezvous in Otaheite, seemed little in our favor.

About two in the afternoon, land was discovered from the deck, appearing like a high island, bearing by compass S.S.E. three or four leagues distant; about an hour afterwards, we had sight of more land lying to the southward and detached from the former; our utmost endeavours were used to weather this land, but finding it impracticable, we bore up for a passage between the high island and the detached land, which was found to be composed of a cluster of small islets and rocks, greater in extent though about the height of the Needles; their tops or ridges are much broken; and from the high island bore by compass N.E. and S.W. forming a passage three miles wide; about one third of the passage over, on the southern side, lies a small black rock just above water; on all these rocks and islets the sea broke with great violence. In this passage we had a confused irregular swell, with the appearance of broken water; large bunches of sea-weed were observed, and the whole surface was covered with birds of a blackish colour. The N.E. part of the island in the

---

[1] 'In the late Gale we labour'd much and shipp'd an immense quantity of Water – there was scarce a man that had a dry Bed to sleep in – or a dry Jacket to put on, even the Captain & the Officer's Cabbins were half full of water.' – Bell, 24 November.

evening, bore by compass north; the S.W. part, N.W. by N.; the passage N.W.; and the rocky islets from N.W. by W. to W. by N. between two and three leagues distant: in this situation we had no bottom at the depth of 60 and 80 fathoms. Some parts of the island presented a very barren appearance, not unlike the S.W. side of Portland, composed of whitish rocky cliffs. The rocky islets are five in number, some of which wore a pyramidical form. On account of the haziness in the atmosphere, the north-easternmost part of the island was seen so very indistinctly, that its extent could not be ascertained. We had no reason to suppose it inhabited, and its desolate appearance made that very improbable. This island, in honor of Captain Knight of the navy, I named KNIGHT'S ISLAND.[1] Its south point lies in the latitude of 48° 15′, longitude 166° 44′, ascertained by the watch the last time the bearings were taken, allowing its error to be 30′ west, as determined at Dusky Bay. Knight's Island, so far as we could see of its extent, and the rocky islets, lie in the direction of N.E. by E. ½ E. and S.W. by W. ½ W. allowing a point and a half variation east: they extend about four leagues.

In the morning of Thursday the 24th, with a fine westwardly gale, we altered our course and made all sail to the N.E. The wind which varied in point of force, veered gradually round by the north. On Saturday the 26th our latitude was 46° 43′, longitude 173° 30′. In the evening the wind shifted suddenly to the S.W. and blew with such violence, that striking our topgallant masts and yards became necessary. A remarkably heavy following sea, kept the vessel constantly under water; but the gale was attended with clear weather. At noon on Sunday the 27th our latitude by observation was 45° 54′, longitude by account 176° 13′. The gale now moderated, which permitted us again to resume our N.E. course, with a fine breeze between west and N.W. Early in the morning of Monday the 29th, low land was discovered, bearing by compass from N.E. to E.N.E.; and being then in 40 fathoms water, we brought to until day-break. About four o'clock we had 38 fathoms, bottom of sand and broken shells, when the N.W. point of this land, which is low, bore by compass S. 7 E. about three leagues distant, and which, after the man who fortunately saw it from the fore yard, I named POINT ALISON;[2] a remarkably rugged rocky mountain that obtained the name of MOUNT PATTERSON[3] S. 60 E.; a sugar-loaf hill S. 84 E.; and the extreme point to the

---

[1] Later Admiral Sir John Knight. Broughton had served under him on several occasions, notably during the American Revolutionary War. In 1776 Knight was second lieutenant of the sloop *Falcon* in which Broughton was a midshipman; both were taken prisoner while attempting to destroy a schooner that had run ashore, but they were exchanged later in the year. The name Knight Island never came into use as Vancouver had already named the islands the Snares. Broughton later named an inlet on the Northwest coast for Knight.

[2] Hugh Alison, an AB who had joined the *Chatham* at False Bay. The name has been retained. Hewett commented: 'Mr Broughton properly encouraged those who made Discoveries.' He 'gave every man his due.' The name is wrongly spelled 'Allison' on Vancouver's chart.

[3] This name has not been retained.

eastward, which formed an abrupt cape, N. 75 E. Two islands N. 3 E. to N.
5 E. two or three leagues distant. The interior land was of a moderate height,
rising gradually, and forming several peaked hills, which at a distance have the
appearance of islands. From point Alison to mount Patterson the shore is low,
and covered with wood; from thence to the above cape was a continued white
beach, on which some sandy cliffs, and black rocks were interspersed,
apparently detached from the shore. To the eastward of these rocks, between
them and a flat projecting point, the land seemed to form a bay open to the
westward. From this point to the above cape, a distance of about two miles,
the cliffs are covered with wood and coarse grass. These cliffs are of moderate
height, composed of a reddish clay, mixed with black rocks. Several large black
rocks lie off point Alison, and the cape, extending to a little distance; and
as we passed within about half a mile of the shore, the depth of water was
14 fathoms, broken shells, and sandy bottom. This cape forms a conspicuous
headland, and is the northernmost part of the island; I called it CAPE YOUNG;[1]
it lies in latitude 43° 48', longitude 183° 2'. The above two islands lie very
near each other; to the eastward of them lies a small rock, apparently
connected, though at no great distance, by a reef; another rock somewhat
larger is situated between them. They are of no great height; flat top with
perpendicular sides, composed intirely of rocks, and much frequented by birds
of different kinds. These, which from their resemblance to each other, I called
THE TWO SISTERS,[2] are in latitude 43° 41', longitude 182° 49'; and bear, by
compass, from Cape Young N. 50 W. four leagues distant. We steered from
cape Young E. by N. keeping between two and three miles from the coast,
with regular soundings from 25 to 22 fathoms. The shore is a continued white
sandy beach, on which the surf ran very high. Some high land, rising gradually
from the beach and covered with wood, extends about four miles to the
eastward of the cape. After passing this land, we opened the several hills over
the low land we had seen in the morning, and could discern that many of
them were covered like our heaths in England, but destitute of trees. The woods
in some spots had the appearance of being cleared, and in several places
between the hills smoke was observed. The beach is interrupted at unequal
distances by projecting rocky points covered with wood. Over the banks of
sand were seen a range of retired hills at a considerable distance, in the direction
of the coast. After sailing about 10 leagues, we came abreast of a small sandy
bay. Water was seen over the beach, and the country had the appearance of
being very pleasant. With our glasses we perceived some people hauling up
a canoe, and several others behind the rocks in the bay. Fearful that so good
an opportunity might not occur for acquiring some knowledge of the
inhabitants, I worked up into the bay, which we had passed before the natives
were discovered. We came to an anchor about a mile from the shore in 20

---

[1] Cape Young is still so named. Its position is lat. 43° 42' S, long. 176° 37' W
(183° 23' E).
[2] Now The Sisters, in lat. 43° 34' S, long. 176° 49' W (183° 11' E).

fathom water, sandy and rocky bottom. The eastern point by compass bore N. 78 E.; cape Young W. 12 S.; the larboard point of the bay S.E.; the eastern point from our anchorage proved to be the termination of the island, to which I gave the name of POINT MUNNINGS.[1]

Accompanied by Mr. Johnston the master, and one of the mates,[2] we proceeded towards the shore in the cutter. The rocks project a little at each extremity of the bay; within them we found smooth water, and landed upon the rocks on the starboard shore, where we had first perceived the inhabitants; who were, at this time, on the opposite side, but seeing us examining their canoes, they hastily ran round the bay; on which we retired to the boat, to wait their arrival.[3] As they approached they made much noise, and having soon joined us, we entered into a conversation by signs, gestures, and speech, without understanding what each other meant. We presented them with several articles, which they received with great eagerness, and seemed pleased with whatever was given them;[4] but would make no exchanges. Yet as we had reason to believe they were very solicitous that we should land, Mr. Sheriff, leaving his arms in the boat, went on shore; but he seemed to excite the attention of two or three of them only, who attended him towards the canoes on the beach, whilst the rest, amounting to forty or thereabouts, remained on the rocks talking with us, and whenever the boat backed in, to deliver them any thing, they made no scruple of attempting to take whatever came within their reach. Having repeatedly beckoned us to follow them round to where their habitations were supposed to be, as soon as Mr. Sheriff returned, we proceeded to comply with their wishes. They had been very curious in their examination of Mr. Sheriff's person, and seemed very desirous of keeping him, as they frequently pulled him towards the wood, where we imagined some of them resided.[5] On meeting them on the other side, they seated

[1] Now Point Munning.

[2] John Sherriff, master's mate. Johnstone described the events of the day in detail in his log, and Bell copied much of his narrative into his journal.

[3] Johnstone tells a somewhat different story: 'The natives, who had quited their station as soon as they saw us land now advanced hastily, and by their threats and gestures plainly indicated their hostile intentions but rather than oppose their tumult we thought best to retire to the boat, where more in safety we might endeavour to engage their friendship. With the Oars we kept her just afloat, they without making the least stop rushed hastily on, some of them up to their knees in water, brandishing their spears and clubs with much vociferation.' – 30 November.

[4] 'At last their violence somewhat abated and they received some presents which we conveyed to them on the ends of their Spears, which they held out for the purpose for we did not yet choose to trust the boat within their depth. They now became to all appearance perfectly reconciled and received every thing we offered with avidity...' – Johnstone, 30 November.

[5] Johnstone states that the natives 'forcibly detained him longer than he wished' but he did not 'think this was done with any other intention than for a longer opportunity of gratifying their curiosity.' – 30 November. Sherriff's own account reads: 'I then went ahead unarm'd & I stai'd with them a quarter of an hour, they did not offer me the least violence, but seem'd to gaze upon me with the greatest astonishment.' – 29 November.

themselves on the beach, and seemed very anxious to receive us on shore;
but as all our intreaties were ineffectual in obtaining any thing in return for
our presents, perceiving many of them to be armed with long spears, and the
situation being unfavorable to us, in case they should be disposed to treat us
with hostility, we did not think it prudent to venture amongst them; and
finding our negociation was not likely to be attended with success, we took
our leave; but in our way off, as the natives remained quietly where we left
them, I thought it a good opportunity to land once more and take another
view of their canoes. Having again reached the shore without any interruption,
we displayed the Union flag, turned a turf, and took possession of the island;
which I named CHATHAM ISLAND, (in honor of the Earl of Chatham,)[1] in the
name of His Majesty King George the Third; under the presumption of our
being the first discoverers. After drinking His Majesty's health, I nailed a piece
of lead to a tree near the beach, on which was inscribed, His Britannick
Majesty's Brig Chatham, Lieutenant William Robert Broughton commander,
the 29th November 1791. And in a bottle secreted near the tree, was deposited
an inscription in Latin to the same effect.[2]

The canoes we examined were more in form of a small hand-barrow
without legs, than any other thing to which they can be compared, decreasing
in width from the after to the fore part. They were made of a light substance
resembling bamboo, though not hollow, placed fore and aft on each side, and
secured together by pieces of the same wood, up and down, very neatly
fastened with the fibres of some plant in the manner of basket work. Their
bottoms flat and constructed in the same way, were two feet deep and eighteen
inches in breadth; the openings of the seams on the inside and bottoms were
stuffed with long sea weed; their sides meet not abaft, nor forward, their
extreme breadth aft is three, and forward, two feet; length eight and nine
feet. In the stern is a seat very neatly made of the same material; which is
moveable. They appeared calculated alone for fishing amongst the rocks near
the shore; were capable of carrying two or three persons, and were so light
that two men could convey them any where with ease, and one could haul
them into safety on the beach. Their grapnels were stones, and the ropes to
which these were made fast, were formed of matting, worked up in a similar
way with that which is called French sinnet. The paddles were of hard wood,
the blades very broad, and gradually increasing from the handle. The nets of
these islanders were very ingeniously made, terminating in a cod or purse;
the mouth was kept open by a rim of six feet in diameter, made from wood of
the supple jack kind; the length from eight to ten feet, tapered gradually to
one; they were closely made, and from the center attached to the rim by cords,
was fixed a line for hauling them up. They were made of fine hemp, two
strands twisted and knotted like a reef knot, and seemingly very strong. They

[1] John Pitt, second Earl of Chatham, First Lord of the Admiralty.
[2] Johnstone gives the Latin text as: 'Navis. Briten. Majest. Chatham. Gul. Robertus
Broughton. princeps. 29th Novembres 1791.'

had also scoop nets, made of the bark or fibres of some tree or plant, without any preparation, and netted in equal meshes. We penetrated a little into the woods, but did not find any huts, or houses, though large quantities of shells, and places where fires had been made, were observed.

The woods afforded a delightful shade, and being clear of undergrowth, were in many places formed into arbours, by bending the branches when young, and closing[1] them round with smaller trees. These appeared to have been slept in very lately. The trees of which the woods are composed grow in a most luxuriant manner, clear of small branches to a considerable height; and consist of several sorts, some of which, the leaf in particular, was like the laurel. Another sort was jointed like the vine, but we did not see one that could be dignified by the appellation of a timber tree. On our return, a few of the natives were seen approaching us, and as they appeared peaceably disposed, we joined the first party, and saluted each other by meeting noses, according to the New Zealand fashion. They were presented with some trinkets, but seemed to entertain not the least idea of barter, or of obligation to make the least return, as we could not prevail upon them to part with any thing excepting one spear of very rude workmanship. On making a bargain with him who had parted with the spear, for his coat, or covering of sea-bear skin, he was so delighted with the reflection of his face in the looking glasses proposed in exchange, that he ran way with them. Previously to this, with a view to shew them the superior effect of our fire-arms, I gave them some birds which I had killed, and pointed out to them the cause of their death. On firing my gun they seemed much alarmed at its report; and all retreated as we advanced towards them, excepting one old man, who maintained his ground; and presenting his spear side-ways, beat time with his feet; and as he seemed to notice us in a very threatening manner, I gave my fowling piece to one of our people, went up to him, shook him by the hand, and used every method I could devise to obtain his confidence. Observing something in his hand rolled carefully up in a mat, I was desirous of looking at it, upon which he gave it to another, who walked away with it; but who did not prevent my seeing that it contained stones fashioned like the *Patoo Patoes* of New Zealand.[2] They seemed very anxious to get my gun and shot belt, and frequently exclaimed *Toohata*.[3] Some of their spears were ten feet, others about six feet in length, one or two of which were new, with carved work towards the handle; whenever these were pointed to, they were immediately given to those behind, as if afraid of our taking them by force. Finding little was to be procured or learned here, we

[1] 'enclosing' in the first edition.

[2] *Patu*. Cook described those seen in New Zealand made of stone: 'they have short Truncheons about a foot long, which they call Pattoo Pattoos...those made of bone and stone are of one shape, which is with a round handle a broadish blade which is thickest in the middle and tapers to an edge all round, the use of these are to knock mens brains out and to kill them outright after they are wounded: they are certainly well contrived for this purpose.' – *Journals*, I, 200.

[3] 'often repeated the word Tohoua' – Johnstone, 30 November.

made signs of going to their supposed habitations, and endeavoured to make them understand we needed something to eat and drink. As they continued very friendly, three men armed attended Mr. Johnston and myself along the water-side; the boat with four hands keeping close by the shore as we walked, lest we might require support, or it should be necessary to retreat. Every one had orders to be prepared, but on no account to make use of their arms, until I should give directions, which, at this time, I had not the most distant idea would become necessary. When our little party first sat off, several of them collected large sticks, which they swung over their heads, as if they had some intention of using them. He who had received the stones from the old man, had them now fixed, one at each end, to a large stick about two feet in length.[1] Not liking these appearances, we had some thoughts of embarking; but, on our suddenly facing about, they retired up the beach to a fire which some of them had just made. Mr. Johnston followed them singly, but was not in time to discover the method by which it had been so quickly produced. His presence seemed rather to displease them, on which he returned, and we again proceeded along the beach, making signs of our intention to accompany them on the other side of the bay. Fourteen only followed, the rest remained at the fire. Those who had not spears substituted the drift wood on the beach for their weapons; yet as our party consisted of nine, all well armed, we entertained no fear for our personal safety, especially as every thing had been studiously avoided that we imagined might give them offence, and the various presents they had received had apparently purchased their good opinion and friendship, until now that we had reason to believe the contrary by their providing themselves with bludgeons. Having walked about half round the bay we arrived at the spot behind which, from the mast head, inland water had been seen. As we proceeded up the beach we found it to be a large sheet of water, which took a western direction round a hill that prevented our seeing its extent.[2] At the upper end of this lake, the country appeared very pleasant, and level. The water seemed of a reddish colour and was brackish, which was most probably occasioned by the salt water oozing through the beach, which at this place is not more than twenty yards wide; or by its having some communication with the sea to the westward, which we did not perceive. We tried to explain to the natives who still attended us, that the water was not fit to drink, and then returned to the sea side; when, abreast of the boat, they became very clamorous, talked extremely loud to each other, and divided so as nearly to surround us. A young man strutted towards me in a very menacing attitude; he distorted his person, turned up his eyes, made hideous faces, and created a wonderful fierceness in his appearance by his gestures. On pointing

---

[1] 'Their clubs were rough pieces of Wood, some as picked from the beach, others as they had been broke from the tree and a very few had two stones lashed to one end which gave them the appearance of a double headed maul.' – Johnstone, 30 November.

[2] The large Te Whanga Lagoon, which lies behind a narrow beach or barrier that divides it from the ocean.

my double-barrelled gun towards him he desisted. Their hostile intentions were now too evident to be mistaken, and therefore, to avoid the necessity of resorting to extremities, the boat was immediately ordered in to take us on board. During this interval, although we were strictly on our guard, they began their attack, and before the boat could get in, to avoid being knocked down I was reluctantly compelled to fire one barrel, which being loaded with small shot, I was in hopes might intimidate without materially wounding them, and that we should be suffered to embark without further molestation. Unfortunately, I was disappointed in this hope. Mr. Johnston received a blow upon his musket with such force from an unwieldy club, that it fell to the ground, but before his opponent could pick it up, Mr. Johnston had time to recover his position, and he was obliged to fire on the blow being again attempted. A marine and seaman near him, were, under similar circumstances forced into the water, but not before they had also, justified alone by self-preservation, fired their pieces without orders. The gentleman having charge of the boat seeing us much pressed by the natives, and obliged to retreat, fired at this instant also, on which they fled. I ordered the firing instantly to cease, and was highly gratified to see them depart apparently unhurt. The happiness I enjoyed in this reflection was of short duration, one man was discovered to have fallen; and I am concerned to add, was found lifeless, a ball having broken his arm and passed through his heart.[1] We immediately repaired towards the boat, but the surf not permitting her to come near enough, we were still under the necessity of walking to the place from whence we had originally intended to embark. As we retired, we perceived one of the natives return from the woods, whither all had retreated, and placing himself by the deceased, he was distinctly heard in a sort of dismal howl to utter his lamentations.

As we approached our first landing place we saw no signs of habitations, although women and children were supposed to have been looking at us from the woods, whilst talking to the natives on our arrival. On tracing some of the footpaths, nothing was discovered but great numbers of ear shells, and recesses formed in the same manner with a single pallisade as those seen on our first landing. We distributed amongst the canoes the remaining part of our toys and trinkets, to manifest our kind intentions towards them, and as some little atonement also for the injury, which, contrary to our inclinations, they had sustained, in defending ourselves against their unprovoked, unmerited hostility. In our way to the ship, we saw two natives running along the beach to the canoes, but on our arrival on board they were not discernible with our glasses.

The men were of a middling size, some stoutly made, well limbed and fleshy; their hair, both of the head and beard, was black, and by some was worn

---

[1] ' In hopes that some relief might be given to his wounds that were probably not mortal with two of the people I went up for that end, but to my utter grief found him dead.' – Johnstone, 30 November.

long. The young men had it tied up in a knot on the crown of their heads, intermixed with black and white feathers. Some had their beards plucked out; their complexion and general colour is dark brown, with plain features, and in general bad teeth. Their skins were destitute of any marks, and they had the appearance of being cleanly in their persons. Their dress was either a seal or bear-skin tied with sinnet, inside outwards, round their necks, which fell below their hips; or mats neatly made, tied in the same manner which covered their backs and shoulders. Some were naked, excepting a well woven matt of fine texture, which, being fastened at each end by a string round their waists, made a sort of decent garment. We did not observe that their ears were bored, or that they wore any ornaments about their persons, excepting a few who had a sort of necklace made of mother of pearl shells. Several of them had their fishing lines, made of the same sort of hemp with their nets, fastened round them; but we did not see any of their hooks. We noticed two or three old men, but they did not appear to have any power or authority over the others. They seemed a cheerful race, our conversation frequently exciting violent bursts of laughter amongst them. On our first landing their surprize and exclamations can hardly be imagined; they pointed to the sun, and then to us, as if to ask, whether we had come from thence. The not finding a single habitation, led us to consider this part of the island as a temporary residence of the inhabitants, possibly for the purpose of procuring a supply of shell and other fish. The former, of different kinds, were here to be had in great abundance: claws of cray fish were found in their canoes; and as the birds about the shore were in great numbers, and flew about the natives as if never molested, it gave us reason to believe that the sea furnished the principal means of their subsistence. Black sea pies with red bills, black and white spotted curlews with yellow bills, large wood pigeons like those at Dusky Bay, a variety of ducks, small sand-larks, and sand-pipers, were very numerous about the shores.

These observations conclude a brief narrative of our visit and transactions at Chatham Island; and I have to lament that the hostility of its inhabitants rendered the melancholy fate that attended one of them unavoidable, and prevented our researches extending further than the beach, and the immediate entrance of the adjoining wood.

On our return to the vessel we got under weigh, with a fresh gale at S.W. About six in the evening, on passing point Munnings, which is the N.E. extremity of the island, it was seen to be a low peninsula, over which, from the mast-head, was discovered more land to the southward; but the weather became so very hazy, that it was impossible to discern how far it extended in that direction. From the bay, which I called SKIRMISH BAY,[1] to point Munnings, the shore is low, rocky, and clothed with wood. Some rocks lie a little way off the point. The extent of the island is an east and west direction, which is nearly the line of the coast, was now considered to be about twelve

[1] This very appropriate name has not survived.

leagues, allowing 14° east variation. The latitude of our anchoring place in Skirmish bay was 43° 49', and its longitude 183° 25'.[1] At eight o'clock the extremities of the land bore from S.W. by S. to W. by S. five or six leagues distant. At day-break in the morning of Wednesday the 30th, we made all sail as usual, and pursued our way to the N.E. In the course of this day, we passed many patches of sea weed, and saw some port Egmont hens and several oceanic birds.

With pleasant weather and a fine gale between the S.E. and S.W. quarters, we proceeded, without any thing occurring worthy of notice, until Saturday the 3d of December, when, in the afternoon, our latitude was 38° 52'; the mean result of eight sets of lunar observations taken the two preceding days, and reduced by the watch, gave the longitude this day 192° 43' 33". The watch, by its rate, and error, as found at Dusky Bay, shewed 192° 45' 37". The mean variation, by azimuths and amplitude, 11° 56' eastwardly. The watch and observations having agreed so well, little error is to be apprehended in the longitude assigned to Chatham Island.

Our pleasant weather was of no long continuance; on Tuesday the 6th, in the latitude of 35° 43', longitude 197° 20' towards evening it fell calm. A breeze next morning, Wednesday the 7th, sprang up at N.E. with which we steered to the E.S.E. between which, and the N.N.W. the wind continued with hazy, rainy, foggy and very unpleasant weather until Sunday the 11th, in latitude 36° 53', longitude 206°: having been visited by few oceanic birds. The wind now veered round by the west to the southward, and brought us tolerably pleasant weather, with which, until Thursday the 15th, we continued to steer north by east; when, in latitude 30° 17, longitude 208° 46', the wind again resumed its northern direction, varying a point or two on either side of north. The atmosphere became dark, heavy, sultry and gloomy; the clouds poured down torrents of rain accompanied with much lightning, thunder, and violent squalls, which obliged the crew to be constantly exposed, until Tuesday the 20th; when the wind changed to the south, blew a moderate breeze, and we again had fine settled weather.

Although every advantage had been taken which the winds afforded, during the last four days, we had not been able to shorten the distance from our destined port, more than six leagues; our latitude this day being 29° 8', longitude 211° 55'. Shortly after noon, some observations were procured for the longitude. The mean of four sets of distances gave 214° 30' 18", the watch, 212° 13' 15". Although the watch was considerably to the westward of the lunar observations, yet in the last of five days, it made 1° 19' more easting than the log shewed.

The wind continued between south, and E.S.E. with pleasant weather; on Thursday the 22d we were again enabled to obtain more observations for the longitude, when the mean of two sets gave 213° 53' 7", the watch 212° 43', the mean of these, and those taken on Tuesday, reduced by the watch to this

[1] The position of Chatham Island is lat. 44° 00' S, long. 176° 30' W (183° 30' E).

day, gave the mean result of the six sets 213° 51′ 30″, which was 1° 10′ east of the watch; our latitude at this time was 25° 26′.

At eight the next morning, land was seen from the mast-head bearing, by compass, W. by S. an hour afterwards it was visible from the deck bearing W.S.W. ½ W. at the distance of about ten leagues. It proved to be a small high island; its northern part formed an elevated hummock, from the fall of which the land continued level, and then gradually decreased to the other extreme point.

The watch, with its error, gave the longitude, at the time the above bearings were taken, 211° 6′, ☉ a ☾ 213° 16′, our latitude by estimation at this time 23° 36′. The sun being within a few minutes of the zenith at noon, our observation was indifferent, and could by no means be depended upon. I did not think it proper, on the present occasion, to give any name to this island. I had some reason to doubt the accuracy of our longitude. On our arrival at Otaheite I should be enabled to determine whether this island might not be Tobouai seen by Captain Cook, or the land supposed to have been seen to the southeastward, whilst the Resolution was off that island.[1]

The wind principally between E.N.E. and S.E. blew very fresh, attended with squalls, a gloomy atmosphere, and an almost incessant rain, until seven in the morning of Monday the 26th,[2] when the weather clearing, gave us a view of Maitea or Osnaburgh island;[3] bearing, by compass, E.S.E. distant only about six or eight leagues. We immediately steered for Otaheite, which was seen about eight bearing W. ½ N. The wind was now eastwardly, accompanied by showers of rain. At noon, the land over point Venus[4] bore west, distant seven or eight leagues. The latitude now observed (being the first time since the 23d) varying only 5′ from the dead reckoning, was 17° 29′, longitude 211° 45′, by the watch 210° 39′. In the afternoon, the wind became southwardly, with dark gloomy weather. Having reached, by five o'clock, within four or five miles of the shore, a little to the eastward of point Venus, some canoes came off, and brought some cocoa-nuts, and two small hogs, which were instantly purchased.[5] Towards sun-set, the breeze died away, and it continued calm until

---

[1] Cook did not go further than to say that 'Some *thought* they saw land' to the S and to windward (i.e., to the E); the nearest land in that direction was Raivavae, about 100 miles away. It seems certain that it was Raivavae that was sighted from the *Chatham*; it is 29′ S and 1° 47′ E of Tubuai.

[2] Neither Broughton nor Vancouver mentions Christmas Day, but it was observed in a modest way, with due regard to safety at sea. 'The 25th being Xmas day the people were allowed every thing in the eatable way that the Ship afforded – but being at Sea had no more Grog given them than their usual allowance the Customary extra allowance was reserv'd till we got into Port.' – Bell, 25 December.

[3] Now Mehetia Island.

[4] The N point of Matavai Bay, so named because it was there that Cook built Fort Venus from which he observed the transit of Venus in June 1769.

[5] Only Heddington notes that this contact was made 'Off Oaitepeha [Vaitepiha] Bay. Several Canoes came off with hogs, cocoa-nuts, Bread Fruit, & vegetables. In one came a Chief nam'd Hero who call'd us his Friends & ask'd if King George was well. himself

midnight, when it again freshened from the eastward; with which, under an easy sail, we plied until the morning, when all our canvas was spread for Matavai bay. About eight o'clock we rounded the Dolphin bank[1] in 2½ fathoms water, and worked up into the bay. About nine we anchored in eight fathom, black muddy bottom; point Venus bearing by compass N. 15 E.; the Dolphin bank N. 70 W.; and One-Tree hill[2] S. 31 W. This being the place of rendezvous appointed by Captain Vancouver, we experienced no small degree of disappointment on not finding the Discovery in port; and our solicitude for her welfare was greatly increased, when we adverted to her superiority in sailing, which had given us reason to believe her arrival would have preceded ours, at least a week.

We scarcely anchored, when the natives flocked around us in the most civil and friendly manner, bringing with them an ample supply of the different refreshments their country afforded. Some trifling thefts being committed by some of our numerous visitors, we were under the necessity of obliging them to retire to their canoes alongside, with which they complied in the greatest good humour. The whole of the afternoon was a continued rain, as heavy as any one on board ever beheld, accompanied with a very severe tempest. On our first arrival, the whole of the shore was one uninterrupted beach; but, towards evening, the torrents of rain which had fallen, caused an inundation of the river, which broke its bank about half way, between point Venus and One-Tree hill;[3] and through the breach an immense quantity of water was discharged, which brought with it a great number of large trees that were scattered in various directions over the bay. A great concourse of the inhabitants had assembled and beheld the bank give way, upon which they all shouted, seemingly with acclamations of great joy; for had not this event taken place, their houses and plantations would probably have been much incommoded by the overflowing of the river.

Our cutter was moored alongside. In the course of the night one of the trees drifted athwart her, broke the iron chain with which she was secured,

& some other men, one a Priest, slept on board. they were very handsome by primitive st[anda]rd.' – December 27. Bell adds a detail: 'One of the Canoes having met with an accident we got it on board – and the 3 men belonging to it staid with us all night.' December. Vaitepiha Bay, on the NE tip of Taiarapu (Little Tahiti) is an interesting spot historically. Cook visited it on all three of his voyages, and in 1774–75 Spaniards from Peru left two Franciscans, a ship's boy and a marine there in an unsuccessful effort to establish a mission.

[1] W of Point Venus; named after the *Dolphin*, the ship commanded by Samuel Wallis, who discovered Tahiti in June 1767.

[2] Now Mount Taharaa. Cook and Vancouver regarded One Tree Hill, about a mile and a half SW of Point Venus, as the S limit of Matavai Bay, but application of the name has since been extended to include two smaller bays to the SW.

[3] The river ran down from the mountains about the middle of Matavai Bay. Ordinarily it swung to the N and ran along behind the beach to a mouth near Point Venus. The freshet caused it to break through directly into the bay.

stove in her broadside and stern; and, on her filling, the furniture was washed away.[1] This circumstance, little to the credit of the gentlemen who had the watch on deck, was not discovered until the morning of Wednesday the 28th, when, after some hours search in the launch, the party returned without finding the lost materials.

From young *Otoo*, I received this morning a present of two hogs, and some fruit. *Otoo* the elder, now stiled *Pomurrey*,[2] we understood, was at Eimeo,[3] whither the messengers requested we would send to acquaint him with our arrival, on which he would instantly repair to Matavai. His absence, however, had produced not the least inconvenience; for notwithstanding we had not been visited by any chief, yet the behaviour of the people was perfectly civil and friendly. They supplied us with as much provision as we could possibly use, on very reasonable terms. The greater part of this day, and all the succeeding night, the tempest continued with unabated torrents of rain.

On Thursday morning the 29th I received from Oparre[4] a very bountiful present, consisting of hogs and fruit, from young *Otoo*, with a message to signify that he might be expected next day at Matavai. In the evening, the weather being a little more temperate, though the surf continued to run too high to admit of our approaching the beach in the bay, we landed at the back of point Venus, and were received by the natives with great cheerfulness and cordiality. They treated us with the utmost hospitality, and vied with each other to be foremost in friendly attentions. The wind having shifted to the eastward, the weather became serene and pleasant; and being informed the next morning, (Friday the 30th) by some of the natives, that a ship was in sight, I repaired instantly on shore, and had the unspeakable pleasure of perceiving it to be the Discovery to the eastward, steering for the bay. About ten o'clock, as she hauled in between the reef and the Dolphin bank, I went on board to congratulate Captain Vancouver; and to inform him of our welfare and proceedings since our separation.[5]

———

It may not be improper to observe, that the separation of the two vessels was occasioned, as was first conjectured, by circumstances unavoidable, which occurred during a very heavy and violent storm. As some recompence,

---

[1] By 'furniture' the oars, masts, sails, &c., were meant.

[2] Cook and Vancouver had both dealt with the elder Otoo on earlier visits. In accordance with Tahitian custom, on the birth of his son the latter had succeeded his father as chief, with the father acting as regent during his minority. Otoo the elder resigned his name as well as his status and was known as Pomurrey. The name is here spelled Pomarre in the first edition, but in all subsequent references it is spelled Pumurrey. The modern spelling is Pomare. Bligh's version of the name is Tynah. Otoo is now spelled Tu.

[3] Moorea. Although both Cook and Vancouver referred to the island as Eimeo, the name Moorea was already in use by the natives in Cook's time. See *Journals*, III, 225n.

[4] Pare, a district W of Matavai Bay at the N end of Tahiti.

[5] Broughton's narrative ends at this point. In the first edition it is within quotation marks.

however, for the anxiety attendant on losing the company of our little consort, we had to reflect, that, eventually, the gale had been the fortunate means of our making some additions to geography.

The islands first discovered by the Chatham, and named Knight's island by Mr. Broughton, were the Snares,[1] which we had passed in the Discovery a few hours before. As Mr. Broughton considered our means for ascertaining their true position superior to what he possessed, their positive situation as placed by us may be received as correct; but as the Chatham passed through them, the relative situation to each other, according to Mr. Broughton's observations, is to be preferred.

The Discovery passed about twenty leagues to the north of Chatham island; as did Captain Cook in March 1777, who also passed, about the same distance to the south of it, in June 1773: on all these occasions, it was not observed, nor did we, in the Discovery, see the islands discovered by the Chatham on the 23d of December, lying more to the eastward than Tobouai, and in latitude 23° 42′, longitude 212° 49′.[2]

---

[1] Bell made a curious error when he recorded the sighting of Raivavae: 'On the 23rd [December] we discover'd an Island...as this Island had never been seen before by any navigator we know of Mr. Broughton nam'd it Knights Island after Captn. Knight of the Navy.'

[2] The position of Raivavae is lat. 23° 52′ S, long. 147° 40′ W (212° 20′ E).

CHAPTER VI.

Visit Otoo—Arrival of Pomurrey and Matooara Mahow—Arrival of Taow, Pomurrey's Father—Interview between Taow and his Sons—Submission of Taow to Otoo—Entertainments at the Encampment—Visit of Poatatou— Death of Mahow—Excursion to Oparre.

By the time we had anchored, the ship was surrounded with canoes laden with the different productions of the country. The natives, with every assurance of friendship, and with expressions of the greatest joy at our arrival, were crowding on board. One or two amongst them, although not principal chiefs, evidently assumed some little authority, and were exceedingly earnest that we should not suffer the multitude to come on board, as that would be the best means to prevent thefts, and insure that amity and good fellowship which they appeared very solicitous to establish and support. We complied with their advice, and found no difficulty in carrying it into execution. We had only to desire they would return to their canoes, and they immediately complied.[1] I had the mortification of finding on inquiry, that most of the friends I had left here in the year 1777, both male and female, were dead. *Otoo*,[2] with his father, brothers, and sisters, *Potatou*,[3] and his family, were the only chiefs of my old acquaintance that were now living. *Otoo* was not here; nor did it appear that Otaheite was now the place of his residence, having retired to his newly acquired possession Eimeo, or as the natives more commonly call that island Morea, leaving his eldest son the supreme authority over this, and all the neighbouring islands. The young king had taken the name of *Otoo*, and my old friend that of *Pomurrey*; having given up his name with his sovereign

---

[1] Manby, with an eye for the ladies, gives a more highly coloured account of the arrival of the *Discovery*: 'As we drew near the Bay Canoes thronged out in prodigious quantities and were so thick as we passed the reef that our utmost exersions were in practise to prevent running over them. The Noise they made is not to be conceived, as every one repeated the welcome salutation of Friendship. Canoes of all sizes fill'd with beautiful Brunettes, were struggling to approach the Ship and gain admittance and on finding themselves prohibited until our arrival in Anchorage reproachful glances from their sparkling Eyes, plainly bespoke their displeasure at our refusal.' – Letters, December 30.

[2] Otoo the elder (Pomurrey) is meant.

[3] Potatau (spelled Potatow in the first edition) was chief of the district of Punaauia, on the W side of Tahiti. Beaglehole characterizes him as 'gigantic but good-humored' and in 1777 Cook noted that at a peace conference he 'spoke with much greater fluency and grace' than the other chiefs. – Cook, *Journals*, II, 211n; III, 217.

jurisdiction, though he still seemed to retain his authority as regent. Mr. Broughton had received some presents from *Otoo*, who being now arrived from Oparre, had sent desiring that gentleman would visit him on shore at Matavai. I had received no invitation; but, as some of the natives gave me to understand that my accompanying Mr. Broughton would be esteemed a civility, I did not hesitate to comply, especially as Mr. Broughton had prepared a present in so handsome a way, that I considered it a sufficient compliment to the young king from us both. As soon as the ship was secured, Mr. Whidbey and myself attended Mr. Broughton, with intention to fix on an eligible spot for our tents, and for transacting our necessary business on shore; and afterwards to pay our respects to his Otaheitean majesty.

The surf obliged us to row round the point near the mouth of the river; where we landed, and were received by the natives with every demonstration of regard. A messenger was instantly dispatched to inform the king[1] of our arrival, and intended visit. The station of our tents on my former visits to this country, was not likely, on the present occasion, to answer our purpose; the beach was considerably washed away, and the sand being removed from the coral rocks rendered the landing very unsafe. The surf had also broken into the river, and made it very salt. These circumstances induced me to fix on a situation about a quarter of a mile further along the beach, to the southward. The messenger that had been dispatched to inform *Otoo* of our landing and proposed visit, returned with a pig, and a plantain leaf, as a peace-offering to me;[2] accompanied by a speech of congratulation on our arrival, and offers of whatever refreshments the country afforded. This short ceremony being finished, we proceeded along the beach in expectation of

---

[1] The conception of a king was foreign to Polynesians; they simply recognized chiefs of greater or lesser authority, whose power might wax or wane, depending on such factors as inheritance, marriage and the fortunes of war. But the British and French, accustomed to the role of a king, bestowed royal status upon chiefs who appeared to rule over the various islands they visited. This recognition was often of considerable political advantage to a chief and helped him strengthen or extend his authority. For a recent comprehensive study of Tahiti at this period see Douglas L. Oliver, *Ancient Tahitian Society*, 3 vols. (Honolulu, 1974). Two accounts that draw heavily upon native sources are *Ancient Tahiti* by Teuira Henry (Bernice P. Bishop Museum bulletin 48, Honolulu, 1928), and *History and Culture in the Society Islands* by E. S. Craighill Handy (bulletin 79, Honolulu, 1930). For a most useful summary see J. C. Beaglehole, 'A Note on Polynesian History', in Cook, *Journals*, I, clxxii-cxcii.

[2] The plantain leaf was the symbol of peace and friendship: hogs, dogs and fowl were raised in the islands for food. Bell's comments on their quality are interesting: 'The Breed of Hogs here is far superior to anything I ever saw of the kind, both in size and quality, we got many that weigh'd when dead and clean'd upwards of two hundred weight, and of about thirty that we carried to Sea, there were few that weighed less than 140 lbs. Wt. – the meat is delicious, and that of the largest was in general the whitest and best flavor'd...The Dogs they have are a very poor ugly race, and what is extraordinary are neither docile or affectionate. The Fowls are excellent, and they have them in tolerable quantities – during our stay – I suppose upon an average both Ships were supplied (including what we carried to Sea) with 16 or 18 dozen Fowls.' – January 1792.

meeting the young sovereign, until we arrived near to the place where the river had broken its banks. There we were directed to halt, under the shade of a palm tree, to which we readily consented, the weather being nearly calm, and excessively sultry. After waiting a short time, we were acquainted that the king, having some objection to cross the river for the purpose of meeting strangers, requested we would go to him. A canoe was in waiting to take us over; and having walked about an hundred yards on the other side, the interview took place. We found *Otoo* to be a boy of about nine or ten years of age. He was carried on the shoulders of a man,[1] and was clothed in a piece of English red cloth, with ornaments of pigeons' feathers hanging over his shoulders. When we had approached within about eight paces, we were desired to stop: the present we had brought was exhibited; and although its magnitude, and the value of the articles it contained, excited the admiration of the by-standers in the highest degree, it was regarded by this young monarch with an apparently stern and cool indifference. It was not immediately to be presented; a certain previous ceremony was necessary. Not considering myself sufficiently master of the language, I applied for assistance to an inferior chief named *Moerree*, (who had been useful to Mr. Broughton) to be my prompter. At first he used some pains, but not finding me so apt a scholar as he expected, he soon took the whole office upon himself. He answered for our peaceable and friendly intentions, and requested supplies of provisions, and a pledge of good faith towards us, with as much confidence as if he had been intimately acquainted with our wishes and designs. Our situation on this occasion was similar to that of his Otaheitean majesty, who condescended to say but a few words, a person by his side sparing him that trouble by going through all the formal orations. A ratification of peace and mutual friendship being acknowledged on both sides, and these ceremonies concluded, which took up fifteen or twenty minutes, the different European articles composing the present, were, with some little form, presented to *Otoo*;[2] and on his shaking hands with us, which he did very heartily, his countenance became immediately altered, and he received us with the greatest cheerfulness and cordiality. He informed me, that his father, my former acquaintance and friend, was at Morea, and requested I would send thither a boat for him; for, as the islanders were much accustomed to raise false reports, *Pomurrey* would not

---

[1] He would be carried on a man's shoulders and sit on a man's lap until he was of age to succeed the regent in authority. Menzies thought he was 'about ten years of age'. 'His appearance is firm & graceful, his behaviour affable & easy & his features pleasant & regular though sometimes clouded with a degree of austerity that enables him already to command immediate obedience to his will among these mild people.' – Menzies, 30 December.

[2] Menzies described the presentation. After the speeches 'Mooree, who then divided Mr. Broughton's intended present which was very considerable into four equal parts & each of us [Vancouver, Broughton, Whidbey and Menzies] being then wrapped round in a quantity of Island Cloth separately carried our presents & laid them upon a Mat close to the young prince. After which we were admitted to a conference.' – 30 December. Vancouver mentions the cloth later in the paragraph, but does not explain that it was wrapped around the visitors – a common welcoming gesture in Tahiti.

believe that I was arrived without seeing some of us, by whom he would be convinced. He also added, that if we should sail without seeing his father, he would not only be very much concerned, but very angry. This language being in the mouths of every one around us, and feeling a great desire to see an old friend who had ever conducted himself with propriety, and appeared firmly attached to our interest, I promised to comply with the young king's request. The suffusions of joy, and a readiness to oblige, were evident in the countenances of all whom we met. Their instant compliance with all our requests, and their eagerness to be foremost in performing any little friendly office, could not be observed without the most grateful emotions. Each of us was presented with a quantity of cloth, a large hog, and some vegetables; after which we returned on board extremely well pleased with our visit and reception.

My original intention in calling here was for the sole purpose of recruiting our water, and obtaining a temporary supply of fresh provisions; but on further consideration I was convinced, that we should not find any place this winter, where the necessary duties we had to perform before we could proceed to the coast of America, would be so well done, or executed with so much ease and convenience, as in our present situation. A small boat for the Chatham was to be built, and a great repair was necessary to her large cutter. The timber cut in Dusky bay wanted to be sawn into planks for many other essential purposes. These matters required immediate attention, and could not so properly be executed on board; beside which, the known accuracy with which the situation of this island is settled, made me anxious to land our chronometers, for the purpose of ascertaining their error, and rate of going, which had lately become somewhat equivocal. These reasons induced me to determine on giving the vessels every equipment here they required, which would have the further convenience of shortening our visit this season at the Sandwich islands. Directions were therefore given, that the sails should be unbent, the topmasts, &c. struck, and that a thorough examination of the rigging and sails should take place. The Discovery's carpenters were ordered to assist those of the Chatham, in building and repairing her boats, and sawing out the plank, and all other necessary services that circumstances rendered practicable, were, by the several artificers, put in a train of execution.

Agreeably to the promise made to *Otoo*, Mr. Mudge, accompanied by Mr. Menzies, was on Saturday the 31st dispatched to the island of Morea for *Pomurrey*. *Matuaro*,[1] who we were informed was, under *Otoo*, sovereign of Huaheine,[2] and who was now here on an Ereeoi party,* undertook to be their

---

[1] Now usually spelled Matuaro. Menzies' version is Motooaro.   [2] Huahine.

* Vide Cook's Voyages. [The specific passage Vancouver had in mind cannot be identified. Cook's journals of all three voyages include many references to the ariori, the special and superior sect, skilled in dancing and mime, which travelled about the islands, celebrating both religious and secular festivals, and providing popular entertainment as well. The sexual abandon of some of their dances and their practice of infanticide repelled but also intrigued early visitors.]

pilot. As soon as the boat put off, the crowd about the ship becoming acquainted with her errand, the news was speedily carried with acclamations to the shore, and there received with great demonstrations of gladness.

During the night, the swell in the bay had greatly increased, and conceiving we were nearer the Dolphin bank than was imagined on our arrival, we warped nearer in shore, and moored in 13 fathoms black sand, and muddy bottom: One-Tree hill bearing by compass S. 26 W.; and point Venus N. 14 E. The surf breaking with great violence, had hitherto prevented our landing the camp party; but as I had been accustomed to see this place perfectly smooth, I entertained no doubt that the bay would in a day or two resume its usual tranquillity.[1]

Sunday morning ushered in the new year. The surf had in some measure subsided, though it still broke with great violence on the shore; which induced me to make new year's day a holiday. Every one had as much fresh pork, and plum-pudding as he could make use of; and lest in the voluptuous gratifications of Otaheite, we might forget our friends in old England, all hands were served a double allowance of grog to drink the healths of their sweethearts and friends at home. It is somewhat singular that the gunner of the Discovery was the only married man of the whole party.[2]

The weather becoming pleasant on the morning of Monday the 2d, the tents, observatory, &c. were sent on shore. These were constantly protected by a guard of marines, and our field pieces; which were very properly constructed for our occasions, and answered every expected purpose. Mr. Puget was charged with the encampment, and Mr. Whidbey was particularly to attend the observatory.[3] My attention and residence was divided between

---

[1] The tranquility Vancouver expected failed to come. Mudge commented on 5 January that there was 'a heavy swell, the ship constantly rolling her guns under Water.' Reviewing the visit to Tahiti, Baker wrote: 'We found the Bay of Matavai at this season of the year a most unpleasant anchorage, great part of the time we stayed here, a prodigious swell rolled in over the breakers which form the Bay, sometimes filling the decks with water. Mr. Bligh when he came here...in consequence of this inconvenience, removed down to Oparre, which certainly affords a much better anchorage, but as our time was not likely to be of long continuance, and the passage to that place rather intricate, it was not judged necessary to alter our situation.' – 24 January 1792.

[2] Hewett insists that the surgeon and the sergeant of marines were also married.

[3] Manby was named to 'the Lieutenant Governorship' of the camp, 'much to my satisfaction.' He described his relations with the natives: 'I took up my residence in a snug tent during our stay and very soon got initiated in all the social customs practiced by these generous People. The first step is to select a Chief who swears to be your friend, guide and protector during your stay, with this person you [ex]change names, and according to the term of Otahita he is called your Tio [taio]. One of the greatest Warriors Otahita produces was my declared Tio. I then assumed the name Toubaino and he that of Mappée the nearest they could come to my name and it would be the height of ingratitude did I not acknowledge him a faithful and true friend to me whilst the Discovery remained at the Island....His Wife, Daughter and female relations were at my Command. His House Hogs and everything belonging to him was at my disposal and a large retinue of domesticks were subservient to my Nod – in short he made me Lord of all in return I gave him a Matress in my Tent and made him welcome to what it produced.' – Letters, January 1792.

the ship and the shore. On pitching our tents, a great concourse of the natives in the most friendly and orderly manner attended. Their numbers, in some measure, proved inconvenient, by interrupting our labours; but, on a line being drawn on the ground, denoting the space we intended to occupy, not one attempted to trespass; and those who were permitted to help in the debarkation of our stores, conducted themselves with the utmost decorum, and seemed amply repaid with a few beads for their assistance.

Towards noon Mr. Mudge returned with my old friend *Pomurrey*,[1] who was saluted, previously to his coming on board, with four guns from each vessel, which gratified him extremely. With him came *Matooara Mahow*, commonly called *Mahow*;[2] the reigning prince, under *Otoo*, of Morea. There was however little probability of his long enjoying this honorable station, as he appeared to be in the last stage of a deep and rapid decline; his person was reduced to a mere skeleton, which he was not able to raise without great assistance. He was hoisted on board in a chair, and supported by six people down to the cabin, where, unable to sit up, or to stand, a bed was prepared for him on the lockers. The reasons that could induce a man in his deplorable condition to undertake such a visit, must, without doubt, be not less curious than extraordinary!

Pomurrey had perfect recollection of me; and every expression, and action, indicated the sincerity of the happiness he professed on our arrival. He frequently observed, I had grown very much, and looked very old since last we had parted. In the afternoon, his two wives and youngest sister arrived; the former were the sisters, and the latter the wife of *Mahow*.[3] His two brothers

---

[1] Menzies described the arrival of Mudge and himself at Moorea: 'After spreading several Bales of Cloth on the Beach opposite to us we were then invited to land, & Otoo [Pomurrey] himself received us with open arms....He then introduced us to the Queen & two other ladies & a sick chief who lay on a litter close to him. After these salutations we were wrappd up in such a quantity of Cloth by his own hand that we could hardly move under it. In this situation we made our presents to him which consisted only of two Axes a few knives scissors looking glasses & some beads....He then askd if Mr. Webber [artist on Cook's third voyage] was on board or any one in his place, & when he was answerd in the negative he expressed his concern as he wishd much to send his son's picture to the King of Britanee. He askd if *Bane* was still alive (by which he meant Sir Joseph Banks) & whether he would again visit Otaheite.' Richard Collett, the *Discovery*'s gunner, was with Mudge; he had been with Cook in 1777 and Pomurrey 'recollected him the moment he landed & askd him after a number of old acquaintance & questioned him particularly about Capt. Cook's death whose fate he seemd to bewail with real sorrow.' – 31 December 1791.

[2] Now usually spelled Mahau.

[3] The names of the two sisters of Mahau whom Pomurrey married are given differently, or spelled differently, in almost every account. In his recent study of *Ancient Tahitian Society* (Honolulu, 1974) D. L. Oliver gives the name of the older wife as Itia and states that she was the mother of the younger Otoo (Tu, later Pomare II). Bligh, who knew her well personally, spelled the name Iddeah and stated that she and Tynah (as he called the elder Otoo) had four children at the time of his visit in 1788, the eldest of whom was the younger Otoo. By Pomurrey Whaheine, referred to in the next paragraph, Vancouver meant the mother of Pomurrey's children. Vancouver gives the name of the younger sister as Fier

also accompanied the ladies, with many chiefs and attendants, each presenting me on their coming on board with cloth, hogs, fowls and vegetables, in such abundance, that we had now more than we could well dispense with. This profusion, however, and the manner in which it was bestowed, was very grateful to our feelings, as it plainly evinced the kind-hearted disposition of the inhabitants, and that we could not experience any want were our stay to be protracted far beyond the period of my present intention. It now became necessary that a handsome return should be made to the whole group, agreeably to the rank and situation of each individual. In selecting the presents I was fortunate enough at once to succeed, far beyond their most sanguine expectations.

As *Pomurrey* and *Mahow*, with their wives, were to sleep on board, their donations were not to be exhibited to public view until the crowd was dispersed; and I was instructed, in the event of inquiries being made concerning the presents I proposed to make these illustrious personages, to enumerate but few of the articles. Amongst those intended for *Pomurrey* were two axes. These he desired no one should know of; and to prevent even suspicion, hid them under my bureau, where they remained some days, until he sent his elder wife *Pomurrey Whaheine* for them. This degree of secrecy seemed inexplicable.[1]

Amongst the several chiefs who visited us, was *Poeno*, chief of Matavai,[2] who brought with him a portrait of Captain Cook, drawn by Mr. Webber, in the year 1777. This picture is always deposited in the house of the chief of Matavai, and is become the public register. On the back of it was written, that the Pandora had quitted this island the 8th of May, 1791.[3]

It is natural to suppose we should be very solicitous to become acquainted with the circumstances that had attended the vessel and the unfortunate persons belonging to the Bounty. Captain Edwards, who in the Pandora was dispatched from England in quest of them some months prior to our sailing,

---

re te. Menzies transliterates the name differently: 'Pomarre has lately taken to himself another sister of *Motooaro-Mahou* [Mahau] named *Whaerede* so that he lives at present with both sisters & is very fond of the youngest but has no children by her – indeed I suspect that the cruel custom of the Country [infanticide] would not suffer them to live.' – 31 December 1791. When talking to Bligh, Pomurrey referred to a fifth child, a daughter who had been killed at birth. Pomurrey's brother told Bligh that Pomurrey in his youth had belonged to the ariori, but that he had renounced the society and the custom of infanticide shortly before the birth of his second child, Otoo the younger. William Bligh, *Log of the Bounty* (London, 1937), I, 387, 389.

[1] Hewett offers an explanation: 'Had the Son Otoo known of them they must have been given up to him as a Superior in this Country can demand whatever he knows an Inferior to possess.'

[2] Menzies, who spells the name Poeenoh, refers to him as 'my particular friend'. – 8 January.

[3] Beaglehole states that the portrait was 'snatched from Tu in the wars that broke out about 1782 between him and Mahine [or Moorea]' but was afterwards returned. *Journals*, III, cxi.

had, we understood, arrived here, and taken on board those of the crew who were left at Otaheite, amounting to the number of thirteen, at the time Mr. Christian with the rest of his party sailed from the island, which was some time before the arrival of the Pandora; since which period I was not able to procure any intelligence of Mr. Christian or his companions.[1]

Whatever particulars could be collected from the natives, respecting this no less criminal than melancholy event, I thought it an incumbent duty to procure and transmit to England, lest any accident should befall the Pandora.[2] But as a legal investigation has since taken place, I trust I shall neither incur the displeasure of the humane, nor the reproach of the curious, by declining any further digression on this sad subject: the former will readily find an apology for me in their own bosoms; and the latter may resort to the publications of the day, for any other particulars with which they may be desirous of becoming acquainted.

A large party of royalty, and chiefs, honored us with their company at dinner, which failed of being a pleasant circumstance in consequence of the weather being extremely hot, and the cabin excessively crowded. On this occasion, the wives of *Pomurrey* and the wife of *Mahow* were permitted to sit with us at table, and partake of the repast. This indulgence, however, is by no means common, and, I believe, granted to no other of the women on the island. Our attention was particularly attracted by the great desire which the generality of them, both male and female, exhibited, in their endeavours to adopt our manners and customs, and the avidity with which they sought spirituous liquors.

Pomurrey, in the course of dinner and afterwards, drank a bottle of brandy,

---

[1] Bligh was master of the *Resolution* in Cook's third voyage, but Vancouver, then a midshipman in the *Discovery*, probably had little or no contact with him. The story of the *Bounty* need not be recounted in much detail. She arrived in Matavai Bay on 26 October 1788 and remained there more than five months. Her mission was to secure breadfruit seedlings to be planted in the West Indies, and she had to wait until they had grown sufficiently to be transplanted into pots. Alan Moorehead suggests that this long delay was the principal cause of the famous mutiny: 'No large group of Europeans had remained so long on the island before, and the attachments formed by the *Bounty's* crew with the Tahitian women was something more than those of a sailor's spree. Every man had his girl, and when they came to sail away many of them found the loss of their companions quite unendurable.' – *The Fatal Impact* (New York, 1966), p. 76. The mutiny occurred on 28 April 1789, just 24 days after the ship left Tahiti, and Bligh, cast adrift, began his remarkable voyage across the Pacific in an open boat. The *Bounty*, now in the hands of Fletcher Christian and the mutineers, returned twice to Tahiti, first in June and then in September. She left behind four midshipmen who had taken no part in the mutiny and ten crewmen who preferred to take their chances in Tahiti. The *Pandora*, Captain Edward Edwards, did not arrive until 23 March 1791. Edwards made no attempt to discriminate between the guilty and the innocent; all were seized and carried away. Meanwhile the mutineers had sought refuge on Pitcairn Island. The existence of the unhappy colony they founded there was not known to the outside world until 1808.

[2] This seems to imply that Vancouver sent a report of some sort to London, but nothing of the kind has come to light.

without diluting it. This threw him into such violent convulsions that four strong men were required to hold him down, and to perform the office of '*Roome, roome,*'* which is done by squeezing the flesh of the limbs, and body of the intoxicated person with their hands. On these convulsions subsiding, he slept for about an hour, and then arose to all appearance as much refreshed with his nap, as if he had retired perfectly sober. I expostulated with a desire to convince him that inebriety was highly pernicious to health, but in vain; his only reply was, '*Nowe none,*' a term used for every thing that delights or pleases, such as music, &c. &c. accused me of being a stingy fellow, and that I was not '*Tio tio,*' a phrase lately adopted to signify a jolly companion. This determined me that he should have his own way, and orders were given that he should have as much brandy or rum, as he chose to call for; concluding, that in a few days he would be convinced of its ill effects. In this I was not mistaken; before a week expired he ceased calling for spirits; and a few glasses of wine, at and after dinner, completely satisfied him; frequently saying, that all I had told him of the '*Ava Britarne*' was perfectly true.[1] Spirits and wine are, however, in great request with all the chiefs, as is sugar; and there can be no doubt that these articles might be rendered amongst them considerable branches of traffic.

We were busily employed on Tuesday the 3d about our rigging, sails, and other matters on board; and in landing the chronometers, instruments, and other necessary articles and implements for the execution of our business on shore; from whence the boats returned with some water; and we began salting pork.

The weather continued to be very sultry; the thermometer generally standing between 83 and 86, my royal guests, with a crowd of attendants, still remained on board, and their company became no less unpleasant than inconvenient. I was given to understand they intended to make the ship their place of residence, until they should return to Morea. This arrangement was very incommodious, and to which it was impossible to object: I was therefore under the necessity of resorting to some little address, which fortunately was

---

* Vide Cook's Voyages. [For Cook's description see *Journals*, III, 214–15. Menzies, a surgeon, described the vigorous massage he received when he returned from a journey: 'finding I was very wet and fatigued, they made me strip off my cloathes & wrapped me up in a quantity of dry Oheitean Cloth & in this situation a number of women gathered round to romee me, & continued their operation of pinching, nipping & squeezing till every part of me was so benumbed & torpid that I actually fell asleep under their hands, & when I awakened found myself very much refreshed, by this rough usage, which I am confident might be employ'd to advantage in many lingering chronic & sedentary disorders.' – 8 January.]

[1] Pomurrey was not the only member of the family who developed a fondness for alcohol: 'the only extravagance we were subject to was in wine and spirits Pomurrey and more particularly his two brothers being excessively fond of both. Weytooa [Vaetua] the Younger was looked upon by the Sailors as (what they called) a hearty Soul, his morning beverage when he could get it was seldom less than a pint of the strongest Brandy which he was never long in finishing....the two wives of Pomarri one of them the mother of the young King, partook of it with almost equal prodigality.' – Johnstone, 9 January.

attended with the desired success. I took an opportunity of acquainting *Pomurrey* that my attendance at the observatory would now be constantly required, which would oblige me to dine on shore; but that I had ordered a dinner on board, and plenty of brandy, for him and his friends. A consultation shortly took place, and as I was about to leave the ship, he said, if I would call for him after dinner, the whole party would disembark, desiring at the same time, that he might be saluted on his landing, from the encampment; which in the evening was done accordingly.[1] Our royal friends took up their abode in a wretched house brought for the express purpose to point Venus, where our tents on former visits had been pitched. *Pomurrey* was not in a condition to favor us with his presence that evening; but, in the morning of Wednesday the 4th, we had the honor of his company at the encampment. He regarded with inquisitive attention, and great admiration, the several works in which our people were engaged. A large piece of timber which was sawing into plank, greatly attracted his notice, and drew me into a scrape; he said it was impossible we could be in immediate want of so great a quantity, and did not doubt that ere long we should be in a country where we could again be supplied, having understood that this stick had been cut at New Zealand. These considerations led him to request, that I would order a chest of the plank to be made for him, six feet long, four feet broad, and three feet deep. I excused myself, by replying that I could not with any conveniency part with so much plank, nor could the carpenters be well spared from the business on which they were employed; but that, before we sailed, I would endeavour to have a small chest made for him. *Pomurrey*, however, was of opinion, that a large chest would take little more time to finish than a small one, and offered to find plank for the top and bottom, if I would supply the sides and ends, and allow a carpenter to make it. In short he was so pressing and earnest, that much against my inclination, having great demands for the plank, and constant employ for the artificers, I was under the necessity of complying with his wishes.[2]

Mahow, though extremely feeble, paid us a visit on shore; being unable to walk, he was carried about in a kind of litter. Many other chiefs were now constantly attendant upon us with a numerous party of the natives, who all conducted themselves with the strictest propriety, and seemed highly delighted

[1] 'Pomarre's reason for thus apparently incommoding himself & family was that he might be near to us to preserve good order among his people, as he still administred the government for his son who was considered in some respects a Minor.' – Menzies, 3 January.

[2] Pomurrey wanted the chest to protect his valuables against thieves. In 1777 Cook noted that the Tahitian chiefs 'were extremely desirous of Chests, a few that the Spaniards had left among them [in 1774–75], they seemed to set much Value upon and were continually asking us for some. I had one made for Otoo according to his own dimensions, it was eight feet long five broad about three deep; locks and bolts were not a sufficient security, but it was large [e]nough for two people to sleep upon by way of guard[ing] it in the night.' – *Journals*, III, 222. This chest was lost in the war with Moorea.

with the new mode of spending their time, in observing and animadverting on our different employments.

The wind, since our arrival, had been eastwardly, blowing a moderate breeze; it had now veered to the north with squalls and showers of rain, attended by a very heavy rolling swell in the bay. The Discovery's yawl wanting repair was hauled up for that purpose. In the evening we had much rain, with frequent gusts of wind; which so much increased the surf, that all communication with the shore must have ceased, had not the good offices of our kind friends on the island, enabled us to keep up a correspondence. They successfully contended with the boisterous elements, by swimming to and from the ship; and, to manifest their attachment, supplied us by this means with bread-fruit, cocoa-nuts, and other refreshments.

On the morning of Thursday the 5th, the N.W. wind, which is the most boisterous and unpleasant known in this country, brought with it a sea which broke with such great violence on the shore, as to insulate the spot on which our royal friends had taken up their abode. The wind could not be considered as a strong gale; yet so violent was the sea that accompanied it, that it broke with unintermitted force in every part of the bay, excepting where the vessels rode; and, even there, we did not intirely escape its fury; two seas broke on board the Discovery, although in eight fathoms water, which nearly filled the waist. Towards eight o'clock, the clouds in the N.W. bearing a very threatening appearance, the sheet anchor was dropped underfoot. This disagreeable weather continued all day, and the surf ranged so high on the shore as to make it necessary to remove the observatory further back several paces; notwithstanding which, the kind offices of the friendly natives, regardless of danger, were uninterruptedly continued.

It became calm, and the weather appeared more settled on the morning of Friday the 6th. The sheet anchor was weighed and replaced; and all hands were busily employed in their respective departments. After breakfast, I went on shore, and understood that *Otoo* had, in the course of the last two days, been carried, as when we first met him, about the encampment. On his approach, I invited him into the marquee, and requested he would visit the ships. Both these invitations he declined; and I was immediately given to understand, that should he enter the tents or ships, neither his father, mother, or any inhabitant of these islands, could again be admitted; that every thing is and must be destroyed out of which he should eat or drink, although vessels or utensils belonging to us. As the young monarch was about the encampment most part of the day; whilst at dinner, I demanded of his father if I might send him a glass of wine; he replied, if I chose to have the glass broken, I was at liberty so to do; and enquired if I had an abundance of such articles to spare. Some wine was therefore sent in the shell of a cocoa-nut, which being emptied by the young king, was instantly broken and thrown in the sea. *Pomurrey* had, early and frequently, asked if we had not fire-works on board, and being informed that we had, Saturday evening was fixed for an exhibition, after which the royal party, with their dying chief *Mahow*, were to return to Morea, and having landed him, *Pomurrey* and his wives were to return, and remain here until we should depart. The intended display of fire-works was made known to all around us, and messengers with the intelligence were dispatched to various parts of the island.

Pomurrey's father, who was formerly known by the name of *Happi*, now called *Taow*,[1] had arrived from Morea, on Saturday the 7th, and was on board the Discovery, where he desired to see me; on which, *Pomurrey* with *Urripiah* and *Whytooa*, his two next brothers,[2] accompanied me to pay our respects to their old sire, who had just arrived in a large canoe, laden with the productions of the country as a present. This interview was excessively affecting. It was with great satisfaction that I beheld the affectionate regard with which the three sons embraced their aged and venerable father; who, in acknowledging a grateful sense of their dutiful congratulations, exhibited feelings which drew tears from the whole party. When these filial effusions, which would have done credit to the sensibility of the most polished nations, had subsided, I presented *Taow* with a suitable return; and, on including some articles for his wife,[3] who was still living at Morea, he was highly delighted, and the value of the present in his estimation seemed thereby infinitely increased.

Some of the royal females had now joined our party; and as *Pomurrey* had not yet paid Mr. Broughton a visit, we all went on board the Chatham. Presents were necessary on this occasion; and although I considered that Mr. Broughton had been very liberal, our royal guests seemed of a very different opinion;[4] but on explaining that there was not the same abundance of valuable things on board the small vessel that there was in the large ship, and having some retrospect to the number and value of those obtained from the Discovery, we left the Chatham, and went on shore tolerably well satisfied.

Soon after our arrival at the encampment I witnessed a scene, very different from that which had been exhibited on board on the meeting of three sons with their venerable parent. It was shortly announced that *Otoo* was

---

[1] Hapai and Teu are the modern renderings.

[2] Oliver gives these names as Ariipaea (not to be confused with Ariipaea Vahine, a half-sister) and Vaetua. Ariipaea was regarded as a great warrior and has been credited with bringing about drastic changes in methods of warfare in Tahiti. Inter-island clashes, and even clashes between districts in the same island, had been largely naval affairs. Ariipaea preferred invasion on land, and for the great war canoes of Cook's time substituted fleets of canoes used as troop transports. In view of this reputation, Menzies' description of him is interesting: 'He is very pleasing in his manners, firm & graceful in his gait, communicative in his conversation – pert in his inquiries – quick in his discernment & sincere in his attachment, as we found by that particular veneration he continues to pay to the memory of Captain Clark [Clerke], whose friend he was & whose name he still bears in preference to any other, however honorable...' – 6 January.

[3] Tetupaia.

[4] Hewett comments: 'The Chiefs all declared Mr. Broughton to have been very generous but that Captn. V. was pere pere (close fisted).'

approaching. On this occasion, it became necessary that the grandfather should pay homage to his grandson. A pig and a plantain leaf were instantly procured, the good old man stripped to the waist, and when *Otoo* appeared in the front of the marquee, the aged parent, whose limbs were tottering with the decline of life, met his grandson, and on his knees acknowledged his own inferiority, by presenting this token of submission; which, so far as could be discovered, seemed offered with a mixture of profound respect, and parental regard. The ceremony seemed to have little effect on the young monarch, who appeared to notice the humiliating situation of his grandsire with the most perfect indifference and unconcern.[1] This mode of behaviour is, however, rather to be attributed to the force of education, than to a want of the proper sentiments of affection; as I perfectly recollected that, when I was here with Captain Cook, *Pomurrey* treated his brothers with the most cool indifference, although, on the present occasion, there are few examples of three brothers in greater harmony, or regarding each other with more fraternal affection: it should therefore seem, that this sort of distant deportment is a necessary appendage to the high office of sovereign. Another royal son and daughter honored us with their company. These, with a daughter remaining at Morea, are all the children of *Pomurrey* now living. His family originally consisted of five, but one of his daughters was deceased. All these children were by his eldest wife, known by the name of *Pomurrey Whaheine*, or the female *Pomurrey*; this lady I shall hereafter distinguish by the appellation of Queen Mother. By his youngest wife he has had no children; she is called *Fier re te*. Our new visitors were, each like their brother *Otoo*, carried on men's shoulders; and for the same reasons which interdicted him, they could not enter our habitations. The youth seemed to be about three or four years younger than *Otoo*, and had taken the name of *Whyeadooa*, in consequence of his being the acknowledged sovereign of *Tiarabou*, under his brother *Otoo*; the daughter appeared to be about two or three years of age, to whom, or to the young lady remaining at Morea, I did not understand that any particular titles or consequence were at present annexed; yet this child seemed treated with much respect and attention.[2]

[1] Bell commented: 'we saw no respect paid to any but Pomarre, and Otoo – to these every person whatever uncovered, – that is, both men and women stripp'd themselves as low as the breast, – in this they are very strict, and even Pommare's Wife and mother of Otoo, strip to her Son.' – January. Menzies noted that Teu (or Hapai) was treated with no deference when he went to Moorea to bring back Pomurrey: 'on presenting him with a few small trinkets, he hardly got hold of them when they were tore out of his hand in a squabble by the Multitude who seemed to consider him as their common prey.' – 31 December 1791.

[2] Confusion about the names of Pomurrey's children more than equals that about the names of his wives, but the details need not be given here. Bligh, who knew the family well, lists the four surviving children as the younger Otoo, born about 1783, a daughter born in 1784, a second son born about 1786 and another daughter born in 1787. *Log of the Bounty* (London, 1937), I, 385. Vancouver evidently thought the children were somewhat younger. The second son assumed the name Whyeadooa (Vancouver's attempt

We had a very large party of the royal family and of the different chiefs to dinner at the marquee; after which it was proposed, that the 'Heava no Britarne,' that is, the English entertainments, should commence. Pomurrey requested that some guns from the ships should be fired as a prelude; that the marines on shore should go through their exercise, and fire; and that the efforts of the field pieces should be exhibited. From the latter were fired both round and cannister shot, which the surrounding multitude beheld with surprize, admiration, and terror, manifested by their expressions, particularly on observing the distance to which the small three pounders threw the round shot; and the execution that evidently could be done by the cannister, which was fired at a rock in the sea, lying at a convenient distance. On firing with some dispatch, three rounds from the field pieces, the fear of Pomurrey completely overcome his curiosity, and he exclaimed 'Anteerara,' signifying he was perfectly satisfied.

In the evening, we were very fortunate in our display of fire-works. They had been well prepared and preserved; and were, without exception, of their various kinds, equal to any I ever saw discharged in Europe. A numerous crowd assembled on the occasion expressed as much astonishment and admiration as if these had been the first exhibited in the island. I endeavoured to prevail on Pomurrey to assist in the performance. He once took the port fire in his hand, but his heart failed, and calling his youngest wife Fier re te, desired I would instruct her. She was by no means so alarmed as her husband; and, with a little of my assistance, she fired several rockets, a catharine wheel, some flower-pots, and balloons. Having displayed an assortment of these, together with some water rockets, &c. the exhibition was closed; and the natives retired in the most perfect good order to their respective habitations, excessively well pleased with their entertainment; although it was evident, that the major part had been as much affected by terror as admiration. Pomurrey, with his two wives and sister, came to breakfast the next morning, Sunday the 8th, and expressed great satisfaction and many thanks for the pleasure which the last evening had afforded them. The young king, with his brother and sister, honored the encampment also with their presence. Understanding that our royal party were about to leave us for some days, presents were made them on the occasion; with which, highly delighted with their excursion, and their reception by us, they departed.

The chronometers and other instruments had now been landed nearly a week; but, owing to the very unsettled state of the weather, until this day, we had not been able to get corresponding altitudes. The like cause had operated also in retarding the general transactions at the encampment; where whilst I was busily employed at the observatory, Poatatou[1] arrived; having sent

to transliterate Waheatua, which is now spelled Vehiatua) because he was succeeding Vehiatua III, the young chief of Taiarapu (Vancouver's Tiarabou), who had died in 1790. Taiarapu was the southern part of Tahiti, sometimes called Little Tahiti, separated from the much larger northern part by a narrow isthmus.

[1] Chief of the district of Punaauia, in Western Tahiti.

before him a magnificent present of hogs, vegetables, cloth, mats, &c. I had
been very intimate with this chief on my last visit to this country; we perfectly
recollected each other; and the sincerity of my friend, and his wife also, did
not spare me the mortification of being informed a second time, that I was
grown exceedingly old. He much regretted that he had not arrived in time
to partake of the entertainments of the preceding day and evening; as he had
never been so fortunate as to be present at such an exhibition. This induced
me to promise, that, on the return of *Pomurrey* from Morea, a similar display
should take place.

Poatatou, who was now called *Hidiea*, with his wife and sister, accompanied
me on board. Amongst the valuables with which I presented my old
acquaintance and friend, was an axe, of which his sister became so enamoured,
claiming to herself a part of the present I had received, that *Hidiea* was under
the necessity of using some force to prevent her wrenching it out of his hand;
but, on my making a small addition to the articles she had received, the lady
became reconciled.

Our business in the several departments was now in great forwardness; yet
we were likely to experience an inconvenience in procuring fire-wood, as we
had few trees in our neighbourhood but such as bore fruit. On mentioning
this circumstance to *Urripiah*, he undertook, with *Whytooa*, *Poeno*, and *Moerree*
an inferior chief, to supply more than the ships would contain, provided they
were furnished with two axes each, as, on such an occasion, they could not
afford to wear out their own; which, on my part, was readily acceded to.

The sea had broken so much into the river as to render it brackish and unfit
for use near our encampment; this obliged us to have our casks filled near
a mile off, opposite *Urripiah*'s habitation; who ordered them to be emptied,
and filled, for the purpose of seasoning, as often as we desired; and giving
them in charge to his trusty domestics, they remained in his custody several
days in the most perfect safety. This conduct was not singular; for it is but
justice to acknowledge, that every one of the inhabitants behaved with an
uniform propriety, as deserving of our thanks as of our commendations. In
every transaction, they were emulous to afford us assistance to the utmost of
their power; and seemed amply and satisfactorily rewarded for their exertions
in our service, by the humble return of a few beads, or small nails.

The departure of *Pomurrey*'s family was daily put off, *Mahow* being very
desirous that we should convey him home in one of our boats; but as these,
as well as our men, were too much employed to be spared for this purpose,
we were daily honored at our meals with most of this good company; and
it must be acknowledged, that their deportment at table was now so much
improved, that the major part conducted themselves with great consistency.
Excepting the daughter of *Opoone*,[1] who reigned over Bolabola,[2] and its two
neighbouring isles, we had now the presence of all the sovereigns of this group
of islands. *Opoone* had formerly conquered and annexed the islands of Ulietea
and Otaha[3] to the government of Bolabola; but, on his death, the sovereignty

---

[1] Puni.   [2] Borabora.   [3] Now Raiatea and Tahaa.

of these islands had, in right of natural, or original succession, fallen to a chief whose name was *Mowree*.[1] He was a shrewd sensible fellow, affected to be well acquainted with the English language, and certainly had acquired some words which he pronounced so as to be understood. He was a brother of *Pomurrey*'s mother, was on a visit to the royal family here, and was by them treated with much respect and attention.

Hitherto I had received a few trifling presents of provisions only from *Pomurrey*, who had lately expressed some regret that he had not made me a return for the many useful matters I had bestowed upon him, and had fixed this day to make an acknowledgment.

Towards noon *Pomurrey* came to the marquee, attended by a considerable train. He was preceded by three men, each bearing a *parri*, or mourning dress, esteemed the most valuable present the country can afford.[2] Many of the rest were laden with cloth, fowls and vegetables; these with some very large hogs which brought up the rear, made altogether a very superb and grateful compensation. *Pomurrey* and his wives dined with us; after which they took leave of the encampment to embark for Oparre, there to join *Mahow*, who had departed early in the morning for Morea; for which island the whole of the royal party were to sail the next day; there they proposed to land *Mahow*, and, in the course of four or five days, return; having given them to understand we should, about that time, be on the eve of our departure. They were saluted from our station on shore, on their way on board the Discovery, where a canoe was waiting to receive them; and in which were two large hogs, that *Pomurrey* had desired might be sent me from Oparre. Considering myself, on this occasion, his debtor, I endeavoured to discover what would be most acceptable in return. He had promised to solicit a file for a man in his canoe, and he could not be prevailed upon to accept any other article. After a short stay on board, they bade us farewel, and were saluted with eight guns from the vessels. Most of the chiefs left us, in order to procure such articles as they considered might be acceptable to us previously to our departure.

Mr. Broughton, Mr. Menzies, and several officers of the Discovery and Chatham made an excursion on Friday the 13th to the westward, towards Oparre, and the country in its vicinity; which, together with the absence of the chiefs and their attendants, so much reduced our society, that the encampment had the appearance of being almost deserted.

At day-break the next morning, Saturday the 14th, I received a message from *Pomurrey*, acquainting me with the death of *Mahow*; in consequence of which their voyage to Morea was at an end. Little concern could possibly be felt on this occasion. *Mahow*'s relief from the wretched condition in which

[1] Mauri.

[2] 'The most valuable Artifical Curiosities among them are the *Taoume* [tamai], or Breastplate, and the *Pari* [parae] or Mourning dress, they are both principally composed of the Glossy Pidgeon's feathers, the Pearl Oyster Shell, and the Small Shark's teeth – they are very strongly and neatly work'd, and display much taste & elegance.' – Bell, January.

he existed, was directed by humanity to be esteemed a most happy event; particularly when the very singular treatment is considered, which this poor being endured whilst in our neighbourhood. Almost every evening, and sometimes twice in the night, he was brought in the litter from the royal habitation near the point, and placed in some one of our tents for a short time, and then carried back again. In the day-time he was either visiting the encampment, or, in the heat of the sun, or in the midst of rain was rowed round the ships, and insisted one evening on sleeping on board the Chatham. He was very fond of tea, and extremely desirous that whatever nourishment he took should be dressed in the English fashion. The conduct observed towards this dying man, seemed calculated, if not intended, to hasten his dissolution. This however, was not to be reconciled with the general deportment of the whole royal party, and especially with that of *Pomurrey*, who appeared to regard him with great tenderness and affection. I was particularly inquisitive why he was so harassed about; and they all agreed it was in consequence of his own desire, which, so far as could be learned, seemed dictated by superstitious notions.

I desired the messenger to inform *Pomurrey*, that I would attend the funeral solemnities of the deceased the next day. On the morning of Sunday the 15th he again returned with a request from *Pomurrey*, that I would not visit Oparre until Tuesday, when the religious interdiction under which that district had been laid would be at an end, no communication at present being permitted between the inhabitants of Oparre and those of the other parts of the island. This was made generally known by the display of flags in the several path-ways; not a canoe was suffered to move along the shores; nor was a fire allowed to be made; which produced a degree of solemnity, that was very expressive of the concern felt for the death of this chief, and of his consequence and respectability. Numerous fires had been observed the preceding day all over the district of Oparre. These, we were given to understand, were ceremonies of a religious nature consequent on the demise of *Mahow*; and it is reasonable to suppose that the mourners took advantage of this ordinance to cook sufficient provisions for the time of the interdiction.

Our provisions having been supplied in the greatest abundance, permission was now granted for the purchase of curiosities, agreeably to my promise contained in the restrictive orders of the 25th of December last.[1] And as

---

[1] As usual, Hewett was critical: 'After this time very little could be purchased as no Canoe came near the Ship in Consequence of the Death of the Chief and had we not Smuggled before [his death] we should have gone without sometimes even Provisions as one Day only three fourths of a Bread fruit was given to our Mess (five in Number) for Breakfast so that without breaking Orders we should have Starved in the midst of Plenty and in Consequence dealing privately and in a Hurry we gave double the price for the Articles that we should have done if dealing Openly.' Manby, also frequently critical of Vancouver, termed it 'an unpleasant order'. Even more unpopular was an order that limited shore leave. A few sick men were allowed to go on shore, but they 'were the only people out of the Ships who were permitted to go on shore except on duty during the whole time of their Stay' – an order that Bell considered unjust. 'When we consider for

nothing worthy of attention had occurred in our neighbourhood during the absence of Mr. Broughton and his party, I shall insert such observations made during their excursion, as were communicated to me on their return.[1]

Our gentlemen embarked in a canoe belonging to *Mowree*, the sovereign of Ulietea, who together with *Whytooa* and his wife accompanied them towards Oparre. On their way they landed for the purpose of seeing the morai of *Tapootapootatea*.[2] *Mowree*, who attended them, on approaching the sacred spot, desired the party would stop until he should address the *Eatooa*.[3] For this purpose he seated himself on the ground, and began praying before a watta, ornamented with a piece of wood indifferently carved, on which was placed, for the present occasion, a bundle of cloth and some red feathers. During this ejaculation, which took up a considerable time, the names of the party were twice mentioned. He likewise repeated the names of the several commanders who had visited the island; together with those of '*Keene Corge*' (that is, King George) and '*Britarne*,' which were frequently expressed. When these introductory ceremonies were finished, *Mowree* attended them to every part of the morai, and explained every particular. He appeared to be well versed in all the ceremonials and rites appertaining to their religion, which made the party greatly lament their want of a competent knowledge of the language, as they were unable to comprehend his meaning, except in a few common instances.[4] Having left the morai, and proceeded westward about a mile, they arrived at a house surrounded by a plantation of *ava* belonging to *Urripiah*, who was then at dinner with a numerous company of our Matavai friends; and whilst our gentlemen were taking some refreshment, a messenger arrived from *Whytooa*, whose guests they were to be, and who had gone before them

a moment, how very anxious every person must be to get ashore, – and what a relaxation it must be, after having been five weeks at Sea – and more expecially when at such a place as Otaheite – one of the most charming Countries in the world, – Why should poor Sailors...be debarr'd those recreations which they see every Officer on board enjoy?' But he recognized that 'Captain Vancouver's motive was nevertheless good, – for he was apprehensive of quarrels happening between the Sailors & the Natives.' – Bell, January.

[1] The chief source of information was evidently Menzies' journal, which the account given by Vancouver follows very closely.

[2] The marae of Taputapuatea. Vancouver here follows Menzies, who was mistaken in the name. The marae of Taputapuatea was a considerable distance away, on Point Punaauia, on the W coast of Tahiti, whereas the marae visited was not far from Matavai Bay. Menzies states that 'On passing the first point of Oparre we requested to land in order to see the Morai...' – 13 January. The most likely identification is the marae of Tarahoi, the principal marae of Pare and the family marae of Pomurrey.

[3] atua, the general term for any god.

[4] Knowledge of the language evidently increased rapidly: 'It is surprising with what facility every person on board learn'd the language; we made ourselves well understood in the course of a couple of days, and before we left, there were many that could hold long conversations with the Natives; indeed a Language so easy of pronunciation, there being few Consonants to render it harsh – is easily learn'd, and particularly under such good tutors as these people are...if they observe you have a desire to acquire a knowledge of their Language, they are indefatigable in their exertions to instruct you.' – Bell, January.

from the morai, requesting their attendance at his habitation, which they found situated on the verge of the sea shore. In the front of it was an *ava* plantation, interspersed with sugar cane, and bananas; near the house was a small shrubbery, of native ornamental plants. The whole surrounded by a well constructed fence of bamboo, neatly intersected with clean paths, that led in different directions, produced an effect that was extremely pleasing, and redounded much to the credit and ingenuity of the proprietor. *Whytooa* had taken very effectual means to provide for their entertainment; for a large hog had been committed to the oven, and was nearly ready for the table, with an abundance of other refreshments. The mansion was large and airy. By lines stretched across, they had quiet possession of one half of the building; and this partition prevented the idle curiosity of the assembled natives from interrupting the comfort of their repast.[1] In the afternoon they were visited by *Urripiah* and some of his attendants. He observed, that, in the absence of his royal brothers, and other principal chiefs, it was not improbable that some of the natives might take advantage of this circumstance, and discontinue their present orderly behaviour in the neighbourhood of the vessels and the encampment. He therefore requested Mr. Broughton would, in his name, write to me, recommending the five following chiefs to be admitted into our society on board and on shore; whose presence would be the means of effectually restraining the populace. Their names were *Poeno, Matiapo,* and *Moerree,* of Matavai; and *Tatoah,* and *Arreheah* of Hapino;[2] in the protection and good offices of whom we may[3] place the fullest confidence. *Matiapo* being present, he was charged by Mr. Broughton with this embassy. From our earliest acquaintance with this royal and worthy chief, his mind had appeared to be wholly engrossed in devising the means for our comfort, and for preserving a friendly and good understanding between us and his countrymen; and even here, though retired to his cottage, he was found equally zealous in the same laudable pursuit. They were also complimented by the young king *Otoo* with a visit. His approach was announced by the usual ceremony of all the natives present uncovering their shoulders; and as he could not with propriety enter *Whytooa*'s fence, they paid him their respects on the beach; whence, after receiving some trinkets, he hastened with his royal sister, each carried as before, to meet *Pomurrey,* who was about to land at the morai. Towards the evening, a scene was presented that gave a very different turn to the feelings of the party. On paying their respects to the royal family, who had landed near them, the sorrow and dejection which appeared in the countenance of *Pomurrey,* induced an inquiry into the cause of his melancholy;

---

[1] Menzies noted an amusing detail: 'We now found that three English Geese had been landed...so far were these animals enabled to distinguish our voices or dresses that they kept gaggling about that end of the house we were in & constantly shun'd the natives.' – 14 January.

[2] Haapaianoo, a district E of Matavai Bay; now called Papenoo.

[3] 'might' in the first edition.

he replied in a low tone of voice, that '*Matooara Mahow* was dead.' *Urripiah*
on hearing the news burst into a flood of tears; and a sorrowful gloomy sadness
soon overspread the whole assembly. On advancing a little further, we[1]
observed the queen-mother and *Fier re te* in tears near the canoe from which
they had landed, searching a bundle containing some shark's teeth, with which
the women of this country torture themselves, to manifest their grief on such
occasions. After each had made choice of an instrument for this purpose, they
retired in silent affliction to a neighbouring plantation.

The next morning, (Monday the 16th) they were again honored by a visit
from *Otoo* and several of the chiefs, in their way to the morai. Soon after,
a canoe covered with an awning was seen coming from the westward,
paddling in a slow and solemn manner towards the morai, in which was the
corpse of the deceased chief. On their expressing great anxiety to see *Pomurrey*
for the purpose of obtaining permission to attend the burial ceremony, they
were informed that he was gone to the morai, but would have no objection
to their being present. They proceeded; and, near the rivulet that flows by
Urripiah's house, they saw the queen-mother, *Fier re te*, and the widow of the
deceased *Mahow*, sitting all in tears; and in the paroxysms of their affliction,
wounding their heads with the shark's teeth they had prepared the preceding
evening. The widow had a small spot shaved on the crown of her head, which
was bloody, and bore other evident marks of having frequently undergone
the cruel effect of her despair. Being apprehensive that the presence of strangers
might be unwelcome, they took leave, and repaired to the morai, where the
priests had already begun their funeral solemnities. *Pomurrey*, *Urripiah*, and
others, silently assenting, they moved quietly through the assembly, and were
seated with as little interruption to the duties, as on entering a church in
England after the service is commenced. Five priests were seated before
Pomurrey, chanting a prayer, with their faces towards *Otoo*, who sat on a man's
lap. About ten yards from him was held a bundle of cloth, which contained
emblematically the *Eatooa*; a general name for their deities. The body of
Mahow, wrapped in English red cloth, was deposited under an awning in a
canoe, whose bow was drawn up a little way on the beach near the morai,
and was attended by one man only at her stern up to his middle in water,
to prevent her driving from the spot. The priests continued chanting their
prayers, frequently exalting their voices, until they ended in a very shrill tone.
He who, on this occasion, performed the office of chief priest, was discovered
to be our friend *Mowree*,[2] whose prayer was equally fervent, and continued
nearly half an hour longer than the rest; during which he was occasionally
joined by another priest in a very shrill tone of voice. This prayer of *Mowree*'s
seemed at intervals, like an expostulation with the Divinity, by adverting to
the different productions of the island remaining, and still flourishing in the
greatest plenty, and yet *Matooara Mahow* was suffered to die.

---

[1] 'they' (correctly) in the first edition.   [2] Mauri.

The address being ended they all rose up, and proceeded westward along the shore, followed by the canoe in which was the corpse, to the mouth of the rivulet, where the three royal ladies still continued to indulge their excessive grief; and who, on perceiving the canoe, burst forth into a loud yell of lamentation, which was accompanied by an accelerated application of the shark's teeth, until the blood very freely following, mingled with their tears. The canoe entered the brook, and proceeded towards another morai at the foot of the mountains, where the ceremonies to be performed on the body of the deceased required such secrecy, that, on no account, could our gentlemen be permitted to attend, although it was most earnestly requested. As some alleviation to this disappointment, *Pomurrey* promised they should see the manner in which the remains would be deposited the next day, and earnestly intreated they would desist from following the procession any further on the present occasion. As it was generally suspected that the body was now to undergo the process of embalming, the party much lamented *Pomurrey's* interdiction, as it deprived them of the only opportunity that possibly might ever occur of becoming acquainted with the nature of this operation; whence might be derived not only curious, but useful anatomical information. This prompted Mr. Menzies to renew his solicitations to *Pomurrey* to be admitted alone; but as these were attended with no better success they determined to abandon these melancholy solemnities, and extend their excursion a few miles westward to *Pomurrey's* residence; which they found pleasantly situated near the shore, consisting of two large houses lately erected.[1] Here they were entertained with a heava[2] performed by a number of very young girls, in the wanton manner of the country. At a particular part of the dance, a fellow stept in amongst the performers, and in a very obscene though ludicrous manner entertained the native audience: but, on our gentlemen expressing their abhorrence of such indecorous behaviour, the girls, in finishing their parts, did not expose their persons below the waist.[3] After distributing some presents to the young actresses, they retired; and directing their route back, through the plantations, soon arrived at the house of a chief, where *Whytooa* having provided an excellent repast they were sumptuously regaled.

In the evening, as they returned to our friend's house, they observed many fires were burning at Oparre, as if a grand entertainment was preparing; they however fared as usual; and after supper, on requesting their worthy host would join in a glass of grog, to the health of friends in *Britarne*, he, though

---

[1] 'one of which was 16 yards long by 18 yards wide'. – Menzies, 14 January.

[2] heiva.

[3] Menzies' account differs: 'Here a number of young girls entertained us with a *Heiva* in the wanton manner of their country, at particular parts of this dance a fellow stept in before the Girls who had a large Hernia & exposd it in a ludicrous manner, to the no small amusement of the rest of the Natives, but when we expressd our disgust at this fellows actions, the girls then went on & performd the part by exposing themselves below the waist.' – 14 January.

extremely fond of the liquor, very politely declined the invitation; saying, there was but little for themselves, and he would therefore drink 'Britarne' in a bowl of Otaheitean *ava*, which was immediately prepared.[1]

Before break of day, *Mowree* acquainted them, that, as religious restrictions were laid on all the canoes in that part of the island, his could not be launched; he was informed this would not be any inconvenience, as it was the intention of the party to return by land; and requested, that *Whytooa* would prepare them an early breakfast. This, *Whytooa* hoped they would excuse, as fires were interdicted, and cooking could not be suffered at his house; but that he would endeavour to provide them with some refreshment on their journey, when out of the district of Oparre. Accompanied by their worthy host and hostess, they now set forth on their return, highly impressed with the attentive kindness and hospitality they had received.

On reaching the rivulet, they requested to be shewn the morai to which the remains of *Mahow* had been carried the preceding day. The road was pointed out, but having advanced a little way a message was delivered, requesting they would return. On explaining the promise made by *Pomurrey*, much hesitation ensued; after which *Whytooa* directed one of the natives only to accompany them, giving him at the same time very particular injunctions. Mr. Broughton and Mr. Menzies followed this man, who appeared exceedingly cautious and apprehensive of every step he took. They had not proceeded far when a general solitary gloom prevailed; all the houses were deserted, and not a living creature, excepting two or three dogs, were to be seen until they arrived near the morai; where, in a small house, three men were observed, who, most probably, were the centinels of the sacred place. These questioned the guide in a very particular manner, and then acquainted him, that the body of *Mahow* had been removed to the morai, where it had stopped the day before; and that *Pomurrey* was there also. They now took a cursory view of the holy spot, which afforded little worthy of notice. It was terminated by high perpendicular rocks, whence issued several streams of water, whose continued murmurs, assisted by the wild and gloomy situation of the morai, gave an awful solemnity to the place, and fitted it to the mournful, sacred purpose, for which it is designed. On the return of these two gentlemen to join the rest of the party, they passed the residence of the young king *Otoo*. It consisted of a middling-sized house, inclosed by a railing of wood, situated on the confines of the districts of Matavai and Oparre; beyond which the religious interdictions did not seem to extend any great distance, as they soon afterwards partook of an excellent breakfast that *Whytooa* had taken care to provide. They then returned to the encampment, extremely well pleased with their excursion, on which they had been constantly attended by several of the natives, who were always struggling to be foremost in acts of friendly attention; such as carrying the party over the rivulets; taking charge of their

[1] '& Mr. Broughton's politeness & curiosity together went so far as to drink some of this bowl with his friend.' – Menzies, 14 January.

414

superfluous apparel, and other bundles; which, although comprised of many articles highly valuable to them, yet, in justice to their honesty, it must be recorded that the most trivial article was not missed.

I shall take leave of this excursion by adding a few ideas which, though principally founded on conjecture, may not be unimportant, as they respect these peculiar religious ceremonies. The opinion that the operation of embalming commenced at the morai near the mountains was most probably correct. One of the principal parts of this ceremony I have been given to understand, is always performed in great secrecy, and with much religious superstition; this is the disembowelling of the body.[1] The bowels are, by these people, considered as the immediate organs of sensation, where the first impressions are received, and by which all the operations of the mind are carried on: it is therefore natural to conclude, that they may esteem, and venerate the intestines, as bearing the greatest affinity to the immortal part. I have frequently held conversations on this subject, with a view to convince them, that all intellectual operations were carried on in the head; at which they would generally smile, and intimate, that they had frequently seen men recover whose skulls had been fractured, and whose heads had otherwise been much injured; but that, in all cases in which the intestines had been wounded, the persons on a certainty died. Other arguments they would also advance in favor of their belief; such as the effect of fear, and other passions, which caused great agitation and uneasiness, and would sometimes produce sickness at the stomach, which they attributed intirely to the action of the bowels. If therefore this reasoning be admitted, it would appear probable that the intestines of *Mahow* were deposited at the morai under the mountains; and as it is natural to imagine they would consider the soul most attached to those mortal parts which bore to it the greatest affinity, so wherever those parts were deposited, there they may probably suppose the soul occasionally resorts. And hence it may be inferred, that it is in the places made sacred by the deposit of these relics, that the ceremony of chief mourner, habited in the *parie*,[2] is performed; whose business it is to keep off the inquisitive, and to maintain as far as possible a profound silence over a certain space in which he parades, having a kind of mace, armed with shark's teeth, borne before him by a man almost naked, whose duty it is to assail any one with this formidable weapon, who may have the temerity to venture within his reach. This may account for *Whytooa*'s disinclination to permit our gentlemen to visit the morai; the apparently deserted houses; and the apprehensions of the guide, who started at the least interruption of the profound and solemn silence which prevailed in the neighbourhood.

[1] 'The process of embalming (*miri*) consisted chiefly in first extracting the bowels and the brain, for which was substituted cloth soaked in coconut and sandalwood oil and then drying the body, plentifully and continuously anointed with coconut oil, in the sun.' – Note by Beaglehole in Cook, *Journals*, III, 209n.
[2] parae; the headpiece of the dress worn by the chief mourner.

CHAPTER VII.

*Two Natives punished for Theft—Obsequies of Mahow—Several Articles stolen—
Measures for their Recovery—Towereeroo the Sandwich Islander absconds—
Brought back by Pomurrey—Sail from Matavai Bay—Character of Pomurrey—
His Wives—Changes in the Government of Otaheite—Astronomical and
nautical Observations.*

ON the morning of Tuesday the 17th we were visited by the young king,
his uncles, and several other chiefs from Oparre. Two men had been detected
in stealing a hat from on board the Discovery; and, as several other petty thefts
had been committed at the encampment, I desired the delinquents to be sent
on shore, that they might be punished in the presence of their chiefs, and
countrymen, which was done by shaving their heads, and bestowing on each
a slight manual correction.[1]

A message was received from *Pomurrey*, requesting my attendance at
Oparre, to 'tiehah,' that is, to mourn for the death of *Mahow*. It was
understood to be much wished, that we should be provided to fire some
vollies; and that I should present, on this occasion, a piece of red cloth as an
offering to the deceased. I was informed also that most of the neighbouring
chiefs were to pay their last tribute of respect to the remains of *Mahow*, and
that the ceremony would consequently be attended with many formalities;
but on our arrival at Oparre there did not appear the least foundation for any
such report. Mr. Broughton and Mr. Whidbey accompanied me. On our
landing, we were conducted to a temporary habitation of *Pomurrey*, where
we found him, his wives, and sisters, in readiness to receive us. Some little
concern was certainly apparent for the loss of their friend and relation;
though very unequal to the affliction I expected to have witnessed, from the

---

[1] Cook seems to have originated head shaving as a punishment for thieving at Vaitepiha
Bay, Tahiti, in 1777. When a thief was caught there 'his captors shaved half his head, took
off one eyebrow and half his beard', which made him both a marked man and an object
of ridicule and contempt to the natives. *Journals*, III, 210n. The extent of the 'slight manual
correction' is variously reported. Johnstone states that the thieves 'were flogged by the
Boatswains mate with three dozen lashes each.' – 17 January. Baker reduces the punishment
to two dozen, while Bell states that 'they were flogged with a dozen lashes each.' Shaving
and flogging 'happened in the presence of Otoo King of the Island several of the principal
Chiefs & a numerous concourse of the Natives who all appeared highly satisfied with our
levity in not inflicting a severe punishment.' – Menzies, 17 January.

great care, and tender regard, manifested to *Mahow* by the whole party when alive. The grief of these people is of two descriptions, natural and artificial; it is excessive on the first impulse, but soon moderates and wears away.

The corpse was laid on the tapapaoo,[1] which seemed to have been erected for the express purpose about a quarter of a mile to the eastward of the grand morai; (or as it is called, 'tapootapootatea')[2] and appeared to be then undergoing the latter part of the embalming process, in the same manner as described by Captain Cook in the instance of *Tee*.[3] The body was exposed to the sun; and, on our approach, the covering was taken off, which exhibited the corpse in a very advanced state of putrefaction. The skin shone very bright with the cocoa-nut oil, with which it had been anointed, and which, we understood, was highly impregnated with 'aehigh,' or sweet-scented wood. One of the arms and a leg being moved, the joints appeared perfectly flexible. The extremely offensive exhalations that were emitted, rendered it natural to conclude, that the whole mass would soon be completely decomposed; but, if credit may be given to their assertions, which were indubitably confirmed by the remains of *Tee*, and to which I could myself bear testimony, this will not be the case. *Pomurrey* informed us, the corpse was to remain a month in this place; then a month was to be employed in its visiting some of the western districts; after which it was to be removed to Tiaraboo[4] for another month; whence it was to be carried to Morea, and there finally deposited with his forefathers in the morai of the family. In the course of a few months after its arrival there, it would gradually begin to moulder away, but by such very slow degrees, that several months would elapse before the body would be entirely consumed.[5]

This method of embalming, or rather of preserving human bodies, is certainly an object of great curiosity; particularly, when it is considered that it is performed under the influence of a vertical sun; sometimes in the rainy season; and that the operators are totally ignorant of the properties of spices, salts, &c. &c. as antiseptics. Whether their preparations be simple or compounded, or what may be the peculiarities observed in the process, remains, I believe, intirely unknown to Europeans; and it is much to be regretted, that their religious interdictions precluded our attending the whole of these mysterious obsequies, as many vessels may visit this country without meeting so favorable an opportunity, with persons on board qualified and inclined to direct such enquires to[6] effect.

The boat's crew were ranged before the paling that encompassed the

---

[1] 'The *tupapau* was the corpse; the covered platform on which it was laid was the *fata tupapau*.' – Cook, *Journals*, III, 191n.

[2] Taputapuatea.

[3] See *Journals*, III, 208–9.

[4] Taiarapu, or Little Tahiti, is meant.

[5] Beaglehole states that the 'Tahitian "mummies" lasted about a year, after which they were laid away in coffins.' – Cook, *Journals*, III, 209n.

[6] Misprinted 'into' in the second edition.

tapapaoo; the piece of red cloth was given to the widow, who spread it over the dead body; some vollies were then fired, and I was directed to pronounce ' *Tera no oea Mahow*,' that is, For you *Mahow*. On some rain falling, the body was taken under cover, and carefully wrapped up. We had but a few yards to retire to *Pomurrey*'s habitation, where himself and family had taken up a temporary abode for this occasion; but the exceedingly offensive smell of the corpse obliged us to proceed to an excellent new house of *Whytooa*'s, a little to the westward of *Pomurrey*'s former habitation, which had been destroyed during the late wars, and had not been rebuilt; nor did it appear that he had any other house at present in this part of the district. Here we dined, and returned to Matavai with two large hogs, presented on this mournful occasion by the widow of *Mahow*.

Our friends with their axes made so little progress, that on the morning of Wednesday the 18th, I requested *Urripiah* would point out such trees as we might cut down ourselves. This, with *Whytooa*'s assistance, he shortly did; and we procured of the apple, and bread-fruit, sufficient numbers to supply our wants. Parties for this service were sent on shore, and the axes lent to the chiefs for this express purpose, were directed to be forthwith returned; with which *Urripiah*, *Whytooa*, and *Poeno*, immediately complied.

The mourning for *Mahow* being now at an end, the royal females paid us a visit, and returned after dinner to Oparre. *Pomurrey*, his father, wives, brothers and sisters, with our several friends, were again about us the next morning, perfectly cheerful and in high spirits. As Sunday was now determined upon for our departure, the preceding evening was fixed for a further display of fire-works, in which all our friends seemed to anticipate much pleasure. *Pomurrey* returned in the evening to Oparre, for the purpose of procuring us such supplies as he thought would be acceptable previously to our sailing.

A great number of presents were received on board on the morning of Friday the 20th, consisting of hogs, fowls, goats,* roots and vegetables, from our several friends; who had uniformly conducted themselves with the greatest propriety, and who all appeared to regret that the period of our departure was now so near at hand. In the midst of this happy intercourse and desirable harmony, a circumstance unfortunately occurred, which occasioned much concern. A bag, containing a large quantity of linen belonging to Mr. Broughton, had been artfully taken out of the marquee.[1] *Moerree*, who

---

* Produced from the stock originally established by Captain Cook.

[1] Vancouver does not mention an earlier theft: 'the facility & honesty with which the natives were brought to work & drudge for us in this sultry climate was highly pleasing, for they washd all our linnen, taking on shore a parcel of it in the morning & bringing it on board again in the evening or next day exceedingly well done. But this day a circumstance happend which put us in some measure upon our guard in trusting them at least with much at a time, for some linnen belonging to Mr. Johnstone & about half a dozen shirts & other things belonging to Mr. Walker of the Chatham were run away with.' – Menzies, 11 January. Menzies felt that 'the negligence with which every thing lay

had offered to be a cutter of wood, had neither sent any down since the first or second day, nor had he returned the axes with which he had been furnished. This led me to suspect he intended something unfair; of which, as well as of the theft, I acquainted *Urripiah*, who immediately replied he would go in quest both of the axes and the linen. He seemed, by no means, to be ignorant of the theft, and requested I would apply to *Whytooa*, who, having in a more particular manner attached himself to Mr. Broughton, was the most proper person to exert himself on this occasion; especially as he had reason to believe the linen had been taken to a part of the country where *Whytooa's* influence was very considerable. Several shirts also had been, the preceding evening, reported missing from the people's tents; but as circumstances induced me to believe the inhabitants were little concerned in their removal, no means were pursued for their recovery. Mr. Broughton's linen was, however, too serious a loss, and was a robbery too audacious to be passed over in silence; particularly, as it became evident the chiefs knew of the linen having been stolen before we discovered the theft; which was strongly suspected to have been projected by themselves

Urripiah had prepared a *heava*, close to the lines of the encampment, for our amusement; but, to shew my disapprobation, I deemed it expedient to forbid the performance, and told *Urripiah*, that, whilst his people conducted themselves so treacherously, the less connexion there subsisted between us the more agreeable it would be; and that, unless the articles purloined were immediately returned, I should be under the disagreeable necessity, though greatly against my inclination, of enforcing the restoration of them by the adoption of very serious measures.[1] On this he immediately departed; and about noon returned with one of the axes, and said that he had dispatched people in search of the linen, which he hoped would soon be found; but that *Moerree* would not give up the other axe, alledging as an excuse for with-holding it, that he had left an adz with me to be altered, which when done and sent to him, he would send back the other axe; but this was a kind of bargaining with which I did not think proper to comply. The queen-mother, who was our guest, informed me that *Pomurrey* would be at the tents the next morning, and for that reason I deferred any further proceedings until his arrival.

A favorable opportunity occurred in the evening to send on board the

---

about the Tents especially shirts & linnen' prompted the thefts, for 'these were the articles which they were at this time fondest of from the highest to the lowest, so that it was not surprising that their honesty was not able to resist those alluring opportunities which we ourselves put in their way.' – Menzies, 20 January. Bell states that the bag stolen from Broughton contained 'among other articles upwards of a dozen Shirts' – a serious loss when replacement was impossible. – Bell, 19 January.

[1] 'Captain Vancouver issued his threats to Pomarre & the rest of the Chiefs telling them, that if these articles were not brought back very soon, he would desolate the whole district & destroy all their Canoes.' – Menzies, 20 January. No doubt Vancouver remembered the houses and canoes that Cook had destroyed at Moorea in 1777 when a goat had been stolen. See *Journals*, III, 230–2.

observatory, chronometers, instruments, together with a large quantity of lumber from the encampment; and apprehending that the natives might attempt to commit other depredations on our moveable property, additional centinels were posted; and, as a summary and immediate punishment when caught in the fact, seemed most likely to prevent in future a repetition of crime, orders were issued to shoot any person who might be found in the act of stealing; but, on no pretence, to fire without the presence of an officer, who had the strictest injunctions to be extremely circumspect.[1]

On going on board the next morning, (Saturday the 21st) I had the additional mortification to understand that a much more material circumstance than the loss of the linen had occurred to interrupt the harmony which had so long subsisted.

Towereroo the Sandwich islander had, in the course of the preceding night, found means to elope from the ship.[2] Of this his intention, we had not for some time been free of suspicion; but I did not like to impose absolute confinement upon him without some proof. He had formed an attachment with the daughter of *Poeno*, the chief of Matavai, on whom, by examination, we now found he had lavishly bestowed nearly all he had possessed. This was of no small value, for, independent of his abundant outfit in England, many presents had been made him; to which his want of principle had added, by making too free with some valuable articles belonging to the gunner, with whom he had messed previously to his departure. *Towereroo* was a boy of weak intellect, of a sullen disposition, and excessively obstinate; and though his condition was so very subordinate at the Sandwich islands, that there was little probability of his services being important to us or to our countrymen hereafter; yet his example was a matter of such consequence, as to render it highly expedient that his return should be insisted upon; lest the crew might suppose I had not sufficient influence with the chiefs to procure it, and some of them be tempted to abscond from the vessels.[3] On my return on shore

[1] Some natives were in fact found 'lurking within the lines after the watch was set, in consequence of which two of them were this night fired at but they effected their escape unhurt.' – Menzies, 20 January.

[2] Bell describes the escape of Towereroo (Kualelo) from the ship. He had managed to get most of his possessions ashore, 'reserving to the last a Broad Sword, a pair of Pistols, &c. [and a] Rifle Barrall'd Gun...and with all these articles – in the dead of Night he dropt himself over the Ship's Bows, and attempted with these in his hands to Swim ashore, but finding them too heavy and the distance considerable, he was obliged to let them all go to the Bottom.' – January.

[3] Most of the officers of both ships sympathized with Towereroo's ardent wish to remain in Tahiti, and Vancouver's insistence that he must be captured and taken to Hawaii was highly unpopular. But Vancouver was simply obeying his instructions, which, as noted in the first pages of his narrative, included an order 'to receive on board and convey to his native country *Towraro*, an Indian, from the Sandwich Islands.' The fairest of his critics accepted this as the reason for his action. Baker, for example, thought that Towereroo deserted 'thinking with good reason that he should lead a much happier life [in Tahiti] than in his own Country' but added that 'as Capt.ⁿ Vancouvers orders respecting him were of a different tendency he positively insisted on his being returned...' – 24 January. No

Pomurrey and his wives were at the encampment, and seemed not at all ignorant of what had happened, therefore little explanation was necessary. A servant of *Moerree* being sent for by *Pomurrey*, delivered the same message *Urripiah* had brought respecting the wood axe, and with which *Pomurrey* requested I would comply. I shewed him the adz, but insisted on the restoration of the axe before it should be returned. A short conference now took place, on which he said he would himself go for the wood axe, and gave directions that proper persons should be sent in quest of *Towereroo*, who he most solemnly promised should be given up; and added, that he would immediately take measures for the recovery of the linen, but requesting, as *Urripiah* had before done, that I would resort to *Whytooa* for this especial purpose, as it lay in his particular department. About noon *Pomurrey* returned with the wood axe, and the adz was accordingly restored to its owner.[1]

In the presence of *Taow* his father, his two brothers, *Poatatou*, and several other chiefs, *Pomurrey* inquired if, agreeably to my promise, I intended a display of fire-works that evening; to which I replied in the negative, and explained, that when that promise was made there was no reason to expect the treatment we had since experienced, from those whose duty it was to have observed a very different conduct with respect to the theft of the linen, and the elopement of *Towereroo*; in both of which unpardonable transactions many of the principal chiefs were materially concerned. *Pomurrey* instantly replied, that *Towereroo* should the next day be brought back, either to the tents or to the Discovery; and, on interrogating him respecting the linen, a very warm argument took place between the three brothers, in which *Pomurrey* in particular accused *Whytooa* of a want of exertion and friendship on the

---

one seems to have realized that Vancouver feared that a successful escape might well prompt desertions amongst the crews. Menzies was convinced that Pomurrey and Urripiah (Ariipaea) had urged Towereroo to stay in Tahiti; Bell agrees and suggests an interesting motive: 'their reasons for this step were that he wou'd be of service to them in their Wars, not only from his possessing such a stock of Fire Arms &c. but that they conceived that he could repair and put in order the fire arms they possess'd; – if this account is true, I really cannot blame these poor people for wishing to have such a man among them, nor upon reflection do I think Towerooo to blame . . . it was very well known that he anticipated no great happiness from going home to his Native Country, where therefore cou'd he be happier than at such a charming place as Otaheite.' – Bell, January.

[1] Bell states that Moerree had been given three axes but 'only return'd one, & positively refusing to give the other two up, reserving them for payment of his trouble – as this was a piece of presumption and impudence not to be pass'd over, Captn. Vancouver sent to him to inform him, that if he did not immediately return them, he shou'd take them from him by force, on this – One more was return'd with a declaration that he would not give up the other. Captn. V. being determin'd to have them all, again sent him word that if he did not instantly send back the other, he wou'd burn his house down about his Ears and every thing belonging to him, – he refus'd – but hearing that preparations were making to really burn down the House that night, he very quickly sent the Axe back – and never after shew'd his face on board tho' he had before been on very intimate terms with both the Captains – and had he acted as the other Chiefs did would have been handsomely paid for the trouble in Cutting the Wood.' – 19 January.

occasion. In the course of this debate, the name of *Arreheah* was frequently mentioned; and so far as I could understand, *Pomurrey* seemed convinced that he was very principally concerned. This man was an inferior chief in Hapino,[1] one of the districts belonging to *Whytooa*, who, as well as *Urripiah*, had recommended him[2] to our notice; in consequence of which, he had lately been a constant attendant on the encampment: a man, who had also been recommended by some of the chiefs to assist in cooking, had been observed with *Arreheah* to have slept near the marquee on the night the robbery was committed. On this circumstance being made known to *Pomurrey*, he replied, that one, if not both, were certainly guilty. The dinner being now served, ended the debate; after which the three brothers sallied out in quest of the stolen linen, and soon returned with the servant who had absconded. On his being examined he accused *Arreheah* as the thief; but being conscious of the robbery, he had fled, lest he should be suspected and punished. This man's evidence although tending to acquit himself, as the principal, clearly proved him an accomplice; and, not being without my suspicions that he was in reality the thief, I ordered a halter to be put about his neck *in terrorem*, and sent him on board the ship, there to be confined in irons; with the assurance, that if the linen was not restored, he should certainly be hanged.[3]

A short debate, nearly to the same purport, again took place between the three brothers, in which *Whytooa* seemed much affected by *Pomurrey*'s rebuke. As the thief was now known, I embraced this occasion to inform the royal party, that very considerable presents were intended to have been made to them and the several chiefs; but not one single article would be presented unless *Towereroo* and Mr. Broughton's linen were forthcoming. On this they again departed, saying every thing should be restored.

The surf being tolerably smooth in the afternoon, the large working tent, with various other articles were sent off; leaving the marquee, the guard's tent, and cannon, only to be embarked. Whilst thus employed, the chiefs had all, imperceptibly, withdrawn themselves; towards sun-set, most of the canoes that had been on the banks of the river were observed to be moving off, and the houses on the opposite side, which had been fully inhabited, were intirely stripped and deserted. We were soon given to understand that the Erees and people were '*mattowed*,' that is, alarmed,[4] because I was angry; which intelligence a man named *Boba* was extremely urgent to communicate. He had, on the evening the linen was stolen, come over the river under a flimsy pretence, with which at the time I was by no means satisfied; and since then he had not been seen. Suspecting him to be an accessary, I gave directions

[1] Haapaianoo, now Papenoo; a district E of Matavai Bay.

[2] Misprinted 'himself' in the second edition.

[3] Hewett charges that Vancouver 'in a Passion snatched hold of the Halter himself and drew it so tight as nearly to deprive the Man of Life…'

[4] matau, to fear or to dread. Menzies states that the 'general alarm' amongst the natives was caused by the 'harsh manner' in which the native prisoner 'was threatened with instant death'. – 21 January.

that he should be secured; and that the remaining canoe, which chanced to contain many of their most valuable articles, should be detained; that we might have something in our power in case the chiefs should have deserted us, which I began to apprehend, as a general *mattow* seemed to have taken place. Mr. Broughton, who had been with the natives on the other side of the river,[1] informed me that the principal cause of the *mattow*, was the confinement of *Boba*; and that they conceived, I had also confined the queen-mother. This good lady had been our constant companion, even in the absence of her husband; and was, on all occasions, very solicitous to imitate our manners. Having carried her politeness rather too far, in taking a few glasses more at dinner than was quite agreeable, she had been sleeping in the marquee most of the afternoon. On this information, I requested she would instantly repair to *Pomurrey*, who, with several chiefs, and a large concourse of the inhabitants, were assembled on the opposite shore of the river. She complied, though greatly against her inclination, saying she well knew that I was the friend of her *Pomurrey*, and all the chiefs, and it was his and their business to come to me. This conversation took place at the river side, whilst *Pomurrey* and the natives were accusing me of detaining his wife, who, with all imaginable spirit contradicted the assertion. The crowd replied, she was instructed by me to say so; asserting that I well understood their language. Matters thus situated I insisted she should cross the river, with which at length she complied, and was received on the opposite side with great demonstrations of joy. On her assuring *Pomurrey* that I was still his friend, and that I earnestly wished to confer with him on the unpleasant circumstances that had occurred, he attempted to come over the river, but was prevented by the crowd. On his assuring them his intentions were not to cross, but to be sufficiently near to understand me perfectly, he was allowed to advance a few paces, when he again questioned my pacific intentions, and whether I would confine him if he crossed the river. After receiving the most unequivocal assurances of a continuance of my friendship, and his own personal liberty, he disengaged himself from those who forcibly attempted to stop him, and came over to us much against the general voice and opinion of the multitude, who murmured excessively on the occasion; but this shortly subsiding, his wives soon followed his example. I acquainted *Pomurrey* with the detention of the canoe, and the man I had confined. The instant he saw it was *Boba*, he assured me he was innocent, and requested he might be released; and, as he had been arrested on suspicion only, I did not hesitate to comply with the request of *Pomurrey*, who had gratified me exceedingly by the confidence he had so recently reposed in my integrity.

Our royal guests became perfectly reconciled, spent the evening with us, and slept in the marquee. Early on the morning of Sunday the 22d they departed. *Pomurrey* informed me, he was then going to Oparre in quest of

---

[1] 'In this situation Mr. Broughton went singly and unarmed across the river (though Capt. Vancouver had entreated him to the contrary) – to endeavour to reconcile the Natives & bring them back to a state of confidence.' – Menzies, 21 January.

Towereroo, who, it was reported, had secreted himself in the mountains of that district; that in the course of the day he would be taken, and that, with him, he would return to Matavai; he further added, that *Whytooa* was going in search of the linen, which would likewise be restored.

It was an excessively mortifying reflection, now that we were in every respect ready for sea, after having lived three weeks on terms of the strictest amity with these good people, that just on the eve of our departure, they should so conduct themselves, as materially to incur our disapprobation and censure, and prevent our bidding them farewell with that cordiality and good-will, to which they were so highly intitled by their former good behaviour.

Having nothing further to transact on shore, every thing was sent on board excepting the marquee, at which, with a guard, Mr. Puget remained for the more easy communication with the chiefs, should they be inclined to renew their visits; as no one person of any distinction had appeared since the departure of *Pomurrey* in the morning. Mr. Broughton having strolled over the river, found *Whytooa* in soft dalliance with his wife at home, instead of being in search of the linen. Mr. Broughton invited them to the marquee, but *Whytooa* replied he was '*mattowed.*' After some persuasion he complied, and having come opposite the encampment, he requested some assurance of friendship on my part; which being complied with, he consented, and having gained about the middle of the river, he was compelled by the natives to return. Another conversation now took place; and on Mr. Broughton proposing to remain with them during *Whytooa*'s absence, he came over, and being soon reconciled after his arrival, to this situation, he sent a servant to desire Mr. Broughton would cross the river. On this occasion *Whytooa*'s wife accompanied him, and we afterwards went all on board to dinner. On my enquiring, he said *Pomurrey* and *Urripiah* were at Oparre, but would return the instant *Towereroo* was taken. With respect to the linen I could gain no satisfactory account; and, as I wished to encourage him in the confidence he had manifested, I did not think it right to push this inquiry further; wishing to detain him and his wife, in case their imprisonment hereafter should be deemed necessary to effect our purpose; but desisted from any further measures, until I should see or hear something of the other royal brothers. The canoe and goods we had arrested the preceding evening now appearing to belong to a chief of Ulietea, who could not have had any concern in the late improper transactions, justice dictated its restoration to the proper owner, and directions to that effect were accordingly given.

Neither *Pomurrey* nor *Urripiah* having arrived on the morning of Monday the 23d, Mr. Broughton proposed that *Whytooa* and his wife, who were still with us, should accompany him to Oparre, in order to procure an interview with *Pomurrey*, and learn how our affairs stood in that district. To this *Whytooa* readily agreed, and whilst the boat was preparing for their conveyance, the royal females paid us a visit. They said *Pomurrey* was still at Oparre, but would return to the ship the instant that *Towereroo* could be found. The ladies were immediately informed of Mr. Broughton's errand, and told, that, until his return, they were to remain on board. With this arrangement they seemed perfectly satisfied; and from their mirth, and joking with each other as to their being carried to sea, their reception in England, &c. &c. I began to conjecture that *Towereroo* was in reality taken, though it was their pleasure to keep me in suspence. We did not long remain in this state. About noon, the boat returned with the three royal brothers, and *Towereroo*.[1] Mr. Broughton met them on their way towards the ships, attended by a fleet of canoes, laden with every species of provisions as presents from the royal family and our several other friends, who all flocked on board with such a profusion of their various valuable commodities, that unable to dispose of their bounty, several laden canoes returned to the shore.

Pomurrey and *Urripiah* observed, on the delivery of *Towereroo*, that they had now restored every thing in which they considered I was particularly interested, and that it was *Whytooa*'s business to recover the linen for Mr. Broughton. *Whytooa* protested that, if we could remain until the morning, it should certainly be brought on board; but as we had been repeatedly instructed to place little reliance on assurances of this nature, had the wind been favorable, we should not have waited to put his integrity to the test.

Poatatou, with many other chiefs of the distant districts, were made extremely happy by the presents which each of them received; and, finding we were to sail with the first favorable wind, took their leave in the evening, with much apparent regret for our departure; which was evidently increased by their being disappointed of a second display of fire-works. From the inordinate love of pleasure which these people possess, I do not believe it were possible to have caused, by any other means, so general and so great a degree of mortification. Many chiefs, and numbers of the inhabitants, had come from the most distant parts of the island, and from Morea likewise, for no other purpose than to gratify their curiosity, and to be present at the expected exhibition. These, in particular, complained much of their disappointment; to which I replied, their concern was by no means unpleasant to me, as it gave me reason to hope it would operate to prevent the cause of it in future; and that, if thefts, and other breaches of confidence had not been committed, and sanctioned, as I was confident they had been by the chiefs themselves, I should not have been under the painful necessity of denying them the

---

[1] Menzies regretted the way in which Towereroo was treated after his return: 'the punishment...suffered for his imprudence, for in him it could scarcely be called any more, was far too severe, for he was kept in confinement till we past the Island of Techteroah [Tetiaroa], & the Captain in a manner discarding him, he was thrown out of the Gunners Mess where he had livd since we left England, so that he was obliged to make it out the best way he could among the common people all the passage to the Sandwich Island, with scarcely any clothing except what the generous pity of his Shipmates supplied him with.' – 23 January.

promised entertainment, and we should have parted much better friends. On the arrival of another ship, I trusted, from this disappointment, they would all be taught to conduct themselves with more fidelity.[1]

Pomurrey and his wives remained on board all night.[2] The next morning, Tuesday the 24th, brought no tidings of the linen. On reflecting that, without using rigorous measures, which, in all probability, would fall more on the innocent who were in our power, than on the guilty who were at a distance, there did not appear the most remote prospect of regaining this property; and as we had now a favorable breeze from the eastward, and could ill afford a longer detention, about ten in the forenoon we sailed out of the bay. *Pomurrey* and his wives were our guests until we were beyond the reefs:[3] they were now presented with an assortment of valuables, which afforded them the highest satisfaction; and *Pomurrey* requesting as a particular favor that they might be saluted on leaving the ship, they took a very friendly and affectionate leave, and were complimented agreeably to his wishes. *Whytooa* had also accompanied Mr. Broughton in the Chatham; who, after we were out, brought him on board the Discovery, with an assortment of such articles as he conceived *Whytooa* intitled to, for his hospitable attention, and the large quantity of provisions, &c. &c. which he had supplied, without having as yet received the least return: but as I had repeatedly declared *Whytooa* should receive no present, unless the linen was restored, my ultimate decision was now requested. On considering, that possibly it might not have been in his power to recover the linen, and that equity demanded he should be paid for the supplies which he had furnished, I consented to his receiving in return, such articles as were deemed fairly equal in point of value; but he was not presented with any thing from me, although I had promised him several valuable implements. These were again enumerated, the reason of their being with-held fully explained, and shewn to have arisen from his not having acted towards Mr. Broughton with the propriety which had been observed in the conduct of his royal brothers towards me.[4]

[1] Bell took a more charitable view of the behaviour of the natives: 'In all Societies there are some bad members, – Some few thefts were committed, but they were fewer than might be expected, considering of what great value the most trifling article of ours is to them and the opportunities they had.' – 24 January.

[2] Urripiah and his wife were guests on the *Chatham*, where they spent the night in Broughton's cabin. Bell, 23 January.

[3] Peggy, the Tahitian wife of midshipman George Stewart of the *Bounty*, who had been carried away in the *Pandora*, was on board the *Chatham*. She was 'one of the last who left us...Just before she went away, she came into my Cabbin – and ask'd me the same question she had often done, whether I thought Stewart would be hung. I told her I cou'd not tell, – perhaps he would not – she then said "If he is alive when you return tell him that you saw Peggy and his little Charlotte, and that they were both well and tell him to come to Otaheite, and live with them, or they will be unhappy."' – Bell, 24 January. Unfortunately Peggy's story was to have a tragic ending. When the *Pandora* foundered after striking the Great Barrier Reef, Stewart and three others were still manacled when the ship sank, and all were drowned.

[4] Bell, defending Whyatoo, was 'perfectly confident he knew nothing of the business' and that his inactivity 'merely arose from an indolent disposition, – he cou'd not take the

I am well aware that our visit to this country will fill the inquisitive mind with the expectation of acquiring much additional information, relative to a people whose situation and condition have been long the subjects of curious investigation; but the shortness of our stay, and various concurring circumstances afforded little opportunity to gratify such desires.

The veneration these people entertain for the names of their sovereigns, has been already very justly related by Mr. Anderson.[1] But no example, I believe, had then appeared to that judicious observer, of the extent to which this respect is carried. On *Otoo*'s accession to the *Maro*,[*] a very considerable alteration took place in their language, particularly in the proper names of all the chiefs, to which however it was not solely confined, but extended to no less than forty or fifty of the most common words which occur in conversation, and bearing not the least affinity whatever to the former expressions.[2]

This new language every inhabitant is under the necessity of adopting; as any negligence or contempt of it is punished with the greatest severity. Their

trouble, his whole time & thoughts being taken up in Eating & drinking &c.' 'Even his Brothers shew'd their displeasure at his behaviour.' – 23 January.

[1] In James Cook, *A Voyage to the Pacific Ocean* (London, 1784), II, 169–70.

[*] Or girdle of royalty.

[2] No definitive study of this practice seems to have been made. For an interesting discussion see Ralph Gardner White, 'Onomastically induced word replacement in Tahitian', in *Polynesian Culture History* (Bernice P. Bishop Museum Special Publication 56, Honolulu, 1967), pp. 323–38. The *Tahitian and English Dictionary* published by the London Missionary Society in 1851 defines it as 'the custom of prohibiting the use of a word, or syllable, which had become sacred by its having been adopted as the whole or part of the name of some chief, when another word was substituted in its place'. Use of the name itself was not forbidden, but the sound of the name could not be used in other contexts. Violations of the taboo could result in drastic punishments, including mutilation and death. Menzies, a shrewd observer, noted the changes, but seems not to have understood the rules that governed them: 'all the principal chiefs on the Island' changed their names 'on young Otoo's accession to the regal dignity when he was invested with the Maro ooro [in February 1791] & what is very singular on this occasion a great number of words in their language were changed and new ones adopted in their stead; even words expressing the most common & familiar things sufferd this mutation...& the words which were thus laid aside are forbidden to be used by any one on the Island under the severest punishment; so that if these changes happen frequent[ly] there can be no stability in their language, but what depends upon whim & superstitious caprice'. – 11 January. The custom seems to have been at its height about the time of Vancouver's visit. While authority in Tahiti had been divided among a considerable number of chiefs, word changes were frequent, but were usually regional and often temporary. But when Otoo the elder (Pomare I) extended his authority over most of Tahiti changes became fewer, but applied over a wider area. Presently two circumstances tended to make them permanent. Otoo the younger (Pomare II) was king for the unusually long period of 30 years, and in 1797 the first missionaries arrived and immediately set about reducing the Tahitian language to writing. By the time Pomare II died in 1821 a well established written vocabulary was coming into existence. But if the custom of word changing declined, the names of kings continued to be highly respected and considered by many as sacred. The missionaries in Moorea discovered this when they built a schooner and it became known that they intended to name it Pomare. 'The day when the boat was to be launched, the Natives gathered by the hundreds, armed with axes, for the purpose of smashing it up, and they had to change its name'. Quoted by White, p. 331.

former expressions were, however, retained in their recollection; and for our better communication, were, I believe, permitted to be used in conversation with us, without incurring displeasure. *Pomurrey* however would frequently correct me on my accidentally using the former mode of expression, saying, I knew it was wrong, and ought not to practise it. Were such a pernicious innovation to take place, generally, at the arbitrary will of the sovereigns throughout the South-Sea Islands, it would be attended with insurmountable difficulties to strangers; but it appears to be a new regulation, and, as yet, confined to these islands, or it would be impossible to reconcile the affinity which has been hitherto found to subsist in the language of different parts of the Great South-Sea nation. The new-fashioned words produce a very material difference in those tables of comparative affinity which have been constructed with so much attention and labour; and may, possibly, when the reasons for the alteration are known and developed, be a matter of interesting political inquiry. This, however, required more leisure, and a more intimate knowledge of the language, than I possessed. Circumstances of greater importance to the expediting the various services here, which the grand object of our voyage demanded, and on which my mind was every hour anxiously engaged; augmented by the difficulties we had to encounter, in the new modification of so many terms, rendered most of my inquiries ineffectual. These perplexities and disadvantages were also materially increased, by the difficulty of obtaining the truth from a race who have a constant desire to avoid, in the slightest degree, giving offence; insomuch, that, on the least appearance of displeasure, even in conversation, to disengage themselves from any such inconvenience, they would often, by that extensive and specious comprehension, which their language admits of, seemingly so qualify, what they before had asserted, as to contradict, according to our acceptation, a positive matter of fact; or, what amounted to nearly the same thing, a completely different construction was by us very frequently put on a second conversation, from that which we had conceived from, or had attributed to, the first. Had we been more competent linguists, we might, in all probability, have found both their modes of expression tending to the same point, and differing only in the figurative relation of the circumstances, to which these people are much accustomed. This deception I have more than once experienced, and have on reflection, thus reconciled the apparent incongruity. Such, and various other important circumstances must ever occur, to render the acquirement of knowledge in the language, manners, and customs, of newly-discovered countries (beyond a certain superficial extent) a business of much labour and study, although aided by a series of minute observations. Under such evident disadvantages, how far my abilities might or might not have empowered me to direct such inquiries to effect, had time and other objects permitted, must still remain to be proved. I shall therefore resign the palm to those gentlemen who have preceded me, and to whom the world is indebted for many pertinent and judicious observations contained in their general description of this country.

Notwithstanding I must concur with Mr. Anderson[1] in opinion, that much information remains to be acquired which would be extremely acceptable to the contemplative mind, yet it only remains with me to record faithfully those circumstances which arose in our transactions and intercourse with these people.

The changes which have taken place in their government, so far as I have been able to understand from the chiefs, with such other matters worthy attention as have fallen under my own immediate observation, I shall proceed to relate; as the preceding narration would be incomplete without such an explanation.

We have become acquainted by subsequent visitors, that, shortly after the last departure of Captain Cook from these islands, considerable disputes had arisen between *Maheine*[2] the usurping chief of Morea, and *Pomurrey* (then *Otoo*) in some of which wars (for there had been many) *Maheine* was joined by *Towha*,[3] and other chiefs of the western districts of Otaheite; by which means, for a considerable space of time, *Pomurrey* was materially worsted, and his own districts laid intirely waste.[4] Thus His Majesty's benevolent intentions of adding to the comforts of these people, have been nearly frustrated. Most of the animals, plants and herbs, which had caused Captain Cook so much anxiety and trouble to deposit here, have fallen a sacrifice to the ravages of war.[5] The black cattle were carried to Morea, where they still remain; and having bred, are now five in number, four cows and a bull. The latter has very unfortunately received a hurt in his loins, which renders him an intire cripple; consequently their further propagation will be at an end unless some additional assistance is afforded.

In the midst of these hostile engagements, *Pomurrey* married the queen-mother, a near relation of his most inveterate enemy *Maheine*.[6] This lady having taken a very material part in the advantageous change of *Pomurrey*'s government, I shall obtrude a few lines as a sketch of her character, and also that of *Fier re te* her sister, and conjugal partner in the royal affection.

[1] See Cook, *A Voyage to the Pacific Ocean*, II, 141–2.

[2] Mahine.

[3] Tetoofa, chief of Faaa, the district W of Pare in the NW corner of Tahiti. He was a leader in naval warfare and was referred to by Cook and others as 'the admiral'.

[4] This occurred in 1782. Otoo related the details to Bligh in 1788. See *Log of the Bounty*, I, 378–9.

[5] Menzies relates that while exploring a valley near Matavai Bay 'the Natives pointed out to us some shadock trees...in a very flourishing state, loaded at this time with plenty of fruit but none of them were ripe. They told us that they were planted here by *Bane* (Sir Joseph Banks) [in 1769] & from their size and apparent age we had no reason to doubt this assertion.' – 17 January. Menzies also saw orange trees that had been planted by Bligh; some were two feet high. Menzies himself planted 'in different parts of the Plantation a number of young orange seedlings which I had reard in the frame on the quarter Deck since we left the Cape of Good Hope.' In addition he 'cleard a small spot...for a garden, where we sowd a variety of English Garden Seeds, many of which were above ground & in a thriving way before we left the Island.' – 9 January.

[6] She and her sister were nieces of Mahine.

The queen-mother, although destitute of any pretensions to beauty, and having in her person a very masculine appearance, has yet, in her general deportment, something excessively pleasing and engaging; free from any austerity or pride, she is endued with a comparative elegance of manners, which plainly bespeaks her descent, and the high situation in which she is placed. Although her figure exhibited no external charms of feminine softness, yet great complacency and gentleness were always conspicuous; indicating, in the most unequivocal manner, a mind possessing, and alone actuated by those amiable qualities which most adorn the human race. All her actions seemed directed to those around her with an unalterable evenness of temper, and to be guided by a pure disinterested benevolence. Self, which on most occasions is the governing principle in the conduct of these islanders, with her was totally disregarded; and indeed, such was her very amiable disposition, that it counterbalanced any disadvantages she might labour under in a deficiency of personal attractions.

The portrait of *Fier re te* on canvas would most probably be generally thought intitled to a preference; yet she appeared by no means to possess either mental endowments, or other excellent qualities, in the same degree with the queen-mother; if she had them, they were latent, and required some particular exertion to bring them into action. Her softness and effeminacy afforded her some advantage over her sister; yet there was a shyness, want of confidence and manner in her general demeanor, that evinced her motives to be less disinterested. We were however led to believe, that she was not destitute of the amiable qualities, though to us they did not appear so conspicuous as in the character of the queen-mother. Of the two ladies, *Fier re te* was now the favorite of *Pomurrey*, at least we had every reason to think so by the general tenor of his conduct. Notwithstanding this preference, he was observed in several instances to abide implicitly by the advice and opinion of the queen-mother, and to treat her with great affection and regard;[1] who in return never appeared jealous or dissatisfied at the marked attention, or evident partiality, with which her sister *Fier re te* was treated by *Pomurrey*.

In consequence of the very superior rank and condition of these two ladies, they possessed privileges which I had never before seen conferred on any of the women of the Great South-Sea nation; as they were not only permitted to eat of all the good things of the country, but allowed to partake of them in company with men; as well the chiefs of the island as ourselves; and of the identical dishes at any repast of which men had eaten, without incurring displeasure or disgrace; these were honors to which we had reason to believe no other females of the island could aspire.

[1] 'She also appeared to posess great sagacity & penetration aided by a quick & clear comprehension of whatever was laid before her, so that she was not only usefull to Pomarre in his domestic concerns, but even in the management of the most important affairs of Government, for her councel had great weight with him on all occasions & he seldom transacted any business of moment without first obtaining it, by which she always seemd to have great ascendancy & influence over his conduct.' – Menzies, 23 January.

These two ladies, with the deceased *Matooara Mahow*, were the children of a sister of *Maheine*,[1] and his only near relations. *Mahow* I considered to be the same person mentioned by Captain Cook, under the name of *Tiareetaboonooa*,[2] as, on our first arrival, he was introduced to me by the name of *Areetaboonooa*, which appellation was almost immediately dropped, and he was afterwards called *Mahow*; occasioned most likely by the recent alteration in their language, which has before been stated to have taken place on the accession of the young king *Otoo*.

As *Maheine* was an Ereeoi,[3] whose advanced age precluded the expectation of his having children, little doubt was entertained that his consequence and power would soon descend to his family, which had become more firmly attached to the Otaheitean authority by the intermarriage of the late *Matooara Mahow* with *Pomurrey*'s youngest sister.[4] This connection appears to have been an important political measure, to insure a permanent establishment of peace and tranquillity between the two islands, on the conquest or death of *Maheine*. The event was however long looked for before it arrived, for we understood it did not happen until about fifteen months previous to our arrival; at which time *Maheine* was killed in a battle fought at Athoora[5] by him and some of the western chiefs, against the partizans of *Pomurrey*, who, I believe, then for the first time came off victorious.

Maheine having fallen in this conflict, and *Towha* being dead, little was necessary to complete the conquest, which was finally accomplished by the excursion of the *Bounty*'s people in a vessel they had constructed from the timber of the bread fruit tree;[6] and as good or bad fortune is generally attended with corroborating events, other circumstances intervened to foster and indulge the ambition of *Pomurrey*. At this time *Whyeadooa* the king of Tiarabou died,[7] leaving only a very distant relation to assume his name and

---

[1] Oliver gives her name as Vavea.

[2] Tieratabunue. Beaglehole perferred the spelling Teriitapanui. See Cook, *Journals*, III, 198, 198n.   [3] arioi.

[4] Auo, according to Oliver; Henry gives her name as Tetuanui.

[5] Atehuru. Oliver states that Vancouver 'recorded, mistakenly I believe, that Mahine was killed in the battle of Atehuru [in 1790], whereas other evidence places his death sometime earlier.' – *Ancient Tahitian Society*, III, 1360.

[6] Henry describes the building of the schooner, in which the *Bounty* men hoped to reach Batavia, whence they could return to England. She states that the vessel 'served occasionally as a man-of-war in Prince Tû's fleet' and that 'fourteen of the white men ultimately aided him greatly in subjugating all Tahiti.' – *Ancient Tahiti*, p. 28. But James Morrison, one of the *Bounty*'s seamen, who wrote an account of his sojourn in Tahiti – the only contemporary account – states that the mutineers provided Pomurrey's supporters with arms, but did not themselves take part in the expedition to Moorea. See *The Journal of James Morrison* (London, 1935), 92–3.

[7] Vehiatua, chief of Taiarapu (Little Tahiti). Vancouver does not mention that Churchill, the *Bounty*'s master-at-arms, and Thompson, a seaman, had established themselves in Taiarapu, and that Churchill was actually elected to succeed Vehiatua. Soon, however, he quarrelled violently with Thompson and was killed by him. Thompson in turn was then killed by Churchill's supporters. See Oliver, *Ancient Tahitian Society*, III, 1258–9.

government; who was by *Pomurrey* and his adherents obliged to relinquish all pretensions to such honors, and with the people of Tiarabou to acknowledge *Pomurrey*'s youngest son as their chief, under the supreme authority of his eldest son *Otoo*; which on their assenting to, the youth assumed the name of *Whyeadooa* as a necessary appendage to the government. By this acquisition it should appear, they have more effectually established a firm and lasting peace amongst themselves than has been enjoyed for a long series of years; and to insure this inestimable blessing to their dominions, the royal brothers have so disposed themselves as completely to watch over and protect the two young princes during their minority.

Urripiah, the next brother to *Pomurrey*, having acquired the reputation of a great warrior, has taken up his residence on the borders of Tiarabou, to watch the conduct of those people in their allegiance to his nephew *Whyeadooa*; and on the least appearance of disaffection or revolt, to be at hand for pursuing such measures as may be required to bring them back to their obedience. *Whytooa*, the next brother, resides for the like reason at Oparre, near the young monarch; and *Pomurrey* with his wives has retired to Morea, where the inhabitants are, in all respects, perfectly reconciled; firmly attached to his interest; and ready to afford him and his children every support and assistance they may require. From the relative situation of this island with Otaheite, there is but little probability that *Pomurrey* could long remain ignorant of any dissentions that might take place, or that he would be prevented affording such succour as the nature of the occasion might demand.

There is yet a fourth brother whose insignificance has hitherto precluded his name, which is *Tapahoo*,[1] from appearing in any of our transactions with these worthy people. Although in the possession of a very considerable property, *Tapahoo* seems little regarded by his family, and less esteemed by his people. This want of respect is greatly, and possibly wholly, to be attributed to a natural imbecillity of mind; as, to all appearance, he is a young man of an exceedingly weak and trifling character.

On the late decease of *Mahow*, his daughter by *Pomurrey*'s sister succeeded to the sovereignty of Morea, under the supreme authority of her cousin *Otoo*. To this young princess *Pomurrey* became regent, and in course, the inhabitants of Morea were intirely at his command. In consequence of *Pomurrey*'s connexion with *Mahow*'s family, his son *Otoo* in right of his mother was acknowledged as the supreme sovereign of Huaheine; and *Matuarro*[2] the king of that island, had consented to the superiority of *Otoo* over him, as 'Aree Maro Eoora;' but that he *Matuarro* was 'Aree de Hoi.'[3]

Omai[4] having died without children, the house which Captain Cook had

---

[1] Tepau.

[2] Matuaro is the usual spelling. He has not been clearly identified, but should certainly be described as a tribal chief and not as a king.

[3] 'arii maro ura' and 'arii rahi'.

[4] Omai, a young native of Huahine, had been most anxious to go to England, and Captain Furneaux took him on board the *Adventure* in 1773. Having spent a year in

built for him, the lands that were purchased, and the horse which was still alive; together with such European commodities as remained at his death, all descended to *Matuarro*, as king of the island; and when his majesty is at home, *Omai*'s house is his constant residence. From *Matuarro* we learned, that *Omai* was much respected, and that he frequently afforded great entertainment to him, and the other chiefs, with the accounts of his travels, and describing the various countries, objects, &c. that had fallen under his observation; and that he died universally regretted and lamented. His death, as well as that of the two New Zealand boys left with him by Captain Cook, was occasioned by a disorder that is attended by a large swelling in the throat, of which very few recover, but die a slow lingering death. During the latter part of our stay several persons were pointed out who seemed much afflicted with this fatal malady, particularly those belonging to Tiarabou, who said the disease had been imported by a Spanish vessel which had anchored near the south part of Otaheite.

Otoo, in right of his grandmother by his father's side, on the death of *Mowree* will claim the sovereignty of Ulietea and Otaha.[1] *Mowree*, who is brother to *Pomurrey*'s mother, is an Ereeoi of an advanced age. He seemed extremely fond of *Otoo*, and proud of his succeeding him in the government of those islands; saying, that, at present, there were two sovereigns, that '*Maw ta Tarta*,' but when he should die then there would be but one, meaning *Otoo*. This expression, in its literal signification, means '*to eat the Man*;' the idea, however, which in this sense it is intended to convey, is to point out those, whose rank and authority entitle them to preside at human sacrifices; a power which at present is possessed only by *Mowree* and *Otoo*.

In consequence of the extensive dominion that has devolved upon this young monarch, he is not now distinguished by the title of *Aree de Hoi*, but by one which is considerably more eminent and comprehensive; since they say there may be many *Arees de Hoi*, but there can be but one *Aree Maro Eoora*; which means the chief of the red feathered *Maro*;[2] and under which title, *Otoo*'s authority is acknowledged in Otaheite, Morea, Mattea, Tetero, Tupea-mannoo, and Huaheine.[3] But the people of Ulietea and Otaha,[4] seem much averse to this submission; and it does not appear, that even *Mowree* himself has much influence in those islands, notwithstanding that he is their acknowledged sovereign. Since the death of *Opoony*,[5] the government of the islands under his late authority appears to have been ill administered; the inhabitants having

England, he sailed home in the *Resolution*, and Cook did his best to establish him comfortably in Huahine in November 1777. He died only three or four years later.

[1] Raiatea and Tahaa.

[2] The 'maro ura', the emblem of a preeminent chieftain. Partly by inheritance and partly by a complicated series of wars, Pomurrey had become possessed of two of these, which gave him primacy in almost all Tahiti. See Oliver, *Ancient Tahitian Society*, III, chapters 26–28.

[3] Tahiti, Moorea, Mehetia, Tetiaroa, Tubuai-Manu and Huahine.

[4] Raiatea and Tahaa.   [5] Puni, a chief of Borabora.

been very turbulent and much disposed to anarchy: and in consequence of the disinclination which the people of these islands have manifested to subscribe to the supreme authority of *Otoo*, an expedition was in contemplation from Otaheite, to enforce the power of the *Aree Maro Eoora* over them, and little doubt was entertained of its success. Another favorite object was the annexing to *Otoo*'s present dominions by conquest, (for no right was set up) the islands of Bolabola, Mowrooa, and Tapi, [1] which, since the death of *Opoony*, had been governed by his daughter, and were said, in a great measure, to have lost their former high reputation as a martial and warlike nation. [2]

Pomurrey and his brothers having procured from the vessels which had lately visited Otaheite, several muskets and pistols, they considered themselves invincible; and the acquiring of new possessions for *Otoo*, now seemed to occupy the whole of their study and attention. They were extremely solicitous that I should contribute to their success by augmenting their number of fire-arms, and adding to their stock of ammunition. Of the latter I gave *Pomurrey* a small quantity; but of the former I had none to dispose of, even if I had seen no impropriety in complying with his request. Finding there was no prospect of increasing their armory, they requested that I would have the goodness to conquer the territories on which they meditated a descent, and having so done, to deliver them up to *Otoo*; and as an excuse for their subjugation, insisted that it was highly essential to the comfort and happiness of the people at large, that over the whole group of these islands there should be only one sovereign. On satisfying them that the islands in question were quite out of my route, and that I had no leisure for such an enterprize, *Pomurrey*, in the most earnest manner requested, that on my return to England I would, in his name, solicit His Majesty to order a ship with proper force to be immediately sent out, with directions, that if all those islands were not subjected to his power before her arrival, she was to conquer them for *Otoo*; who, he observed, I well knew would ever be a steady friend to King George and the English. This request was frequently repeated, and he did not fail to urge it in the most pressing manner at our parting.

I cannot take leave of my friend, for to such an epithet from me *Pomurrey*'s conduct justly entitles him, without adverting to the alteration which seemed to have taken place in his character, since my former visits to this country. At that time, he was not only considered as a timid, but a very weak prince; on this occasion, however, he did not appear deficient either in discernment, or intrepidity; although it must be acknowledged his fears were exceedingly awakened at the display of our fire-works, and that he always appeared to regard fire-arms with a considerable degree of terror; which possibly might arise from his knowledge of their destructive powers, whilst at the same time

---

[1] Borabora, Maupiti and Tupai (now Motu-iti).

[2] In volume III of *Ancient Tahitian Society*, entitled 'Rise of the Pomares', Oliver describes at length the complicated kinships and political relationships that linked Pomurrey with these and other chiefs.

he remained ignorant of the extent to which they were capable of doing execution; but this description of weapons out of the question, we had reason to believe his courage was equal to that of his neighbours, of which he certainly gave an undeniable proof by joining our party alone and unarmed at the encampment; in direct opposition to the counsel and apprehensions of his surrounding countrymen. On former occasions, I had also considered his general character to be haughty, austere, and combined with much low cunning.[1] When he condescended to speak, or converse, which was not frequent, little or no information could be derived; whilst the questions he asked in return, did not tend to the acquisition of useful knowledge. His conduct and deportment on the present occasion, were extremely different; and, when compared with that of his associates, were marked with an evident superiority, expressive of the exalted situation he filled; and indicated that he possessed a just knowledge of himself, and an open, generous, and feeling heart.[2] In conversation, there were few from whom better information could be acquired; nor was he now deficient in directing his observations and enquiries to useful and important objects. For this purpose only, he would remain whole days in our working tents, observing with the strictest attention the different transactions going forward; and frequently interrupting the mechanics, to require explanations of their several operations. The whole tenor of his behaviour towards us was so uniformly correct and meritorious, that, on his taking leave, I could not resist making him, and his wives, such acknowledgments in useful articles, as he conceived they could have no possible claim to; and suspecting I was about to make some addition, he caught my arm, expressed how highly repaid and gratified they were with what they had received, and observed, as I was going to visit many other countries where such things would be equally valuable; I ought to be careful and œconomical.

How far these disinterested sentiments had actuated the conduct of the royal party in all their former transactions, is not easy to ascertain; but certain it is, they took great pains to keep up the value of our commodities, and, by their own example, established the price of three large hogs, weighing from an hundred to an hundred and fifty and two hundred pounds each, at an axe; under which they desired we would not part with our axes; and would

---

[1] Beaglehole notes that when Cook visited Tahiti on his third voyage 'The sly and even mean side of Tu's character was generally recognized' and quotes Burney to confirm this. Cook, *Journals*, III, 219n. It is confirmed further by an entry in King's journal for September 1777: '...Otoo and I walked to Matavai. I ought to do justice to this Eireedehoi in acknowledgeing the great care he took of me & his very civil treatment; but as I have thought him a selfish & cunning Monarch this conduct of his will not suffer me to alter my Opinion altogether'. *Ibid.*, III, 1381.

[2] 'Pomarre is at present about 6 feet 5 inches high, very muscular & well proportioned, he walks firm & erect with that majestic dignity of deportment becoming his high rank & station. Those on board who have seen him formerly say that he is much improved in every respect, not only in his personal appearance but in the firmness & steadiness of his actions & general behaviour.' – Menzies, 23 January.

frequently admonish us, when they considered we were about to pay extravagantly for our purchases. In our traffic, axes were the most valuable; next to these, red cloth, and all kinds of European linen; files, knives and fishing hooks, were in great request; as were scissars and looking-glasses by the ladies; nails were of little value, and such things as were only of an ornamental nature were accepted with indifference, red feathers excepted, which I believe would still find a ready market.

So important are the various European implements, and other commodities, now become to the happiness and comfort of these islanders, that I cannot avoid reflecting with Captain Cook on the very deplorable condition to which these good people on a certainty must be reduced, should their communication with Europeans be ever at an end.[1] The knowledge they have now acquired of the superiority and the supply with which they have been furnished of the more useful implements, have rendered these, and other European commodities, not only essentially necessary to their common comforts, but have made them regardless of their former tools and manufactures, which are now growing fast out of use, and, I may add, equally out of remembrance. Of this we had convincing proof in the few of their bone, or stone tools, or utensils, that were seen amongst them; those offered for sale were of rude workmanship, and of an inferior kind, solely intended for our market, to be purchased by way of curiosity. I am likewise well convinced, that, by a very small addition to their present stock of European cloth, the culture of their cloth plant, which now seems much neglected, will be intirely disregarded,[2] and they will rely upon the precarious supply which may be obtained from accidental visitors, for this and many others of the most important requisites of social life.

Under these painful considerations, it manifestly appears that Europeans are bound by all the laws of humanity, regularly to furnish those wants which they alone have created; and to afford the inhabitants from time to time

---

[1] These sentiments are not expressed in Cook's own journals, but they appear in the official version of them edited by John Douglas, Bishop of Salisbury: 'I own I cannot avoid expressing it as my real opinion that it would have been far better for these poor people, never to have known our superiority, in the accommodations and arts that make life comfortable, than, after once knowing it, to be again abandoned to their original incapacity of improvement. Indeed, they cannot be restored to that happy mediocrity in which they lived before we discovered them, if the intercourse between us should be discontinued. It seems to me, that it has become, in a manner, incumbent on the Europeans to visit them once in three or four years, in order to supply them with those conveniences which we have introduced among them, and have given them a predilection for.' – A Voyage to the Pacific Ocean, II, 136–7.

[2] Hewett denied that the natives were losing their skills: 'They had both Bone and Stone Tools exceedingly well made which they commonly used but great numbers were also made during our stay here...only to Sell [and those] were bad enough. there is no fear of their forgetting how to make them nor of their neglecting the Culture of the Cloth plant as the little European Cloth among them can only be worn by the Chiefs and that not in the presence of any one who is Superior in Power. of this Captn. V. had a proof when Pommurrey ws dressed in a Check Shirt on hearing his Son was approaching he in a great hurry pulled it off and hid it for fear of being asked to present it to him.'

supplies of such important useful articles as have been already introduced, and which having excluded their own native manufactures, are, in most respects, become indispensably necessary to their whole œconomy of life: in return for which a valuable consideration would be received in provisions and refreshments, highly beneficial to the traders who may visit the Pacific Ocean.

The various manufactures in iron and in cloth have become so essentially requisite to their common concerns, that instead of these commodities being reduced in their value by the frequent visits of Europeans, or their supplies of food and refreshments being less plentiful in return, we were served with every article in the greatest profusion. Six hogsheads of very fine pork were cured; and had we been better provided with salt, we might have secured ten times that quantity,[1] and sailed with a large supply for present use, which comprehended as many live hogs and vegetables, as we could find room to dispose of;[2] the whole procured at least 200 per cent. cheaper than on any of Captain Cook's visits, notwithstanding the recent departure of the Pandora.

Great alteration has taken place in the military operations of these people. On our first discovery of these islands their wars were principally of a maritime nature; but at present it should seem they were conducted in a very different manner. For although some of our gentlemen extended their excursions to a considerable distance, not a single war canoe was seen belonging to *Otaheite*.[3]

[1] There was a sharp difference of opinion on the salting of the pork. 'As we had now a good stock of Hogs we began Salting Pork and follow'd the method pointed out by Captn. Cook; but whether from the rainy weather, the great heat, or from being our first attempt – I cannot tell, we however did not Succeed at first – and our Small Stock of Salt prevented our Curing more than 2 *good* Casks of Pork.' – Bell, 4 January. 'Capt. Vancouver had built a large press for salting Pork previous to our arrival, therefore being all ready it is natural to suppose that no time was lost. twenty or thirty of the largest Hogs were daily Killed and after undergoing the necessary process of rubbing, pressing, squeezing and salting it was Cask'd for Sea Store. after being kept some time it was by no means a pleasant diet, as the Bones being all extracted left little else but skin and Fat. to speak candidly, no one approved of it but those that received the emoluments of pursurage [meaning Vancouver].' – Manby, letters, January. Hewett contends that 'The Pork Salted here was both Putrid and Rancid.'

[2] Hewett states that 'Lord Camelford and his Messmates had at the Island six Hogs presented to them which were as soon as they left the land taken from them by Captn. Vancouvers Order killed and served to the Ship as one Days allowance for which Captain Vancouver [as acting purser] received the Money – without any reason being given [other] than *they had no right* to have Hogs.'

[3] Hewett contradicts Vancouver and notes that he and Barrie 'saw at Oparre several War Canoes this therefore must be a Mistake.' Baker believed that the big war canoes had either been 'totally destroyed or sent to the other Islands, as during the whole of our stay we saw only one, which was by no means remarkable for its size, and even this, we were informed, belonged to Ulitea [Raiatea].' – 24 January. Vancouver's statement was correct. There had been a marked decline in naval strength since April 1774, when Cook, then on his second voyage, had seen a great fleet of 160 war canoes, supported by 170 lesser craft. In September 1777, when he visited Tahiti on his third voyage, a fleet had been mobilized in anticipation of hostilities breaking out with Moorea, but it was evidently a much smaller force. William Bayly, the astronomer, refers in his journal to '30 Sail of War Canoes'. – Cook, *Journals*, III, 211n. James Morrison, a *Bounty* crewman who spent most

437

I had much conversation with *Urripiah* on this subject; from whom I learned, that in their late contests they had found them so unmanageable, particularly when the wind blew at all strong, that they had intirely given them up, and now carried on their enterprizes by land, using the larger sort of their common canoes, when their wars were offensive, to convey them to the place of their destination, which was generally effected under cover of the night, or in dark rainy weather.

The youth of *Otoo* authorises us to say little more, than that he bore every appearance of becoming a very promising man. Some circumstances attendant on this young monarch were so very peculiar and extraordinary, as to make a few observations indispensable. Amongst the first was the curious restriction which prohibited his entering any of our habitations. His father, when *Otoo*, and king of the island, was under no such interdiction; but, as frequently as his inclination prompted, visited our ships and tents without attaching the inconvenience which would now have fallen upon the people had the young king done the same. Nor was the grandfather *Taow* then treated with that degree of obedience and respect, which is at present paid to him on all occasions. The origin of the above mysterious restraint, or the reasoning on which it has been founded, I could not satisfactorily learn. The result, however, of my enquiries on this head induces me to believe, that a ceremony very similar to the *Natche* of the Friendly islands described by Captain Cook, on *Poulahou*'s son being permitted to eat in company with his father, will be performed here.[1] This ceremony will occupy a considerable space of time, after which he will no longer be carried on men's shoulders, but be at liberty like others to walk about; but when this was to take place in respect of *Otoo*, I could not discover; for as often as the question was put, so often the period

of the years 1788–91 in Tahiti, and who participated in some of the naval activities of the time, comments: 'Their Chief Strength consisted formerly in their Naval force, which at present [1791] is but triffling, their Navy being put on a very indifferent footing, oToo [Pomare I] thinking it better to keep peace then [sic] make war. At present the whole Naval force does not exceed 20 sail of War Canoes & for the most part of these he is beholden to his Sister Areepaeoa Waheine who brought them from Ryeataya'. He adds that Otoo 'stands in no need at present of large Canoes as Morea is now under him' – thus linking the decline with the widening and strengthening of Otoo's authority. – *The Journal of James Morrison* (London, 1935), p. 171. James Wilson, one of the first missionaries to arrive in Tahiti, who spent the years 1797–98 in the island, 'knew of the existence of only five war canoes in all Tahiti.' – Oliver, *Ancient Tahitian Society* (Honolulu, 1974), I, 405, citing James Wilson, *A Missionary Voyage to the Southern Pacific Ocean performed in the years 1796, 1797, 1798 in the Ship Duff*...(London, 1799), 405.

[1] The precise nature of the ceremony (inasi) Cook witnessed in July 1777 at M'ua, a village in Tongatapu, remains somewhat of a mystery. It was held by Paulaho as some form of initiation or installation of his son. For a discussion by Beaglehole see *Journals*, III, 145n, and for Cook's own extended account, *ibid.*, pp. 145–54. Anderson's conception of it seems to have been fairly definite: '[We went] to see a Ceremony which Poulaho told us when we went last to visit him was to happen about this time. We understood then that it was to be an initiation of his son and heir into some privileges, amongst which was that of eating with his father which he had not yet done...'– *ibid.*, III, 913.

when the event was to take place varied. It was likewise very remarkable, that
we never saw any person of consequence or respectability about the young
monarch. His nearest relations, though they paid all respect to his high office,
did not appear to regard or converse with him; and those whose duty it was
to attend him on his journies between Oparre and our encampment, were
servants from the lowest order of the people. Amongst these was a man named
Peterrah, who apparently was a very shrewd, sensible fellow, on whose
shoulders the young king never rode, but who, on all occasions acted as
messenger, and bore no higher office than that of a butler, or upper servant.
I had originally taken this man for a priest and sort of preceptor; but, on
repeated enquiries, they always pointed to my steward as bearing the same
office with that of *Peterrah*.

Much encomium, and with great justice, has been bestowed on the beauty
of the female inhabitants of this country. I cannot avoid acknowledging how
great was the disappointment I experienced, in consequence of the early
impression I had received of their superior personal endowments. The natives
themselves freely admit the alteration, which in a few years has taken place,
and seem to attribute much of the cause to the lamentable diseases introduced
by European visitors, to which many of their finest women, at an early period
of life, have fallen sacrifices.[1] Beauty in this country, especially amongst the
women, is a flower that quickly blossoms, and as quickly fades: like the
personal accomplishments of the Creoles of America, theirs soon arrive at
maturity, remain but a short time stationary, and as rapidly decay. The
extreme deficiency of female beauty on these islands makes it singularly
remarkable, that so large a proportion of the crew belonging to the Bounty,
should have become so infatuated as to sacrifice their country, their honor,
and their lives, to any female attachments at Otaheite. The objects of their
particular regard, by whom they have children, we frequently saw. Whatever
superiority they may be entitled to from their mental accomplishments, we
had no opportunity of ascertaining; but with respect to their personal
attractions, they were certainly not such as we should have imagined could
possibly have tempted Englishmen to so unpardonable a breach of their duty;
nor were any of the women they selected, persons of the least power or
consequence in the island.[2]

[1] When and by whom venereal diseases were introduced into Tahiti is still a matter
of discussion. Wallis, Cook and Vancouver all took what precautions they could to prevent
infection spreading from their crews, with varying success. Early visitors could easily have
mistaken yaws, an endemic disease, for syphilis, which in some respects it resembles closely.
Some hold the view that gonorrhea was widespread in Tahiti and the other islands long
before any Europeans arrived.

[2] Hewett comments that he never heard 'that the Women were more beautiful in former
times' and shrewdly adds that at the time of Vancouver's first visit 'he was a Young Man
but that not being now the Case the Ladies of course were not so Attractive.' Bell recorded
his impressions: 'The Women are about the middling size of European women, have fine
delicate regular features. their faces in which in general we could not observe all that
wonderful degree of Beauty which the different visitors have described, were nevertheless

The European animals and plants deposited here by Captain Cook, and other navigators, with the hope of their future increase, I have already had occasion to regret, had been almost intirely destroyed in the late conflicts of the contending parties. My concern at this circumstance was greatly augmented, not only by my having little in my power with which I could replace them, but in the confidence of their now succeeding could I have furnished a supply; as the recent alteration which has taken place in the government, afforded reasonable grounds to believe that, whatever I might have bestowed on the present occasion, would have been carefully protected. To the race of animals, I could add but two Cape geese and a gander. We planted some vine cuttings that had flourished extremely well on board; with some orange and lemon trees; and an assortment of garden seeds; but as nature has been so very bountiful in the variety of vegetables she has bestowed on this country, the natives seem to possess little desire for any addition; and, if a judgment is to be formed, by the deplorable state in which we found the several spots where foreign plants and seeds had been deposited, we had little reason to be sanguine in the success of our gardening. Nor do I believe such attempts will ever succeed until some Europeans shall remain on the island, and, by the force of their example, excite in the inhabitants a desire of cultivating the soil by their manual labour, to which at present they are almost strangers.

The *ava*, and the cloth plant in a small proportion, are the only vegetables which the Otaheiteans take the least trouble to cultivate. Some few indifferent shaddocks, a little tolerably good maize, a few pods of the capsicon, [1] and some very coarse radishes, were the only productions I saw from the various and numerous vegetable exotics, that, from time to time, have been introduced into this island.

pretty, and several that I saw were very handsome; – their Countenances bespeak much Sweetness, sensibility and expression, they have fine sparking black Eyes, – their Teeth are beautifully white and regular, – their hands and Fingers remarkably delicate, tapering to the ends Small & neat.... Though I say we were in general disappointed in the Beauty of the Women, yet had not *so much* been said of them, by the different people who have written about them, some of whom have compar'd them to Europeans, we shou'd certainly have thought them very handsome.' – January 1792. It should be remembered that Tahitian ideas of beauty differed markedly from those of Europeans. They favoured broad flat noses, tried to bleach their complexions, and 'admired corpulence in both males and females...it is a well-established fact that they went to considerable pains to become corpulent.' – Oliver, *Ancient Tahitian Society* (Honolulu, 1974), I, 358. It is quite clear, nevertheless, that the crews of Vancouver's ships found the women highly attractive. We have comments on Peggy, the Tahitian wife of midshipman George Stewart of the *Bounty*, by both Bell and Hewett. 'Poor Peggy', in Bell's opinion, 'was not a Beauty, nor had she that in her appearance that I shou'd suppose cou'd ever tempt a man to turn Pirate; – but she was possess'd of much sensibility, an affable agreeable disposition together with a sweetness of manner that upon a short acquaintance made up for the deficiency of personal Beauty.' – January 24. Hewett came to Peggy's defence: 'The Wife of Stewart was a very fine Woman noble in her manner her Voice lofty (like Siddons) another of the Wives called Jenny Baker was as pretty a little figure as I ever saw extremely lively Chatty and pleasing.'
    [1] capsicum.

The milk of goats not having been appropriated to any use, and the animal not being sufficiently fat for the taste of these people, they have fallen into disrepute, and become scarce. I collected, however, a sufficient number to establish a breed of those animals on the Sandwich islands, in case I should there find them acceptable to the inhabitants.

The few atronomical and nautical observations, here made, tending only to our own useful and necessary purposes, will conclude our transactions at Otaheite, and are as under, viz.

Eighteen sets of meridian observations of the zenith distances of the sun and stars, gave the latitude of the observatory by their mean result   17° 30′ 20″

Its longitude, by the chronometer, allowing the Dusky bay rate, to the 19th of January at noon   209 58

Its longitude to the same time, allowing the Portsmouth rate   211 18

Its longitude by eighteen sets of distances, by my sextants, of ☾ a ☉, east of her   210 31 53

Its true longitude, as determined by Captain Cook   210 24 15[1]

By our observations made at the observatory the first day, viz. the 7th of January, on allowing the Dusky bay rate, the chronometer gave the longitude 209° 55′ 45″, from which day to the 19th instant inclusive, being twelve days observations of equal altitudes, it was found gaining at the rate of 4″ 2‴ per day, and fast of mean time at Greenwich, on the 20th at noon, 31′ 42″ 46‴. Allowing the chronometer this error, and the above rate of going since we discovered the island of Oparre,[2] the difference of the longitude between it and point Venus, will by such means be 5° 14′ 45″ west, and consequently its longitude, by that mode of calculating, would be 215° 39′; my observations however place it in 215° 58′ 20″; the mean between the two 215° 48′ 40″, I should suppose can be liable to little, if any error; and as such I shall adopt it for the true longitude of that island.[3] This is further authorised on finding, that by nearly the same number of observations, made with the same intruments at point Venus, and the sun on the same side the moon as when the observations were taken off Oparre, I placed that point 7′ 38″ to the eastward of the truth.

Mr. Arnold's chronometer on board the Chatham, when taken to the observatory, was found to be fast of mean time at Greenwich on the 20th of January at noon 2 10′ 25″ 46‴, and to be gaining at the rate of 19″ 51‴ 24″″ per day.

The variation of the magnetic needle, with all our cards, and compasses,

---

[1] The correct position of the observatory on Point Venus was lat. 17° 29′ S, long. 149° 30′ W (210° 30′ E).

[2] Rapa Island.

[3] Its 'true longitude' is 144° 25′ W (215° 35′ E); lat. 27° 35′ S.

in fifteen sets of azimuths, varied from 7° 30′ to 5° 30′ east variation, giving their mean result 6° 12′, and the vertical inclination as under:

Marked end,	North face	East,	30° 15′
Ditto	ditto	West,	31 13
Ditto	South, face	East,	30 43
Ditto	ditto	West,	30 47

The mean vertical inclination of the south point of the dipping needle   30 53